From a
White Rose
and a
Butterfly

My life and the ambulance service

From a White Rose and a Butterfly

Copyright © Ian Firth 2018 All Rights Reserved

Spiderwize
Remus House
Coltsfoot Drive
Woodston
Peterborough
PE2 9BF

www.spiderwize.com

A CIP catalogue record for this book is available from the British Library.

ISBN: 978-1-911596-65-3

From a
White Rose
and a
Butterfly

My life and the
ambulance service

Ian Firth

CONTENTS

FOREWORD.

Mum had written some of her memoirs down, she had tried to get dad to do the same. He did try, but he only managed a few pages. Mum had written quite a lot.

It was only after mum passed away, that I realised that I was the eldest in the family. I had nobody left to ask for information regarding previous generations, and their lifestyles.

I thought that I was a hoarder, but mum well. She had kept everything, when it came to important receipts, certificates etc.

It wasn't until early in 2016, that I felt that it was the appropriate time to go through mum's personal things. I had kept them at home, in two large baskets since she died in January 2011. I hadn't felt able to do before.

I found all sorts of things. There were even birth certificates of her grandparents. A receipt for her own engagement ring and even funeral receipts of past family members. It was upsetting to rummage through her personal things, but at the same time, it was amazing and enlightening.

I had already copied mums book, and dads story years earlier. I had given each of the family a copy of them both.

This though, was the first time that I had actually read it all properly.

My wife Wendy and my boys Adrian and Ben, had mentioned it to me before about me writing a book. My sisters were also encouraging me. I never thought I would be able to, I have always been a practical person.

I hated writing essays when I was at school, but a book, come on! I imagined that I would only be able to do something like my dad, short, but perhaps very informative.

The time did feel right to have a go, to jot down my life's memories while I could still remember them. Then my children, my grandchildren, and hopefully some future generations might be interested to see what this daft old bugger had got up to in his life.

I started this book, late on the night of the 23rd of February 2016. I worked into the early hours of the next day, it happened to be my dad's birthday, if he had still been alive, he would have been 86 years old.

It took the best part of five and a half months to do the main draft and it turned out to be such an enjoyable task as well. It brought back so many memories, I went through such a variety of emotions in doing it. I had very happy memories and also some really sad or depressing thoughts whilst writing, as I have got older it seems the more emotional I have become.

There were times when I would suddenly start chuckling to myself, there were others where I would find myself with floods of tears running down my face.

I wasn't bothered though, these were MY memories and it was MY life, nobody else's. If I was emotional, then that was meant to be. Even if most of the writing was done in public.

I had been sat at a table in the Huddersfield Leisure Centre's cafe for most of the time, while Wendy was swimming in the centre's pool. That was the start of her new life and weight loss programme.

This was going to be mine.

I hope you will find some interesting things to come.

Cheers

Ian Firth

OPINIONS.

All the words that you are about to read in this book. Are purely the personal memories, ideas, thoughts, feelings and opinions of one man, one man alone and that one man, is me.

These words may not be to the full agreement of everyone, but that is up to the individual. If we didn't have personal ideas and opinions, the world would be an extremely strange place.

I have not intentionally set out to offend anyone in the process of writing this book. Although there are some individuals and the organisation that I have worked over 36 years for. That I have criticised strongly in places, for their behaviour or attitude. The reason being that, that is how strongly I feel, of how their actions have affected me personally.

For that I do not make any apologies.

I am aware that some of my words may cause a conflict of interest, again though in my defence, these are my opinions, and they are there to invoke discussion if required.

I have since writing, found that a couple of the items that I have written about, are not 100% accurate. However, they are my memories, and how I personally have remembered the people or events as I believe that they happened. I have decided not to change them.

Again, other people may perceive certain aspects of my recollections slightly differently. If in doing so, I have upset or offended anyone, it was not intentional and for that I do sincerely apologise.

Names have been changed for legal purposes. I simply could not get individual written permission of the many involved for inclusion. If you do read this, and are included, I am sure that you will recognise the part that you played.

Thank you for your time.

DEDICATION.

This book is dedicated to all of my family. Without them I wouldn't have had a life to write about.

To Brian, my father. A true and proud, hardworking Yorkshireman. He was a white rose through and through, who I miss immensely. Also to Sylvia, my mother. Very much loved, missed and remembered with the symbol of a butterfly. A creature that has seemed to be around all the family since my mum passed away. A symbol that appropriately has been adopted by over a 100 hospitals in Britain, who are helping patients and families suffering with Alzheimer's.

Without them, obviously I wouldn't be here, and had the start in life that they gave me. They brought me up to be true and honest, and to be there to help others. As such, I have always tried to do so.

To my two sisters, Lindsay and Diane. I had to rely on them both for helping me, mainly in the later stages of our lives. Particularly by looking after dad, and then mum in their hours of need. And of course in the writing of my book. I am now the eldest of my family, I have no one else to ask of my history and my own memory hasn't been as good as I would have liked it to be.

Of course, it goes without saying that I have to thank my beautiful wife Wendy. She is the one that has put up with me, and supported me since we first met in 1980. She has been right by my side through thick and thin, the good times and the bad. I can't think of anyone else who could have been so strong and understanding for me. In the times that I just couldn't bring myself to put down in writing, due to being far too painful to write about. Wendy is the only one that knows me fully. I love her and respect her far more than I have ever been able to put into words.

Wendy and me have two sons, Adrian and Ben. They have both given me some heartache over the years, but they have also given me an immense amount of pleasure too. They will probably never know how proud I am of both of them.

My sons have also provided us with five beautiful grandchildren between them, I can never thank them enough for that.

I have quite an extended family that includes my cousins, and I include my in-laws in that. I thank them all for the help that they have given to me and my family.

I have had many friends from school, from scouting, and from life itself. I thank them all.

Last, but certainly not least. I would like to give a very big thank you to all my work colleagues, past and present. Without their help and support, I would not have been able to face some of the extreme life experiences that I have.

Please, please, all of you accept a big round of applause. A great pat on the back and the thanks from the bottom of my heart, because you have all helped to make my life, the life that it has been.

Thank You so much.

CHAPTER ONE.

THE EARLY YEARS.

1958 What a year.

There was a conservative Prime Minister, Harold Macmillan.

In January. The European Economic Community (EEC) was founded.

In February. The famous Busby Babes. The Manchester United team was hit by tragedy, where 23 members were killed in the Munich air disaster.

In March. The Planetarium opened in London and work began on the first full length motorway. The M1, from London to Leeds. Opening in the early sixties, over 200 miles.

In April. The first Campaign for a Nuclear Disarmament (CND) march took place.

In May. Dracula starring Christopher Lee made its debut. In the same month, Alfred Hitchcock's film Vertigo was released.

In June. The first Duke of Edinburgh's Award was presented.

In July. Our Queen gave her eldest son Prince Charles, the title Prince of Wales. Also in July the first parking meters were installed.

1st of August. That saw the premiere of Carry on Sergeant, the first of the Carry on Films. 29th August, Cliff Richard launched his debut single "Move It". It reached number 2 in British pop charts.

In September. Jack Kirby invented the first Integrated Circuit Board.

In October. British Overseas Airway Corporation (BOAC), became the first airline to fly jet passenger services across the Atlantic. (Comet jets).

October also saw the first episode of the long running TV show, Blue Peter.

In November. Donald Campbell set the World Water Speed Record, of 248.62 mph. Also in November, Paddington Bear was first published.

In December. Subscriber trunk dialling (STD) was inaugurated by Her Majesty the Queen. The call was from Bristol to Edinburgh, where she spoke to the the Lord Provost.

My arrival on the scene.

In December 1958. That was to be the first year that Mrs Sylvia Firth of Paddock and wife of Brian, would not be cooking a Christmas dinner, for as long as she could remember.

That year, she would be an in-patient at St. Luke's Maternity Hospital in Crosland Moor. She would be giving birth on the 22nd. To her firstborn, a son, that's me.

Mum had spent most of her life looking after others, her mother Florence was very ill for most of my mums young life. Mums brother Derek was also very ill, dying at the age of just 24.

My grandma Florence died when mum was only sixteen. My mum at that time, still lived with her dad, my grandad Fent (Fenton) Woodhouse. He was a street cleaner in Huddersfield's town centre, he had two dustbins on a cart, along with his brushes and shovels.

With his ultra modern state of the art equipment, he would take pride in keeping the streets of Huddersfield clean. He was only short in stature, and had extremely bowed legs. Mum used to say that "he'd never catch a pig in a ginnel"

Mum met my dad, Brian, whilst he was home on leave from the army in 1949. He was doing his two years National Service. Bring it back!

Dad was a textile mill worker in Milnsbridge at James Sykes' along with his brother John. Dad lived at the top end of Paddock, at Victory Avenue by Royds Hall School. He lived there with his mum and dad, my grandparents John and Mary-Anne Firth.

After they got married, on the 14th February 1953. Mum and dad lived at her family home on Longroyd Lane, at the bottom of Paddock with grandad Fent.

I was born at St. Luke's Hospital at Crosland Moor, on the 22nd. Mum had to stay in for a few days. Taking me back to the family home on New Years Day, 1st of January 1959.

The 3rd of January 1959, that was my first outing. Mum and dad took me in the pram to see my grandma and grandad Firth. At the top of Paddock, on Victory Avenue. A walk of just over three quarters of a mile, each way. It had snowed heavily all the time that they were there, making it quite a struggle to get back home. Even though it was downhill every bit of the way.

Washing machine.

9th of January 1961. At home on Longroyd Lane. My mum was doing the washing and for some unknown reason, I put my hand in between the rollers of the electric mangle. I got stuck!

That was to be my first dealings with the fire service. They were called to dismantle the rollers of an ADA Coronation washing machine and free little old me.

Ever since that incident, I have had some nerve damage in my upper right arm. That leaves my hand with a permanent tremor, on some days it is far worse than others. If the adrenaline is kicking in, my hand can be totally wild. It has never caused me any real distress though.

My earliest memory of any difficulty, was when making models of Airfix planes. I could stick the body of the plane together, and I could add the wings, but could I 'ellerslike get the little pilots into their seat.

As I got older, I couldn't, and I still can't carry a cup and saucer without making a right mess. But more importantly, I have always managed to keep a good head on my beer.

I wanted to be a paramedic when they were first starting out, but I couldn't cannulate, (place a needle into a vein). So I went no further with that. It didn't stop me doing my job though, I carried on working for the ambulance service for well over thirty five years.

New house, new start.

We moved house to Crosland Moor in the summer of 1961, I think it was July.

I started at the nursery school at Mount Pleasant, probably early in September of the next year, 1962. I was under the watchful eyes of teachers Mrs Ramsden and Mrs Mettrick.

One of my early memories there, was when the whole school gathered around a television in the main hall to watch the funeral procession of Sir Winston Churchill. It was on a small black and white television, probably only around a ten inch screen. Not like the monsters available today. I was sat with a schoolmate I'll call him Dennis, his mother ran a local dancing class. I still see him about occasionally.

In fact, in 2010, I picked his daughter up following a fall in King Street in the Town Centre. When her mother arrived, I recognised her, I explained to them both, that I used to go to school with Dennis. Wow! What an unexpected reaction. "We don't talk about him!" They both said in unison. End of that conversation.

Only a few months later, I saw him in one of the larger stores in Huddersfield. He had changed. The last time I saw him, he had put on a lot of weight. Then, much, much thinner and dressed to the nines. He was in the make up department working as a manager. I was shocked, he looked so feminine, mincing about the store. Not the Dennis I knew, but it was definitely him. His name was called on the tannoy, the way he responded to it. Other than the immortal words "I'm free!", he was Mr. Humphries from TV's Are You Being Served. Just as camp!

First Holiday.

August 19th 1961, mum, dad, and me, had a holiday, we all went to Pwllheli in Gwynedd, North Western Wales, for a week self catering. In a furnished flat. We went with another couple of mum's and dad's friends Harry and Barbara, with their daughter of a similar age to me Jeannette. I think that it was my first holiday, it was certainly my very first holiday on foreign soil.

Close Neighbours.

At Crosland Moor. I can remember some of my neighbours. Next door, there was Doris and George, he was then the manager at the Home and Colonial shop on Shambles Lane in Huddersfield. They had one son Kenneth, he married a girl called Anne. They both lived where the family had come from in Grantham. I got on great with the younger couple, when they came to visit. I used to keep asking when "Kennerfannan" were coming.

Next door to them were another family, Pat and Derek. They had two sons, Peter my age and a younger brother Jack. They also had a younger child, a daughter Sara. Jack amongst other jobs retired from the Fire Service in 2014, he now works for the Yorkshire Ambulance Service on PTS. Across the road, were Doreen and Frank. They had some children, Michael the eldest, was the one I remember most from school.

Other schoolmates of the time were Colin, Peter, and Bhader, he was the only Asian I had ever met at that time.

A sister for me, Lindsay.

On the 22nd of October 1962 my sister Lindsay was born. Lindsay, like me, was born in Hospital. Only a couple of days later, she was brought home. To our home in Crosland Moor, to Grandad Fent and me.

Family Holiday.

August 15th 1964 we had a holiday in Mablethorpe, we went for a week self catering, the main thing that I remember about that holiday, was that we went on a train. I believe that it was my first rail journey. I have seen a couple of photo's from then. There was mum, dad, my sister Lindsay and me. I don't think grandad Fent went with us that time, he was happy to stay at home. His sister, mum's auntie Polly only lived a short distance away.

Pigeon toes.

For a long time, I had been having a lot of problems walking. I used to walk with pigeon toes, my feet were really pointing inwards. It was down to a problem with my knees.

In 1964, I had to attend at a special clinic. I think it was at the Princess Royal Hospital in Greenhead Road. I went there for weeks, where I had to have a lot of exercises and manipulation.

The main exercise was to pick up some plastic sticks, with my toes. They were green, about six inches long and around half an inch thick. The cross section being the shape of a cross.

I had to place them on the floor, I then had to pick them up with my toes and place them in a tin. Alternately with each foot. I even had to pick pens or pencils up and to try to write my name. With the accompanying physiotherapy, they eventually got me sorted.

I seem to be fine now. In fact, up and till recently I could get my feet to turn right round the other way. Instead of standing with my feet pointing forward at 12 o'clock I could stand at twenty five to five, work that one out.

And I could walk like that!

A couple of times when in the pub, if it was busy and I was feeling that way out. I have been known to go to the gents, remove my trousers and put them on back to front, and swapped feet with my shoes. I have then stood at the bar with my feet that way, caused one or two shocks that!

I have great dexterity with my feet, I am very proud of that. Whenever possible, I am in bare feet around the house and I can still pick things up with my feet/toes.

One such item, dad asked me to pass him his old Ronson lighter, I would have been around thirteen at the time. I picked it up with my foot, and passed it to him. He said "ok, clever bugger, can you light my cigarette with your feet?" I could, using both feet. I was able to grip the lighter with one foot and depress the trigger with the other, but the flame would not ignite.

Just to prove a point, I then opened the base of the lighter, and took out what was left of the flint. I then removed a new flint from a packet, and inserted it in to the lighter and closed it all up again. All with my feet and toes.

Then I tested it, it lit as good as new.

I then picked up the lighter, reached across with my feet, I depressed the trigger and lit a cigarette for dad.

Grandad Fent.

It was whilst living at Crosland Moor, that my grandad Fent passed away, it was the day after Boxing Day 1964. A very sad day for all of us. I had always been very close to him.

It was just after lunch, I was sat on his knee in the front room and we had both gone to sleep. The next thing that I knew, I was carried into the kitchen and then I was sent to sit with George and Doris next door.

When I got home, grandad Fent wasn't there, he had died.

I never saw him again.

Land Owner.

Since my mum died, I have been looking through her things. She collected receipts, certificates and family documents for just about everything. Within those items, I found a receipt for grandad Fent's grave with grandma Florence.

Wendy and I went to find the grave. It is in Edgerton Cemetery, not too far from the Cemetery Road entrance.

I don't remember ever having been and visited before. Wendy had found out the location from work, using the reference numbers. We both went on a cold March day this year of 2016. It wasn't as clear to find from the council instructions, as I would have expected. We had struggled and were just about to call it a day. Then there it was, as clear as day.

The grave is marked with a fully engraved and ornate headstone for them both, only a low stone, so it is still standing proud and doesn't need any maintenance. I stood there for a while, I just couldn't speak. I found it very emotional after all those years, that I had found them again.

Thank you Wendy, you have helped me out yet again.

Along with the documents, it states that it is a family plot and that as the deed holder, I have inherited the rights to it. That being one burial plot, or more significantly up to six interment of ashes. To be buried along with grandma Florence and grandad Fent.

I have an inheritance, a plot of land, I am a landowner. I can't build on it, but hey ho! A landowner I am.

Another Holiday.

On August 7th 1965. We went to St. Anne's for another week self catering holiday. Mum, dad, Lindsay and me. I would have been about seven and a half, I can't really say that I remember much about it. It's a damn good job that mum wrote all those things down. I would be lost without her and her memories!

Junior School.

After leaving Mount Pleasant Infants School in the July of 1965. I then attended Dryclough Junior School at the top of Walpole, from the end of the summer break in September.

I didn't go there long, I was just there for the Autumn term, before the family moved to Paddock. That was during the Christmas break.

Of the teachers, I only remember the headmaster there, his name was Mr. Wallbank.

CHAPTER 2.

ANOTHER NEW HOUSE.

Another new house, another new start.

We moved to Paddock, on 10th of January 1966. It was a two bedroom house. The front bedroom was massive, it had two front facing windows, dad made a corner of that room into a bedroom for me. My sisters shared the rest of the big room. Mum and dad had the back bedroom. It served that purpose right up until I moved in with Wendy.

When my sisters moved out, the little room was removed, mum and dad used the whole room then as a large bedroom. Dad could have his own bed, but mum could still be in the same room and keep her eye on him after his slight stroke.

The main difference with that house, from our council house at Crosland Moor, was dad's beloved garden. There we had a front garden, it was edged with privet and lots of small flowers, all around a gently sloping lawn. There was a fairly large lawn at the back, ideal for kids playing and there was also a narrow strip of garden down the side between our house and that of Doris and George. That bit was only small, but dad made it look good. He took great pride in his garden, each year the council gave prizes for the best garden in each area, dad won three out of the four years that we lived there.

The new house was at the road side, with no garden or even any room for flower boxes at the front. At the rear, there was a communal yard. In the yard, was our back door and porch, and the rear of a shop. There was one house, a back to back and there was the access arch through into the yard. Then there were the back of three more houses, after the corner, was the back of the houses going down the next street. Three of them were elevated, so had steps leading up to a long balcony. All looking down in to the yard.

Inside the yard, there was one single garage, it was facing the arched passageway and then there were six useable working outdoor toilets. All brick and stonework. The yard itself was all tarmac. No garden area.

There was a high wall separating our yard from the yard at the back of a pub. Dad painted the wall white, it lightened the area from being the plain dark brick.

He then built a low wall with an irregular edge, all the way from the toilets to just short of our back window, approximately twenty five feet in all. That when back filled with rubble and soil, created a raised bed.

In which he was then able to fill with all the colours and the smells of his favourite flowers. Not forgetting his beloved his white roses. We had a glass walled porch at the back door, not big, but enough to act as a small greenhouse.

The garden was not anywhere near as big as at Crosland Moor, but it had become a garden nonetheless.

Neighbours at Paddock.

Mum and Dad rented the house from Frank, an elderly man who lived higher up Luck Lane, he owned all the houses in our block. He was a former dispensing chemist before retiring. Frank used to let mum and dad live at the house for a reduced rent. In return dad did most of, if not all, of the every day handyman jobs. Including painting and decorating, for all of the other houses in the block.

Not long after we left Crosland Moor and moved to Paddock, George and Doris moved back to their native Grantham in Lincolnshire.

We took over the house from another couple, I'll call them Henry and Mary. I was always led to believe that the couple were friends of mum and dad, they certainly knew them before the sale. They had two sons, one is now a conservative councillor.

From just recently reading the book that mum had written, the truth has to be told. It turned out that the couple were not really friends at all and they left dad with a large debt to pay for a gas fire that had just been fitted.

Dad, normally a very proud man, had to turn to another "friend" to borrow the money. It would save him the shame of going to court for non-payment. That "friend" was, I'll call him Gerald. Again, I thought he was a friend of dad's. It turned out that instead of paying the loan back, the whole incredible twenty five pounds! Dad would have to work for it.

For years we used to walk, or bus part way and walk the rest, to Gerald's on the hillside in the Holme Valley. On a Sunday morning, dad would spend at least two hours washing the family cars. Dad did that for as long as I can remember.

Oh what it must be like to have power and money! Then have skivvies like dad to do your work for you! It makes me sick! That family weren't friends, they exploited dad and his predicament.

Our house was sandwiched between two shops, neither of them were lived in. There was Frank's electrical shop, he was a TV engineer, and sold small household electrical items. I seem to that think he lived over in Halifax somewhere. A nice enough chap, he always used to give me the large powerful magnets from the back of the old tv tubes. (Look it up on google).

I remember someone once threw a brick and smashed the large plate glass front window! They stole some small items, including a "Dansette" record player. It was a basic wooden box shape, with an opening and removable lid.

Frank thought it would be funny to put a notice in his new window. It read "whoever stole the record player from my window, please come back and see me, you forgot the lid". He prominently attached his notice to the lid in the middle of the shop window display. Yes, you guessed it. Some smart Alec came back that very same night, smashed the window yet again and they took the lid. Not only that, the cheeky bugger left Frank a note, simply saying "Thanks for that!"

Next door on the other side of us, was Kenneth the dispensing chemist, ably assisted by Betty. That shop was also broken into several times over the years, Kenneth had never had an alarm fitted. The best he ever managed, was to stack row upon row of glass bottles leaning against the windows at the back.

The burglars simply removed the old putty from the outside of the single glazed window! And then they stood all the bottles in a line outside the rear of the shop. Dad had called the police on several occasions. Once the intruders were actually caught inside, and one of them had a gun!

Kenneth was advised that time by the police to get a substantial alarm system. He did, it was too sensitive. If a bluebottle fly, or a bee or a wasp had got into the shop, the alarm would go off. It was always in the middle of the night.

Kenneth had a wife, Jennifer, both of them were very keen golfers. Along with Denis from the green grocers round the corner, where mum worked. Kenneth lived at Outlane. They also had two daughters, then a few years later along came a son. The daughters were of a similar age to my sisters. We didn't see a great deal of them.

The son however, could be a little sod as a child. One vivid memory I have, was when his dad Kenneth was painting the shop front. It was a deep maroon colour.

The little lad was helping! He would have only been two, going on three at the most. He had been dipping a two inch brush deep into the gloss paint, no wiping the excess off on the edge of the tin, and then "applying it" to the woodwork on the shop front.

There was just as much paint on the stone flags, (before it was all tarmac) as there was on the wall.

Suddenly mum was screaming, if a mad axe man had walked in, I don't think that she could have been as afraid.

Mum and dad had just nicely got a brand new three piece suite, it was a sort of kingfisher blue, leather one. The little bugger was just stood there in the middle of the room, with maroon gloss paint dripping off his elbows, and onto the carpet. His brush was fully loaded with paint, Kenneth said, "he wants you to look at what he has been doing". Mum was screaming, "get him out! Get him out! For God's sake get him out!"

Dad and me, on the Golf Course.

Denis and Kenneth used to both be mad keen on golf, both playing regularly at a well known Huddersfield Golf Club. They were just everyday blokes, enjoying their time off from running a small business.

If either of them were involved in a competition, they would always caddy for each other. One year, I think it was 1975, I had just gone sixteen. Both Denis and Kenneth had got through to the grand final of the same competition. They were playing together in a pairs tournament. As they were both in the same competition, they would each require a caddy. They asked dad and me. I had to be sixteen to be involved. We agreed, even though we didn't really know what was expected of us.

He wasn't always the first to show it, but dad had a similar wicked sense of humour to me.

That was to prove our downfall.

We had been on the course for around three quarters of an hour. It wasn't mine nor dad's cup of tea, there were too many stuffed shirts, some proper toffee nosed pillocks. All patting each other on the back, all lovey dovey, I thought I would be sick.

Then it happened, one of Denis's opponents shot landed right at the edge of a quarry. Everyone gathered round, a lot of "oh bother!" "Bad show old chap!" Etc.

What a load of crap!

As they were all buttying each other up, the ball moved and rolled off the edge of the disused quarry. It fell and stopped on a ledge only about six inches from the top, but impossible to hit with his golf club. I thought that was funny, and I started laughing. Everyone else, in unison went "shush!" That made me laugh even more.

The player elected to drop a shot, as it was impossible to take his shot from that position. He picked the ball up, then to place his ball, it apparently was custom to drop it backwards over his shoulder.

As he did so, the ball hit the only stone that wasn't in the quarry, it bounced violently off the stone and then dropped right down into the very bottom of the quarry.

That was it, I completely lost it. I was in tears of laughter, and dad had also joined in. All the other players and caddies, and a crowd of spectators were silent. Their looks of disgust, instead of stopping us from laughing, only made it worse.

The player then, in a mad hig, threw down his club. That also went down the quarry and then bent at ninety degrees.

Laurel and Hardy couldn't have done it better!

Dad and me were then promptly removed from the Golf Course, due to "ungentlemanly conduct". Denis and Kenneth would have to caddy for themselves throughout the rest of the competition.

They didn't do bad though. Out of a starting field of forty eight teams, the caddy less duo finished fifth over all.

Dad and me were never asked to caddy again!

Back to the neighbours.

Next door to the chemist, at the other side to us, at the front. There was a small one up, one down house. It was rented by a funny, dirty little man, a really heavy drinker and even heavier smoker.

He was called Mickey. I only went into his house once, that was enough for me. I do remember though, that he didn't have any wallpaper on his living room walls. They were completely covered from top to bottom, originally with black and white pictures. But by then they had become more of a sepia tint, from the amount of nicotine. They were all newspaper cuttings of the Sun's topless page three girls.

If it was a warm day and Mickey had his front window open. Sat just inside it, on a table, was his pet. It was a caged bird, a Mynah bird, a black crow like creature that was well known for mimicking people and voices. It was good, that one always swore at anyone passing. It was so clear, with the most extreme profanities.

As a lad, I thought it was great!

To the rear of him was a lovely little woman, Kathleen, she lived there with her son Paul. He had an older brother Terry, who had long since left home. Kathleen used to give me some empty bottles to take back to Colin's the bakers shop across the road. The sterilised milk bottles had a penny deposit, but the Ben Shaw's pop bottles had a wapping threepence on them. Some times it was quite lucrative, I could earn twelve pence, a whole shilling. (Five pence in today's money).

Then there was a passageway, above that, lived a strange old couple called Fred and Gertie. They weren't the cleanest couple you would ever meet, the house was "loopy". Gertie worked behind the bar in a couple of the local pubs. We had only been in Paddock a couple of years before she died, not too long after that, so did Fred.

He hadn't been seen around for a while, if I remember right, it was for over three weeks. Everybody thought that he was in the hospital. He had been, but only for just one day, he had then been discharged home in the middle of that same night and nobody knew.

Dad was the one to have to kick the door in, the first thing that I remember seeing were the flies, thousands of bluebottles flew out of the front door. Then the smell, my God! It was horrendous. I had never smelt death before. I didn't really know at the time what the smell was.

I do now!

Fred had a couple of dogs in the house, they hadn't been fed, or been walked. They hadn't been out for nearly a month, they had therefore had to help themselves to some "long pig" as the cannibals call humans. They were usually looked after by his sister when he was in hospital.

It wasn't nice! I saw things that day that I'll never forget. I was only eight.

Once the house had been cleaned and all done up. Ada, the mother of George, a local painter and decorator moved in.

Above them were Edna and her daughter Diane. On the very rare occasion that mum and dad went out, Edna, or as we three called her aunty Edna would look after us. Her daughter Diane, then became one of my younger sister Diane's Godparents.

The next house was a strange house in the corner. At the back, it had a door and some steps, nothing else. There wasn't even a window. The house was a large wedge shape on the corner of two streets. It had two bedrooms and a box room, just big enough for a single bed and nothing much else. The front of the house had a curved wall, it was the full ninety degrees of the corner.

A widow, called Milly lived there with her two sons Stuart and Keith. When the boys left home, Milly married Philip, he had a daughter Susan.

Stuart used to deliver bread for Colin's bakery across the road. During the school summer holidays I occasionally went with him on his early morning deliveries. The smell of fresh bread was gorgeous, but in a little van, it could be overwhelming and sometimes made me feel sick.

The next three houses in the back yard were at the top of the steps, and along a verandah. They were actually situated in the next street.

In the first house down lived an elderly couple Doris and Frank. Next door to them originally was an elderly spinster on her own called Tilley. After she died, another widowed elderly lady moved in. Clara, she was aunty Clara to Kenneth the chemist. Shortly after, her brother John was widowed and he moved in with her. The last house in the corner of the yard was another old couple Mary and her husband, he was Tilley's brother Derek. He also died not long after we had moved in, Mary lived there for many years on her own. My sister Lindsay and I used to help out most of our neighbours with bits and bats of local shopping.

Across the road at the end of Lowergate was a very old lady, Frances. I did a lot of shopping for her. When she was 95 she had a fall at home, unfortunately she broke her hip. Following that injury, Frances never came out of hospital again.

Nine years in St. Luke's Hospital, she was 104 years old when she died. Her latter years were a sorry existence. She was unable to get out of bed unassisted, she would be lifted out into a chair in the morning, and then put back to bed at night.

I remember how clear she was in her mind though. In her own words, she described it "as living on a train, that was stationary". But when she was put back into bed and the sides were put up, "the train would set off into what seemed to be a never ending featureless tunnel".

The landlord of the Angel Pub at Paddock, was Leonard, along with his wife Mary. They had a large boxer dog, Butch. They retired, in 1979. Then ex Huddersfield Town player, Bob and his wife Pat took over. In 1989 the pub was then taken over by Brian and his wife Elaine.

Brian was related to me, the exact relationship to him and his brother Harry, I have no idea. Their dad was brother to my uncle Norman, who married my aunty Joan, she was mum's sister. Brian and Harry, were cousins of my cousins Geoffrey and Philip.

If you know what the family connection is, please tell me.

When we moved to Paddock, the landlord of the Royal Oak was called Stephenson, (I never knew his first name). He was replaced by ex policeman Alan and his wife Sylvia in 1973. They had two daughters and a son, Dawn, Wayne and Deborah.

When Frank the electrician retired, Tetley's Brewery bought the shop, and extended the pub into it. Even though the pub was then next door to mum and dad's, the soundproofing that had been installed, made it a lot quieter than before. Worries that mum and dad had, were unfounded.

New School.

Starting later in January of 1966, I went to Paddock Junior School. I clearly remember some teachers there. The headmaster was Mr. Richardson, replaced by

Mr. Chambers when he had retired. There was Mrs. Mellor, Mrs. Hubbard and Mr. Singleton.

I had friends there called Andrew, David W, Billy, Michael C, Michael M, David H, Neil, Helen, Tracy, Sharon, Paul K, Paul S, Paul M, Barry, Mohammed, Abdul, Guy, Tommy, Trevor and Jonathon, just to name a few.

Abdul always greeted everyone with "Salaam Alaikham" We had to respond "Wa Aalaikham Salaam". I think I got that right. I believe it means peace be with you, and the reply, you be with peace.

We went to London with Paddock school once, I was in the third year then. It was my first school trip and my first experience of London. We went for three days and two nights. We were on a coach trip and saw all the general sights. Including a day trip to London Zoo. I shared a room with two other lads, Trevor and Jonathon. Jonathon fell on a slide in the zoo and broke one of his front teeth, he kept us up all that night, he was in such pain.

Playing Hooky!

I only ever got the guts to "leg it" off school for one afternoon, what a disaster. David and myself decided to not go back after school dinner. We crept out of the dining hall building, which was across the road from the school and upstairs, above the youth club. We went a hundred yards down the road to where the railway line runs under Branch Street.

We scrambled down the banking at the side of the bridge, to a little ledge where we could sit and watch the trains.

We had only been there five minutes, when David fell off the ledge and split his head open.

A quick sprint back to school, the teachers fussed so much over David's cut that we hadn't even missed the school bell. Nobody ever knew.

I didn't try that again!

CHAPTER 3.

OUR FAMILY.

Another sister, Diane.

When we moved to Paddock, mum was already heavily pregnant with her third child, my youngest sister Diane.

Diane was born at home on mums 34th birthday, it was on the 1st of March 1966. It was a planned home birth, they had a bed downstairs and at that time they had an open fire in the kitchen cum living room, it was an ideal setting.

A community midwife arrived at the house when the need arose.

Dad's older sister, my aunty Winnie was also there every step of the way.

Aunty Winnie had eight children of her own. George, James, Eileen, Terry, Colin, Valerie, Barry and Susan. We as a family drifted apart, and don't see much of any of them now.

Sadly, Aunty Winnie died of cancer, just three weeks before grandad Firth gave up his fight for life. Auntie Winnie's husband was called McGregor Hirst, or as we knew him uncle Mac. Uncle Mac, cousins George, Terry, Valerie and Barry are now no longer with is.

When Eileen still lived in Huddersfield, we would see her at least once or twice a year. Colin and his wife Marlene lived down at the bottom of Paddock, we would see them knocking about now and again. I have seen Susan occasionally through work, but not for a while though.

Uncle Bill, Auntie Sheila and Cousin Alan.

Every year, one way or another. We either went to Uncle Bill's or he came to us, to watch the F.A. Cup Final, it was just the same for the rugby league Challenge Cup Final. Whoever's house, they never missed.

One year, 1966 was to be a special year. Yes it was the World Cup, held in England. The big day arrived, and in the final it was England v West Germany. I have special memories of dad, uncle Bill and me sat in our front room, glued to the tele.

The television was quite large and extremely bulky, none of your big and flat screens then and it was only only black and white!

I seem to remember that we had just borrowed a big twenty six inch television. Our own, was only a twelve inch one, tiny!

Frank next door loaned the big one to dad just for the final.

It was a gripping game, two each at full time. Then extra time, and another two goals for England. England won 4-2, fantastic!

I will never forget that day, and I actually heard and remember Kenneth

Wolstenholme's famous words live on television. "Some people are on the pitch, they think it's all over". Geoff Hurst scored his third goal, in injury time, "it is now!"

Fantastic!

The end of game celebrations will always stick in my memory. Particularly a completely exhausted Nobby Stiles, socks around his ankles, dancing around with the "Jules Rimet Trophy". He had half of his teeth missing, but his grin said it all.

England's football team had won the World Cup.

On Boxing Day, when we were all small, we always used to go to Uncle Bill and Aunty Sheila's in Thornton Lodge for the day. We always had a salad for tea, a bowl of salmon on the table and that was the first time that I remember having brown bread.

Their son Alan would be there, he was a little bit older than me. We would play games, cards, it was always Newmarket for pennies. Dad always told me to pay uncle Bill by putting the penny flat on the table, and not to give it to him in his hand. The reason being, uncle Bill had lost the tip of his middle finger in an accident many years ago, but the nerve was still there. He used to struggle like mad, his middle finger going ten to the dozen trying to pick the penny up. Sick, but funny.

Alan grew up into a proper hippy, I remember his wedding at Huddersfield Register Office. He married a Welsh girl called Gerry, (I think short for Geraldine, although I have never heard her being called any other). Alan was dressed in a white suit, he had very long fair hair at the time, and a beard to match. Now like me, he has hardly any hair and sometimes sports a goatee beard.

Once married, they moved into a house at Netherthong, on the hillside above Holmfirth. They still live there now.

They were blessed with two children, a little boy Stefan and a little girl called Delyth.

Uncle Bill and aunty Sheila eventually left Thornton Lodge, and they moved to a ground floor flat near to where Alan and Gerry were, above Holmfirth. It was the same street, about a hundred yards away round the corner.

Uncle Bill had become disabled, and had great difficulties walking, I think it was due to diabetes. It had caused him all sorts of complications, and eventually he had to have both of his legs amputated above the knees. He always had a wonderful beaming smile whenever we visited. I don't know how he was in private, but he never let us see him feeling down.

Uncle Bill had fought with the Gurkhas in World War 2, and I always remember that he had been given an original kukri knife.

We played two other games regularly with them. One was a quiz based board game, it was called Magic Robot. You were asked a question, the robot was then stood on a mirror in a circle of answers and you would point it's pointer to the answer that you thought was correct. When you let go, the robot would let you know if you were right by spinning around and then pointing to the correct one.

There was also another game called Tell Me. That was a little disc that you had to spin. There was a hole in the disc, it was spun around on top of a plate with the alphabet on. You then picked a card with a question on it, your answer had to begin with the letter that the spinning disc had revealed.

I recently bought one of them from Amazon, it cost me £8.99, and it's rubbish, it's made of a cheap plastic. I wasted my money, I'll have to look around antique shops for an original. I have got a magic robot game as well now, I paid a staggering £1.49 for it from a charity shop, an absolute bargain is that one.

Since buying those, I have managed to track down a better Tell Me, it's an original metal one, much better quality and it was only £5.99. Not only that, I found a brand new Magic Robot for under a tenner.

Amazon strikes again.

It was my sister Diane that had reminded me of those two old games, so I gave her the other two spare games. Although made of a much cheaper quality, I'm sure she'll have a lot of fun with them

Grandma and Grandad Firth.

We all as a family went to grandma and grandad Firth's on a Friday, after dad finished work. Grandma traditionally baked all her own bread on a Friday. She had an old black leaded cooking range in the living room, it was always highly polished with Zebo, a specially made polish for that purpose.

There would always be some extra special teacakes, little ones for us kids. Fresh out of the oven with real butter.

When any of the grandchildren went, there weren't any toys at their house. But on the sideboard at the back of the room, was a silver/chrome cruet set, it was in the shape of a ship.

Every single one of the grandchildren had played with that ship for many an hour over the years. It was only fairly recently that I was sharing the memory of it with cousin Alan.

The week after that conversation, I went to Elsecar Heritage Centre with Wendy. Where there is an Antiques Centre, it is packed with shops, alcoves and cabinets selling all kinds of curiosities. I saw "the ship", I had to have it, whatever the cost.

It was just as I remembered and it was complete. The price, a massive twelve pounds.

Get in! I had been looking for one of those for years.

Day trip with grandad.

I only ever remember one day going out with grandad Firth. That was also in 1966.

We had travelled to town on a trolley bus. As we had been walking around Huddersfield town centre, we had ended up on Cloth Hall Street.

There was a large crowd that had gathered, near to where the new Halifax Building Society was being built.

There was a super tall tower crane and everyone was pointing at it, up on top of the crane, right at the end of the jib there stood a man.

Suddenly there was a gasp and a scream from the crowd, the man had jumped, my grandad threw me over his shoulder and ran all the way down the street. He was off, he prevented me from seeing anything.

Later, almost fifty years later and after I started working for the ambulance service. I was talking to a fellow Paddocker, Thomas. He was a mechanic for the service. He worked there for an impressive 46 years before his retirement.

We had been talking about the history of the old Huddersfield Royal Infirmary. He told me that during the last few days before the new hospital had opened, any ambulance staff who wished, were given a guided tour of the new building. Trevor had attended that tour.

All areas of the new hospital were deserted.

The theatres, the casualty department, x-ray, even the wards were shown and their facilities explained to them.

Then they went down into the bowels of the hospital, they were shown the staff canteen and dining room.

Following that they went into the service area where behind the scenes, the daily running of the hospital would be taking place. The boiler house, the pathology laboratory, the laundry and the main hospital kitchens.

Down there in the sub basement was also the mortuary. All of its facilities were shown to them, including the post mortem room, the marble slabs and even the fridges were opened and shown.

All except for one. That one was occupied.

The visitors were told that in that fridge was the only resident in the hospital, he had died a couple of days earlier.

The old hospital had seen him in their A&E, but his injuries had been so severe, that they hadn't been able to save him and he had passed away. The old mortuary had already closed down, so they had to transport him up to the new one.

That man, they were told, had committed suicide. He had climbed to the top, and then jumped off a tower crane on Cloth Hall Street, Huddersfield.

How strange, what a coincidence.

My first solo shopping experience.

As I got a bit older, I believe I was nearly ten years old, I occasionally went to town for my grandad Firth.

He used to give me a sixpence, a tanner, nowadays that would be two and a half pence.

The bus fair was one old penny each way, I had to go to Victoria Lane, at the back of the Woolworth's store. There was an old traditional style tobacconists shop. From there, I had to get three rubber capsules, each one contained enough lighter fuel to fill a Zippo lighter once. They were a penny each. Each one would last grandad for around a week. When I got back, I could keep that last penny for myself.

No wonder I'm not a millionaire. At that age though, I felt that I wasn't far off.

Fighting beers.

Grandma and grandad Firth used to go out for a drink most nights of the week.

They would always go to the Angel pub at Paddock Head, have one drink, then they would cross the road to the Royal Oak. There they would have another and then go back to the Angel for one more before returning home.

They always sat at the same table in each pub, always near the door.

I do remember my grandad telling me to steer clear of Wilson's bitter, as was sold in the Angel and Stone's bitter as was sold in the Commercial and Tam O'Shanter pubs lower down Paddock. He said they were both "fighting beers".

As I got older and able to drive, I would have loved to have been able to take grandad Firth to some of the pubs that I had been to and to try some of the real ales that I have found and enjoyed. I am sure that he would have been in his element.

I would occasionally go to the shop for grandma Firth after grandad died, I used to go to Mrs. Kale's off license in Longwood Road, a little corner shop and get her a couple of pint bottles of Guinness. She would have one a day, for just about the rest of her life. When I got back with them, she always made me have a small glass. She said it would do me good. I hated it, actually I still do. I cannot stand the stuff.

Everlasting soles.

During his working life, grandad Firth worked on the roads. I'm not sure of his actual job, but he was part of a gang of road construction workers. He wore heavy leather and wooden clogs, originally they were fitted with irons underneath (almost like a horse shoe), to work in.

He told me that one of his jobs was the resurfacing of Bradley Road, from the top to the bottom. That must have been in the late nineteen forties.

Bradley Road was unusual in construction, I wonder if perhaps we should go back to that method, but who am I?

The surface was made of old cobbles.

Most cobbles or "sets" were made of granite, really hard wearing, but it was a really rough surface to drive on.

Bradley Road was made of wooden sets. Solid oak cobbles that had been set with the grain pointing upwards, into the surface.

They were that tightly packed together, that if any water had got into the surface, the wood would swell. They would be compressed against each other so much that it would squeeze the water right back out again, ingenious.

The only version of a road in Huddersfield now with wooden sets, is a short length of road near to Lloyds bank in Huddersfield Town Centre, it is called Chancery Lane. Have a look before some council boffin gets rid of them.

Somebody had gone one better though with Bradley Road, because it was used as a coaching road. At some stage, to deaden the sound from the horses hooves and the metal wheel rims of the coaches. It had been decided to cover the wooden sets with a thick layer of rubber. Each one of the sets had an individual cap on.

The road surface was due to be covered in the more modern tarmacadam, (Tarmac) like most roads nowadays. That where grandad came in.

As the men had dug up the sets, they had also removed the rubber from the tops.

The wood had gone home to burn on their open fires. Now, the rubber, could that be any good to anybody?

One of the gang had an idea. Rubber was replacing leather on the soles of shoes, perhaps they could replace the irons on the bottom of their clogs, with a non slipping rubber. One set, had enough rubber to sole one clog, perfect.

The job was done, every man on their gang and every gang that they could contact, got rubber soles for their clogs. That rubber was around a half inch thick in the middle, but tapered off to each corner. That gave a natural rock to the clogs as the man walked. He became silent, not the usual ringing of the irons as he walked. His clogs suddenly had a good grip as well.

Fantastic, recycling in the making!

Grandad had a great pile of those rubber tops at the bottom of his garden. As you can imagine, that rubber was there to protect the road surface from the wear of the traffic. I know the amount of traffic then, was nothing near what there is now. Once it was placed on the sole of a clog, the rubber never needed to be replaced, they would last forever.

The only time that grandad ever had to replace one, was when he had been stood near some hot coals. Some cinders had melted into the bottom of his clog.

Between them, grandad's road gang could have resoled every pair of clogs in Yorkshire no doubt!

The road stretched from Bradford Road at the top, all the way down to Leeds Road at the bottom, at least a mile and a half long and it was one of the widest roads in Huddersfield.

Fractured skull.

One of the other jobs that grandad Firth worked on with his gang, was the large paddling pool at Ravensknowle Park, in Moldgreen. It was a large feature of the park, and could be seen just over the low wall from Wakefield Road. A large stone feature, with a concrete base, made in sections and then fitted together. It had a fountain in the middle, not dissimilar to the one at Greenhead Park. It has since been removed and is part of a larger grassed play area.

The gangs in those days were paid for a job on completion. They would put in a tender, and then agree to a price for the job. That fee would then be paid whether the job took one week or two. The good gangs could rattle the jobs off and earn the most money. The job had to be done to a good standard of course, they wouldn't get paid for shoddy work. That was the case with the pool. They had finished the job early and were paid handsomely.

As was tradition, on finishing a big job, they would all go to the local pub to celebrate its completion. They went to the Stag, a Tetley's house just down Wakefield Road, at Waterloo. When it came to going home, they would all pile onto the back of the truck, and then get dropped off one by one at home. He told me that there was about a dozen of them in his gang.

That time tragedy struck, I think a little too much Tetley Bitter had been flowing and the legs of some of the men in the truck had gone rather wobbly. So much so, that three of them including grandad fell out of it. They were not far from the new University buildings at Shore Head, it was as they went round the roundabout.

A couple had got broken bones, but grandad came off worst, he managed to get a fractured skull. It had him off work for a while, but in his own words he was "a bit thick headed then, and no harm done". He was back at work before too long.

Bred them tough in them days!

CHAPTER 4.

LOCAL EARLY MEMORABLE EVENTS.

Longwood Sing.

There is local tradition on the hillside above Longwood. Each year there is an annual "sing". It still takes place in the man made "amphitheatre" that was built specially for the first event in 1873. It was then rebuilt in 1930. It is situated very close to the famous Longwood Tower, or Nab End Tower as it should really be known.

The "tower" is actually a folly, that was built in 1861, by unemployed local woollen mill workers.

The annual event, would attract people from near and far. There would be an orchestra at the bottom on the main platform. The first row of the concrete seats would be cushioned and occupied by invited dignitaries, local MP's and councillors.

Behind them would be several rows taken up by members of local Churches and schools, to form a choir. Then all around, members of the public would gather on the hillside to watch and join in the singing.

The proceedings would start, with a short blessing by the vicar of Longwood, maybe the Vicar of Huddersfield and from various other religious denominations. There would then be a speech by the invited guest, who would officially announce the start of the performance.

When I was a nipper, we as a family used to go every year to watch. We would walk up to Longwood, then take the path between the Rose and Crown Pub and the Church, we would climb all the steps through the trees up to the top. So that we could watch and join in.

Oops!
It was September 1965, as usual I was full of beans, I never, ever stopped running around, I had untold energy back then. I don't know where it went, but when it went it never came back!

I was running up and down the last couple of sections of the stone steps leading up to Longwood Tower. It was on one of my downward journeys, I ran straight into a very smartly dressed man smoking a pipe.

Bang!

I bowled him clean over and I then ended up on the floor at the side of him. Within seconds, half a dozen men in suits came from all over to pick him up.

Never mind me. I was in shorts and I was bleeding, I had taken the skin off my knees and elbows.

Once the chap had been dusted down and made presentable again, it was him that came to see if I was ok. I was fine really, they were only grazes and he helped me to my feet. I apologised for my actions. He looked at me and said "no matter lad, I was your age once! I could fly up and down these steps as well!" He shook my hand, and I took off again back up the hill.

When I got back up to the top, mum and dad wondered what the hell had happened. I was still bleeding a bit, from the cuts and grazes. I told them what I had done, I got the usual "well bloody slow down, you'll really hurt yourself one day!"

Then everybody stood up, the orchestra played a bit of a fan fair piece. It was to signify the entrance of the dignitaries. At the front of them, there was the man with the pipe. "That's him, that's the fella I knocked over!" I cried. My dad nearly died, "you didn't did you?" He asked.

Why?

It was only our Prime Minister at the time, a local lad from Milnsbridge, Sir Harold Wilson.

For some reason, mum and dad were mortified by the event, and it was never to be spoken of again. It was as though they were so ashamed that it would ever come to light, that one of their children could have possibly caused an injury to a national statesman.

I hadn't, but they were badly affected by the incident.

Hailstones, bigger than golf balls.

One day while we were at Paddock School, the sky went dark in the middle of the day, it was July 2nd 1968.

All of a sudden the hailstones started falling, they were giant lumps of ice, even bigger than golf balls. Some of the windows at the school were getting smashed, we were all told to hide under the large wooden desks to escape the worst of it.

Then the storm stopped just as quick as it had started, it had lasted less than an hour. The school yard sloping towards Branch Street had become engorged with the hailstones, up to about three foot deep at the bottom, tapering to nothing halfway up. After a brief respite, the heavy rains started.

When I got home from school, the scene at our house was devastating, I had never seen anything like it.

The hailstones had blocked the one and only drain in the backyard. The rain water had gone into our house via the back door, it had cascaded down the cellar steps and some of it ran straight out of the front door and into the road.

Dad had had to come home from work early, he had taken the carpets up and laid them out on the garage roof to dry. That sounds daft, but at the time, there was nowhere else to put them. Even though it was still raining heavily at that stage, it would have to stop eventually.

The windows in my bedroom had shattered and showered glass all over my bed.

Guy Chapman.

One July morning in 1968, at Paddock Junior school assembly. It was just before the summer holidays.

The headmaster Mr. Richardson, announced that he had some bad news for all of us. Tragically one of the pupils who was a friend of mine, Guy Chapman, of Paddock, had died.

He didn't tell us the part that Guy's mother had committed suicide, and she had also taken the lives of her children, Guy and his two younger sisters.

She had gassed them all using fumes from the oven. It was in the days of coal gas, it was highly toxic/poisonous. That is why we now have the newer safer, natural gas in all our gas appliances.

James Mason.

For Christmas in 1968, amongst my presents, I had been given some book tokens for W.H. Smith on John William Street in Huddersfield. The shop was then almost opposite where McDonalds is now.

I went into the shop on one of the first days in January of 1969.

One of the books that I had been interested in was The Story of Huddersfield by Roy Brook. It was to celebrate the Centenary of Huddersfield. The story of a hundred years of the Huddersfield County Borough.

That book with its local history, features and maps. Helped me through many many years of school work and research in later life. Even today. All for the amazing price of 45 shillings, or £2.25p in today's money.

As I was in the queue to purchase my book. I noticed in front of me, a tall, very distinguished man with a grey beard wearing a long brown camel haired coat. His voice was instantly recognisable. It was the late great Huddersfield born actor James Mason.

I asked him to sign my new book, he did so willingly. He told me that I had made a remarkable choice of book to purchase.

I still have the book, the cover is well worn and a bit dog eared. But it is probably the best, and most used reference book that I have ever had.

Neuralgia Pain.

When I was on my journeys on a Sunday with dad, we often went to see Gerald and his family at Honley. It would probably be once or twice every month or so, for dad to repay his debt.

We would walk to town and then catch the bus to the Alpine Garage, just before Honley Bridge.

It was on one of those Sunday morning journeys, that an incident that would then affect me for years to come, was to happen.

Dad and me were upstairs on the top deck of a double decker bus. I had claimed the front seat. I always wanted to be at the front and I would stand up there, watching the view.

We had only just set off from the Huddersfield bus station and were on our way down Chapel Hill. When a car pulled out of Milford Street, the bus driver had to brake suddenly, I fell forward and hit my face on the chrome bar that ran across, half way up the window.

I was battered, bruised and bleeding. So we returned to the bus station and went back home to Paddock. That was either late1967 or early 1968.

It would have been worthwhile putting a claim in today. In those days, claiming never happened, but "accidents" did.

All through secondary school, I used to suffer with terrible pains in my face, the left side would swell enormously. I had many repeated visits to doctors, they put it down to neuralgia, nerve pain.

It went on for many years, every three or four months or so. I had to take strong painkillers, and use heated salt bags pressed against my face, to ease the pain.

The incident on Chapel Hill, had long been forgotten.

It was shortly after moving to Lindley in 1982, that I finally went to see a dentist. It was a Mr. Breare, he and his wife had shared a dental practice near to the Bay Horse roundabout.

I hadn't been to a dentist since going to the school dentist at the Civic Centre. Probably not since my accident, around 1967 or '68, it had been almost fifteen years.

Mr. Breare did the works, a full MOT as a new patient. I needed nineteen fillings, and four extractions. He must have been wringing his hands with delight.

He did some x-rays as part of the routine examinations, he told me that he was shocked. When he showed me the x-rays, there were broken bits of teeth all along my lower left jaw line. He asked me if I had ever been badly beaten up, as they were signs of a very serious, but also very old injury.

I couldn't remember the bus accident, at the time.

I did tell him about the neuralgia pain that I had suffered from. He asked me if they had ever done any x-rays in the past. He was surprised when I hadn't had any done.

He told me that some of the bits were rotten and infected, that they all looked like bits of root belonging to my first teeth. My second or adult teeth had grown through and between the set of old roots and no wonder I had been in severe pain.

Each time that the infection had flared up, it had caused my face to swell up and I would have had many abscesses all along my jaw.

I had to go to hospital for the infected bits removing, they really had to dig deep. It was an awful ordeal, but, when my jaw and gums had healed, all of the neuralgia pain had stopped.

I have been to the dentist religiously for every six month check up ever since then. I hate going, but after what I had been put through, I didn't want to go through it again.

It was only when I mentioned the hospital treatment to mum and dad, that they had reminded me of the incident on the bus.

CHAPTER 5.

GROWING UP.

Off to big school.

I took my eleven plus exams at Paddock Junior School, out of my year group only six boys passed. Two went to King James' at Almondbury, the other four, including myself went to New College at Salendine Nook.

At New College, I got to know a lad in my class Gavin, we became life long good friends.

There, I found that my sporting ability was very limited. The school loved cross country running, I hated it. They played rugby union, I always got crushed in the scrum. Soccer, I loved it. But unlike my dad, I had two left feet. Being small though, I could sprint. So as far as running went, the 100 metre sprint and hurdles were my absolute limit.

It was then that I found that I was good at hockey, really good, I managed to play for my school and county.

Gavin was my training partner, we played really well together and we practiced every night after school. We were seen by our nightmare teacher, Mr Tom, he was our Latin teacher. Generally, nobody really liked him, he was a very imposing figure with a violent reputation.

He had been the Scottish International hockey team's goalkeeper, and took us under his wing, he really helped. He wasn't such a bad bloke after all.

The Head was another Mr Tom and his deputy Mr James.

Travelling to school I was with some older lads, Peter, Graham, Kevin and Bohdan. We would catch the Newsome - Lindley bus. It was locally called the cross country bus. It would travel from Newsome via Lockwood, Crosland Moor, Milnsbridge, Paddock, Quarmby, Oakes, and then on to Lindley, before doing the reverse journey.

We all got on near to Royds Hall Printers at the bottom of Quarmby Road, then we would get off on Tanyard Road at Oakes. We walked on Wheatfield Road and at the end, instead of the long walk around the streets to the main school entrance. We would hop over one perimeter garden wall, and we were there. If the man saw us, my God did he go mad.

It was a daily quest for us to avoid him.

Paper round.

When I was a young lad. I think I started when I was eleven years of age, I started my paper round. John owned the Post Office and Newsagents shop in Church Street at Paddock.

I was offered the choice of any one, or if I wanted, all three of the following. Six days a week starting at 5:30am, or six days a week early evenings anytime before 6:00pm. Or the final choice was 6:00am on a Sunday.

I just couldn't bear the thought of having to get up at 4:45am everyday, I stayed after school regularly doing hockey practice, so that ruled out the evenings. I opted for the Sunday morning.

It suited me, and put a few pennies in my pocket. Within six months, I was delivering four individual paper rounds around the local streets of Paddock. Come rain or shine, every Sunday morning, I was up and about. I really enjoyed it, I was always happy when I was walking.

The only problem for me, was that I was very small for my age and I mean small. When I started as a Cub Scout Leader later on, some of the kids were bigger than I was. They all called me "Mini" a nickname that stuck with me for many years in Scouting circles.

At the wedding of the main Cub Scout Leader, Malcolm. We formed a guard of honour for the happy couple. In the photo's, it showed clearly that some of the cubs were a lot taller than me.

To really put it in perspective. I was so small, that when I left school at sixteen.

I was only four foot ten inches tall (147.3cm), and I only weighed four stones and ten pounds (29.9kg), figures that I will never forget.

How the hell did I get to over sixteen stones this year? My God!

Why did my size matter for a paper round?

Well, I never had a paperboys bag. I had to carry each round as a bundle under my left arm, all of them numbered in order of delivery. I removed them one at a time from the top of the bundle which was nestling against my side.

At that time, the Sunday papers were just starting to add colour supplements to their editions, that meant that my bundle was getting bigger.

I was advised by my predecessor Stuart, (stepson of Ernie, one of my future ambulance service colleagues) to get a different coat and to get a traditional fishtailed parker.

Then, if I grabbed hold of the left hand tail, I could put the full newspaper bundle underneath my arm, my "reach" had increased by a mile.

Brilliant.

That then had to be the coat I wore for that job and nothing else, due to the very large black mark all down the left side of it from the printers ink that rubbed off as I slid each paper out.

I did that until I started my apprenticeship at sixteen, then I handed over the round to my good mate Paul, my Assistant Patrol Leader from Paddock scouts, a friend for many years.

Paul.

Paul was a hyperactive kid, always on the go. He had the cheesiest smile you have ever seen, it was permanently etched on his face.

He got married and had a daughter. He managed a very successful pub on the outskirts of Huddersfield for a few years.

Then sadly, for whatever reason, a deep dark cloud loomed over him. He disappeared into the deepest darkest depths of despair, depression and alcohol.

He lost everything including his home, his wife and his daughter.

He only very rarely appeared out of his black hole, he was brilliant when he did, but he would drop back down again very quickly.

He sadly decided whilst on a shock visit to America, to take his own life. It was devastating for everyone who knew him, especially his mum and sister. They had been by his side without fail through his dark days, so sad that they weren't able to be with him at the end.

God bless Paul, I really hope you are in a brighter place now mate.

Holiday time in Bridlington.

July 25th 1970. All of the family, mum, dad, Lindsay, Diane and me, went off for a week, I think it was Diane's first holiday. We went to Bridlington for a weeks self catering in a self contained flat. I remember some things about this one. We spent a lot of time on the beach, the flat wasn't far away.

The one thing that let us down, there wasn't an indoor swimming pool then. The weather was fine for the full week, but some of the days it was too cold to go in the sea. An indoor pool would have been a great addition.

10th Paddock Scouts.

When I was twelve, nearly thirteen years of age. My school friends Kevin and Bohdan encouraged me to join the 10th Huddersfield, Paddock Scouts.

That was unknowingly then, to be the start of a journey that would be the major foundation stone for the rest of my life.

Shortly after joining the scouts, my cousins Philip and his older brother Geoffrey supported me. They both had a long and happy connection with the 43rd Crosland Moor scout group. Between them, they gave me lots of badges to start making a camp fire blanket.

They also gave me some of my first camping and outdoor clothing as well.

Including a couple of wind cheater jackets. They were made of a very lightweight wind and waterproof material and could be rolled up small, or screwed up, whatever and stuffed into a rucksack pocket. They pulled on over the head and were hooded. They had a large zipped map pocket on the chest, with two smaller pockets for the hands. I was so disappointed when I grew out of them, they were the best outdoor jackets that I have ever owned.

The leader of Paddock Scouts, always known as "skip" was a lovely gentleman by the name of Ken.

He was the husband of mums best friend at Denis and Brenda's green grocers shop Joyce, he was also the father of David. Ken had two assistants, Terry and Peter.

When Ken retired, Terry took over as Group Scout Leader. We then had Cliff join us as an assistant leader.

I made many friends at scouts including Paul, Nigel, Stephen, Steven, Chris, David (Kevin's brother), Melvin, Richard, and many others.

We went camping, hiking, and learning many of the skills required to be able to fend for ourselves.

Terry was the first person to teach me first aid, who would have known how that could have become such a major factor in my later life.

Every year we had a week long scout camp, always during the spring bank holiday. Wherever we went camping, it was never an organised, or official campsite. We always stayed on a farm. To get there, we had the use of some unique transport. It was ideal at the time, but would never be allowed now.

Terry was a director at Shaw's Pickles, in Huddersfield, we would use the pickle wagon to travel in. We went all over the country in that wagon. It had sides that folded up to around two foot six inches high. For safety, we had some extra panels that would fasten on with a toggle system.

We would put all of the equipment, tents, gas bottles, personal kit, everything, at the front of the wagon against the back of the cab and then we would sit on wooden benches all around the edge of the back. That was always an adventure in itself. Rain or shine, we travelled in the open sided wagon. I am so glad that it had a roof fitted. It was also fitted with side curtains, we could slide them on if it rained.

As we always camped on a farm, it was then a tradition with us. That for one of the days, the whole troop would offer their services and help the farmer for the day.

It was 1973, we were camping in Wales at St. Asaph, I was fourteen. It was my turn for an unexpected trip to hospital. To help the farmer, we were given the job of erecting vertical fence posts, ready to have a roll of wire netted fencing applied.

It was an extremely warm day, the sun was cracking the flags. We had all been hard at it from eight thirty in the morning, knocking the stakes in all around the perimeter of a large field. It got to about three thirty in the afternoon, then apparently I started talking jibberish, nowt new there. I was shaking, almost like an epileptic seizure, then I collapsed.

A trip in an ambulance for me. I had suffered from severe heatstroke, I had not been taking in anywhere near enough fluid and so had become dehydrated.

After spending four hours on intravenous fluids, I was deemed safe and well enough to return to camp. No more fence posts for me.

Once in 1974, whilst staying at Walter's farm at St. John's in the Vale near Keswick in the Lake District. Which was a regular haunt of ours, it was hay making time. The crops had been cut and dried, all the hay bales were laid where the baling machine had left them the day before. Walter wanted us to collect them and stack them in the barn.

Another new adventure. He had a large tractor with an even larger flat backed trailer. We were to take turns in driving the tractor around the large flat field, collect as many bales as we could onto the trailer, then drive them to the end of the field. There one of the adults would take over the driving and continue up to the barn, we weren't aloud to drive on the road, even if it was only a couple of hundred yards. The kids then all piled on top of the bales onto the trailer for that short journey.

Yes, each and every one of the kids had a spell of driving a tractor, where else could you get that.

We then stacked all the bales in the barn, under the close supervision of Walter the farmer.

All was going well until the fool of the group, Paul, jumped from one stack of bales to another. He hadn't seen the roof joist. Bang!

His head cracked into the beam and split his forehead.

A trip to A&E for some stitches.

On a farm in 1975, on the North Yorkshire Moors above Scarborough. Not far from Goathland (Aidensfield), the village where they filmed the long running police TV series "Heartbeat". The weather was absolutely atrocious, it rained, then more rain and high winds.

That time it was the turn of Steve, to have a trip to A & E. Steve, a nice lad, he was not the sharpest knife in the box at the time. But he was blessed with sheer determination. He was given a task using knots and lashings, and he was going to complete it no matter what the weather threw at him.

All the tents had become flooded, most of us were sat in the back of, or even underneath the Pickle Wagon. Anywhere to keep dry. Steve carried on, despite being told numerous times to give it up. He wouldn't, he ended up in hospital with mild hypothermia. He from then on became known as Bionic, it has stuck with him ever since.

Another year in 1976, on Walters farm again in the Lake District. Linda, married to one of the leaders Peter, fell and broke her ankle. That time an ambulance journey to Carlisle Hospital.

I became an assistant patrol leader at Paddock, and then I led Tiger patrol myself, before becoming Paddock's one and only senior patrol leader. Finally leaving the scouts, and joining the venture scouts at the 43rd at Crosland Moor.

During my time with the venture scouts, I was helping Malcolm, Cub Scout leader at Paddock. I did that for some years. Jane and Annette from the Ranger Guides came to help. Annette married my friend Richard. They had young children when she died suddenly, she was only in her mid thirties.

Jane eventually took over from Malcolm for a few years and then became a District Leader herself under District commissioner for Cub Scouts, my cousin Philip. Eventually when Jane became a District Leader, one of our ambulance managers Jean, took over the Cubs.

Unfortunately Paddock Scout Group folded early in the new century, and so merged with Milnsbridge Scout Group. There used to be eleven groups in the Colne Valley, the number of groups have diminished to six. The remaining ones are thriving, with the numbers of children increasing. It seems to be the adult leaders that they are short of.

I did a lot of hiking with either the scouts, or my cousin Philip, long distance ones as well. The Lyke Wake Walk, Coast to Coast. I even did the Pennine Wa. My only regret, is that I never got the chance to do it all in one go. I did it in many short sections over the years.

I heard through the grapevine, that a new walk around Huddersfield was being launched, I had to tell Philip. It was then with him, that we took part in the Cuckoo Walk around Marsden Moor, approximately twenty miles of good hard slog.

We were the first people to officially take part, and subsequently complete the walk. For that, we were awarded certificates numbered two and three. Of course number one being held by the walk originator, a Marsden Scout Leader named David.

There was a cuckoo on the emblem, complete with woolly hat, scarf and walking boots. It was surrounded by the reef knotted rope symbol associated with the Scout Movement.

On the reverse of the certificate a poem written, and had to be read, in a broad Yorkshire accent.

"Tha's walked ovver t'moors along this 'ere course, ovver peat bogs 'n bracken, 'n eather 'n gorse, to certify that, well it fills mi wi glee, for tha's dun t'cuckoo walk, well dun thee".

Then there followed a short description of the "legend of the Marsden Cuckoo". How the local people were led to believe, that if they managed to capture a cuckoo, they would be able to hang on to spring all year round.

They supposedly built a tower around the nesting cuckoo, but it simply flew out over the top. Legend says that one of the men said that it would have worked, but that the tower "twas nobbutt a couple o' courses o' bricks too low!"

Paddock Village Hall.

I also helped my dad (minimally, but heart and soul) with the men of Paddock, to create the village hall from a run down Church. It was whilst working on the building of the concert stage, that I injured my knee, damaging my cartilage on my left leg.

The men of Paddock did some tremendous voluntary work on the conversion. The women did too, they made all the soft furnishings themselves. Mum's responsibility was all the curtains. They were all the same, made of a very heavy, grey woollen fabric, with a series of four pastel coloured horizontal stripes near to the bottom.

Some of those curtains were massive, particularly the stage curtains, and the ones for the high old style Church Windows at the Church Street end of the building.

I was chosen to present flowers to the Mayoress of Huddersfield, following completion, at the opening ceremony in 1969.

Paddock village hall hosted all kinds of functions, community groups, and anyone who wished to hire some of its facilities.

It held the monthly meetings of the Paddock branch of the old age pensioners organisation. It was an hour of discussion, regularly attended by fifty or sixty members, followed by a short half to one hour concert by invited artistes.

I used to climb a Jacobs ladder to a vantage point above the concert stage, from there I used to operate the opening and closing of the curtains, and the lighting systems for each of the performances.

Diane horsing about.

Another family day out, in 1972 I think I would have been thirteen then. Was a day trip by train to Southport. Well known for the massive expanse of beaches. Once the tide went out, the sea appeared to be miles away.

I really remember the "sand yachts", similar to a large go-cart, with a single large sail. Those things were driven and raced along the beach at ridiculous speeds. Now instead of sails, they are still powered by the wind, but are harnessed by using large kites attached to many long strings.

Another thing I remember of Southport, they didn't have donkeys, they had pony rides. My sisters Lindsay and Diane both went on a ride. It started off well, a group of people were walking with the children sat on the ponies, similar to a donkey ride elsewhere. Mum, dad and me were stood on the promenade watching.

For whatever reason, I can't remember, but something spooked the ponies and they got a bit restless. The one carrying Diane set off, bucking and kicking, out towards the sea. When it hit the waters edge, it started spinning round and bouncing.

Diane was still clinging on to its back.

I remember jumping off the prom and chasing down the beach after the pony, eventually catching up to it at the waters edge and grabbing hold of it. Diane was able to get off safe and unharmed. She would only have been about five years of age at the time. I think she still has a fear or dislike of horses. She obviously remembers that incident far clearer than I do.

She has a love of donkeys though!

CHAPTER 6.

MEMORABLE TIMES WITH MY DAD.

A day spent on Morecambe Bay.

Later in the year 1972, the family went on a holiday to Heysham, near Morecambe. We stayed at a guest house, run by my cousin Michael and his wife Marjorie and their two boys. Michael worked at the nearby Heysham Power Station.

It was to be a strange holiday, we were only there for about three or four days. My only real memory of it, was of a full day spent on Morecambe Bay with Michael. He had a motor boat, he let me drive it around the bay for what seemed like hours. Dad was with us. Michael was sprawled out at the back of the little boat, his feet dangling over the edge.

When it was time to go, we had some major problems. The sun had been beating down all afternoon and it had been reflected off the water. It had severely burnt the soles of Michael's feet. He was in agony, he couldn't stand on them, let alone walk.

We had a devil of a job hitching the boat back on to the trailer. I believe, that dad, who hadn't even got a real current driving license had to drive us back to the guest house.

The only previous driving that he had done, was whilst on his National Service, it was only an army driving license and a provisional one at that.

He had driven ambulances at the army base. Not in anger though, he would only be moving them around the base, to his place of work.

Dad had the job of repainting the Red Cross, the white background circle, and the hand written word ambulance on the side.

He had also driven a DUKW whilst in the army, a six wheeled amphibious vehicle affectionately known as a "duck".

Dad's Uncle Wilf.

Uncle Wilf, he was grandad Firth's older brother.

In his younger days, he was a circus trapeze artist and a bare knuckle fighter.

When he had left the circus, he came back to live in Huddersfield.

He had a very popular party piece, that he would perform regularly in the pubs around Turnbridge, and the Town Centre.

He was a gambling man and liked to take bets. One idea was to get himself arrested and the bet would be, how long before he would be back in the pub with a beer in his hand.

He was only a small bloke, I believe only around five foot tall. He was known as wiry at the time, thin in stature, but extreme muscles and as strong as an ox. His upper body strength, from his time on the trapeze, was phenomenal.

He could easily free himself from handcuffs, and I believe he also had a routine where he could escape from a straight jacket.

Another of his bets, would involve picking on the larger blokes in the pub and challenge them to an arm wrestle. A lot of money would change hands over the "bouts".

He wasn't a bad bloke, although he had the reputation of being a loveable rogue. He took enough money from the bets, to more than cover the cost of any of his fines.

When I knew him, he lived in some tenement flats at the bottom of Huddersfield, on Southgate. It is where students now live after a full refurbishment.

At the time, in the early sixties, they were the cheapest of cheap living. I only remember going to visit him a few times before he passed away. I would only have been five or six years old then.

It was on one of those visits with dad, it would possibly have been early in 1964, it was definitely winter time. The buildings were always in disrepair, some part of them was always surrounded by scaffolding.

The living room was furnished with a sofa, a small table and two small buffets. He owned a small radio, but no television. There was an open fire burning in the hearth, a tiled floor and he had no carpets or rugs.

The fire, was simply a builders plank burning in the fireplace. He would just give it a kick every so often as it slowly burned away. When the plank was nearly burnt, he would simply scale the scaffolding and get himself another.

Walking with Dad.
Dad and me did a lot of walking, he never had a car.

We sometimes walked to his uncle Joe's in Copley, near Halifax. We would walk from Paddock, up through Lindley to Lindley Moor, to the Wappy Springs Pub. No, not to stop. In those days, the M62 wasn't there, so we would walk down the other side and into Copley via the old "Toll Bridge". The Toll House itself, is still lived in. There is a board displaying the original prices to go across the bridge, which has recently been renovated. It stands prominently outside.

In 2016, there were horrendous rainfalls in the Calder valley. The severe flooding that followed, caused tremendous damage. Including the collapsing of the very famous and well publicised Elland Bridge. Less publicised, was the collapsing of the old bridge at Copley.

Over twelve months later, the Elland Bridge has been very publicly replaced. Not the bridge at Copley, there are still arguments as to who will pay for the repairs.

Scammonden Dam hadn't been built then either. Another treck that dad and me went on, we took the path that went from the car park of the now closed Nont Sarah's pub. We walked down the valley, which was flooded for the dam. Over the stream in the bottom, was a footbridge, at each end of which was a turnstile. That kept two different farmers animals, at their own side of the valley. We would walk over the little bridge, and then back up the other side to where the big bridge over the motorway is now.

It would not be until the drought of 1995, that the valley would be seen in its entirety again. We had booked the Scouts Activity Centre at Scammonden for a sailing weekend for Paddock Scouts.

Oops, no water!

Hundreds of tankers were ferrying millions of gallons of water from Keilder Dam in the North East, and others in the north of England, to a temporary base near to Nont Sarah's. There they unloaded their precious cargo down to what was left of the dam, via large bore pipes.

It was a huge operation to do.

Because there was no water, we had somehow managed to borrow some "carts" from Shibden Park at Halifax. They were green plastic sledges fitted with caterpillar tracks.

They were fantastic!

The kids soon found out that they could reach great speed going down the concrete slipway, normally reserved for launching the boats, before dropping off the end and landing in three foot of sloppy wet mud.

They loved it!

We had to hose the mud off them before allowing them back into the Centre.

One of the mornings, we walked to what was normally the deepest part of the dam and there was the little bridge. The turnstiles were silted up, but with a little bit of digging, both of them still rotated.

Brilliant!

In Scouting, vandalism and graffiti are absolutely frowned upon, but not that day. All the kids were encouraged, including every one of the adults, to scratch their name and or a message onto a stone under the bridge.

After all, the powers that be, promised that the drought would never happen again. Who knows when, or if, the bridge will ever be seen by people again. It shouldn't be.

There will be some shocks if it is. Some home truths were written underneath that bridge.

Storthes Hall Hospital.

Another walk, on most Sunday's for several months in the 1970's, was to Storthes Hall Hospital at Kirkburton.

My grandma Firth had suffered a fall and had broken her hip. She had then been convalescing in St. Luke's Hospital at Crosland Moor.

The building of the fifties, was one of architect Geoffrey Poulson's debacles. He had scammed many thousands of pounds from public services. On all the roofing projects that he had been involved in, he had cut corners.

Famously charging for five roof trusses, but only fitting three, pocketing the excess money. It was a major public scandal in the 70's and 80's.

When the roof had to be replaced on grandma's ward, she was transferred to

Storthes Hall. Known for being a massive, former Lunatic Asylum, then home to people with long term psychiatric illnesses.

Just after the Second World War, it was full, with nearly five thousand patients. Or inmates, as they were known then. The people, clients, service users or patients. Whatever the name, they were all vulnerable people. At the time when grandma was there, it was nearer to five hundred residents.

It was a long walk of at least eight miles each way.

Once on the wards, I as a child, was very frightened. Some of the patients/ inmates had severe mental disabilities. They paced up and down the ward, they were staring and had very strange, zombie like walks. All drug induced, known as the "Largactil shuffle".

There were long, long corridors linking all of the buildings together. The patients would walk those corridors endlessly, both day and night. It really was a most unnerving place.

Certainly not a place for sane, normal people.

Although dad was on edge, he felt really sorry for them. I remember that in those days, nearly everyone there smoked. They would be scouring the ashtrays, bins, floor and anywhere they could think of. Looking for tab ends to smoke. Dad would buy a pack of twenty untipped cigarettes from the hospital shop, he then cut each and everyone of them in half and gave them out to everyone that wanted one.

He didn't have much didn't dad, but what he had, he was very generous with.

Fox hunting.

It was on one of those walks to see grandma, that we spotted another of my pet hates. A fox hunt. I detest them! Stuck up toffee nosed prats, prancing about all over the place on horseback, thinking that they are God's gift.

We had almost got to the Golden Cock pub at Farnley Tyas, where we could see the crowd of red coated hunt followers. There was a lot of cheering and clapping, the dogs had cornered the fox. They were baying for blood.

The people that was, not the dogs.

As the dogs were ripping into the poor animal, the Master of the Hunt stepped down from his horse, he picked up the poor thing, held it aloft and then cut off its tail.

He then went up to three of the younger members, two teenage girls and a boy, he smeared the foxes blood across their faces and tossed the animal over the wall.

They all then trooped into the pub for lunch.

As we approached, the fox was still alive. It was making the most horrendous noise, almost like a baby screaming.

I couldn't resist, I climbed over the wall and I picked up the bleeding animal.

It had been ripped to shreds by the dogs, one of its back legs was completely missing.

Dad and me walked into the pub and I placed the screaming mess onto the bar, and shouted, "you forgot the rest of it!"

Bloody hell!

The whole place erupted. We were pushed, threatened and hit. At least two of the toffee nosed morons struck us with riding crops, across the face and shoulders. I thought we were going to be killed. I was only fourteen or so at the time.

As we were escorted out, I do remember the Landlord screaming at us to never come back and that we were "barred!"

That was the one and only time that I have been asked to leave a pub.

To be true to myself, I have never stepped inside the establishment ever since.

I was once actually called to attend there in an ambulance, the call was for someone under twenty years of age, with a "bruised, finger injury!"

A bruised finger, for God's sake!

I got the people in the pub to bring the patient outside. It was occupied by the same supercilious mentality of customer, nice to see that some things hadn't changed.

Although we had been battered and bruised, dad and me still had a grin on our faces when we reached grandma. Actually we were quite proud of our actions.

If only I could have got pictures.

After dad and me arrived in the pub with our "gift", the women especially, were screaming again. It was different scream then, they weren't baying for blood. No, but for the screaming, writhing and bleeding mess to be removed. They didn't want to see our surprise, firmly placed on the bar and in prime view of everyone, especially for the diners.

A special moment in my life! I miss you dad.

CHAPTER 7.

SOME OF LIFE'S LITTLE MISHAPS.

Accident prone.

When I was fourteen, in 1973. I was on my way home from school with my friend Martin, from higher up Luck Lane. We were running down the hill and I jumped over a hole in the pavement. I landed really awkwardly and I felt a searing pain in my right thigh.

Ambulances in those days were "genuinely" only called by the public for real emergencies. Not, for what we thought at the time may have ONLY been a broken leg. Martin hoiked me up onto his back and carried me down the rest of the hill to my home.

My parents agreed that I did need to visit the hospital for an x-ray. So we waited for Kenneth the chemist next door to close his shop at seven pm, he then gave us a lift.

My resulting injury actually being quite severe, it was a well and truly torn hamstring.

Hyphema.

When I had just gone 16, it was 10th January 1975. I was playing in a five a side football competition at Newsome School, for Paddock scouts.

I saw an opportunity to score a goal, I volleyed the ball with all my heart, only for the goalkeeper to punch it clear.

I was hit clean in the face with the ball, I went blind instantly, I couldn't see out of either eye.

Dad was watching me play, he and one of the scout leaders ran on to the pitch. I was immediately taken up to the casualty department at HRI. Not in an ambulance, but in a car.

I had suffered a left eye injury, known as a hyphema, that is bleeding into the anterior chamber of that eyeball. The front of the eye fills up with blood, between the iris and the lens. The total blindness, fortunately was only temporary.

Two full days though, of total blindness, it was a very frightening experience. It meant that I had to stay in hospital until the 16th.

I was bed bound and had to lay flat for three days solid, only then I was allowed to sit up. I was fitted with some extremely dark glasses, they even went around the side of my eyes, they were not unlike the welding goggles that I had seen.

There was a pinhole in the middle of each lens, to let the minimum of light in. Each day the hole was made slightly bigger. It was very difficult to come to terms with them. There was the refraction to deal with. It was ok looking at something, but if you needed to touch it, it wasn't where you expected it to be. Light was being bent, by the pinhole.

If you imagine how a stick appears when placed into clear water, it bends at the point of entry. Refraction.

My vision was like that.

So when I got my meals, the plate was on a tray over my bed, I could see it clearly, but when I tried to stick my fork into my dinner, the plate wasn't there. There was almost a six inch difference in seeing, and being.

It took some getting used to I can tell you. I had to wear the glasses all the time, for about three weeks in total.

I was told that I would probably have to wear glasses permanently, following the accident, as I had also suffered a partial detached retina on my left eye.

I needed laser surgery to reattach it.

That was done by a top eye surgeon called Mr. Wilson. I was one of the very first people to have laser eye surgery in this country, I believe I was actually the first in Yorkshire.

Whatever, it was a success, I haven't suffered any lasting effects.

Did he just wink at me?

Whilst in the eye ward, it was Ward 8 at the time, down on the lower ground floor of the infirmary.

I met another young man, he was about three years older than me. He was a trainee chef at a local Hotel and Restaurant in the Huddersfield area.

He had been in a car accident, in those days seat belts were not worn as a matter of course. (He wasn't). He had been driving his first car, following his shift at the hotel. It had been late on a freezing January night.

He lost control and crashed. As was quite common in the sixties and seventies, he had been thrown through the front windscreen of the car, suffering from the most horrendous facial injuries.

He was laid in the next bed to me.

We talked a lot, especially at night. He told me all about the crash, it was a good job he had been on his own, any passengers in the vehicle would have come off even worse than him.

He wasn't sure how many, but he had been told that he had well over 100 stitches, just in his facial wounds.

He looked a right mess. He had already been in hospital for nearly a week when I met him. By that time, most of the bruising had come out, and most of the swelling had settled.

He kept being taken down to the day clinic to have some of the stitches removed.

On the third or fourth day of my stay in hospital, I remember the doctors rounds, there was a circus of people all gathered around the bed discussing your case.

Several junior doctors and nurses, with Mr. Wilson leading the conversation and discussion. After he had made the hole in my lenses a little bigger and he was happy with my progress, the circus moved on to the bed next door.

As was traditional, they pulled the curtains around the bed to give privacy, but conversation wasn't muffled. Particularly when several people are discussing your case, every word could be heard, and clearly.

Mr. Wilson seemed concerned about some of my neighbour's injuries, particularly around his left eye. I had seen it, it had been stitched so that his eye was closed. The reason apparently was because his eyelid had been completely ripped off in the accident and it was to keep out any dirt or dust, so to prevent infection.

It was the time to think of some form of repair, it would be classed as plastic surgery.

I remember Mr. Wilson asking his entourage what they would do to reconstruct an eyelid. The responses varied, but were all deemed unsuitable.

Mr. Wilson dropped the bomb, he asked my neighbour very clearly. "Now then my young friend, when younger, were you ever circumcised?"

He must have shook his head, as I didn't hear a reply.

Next Mr. Wilson said to him. "Brilliant, that's perfect, we will do the operation tomorrow".

He then explained to all his followers that the foreskin is just about the right consistency of flesh and skin to form a new eyelid.

"There is only one thing", he told him, "there will be no eyelashes on the eye concerned". He then said to all around, "he will just be left a little cock eyed!"

He laughed loudly at his own remarks, and the circus moved off to deal with the next patient. As he passed my bed, Mr. Wilson, winked at me. He knew that I had heard every word.

They did the operation, and at the same time nearly all the rest of my new friend's facial stitches were removed. He would have to wear a flesh coloured patch over his eye for a few more days. He was discharged the day after his operation.

I have seen him since, but I didn't mention it to him. I don't know who would be most embarrassed, me or him. He still has a lot of deep scars around his face, and yes, his eye did look slightly different. It was probably down to the eyelashes issue.

Something in my eye.

I did have another injury, in 1977 and it was to the same eye.

It was when I was an apprentice at Brook Motors. We had to wear safety glasses all the time in the workshops.

I was working at a bench. I had made a cold chisel using the forge, hammer and anvil. I had then hardened and tempered it using a heating and rapid cooling process.

Following that, I was just honing the edge with a draw file, when I felt some dust on my nose. I lifted my safety glasses and brushed the dirt away with my sleeve.

Big mistake.

I must have brushed a sliver of meta into my eye.

The day after, I couldn't even open my eye. I forced the lid slightly, it was completely bloodshot, another trip to A&E. They had to put some drops in to numb the eye and to dilate the pupil. When they looked at my eye under black light conditions, the dye/drops that they put in showed the sliver of metal.

Due to the steel being in my eye. My body had tried to fight it and had formed a skin over it. It had caused severe irritation and had become infected.

The offending foreign body was removed easily in A&E, I had to wear a patch for another couple of days. My only setback, was that I needed prescription sunglasses. To wear when in bright lights for some time.

I didn't need to wear proper glasses for about thirty years, not until I was forty seven. Then it was an age thing for reading. I'd got to the stage where my arms weren't quite long enough to see the date on my watch. I got some with varifocal lenses.

I have needed them ever since.

This month April 2016, at my annual check up, I was diagnosed with the first stages of cataracts. I need to watch out, and keep my eyes safe.

I will need to wear prescription sunglasses wherever possible. I have got the type with transition lenses. They go dark extremely quickly, it's a shame that they don't return to clear as quick.

Still you can't have everything.

Next year I will get permanently dark prescription lenses.

CHAPTER 8.

––––––––––

MAKING WAVES FOR MY FUTURE.

Venture scouts.

I joined the venture scout unit at Crosland Moor in 1974.

There I made many more lifelong friends. The leaders were David, John, Patricia, and Mary.

Friends were Graham, Richard and his future wife Annette, sadly she passed away at a very young age, Christina, Christopher, Nick and Andrew T, Andrew C, Diane, Alison and Jill, Jane, Russell, Alex she went on to marry Mark, best man at my wedding, Sally, Helen, Alan and Annette, Julie, and many many others.

Other leaders within the 43rd Scout group, were Group Scout Leader Geoff, Scout Leaders Dave and John. Cub Scout Leaders Peter and Yvonne. Also based at the 43rd was Assistant District Scout Commissioner Jim. The District Commissioner was another Geoff, he was based with the 4th Golcar Scouts.

I worked hard for my Queens Scout Award, it took years of hard work and sheer dedication. It involved many expeditions, hikes, camping, first aid, leadership etc.

One of our expeditions was a life changing experience of a trip to Switzerland, two weeks under canvas, of highly exhilarating challenges never before thought of.

I was always deemed to return to Kandersteg.

We did the Three Peaks of Yorkshire in 1976. A gruelling twenty five miles or so, combined with over five thousand feet of climbing. Achieving a personal best of just over six hours, two of our party ended up suffering from heat exhaustion.

The Masters Hike around Huddersfield was an annual event that was always held in November, it was always around the Remembrance Sunday weekend. The competition started at my old school, New College. That walk had been run by the Holme Valley Scouts since the early sixties.

The route was a hard walking forty miles, from the school to Emley Moor mast, via the masts at Pole Moor, across the hills to the one at Holme Moss mast and then across the rough moorland to finish at the mast at Emley.

Then a well earned bus ride back to the school.

There were teams of four from scouting all over the country, many teams even came from abroad. A full pack on your back had to be carried at all times, with a full set of spare clothes, and support equipment including tent and sleeping bag. Just in case of emergencies.

As with the Four Inns walk, it was a team event, all four of you had to stick together for safety reasons. The time given was when the last of your team crossed the finish line.

The Four Inns walk from Huddersfield to Derbyshire, was annually over the High Peak. That was around Easter time.

Forty five miles of open moorland walking. That one had been run by the Scouting Association in Derbyshire since 1957.

Again teams of four and they set off from Holmebridge. Up to the old Isle of Skye above Meltham, an inn used to be there. Over the tops to the Old Nags Head at Edale and to the Snake Inn on the Snake Pass. Across into Derbyshire and then on to Buxton via the Cat and Fiddle Inn.

We had several camping adventures in the Lake District, including one gallivanting around the area for two weeks in an old ambulance belonging to the Cambodunum venture scouts.

That Venture Scout Unit was based at the Beechwood Cheshire Home in Edgerton. The old ambulance was driven by one of them, he was one of my old mates from Brook Motors, Paul.

Fourteen of us went on that trip, ten of us in the ambulance and four in Richard's car.

Formal school exams.

In 1975, whilst at New College, I took my GCE O levels. I got three grade C passes, in Biology, Chemistry and Engineering (Technical) Drawing and I had three at grade D. They were borderline passes in English Language, Maths and Physics.

I took two other exams, English Literature and French. Both of which I had studied for six years, and hated. It showed, I got a U grade in both subjects. A fail of such proportions that they were both registered as "unclassified".

Fatal road accident and broken dreams.

When I had been to the Venture Scouts at Crosland Moor, I nearly always got a lift home. One night in autumn 1976. Richard was giving me a lift. He had a fairly new car, it was a Vauxhall Viva.

Just as we were coming down Park Road West to join Manchester Road, that was when we heard it. A noise that cannot be mistaken for anything else.

It was the screech of tyres, tyres skidding along the road, then the loud sickening crash and breaking glass of two cars colliding.

It was only fifty yards away from us.

One car heading from Huddersfield towards Cowlersley, had to move to the middle of the road to pass a parked vehicle on the near side. Another car heading from Cowlersley from Huddersfield also headed for the middle of the carriage way, it was passing a mobile fish and chip van parked at their side of the road.

The inevitable had happened, both cars had hit each other head on. The sight was horrific, something directly out of a horror film.

Richard and I raced to the stricken vehicles. We were told that 999 had already been called, and was still being done.

The first car was totally unrecognisable, the driver had already got out relatively unscathed, he had been taken into a nearby house. The passenger though, well, that was a different story. I will, as I did then, come back to him.

The second car heading towards town, had been totally destroyed, it had virtually exploded on impact.

Don't forget, in January 1975, cars didn't all have seat belts. Never mind airbags, they hadn't been dreamed of. No crumple zones either.

It had been a full high speed head on smash.

The driver of the second car, had been turned through ninety degrees on his own seat. There was no front windscreen left, he had his face pushed up against the drivers door window. He was fully conscious, he told us that although he was trapped by wreckage, he hadn't been physically hurt.

"Please make sure that the wife is ok" he pleaded. The sight I saw next has always been there in the back of my mind. It was horrific.

Miss the next bit out if you wish, the worst bit is between the asterisks.

*******The lady, around fifty years of age, was sat in the passenger side. The dashboard and engine compartment had been forced right back into the passenger area. It was up against her chest. Her head had flopped back over the back of her seat. No head restraints were fitted either. Her neck had obviously been broken on impact. I moved around to the side, the car had been ripped apart. I could see that the lady's throat had a gaping hole across the front, she had been bleeding profusely, but it had stopped!

She was dead!

I could also see from there, the damage that body work could do. Both of her legs had been completely amputated and very roughly, at the knees.*******

There was nothing we could do for her. I couldn't tell her husband. At that time, he was blissfully unaware. Another couple were comforting him, they were distracting him all the time.

I went back to the first car with Richard. It was a two door car. The passenger had hit his head on the then none existent windscreen, his face was unrecognisable. It was full of deep, wide lacerations and he was bleeding profusely.

At that stage, he was semi conscious.

Somehow, it must have been an adrenaline rush, but I was able to yank the mangled car door open. I could see that the male also had an extremely serious abdominal injury.

The car had chrome strips, they were common in those days for decorating car body panels. (Now removed from vehicles due to the damage and injury that they regularly caused). One of them had come in through the windscreen and entered the lads abdomen just below his ribs. It had then continued through his body and was protruding out through the back of his seat.

I climbed into the back of the car to, if nothing else, support his head and neck.

To try and prevent further spinal injury. (First Aid training in the Scouts). I was also talking to him to try and keep him conscious.

That was my first true recollection of being present at any real emergency situation.

Whilst I was sat there, the ambulances arrived, two of them. The place was also crawling with firemen and police.

The first ambulanceman to speak to me, I now know was Ray, a then rookie to the job. He has since retired in 2014. He asked me if I was ok doing and carrying on exactly as I was. I was fine. I was asked to help by staying just like that.

Duly done, the fire service set to work and they cut the roof off. Surprise, surprise! Some things never change!

I was given a fire service helmet to wear for my own protection during that operation. Once the roof was off, more could be seen of his situation.

It was decided by all the emergency services, that the best option for the patient was to remove the car seat, complete with its passenger and put them both directly into the ambulance.

They would then be able to sort him out properly at the hospital.

That fascinated me at sixteen year old. I saw the haunting sight in my minds eye for many, many months afterwards. Occasionally, but rarely, some things come back and provide explanations later.

Several years later it was, nine years to be exact. I was having a drink in the Royal Oak at Paddock. A few of us from our younger days were in there. Mike, Michael, Barry, Tommy, Stephen, Paul (Mazda), John and me.

John was asking Mike about his exploits working for the ambulance service, then Mike told him that I was working for the service as well.

As he looked at me his face changed, he then made a statement that I have never heard either before or since. "Broken my dream".

He took a large drink of his beer, and then he said "shit! You have just broken my dream! I have had the same dream for nine years, you've just broken it!"

All of us were at a loss.

He then explained that he had been involved in a serious road accident, and that he had undergone major surgery on his stomach. It had taken seven hours, followed by many years of plastic surgery on his facial injuries.

He said that for some reason, one that he didn't understand. Whilst he had been in the hospital for many weeks, he had kept repeating the same dream of the accident. He was still occasionally having that dream. It had been of his time in the car, and the friendly voice at the side of him, keeping him safe.

"Bloody hell! It was you! Wasn't it?" He exclaimed, "it was you that was sat in that bloody car with me!"

From being around twelve years old, we had lost contact. That was the first time that we had knowingly met since, thirteen years had passed since last really seeing each other.

He said that he remembered it as though it was yesterday, but hadn't been able to put a name to his companion until now.

I hadn't been aware either at the time of the accident, due to his horrendous facial injuries.

It was great to be able put it to bed, it helped both of us.

How weird was that!

CHAPTER 9.

_____

STARTING WORK.

Apprentice Engineer.

On the 1st of September 1975, I started my first proper job, it was an engineering apprenticeship at Brook Motors Ltd. On St. Thomas' Road, Huddersfield.

Nick, was one of the first people I met, he started his first day with us, he was also one of the members of the Venture Scouts.

Instructors there were, Vince, Brian and Bob, Bob still lives just on the road from me now. Unfortunately both Vince and Brian have passed away some time ago.

Other new starters with Nick and I were, David, another David, Alan, Michelle, John, Michael, John, Linda, Anthony, Stephen, Kevin, Malcolm and then David from Barnsley.

Linda and Michelle were the first females to start a mechanical engineering apprenticeship at Brook Motors. They were highly regarded as a trial in engineering circles.

As much as they were a prototype and someone to watch, it didn't do them any favours. They were both made redundant at the same time as I was.

I thought I had enjoyed my time there but in hindsight, it wasn't all it was cracked up to be. I did have some good time, don't get me wrong. It just wasn't for me.

I didn't see it at the time, but my redundancy was probably the best thing that could have happened.

Wonderful thing that hindsight!

I had wanted to become a fireman when I left school, but was nowhere near the minimum size requirement.

When I had left New College on the 20th of June 1975, I was 4'10" tall, and I weighed only four stone and ten pounds. For my apprenticeship I had to have specially ordered overalls, the smallest they had available were a size 28" chest.

They were still massive on me.

They did have an industrial fire brigade at Brook Motors, who were highly regarded and were very successful in competitions with other industrial brigades.

Size was not an issue with them, there I was in my element. I did six weeks of the twelve weeks basic training that a full time fireman would have done. My time in the fire brigade at Brook's was the best.

We even got paid a retainer by the fire service.

I took part in many competitions, our team winning most of them. My best mate there was Mark, another Paddock lad. He went on to become my best man. In our team, there was also Bob, Stuart, David, Gordon, John, another John, Fire Chief Andy and his assistant Bernard, (I was at school at New College with Bernard's son Peter).

All the competitions were of a similar format with up to ten teams competing in a series of around seven events. Two teams would be running against each other in knockout heats. The prize for each event was £5 for first, £3 for second and £1 for third place. We had two teams in most events, we were good and came first and second in nearly all of them.

My God did I get drunk on the way home from the first one.

Norris was the health and safety officer at Brook Motors, also a fellow Paddocker. He once saw me assist a pedestrian, who had been knocked down on St. Thomas' Road. He was impressed by my actions, and got me enrolled on an adult first aid course.

Passing that course, entitled me to be a registered works first aider. It got me an extra one pound and fourteen pence added to my weekly wage.

Thanks Norris!

Practical jokers at Brook Motors Ltd.

I spent a large chunk of my apprenticeship, In the tool room of number 12 works. It was a large room where five of us worked. There were several large machines in the tool room. Including a large and a small lathe, there was a shaper and a grinding machine. As well as a large milling machine and three large work benches.

Raymond was the charge hand, Stanley was the labourer, then there was Jeff from Barnsley and Ian.

Ian played in a band from Huddersfield Ukrainian Club, they were called Euro Sounds. I travelled with them all over Yorkshire and Lancashire, to events. Mainly as the entertainment in various Ukrainian Clubs, or to perform at Wedding Celebrations. They were predominately a dance band.

It was at a Wedding, that we had an extremely drunken weekend at the Ukrainian Club in Edinburgh.

After redundancy, Ian left and went to live in Canada for a while. It was around twelve years I think. Then he came back to Huddersfield, as I write this, he now is a partner in a fish and chip shop at Linthwaite.

Despite my feelings, I did learn a lot at Brook's and I had a lot of fun there as well. Practical jokers the lot of us, perhaps that is where I got my warped personality and sense of humour from.

We had a man on the board of directors Stanley, what a gent. He had started at the company as an apprentice like me and then he had worked his way up. He was one of the most respected man that I have ever met. Everybody who knew him spoke of him with extremely high regard.

As an apprentice, you are expected to be the butt of all jokes and to put up with them with a smile. Or you will get hammered. "Fetch a bucket of steam, go to the stores for a long stand, get me a left handed screwdriver, ask for a tin of tartan paint, all the usual".

Stanley approved of banter in the work place, but woe betide anyone who did something that was, or could have been deemed as dangerous.

I remember I was welding the floor of a full sized steel skip, it had been laid on its side for access. Whilst I was working in it, some of the lads pushed it over trapping me underneath.

They all went off to lunch with me left inside, all of them banging on the side with hammers as they went past on the way to the canteen. They let me out straight after lunch.

When Stanley found out about it, he went mad. He eventually found two of the culprits, they were both suspended for two days without pay.

He was not averse to his own jokes and pranks either. He once came to me with a set of expertly done, engineering drawings of certain items to be made with absolute precision.

That was going to be my monthly "phase test". A task to see how I was progressing.

It took me ages to finish all the components. Then once they had all had been duly tested and measured Stanley assembled all the parts into a most bizarre shape. It was fastened together, using man made (me) nuts and bolts.

Totally hand threaded.

What was it? Only a luxury carrier for his dachshund dog.

The nose of the dog fitted in the specially made funnel, a number six morse taper. The other end a twin start left handed threaded screw, of exactly four and a quarter inches long with a softly rounded point on the end, screwed into the dogs backside. It was all completed with an ergonomically designed carrying handle.

I felt a right clown. But, it was made with exacting precision. I passed that test.

Stanley and my charge hand Raymond were helpless with laughter, they had got yet another apprentice to make one.

Christmas in Barnsley.

December 22nd 1976, that was the day of my eighteenth birthday. It would be a day that I will never forget, for several reasons. I was still working at Brook Motors Ltd. serving my engineering apprenticeship. As part of it, I had to work in lots of different departments. The particular Christmas placement, for my sins, was at the dreaded Barugh Green factory near Barnsley.

Ever since starting as an apprentice, all of us were warned about the Barnsley women. About what they like to do to young apprentices, the stories were enough to make your eyes water.

Well, there we were and at Christmas. The stories were becoming even more frightening. One of the lads that I started with Dave, he lived at Barugh Green. He and me were both on the placement together.

It was a large factory, predominantly run by women staff and most of the managers were women as well. They operated the highly dangerous winding machines. Which were well known for catching wedding rings and ripping fingers right off. The only male staff at that factory, were a couple of senior managers and one director.

We always finished at lunchtime on the last working day before any Christmas break. Even though it was only Wednesday the 22nd, that was to be the last day for 1976.

We expected to be knocking off at 13:00hrs.

As apprentices working with the women that we had been warned so much about. I can say that we had been looked after pretty well over the previous couple of weeks, what were people talking about?

We would soon find out.

It was only 12:00hrs, when the lunch break klaxon sounded.

All the machines were switched off within a minute or so. We would normally be heading off to the canteen at that point, but not that day. We were told it that "we're off to 't pub, it's tradition".

The klaxon at 12:00hrs though, that was an hour early. Dave and I were a bit lost, what was happening?

Then the shop steward, Barbara. Only a small, but loud voiced lady, who would be around her mid forties. Stood on one of the wooden workbenches. They usually did that when they had an announcement to make.

She stood there and started her speech. She was thanking everybody for their hard work. Wishing everybody complements of the season etc.

Then she said it.

"Before we leave ladies, we will be having our carol concert. As you know it's tradition". She carried on with "this year our two young men to provide the entertainment are, a young local lad who lives just down the road. Please welcome up on stage, David".

There was a round of applause as he was dragged up to the bench in front of her. I was just about to make my escape when I was held. "And his good friend from Huddersfield, please put your hands together for Ian".

Another round of applause as I was pushed to the front.

"Right lads" she said. We need a couple of songs off you two, before the holiday".

She then said "and when you have finished, we're all" and the whole room cheered in unison "off to 't pub!"

Dave stood there, like a pillock. He was just like me, he couldn't sing to save his life either.

After a couple of minutes in complete silence, it probably wasn't even that long, but it seemed like a lifetime. Two of the women stepped forward with a can of shaving foam and a razor.

Then Barbara spoke again. "Come on lads it's f-ing Christmas, don't be shy. If you don't bloody perform, Dolly and Shirley are going to give you both a shave".

The women all started cheering again. "And it won't be your bloody face they'll be doing". That raised even more cheers.

Then Dave had to open his bloody big mouth, didn't he. "Don't pick on me" he said. "It's that buggers birthday today, he's 18, let him do it".

That was his big mistake. Barbara said "we don't like big gobs 'ere". The women pounced and pinned him down, they whipped his trousers and undies down. Then they quickly covered his nuts in shaving foam. Before they could shave him, a couple of Polaroid cameras appeared.

"Flash" and a couple of pictures later they let him up. He was embarrassed enough, even though he hadn't been shaved. "Now you buggers had better sing, we won't bloody pretend next time!"

Together, we gave the world's worst rendition of Once in Royal David's City. Quickly followed by the start of an even worse Silent Night. Half way through the second Christmas Carol, all the women joined in.

When finished Dave and I were smothered in kisses by those Amazon women of all ages. They would have been between 18 and 65, most were of the latter.

They all joined in "Happy Birthday" for me.

Then we went "off to 't pub".

As soon as we reached the pub, there would probably have been about forty of us all together. Barbara the shop steward stood on one of the picnic tables outside, she started spouting again. Only this time, she said that she had a present for us.

What could that be?

The women had been having a whip round for us, apparently "it's tradition". We were given an envelope each. When I looked, I had got thirty five pounds. That was nearly double a weeks wage, at that time I think I was on just under £18 a week.

I had to spend the night at Dave's house. I had that much to drink, I would never have made it home. I had absolutely no idea how much we had to drink. I only know that I hadn't spent one single penny of my gift, over the bar.

Those women, no matter what was said about them. They were bloody fantastic! As the saying goes, "it was as though all my Birthdays and Christmas's had come at once".

Birth neighbours.

As an apprentice, I had to go to Huddersfield Technical College. I had to attend one full day a week, nine in the morning until nine at night. Plus another evening six until nine, I hated tech with a passion.

We had to memorise and learn dozens of formulas for drilling and cutting speeds.

I never even needed them, as they were all printed on every machine that we operated.

I must have done ok though, I passed every one of my exams.

I met a lad in my first year at tech, he worked for the ICI, his name was Paul. I just happened to mention his name and surname in conversation at home once, mum said, "ask him when his birthday is?"

As it turned out his mum was in the next bed to mine at Christmas 1958, he was born the day before me on the 21st.

Funnily Brenda, who was in the bed on the other side, gave birth to Gillian on the 26th.

Gillian and I were friends at junior school, and travelled home together on the bus from secondary school. Mum had also worked for Denis and Brenda (Gillian's parents) in the greengrocers shop at Paddock Head, along with her best mate Joyce. A small world or what.

Driving lessons.

I took driving lessons with Glynn from Slaithwaite, a fantastic man with walking difficulties. He became a good friend as well, meeting up on several occasions in later life.

I only took eleven lessons. Glynn's way, was to match you with students of a similar ability. You would be picked up part way through their lesson, then sit in the back, to watch what they did and to listen to what Glenn told them. During your drive you would drop them off and pick up the next student, they would do the same.

It worked for me. As no one in our family had a car who could assist me. I managed to pass on the first attempt. My driving test examiner was a Mr Greenfield from the Huddersfield test centre.

There was a three month delay in taking my test, as that was the time that I had an operation on my knee. It was the one that I had hurt when helping at Paddock village hall. I had the damaged cartilage completely removed, along with a lipoma, a benign tumour attached to the damaged bit.

The orthopaedic surgeon was called Mr Hird. I got all the usual ribbing prior to my first surgery from friends. Including, "hope you are first down, whilst the knife is still sharp". Another comment (untrue), "you know he's alcoholic, (the surgeon) if it's in a morning his hands will be shaking" etc.

You can imagine my face when sat on the bus I was travelling to hospital on. Sat on the seat directly opposite me, was Mr. Hird himself. What a shock.

By the way, he did a great job. They were all winding me up.

Blood donor.

It was March 1977. While I was working at Brook Motors, our Fire Chief Andy had just passed away. Bob picked me up at home, we were going to Andy's funeral.

We were very early, he asked me if I wanted to go for a pint first. I had just gone eighteen.

I thought it would have been rude not to.

We pulled up on King Street in Huddersfield, before the Kingsgate Centre had even been thought of. We were parked outside the Methodist Mission Hall. I started to feel rather uncomfortable, after all, Methodists don't drink, do they?

As we went inside the building, we were made very welcome by some nurses in uniform. Bob went to the reception and they gave him two clipboards. One was for him and one for me. Bob asked me to fill the questionnaire in.

The penny finally dropped, we weren't having a pint at all. We were going to donate a pint, a pint of blood, my blood! Hang on a minute.

I wasn't sure about that. Bob said that it was a painless procedure, it was Andy that had got him started and he was donating in memory of him.

After that explanation, how could I refuse.

That day I gave my very first pint of blood, I must admit that it did make me feel good. I regularly gave every six months after that, until I had been working for the ambulance service for a couple of years.

I was on a routine trip to the hospitals in and around Leeds, I was working with Karl. Now normally, Karl was a very private chap, you couldn't really get to know him. That day was would be slightly different.

Our last drop off, was at Seacroft Hospital. We would normally go to the tea bar for a drink at that point. Karl decided that instead, we would go for a walk. On our way, he began talking about blood donations, he knew that I was already a donor. He said that he used to be a blood donor, but now he did something a little different. He said that he was going to explain everything.

Seacroft Hospital is the home of the National Blood Transfusion Service in Yorkshire, it was into their unit that we were going. We grabbed a cup of tea from the "League of Friends" tea bar.

Then we went into the Plasmapheresis Unit. As we walked in, the nurses there were all on first name terms with Karl. It seemed a very friendly place. Karl spoke to the nurse in charge and asked if she would show me around. After all, I could be a potential donor for them.

The lady was very passionate about her work and most of all, the wonderful work of the unit. We began watching a patient. Instead of blood going down a pipe from his arm and into a bag, like mine had always done.

His blood went into a machine, every few minutes the centre of the machine would start spinning at high speed. You could see the blood separating into different colours.

There was the red cells on the outside, the ring of white cells and then in the middle, the straw coloured liquid that was plasma. When the plasma reached the centre, it overflowed and into a bag. Then it would stop spinning, and go into reverse.

At that point the patient's red cells were being returned up the tubing, and back into his own body. That happened three times, until there was half a litre of plasma in the bag.

It was actually measured by weight. One litre of water weighs one kilogram. I was absolutely fascinated by that. Blood is ever so slightly heavier, 1.04 times heavier.

She also explained about the protein known as "factor eight", that was contained in the plasma and how easily it could be removed. That was the clotting factor that is so desperately needed by patients suffering with haemophilia.

I was hooked, they had got me. I signed up for it there and then.

With getting the red cells back, it meant that you could donate a lot more frequently than six months, you could go every four weeks if you wished. I went every four to six weeks, shifts permitting. It was very rewarding, you also seemed to be able to find out a bit more of what was happening with the products of your donation.

It was on the 11th of November 1991 that I gave my 100th donation. I arrived at

Seacroft Hospital and went in to the Unit as usual. I had only just set foot inside the doors, I was greeted with a standing ovation from all the staff and a huge cheer and round of applause from everybody. That is how you are treated there.

In the October of the following year, Wendy and me were invited to a presentation by the Lord Mayor of Leeds at the Leeds Town Hall. Where I was presented with a Wedgewood China plate to honour my 100th donation.

It was a boxed, full sized bone China dining plate. In the middle in gold, was the entwined hearts logo of the Blood Transfusion Service and the figure 100. The outer edge of the plate had a reddy coloured patterned border, this pattern was about an inch deep, enclosed on both inside and outside by a thin band of gold.

The redness I was told later, was a representation of what blood looked like under a high powered microscope.

Perfect.

It wasn't long after that, that I received a letter from the BTS, informing me that I wasn't really required any more. My blood group wasn't required as much as the other groups, but I was asked to still remain on their list.

I was occasionally called in at short notice to donate plasma for patients suffering from the debilitating Guillaume Barre Syndrome. I was only called a few times for that, because now the patient can be given an IV injection of immunoglobulin direct.

It is still obtained from donors, but technology has advanced by leaps and bounds. That it is so much easier to obtain from already built up stocks of whole blood.

I once got the call from Seacroft Hospital to attend straight away, to leave work and go at once. Once it had been cleared with my bosses I had to go, a car was waiting outside the ambulance station to take me there, blue lights as well.

On the Unit was a small child, he was "moribund" he was expected to die imminently. There were two other adult males there donating for the same patient. He was three years old and unconscious.

The three of us possessed a protein in our plasma, it wasn't there at every time of donation, they were gambling that one of us would have had it present that day. It paid off. Two of the three of us were showing the protein present.

They didn't say which ones.

Our plasma was being taken straight from our bedside, across the room and infused straight into to the little boy.

Before we left to go home, the three year old dying little boy was sat up, on mum's knee enjoying some ice cream. I do hope he made a full recovery. Hey weren't allowed to go into too much details, down to patient confidentiality.

No further comments required here, just some tissues. That moment was absolutely priceless!

I had even put my name down on the Anthony Nolan Register for possible bone marrow donations.

The Anthony Nolan Register was formed in 1974, by Shirley Nolan. Her son Anthony was born in 1971 but died shortly after in 1979. He didn't suffer from

Leukaemia, but had a very rare inherited blood disorder known as Wiscott-Aldridge syndrome

When Adrian was five years old, it was late in 1991.

I was called to attend Seacroft for further tests, I had been found to be a close match for a five year old boy. A bone marrow transplant was his only hope of survival.

I attended and had several more blood tests, the whole procedure was explained to me and I was told that I could back out at any stage of the proceedings.

How could I?

If that child was depending on me for a bone marrow donation, there was no way on earth that I could back out.

The whole of the Anthony Nolan list, and all of the members of our British Armed Forces had been checked. I was a near match at 97.4%.

It was explained that when it was time, I would be provided with transport to Bristol Royal Infirmary. I would spend the first day having further tests on my own wellbeing and fitness, the procedure would be carried out the secon day and then I would be brought home on the third day. All this time, my wife Wendy would be housed in a nearby hotel.

I was very excited at the prospect, although I must admit that I was absolutely petrified at the same time.

The date was getting nearer, I was kept informed of the little boy's condition. Poor little chap, he had leukaemia. He had to have all sorts of radio and chemo therapy, to totally irradiate his immune system prior to the life saving transplant.

He was gravely ill.

Sadly, the radiation had made him even worse and he passed away only three weeks before it was all due to happen.

I was devastated at the news, I can't even begin to understand how the little boy's parents must have felt. I was so sorry for them.

That was the end of that little saga in my life and I didn't hear any more, it was so sad.

All of that happened just from going to a funeral. I know that our ex Fire Chief at Brook Motors, Andy, was a great ambassador for the BTS in Yorkshire. I hope I did him proud too.

Director of Brook Motors, Stanley.

In my last year at Brook Motors, I unwittingly got my own back on Stanley, for his prank on me.

He had not been the intended victim of my plans.

We had a just got a junior apprentice that had started with us for a four week placement, he was a right character, Graeme.

He ended up running his own pub and brewery in Batley, the last I saw of him.

Anyway, one day for some reason that I can't remember, Graeme had shaved his head. I had a plan. In the tool room, the phone was a big old heavy black bakelite thing. I covered the earpiece with engineers marking blue.

A very dark, navy blue ink gel, it was designed to mark and stay, on even oily surfaced metal. It would not to rub off. If you got it on your hands, even with "Swarfega" it was a devil to get shut of.

I went down to the storeroom from where I rang that phone and waited for Graeme to answer. The phone rang twice, it was picked up and I was busting to laugh. When it was answered, it wasn't the gruff voice of Graeme, but the Queens English of a very well spoken Stanley!

I nearly died, I daren't speak, I couldn't I had froze.

I sat alone in the store room for ages, how do I get out of this one? What the hell was I going to do?

Eventually I returned to the tool room, Graeme was sat in the corner, crying with laughter. "That were fer me want it" he said.

Stanley was always very smartly dressed in a well pressed suit, white shirt and always a tie. His hair was almost pure white and he had a lot of it for his age. He also had a well defined, precision trimmed, military style white moustache. Other than the colour, it was like the one that actor David Niven had, if you are old enough to remember.

The black toolroom phone rang, it was the company secretary asking for me. Graeme had spragged, he had told Stanley that it was me that had rigged the phone.

I had to go to the boardroom immediately.

The walk from the tool room was probably only a couple of hundred yards, it seemed to go on forever, I didn't want to go, but I daren't not do.

I got to the boardroom, it was full, all the directors of the company were sat around the great oak table. Stanley was stood at the blackboard at the far end of the room. All the left hand side of his face and some of his white hair was stained a really vivid shade of royal blue. (It went like that when you tried to wash it off). I desperately wanted to pee there and then.

His only word was "WELL?"

What could I say? I stood there shaking and biting my bottom lip, I wanted to die.

I looked around the room all the faces were contorted, their shoulders jiggling up and down. Every one of them a company director, and they were all in hysterics.

Stanley then said that "all these people are usually the most boring, miserable set of bloody individuals that you would ever be likely to come across, today they were giggling like a load of school kids".

He hadn't been able to understand it. Not until he had moved his old freestanding blackboard away from the window, to be able to start his presentation. Then he had caught sight of himself in the mirrored windows and what a sight he had seen.

He then started laughing, it was a proper, full blown belly laugh. It was closely followed by the rest of the board members. They could then let it go.

"I look a right pillock" he said, followed by "and it'll take weeks to shift this" pointing to the blue. Then he surprised me and said that despite that, it was the best board meeting he had ever attended.

He told me to "get your coat, and get off home, you have made my day".

Then he said, "when you get back to the tool room to get your stuff, don't tell them anything. Make out that you've been sacked, it'll do them good. See you tomorrow".

What an experience and what a man!

One of my heroes.

CHAPTER 10.

PROUD MOMENTS.

Queen's Scout Presentation.

I received the Queens Scout Award in 1977. Being presented with my certificate at St. Georges Chapel, Windsor. That being the Queens own Chapel in the grounds of Windsor Castle. A truly fantastic building.

It was on St. George's Day, 23rd April 1977.

Prior to the presentation by the then Chief Scout, Sir William Gladstone. Hundreds of us took part in a massive parade through the main streets of Windsor, through the main gates into the palace and formed up around the lawns in the centre of the Palace yard.

The Royal Marines Marching band at the front of the parade and at the rear were the Coventry Scout Band, the National Champions for several successive years.

That year being her majesty's silver jubilee year, all Queens Scouts were invited to Buckingham Palace on the actual day of her celebration. Watching the parade pass and ultimately a flypast of hundreds of planes from the Royal Air Force, from inside the grounds of the palace.

Another once in a lifetime experience.

Paddock Carnival Queen Lindsay.

Not only was 1977 her majesty Queen Elizabeth 2nd's silver jubilee year, it was also to be the year that we had one of our own family members crowned into a royal family. My sister Lindsay was chosen as Miss Paddock, she was to be that years Carnival Queen.

Mum and Dad were so proud, but it is still a moment that Lindsay cringes about every time it is mentioned.

Ford Anglia, "the Beastie"

I had recently passed my driving test and had got a 1967 "E Reg" Ford Anglia car. My first, and a first for our immediate family.

It was a great little car known as "the Beastie".

I don't know why, or where the name came from, but it was a name that seemed to fit.

My uncle Fred, although he was not really my uncle, he had worked in the mill where dad did. James Sykes' in Milnsbridge.

Fred's wife Amy also worked there. They had taken dad under his wing when he first started working in the mill.

He had always simply been known to us as uncle Fred.

He went with me to pick the car up from Molly, another friend that dad worked with.

It was her dads car.

Later on Molly's son Nick started at the mill, at times he worked with my dad. He went school with my sister Diane. Little be known then, he then went on to work for the ambulance service and he worked with both my son Adrian and me, three generations of my family.

A small world eh!

After uncle Fred retired from the mill, he was still very active for his age and he wanted a part time job.

I talked to Terry, my old scout leader, in his Shaw's Pickles director capacity. They were after a handyman. I managed to get uncle Fred a job.

Because of how I talked about him and called him uncle Fred, at that time I didn't even know his last name. Everybody there at Shaw's took to him immediately. Everyone affectionately called him "uncle Fred", even the directors.

It was great.

I went all over in the little "Beastie". I had never been on a motorway until that Easter Monday, I had to use the M62 to get home from Leeds, I couldn't find any other road out.

On the Friday of the same week, I drove all the way to and across London to Epping Forest. To Gilwell Park, the home of Scouting in England. Then across central London again to Windsor Castle for my presentation.

Mum was not a seasoned traveller, but she loved that little car. I even managed to get her to travel on a motorway, that was something new.

The only thing, I could not go up Birchencliffe Hill in the "Beastie" without stalling the engine. I don't think I ever managed it with that car.

I took the little car all over north of England.

I had a Corsair 1500 engine fitted. Then I swapped the great big bus sized steering wheel for a super cool seven inch diameter sports wheel.

I thought it was fantastic until I had a blowout on a front wheel whilst travelling at speed on the A66 towards Keswick. It ripped the steering wheel right out of my hands and I ended up doing a 360 degree turn in the middle of the busy dual carriageway.

As soon as I got home, I changed it back.

Radio One Roadshows.

Again, another road trip in the "Beastie". In 1977 for almost a full week, Monday to Friday anyway. I followed one of the Radio 1 roadshows across Lancashire and into Yorkshire with my friend Alan. We were lucky enough to meet many of the then top radio DJ's. We got loads of freebies from Noel Edmonds, Dave Lee Travis and Mike Reid.

We were even heard several times sounding the distinctive horn of my Ford

Anglia. It was live on Radio One as we followed a charity bed push all the way from Rochdale to Huddersfield.

My cars over the years.

Over the years I have had several cars, both old and new. Some have given me better service than others.

I have very fond memories of a lot of my cars, but other than my very first, the "Beastie". I can't really say that any have held any emotional attachment.

Cars;

Ford Anglia "E" Reg. 1967. It was white, with a very dark green "pine forest" roof. It should have had a 1200cc engine, but it had been stood dormant for two years prior to my acquisition and the engine had seized solid. So it was fitted with a Corsair 1500cc engine. A little rocket.

Peugeot 104 "P" Reg. 1975. A very deep red almost maroon colour, a little hatchback. That one had an 1100cc engine.

Mark 1, Ford Capri "K" Reg. 1971. That had a 1600cc GT engine. It was originally a light metallic green with a black vinyl roof. It was damaged by a cyclist, and had to be resprayed following repairs.

I kept the traditional black vinyl roof and the green should have been the original colour. But due to costs, I was told that it would be the same green colour, but I couldn't have metallic.

It came back the same green as Kirklees busses. Wendy hated it after that, I quite liked it if truth be known.

I had bought it off a lad at Brook Motors, Mick. He had owned the car at the time when he was getting married. It was when I was working in the drawing office. He was marrying one of the girls from the office.

The car was in the car park under the office windows, he had left the sun roof open a little. Some machines on the shop floor, were computer operated, they were controlled using a ticker tape. That was a long reel of paper, with a series of holes punched into it. The dots were only very small, perhaps one and a half millimetres diameter.

In our office, we had bags upon bags of the little dots, they were kept until a large amount were ready for dumping. One of the girls suggested that we could fill the car with dots, for a laugh. After all, it was the day before the wedding, but who would be daft enough to do it.

Can you guess?

It took thirty four bin liners full of the damn little dots, the car was absolutely full to the top. I just couldn't get any more in. It was just a shame that I didn't manage to get a picture of it, or of Mick, when he and his future wife opened the car.

It looked like there had been a wedding on St. Thomas' Road, it was like confetti. It blew all down the road, even across the bottom of Chapel Hill, and onto the front of the Changing Lights Pub. They even found some that had been trailed inside the pub and lots more were all over the forecourt of Colin Appleyard Cars.

I had no idea at that time, that three years later that I would be buying the car.

I owned it for another two years. Every time I put the air blowers on to clear the windscreen, there were still bloody dots flying out. Five years after the event, I was still vaccing up the little buggers!

VW polo "V" Reg. 1979. Another deep red and another hatchback, with a 1000cc engine.

Wendy was heavily pregnant in 1984 with Adrian, when I had the Polo. I was on my way home with her when we had an accident. As I pulled out of a side road into Morley Lane, Milnsbridge, I hit a car coming up the hill.

Although it frightened Wendy, there was minimal damage done to the cars, and the baby was fine. The lad whose car I hit back then, is the brother of a paramedic that works at Honley ambulance station now. Tom.

Ford Escort van "W" Reg. 1980. That one was pillar box red, and it had an 1100cc engine. It only had two front seats and as the children were little, I needed somewhere to fasten their child seats.

Thomas, one of our mechanics from work, had connections with a bus preservation society. He got me a seat from an old Huddersfield Corporation double decker bus. We fitted and bolted it into the back of the van, and the child seats fitted in perfectly. The van even passed its MOT with it fitted.

At the same time as the van, I had a bright yellow Honda Melody 50cc moped "Y" Reg. 1982. I travelled all over on that little machine, it had a top speed of 30mph and that was only downhill with a following wind. I even went to the RATC at Keighley on that.

I had a rucksack with all my kit for the week. It was fine, I did the journey twice. On my return to Huddersfield, I got a puncture in the rear tyre. I was only a quarter of a mile from home on Manchester Road. It was outside D and M cars at the top of Factory Lane.

How lucky was that!

A light blue Lada estate "B" Reg. 1984. 1500cc engine.

A brown Lada estate "D" Reg. 1986. 1500cc engine.

A white Lada estate "K" Reg. 1992. Another 1500cc engine. Although Lada's were a laughing stock, I loved mine. They were comfortable and they were workhorses. You could carry anything in them, or on top with roof bars. They always passed an MOT first time as well.

A blue Lada Samara "N" Reg. 1995. 1300cc engine. That was the new Lada shape, I bought it from Colin Appleyard's at Chapel Hill. It was almost the worst car that I ever owned, but not quite. I had a warranty with it and it spent more time in the garage than I had it.

Even the mechanics at Colin Appleyard's named the car the "boomerang" because it was "always coming back".

Austin Montego estate seven seater "M" Reg. 1994. That had a bigger 2000cc engine and was the only diesel car I have owned. It was white. I had got it, because it would ideal to take us all out and for mum and dad to be with us at the same time.

Unfortunately dad died before he even got a chance to have a single trip in it.

That car let me down, the engine blew up. I needed a quick replacement and so I got the next one.

Skoda Favorit "N" Reg. 1996. A 1000cc engine. That was a kind of coffee colour. It was rubbish, absolutely bloody awful. It not only looked bad, it rode badly, it was a rattling tin can. I only had it for two weeks, it had to go. My worst car ever without any doubt.

Ford Escort estate "J" Reg. 1991. That one had a 1600cc engine. A lovely car in a metallic light blue. It was unlucky though. In all the years I have parked outside my house, that was the only car that ever got run into and damaged. Three times it was hit whilst parked outside our home. All within a period of six months. I had to get rid of it.

Suzuki Swift "W" Reg. 2000. It was my first ever, brand new car. A 1000cc engine. I needed a change, the opportunity arose for a new car. It was a lovely, slightly deeper blue metallic. A little small, but fine. At the time, I had been looking at the Ignis, but it had very little boot space, and we had the two dogs at the time.

Suzuki Ignis "03" Reg, the new shape. Another brand new car. A 1300cc VVT (variable valve timing) engine. Cliff who worked at Colin Appleyard's told me about the new Ignis being launched.

It came in to store the day after he had told me about it, I went for a test drive and ordered one there and then. It was ideal for us. A deep blue, almost metallic, called pearlescent.

An economical and practical car, it could be a little uncomfortable at times. With the seats down, it had the biggest boot space that I have ever had. I even collected a washing machine, and didn't even need to remove any of the packaging. It had a flat square back, it was classed as an estate.

Suzuki Ignis "56" Reg. Brand new again. I had that one for ten years. 2006. It was exactly the same as the first one, engine size, everything. Even down to the colour. It had to have a replacement gearbox and clutch at five years old. Wendy and I really liked the car, but it was starting to cost us money and it was going to need another gearbox before long. It was a very practical car, but it was a harsh ride.

Ford Focus Zetec, hatchback. „07" Reg. 2007. It was not new by any means. One of my oldest cars for a long long time. Another deep blue metallic finish. It is a much more comfortable ride than any of the cars I have ever owned.

That, my latest car, has a 1600cc engine fitted.

CHAPTER 11.

MEMORABLE HOLIDAYS.

Paris in springtime.

Spring Bank Holiday 1977. I went to Paris with my mate Richard from venture scouts. We had the itinerary of a four day, three night coach tour, but we did it on foot.

The whole trip was sorted out by one of our district scout leaders, Miss Ann. She ran her own small travel agency. Small being the word, it was a "lean to" shop on the corner at Cowlersley traffic lights. Directly opposite Taylor Funeral Service where my wife Wendy works.

The whole trip cost us a staggering £38 each. Excellent value, even for 1977.

We stayed in a small bed and breakfast hotel, near to the famous Moulin Rouge. Breakfast was great, with the freshest bread imaginable. The Chinese hotelier would open the window and ask the baker across the road for whatever he needed. The road was so narrow, more of a footpath really, cars weren't able to use it. Once ordered the baker could lean out of the window and pass it to him. A bit like the Shambles in York.

We went to all the usual touristy places and climbed the Arc de Triomphe, the Eiffel Tower and the Sacre Coeur. We went to see the Palace of Versailles. We went on night trip on the Seine.

We covered just about everything of interest.

We had some excellent meals, including horse steak.

I always said that I would to go back there some time. Paris is a marvellous city with some fantastic sites of beauty and historical interest.

Kandersteg Scout Centre.

Later that same year, in August. A party of us from the venture scouts went on an expedition to the international scout centre at Kandersteg, in Switzerland. The twelve of us were travelling from Huddersfield to London by minibus.

We had just got to Bretton roundabout, Graham had bought a Huddersfield Town scratch card with his morning paper.

He was bouncing around like a lunatic, he had good reason though, he had only just won a thousand pounds. It was a massive amount of money back then. But he only had seven days to claim his winnings, we were going away for 14. Graham had to ring from a pay phone and get his mate to meet us. We had to wait for his friend to arrive on a motorbike, he took the ticket and collected the money on Graham's behalf.

The rest of the journey from London was by overnight train to Zurich and then on to Kandersteg.

It is a wonderful place, there the scouts came to visit from all over the world. There is a 400 bed, 4 star hotel on site. We opted for the outdoors. We were one group out of hundreds camping. A massive site, virtually a town all of its own.

The toilets though, they were something else. It was a shed, there were handles at each end and it had no floor. The shed would be picked up and placed over a large trench. Inside were two poles running the length of the shed, there was one just above floor level and another one about eighteen inches higher. Above, were three knotted ropes hanging from the roof.

To use the facilities was something to behold. You were to stand on the first pole and turn to face the wall. Then you needed to drop your pants and carefully sit back over the second pole, until it was against the back of your knees. Once in that position, you had to grab hold of a rope, lean back and do the necessary.

Three people could "perform" at the same time. You needed to be good friends. There wasn't a Ladies or Gents either, everything was unisex.

As the trench filled, there were plungers to compact the waste. Once it was nearly full, then a new trench had to be dug and the shed was lifted and moved to the new trench. Soil dug out was thrown in to the previous trench to bury the contents, red flags were then inserted as a warning to future digging. An education in itself.

Thankfully there were some more traditional toilets a little further away, that were permanent and had proper plumbing facilities.

I went in some cable cars, my fear of heights meant that although I had some good photos, they were actually taken whilst sat on the floor and reaching up to the window. I never actually saw the view, until the photographs had been developed.

We went on hikes to some of the really remote mountain huts.

On one of those trips, with a mountain guide, we heard what we thought was thunder. The guide shouted at us to "dig in!" We did, frantically digging deep into the snow on the mountain side. We managed to dig a massive hole, thirteen of us were then huddled together, it was an avalanche.

None of us had experienced one of them before, it was frightening. The thunder was just getting louder and louder. The guide looked out and called for us to follow, the avalanche had passed us by, about a hundred yards away. We could feel the vibrations of the mountain all around.

The sight was fantastic. As well as thousands of tons of soft snow sliding down the mountain. There was the ice, huge chunks of it, some as big as a house. The ice was a fantastic blue colour, a shade that I have never seen before, it looked amazing. It only lasted for a few minutes, but what an experience.

The highlight for me though, was a train journey to the top of the Jungfrau mountain, via tunnels carved right through the inside of the Eiger Mountain. Then even stopping at a railway station somewhere in the middle of the mountain. There were tunnels that left the railway track side and stopped at large glass windows. They were set into the rock, looking out of the North Face of the Eiger. Fantastic!

At the top we were at an altitude above 11,000 feet, the air up there was a lot thinner than anything I had ever experienced, and the views beyond description.

At other times while on the campsite itself, we brushed snow off the sun beds and lounged in the brilliant sunshine or swam in the open air swimming pools.

Mad!

There was a hotel bar just down the road, the beer was a pound for a half pint bottle, much much more than you were paying at home. I seem to think it was still less than 50p for a pint in 1977.

Coffee was a pound a cup and a small cup at that.

You didn't pay for each round of drinks, you were given a ticket that was placed in a little cup on your table, you then settled your bill on leaving the establishment. Either a small cafe, bar or restaurant, they all did the same.

That was fine for the first few nights, but on the Thursday, there was an old bloke playing the piano. We had been drinking all evening, what a shock when it came to settling our bill. All of the drinks had been charged at double the prices, due to the "entertainment".

We wised up very quick. In the next group of tents to ours, were two lads from Holland. One of them was always strumming away on a guitar, our cogs were turning, we quickly befriended them and encouraged them to tag along with us.

We were then the entertainment, singing along to traditional campfire songs. Drinks half price for the "entertainers".

A fantastic holiday, it was very expensive, but Switzerland was a place I had dreamed of since early childhood.

I vowed to myself that I would return one day.

Later, you will see what happened.

CHAPTER 12.

VOLUNTEERING.

Countryside Rangers.

In 1979 my cousin Philip and I joined up as West Yorkshire voluntary Countryside Rangers. It was a trial project to help run the countryside in the local area. I was able to volunteer until early 1981. It was a project that involved lots of people all over West Yorkshire.

Our first incentive was based in an old quarry above Haworth at a place known as Penistone Hill. The quarry areas were being turned into a series of free car parks, away from the already limited parking in the town of Haworth. It was to be a true country park. Picnic areas and well defined marked footpaths.

It was also an area set up to be used as a base, for the more serious walkers. With easy access to the open moorland, including the famous Bronte areas. Top Withins, the ruins made famous from the book Wuthering Heights. The Bronte Waterfalls, another beautiful part of the area. A little off the beaten track, but not too far for everyday walkers.

Other aspects of the "Ranger Service" were to organise and run guided walks around West Yorkshire. Anything to encourage people to use the surrounding land and facilities for leisure activities.

We promoted the Pennine Way where it goes across our area. Including improving access to the well established long distance footpath. We made improvements to already well worn moorland pathways, by introducing hardy fast growing heathers.

There were areas of the path that had been completely eroded away, they were reinforced by laying down long lengths of wooden fence palings and then adding heathers to the top. The idea being, that the heather would grow through the wood palings and bind it to the soil below. That was to encourage a living fully supported pathway.

We added stiles over the fragile dry stone walls along some of the major footpaths, that would encourage correct crossing points and reduce the damage caused by people just clambering over walls.

There were opportunities for the "Rangers" themselves, to learn new skills taught by some of the other volunteers. We had been shown the art of dry stone walling, so we were able to help with some of the repairs. I was involved in building a stone clapper bridge, over a stream across the Pennine Way. That was just along the border between Lancashire and Yorkshire at the other side of Buckstones. That was an experience, very heavy work with some very large Yorkshire stone slabs.

We developed the old abandoned Tunnel End Cottages at Marsden, those cottages, then became my local base. We had people with all sorts of skills, and we all helped each other.

The cottages became an activity centre and tea rooms. There were some rooms available for use as classrooms for the local schools. The rooms were also used for regular talks by the volunteers to groups of adults, or children.

We would encourage young people in the ways getting the most out of the countryside.

Not forgetting the Huddersfield Canal Society, and the work that they were doing with Huddersfield narrow canal. There were massive works going on to reopen the Standedge Tunnel to the public. We all used the cottages together.

The old warehouse just further down the canal then became a larger but ideal venue for the visitors centre.

Our cottages eventually became a pub.

Unfortunately, due to me starting work for the West Yorkshire Metropolitan Ambulance Service, I was unable to commit myself to the weekends required for volunteers.

As I worked relief shifts I would not know where, when, or if I was working. To make the Countryside Rangers work, they needed advanced availability of the volunteers, to be able to plan in the activities.

In the summer of 1981, I reluctantly had to give in my notice to the ranger service.

CHAPTER 13.

LIFE CHANGING.

Home alone.

In the summer of 1979, I think it would have been during the school holidays. The rest of the family went to spend a few days with one of mums friends, up in the north of Scotland.

It was a lady that she had met several times, through the Tom Jones fan club, that mum was president of. The Tom Jones Appreciation Society. (TJAS).

Mum had been a member of a couple of Tom Jones fan clubs, but they were both based in America. She got together with a group of her friends and decided to form their own. Mum ran that fan club for over 30 years.

Where the family were going to stay, was not far from Elgin, at a little place called Port Soy. Mum's friend was Margaret. I think I recall this as the first time they had all been away without me.

It was going going to be a very long train journey for them.

I can't remember the exact time, I think it was around half past seven and they should have got there at half past six. Anyway, Margaret was eagerly waiting for them to arrive, just as much as I was. I had been awaiting a phone call from them, to say that they had.

There were no mobile phones in everybody's pocket then. You had to use those red boxes that used to be up and down on most street corners.

Remember them?

Anyway, an hour after they should have arrived, the house telephone rang. It was Margaret, after she had introduced herself, she made a statement. It wasn't to be the first time that I would hear that statement, it was "where's your mother?"

I couldn't answer that. They should have arrived at the train station, and had plenty of time for the short taxi ride.

We had to wait.

Half an hour later, "where's your mother?" She had rung the local rail station and she said that they hadn't been much use.

On the ten o'clock news, there was the reason. A train crash had happened, a particularly nasty one. Two trains had collided on the East Coast Line, close to the Scottish Border.

Details were very sketchy at the time.

I rang Margaret, she hadn't seen the news. She had never had a television and radio signals were poor where she lived. We were then both more than a little worried. There was no way to find out if they had been on that train heading north, or not.

I rang the number given out on the news programme, it wasn't much help at the time. That was more for people with definite confirmation of passengers travelling, I couldn't say for sure that they were on on the north bound train.

I would have to ring back after midnight.

Margaret rang again, it was by then nearly midnight, "where's your mother?" There was still no news.

It was just after midnight, about ten minutes past and the telephone rang again. That time it wasn't Margaret, it was dad. I was so relieved. The long train ride that they had been so looking forward to, had turned into an absolute nightmare.

They had all been delayed due to the accident, that had involved the previous train. Then they had been diverted all over the shop and had to change trains on numerous occasions to accommodate that.

Eventually though, they had a great time in the end. Port Soy was a lovely place.

Margaret owned two little cottages that were next door to each other. One she lived in, the other she let out. Mainly to climbers and ramblers. Famous climbers had stayed there including Sir Chris Bonington and Dougal Haston, two of the world's most famous climbers at the time. Dougal died in an avalanche whilst skiing in Switzerland. Also known for his climbing interests, as well as his acting abilities. Another famous guest of Margaret, had been Brian Blessed OBE.

Redundancy!
I completed my apprenticeship at Brooks, I was not the best academic, but I was very good at the practical side of things.

I was a competent welder, a skilled turner and a jig and gauge fitter. I had also had fourteen months in the design and drawing office, (I loved that bit) it was extremely clean as well.

All my exam papers throughout my years at Huddersfield Technical College, were passed with a distinction grade.

Not bad eh!

My apprenticeship was completed at the end of August 1980. Then I was made redundant early in September of that same year.

Just prior to the many redundancy notices being issued, we had a visit to Brook Motors from the then Minister for Industry, Mr. Michael Foot. All of the last four years intakes of apprentices were gathered in the canteen to hear him speak.

It was on a Monday, that was the very same week that my actual apprenticeship was due to finish on the Friday. He gave us all his personal assurance that not a single one of the last four years intake of apprentices would be made redundant.

Three days later, I received my buff coloured envelope on Thursday, it confirmed that I was being made redundant the next month. Along with around seventy per cent of the last four years intake.

Some promise there!

Was it time wasted?

I don't really think so, it did set me up in some ways for life, to tackle situations with practical and logical methods.

Drink!!!

Following redundancy, I was out of work for about six months altogether. I had some money in the bank at that time, I had been awarded nearly £2,500 redundancy money and it was all tax free. It included a severance payment in lieu of twelve weeks notice.

That meant that I couldn't "sign on" for three months. Then I had to spend the second three months on the dole.

While I was looking for work. I spent most of my redundancy money in the Royal Oak, the pub next door to mum and dads'.

I'm sure I helped keep Alan the landlord in business, being a customer seven lunchtime and evenings a week. It got to the stage where I was drinking between 15 to 20 pints a day.

On an evening my mate from Longwood Road, Mark would come down and accompany me.

We were addicted to the pub video games at the time. Each Friday there was a gallon of beer up for grabs for the highest score. Nine times out ten it was one of us two that won, we would get four free pints each.

Rock stars.

It was sometime in 1980, an exciting time locally, everybody was talking about it. A world famous rock band was due at Paddock Head and they were bringing a film crew with them. They were going to be shooting a music video for their upcoming release.

Kenneth the chemist next door, had been asked for permission to have his shop used, to film both inside and out for the video. The bands name hadn't been disclosed at the time.

There was a lot of commotion during the filming, it went on for most of the day. Fans of the band had got word of it, there were more people at Paddock Head than I had ever seen.

The name of the band "AC/DC".

Traffic was stopped around the roundabout. Crowds were kept at bay and moved out of shot. They used a lot of shots outside at Paddock Head and other locations around Huddersfield.

The video can still be seen on "YouTube". It is under AC/DC, "You Shook Me All Night Long"

On the dole.

During my time out of work, I must have written hundreds of letters/job applications and I always enclosed a stamped, self addressed envelope. But I was lucky to get maybe one reply per week.

I was in an awkward position, as I was classed as too old to train, but way too young to have any practical experience.

I passed an entrance exam to join the West Yorkshire fire service. I was by then just tall enough to get in.

Only to fail the medical at the last push, due to having my cartilage removed within the last two years.

There were that many people applying for fire service jobs at the time, that any reason to whittle the numbers down had to be used.

I wrote to numerous fire extinguisher companies, due to my training with Brooks' fire team. After all, I knew everything there was to know about extinguishers (at that time). The only firm to write back was Nu-Swift at Elland.

Even though they didn't have any jobs going then, they asked me in for an interview.

They were very impressed with my skills, but were unable to offer me a position. Though they did say that they would keep me on file, until such time as they had.

True to their word they did contact me a few months later.

They were the only company to do so.

By that time, I had been given a job with West Yorkshire Metropolitan Ambulance Service (WYMAS). The job with the ambulance service could be a firm career, providing I passed all my exams and then completed my twelve month probation period.

Nu-Swift even kept me on their files until I had passed and got my qualification for the ambulance service.

When I had qualified, I rang them out of courtesy. They wished me well in my future and said that it would be their loss. They would then remove my name from file.

The company spokesman also said that if ever I had a change of heart, I would always be welcome there. I had made such an impression at the interview.

Nice of them to say that!

It's hard to put to words how much that meant to me. Particularly as so many of the companies in and around Huddersfield didn't even have the decency to reply. Not even in the envelopes that I had paid, addressed and already put stamps on for.

That bit was absolutely soul destroying.

CHAPTER 14.

WITH A LITTLE HELP
FROM A FRIEND.

David.

Whilst bored, drinking and getting depressed. My neighbour and friend David, another from scouting. He was Ken's son (skip), offered me some part time work, it would be cash in hand.

He was a former Postman, who also did disco's for extra pennies. He then became somewhat of an entrepreneur, doing anything and everything to earn a bit of money.

He had bought two vans and he shifted rubble, rags, anything. He was even a grave digger for Kirklees, you name it, David would have a go.

He certainly wasn't frightened of hard work.

He had a contract where he visited all the Oxfam shops in Yorkshire and Lancashire. He would collect all the unsaleable items, in black bags and then transport them to Oxfam's large waste saver plant for recycling. It was in an old mill on Britannia Road in Milnsbridge.

Not long after that, Oxfam moved to their present site on Colne Road off Chapel Hill.

To occupy some of my time, David asked me to do some of the collections for him. He gave me ten pounds a day. Some were long days as well and he paid for my lunch, generally for three days a week.

It was a great help.

World Cruise.

One of the funniest memories I have of David. Was going to Thomas Cooks' travel agency, on High Street, Huddersfield. We had just removed the rubble from a fireplace and taken it to the tip, we were nearly as black as the fire back that we had just removed.

David had on a sheepskin coat, it had only one sleeve, no buttons and was tied together with a length of dirty rope around his waist.

Already in the shop was a man wearing a trilby hat, a camel hair coat and he was smoking a large cigar. (A lot like Boycey from Only Fools and Horses). He was an arrogant man trying to arrange a weekend away in Scotland.

When David and I arrived, straight from disposing of the fireplace. He gawped at us both in disgust. Then he was chuntering to himself to the effect that we should have been removed from the premises, we were an embarrassment and shouldn't be allowed in, etc.

When the staff at the travel office saw David, they almost fell over each other to be able to assist him.

The man in the coat was far from happy. He even stood up and complained at the top of his voice, but his complaints simply fell on deaf ears.

David was no doubt a VIP that day, he was paying the outstanding balance on his world cruise.

When the agency cashier announced that there was a balance (don't forget this was 1980) of £3,990 to pay, the man leaned over so much to our cubicle area that he nearly fell of his chair.

Nosey git.

Then, David being David announced loudly that he would be paying the balance in cash. Then he brought out of that tatty coat's pocket, the biggest wad of cash I had ever seen, the man choked and almost swallowed his cigar.

It was priceless!

Freemasons Arms.

David did the disco/dance music, at the weekend dinner dances for landlady Eileen at the Freemasons Arms at Upper Hopton. Particularly over the Christmas period.

Wh I could, I would join him.

We would set the gear up in the function room and then go off for a couple of pints at other hostelries around the area. The Travellers Rest, the Flowerpot and the Navigation Tavern were the best.

We would then come back to do the disco and then fall into David's little caravan at the bottom corner of the car park. Heaven.

That was both on a Friday and repeated on a Saturday night.

It was at the Freemasons Arms, that we used to see the Yorkshire Ripper copper George Oldfield. At that point in his career, he was the Assistant Chief Constable for West Yorkshire.

He was a detective Chief Inspector at the time of the 4th of February 1974. That was when there was the infamous M62 coach bomb, planted by the IRA. That bomb exploded on a coach near to the service station at Hartshead Moor.

Twelve people, nine of them soldiers, three were civilians were killed on their way back to Catterick Garrison in North Yorkshire. More than fifty others were injured.

George was praised for his prompt actions leading to Judith Ward being convicted and then sentenced to thirty years on 4th November 1974.

Mum was directed to do jury service, once she found out what the case was, she asked to be discharged from duty.

It is very rare to be excused jury service, but due to the evidence that would have to be looked at. Including pictures of the horrible injuries of the survivors and some of the ones who hadn't, mum was allowed to step down.

She wasn't asked again.

CHAPTER 15

A NEW CHAPTER IN A NEW LIFE.

A chance meeting.

Saturday 27th September 1980, that day without doubt was to change my life forever. It had started out two nights before at the venture scouts, my friend Christina had been wanting to go to her best friend Wendy's 21st birthday party on the Saturday night.
Her boyfriend at the time, now husband, was working a night shift. He was a policeman, also a venture scout and friend of mine, Graham.

Could I please take her to the party? I agreed, although I must add a little reluctantly. As other than Christina, I wouldn't know anybody.

As I had just been made redundant, I was conscious of the fact that I would soon have to start watching the pennies. I walked from Paddock to Lockwood to meet Christina, then we walked together. All along Lockwood Road, then all the way up Chapel Hill and then from the ring road uphill again to the party. It was on Trinity Street, near to Greenhead Park.

What a trek!

The atmosphere at the party was great, it was taking place at Wendy's home, which was a one room bedsit flat. That room though was packed with people. The birthday girl Wendy welcomed us with open arms.

Wendy had the most wonderful smile, I'll never forget it, I was attracted to her immediately.

The Eagles track "Witchy Woman" was playing at the time when Christina and I walked in. Who would have guessed then, what the future would hold.

All evening, every time the beer in my glass got a little lower, Wendy would come along and fill it again.

It was fantastic.

Late in the night, Christina was wanting to go home. True to my word, I had promised to see her home safely, I bade my goodbyes at the party and walked back to Lockwood with Christina.

I left her safe at home.

Yes, you guessed it. I walked all the way back to Trinity Street, back to the party and of course, to Wendy.

Durker Roods.

It was over a month before I saw Wendy again. I had asked her to accompany me to our Scout Group Christmas do, at the Durker Roods Hotel near Meltham.

She accepted my invitation, I was over the moon. It was on the 8th November 1981.

The dinner was quite a formal affair and one memory I'll never forget, was when the waitress was putting roasted potatoes onto the plates. She gave Wendy one too many and then proceeded to remove it from her plate. She just put it back on her serving platter to give to someone else.

Not one word of apology, nothing.

After the dinner was over, I was able to give Wendy her belated birthday present. Which was a large teddy bear, shaped like the cartoon dog Snoopy, it was dressed in a Scout Uniform.

I thought it was appropriate.

By the number of smaller Snoopy's all over Wendy's flat, I knew I was onto a winner and that it would be something she liked.

From that night we were inseparable, I saw her at every chance I could.

Adam?

A couple of weeks later, 22nd November 1981. I remember going to pick Wendy up from her family home in Lockwood, it was early evening. I pulled up outside the house in my green Ford Capri, Wendy was in the garden with her younger sister Lynne. She told me that her mum wanted to meet me.

I got out of the car and went into the front garden, Wendy's mum came down the path to meet me. As she was walking towards me, she said, "Oh, you must be Adam, pleased to meet you".

What do you say to that, I thought who the bloody hell is Adam?

Wendy had to put her mum right straight away. What a conversation stopper, I couldn't wait to leave.

During the following months I met most of the family, it was a big family, but I didn't meet Adam though.

The first Adam that I did meet, would be many years later and that was Wendy's brother Raymond's second child. They named him Adam.

My Birthday.

My birthday the 22nd of December 1980 was on a Monday that year. It didn't matter though, the others had all finished work for Christmas. It was a good excuse for another party at Wendy's flat.

After the party had finished, most of the guests went home, but we ended up staying at Wendy's flat. That was Mark, his future wife Alex, and me. It was only a one room bedsit, but it was a very big room. We had all been drinking copious amounts.

All four of us collapsed at the end of the night into the one large bed.

Is there any more of them?

It was Christmas time that my eyes were really opened, I met all of Wendy's family at once and there were loads of them. They all went to her family home for Christmas.

There was of course Wendy, mum Dorothy, dad John, grandma Yvonne and grandad Raymond. Wendy's aunty Linda (mum's sister) and her husband Brynn. Oldest sister Julie and her husband John, next was sister Suzanne and her husband Michael, then her brother Raymond and his girlfriend Linda. Then of course was Wendy's youngest sister Lynne and her boyfriend at the time, a DJ and radio presenter called Jon.

A daunting experience for anybody.

CHAPTER 16.

JOB OPPORTUNITY.

Shortlisted.

In early February of 1981, in the Huddersfield Daily Examiner. There was a job advertised. It was to join the West Yorkshire Metropolitan Ambulance Service. I thought about it briefly and I applied, after all, what did I have to lose.
Only a couple of weeks later, I received a letter saying that I had been shortlisted for an interview.

That meant that things were getting serious, my dad rang an old mate of his, Trevor who lived at Fartown. Trevor's nephew Mark was a Leading Ambulance man at Huddersfield Ambulance Station. He agreed to show me around the station prior to my interview.

Dad and me went to meet Mark one evening, my first impressions were of his size, was he fit to do the job?

He was rather rotund.

He told me that he was in charge of Huddersfield Ambulance Station. He showed me all around the buildings, the different type of vehicles used and gave me an overall insight of the job that I had applied for.

It was an extremely valuable visit.

An interview at last.

The next week, it was Thursday 5th of March. I duly turned up at the Ambulance Station at Gledholt for my interview.

There I was at the front door, I was all suited and booted, shaking like a leaf in a wind tunnel. The next couple of hours could change my life forever, I had never been as nervous in all my life.

I rang the bell to be met by an Ambulance Officer, who I now know to have been the Divisional Officer, a chap called Donald. I asked "could I speak to Mark, the officer in charge, please? I have come for an interview".

It was at that moment, that Donald stopped me. He laughed and said that "Mark is not in charge of the Ambulance Station, and as long as he has a hole in his backside he never will be".

Oops!

I felt like just turning around and going home. I thought there and then, that I had blown any chance that I might have had. I was shown down to the mess room by Donald. I was told to sit and wait and that I would soon be called, for my interview, a practical assessment and also a driving assessment.

It was in that mess room, I was reunited with one of my former Paddock Junior School mates, Mike, he had been in the service for around six months. Unbelievably, my hockey mate from New College, Gavin, was also there for an interview.

Sat nervously with us was a third candidate

The door opened and in came a very smart, tall blonde lady, she had two silver pips on her shoulders and introduced herself as Angel, she was to be our driving assessor.

Angel asked for a volunteer, the third lad offered to go first, then not even ten minutes later he returned and very sheepishly sat back down beside us.

Angel followed in shortly afterwards and curtly told him to go home. She said not to waste any more of her, or his time.

Gavin had just gone upstairs for his interview, so I was next for the driving. What the hell had I let myself in for?

In the garage area, I got behind the wheel of ambulance fleet number 202, it was a Ford Transit "S Reg".

As I struggled in adjusting the seat, being a little shorthouse. An ambulanceman, very smartly dressed complete with his hat on, offered to help. Fleet 202 was his regular ambulance, he told me that the seat was seized up and he and his partner never needed to adjust it.

That was my very first meeting with a man who would really turn my life around, his name was Tommy.

Angel explained to me, that on the route I had got to stick to 30 mph. No matter what speed the road signs went up to. She told me that if I exceeded it once I would be told, a second time and it was home time.

She then asked me to leave the station by going through the the electric sliding garage doors at the front of the building. She then said "please wait for them to open fully, before proceeding".

I thought that was strange, until she explained that in his nervous state, the other lad had run straight into the doors before they had even started to move.

Hence his quick return.

I did okay on my drive. It wasn't good, as some things needed to be improved upon, but Angel said it was okay but more practise was required. She told me that as I had not had much experience of large vehicles, that I had passed, but advised me to gain some more experience if I could.

I was given a short practical test of assembling some medical equipment by following written instructions.

I was also given a written exercise, I had to listen and write down some information. The information had been pre-recorded as if I was receiving a radio message.

That was to see if I had read the instructions that I had been sent to my home prior to interview. It had several simple short cuts to minimise the messages.

For example, the status of "an ambulance on route to hospital with one emergency patient". Could be written simply as "red one" followed by the named of the hospital. Another message generally used at the hospital, was "ambulance now clear at hospital, and available for further work". The shortened version "green at hospital". The hospital wherever it be, again being named.

Although I was writing the message down. It was a way of reducing the time using up the airways on the radio and it was the best way of showing that I had read, and understood my instructions.

I then went upstairs to be interviewed by Divisional Officer Donald, Huddersfield Station Officer Geoff and regional ambulance Training Officer Nora.

It all appeared to have gone fine.

That afternoon, I was at home with mum and dad, my friend Mark had just called down to check on my progress.

When the telephone rang, it was Donald, he told me that I had been successful on my interview and that he was therefore in a position to offer me the full time position. Not only that, I had the choice of Huddersfield or Dewsbury.

To a Paddock lad, that was not really a choice. I told Donald that Huddersfield it was. Donald then told me that my mate Gavin had also been selected for the other position.

The panel had interviewed sixteen people over the last couple of days, out of an original 176 applicants, for just the two positions.

He told me that it was the fact of us both getting the Queens Scout Award that had sealed the deal above anything else.

The whole panel were very impressed with that, it proved that we were trustworthy, reliable and dependable. He then said that "they are the main characteristics required to be an ambulanceman".

CHAPTER 17.

A NEW CAREER.

I am an ambulanceman.

On the 23rd of March 1981, I started my new career with the West Yorkshire Metropolitan Ambulance Service and I would be based at Huddersfield Ambulance Station in Marsh.

It seems such a long time ago now. I don't know if then, I expected still to be driving ambulances under blue light conditions, over thirty six years later.

My first emergency call!

When I started, there was no such thing as A&E or PTS (patient transport service) at that time, all staff were qualified ambulance men, or women.

I was to start a twelve month training programme, for the first three weeks I would be third manning. That meant going out observing with a qualified crew. I didn't even have a uniform.

For the fourth week. I was put out on a mini bus. I was going out to collect and drop off patients at pre-planned clinics at the hospitals and then return them back home.

The purpose of that, was to help to familiarise me with the area. There was no sat nav then, we just had an A to Z of Kirklees. If we wanted a map book of all West Yorkshire, for when on a run to five or six hospitals in Leeds and Bradford, then we would have to buy our own.

It was during that fourth week, when a radio request went out. Then, all the messages went out on open speech. All the crews could hear every one of the outgoing messages. The call was for a crew to attend at a works accident. It was on Brooke Street in the town centre, near to the Monday market. The call was for a female whose hand had become trapped in a machine.

I had just dropped a patient off at Bath Street, it would have been around a 100 yards away. I waited for someone to answer, there was nothing, the control room called again, still no one acknowledged and then a third call.

I responded via the radio, I explained to Comms that I was in the vicinity, but that I was untrained. Therefore unqualified and I still didn't have a uniform. (Comms probably thought I was a bit of an idiot) but that if it was ok to do so, I was prepared to attend.

It was fine, and I was despatched to the address. Comms told that the Leading Ambulanceman (LA) from Huddersfield Station had just set off on his way and he would only be two or three minutes behind me.

When I got there, the address was a machine shop above an Asian fabric store. In the machine shop there were a couple of dozen young women, using industrial sewing machines to make traditional Asian garments.

The manager of the factory took me towards one of the young women, she was sat on the floor in the corner of the workshop. She looked extremely pale and clammy. I could see that she had a large bore needle, about 1/16th of an inch in diameter, it was stuck right through her index finger between the base of the nail bed and her first knuckle joint.

The man told me that every time he had tried to pull the needle out, the girl had fainted. I am not surprised. At the bottom end of the needle, there was a hooked barb to collect the thread from underneath the garment.

No wonder she looked pale and clammy.

There was no bleeding. The needle needed surgically removing. There the barb would have been cut off, then the rest of the needle could have been pulled straight out.

All I could do was to place her hand in a clean pillow case, that would hide the offending digit from view and would help by trying to alleviate the shock.

Horace was the LA, he agreed with the treatment I had given and left me to deal with it by myself.

I then only had to transport the young woman to HRI, with a friend for support. There the needle was removed under a local anaesthetic.

Training, what training?

Officially the formal training involved a four week familiarisation/induction, at local level in Huddersfield. That would be followed by a two weeks residential intensive driving course and then the Millar training. A six week residential anatomy and physiology, medical and first aid course.

Both of those to be undertaken at the Regional Ambulance Training Centre (Elm Bank) at Keighley. All of that training to be done during the first twelve months of service. The order and timing in those days was not crucial.

Now, all of the training is done in a block and prior to starting at a station. I didn't do mine until very late on in the first twelve months.

What an eye opener!

A few weeks later and in my brand spanking new uniform. It was almost like the police one. A navy coloured tunic and trousers, a light blue shirt with two breast pockets and dark blue epaulettes and a black tie. All finished off with highly polished shoes and a peaked cap.

I was single handed on an outpatient minibus ambulance. I was empty and clear, known as situation green. I was on my way to St. Luke's hospital at Crosland Moor, to collect some patients to return home.

As I was driving up Nabcroft Lane at the back of David Browns at Lockwood. I heard a horrendous noise, a long low pitched whooshing noise followed by something like a really loud thunderclap.

It was a gas explosion at a house on nearby Sunningdale Road.

I was the one that called it in and then I approached the area with extreme caution. I was still, unqualified.

I could see that the house had no windows left, not only that, the complete window frames had been blown all across the full width of the road.

A man in his early sixties was stood on the doorstep shivering. He said that his wife was upstairs. He assured me that there had been NO fire.

The gas supply was still turned on. I went to the back door as he instructed, just inside the door there was the gas meter and mains, I turned it off.

I asked the neighbours who were all out in the street, to make sure that all their immediate neighbours were safe, and out of the houses. Another neighbour down the bottom of the road, held open house, tea and coffee for all.

I looked around for the stairs, they were at the opposite side of the small scullery kitchen. As I got closer, I could hear the wife crying upstairs, I went in.

The bedroom had a strange appearance, the ceiling had lifted maybe three to four inches and had exposed all the underlying woodwork. Every one of the wardrobe and cupboard doors had opened, all the clothes had come out all over the bed and onto the floor.

The lady was petrified, she was buried under the pile of clothes. There were no windows back or front of the house and an icy blast was blowing clean through.

Although shaken, she was completely uninjured. The lady walked downstairs with me to join her husband, they both sat in my warm mini bus wrapped in nice thick warm blankets.

There was no physical treatment required, by either of them at that stage. We didn't have machines to monitor heartbeat, oxygen levels and blood pressures in those days.

You looked at the patient.

If they were blue, you would give them oxygen, if not you left well alone. If they were talking to you, then you had established that they were conscious and breathing. If they didn't respond, then boy you were going to be busy.

Shortly afterwards, the police and the fire brigade arrived. Followed by another ambulance crew. My patients were safely taken to hospital.

The gas board arrived, and the house was checked for safety. Fellow neighbours were all allowed back in to their own houses again.

Before going to hospital. The man had told me that it was an old cooker and the grill was at the top of the oven behind a drop down door. It had to be lit with a match. He had opened the oven door and lit a taper to reach the grill, as he did there was a large bright flash. The oven door had been blown clean off its hinges and was actually embedded in the kitchen wall, opposite the cooker.

The happy and smiling man had a bright glow about him as though he had been out in the sun too long, apart from white around his eyes where his glasses had been. The lenses of his glasses were pitted with little bits of what appeared to be grit. It had actually been melted into the glass, they had done their job and certainly saved his eyes. They were his safety glasses that he wore for his day job at David Browns.

The couple were actually supposed to be going to Spain later that evening, for their two week summer holiday. When the rest of the family arrived at the house, the insurance assessor was already there. The couple were advised to carry on with their plans and to go on holiday. The house repairs would be completed by the time they returned.

The man had already got a good start on his facial tan.

I'm part of an ambulance crew now.
My fifth week, I was teamed up with a qualified member of staff, only just fully qualified by one month himself. A man by the name of Ivan, I worked a lot with him in the early days. Ivan was ex RAF, he had a very precisely trimmed moustache, typical of the RAF or David Niven types seen in the old films.

We received a call to Berry Brow, where a man had suffered an injury at the bottom of his garden. It was very vague.

What we actually saw was very shocking, we thought the patient was going to die. We had to be extremely careful.

At the bottom of the man's back garden was an unsightly electrical sub station. One side of it backed on to his garden. The rest of it was accessed from a back lane.

The patient had decided to disguise the view, by putting up a series of fence panels. They would be fitted on top of his garden wall, all across the bottom end of his garden. Thereby removing the sub station from view. Each one of the panels was six foot wide by three foot high.

He was stood on the wall and about to put one of the panels into place, when a gust of wind had caught hold of it. The panel lifted like a sail on a ship, causing the man to fall. As he had fallen, he had landed and impaled himself onto the metal railings, that were surrounding the sub station.

He had been suspended, six foot off the floor and sat on top of the railings.

From the top cross bar of the railings, the uprights were topped with spikes. The spiked protruded 8" from the bar, to stop trespassers. Each of the spikes was a continuation of the uprights. A piece of three quarter inch diameter steel.

One of the spikes had literally gone right up the hole in his backside. His family had removed him from his predicament. They had not realised the seriousness of his injuries, or the complications that could have arisen by moving him.

When we arrived on scene, the man was laid on the floor of his kitchen and he was screaming in agony. His trousers were absolutely soaked through with blood. We had to remove his pants to treat the wound.

When we looked, there wasn't an actual wound to treat.

The spike had gone straight up his anus.

Blood was pouring out, including large clots, they were like like large lumps of fresh liver. All we could do was to place large sanitary towels against his backside and pull his pants up tight to hold them in place with some pressure applied.

He travelled to the ambulance on the stretcher, he was face down on his hands and knees. It was the only position that he got any respite from the pain. He was using the entonox, gas and air like it was going out of fashion.

I was driving and raced through the streets with lights and sirens, as fast as I could manage. We needed to get him to waiting medical staff. He required lots of fluid to replace the amount of blood lost.

We would be able to do some of that fluid replacement ourselves nowadays.

He survived, after many hours in surgery. The spike had gone up so far inside him, that it had ruptured not only his bowel, but it had also severely damaged his liver.

He was lucky not to have bled out.

Zebra crossing at Lepton.

In May 1981. There was a little girl knocked down on a children's crossing on Wakefield Road at Lepton. The patient was five year old I'll her Chloe, her grandad, ran the butchers shop at Paddock where I had grown up.

I was working with an old hand, Jack, a single man who lived with his sister. But he turned up for his shift from a different direction every single morning.

He had a lot of "girlfriends".

After getting her safely to HRI, we also got the job of transferring little Chloe to the neuro surgical unit at Pinderfields.

For the transfer, we were using the special care ambulance, bought by the people of Huddersfield in 1974. It had a gyroscopic stretcher in the middle. Once elevated, no matter what movement of the ambulance, the stretcher stayed perfectly still and level.

We were escorted to Pinderfields by four police motorcycle outriders. All with blue lights and sirens, leapfrogging each other. They were closing each and every junction as we were approaching.

Chloe, was unconscious from the accident. To transfer her to Pinderfields, the doctors had ventilated her. Injury wise, Chloe only had what appeared to be a small wound in the centre of her forehead. Other than that there was nothing else visible.

The hole was actually caused by the clutch lever of the motor cycle, it had hit her in the middle of her forehead and snapped off. It had become fully embedded in the centre of her skull. It had actually lodged between the two hemispheres of her brain and was pressed up against the back of her skull. It's a wonder that it hadn't gone right through.

Unbelievably, following surgery and a long stay in intensive care at Wakefield, she recovered. Chloe had to endure many weeks of intensive treatment in Pinderfields, some of the other children who were patients at the same time were not so lucky and had died.

Chloe was a survivor.

It turned out that Chloe had gone to school with one of Huddersfields first to qualify student paramedics, Rhian.

I didn't know that, until an off the cuff remark, brought things to light when working with Rhian. That was late in 2012.

My first dead body.

It was in 1982. Another shift when I was working with Jack, that we were called to an elderly lady being admitted to hospital. She was going for terminal, or as it is now better termed as, palliative care.

Just as we pulled up outside the address, Comms told us that the doctor had just informed them, that the lady had passed away. He was still on scene with the patient and her sister.

We did in those days transport deceased patients to the hospital mortuary. Nowadays, that would be done by the funeral director.

When we got inside the house, we were met by the lady's sister. She was obviously very distressed.

The GP had stayed with her until our arrival, it would be unheard of now, they are far too busy.

To get the lady outside we were going to sit her on our carry chair. To stop any neighbours seeing, and asking any awkward questions. Jack asked the sister if the lady had a favourite headscarf.

She had got a new one recently for a birthday. Jack placed it on her head, gently tying a bow under her chin. He pulled the headscarf well forward, all the time talking to her and apologising for disturbing her.

It was a beautiful thing to see. (If you can understand that). I vowed that in the future, I would like to be as professional as that. It really impressed me.

The doctor remained throughout. It was as we were leaving. He nodded his head quietly and respectfully, his only comment was. "Nice, I liked that".

We moved the lady out of the house, wrapped in a blanket. Her headscarf was forward, nobody suspected. The sister travelled with us on the patients final trip out.

There is not much dignity in death, but Jack taught me a lesson there. To always treat the patient, or more importantly the relatives, with the most utmost respect. To always maintain as much dignity for the deceased, as could be humanly possible.

I have always tried to follow his teaching and I hope that I have done that part of my job well.

Amsterdam Bar.

Another time with Jack in 1983, he was suggesting a night out. "Come on, let's go for a few bevvies" he said.

Some of us decided to take him up on it. There was Jack, Patrick, George and me.

We met up as planned at the West Riding Pub on Albion Street. It used to be underneath the still going, Mandarin, Chinese restaurant.

We then walked down Chapel Hill, on Milford Street towards Queen Street South. We were going to Huddersfield's, very famous Amsterdam Bar.

It was a well known "gay bar" and it was always having "turns", performing on the stage area. It was a "fun pub" in every sense of the word.

George was getting worried, he had a reputation as a lady's man. He didn't want to be seen with just male colleagues in a gay bar, what would people think?

Nothing actually!

In the early eighties the Amsterdam, was THE PLACE to be. Gay, straight or lesbian, it was packed every night.

As we were walking along Queen Street South, a large old style Jaguar pulled up alongside us. It was a dark night, and the driver got out of the car. We were all a little apprehensive at the time, but we thought we should be ok. After all, there were three of us, he was alone.

He was tall, very tall and well built. A West Indian man with a really strong "Brummie" accent.

He politely asked us if we knew where the Amsterdam Bar was, he was to be the entertainment for that night. We were able to point to it from where we were.

He had almost made it.

Once inside and we had quaffed a couple of beers. Kees one of the owners and partner of Philip, stood on the stage and he made the following announcement. "Everyone please give a grand Huddersfield welcome, to an up and coming comedy impressionist, please put your hands together for Mr. Lenny Henry".

He was really just nicely getting going, on what turned out to be a very promising and successful career.

It was a damn good night for us as well.

Working in a hospital.

One day in the summer of 1981

I was working with Mike, my old mate from junior school. We were asked to go up to HRI, a crew and an ambulance were required to take part in a photo shoot.

Someone was making a book about the Huddersfield Royal Infirmary.

We had to go in and out of the A&E department umpteen times. The patient on our trolley was actually one of the porters, Daniel. He was a big lad in those days.

We lifted him in and out of the ambulance several times, no lifts or ramps then. Each stretcher had to be side lifted and then fed into the ambulance.

There was no other way of doing it.

Inside the hospital we were met by Norris, the ambulance liaison officer, (he retired just before Christmas 2015). These photo's were for the section of the book that was about his job. There was also Sister Jackie and Staff Nurse Harriet.

It wasn't strictly true, but to describe each and every job within the hospital would have been impossible. The way it was done, I truly believe that it has given an insight in to aspects of most of the jobs within a hospital environment.

The book was eventually published, I have a copy, it is a careers information book called "Working in a Hospital" by S.D.Storr.

The book describes all potential careers available within a busy general hospital.

CHAPTER 18.

OUR FIRST HOLIDAY TOGETHER.

Luxembourg.

July 1981, it was going to be our first holiday together. Wendy and I were going away to Luxembourg for two weeks. Wendy had not been abroad before. A new experience for her, and what an eye opener she got.

We would not be going alone. We were going along with the 43rd scout group.

The holiday started off by everyone meeting at the Crosland Moor scout headquarters, there we boarded a 19 seater bus from Ivy Coaches at Linthwaite.

All of us, kids and adults were crammed inside. After packing the luggage in, there was not much leg room left, I can tell you.

Our driver was a smashing bloke and I'll call him Reg.

We were not going to be staying in a hotel, we were staying in a scout hostel. A long single storey building with a large room at one end for relaxation or recreation, a large kitchen and dining room at the other. In the middle, there were smaller rooms packed with bunk beds. They were very basic, they had a bed or bunk beds and a mattress. You used your own sleeping bag.

There were male and female toilets and one bathroom with two showers. (19 of us to share, 20 if you included Reg).

This building was not too dissimilar to our own original scout headquarters on Moorside Avenue. That had some small rooms and a kitchen, but no beds.

The 43rd, have a brand new state of the art building now. It is a true fitting legacy for the group scout leader. The late Geoff, who worked tirelessly for the group. It was opened in late 2012.

Reg was sharing a room with Graham, Pete, and me. At bed time, Reg was in the next bunk to mine, I'll never forget him asking me if I was squeamish.

A strange thing to ask I thought, particularly as I was just about to go to sleep. It was then that he removed his glass eye, and put it on the shelf between us.

A continental coach driver with only one eye, a first for me.

He then explained all the trials and tribulations that he had gone through, to get a continental PSV license.

We travelled all over on that bus, seeing all the sights, visiting castles, and viewing the many bridges that make up Luxembourg. A very beautiful part of the world.

Each day a couple of the adults had a day off, time for themselves instead of looking after the kids. Wendy and I got ours, it was on the Wednesday.

86

We decided to go across the border and in to Germany. We had been told that the border town was an absolutely beautiful place to visit.

The sun was really beating down, it was a glorious day and so, we the intrepid duo set off on our adventure.

Little did we know what an adventure it was going to be. It was around 18 miles to get to the border, a long walk and so we decided to try and hitch a lift. There were two of us, it should be safe enough.

After ten minutes of trying, a van stopped, it was transit sized. There were two young lads in the van, a similar age to us, they both spoke perfect English. They were going our way, across the border into Germany to the town we had set our sights on, magic.

They welcomed us, only there were no seats in the rear of the van, we had to sit on the bags of soft items. There were loads of the bags, maybe rags or something.

Everything was going to plan. They talked to us all the time, a general chat, they were pleasant enough. Then we arrived at a queue of traffic. It was the border crossing, a check point/passport control at the end of a long bridge over the river.

Then, suddenly the mood changed, they told us to "get down" to "lay still and be quiet".

What was happening?

They didn't declare us as their passengers, we didn't show our passports, nothing. We were petrified, what next? We have seen the films. We were going to die!

An awful feeling of impending doom descended. At the other end, they didn't even stop, they went straight through the gates. Again "keep down! don't move!" they shouted.

Once away and over the bridge into Germany, things were suddenly back to how it was before. With pleasant conversation. No mention of the previous ten to fifteen, long agonising minutes.

They got us exactly to where we had planned, a small town called Perl, there they pulled up and dropped us off as though nothing untoward had happened. We were just thankful to be getting out alive.

We waved as they left, I'm not sure whether that was out of fear or of relief.

We spent some time looking around, it was a typical German market town, just very small. We looked round for a couple of hours and then it was time to make our way back, on foot.

A long slow progress, but we were taking in all the sights at our own speed. We managed to catch a bus for a long part of the journey, as we would not be hitch hiking again. Sod that for a game of soldiers!

We would be having a relaxing holiday.

As we were getting towards our hostel Wendy wasn't feeling well, she had severe stomach pains, we rang the hostel in the hope that Reg may be able to collect us. It wasn't to be, his driving hours had been reached, (tachographs don't allow any leeway). We had to trudge on the last few miles, with Wendy in pain, we managed it though. What a wonderful welcome sight the old and dilapidated, run down hostel seemed to be.

After a very long day, we had got sunburnt and had an experience that will never be forgotten.

I know Wendy will never forget it, our first holiday together. It must have been alright though, she is still with me, we have been on other holidays together where we have been totally unscathed.

CHAPTER 19

ISSUES WITH THE FIRE SERVICE.

Dislocated knee.

Working with our original Cliff, what an absolute legend he was. He at the time, was the longest serving member of the ambulance service in Huddersfield, just like I am now.

He started down Leeds Road, working for the old Huddersfield County Borough Ambulance Service. They were based at the back of the Peacock Pub.

The pub is still there and the building is still standing, but the ambulance station is long gone.

Cliff was noted for his no nonsense approach.

One particular shift, when we were working together, it must have been in the early 1980's.

We received a call to attend at a building fire in Brighouse.

On arrival, it was an old coach building works, on the site of where the big modern Sainsbury's supermarket is now. That call was for a fireman who had been injured on the job.

His name I cannot say for fear of repercussion, I will call him Sam, an apt name for a fireman! He was to turn up later in my life on numerous occasions.

At the Brighouse incident. He and some of his colleagues had entered into the burning building, but somehow they had not seen the workshop pit.

The pit that was used for the MOT's of coaches. It was about three foot wide and about twenty foot in length, I would safely say it was at least four foot six to five foot deep.

Needless to say Sam had fallen in.

His colleagues had got him out, he was rescued using some vintage equipment. Not like the modern technical rescue services that they would call upon now.

No, they used something called a "ladder".

On our arrival, he was sat outside and in some considerable pain. For the pain, he was using their own entonox. (Nitrogen and oxygen based analgesic gas).

On examination, he had definitely dislocated his kneecap. That one, was to be the first of perhaps hundreds that I have seen.

Cliff, ever the tactician, said "surely it's first rule for you watter fairies, allus look where tha puts thi feet! Tha wunt ave dun that if tha had!" Brilliant.

That was said before taking him to hospital. I will never forget the incident.

Perhaps Sam didn't forget that one, or us either.

That might explain the abrupt attitude that he displayed towards Carl and myself.

Station Officer Joe.

In 1993, a man I'll call Joe was the Station Officer of Green Watch at the Huddersfield fire station.

He was a true leader of his firemen. All of his staff respected his way of working. He could get them to do anything.

When paramedics were starting in the ambulance service, Joe was fighting for his own staff. The fire service originally thought that paramedics should have been themselves. After all, the paramedics in the United States were all fire service.

It caused some conflict initially.

The ambulance staff didn't get a look in at jobs, if the fire service were present. They really thought that the paramedic role was in rescue and extrication. More like the HART unit now. (Hazardous Area Response Team). A specialist unit of paramedics to do just that. Ambulance Service paramedics.

Everyone at the ambulance station used to chunter about Joe, but nobody ever did anything about it.

I decided that enough was enough, as a Station Officer with the ambulance service myself. I arranged to meet up with him at the fire station for an informal discussion.

Following the meeting, I came away with a totally different impression of Gentleman Joe, as he was known to his staff.

Yes, he stood up for them at every turn, yes he hoped that they would get the role for themselves.

In the mean time, Joe had attended at a preliminary paramedic training schedule. There, he had realised that it was nearly all medical procedures and was definitely not for the fire service.

Not, at that time anyway.

If only our bosses in the ambulance service fought for our rights, like Joe did for the fire service, we would all be better off.

He was a true gentleman in every sense of the word.

It is good to talk!

Carl.

1994, and even more rota changes, we would then be working with permanent mates. The same partner every day, every shift for the foreseeable future.

I was teamed up with Carl, one of my heroes. During the previous rota, Carl and I had been working together for seven out of each of every eight weeks.

The new rota meant that we would work every day together. It turned out to be for fourteen and a half years, until Carl retired.

Only a little fella, but what a guy. I could not have wished for anyone better. We worked well together, we had a similar sense of humour and we were very similar in personality. Carl was about twelve years older than me.

We worked together for all that time, until "Carl" knew that his time to retire was due. In that time we saw all spectrums of the emergency care process.

We brought new life into the world, delivering several babies and we attended many tragic incidents involving loss of life.

We had many many letters of appreciation, many from patients whose life would have definitely ended without our intervention. A feeling that can not be put into words.

We didn't have any complaints filed against us in all that time, that were found against us anyway. Any complaints came back as either "no claim to answer", or "claim unjustified".

You will see some in the following passages.

Incompetent with faulty equipment!

Over many years with Carl, we came across numerous incidents involving the fire service.

All our poor experiences seemed to involve the same person, and that was Sam. He was then a fire service Station Officer at Huddersfield, as I was Station Officer with the ambulance service.

Whenever we had to deal with an incident involving his "watch", we would always have some degree of conflict. He reported us and our actions on several occasions, but I can be very pleased to report that "allegations unjustified" (or similar terminology), was the result of enquiry in every single case.

One such incident was early on a January morning, around fiveish, we attended at a house fire on the outskirts of Huddersfield.

A young female had been dragged out from a burning house, she was being resuscitated in the street by some firemen.

Carl and I took over resuscitation, she was not breathing and didn't have a pulse. Carl began using a bag and mask, to try and ventilate her, (to force air and oxygen into her lungs). A fireman was still doing cardiac compressions, as I got the defibrillator ready.

I placed the large paddles directly against the skin on her chest, firstly to see if there was any form of electrical cardiac activity.

The machines cannot be used to shock a heart, if there isn't any electrical activity present. They do not start a heart that has stopped, (contrary to popular belief).

There was some very fine movement, but, was that the patient. Or was it due to my hands shivering in the freezing cold January air.

I pressed the charging button, then I shouted the standard warning "stand clear!" I then pressed the button which delivered a shock of 200 joules, the equivalent of something like 3,600 volts.

Nothing happened, our patient never flinched. I checked her again, there was nothing.

We moved the patient into the ambulance and took her to hospital, she had died.

Prior to leaving the scene of the incident, we went and told the firemen of the situation.

Station officer Sam immediately put a complaint in. He told our management that we were incompetent and had gone out on the road with faulty equipment, or that we had been negligent in not having fresh batteries.

Neither statement was true. I was the one that went with my manager Janet, we had an interview with a Fire Station Commander, I'll call him Don.

I was blazing, (no pun intended), how dare Sam send in a complaint like that without even having the courtesy of speaking to us first?

He had had ample opportunity.

I had to explain to the fire commander how a defibrillator works, Sam had just said to him, that "the patient hadn't jumped so it must be faulty".

The young woman had been dead for some hours. Rigor mortis had already set in, she was as stiff as a board. The firemen were working on her, so at the time we carried on. It was on checking the patient fully, following the shock, that rigor mortis was found.

An electric shock whether it be from a household appliance, or a medical device, causes an involuntary contraction of all muscles. Those muscles have to be relaxed and uncontrolled, as is in unconscious states, to be able to react.

When rigor mortis is present, all the muscles are already rigid. There is no muscle tone, so there can be no contraction whatsoever.

The young lady had died, no amount of resuscitation could have helped her at that stage.

Get your facts right and do some research first Sam!

Soda stream.

On another occasion. Carl and I were first on the scene at a road traffic incident on the M62, it was just after the entry slip road towards Leeds from junction 24 at Ainley Top.

The incident, was for a Land Rover discovery, a first edition. It had actually left the carriageway and had gone over the barriers. It had rolled quite some way down the embankment towards the A629 Elland bypass.

A young unrestrained girl passenger from the rear seat, had been ejected from the vehicle partway down the embankment. The vehicle had then bounced and rolled right over the top of her, that had caused injuries that were incompatible with life.

She was deceased.

The other two occupants from the rear seats, had been wearing their seat belts. A young male and female, had both escaped from the vehicle with minor injuries. They had clambered back up to the motorway hard shoulder, where they flagged other motorists down and had raised the alarm.

The female driver and her female front seat companion were still sat inside the vehicle, both of them were suffering with severe injuries.

The fire service arrived, and as can be their wont, they tried to take over. They tried telling us what they were going to do, and how and when they were going to do it.

Carl and I were having none of it. We didn't want the roof cutting off!

A poke in the eye for some firemen. We wanted to stabilise both our patients before doing anything and then we would be putting them on a spinal board. Once that had been done, we had planned on taking them both out of the back door, with the rear seats laid flat.

No cutting would be required.

One of the patients had to have an intra venous line inserted, with saline running through. That was due to her having severe blood loss, leaving her with a dangerously low blood pressure.

Because of the blood that had been running free, before we had chance to dress her wounds. Carl and I were covered in the red stuff, particularly all over our hands. To move the patient the fluid would need to be turned off, our hands were too wet to do so.

We asked a fireman to simply roll the wheel down on the valve to stop the flow of the saline, he looked at us as though we had just asked him to perform a major operation.

He hadn't been asked by his officer, so no, he couldn't help. Sam came along to see what was going on. Carl then asked him to turn it off. Sam said that he didn't need to and that she could be moved without. "What's the problem with that?" He said.

Carl then explained to him that it needed to be turned off, to prevent any air embolisms getting into the patient's bloodstream. The tubing and the bottle needed to be completely clear of air bubbles.

What happened then just beggared belief, Sam got hold of the bag of fluid. He roughly put it under the patient, around the back of the spinal board and then under the patient again. "There" he said "easy".

Looking at the bag of fluid, he couldn't have got any more air bubbles in it if he had used a "soda stream".

Carl screamed, "what the hell are you doing, are you trying to kill her?" We had to remove the fluid and start all over again.

Another complaint went in from station officer Sam. Apparently we had been unprofessional yet again!

The two women from the front seats, we had been treating for suspected spinal injuries. It turned out that the lady passenger didn't have a spinal injury, but had some serious internal and external bleeding. The driver had not been so lucky, she had got spinal injuries, in fact there were four of her vertebrae that had been badly fractured.

Man on fire!

On yet another occasion, Carl and I received a call to an incident in Huddersfield. It was to attend at a house fire.

As I pulled round a bend into the narrow street, I could see a lot of thick, black smoke. It was coming from one of the first floor windows of the corner house. Just as I was about to pull up at the side of the road in front of the property, a man ran out of the garden and into the street in front of me.

I was shocked, he was on fire.

His hair and shoulders were in flames. We both jumped out of the ambulance, Carl grabbing a blanket. We had to drop the man to the floor, and roll him in it to smother the flames. The flames had been all around his face and upper body, his airway was our major concern.

I ran to the rear of the ambulance to get some burns treatments, and some oxygen. As I arrived at the back of the motor, a fire engine appeared around the corner, guess who?

Station Officer Sam, he alighted from the tender. He shouted at me, in fact he was almost screaming. "Get that ambulance out of my way!"

I tried explaining to him. That he, would have to back the fire engine away, so that I could get our kit out.

He screamed again, "get that ambulance out of my way, or I will shift it!"

He was then beckoning to his driver to pull forward.

I had to shout back "back off, are you mad?". I then said "I've got a man on fire, he's in the road in front of the bloody ambulance".

His only reaction was, "and I've got a fire to put out! Shift it!"

Then Carl appeared, he was wanting to know where I was with the life saving kit.

He was shouting at Sam, to "stop behaving like a bloody spoilt child, just 'cause we got here first, get over it!"

He then physically pushed Sam in the chest and said "get away from me, now!"

Then we both got the kit and were able to put the shocked and burnt patient onto the stretcher and into the ambulance.

His burns were from the fire in the bedroom, there, he had polystyrene roof tiles fitted. As he had tried to put his own fire out, the tiles had caught alight and were melting and dripping down on to him whilst still in flames.

His burns were very severe and his breathing was getting compromised, we had to rush to the awaiting trauma team at HRI.

There he was immediately put into a drug induced coma and ventilated to prevent any further damage to his airways. He was then blue lighted to the specialist burns unit at Pinderfields General Hospital in Wakefield.

The driver of the fire engine, was a mate of mine I'll call him Hugh. I saw him in the pub the very next night. He was asking about our victim, how bad was he?

When I had explained to him where the patient had ended up, he said that true to form, Sam was putting another complaint in.

Back at the Fire Station, he had said to his senior Officer, that we had been abusive and obstructive and had been preventing him from carrying out his duties.

That time he was out for blood. He wanted us to be "charged with a criminal offence".

I went barmy, of all the low life underhanded tricks!

The bastard!

Then "Hugh" made another statement. He said, "you know that we now have a live video camera in the front of the fire engine, don't you?" I said that I was aware of it.

That would have been the proof of exactly what had happened.

The very next morning, first thing. I rang my manager Janet and asked her to sort it out once and for all. I was not having it any more. She said that she would meet with Station Commander Don.

I told her of the events of a couple of nights ago and I told her all that Sam had done.

Then I asked her to view the tape, I said that it would prove beyond any doubt that we were innocent. Janet didn't want me to make the complaint formal, she asked me to try and keep it low key.

We never got to see the tape.

Shortly after that incident, Station Oficer Sam decided to retire from the fire service.

That was the end of our issues with him.

Following Sam's retirement. The Huddersfield Daily Examiner ran a feature on Station Officer Sam's distinguished career with the fire service. There was even a story of how in his early days, he was injured at the scene of a fire. He had damaged his knee and hurt his chest.

He said that whoever had dug the hole that he had fallen in, had not done their job correctly and had not put warning cones or barriers around it.

CHAPTER 20.

WENDY AND ME.

A frightening time for me, and Wendy.

It was August 1981. My sisters were both at home all day as it was the school holidays. At the time, I was working a lot of night shifts (it seems that nights are all I do) and I couldn't sleep.

Wendy suggested that I slept at her flat, after all, she would be at work all day. I did, it wasn't planned but I never moved out and she has been stuck with me ever since.

It was there that a former boyfriend came looking for Wendy, (hers, not mine), he was waiting for her as we returned to her flat. He came out of the hedge, he grabbed hold of her and took off in his car, I remember it like it was yesterday.

I'll never forget that car either, it was a white Ford Granada with a black roof, it's registration number permanently etched in my brain.

I panicked, I had no idea who he was, or where they were going. So I rang the police from a telephone box near to Gledholt roundabout.

By the time I had got to mum's house at Paddock Head, only about a mile or so away, there were eleven bobbies already there.

From my call and description, they thought at the time that he may have been the Yorkshire Ripper. I had told them that he had a lot of black hair and a beard.

Police tracked them both to Hartshead Service station, Wendy was safe and unharmed, he said that he just needed to talk. The police assured me that they would be keeping an eye on them. They did, all night long, they were under a police observation programme.

Not long after that, Wendy and I got a flat together on the first floor of a house in Cambridge Road, another single roomed bedsit in an old terraced house. It was just right for the two of us, even if it did only have a single bed.

It was right opposite the main entrance of the well known swimming baths. Inside the large building, were two swimming pools and a small shop. The smaller of the two pools could be covered over by a hard floor. It doubled up as a dance floor for one of the function rooms. There were two function rooms used for weddings and parties, both with a fully licensed bar. It was a very well used location, for all sorts of community events.

Most of the local schools used it's facilities.

It was in full swing until the mid eighties. Then the new Huddersfield Sports Centre became the main swimming pool and sports facility, along with a bar and function rooms.

Shortly afterwards, all the old buildings on Cambridge Road were demolished.

Wendy and I held our engagement party in the main function room of the Cambridge Road swimming baths.

Now we have a new state of the art building, the Huddersfield Leisure Centre. As well as a competition sized swimming pool, it also has a fun pool. That has large slides, for the adventurous and fun facilities. There is also a beginners area for non swimmers.

The new Huddersfield Leisure Centre opened in May 2015. The old sports centre was closed ready for demolishing.

The old sports centre and the two tower blocks of flats adjacent to it on Southgate, were all demolished in March 2016.

Raising money.

Charity events. The Krypton Factor was on television, a show that involved four contestants battling against each other in a series of mental and physical challenges. The finale was the completion of a full sized, actual army assault course.

The assault course was at Holcomb Moor, army training camp near Bury.

Over the August Bank holiday weekend in 1981, we found that you could tackle the famous assault course. Providing that you got yourselves sponsored for charity. Each year there were four or five different charities that benefitted from the participants.

A team of four of us from work duly attended. Patrick, Tommy, Garry and me. Garry was 64 years old at the time, and so we had to take out a special insurance for him. He was very fit for his age, he lived to be 95. He was still playing football at seventy.

We did the assault course, for three years on the trot. The third year, Wendy also competed with some girls from GSM Syntel where she worked. Our team was Mike, Patrick, Joseph and me, Joseph was the current boyfriend of Wendy's younger sister Lynn.

Our time time to finish that last time, was much better. We had managed to improve each year.

We went to the Royal Fusiliers barracks in Bury, later on in the year to be presented with certificates. Wendy got her picture taken with Krypton Factor presenter, Gordon Burns.

Her hand in marriage.

I actually asked Wendy to marry me in late July 1981, she said yes thankfully.

We didn't announce anything straight away. We didn't even tell any close friends, we had decided that we wouldn't say anything until we had bought a ring. Then we could tell everybody and we would arrange a proper do.

We chose the ring together, and then I bought it, a beautiful platinum and diamond engagement ring.

In my family, I had been brought up traditionally. So even before I had asked Wendy, I had asked my mum and dad what they thought of the idea of us getting married, they were absolutely made up.

Both mum and dad really made Wendy one of the family. I couldn't have wished for anything more, Wendy was thought of very much as one of the Firth family for the rest of both their lives.

My two sisters both thought of Wendy as an older sister that they had never had, and they still think like that today.

Because of that upbringing, again on the quiet and Wendy had no idea. I decided to go and ask Wendy's mum and dad for their blessing too.

I knocked unannounced, on the door of their house one tea time, the first week in August it was. Wendy's mum answered, I asked if I could speak to John, Wendy's dad.

They must have thought my visit was because something was seriously wrong, I was ushered into the front room. Wendy's dad sat me down while her mum went to the kitchen to make a brew.

I remember him saying to me "Whatever's the matter lad? You're shaking like a leaf. What's happened?"

I was sat there stammering like some daft mute, but it came out in the end, the true reason for my visit.

I asked him for his permission, to ask his daughter for her hand in marriage.

His first reaction was to burst out laughing. I thought charming, that's all I need. He stood up, stepped towards me, he raised his hand and shook me by the hand.

Then he threw his arms around my shoulders. "Of course lad, of course you've got our blessing. Welcome to the family" he said.

Dorothy came in at that stage, she appeared shell shocked, I don't think she had any idea what was going on.

I didn't need to say anything though, John said it all for me. Dorothy gave me a hug, she said virtually the same. We drank our teas in almost silence.

Thank God she made my tea in a mug, my hands were shaking like a "sh***ing dog" (another charming phrase of Tommy's).

If it had been in a cup and saucer I would have probably thrown it all over the carpet, that would have been the shortest family blessing ever.

I then went back to Cambridge Road and to Wendy, then I told her where I had been.

I think it met with approval.

Engaged.

It was Saturday September the 26th 1981. Wendy and I got engaged to be married on her birthday, we had a big do for family and friends in the function suite of Cambridge Road baths.

I was over the moon that Wendy was happy to be with me, it was our commitment to be together for the rest of our lives. She was and still is, without any shadow of any contradiction. The true love of my life, my soulmate and my best friend.

Our first house.

Not long after we had got engaged, the landlord of the Cambridge Road flat, told us that he had found a lovely little house for us. It was at Lindley, if we were interested.

It hadn't even been put on the market then, he lent us the keys to go and have a look. It was perfect for us. A front facing, two bedroomed property. A double fronted, back to back property in Lindley. It was situated almost across the road from the hospital.

It was an ideal location for us and a nice area to be in. The asking price, £4,000.

The house needed a lot of updating work doing to it, it had been lived in by a lone elderly female.

When we moved in, we kept the massive wooden and iron antique bed, it just needed a new mattress. It was heaven from the single bed at Cambridge Road.

My mate from Paddock, Mark, rewired the house for us as a wedding present. Most of the walls had to be re-plastered and all of the ceilings had to be re-plastered as well. The only ceiling that wasn't done was the landing, it was a large double landing.

The house had to be decorated throughout. We needed a complete new kitchen and so we fitted it in ourselves. All the time that we were doing the work, we were living in just one of the bedrooms.

Tommy taught me all sorts of building work, cement mixing and stone cutting to be just a couple. We with his help, built a stone/marshallite fireplace and we extended it into the corner for the television to sit on. Then we went around the corner and along the side wall, where we built a seat into it. It would be an ideal place for a carrycot when the time arose.

We didn't even have any carpets for quite a while.

We had just about finished all the main works, decorating done and had the carpets fitted.

When one afternoon, I was sat in the front room with our dog Gem. He started pacing up and down near to the door. Then I could hear what sounded like water dripping down the staircase. I went to investigate, the sound was actually little bits of plaster dropping from the landing ceiling and falling down the steps. Then the lot came down. Me and the dog ran outside followed by a great black cloud of dust. It was all the black lime from in the loft area.

It took many weeks to clean up after that!

The fine black dust had got everywhere, even into sealed packages, it was horrendous.

Gem.

The house at Lindley, was a perfect place to live for us and our first dog, a border collie pup called Gem. He had a wonderful attitude, he was a perfect pet.

He was very timid though. He didn't like anyone with a walking stick, or a flat cap. He used to growl at dad if he had his cap on.

We once came back from the shops, on the floor was a cardboard half moon. It wasn't until a couple of days later, when I tried to find my cap, that we realised what it was. That half moon was all that was left of my flat cap.

Gem had eaten it all except for the cardboard insert of the peak.

When Adrian was born, originally we had been worried in case Gem was going to be jealous of the new family addition. There was no need. He was wonderful.

We would put Adrian in his carrycot, on the special place on the back wall. That is where Gem would lay, on the floor beneath him. He would remain between any visitors and Adrian. He would not let anyone near the Adrian, unless we were there to pick him up and hand him to them.

He moved with us to Manchester Road, he loved it even more then, he had a large garden to call his own. He could run around for hours.

Both our sons use to play, to fight and generally run riot with him, he loved it.

As with everyone, he started to get old, he would struggle to get out of his basket in a morning. We went to the vets, they gave him an injection for his arthritic hips. It was as though they had put a lubricating oil into his seizing joints. He was like a pup again, jumping and running around.

They told us that the injection would be required regularly. It started off around every six months, but as he got older, they were needed more and more frequently. Until they were every couple of months. Whatever the injections were, they gave him a new lease of life and many more good quality years.

It was June 1997, we had been living at our present home on Manchester Road for about eleven years. When as a family we were all devastated, our beloved dog Gem collapsed.

There were no options available to us, he had to go to the vets and we knew what the outcome would be. There was no real choice, it was much kinder for him. He had been ill for a while. He suffered from arthritis, weight loss and he was incontinent, he was getting old.

Gem was put to sleep that evening, it was awful. We were all absolutely devastated. But when I got home, I wasn't ready to be called a murderer by the boys. Adrian and Ben had never known a time without Gem.

At the time they hated me. It took a while for them to accept that it had been the kindest thing to do.

We had no plans to get another dog.

Ren and Stimpy.

August 15th 1997. We went to the pet shop just on Manchester Road, we had some tropical fish and needed some food for them. The shop at 404 Manchester Road, has been all sorts over the years, I believe it was a school to start with. It is now occupied by O'Neills' sports supplies.

It was always an event to go to that shop, they stocked all sorts. Including a couple of spider monkeys of their own. There were fish of all kinds, cold water and tropical. A selection of reptiles, lizards, snakes, and some spiders. There was also a collection of domestic pets, the usual, mice, gerbils, rats, guinea pigs and rabbits. Occasionally a litter of kittens.

That day, we hit jackpot, there had been a litter of thirteen pups born. One unfortunately didn't make it. The pups had been born on the 28th of June, and were looking for a home.

All the cute pups were in a large pen, it was like being a kid in a sweet shop. I knew we wouldn't be going home alone. Wendy let the boys pick one each. Adrian picked a lively, long haired one. It was mainly brown, with a lot of white and a little black. Ben picked the runt of the litter, it was a quiet one. It was very cute, with short black and white hair.

We went home with the two pups, baskets, bowls, leads, toys etc.

The pups although they were from the same litter. Were nothing like each other, neither in looks nor personality but they were brothers. (That sounds like Adrian and Ben).

The boys named the pups after a cartoon series, Ren and Stimpy, it worked.

Mum to the pups had been a border collie. Ren was almost a traditional lassie type collie. Stimpy became a stocky, well made dog, he had more Labrador style features.

Perhaps mum had been a busy girl, we'll never know.

The dogs were inseparable, we had two baskets for them but every morning, they would both be squashed together in one.

We ended up buying one giant basket for them. They never spent a night apart. As they were getting older, Ren became blind and Stimpy was deaf, but together they supported each other.

Eventually, they both became very frail, they were both losing weight rapidly and they were both becoming incontinent.

That time, we had some time. Even though they had both left home, we discussed the inevitable with both of our sons. The decision was a joint effort, that when the time came, we would not let the dogs suffer.

The time came a lot sooner than expected though. It was within a fortnight of our discussions. I came home from work, Stimpy couldn't stand up, he couldn't get out of his basket. I lifted him up, he collapsed again.

He had been incontinent.

The time had arrived, I had to ring the vets there and then. The journey to Donaldson's was a sombre one. I rang my sons. Ben was living in Selby, there wasn't enough time to get him, Adrian came straight over.

I went in and spoke to the vet first, away from Wendy and Adrian, I needed to ask her a question. "Do you think that I am being callous asking for both dogs to be euthanised, together?" I explained their age, condition and that they had never spent a single night apart. The vet, she was lovely, agreed to look at both dogs.

The decision was almost immediate. Stimpy's heart had failed, the vet thought that he had also possibly had a stroke. Ren was already pining for him, they know when something is wrong, don't they?

The lady vet answered my question, "yes, it is the right thing to do".

The lady vet explained to us that Ren was also very ill and that he might only have lasted another couple of days, if that. That evening, as usual they went to sleep together for the very last time.

We had arranged for them to be cremated, at a special animal crematorium in Rossendale in Lancashire. The vet, without our knowing, must have been in contact with them.

I had a phone call, "would we like for Ren and Stimpy to be cremated together?"

No question, that would be perfect.

That vet was so compassionate, even after we had left the surgery, how thoughtful of her to think of that.

That then happened, they were together all their lives, and still are now in death. We had their ashes returned, and have them in a wooden funeral casket.

Beautiful.

CHAPTER 21.

BACK TO AMBULANCE WORK.

Relief rota.

At the start of my ambulance service. Like everybody else, I started on the relief rota. That meant that I, along with six others, covered holidays and sickness.
When we picked a shift up, we would stay on that line until one of two things happened. Either the staff member returned to work or we took a holiday or break in the shift pattern ourself.

That system worked well most of the time.

When there were no shifts to cover or allocated, we would work Monday to Friday from 09:00 until 17:00. (A nominal shift). The drawback being that it was not unusual to have a phone call or a visit, when someone had "rung in sick and we need you in to work, now!" Even on Christmas Day morning, but that's the way it was.

There are "rights" for staff now. Relief staff in the early days didn't have any option. They hadn't got any "rights", they weren't even allowed a vote on any station matters.

Eventually we had Baz and Daz, both of them were ex Station Officers and knew the job inside out. They started the manpower office, then known as the resource department and now known as scheduling. Whatever the name, they do the same job.

Baz and Das, worked from a central office at our headquarters. It used to be at Birkenshaw, now it is in Wakefield. They were the ones that allocated all of the relief shifts, giving as much notice as possible.

No computers for those boys, lots of A3 sheets of paper holding rota's, hanging on 8' x 4' boards. The boards were on runners, sliding past each other, just like the rugs in a carpet store.

Pencils, at the back of their ear, not a pen in sight and a rubber at the ready. The two of them managed all of the shifts, holidays, sickness and cover for the whole of West Yorkshire ambulance staff. That was for PTS as well as A&E.

Now there are several resource staff in each of the divisional offices and they have managers. Everything is computerised now and it still gets messed up on a regular basis.

Come back Baz and Daz.

Since my original writing, I'm sad to say that Baz has passed away, another one of the good guys has been laid to rest.

Broken neck.

It was back in August 1981. I was working with Ivan again, we were called to what was only given to us as a "works accident" on the outskirts of Huddersfield. As we approached the old Huddersfield Town Ground on Leeds Road, people were actually stood in middle of the road waving handkerchiefs, the road had been blocked completely to traffic by these people.

It didn't look too promising.

We were escorted right round to the rear of Learoyds Mill, it is where Walkers Windows reside now. There we were met by a group of people from the works, they were all pointing to the cab of a tractor unit from an articulated truck.

It was explained to us that a man had been working on the engine and the cab had been tilted forward for ease of access. Then somehow the cab had dropped back down shut, trapping the man underneath.

The factory forklift driver had lifted the cab forward taking the pressure off the patient. The forklift was still in situ, supporting the cab to keep us all safe, as we tried to help.

The patient was stood in the engine area, between the wheel and the engine block, he was leaning forward and appeared to be resting on the tyre. His hands were clasped together in a relaxed manner, his chin resting on top of them.

The patient was a large muscular built West Indian man, for the purpose of this article, I will call him Tom.

As I spoke to him he was so matter of fact and he simply said "I think I have broken my neck".

I asked him what made him think such a thing.

Then, he answered with a statement that I will remember for the rest of my life. I still go cold just thinking of his words.

He said "I can feel my hands touching my chin, but I can't feel my chin touching my hands".

I ran my fingers down the back of his head and neck, I felt a hole, my finger could slip right into the gap. It was just below the base of his skull, that wasn't a good sign. He was right, he had broken his neck. I have never come across a neck injury as blatantly obvious since.

We slowly eased him out from his position and laid him onto a scoop stretcher. There were no stiff neck or extrication collars then. We made a horseshoe shape out of a blanket and we wrapped it around his head to support it. It would help to keep his head immobilised in that position.

Then we had to fasten him to the scoop stretcher. We were able to load him feet first into the back of our vehicle, hopefully that would ease some of the pressure applied to his neck on braking.

That was the procedure then.

A really slow transfer was required to get him safely to HRI to awaiting staff on stand by. No bumps, no sharp acceleration or braking.

I also had to travel on the crown of the road, stopping other annoyed and agitated motorists from overtaking me. If they had, especially at speed, the sideways rocking of the vehicle would almost certainly have killed him.

Thank God it was in the days before the dreaded speed humps, any one of those would have been enough to finish him off.

Following his x-rays, it revealed not only a broken neck, he had snapped his "odontoid peg". Also known as the Atlas and Axis, where the skull is attached to the top of the spine.

That type of neck fracture, was Albert Pierrepoint's speciality as a hangman. Normally the injury would result in instant death.

The spinal column consists of a series of ring shaped bones (vertebrae) inside which, runs the spinal chord, the nerve centre.

In the neck there are seven of those bones, all numbered "cervical, or C",1 to 7. There is a rhyme which is so true that "3, 4 and 5 keep the diaphragm alive".

In short, the nerves that pass through those three bones are responsible for the control of respiration and circulation (the breathing and the heartbeats).

Tom's neck had been hit with such force that C4 had been pushed forward so hard and far that C3 was then sat directly on top of C5. His spinal chord had been stretched to almost breaking point.

A man of slighter build would have been guillotined, possibly decapitated. Due to Tom's powerful muscular shoulders, his build had saved his life.

The transfer to Pinderfields spinal unit was again extremely slow, the journey was made under a police escort, with four motor bikes leapfrogging each other at every junction. You never see the motorbikes on general duties now. We didn't have to stop once.

The patient was on a spiker bed. A special type of bed that had a mattress above, as well as below the patient. They can then be sandwiched between the two mattresses and then turned to relieve sores etc. The mattresses can be separated again following the procedure.

Another simple idea, but they are no longer in service.

On arrival at Pinderfields, another patient was being admitted to the same ward, by ambulance. He was a patient that had been transferred from the Leeds General Infirmary. He too had suffered the very same odontoid peg injury.

Two people had an accident within ten minutes of each other, they had suffered one similar and usually an instantly fatal injury, that they had survived. Then they were in the next bed to each other recovering, fate, perhaps.

I'm a great believer in fate.

The other lad was a 21 year old student at the Headingley Campus of the Leeds University. He had suffered a fall down some steps at one of the entrances to the university, whilst on roller blades.

It took Tom a long time to get anywhere, but he did manage to make some progress. He got the use of his arms back, and he was able to propel his own wheelchair for short distances by himself. He was able to sit unaided and have a full and eloquent conversation. Similarly the other patient had the same striking level of recovery.

Six months after that incident, I was with Ivan again and we saw Tom at the spinal injuries unit at Pinderfields. He told Ivan and myself that since his accident, he had lost a lot of "so called friends", but that he had "gained some true friends". More importantly, that his two "little girls had grown in to two wonderful young ladies".

He and his wife, were in the process of separating and she was about to leave him at around the time of his accident.

She still left him and they had since become divorced, but they have remained great friends. As with many couples, they seemed to have got on far better since separating.

The girls spend as much time "looking after" dad as they can.

Tom's wife's job, was was as an "instructor" in transcendental meditation, running her own practice. Using those techniques, she had taught him to come to terms with his condition.

What a man!

As we were talking to Tom, all of a sudden he appeared to be struggling, he started shaking and then he was sweating. We didn't know what was going on, but then raised his right hand and he wanted to shake our hands to thank us both.

I still hauntingly remember hearing Tom talking to Ivan whilst in the back of the ambulance as we were coming up Trinity Street. He actually asked Ivan to tell me to find a large pothole in the road, to "finish me off", he then said "I don't want to live like this".

I was already driving blue light ambulances and I was attending to poorly patients. Including those with injuries such as Tom's, that were classed as impossible to survive. Even though I hadn't even attended my formal training at that stage.

I always had someone qualified working with me. It was to be like that for most of my first year. That practise would not be allowed in the modern day and age, all formal training has to be done prior to going out "on the road".

CHAPTER 22.

MY FRIEND AND MENTOR.

Tommy.

On the relief rota, it wasn't long after I had first started, I was covering for Leo. He had had to have a hernia operation, unfortunately something had gone wrong and he had suffered from a severe infection. He was going to be off work for quite some time.

As a result of that, I was covering his shifts and I worked for quite a long time with his regular mate. Who became my good friend. Tommy, was a very smart bearded man, who always wore his uniform cap.

I had worked "third manning" with Tommy and Leo, several times in my first few weeks.

One of the first jobs with them, that I remember clearly, in 1981. Was when we had been called to see a hysterical woman in Almondbury. At the time there were no further details, she had been too hysterical to give any more information.

We arrived at the house, a fairly large semi detached, in one of the more affluent areas of Huddersfield.

Leo spoke to the woman, she was of around the mid to late forties. She tried explaining, but couldn't get any words out. She handed Leo a note. It was a suicide note that had been written by her husband. He was saying how sorry he was and that he couldn't go on any more.

She then pointed to a door in the corner of the kitchen, "he's down there" she said. It led into the cellar.

Leo went down into the darkness, he had only been down the steps for five or ten seconds, then the noise was horrendous. Leo was gipping and retching, I thought he was going to be sick.

He ran up out of the cellar and into the garden. His uniform cap had already been tipped up and perched on the back of his head. He went outside and lit a cigarette to calm himself.

Tommy then disappeared down into the darkness, sure enough and within seconds, he too began retching and heaving. What a noise? What the hell was in that cellar?

Instead of running upstairs though, there was a bright flickering of light at the bottom of the cellar steps, followed by a red glow. Tommy had only lit a cigarette, whilst still in the cellar.

Suddenly and very loudly, we heard Tommy shout "Jesus bloody Christ!" Just then, the cellar light came on.

At the bottom of the steps, just in view, there was a figure. It was that of a man, the lady's husband. He had hung himself from a large hook, that was fastened into the cellar ceiling.

Tommy eventually came back upstairs and then he went outside, where he finished his cigarette.

The police were duly called.

On their arrival, they took over and we left.

Parked just around the corner, my dynamic duo of friends smoked yet another cigarette.

I asked them "why the retching?"

They both laughed then.

In the pitch black of the cellar, they had both been feeling around for where they thought a light switch might be.

They had both done exactly the same thing. They had stuck their fingers right into the wet, drooling, mouth of the hanging man and then realised what they had done. That would have been enough to make anyone feel sick.

Thankfully, as I was only third manning, I didn't have any contact with the deceased.

Steeplejacks.

Tommy had twelve years of ambulance experience before me. He was a member of a large family of old time steeplejacks, he had some right tales to tell of his former career. Here are just a couple of his quick anecdotes.

One day, Tommy showed me an old post card photograph, that he kept in his wallet. It was of a mill disaster taken in Lancashire. It was a black and white photograph of an event that had taken place many years ago when Tommy had been a young man.

The photograph clearly showed several people, really running for their lives. In the background, the large mill chimney was not quite upright, it had already broken into three sections and was falling towards all those workers.

Tommy and a young apprentice lad, had been given the task of demolishing that very chimney. The chimney was in the middle of a built up village and attached to the side of a textile mill.

The safest method of demolition, was for the steeplejacks to climb up to the top of the chimney. Then using special chisels and hammers, they would break up the large coping stones that ran all around the edge or rim of the structure. Once into much smaller and manageable pieces, they would drop them individually down the inside of the chimney stack.

When they had arrived at the top, Tommy opened his toolbag. He had left their large, wedge shaped "splitting chisels" back at the yard. The young lad stayed up top to have a brew, whilst Tommy went back to their base to get them.

All alone at the top, the young lad must have got a bit ambitious, he found that one of the large stones was loose. He had then loosened some of the bricks on the inside, and he was able to tip the whole of the extremely large stone down the inside of the chimney. He must have thought that he was helping out, how wrong he was.

Unless you come face to face with one of the topping stones, it is difficult to gauge the size of one of those monsters. Although curved, they have a cross section of around 24" square and are around four foot six inches long. They can weigh more than a ton each.

That's a hell of a weight.

It had been a very naive decision, for the young apprentice and with tragic consequences.

There is a real science to demolition, that mistake was just down to his pure immaturity and lack of experience. Small stones don't cause any damage.

The large one, on its way down the inside of the chimney, had ricocheted off each of the side walls. Each time it had bounced, it had gained some momentum. Inevitably it had broken the integrity of the structure on the way down. When the walls have been weakened, there is only one consequence, the chimney will collapse.

The chimney had fallen towards the onlooking mill workers and into the mill itself, as dramatically was captured on the postcard. The young lad, along with two female mill workers had been killed instantly.

The latter part, was from the summarised decision of the inquest.

A shocking tragedy.

Another story that Tommy told with relish, was of around the same era and a favourite trick of the steeplejacks. It was during the summer months, particularly when they were working high up on the textile mill chimneys.

The mill women were notorious for their wolf whistles and cat calls to them. The men in turn would strip off their shirts and strut their stuff around the top of the chimneys.

Once they had got the women's attention, the men would have a readily prepared spare pair of overalls, the shirts that they had removed had been stuffed into them. They would then stand at the edge and would listen to the screams of the women, as they "accidentally" knocked that pair off the top. They would fall to the ground causing sheer panic.

Tommy told me that if "our Ernie (his older brother, and boss) found out, we would have lost a week's pay for that".

M62 fatality.
It was whilst I was working with Tommy, that we received a 999 call to the M62. We were going to pick up a fatality from an RTC, (road traffic collision) formerly known as RTA (A for accident). At that stage we new nothing more. I had never seen a badly injured body, alive or dead.

The incident was on the Eastbound carriage way towards Leeds, right opposite the end of Scammonden Dam.

The problem was, that the driver of a broken down car, had stopped her car only just off the carriage way. The offside wheels were still actually on the solid white line. She had then got out of the car and stepped right into the path of an eighteen wheeler 38 ton truck.

The original ambulance crew called to the incident, Dotty and Fred, had taken the truck driver, in a severe and obvious state of shock, to the hospital at Lindley.

On our arrival, the other services were already there in abundance. There were fire and police personnel everywhere. On the hard shoulder just past the car was a fire service tarpaulin and underneath that we were told was our patient. Parked on the hard shoulder, fifty yards away from that, was the truck.

I cannot reveal the injury details, because they are too graphic. They have been in my head for over thirty years. I can still see the image of that lady when driving across that particular stretch of the motorway. It was a horrendous sight.

Tommy went first, he lifted the tarpaulin and promptly bolted over to the barrier where he was violently sick.

He told me that if I could manage to look at her "you'll do alright cock".

I tentatively lifted the sheet, nothing could have prepared me for what I saw. Half an hour previously, what I was looking at, had been a perfectly healthy living human being.

The only fault found with the car, after extensive and detailed forensic examination later, appeared to be a blocked windscreen washer duct.

Then, all I was doing was staring. Tommy came over to me. He told me to "step back now" and "come on have a minute lad, you've been there long enough". Apparently, in his words, I had "gone to every shade of green ever seen on a Dulux Colour Chart".

To move the lady we had to carefully slide a scoop stretcher (it splits in half lengthways and then slides together and locks) underneath her. Then we placed her with as much dignity as possible, if there is such a thing, into a body bag.

We then took her to the mortuary at the Infirmary.

Arnold, the mortician at that time, was a fascinating man. He was very good at his job, but he certainly wasn't the most hygienic. He was the master of the darkest humour that I have ever come across.

He kept his sandwiches in the fridge with the bodies, he said "who's gonna nick em from in there?"

I do agree.

They were perfectly safe as far as I was concerned.

He had been given the task of looking after our RTC victim. Only the next day, our paths crossed again with Arnold. That time we had brought in a very elderly gentleman, who had died suddenly at home, of a suspected heart attack. (We don't transport the deceased now, unless from a public place. That wasn't the case years ago, we transported everyone).

Whilst round at the mortuary, Arnold called us over.

On a moveable table was the body of the lady from the previous day.

He had just finished preparing her body for viewing. Yes, viewing, her family had insisted on seeing her.

He was about to move her to the Chapel of Rest viewing area.

Arnold had applied some form of make up to the lady and she looked amazing. He had been given a recent photograph of her, the likeness was uncanny, what a comfort it would be for the family.

Only twenty four hours earlier, after what Tommy and me had seen. I would have said, that it would have been absolutely impossible, for the family to be able see her and for them to say their goodbyes.

Well done Arnold, well done.

Funeral home.

Wendy does some cosmetic work now on a regular basis, as part of her job at Taylor's Funeral Services in Cowlersley.

To do the hair and make up of someone who is deceased, to the satisfaction and appreciation of their loved ones, is an art. I am so proud of her.

When I met Wendy and even after she started working at the funeral home over twenty years ago, I couldn't have seen her doing that.

A major achievement!

Who's that knocking?

It was in September of 1981, that I had been called to a flat on the top floor of Richmond Flats. That was one of a trio of tower blocks near to the old Huddersfield Sports centre at the end of Leeds Road.

Working with Tommy again, we had gone to pick up an elderly lady for a routine outpatient appointment.

We were inside the top floor flat, when there was someone knocking on the outside of the windows.

It was Paddock painter and decorator George.

He was actually stood right on the top edge, of the window cleaners swinging cradle and he was leaning across to paint the edge of the window frame.

He had recognised me in the flat and had knocked to wave. What an unexpected greeting so high up on the eleventh floor.

I saw George on the night of the 16th December 2016. He had been brought into hospital by some colleagues of mine.

He is now 83 years of age, he didn't look a day older than the last time I saw him and that must have been well over twenty years ago.

In the days that I remember him from the Royal Oak, he was a heavy drinker. I never saw him really drunk, but then again I don't think I ever saw him what you would call sober.

He was a well known character around Paddock. He always had his white decorators overalls on, whatever time of day. He always wore a flat cap and was always perched on his head, predominantly tipped over to the right side, exactly like my grandad Firth.

Last night he was laid on an ambulance stretcher, he was only wearing his vest and a pair of pyjama bottoms, but he still had his trademark cap on the side of his head.

I had a short, but pleasant conversation with him, it was great that he still recognised me, and talked affectionately of mum and dad.

Protective Gear.

Whilst working with Tommy, we were always smart. We had a proper uniform, ironed shirts and always with a tie. We had sharp creases pressed down our trousers and polished shoes. To finish off we wore a really smart tunic.

Tommy always wore his uniform peaked cap, the qualified staff wore a white cover on it so that we could be spotted.

After I had qualified, he got me into the habit of wearing mine.

One day we had received a call, it was to a hostel on Portland Street in Huddersfield, at the back of the technical college. The hostel was run by a charitable group known as the Syrenians, it was a temporary respite home for homeless men, who mainly had alcohol problems.

It was very basic, they would have a clean dry bed for the night, with four beds to a room. Rudimentary food was served when available, but it wasn't guaranteed. It was usually donated by local takeaways.

Most of the hostel's residents were only there for a matter of a couple of weeks at the most.

Our call was to attend to a man who had been coughing up blood for a few days, he was not very well at all. The charity workers had called for the doctor to visit.

Following his examination, the doctor had diagnosed a very virulent and active case of TB, (tuberculosis). A nasty lung condition which could well be fatal, also known as consumption many years ago. That disease had become almost totally wiped out in this country.

The condition can be very contagious and needs to be handled with barrier nursing. (Full protective gear whilst dealing with the patients and in isolation, in a side room on the hospital ward).

From our point of view, once the patient had been transported, the ambulance would be completely out of commission until it had been thoroughly decontaminated.

For our own protection, to our level of barrier nursing patients. We had to put on a protective suit. That composed of a j-cloth type material pair of trousers and plastic elasticated overshoes. A full length j-cloth type material smock, complete with long sleeves and elastic cuffs, it tied at the back like a surgeon. We also wore a protective face mask and a j-cloth material hair covering, like the ones seen in hospital theatres. It was finished off with a doubled up pair of rubber gloves.

We must have looked a sight as we stepped out of the ambulance, hundreds of students were all milling around on Portland Street, after all it was the technical colleges' lunchtime.

We walked into the hostel, they were expecting us. As we were being directed by one of the volunteer workers, to a room at the back of the hostel. It was on the ground floor, we heard the sound of glass smashing. We ran into the room and at the same time, a man was making his escape out of the window, he screamed to anyone who might be listening. "They're not f-ing operating on me in 'ere! And off he went.

To say he had such a severe and debilitating lung condition, he was running up Fitzwilliam Street quite well. With Tommy and me in our fancy dress costumes chasing after him.

We had to get him back as he was a massive contamination risk.

We even had to get the police involved, to keep some of the well minded students at bay. The students were only concerned, but unaware of the dangers they could face.

The man was kept in hospital for many months, but unfortunately, he was already very frail. He just didn't have the strength to fight it, it killed him in the end.

Arawak Club.
Another memorable job that I attended with Tommy, was at the Arawak Club. It was a West Indian Club on Brow Road at Paddock.

As we arrived, stood outside to meet us, was a very tall man. He looked like I would expect Bob Marley to be. He had a full head of dreadlocks, reaching half way down his back. He had a long plaited beard and a large knitted hat, in Rastafarian Colour's. He was a very pleasant man with a big beaming smile, he said that he was concerned that his dad was "bleeding all over the place" inside.

We were ushered in to the gents toilets. Sat on a stool in one corner, was another Jamaican man, smoking a cigarette. He was only small in stature. He was dressed in a smart dark coloured suit, complete with waistcoat and he was wearing a dark coloured pork pie hat on his head. His hair was very closely cropped and he was clean shaven.

He had his left leg elevated and resting on another similar stool. When he spoke, he had the strongest Jamaican accent and a highly infectious laugh, he was brilliant.

It was only a small room, there was just enough space for two wall mounted urinals and a sink. The toilet cubicle was at the far end.

The blood was everywhere, it was dripping off the ceiling and running down the walls. The sink was covered, it had even splashed onto the small window above the urinals.

The man had his elevated limbs' trouser leg rolled up to his knee. He explained that every time he put his foot on the floor, blood was pouring down his leg. When he elevated it again, the bleeding not only stopped, but all traces of it disappeared.

I checked his leg over, I couldn't see anything.

Then just as he had explained, as soon as he put his foot at the side of his other, "there ya go man!" He said, sure enough, blood was pouring down his leg and into his sock.

I lifted his leg, again nothing there. I squeezed and wiped the area clean, there was nothing.

As soon as his foot went down and touched the floor, there was a blood bath.

It was doing my head in.

Tommy just stood in the doorway, he had lit a cigarette and was just stood there smiling. It was actually more of a smug expression on his face.

I had a large dressing in my hand. The next time, I would be ready.

I put the large dressing on his leg and bandaged it in place. As soon as his foot went down, the dressing went red, but it was on the outside.

The blood was definitely on the outside of the dressing. No way, that couldn't be right.

It had to be from out of his leg coming up to the surface, but no, it was definitely outside the dressing. I got down on my knees, I had to fathom it out.

When I reached out to remove the dressing, to see what the hell was happening, I got the shock of my life.

My sleeves were rolled up and I had my rubber gloves on. All of a sudden, my arm was covered in very warm, very wet and very red blood. It was all down my arm and running off my hand.

Tommy was laughing. From where he was standing, he could see the mans other "good leg". Between where the top of man's sock stopped and below where his trouser leg started, he had a varicose vein. It was that which had ruptured.

As when all varicose veins "pop", there is a very, very fine jet of blood. It is painless, but it can and will, spray anywhere and everywhere. It can easily reach a distance of three metres.

That one was very fine, almost invisible.

As the man's left leg had been exposed, each time it got in the firing line, he could actually feel the blood hitting him. He had thought the blood running down, like me, was from a small wound on that leg.

Neither of us had even the slightest inkling, that it could have been from the other leg. I hadn't seen one of them before, although I have seen many since.

I was covered in blood.

Another lesson learnt from Tommy, a silent master.

My arse is on fire!

Working on a night shift with Tommy, it was near the end of January in 1983. We were called up to the M62.

At about half past two in the morning, we were sent to a motorcycle "incident" on the Westbound carriageway, between junctions 23 to 22. It was after Scammonden Dam and close to Stott Hall Farm. (The little house on the prairie) where the motorway separates around the farm.

It was a very bright moonlit night, but it was absolutely freezing.

When we arrived where we needed to be, there was a lone police car with its bright blue lights flashing and one police officer. He was stopped in the fast lane.

There was only one other car, with a single occupant, he was on the hard shoulder.

As we got out of the ambulance, the biting cold wind nearly cut through us, it was also very icy underfoot.

The police officer explained to us, that the man in the car had been heading back home to Manchester. When he had come across a motorcycle in the fast lane, it was without a rider. The engine was still running when he had arrived, it was on its side and it was still going round in circles. The marks in the road, suggested that the machine had been on its side for some distance, it must have been shifting.

The police officer had managed to stop it going round and round.

The bike had obviously hit something hard, as there was extensive damage to the front forks and fairing. The front lights had been smashed.

But, then the policeman drew our attention to the speedo. The glass on the dial had broken and the needle was stuck at 83mph. That meant that the bike had to be travelling at least that speed at the time of impact.

The rider could have been anywhere.

The motorist had phoned 999 and had then started looking for the rider, but to no avail. He had only looked nearby, in case he had to warn any other traffic about the bike. In all fairness, he wasn't dressed for the cold weather either, but at least he had stopped and called it in.

The fire service arrived, two full crews. I don't really know why, after all, you can't cut the roof off a motorbike!

Can you?

At least there were now another ten pairs of eyes to help search.

We were all looking up and down the road. Some of us on the hard shoulder, some on the main carriageway and others between the Armco barriers that separate the carriageways.

Occasionally, somebody would shout out, "shh! I thought I heard something!"

Everyone would go quiet, but all that could be heard was the howling of the winds. Fortunately there was very little traffic around at that time of night.

There would have been a damn sight more nowadays.

After about twenty minutes of searching, we must have been a good couple of hundred yards from the bike. There was a definite cry in the distance, it was off the hard shoulder side of the motorway.

We all collected on the same side to search, as we walked further away from the bike, the cries were louder and getting clearer.

When the cries did become clear, it was the same cry, over and over again. "My arse is on fire! My arse is on fire!"

We found him

A man in his late forties, he had all the gear on, it looked good stuff as well.

He still had his helmet on.

He was actually in the rain "run off gulley", a channel for the water to drain away, it was made out of closely laid concrete flagstones. It would be two foot wide at the bottom and of a similar depth.

The man had been thrown into the ditch at high speed, he had then been sliding down the bottom of it, on rough debris, water and ice.

It must have been like going down the "Cresta Run" bobsleigh track. He had travelled a hell of a long way away from his machine, at least 300, maybe 350 yards. All the time he had been on his back.

He was fully conscious, he said that he had been throughout his ordeal and he assured us that he hadn't "broken anything". But he still insisted that his "arse was on fire".

Tommy brought the ambulance up to where we had found our patient and we set the stretcher up at the side of the grass verge. Then with assistance from the fire service, we lifted our man out of the ditch and onto our trolley. We had to lay him on his side, due to the amount of pain that he was suffering.

As we did so, we could plainly see the extent of his injury.

As he had been sliding down the bottom of the gulley, it had actually been rubbing away at his leathers. It then made a start on his flesh, that had been ground away, he had then started to grind away at his pelvic bones.

No wonder his arse felt as though it was on fire.

He didn't have one!

Not one inch of buttock cheek was left, there was a lot of boney damage as well. It was going be a difficult job for the surgeons to sort out, it would take a long time to recover from it too.

Other than that, he was fine.

He admitted to Tommy and myself, that just before he had "lost it" on some black ice, he had been travelling at between 110 and 120mph. He hadn't collided with anything. He had been thrown one way, and his bike was off another.

He wasn't aware of what his bike had smashed into.

Sterile dressings were gently applied and then soaked in sterile water to help to cool him down. Water, not saline, that would really have been rubbing salt into it.

Ouch!

It was the best treatment that we could think of at the time.

For pain, all we had then, was entonox. It did the trick for him though.

Tommy had to drive all the way to junction 22, before turning around and then going all the way back to HRI. Staff had been alerted and were waiting for our arrival.

He's got the look!

Tommy had another silent gift, a look that he could give to someone, a look that would turn them immediately to stone.

Many a time, on arrival at a job, particularly in a town centre or a public house. It is not be unusual to be met by a crowd of people, maybe all in drink. They will all be trying to help, all of them can be budding medical students. And they will tell you in no uncertain terms what you should be doing to, or for the patient.

Tommy would just give them the "look". He wouldn't need to speak. The atmosphere would immediately change, it would go quiet, slowly the crowd would disperse, as they all sloped off one by one.

It was an evil glare!

I was at Tommy's house once, I don't know how it cropped up in conversation, but it did. His partner Jean, said "what do you mean a look".

I asked Tommy to show her.

As soon as he did so, her face went very stern and she shouted at him "Thomas, that's evil! Don't ever do that to me again!"

I have been told since, by others, that I can do the look now. It doesn't always work, but it's great when it does.

Once again thanks Tommy, you taught me a hell of a lot of stuff, mostly good stuff mind.

Sadly, Tommy passed away in 2014, I had a lot of respect for Tommy. Rest in peace my good friend.

CHAPTER 23.

THAT'S FREAKY!

Spooky goings on.

Another job with Tommy, was a call on a Sunday morning in 1982.
It was Easter Sunday.

We had a call to attend at a Baptist Church in the Huddersfield area. A male had collapsed inside the Church. That was the only information that we had received. It wasn't unusual and still isn't to have minimal information.

On arrival we were taken through the doors of the Church, the minister was stood in his pulpit at the front. Mid hymn singing, he never stopped or changed, he just pointed down to one of the pews in front of him.

We approached the pew and there, sprawled across at a bizarre angle was a male of around fifty years old.

He didn't look well at all, he was pale and extremely clammy.

He was all alone.

Not one person in the congregation had left their seat to offer him any help or assistance. Someone had called an ambulance and then it was left up to us.

Tommy left the Church, to go back for the carry chair.

While he was getting that, I put an oxygen mask on the man. That was in the days before we had pulse oximetry (levels of oxygen monitoring) and cardiac monitors.

I gave him a high flow of oxygen, the man was cyanosed and he was rapidly going blue. His pulse was weak and thready, the man was dying.

The second that we sat him up to move him, he stopped breathing and his heart stopped beating.

Having no other options available to us, we had to put the man onto the floor and start CPR.

(Cardio [relating to the heart] pulmonary [relating to the lungs] resuscitation [to make active again]).

A bag and mask, attached to 100% oxygen, was used to force the oxygen into his lungs.

Followed by some hard compressions on his chest to try and get his heart beating again.

It was known as a witnessed (by us) cardiac arrest. He would have been a prime candidate today for rapid intervention defibrillation, with a good chance of a successful outcome.

At that time there was no such thing. Good CPR was the only order of the day.

There wasn't any form of cardiac monitoring available, other than feeling and counting a pulse.

Whilst we were resuscitating him, not a soul stirred. The congregation stopped singing and they all knelt to pray. Then everybody sat quiet and listened, as the minister started on his sermon.

A very surreal experience.

We weren't getting anywhere, Tommy returned the chair to the ambulance and came back in with the stretcher.

I carried on CPR without stopping.

Once we had got the patient in the ambulance, we had a blue light and siren run to HRI, with a full resus team on standby.

Hopefully, because we had witnessed his cardiac arrest and started CPR immediately, they might be able to shock him back into life.

Tommy flew up that road, weaving in and out of heavy traffic for a Sunday, it was the same all the way to the hospital.

As we travelled up Westbourne Road through Marsh, I was still stood up in the back of the ambulance, pounding on the man's chest for all I was worth. I was sweating buckets.

CPR is extremely hard work, if done right.

We had just got level with the end of Reed Street at Marsh, when Tommy braked hard, and I went arse over tit into the cab doorway.

Tommy hurled a torrent of abuse at some driver that had just pulled straight out of the junction, neither seeing nor hearing us.

I picked myself up and carried on from where I had been so rudely interrupted.

We raced into the resus room, staff were waiting.

Paddles at the ready, there they had full cardiac monitoring. There was something on the rhythm, his heart was fluttering, it was fibrillating.

That is the heart muscle in rapid spasms due to electrical activity, but no physical output of its own.

CPR carried on, then the now familiar charging noise, followed by, the "stand clear" Command. The same happened three or four times, at the same time intra venous fluids and drugs were being administered. Including adrenaline, that again to try and stimulate a non functioning heart.

We left at that point.

We were sent back to station to try and get our meal break.

About two hours later, we arrived back at HRI with another patient.

We asked how our cardiac arrest patient had gone on, definitely thinking the worst. "Go and ask him" the doctor said, "he's still in resus, (the resuscitation room) but he's doing fine at the moment".

We were amazed, despite having a full blown heart attack, leading on to a full cardiac arrest. Our patient was sat up on the hospital trolley, eating a sandwich and enjoying a cup of tea.

As we talked, then the shocks came and not of a medical kind. That man totally freaked us out. Nobody else has ever said things to me like he did, either before or since, thankfully.

Before we had chance to speak, or introduce ourselves.

He said "thank you for that fella's, I had gone then". He said "if you hadn't have been on the ball I wouldn't be here".

Then he spooked us even more, by telling us, that he had been there watching the whole situation. From the roof of the Church.

He said "I couldn't believe that nobody stopped to help, even the minister didn't stop the service". How could he have known that?

Unless staff had heard Tommy and me talking and then told him.

Then he said to Tommy, "it was close with that dozy woman in the yellow beetle, wasn't it? I was sure that you were going to hit her".

There was no way on earth that he could have known that. He was laid flat in the back, he was unconscious and not technically living at that point.

I looked at Tommy for confirmation. He said "it was a yellow beetle, but I couldn't have told you who or what was driving".

The man explained that he felt as though he was sat on the roof of the ambulance and watching me working on him, from that position.

He recalled that it was a young woman, that she was smoking at the time and that she had dropped her cigarette when she saw how close we were.

He then asked me if I had hurt myself when I fell over.

Too spooky for me!

Gives me the willies that stuff!

Even spookier goings on.

It was early evening in September 2003. I was working with my regular mate Carl and we were called to the home of a well known local character, by the name of, I will call her Annie. The caller had said that "she was dying".

On arrival at the house, we could see inside a large conservatory that ran along the whole side of the house. Inside, on a chair at the side of the fireplace was the patient, she was talking to someone on the telephone.

We knocked, she didn't even look up. We knocked again, harder the second time. The woman looked directly at us, pointed to the phone and carried on talking.

That, seemed to me a most ignorant thing to do, when she was supposedly needing our help.

We both knocked at the same time, then, she looked furious.

If looks could kill, Carl and me were doomed. We thought that she might be talking to ambulance control, many a time, they do keep the caller on the line until our arrival.

Eventually, she put the phone down and came over to the door. She shouted through the glass window, to ask who we were.

Once Carl said the word "ambulance".

She said "oh, why didn't you say so, I've been waiting for you".

She opened the door and let us in.

The lady, was well known for being a little eccentric. As well as a respected upstanding member of the community, she had been a member of the St. John Ambulance Brigade for many many years and had reached a high rank in the service.

She was always immaculately turned out.

When we asked her why we had been called to her address, she stunned us both. It was nothing like the answer that we were expecting.

She said "I told the ambulance operator that I am dying and that, my young friends, is just what I am going to do. Tonight, right here in my own home".

We asked if we could do a full set of baseline observations.

She agreed to that and sat back in the chair by the fireplace. As she did so, she simply laid back and then slid gracefully out of the chair and onto the floor.

What a strange thing to do!

Not only that, she had stopped breathing, we felt for her pulse, it was almost non-existent.

We had to start resuscitation.

Carl placed an endo-tracheal tube, right down into her throat and he attached an oxygen powered ventilator to it. That would force oxygen into her lungs to help her to breathe.

I was performing cardiac massage.

We carried on working on her for about 45 minutes, but to no avail. She had no pulse and had made no attempt to breathe for herself, despite our efforts.

We had no option, she had died, we had to pronounce her life extinct.

We called for the police to attend, as it was a sudden and unexpected death.

Or was it?

We couldn't class her death as suspicious, in any criminal sort of way, but it was certainly mighty strange.

We needed to find out if she had any relatives, who was her next of kin. I don't think that she had ever been married. I knew of a brother, I'll call him Frank, but I didn't know of any contact details.

When the police arrived, they searched through some of Annie's private papers and they managed to find some telephone numbers.

One of the policemen was writing down her details. He wanted her date of birth, full name, a list of her medication and her past medical history etc.

All of a sudden, the other policeman let out a cry of some sort, we all looked up.

He looked very pale and shocked.

He had a copy of that days Huddersfield Daily Examiner in his hand, (the Examiner, was an evening paper then). It had been opened, folded over very neatly and at a particular place.

It was the page that was known locally as the "hatched, matched and despatched" page. Or officially, births, marriages and deaths.

"I don't bloody believe this" he said, and then carried on with, "this is just far too strange to be true!" He pointed to a name in the deaths section, it had been highlighted and circled in red ink. Annie, it was her.

An announcement of her sudden death, in the evening, on the same day of printing.

It was a long report, it was all about her time in the St. John ambulance and her time in the community. It was actually her own obituary.

I rang 1471 from the house phone, it rang a couple of times and then a female voice answered.

As I was explaining who I was, the woman cried out. "No, not an ambulance, has she died?"

When I asked who the lady was. She said that she was Annie's best friend. That she had been on the phone to Annie, regarding the obituary in the paper and that Annie had been convinced that she was going to die that very night.

It couldn't have been more than five minutes from putting the phone down to her, that Annie had done just that. She had simply collapsed and died.

That was crazy, how could she possibly have known?

He Spooked Them. Guess Who?

In the early eighties when I started the ambulance service, there was a lad I had worked occasionally with at Brighouse station, by the name of Greg.

A nice lad, he seemed to be a loner and he could be a bit strange at times. Mind you we are all a bit strange working for the service.

He was a single lad who lived in a cottage in the grounds of Lord Kagan at Fixby. (Known for being the founder of the Gannex raincoat and his friendship with Harold Wilson).

In exchange for a low rent, Greg used to do some maintenance work in the vast grounds of the home.

It was in 1984, that Greg lent his car to a friend for a few weeks. It was an old, but not quite vintage Jaguar. Greg was unable to drive, while he recovered from a recurring disc problem in his back.

For reasons unknown, the friend who suffered at times from severe depression, took it upon himself to commit suicide. He was in Greg's car.

He had driven up to a secluded car park on the moors, not far from the M62 motorway.

The police were in attendance and had asked for an ambulance, in those days we used to transport deceased patients to the hospital mortuary.

It was Danny and Fraser who were the attending crew.

The car had been there for several days and the man was in a state. He was bloated and he was already starting to decompose, so they quickly placed him in a body bag for removal.

The police then handed the crew, some details found in the car, the details matched the owner, Greg.

The police hadn't been able to get hold of Greg, so 2 and 2 had been put together. They had got 5.

Greg had actually gone away to his sister's address, she lived in the North East, to recuperate. Nobody knew, he hadn't told a soul.

Once back at hospital, Danny informed the duty ambulance officer of the incident and that it was a member of staff that had died.

Brighouse ambulance staff got in touch with Sasha. Sasha was single at the time and used to mother Greg a bit, she would look after him. She came home early from her holiday, to help to organise the funeral for him. The day that she arrived home from her holiday, Greg had also arrived home from his sister's.

The next night, Sasha went to Greg's, she needed to find any paperwork, contact numbers of his family, etc.

It was early evening, around eightish, Sasha was alone when she let herself into the cottage. She had been looking through some drawers of a bureau and had managed to find some family details, when the door opened, there was Greg!

I'm not sure who had the biggest shock that evening.

They had a lot of urgent calls to make. The police needed to contact the family of the actual deceased, the coroner needed informing as a preliminary post mortem had already taken place.

It was an absolute nightmare scenario.

Then to cap it all, Greg and as I have already stated could be a bit strange, had an idea. After all that had happened, he wanted to have a bit of fun!

By that time, it was around midnight, he got Sasha to give him a lift to Brighouse ambulance station.

Outside, the two night ambulances were parked on the forecourt, meaning that there would be four members of staff inside.

He childishly put his hood up and then he started gently tapping on the outside of the windows. As the curtains opened, he jumped up and as he removed his hood, he shouted "GUESS WHO?»

He caused havoc.

He did it again at six o'clock in the morning when the day shift started.

Greg had to retire through ill health, it wasn't too long after the suicide incident. His recurring back problems, that he had suffered with for many years, came back with a vengeance. He had to start walking with a stick, until he couldn't manage without it.

I haven't seen him for many years, but as far as I know he his still alive and kicking. I know that he did move away from the area to be nearer to some other members of his family.

CHAPTER 24.

AMBULANCE CADETS.

Ambulance Cadets Scheme.

In October 1981, the West Yorkshire Metropolitan Ambulance Service introduced a revolutionary new addition. They started an Ambulance Cadet Scheme.
It was to be an annual intake of ten young people straight from school or college. They would receive a military style schooling for the next two years.

During their training, they would spend their time divided between the training school, then based at Keighley RATC and time on the road with ambulance crews.

As well as their ongoing medical training. The cadets were drilled in marching, regularly up and down the tennis courts, at the front of the training school. It was all to help instil self discipline.

They would be taught how to drive and to pass their tests. They would attend outward bound courses. There they would be put through physical stuff, hiking, camping and map reading. All of it team building skills, ways of being self sufficient and ways of standing up for and looking after each other.

After all, a team is only as good as its weakest member.

They would have to do a lot of physical training. In the gym and whilst at the RATC, it always included a three mile run before breakfast.

All to groom them into exactly the sort of ambulance staff, that would be required in the future. Those young people were destined to become West Yorkshire's first paramedics and the officers, or as they are now, the managers of the future.

The ambulance cadet scheme was originally organised and run by a chap called Tony. It was proving to be a very successful venture, it was Tony's baby until his retirement.

It was then taken over by a younger female named Mon. Mon was a former army officer.

Mon, had started the service at the same time as me. A very powerful female. A perfect successor for Tony.

Mon was ideal for the job, no offence to Tony, but Mon was a lot younger and she was extremely physically fit. She wouldn't ask the cadets to do anything that she wouldn't be prepared to do herself and she probably would be doing it with them anyway, particularly the running or the gym work.

They were certainly put through their paces. Nearly all of the cadets that started over those six years, went on to become paramedics and most of them became officers of some kind..

We had three of the cadets that started in the first year, based at Huddersfield. There was Manny, Graham and Aaron. All three of them were clever lads and completed their two year training, all of them then went on to be some of West Yorkshire's first paramedics.

Aaron left after around five or six years, he went on to have a successful career as a drugs representative. Before becoming a North Of England Manager, for one of the biggest companies in Europe.

Jean started at Huddersfield in 1986, she is now the locality manager for Calderdale. Eamon, who is Jean's boss and is in charge over all our district. Which includes Bradford, Calderdale and Kirklees. He was also a former cadet.

Eamon was well liked as a young lad, he is now well respected as a manager.

More water with that?

One of the other girls that started in the same year as Jean, was Lisa, I remember her coming out as a third member of staff on vehicles that I was crewed up on, several times.

Lisa married Eamon (mentioned in the previous story). A nice lad. Right from the start, he showed that he had obvious potential and was going to go far.

One job that I really remember with Lisa, was in her early days, probably in the late spring of 1987. For some reason we were both working out of Dewsbury Station with a local lad there, called Alfie.

We had been sent a call to a child that had been scalded. It was for a young boy of only around eleven months old, I remember he hadn't quite reached his first birthday.

They are a particular type of call that get the adrenaline pumping, you have no idea what you are going to be faced with.

The little nipper, had somehow managed to grab hold of a freshly poured cup of tea, it was even without any milk and he had pulled it over on top of himself.

He had suffered a large area of reddening, (erythema) to the front of his body, and at the top of his little fat thighs. He had very little blistering and fortunately had not suffered from any injury to his face or airway.

Although his injuries would have been extremely painful, they were not life threatening.

Today, we would have been able to give him some pain relief, in the form of Calpol (paracetamol) and Junior Nurofen (ibuprofen). The dressings that we could apply now, contain a highly efficient cooling gel, that is a natural antiseptic. It is a pre soaked dressing, in copious amounts of "tea tree" gel.

Then, it was a matter of applying a sterile cotton sheet, that had been packed specifically for the purpose and then soaking it in saline (a sterile salt solution). I wrapped the little boy in a pre-soaked sheet. It seemed to help straight away. It wasn't long though, before the heat from the burn was apparent again and the sheet was drying out. Lisa, took great delight in, pouring more of the cold salty water over the child.

Her delight was two fold. Primarily and correctly, it was helping the child. But also, she could see that as I was sat on an ambulance stretcher, with the child on my knee, I was sitting in a large pool of cold water. My pants were soaked from top to bottom.

Lisa didn't stop giggling the whole journey in to hospital, as she asked if I wanted "more water?"

I have never let her forget it and I keep reminding her, that "one day, one day, I will get my own back!"

I wouldn't, but she's not so sure.

Lisa spent many years as a RRV (Rapid Response Vehicle) driver in Halifax. Now, she has recently qualified as an Urgent Care Practitioner. A paramedic with much higher skills, she can actually prescribe some medications and perform minor suturing. She can do urine testing, all sorts to try and alleviate the need for transporting patients to hospital and to treat some patients at home.

She's done well for herself, and good on her!

CHAPTER 25.

MY AMBULANCE TRAINING.

Finally, I started my Formal Training. A two weeks driving course.

I did my driving course in the November of 1981. It was a two weeks residential course, based at a former home for the student nurses, who worked at the Airedale General Hospital.

The location, was the Regional Ambulance Training Centre (RATC) a place called Elm Bank, at Keighley. A name of ambulance service tradition. The first ambulance training school at Cleckheaton, that was called Elm Bank, it was the actual name of the impressive detached Victorian mansion. The building is still standing and now houses several private apartments.

The latest Elm Bank, is the training school at Wakefield now, that is housed in the former Stanley Road ambulance station.

The course instructors were, big Jack (temporarily seconded from Leeds ambulance station) he was my instructor. Ex Scottish police driver Jake and locally sourced from within the ambulance service, Keith. The latter two were the full time driving instructors, along with a third, Grant. He was on leave at the time of our course. He was being covered by big Jack.

There were twelve of us started that day. We students were divided into groups of four, three car loads of us travelled the same journey, almost together in convoy.

One day it had snowed, heavily, we went down to Nottingham and including into Sherwood Forest. The home of Robin Hood.

One of the lads was from Rickmansworth near Watford, he had never even seen snow, what a big kid.

The next day, we went through the Lake District in more heavy snow, it was like being in another country, it could have been the Swiss Alps. We stopped at the side of the road for a break.

Any excuse to get out the flasks of tea and sandwiches.

Our colleague "from down south" rolled about in the deep snow, a grown man acting like a two year old. Then he was joined by about a dozen or more of us, including the instructors, in a snowball fight.

Ever the professionals!

On the driving course with me were some of the lads I had started in the ambulance service with. Gavin from Dewsbury, Stuart, Pete and another Stuart all from Wakefield. Greg from Halifax and Mike from Huddersfield, before he transferred to Brighouse.

Of all of those eighteen who started in the ambulance service at the same time as me, from all around West Yorkshire. Only Pete at Wakefield and myself are still in the service, at the moment, anyway.

The course itself, was a great experience. It will never be forgotten and great friendships were made. It was amazing.

It was very intense and extremely hard work. We had to take written exams every morning.

Then there was all kinds of driving, fast driving, slow driving, night driving, motorways, dual carriage ways, rural roads and car parks for reversing and manoeuvering.

We even spent time on a skid pan. That was close to the Burnley football ground. It consisted of a large tarmac area, all around the edge of it were a series of pipes leaking a slippery soapy solution that ran all across the surface.

We were driving Ford Escort cars that had been fitted with extremely bald tyres. Another memorable experience that will stay with me for life.

I had the chance to drive an old former Huddersfield BMC ambulance, fleet 551, affectionately known in Huddersfield by the old "Borough lads" as "Nan".

The engine of the BMC, is partly in the cab, making it very warm. The gear stick is situated behind and to the left of the driver. Me, being a short arse, I couldn't possibly put the vehicle into reverse gear whilst still remaining sat on the driver's seat.

I had to perform a probably illegal manoeuvre. I was depressing the clutch with my right foot and then leaning right over. I had to put the gear stick into reverse and get back into the drivers seat, then I could swap my feet back over and release the clutch.

There was no power steering on those vehicles and so they were extremely heavy to steer, no wonder they were nicknamed "panzers" after the German panzer tanks.

I passed the driving course, then it was back to Huddersfield and back to the job on the road. It would be another three months, before eventually starting my six weeks residential medical course, also at the RATC at Keighley.

More Formal Training. The Six Week Millar Course.

In February 1982 it was to be the start of the main ambulance medical training, if I passed the Millar course, then I was in. My job would be as secure as I made it.

The end of the six weeks would coincide with the end of my twelve month probation. That meant that I would be fully trained and I would have completed my qualifying period. I would then be a Qualified Ambulance Man.

Thanks to the Millar report of 1964, where the first formal ambulance training structures were developed.

No paramedics or other grades then, you were either qualified to deal with emergency calls, or you weren't. Then you would provide transport for routine journeys, now the PTS. At that time PTS wasn't a separate service, qualified staff also provided the routine transport, in and amongst emergency calls.

I started by attending at the training school in Keighley, there were a lot of us, thirty six in all.

We came from all corners of the British Isles. After an initial registration and course introduction, we were split into groups known as syndicates, of twelve.

My syndicate leader was instructor Bill, he was ex RAF. Bill was a lovely chap, but very intense. Everything had to be 100% by the book, but he knew his stuff well.

He particularly specialised in maxillo-facial injuries. That was due to the fact that he himself, had been involved in a serious ambulance crash, Where he had hit and smashed the end of an oxygen valve clean off from the bottle.

He had hit the bottle, full on with his face. From that impact, he had suffered horrendous injuries and had the scars to prove it. His face had to be completely rebuilt, nearly every bone was fractured in more than one place. It was all held together with screws and titanium plates.

During the first four weeks of our course, we covered all the theory aspects and systems of the human body. The course also involved us taking several short written exams every single morning. None of the university pass marks of forty per cent there, they had to be passed, with 100%.

Or a re-sit was required the following morning.

When life is at risk, it is no good not knowing sixty per cent of what you need, to be able to save one.

The last two weeks were more hands on. We had many "incidents" set up for us. The instructors made every effort to achieve realism.

The training school staff, would utilise members of the local community and use them to play the parts of our simulated casualties.

Those local volunteers will never realise, how many ambulance staff that they have helped over the many years, to save countless lives.

They were fantastic!

The instructors called them the visitors.

Some of the visitors had special abilities, some of them were suffering from varying disabilities. The instructors used their abilities regularly, to bring make believe situations to life.

My first incident to deal with, was a supposed motor cycle collision. I was crewed up with a bloke called Jack, he worked out of Menston Ambulance Station, for WYMAS.

On the road just outside the training school, a motorbike, was laid partially underneath the rear of the neighbour's milk float.

The story being that the motorcyclist had been temporarily blinded by the sun and he had run into the back of the stationary truck. The patient was laid at the side of the truck, his legs hidden partially under the back of it.

As we checked the patient, unbeknownst to us, he was a visitor with a special ability. He was a single amputee.

As we tried to move him, his leg came off, the false one had been filled with raw meat. You can imagine the type of verbal comments that were aired by us when that happened.

We used the land on the "Keighley and Worth Valley Railway" sidings several times.

The area was used by us, for getting patients out of some of the old railway carriages, right side up or upturned. We had both day and night exercises and both indoors and outdoors.

We also held some of the exercises in Peter Black's car museum, it was a massive old mill complex that was undergoing some extensive renovations. Part of the situation there was that work was in progress twenty four hours a day, that made for a perfect training environment.

We were able to use some of the already erected scaffolding, to scale and rescue patients from.

A patient that I had to deal with, was stood leaning against the edge, right on top of a scaffold tower. He had supposedly been hit in the face by a falling object from the ceiling.

The job for my crew mate and me, was to go up there and assess the patient's injuries.

Then we needed to plan a way of getting him safely down and back to ground level.

I was teamed up with a lad called Ronnie, he was from South Wales. Our patient had received a facial injury, and was holding a very dirty bloodstained handkerchief up to the side of his face.

We had to climb the internal ladders of the scaffold, to get up to him. Not my favourite pastime, the scaffold tower was shaking like mad as we climbed.

Probably nowhere near as much as I was shaking though.

To examine his injury, we moved his hand and cover away from his face, he only had a sheep's eye sat there in the handkerchief. Then he let it go, it went off the edge of the tower, where it slapped right down to the floor with a most sickening splat!

That one was rough!

We were forty foot above the ground on a rickety scaffold tower, and they did that to us.

Thank God, that once we had dressed his wounds, he was able to climb down the ladders with only a little guidance from us.

I was already bricking it being up there, I didn't need any more adding to it.

What we didn't know at the time, was that the patient, was another visitor and that his ability, was that he only had one eye. For that evenings proceedings, he had removed his false one and to make things look authentic, he had acquired the sheep's one.

After the course, I did really appreciate that those methods were the correct way to do it. To be faced with situations that were as near to reality as they could possibly be.

Many, many thanks to the visitors, particularly the special visitors with their unique abilities.

Thank you!

Although the training was hard work, we had all formed some great friendships. There were many loveable and mischievous characters amongst us.

All of the instructors that we had, were great, Bill, Patrick, Gerald, Guy, Fergus and not forgetting my initial driving tester at my job interview, Angel.

Elm Bank RATC Keighley.

At the training Centre itself, there used to be some fantastic facilities.

The building, was actually the former nurses home for the Airedale General Hospital. We each had our own room and each of the rooms had a single bed, it had a wardrobe, a desk, a chair, a sink and two or three plug sockets.

Perfectly adequate for our needs.

On each of the five floor landings, was a utility room with washing machine, ironing board, iron etc. There was also a small kitchen with tea and coffee making facilities, a fridge and a toaster. A couple of toilets and showers at each end of the floor. If mixed staff on that landing, they would then be designated male or female.

Elsewhere in the main building, there was a fully stocked bar and social club, a library, a gym area, a quiet room and a tv room.

We had a large dining room, all of our meals were catered for, three times a day. There were snacks in between and cheese, biscuits, jam and toast facilities were left out all night.

We had plenty of classrooms, a large garage area for four ambulances. A large car park for both students and staff. There was a full size tennis court at the front of the building, and a basket ball area.

The facility is now no longer, it was closed around 1990, with the intention of being sold.

Unfortunately the building was left empty and neglected and it went to rack and ruin. Lots of undesirables had managed to get into the building, and several fires had been lit, along with other untold damage.

So eventually it had to be demolished. It was sold off, but for land value only, the ambulance service lost hundreds of thousands of pounds on that.

A new junior school is now on the site off Cartmel Road in Keighley.

All of us on that six week basic course, as it was known, had passed with flying colours. It was tradition then to have an end of course celebration, so we had a great party night on the last Thursday night.

The drink flowed freely that night.

Two more people that the training centre couldn't manage without were the head of training, Mr. Bob Lee OBE. The other, one of the most unforgettable ambulance service characters ever. The literally world famous, Leading Ambulanceman Ellis Coates. He was well known to all ambulance students, old and young and nationwide all through the late seventies and eighties.

Students attended the RATC for any course, that was required for any rank of ambulance staff. They attended from all over Europe and beyond, we had a chap from Bermuda when I was there once.

They would all leave talking about Ellis.

He was the technician who got everything ready for the instructors.

Woe betide any instructor to cross him though. Without his assistance the lesson would be doomed.

Ellis, knew every course inside out and upside down, he had a great ability to simplify anything for any poor struggling student. He was so glad to pass on his knowledge and expertise.

We don't have anyone like that anymore.

But it was in the bar on an evening that Ellis came to life, what a character he was. He took the mickey out of anyone and everyone in authority, much to the amusement of everyone else in the bar.

He always stood at the bar with a German stein in his hands, he would put in that, whatever any willing student was prepared to buy him, as a thanks for his help. Absolutely regardless of whatever was already in there.

Ellis, at one time actually lived on site at the school, he undertook the role of a caretaker as well as his other duties.

Once qualified, the procedure was ambulance staff, to re-attend at the RATC every couple of years or so. For a two weeks residential PP (post proficiency) update course. The PP course was then reduced to one week, non residential.

It was then superseded with a four weeks on the job assessment, every two years with an FBA (Field Based Assessor), they would work with you as a crew doing the job as you went along. Three days of it were for updated training in a classroom.

Now you are lucky if you get one day on the job training, the rest of the mandatory training, or extra tuition has to be done in your own time and expense. Either attending a CPD (Continual Personal Development) evening at a station somewhere, or on the computer.

The computers at work would be fine, but we are never there long enough to start a training session, never mind complete one.

In 2012. Wendy and I attended the National Ambulance Service Memorial Service, at the National Memorial Arboretum, in Staffordshire.

A visitor from Guernsey saw my Yorkshire Ambulance badge, he immediately asked if I had ever been lucky enough to meet Ellis. He had known him from his own training, in the seventies. Ellis had helped him by simplifying complicated ideas, into simple facts.

We had quite a conversation around happy memories of the RATC.

We in Yorkshire, now have a number of training establishments.

Elm Bank, is at an old ambulance station in Wakefield and there are others, in Rotherham, Leeds and York.

There is nothing residential anymore, everything unfortunately is a mismatch of facilities.

I've got something for you.

I completed my course and passed all of the examinations. I got back to Huddersfield ambulance station, on the Monday 29th of March 1982.

I had passed the course.

Bert was our Station Officer, he had taken over Huddersfield from Geoff on his retirement, as well as still running his own former station at Honley.

Bert said that he had something for me.

I went to the office and there he had my Millar badge, to put on my uniform. I had become a fully certified, and qualified ambulanceman.

The badge to wear proudly on my left arm, is a white Laurel Wreath on a dark blue navy background. About two and a half inches diameter.

He threw it to me from the other side of the room, closely followed by my prized Millar certificate.

Then he said that he had not given one out before. If that was the best he could do, I'm not surprised.

He was not known for his finesse.

Bert.

Bert was our boss, he was the Station Officer. When Station Officers ran the station, he was also in charge at Honley station. He was a strange bloke, he was very keen on discipline. But when it came to applying it, he was too mild mannered.

He couldn't command any authority.

He always used to remind me of the prison officer Mr. Barrowclough, in Ronnie Barker's Porridge, played by Brian Wilde. The actor also famous for playing Foggy Dewhirst in Last of the Summer Wine.

When Bert had a problem, he would try and give the younger end a hard time, he would raise his voice and stand tall. But where the older staff were concerned, he was a pussycat.

He daren't say a thing to them.

He gave me two real bollockings in my early days, both actually, for using fire extinguishers. The problem, he said, was that I hadn't used the extinguishers to put a fire out on WYMAS property or vehicles.

The first incident that occurred, was when I was working single handed on a minibus ambulance. I had just dropped a patient off at Hartley Manor, a residential care home for the elderly. (Newly rebuilt and renamed as Bradley Court).

As I was about to call up clear via the radio, an emergency call was broadcast.

It was for anyone to help, a little girl was "still being savaged by a large dog". The emphasis was on the words "still being".

The location given, was outside the shops on Copthorne Square, on Keldregate at Bradley.

It was across the road from where I was. I drove literally a hundred yards, I didn't even have chance to call it in, I was there.

There was the most horrific sight, of a large Rottweiler dog, in its mouth was a little girl of around three years old. It had its mouth clamped very firmly around her thigh, it was shaking her violently. Up and down, and from side to side, just like a rag doll. She was bleeding badly, and she was screaming. It was a terrifying, ear piercing scream.

She had just left one of the shops with her mother.

Several people were trying to grab the dog, but to no avail. The more they tried, the more the dog seemed to shake her.

Even the attending police officers were powerless to intervene. They had their batons drawn, but were scared not to hurt the little girl, or to set the dog off running away with her.

The people were trying to corner the animal and back it into a walled area, near to the corner of the buildings.

My first thought was to suddenly shock the dog. In the ambulances at the time were two fire extinguishers, one in the cab, between the seats and the other near the back doors.

Those extinguishers were known as BCF, they were a chemical called "bromochlorodifluoromethane". They could be used on any type of fire, but they were toxic in an enclosed environment.

It was a pressurised liquid in the container and it would turn to gas when released into the air, excluding the oxygen from the fire.

I grabbed one of the extinguishers and I ran towards the dog. As I got near enough, I squeezed the trigger and blasted the dog full in the face.

It worked, the dog screeched, it opened its mouth wide and dropped the girl. As the dog backed away yelping, it was cornered by some members of the public.

I grabbed the girl and got her into the ambulance.

Although it was only a minibus, it still had some equipment. I put the screaming and frightened child on oxygen straight away, then I started to treat her many deep and ragged lacerations. A double crewed ambulance arrived, it was Keith and Norris, they took over from me.

Just before they left, a hysterical mother arrived. The police had been sat with her in a police car, so that she couldn't see what was actually happening to her daughter. She jumped into the back of the ambulance, and they set straight off to hospital.

I got back to the ambulance station, I was reporting that I had used the extinguisher and that a replacement was required.

Then, as I explained what I had done, instead of a pat on the back for initiative. Bert went berserk, telling me that they were ambulance equipment and for use on ambulance property only.

"Nothing else, do you understand?"

I did get a thank you from a Police Inspector, he thought my actions were "superb, and that they had been immediately effective". He had also checked on the effects, that the chemical formula of the fire extinguisher may have had on the little girl. The only possible side effect in an open environment, would have been a slight irritation to her eyes and maybe some slight difficulty in breathing. That would require oxygen as soon as possible, which she got.

The police inspector told me that the dog had been euthanised and that the little girl had been transferred to Bradford Royal Infirmary. There she had received the first, of many extensive plastic surgery operations for her wounds.

It transpired, that she apparently had a long but successful recovery.

A second time when Bert had played hell with me. I was on the M621 near Leeds. I was crewed up with Don in an emergency ambulance, a lad from Elland.

We saw a small van on fire, it was just pulling on to the hard shoulder. As we approached, the driver leapt out of the cab and ran across the full width of the motorway. He jumped over the central barriers and then right across to the other side.

We had a couple of routine patients in the back, they were on their way to the Leeds General Infirmary for outpatient appointments.

I grabbed the fire extinguisher, and proceeded to put out the fire. I managed to confine all the damage just to the engine compartment.

The fire service arrived shortly after us and instead of the usual hassle that I got from Huddersfield crews, I was personally thanked by the Station Officer.

As his crew were making everything safe, isolating the battery etc. He said that I had saved further damage and that if it had been left much longer, the gas bottles in the back of the van could have exploded and caused some major problems.

I knew what was likely to be in the back, from the labels on the van. I also knew that if there was, then time was critical, from my training with the fire brigade at Brook Motors.

He shook my hand. Don and I left the scene, we continued our journey to Leeds.

On our return, Bert went barmy with me.

"Don't you ever listen?" He said. "I've told you before about the misuse of ambulance equipment, I'm taking this further young man. You will listen to me!"

I had to sit in front of our Divisional Officer called Brian. After giving me an almighty telling off, he gave me the opportunity to give him my version of events.

After that, he said "Ok, that's fine, well done, now go back to work".

A strange lot work for the ambulance service.

A variety of staff.

Over the next months and years, I have worked with every one of the staff at Huddersfield's ambulance station and I have attended to all kinds of emergency calls.

I was on the relief rota initially and so I also covered shifts all over the West Yorkshire area. I think that I have probably worked at every one of the 22 old West Yorkshire Metropolitan Ambulance Service Stations at some stage.

I am still working with new people all the time, and that's over thirty six years later. We seem to have a massive turnover of staff at the moment, nobody seems to stay settled anywhere now.

CHAPTER 26

A VERY MOVING EXPERIENCE.

A Police funeral.

During my life, I have been to lots of funerals. The older I get, the more I seem to have to go to. A lot of the funerals that I have attended, have been for my ex colleagues.

One of the most moving funerals, that I have ever attended, was to that of a young Motorway Policeman. It was in 1982.

A middle aged lady's car had broken down, it happened just as she had joined the M62 from Cooper Bridge at Junction 25. She had managed to get the car onto the hard shoulder, it was just after the top of the Westbound access slip road.

The police had seen the car on the CCTV cameras and they had gone to assist. The car had a flat tyre. There were two male officers in the police car. The police officer from the passenger seat got out to help by changing the damaged tyre.

The driver placed his car behind the broken down one and put his rear facing red and blue lights on for safety. That should have provided a safe cordon in which his mate could be able to change the tyre.

The lady and her two passengers had been instructed to get out of the car and to sit at the other side of the crash barrier, "just in case".

It was a glorious sunny day.

What happened next, must have been witnessed by the lady and her passengers. A large fully loaded articulated lorry was powering up the hill from the Brighouse junction, it drifted slightly onto the hard shoulder, not a lot, but enough.

The lorry hit the back of the police car with such force, that it in turn hit the broken down car.

The police car burst into flames. The passenger from the police car, fixing the tyre, was thrown forward by the impact, far enough to be clear of the wreckage. Fortunately he only suffered from some relatively minor injuries.

He raced back to help his stricken colleague, trapped in the police car. It was badly damaged, the door wouldn't open. It was already totally engulfed in flames.

The passenger policeman, was smashing at the windows with the car jack handle. To no avail, he was beaten back by the heat and the flames.

The driver died.

The surviving policeman had to be taken to the burns unit at Pinderfields General Hospital in Wakefield, he had suffered from some severe burns to his hands and arms.

The female driver and her passengers and the wagon driver, although in severe shock, were uninjured.

The police officer's funeral was held at Gledholt Methodist Chapel, next door to Huddersfield ambulance station.

It was a full ceremonial Police Service funeral, with honours. The police do it right, they look after their own.

Tommy and me attended the funeral. We knew the officer, both from the job and from drinking in the Globe Pub (then Nightingale's, now known as the Old Wireworks) at Lindley, opposite the hospital. Sasha and Stuart from Brighouse also attended, they were the crew that had been sent to the incident and had then taken him to Pinderfields.

We were all looking smart, in full bib and tucker uniforms. Complete with our hats, including a white cover, the cover was only worn by to 999 staff.

It was a full "dress uniform". Not like the miserable uniforms that we have now.

As we were outside the chapel, on the grass in front of our station. A police superintendent slowly approached us. He asked us politely if we would mind removing the white tops off our hats. It was a sign of respect that the police used, it made everybody equal.

We immediately complied without question.

There were about a hundred and thirty police officers all in uniform, from all ranks and they were all mingling with each other.

The fire service were present, they sent one member of staff from each rank up to Assistant Chief Officer.

Our boss Bert, and Assistant Divisional Officer Brian were in the station office, they were looking out of the window I asked them if they would like to attend, to represent the management of the ambulance service.

"Too busy" was the answer. They also told us sternly that we had to put our white tops back on.

We refused.

We said that we would explain the situation later, at a more appropriate time.

When the hearse arrived, there was total silence. The bearer party stepped forward. Under guidance of the funeral director, they eased the coffin out of the back. It was draped with the blue flag of the West Yorkshire Police.

Then the police man's wife stepped forward, with the utmost dignity, she placed her husbands hat and gloves on top of the coffin. The bearers then gently and with military precision, lifted the coffin onto their shoulders. They began a slow march into the Chapel.

There were two lines of police officers all around the perimeter walls of the Chapel, as a mark of respect, they were all stood to attention and saluted until he had gone past.

They then silently filed in and filled the Chapel to its full capacity. We from the ambulance service were stood quietly and respectfully at the back.

All through the service, you could have heard a pin drop. It was so quiet, and so respectful. The service was a very personal and moving one. It was a very emotional experience.

At the front of the Chapel was the coffin and on a table at the side of it, a large framed photograph of the deceased officer.

There were about eight seats immediately in front of the coffin, there sat the policeman's wife and their two small sons. They were aged two and four. Sat with the children, were the police officer's parents.

Just before the committal, the minister announced a minutes silence, that was signified by a bugler from the police band playing the last post.

That obviously was a very sombre part of the service, anyway.

Part of the way through the silence, the little four year old, in all innocence stood up and loudly asked his mum a question.

That question still haunts me today. It managed to reduce the whole congregation to tears, there was not one dry eye anywhere.

He asked, "what are daddies hat and gloves on that box for?"

He did not get an answer at the time, I don't know if he ever did.

How can anybody answer that?

CHAPTER 27.

EARLY DAYS OF MARRIED LIFE.

Getting Married.

April 30th 1983. It was our wedding day.

Ever the skinflints, the Firth side of the family were stood waiting for the bus. We were at the bus stop, at Paddock Head, ready to go to Huddersfield Register Office.

Across the road from the bus stop was the butchers shop. The father of little Chloe, the young girl who had been knocked down on the school crossing at Lepton. He had seen us, he came across to us and asked what we were up to, all dressed up to the nines.

When we explained where we were going.

He said "I told you that I owed you one, for looking after his Chloe. Now, it's my turn".

His dad, had just got a new Granada car. He trooped us all through the shop. Then he took a crepe bandage out of the first aid kit and strung it across the bonnet like a wedding car ribbon. Then mum and dad, Lindsay, Diane and myself piled into the car.

He then put on a white coat, there was some blood on the shoulder, from carrying sides of meat.

He said "it doesn't bother you, does it?"

It was a wedding we were going to, but, hey ho!

He then took us all down to the register office and he stayed with us. He ferried us on to the reception, where he stayed a little longer and then ran us both up home, to get ready for the night do.

What a thank you! I certainly appreciated it.

It was a shame our wedding photographer didn't feel the same. He would not take his picture. Our photographer thought it wasn't appropriate, with him having blood on the white coat.

In fairness, I was paying the photographer for his services and in my mind, it shouldn't have been his decision.

I do believe, that under the circumstances, it probably was appropriate and apt for the occasion.

It would certainly have been a talking point at album viewings.

I vowed from that moment, that any weddings that I photographed, I would include all or any that the family may have requests for.

That night we had a party for all of our new extended family and friends, at the Commercial, on Church Street at Paddock.

It was a small local village pub, with a large function room and separate bar facility at the back.

It was ideal for our requirements.

Sadly the Commercial has also bit the dust and has been closed down, along with all of the great local pubs that Paddock used to have, in my early days of drinking.

The butchers.

I know it's out of sequence, but, early in 2014. My younger sister Diane started working for the butchers at Paddock.

Chloe's dad was still working there. He asked Diane, if her brother used to work for the ambulance service. When she told him that I still did.

He said that he wanted to meet up with me and buy me a "well earned pint, as a thank you for looking after my little girl all those years ago".

We met up for a couple of hours, he couldn't remember anything, of what he had done for our wedding day.

He did get very emotional talking about Chloe and her life. He remembered every single detail of her accident, her trip to Pinderfields and her injuries.

He could also vividly remember each and every one of the other children, who were in the intensive care at the same time as Chloe.

It was a very emotional experience for me as well.

More often than not, once we have delivered a patient to A&E, that is the last we would hear of them. It is very rewarding to find out now and again how the patient went on.

It would not be professional to find out all the time and we would probably be getting too emotionally involved.

If it was an unusual job, extra feedback would be great, just to know whether the patient had survived and gone on to make a complete recovery, or not.

Our Honeymoon.

We went on honeymoon to Sandown on the Isle of White.

Where we had a brilliant time, we travelled with Shearings coaches. We were the only couple on the trip who were not drawing our old age pension.

Never mind though, we had a wonderful experience.

The others on the trip were an education. One couple we met, were from Dalton, in Huddersfield. The couple were very quiet, the wife especially, was so timid. She would sit at the table all through breakfast and not say a word.

On a night time though, well, she would put on a wig. It was not a vastly different one to her own hair, but it was a wig. She would have more make up on and she was the life and soul of the party. An unbelievable change of personality, what a difference.

At the bar, the pensioners would always buy us a drink. There was some form of entertainment at the hotel bar every night. Sometimes it was only bingo, and so the other travellers would arrange something. They enjoyed their fancy dress evenings. One night, one of the older and larger women did a striptease, that was an eye opener.

We saw some beautiful places, including some picturesque thatched villages. We went on a boat trip to Portsmouth, where we saw the remnants of the Tudor ship the Mary Rose.

Even the royal yacht Britannia was in port.

We saw all the British warships, including the famous Ark Royal, Britain's largest aircraft carrier.

Our little 100 capacity passenger vessel was absolutely dwarfed by that most fantastic of beasts.

When we got home, my sisters and my cousin Philip had decorated the whole front of our house at Lindley. They had hung a large banner, welcoming home the newly weds.

I think that our elderly neighbours on the street had thought that we were married already.

There would be no hiding the fact then.

Neighbours at Lindley.

We had good neighbours at Lindley, there was Mrs. T next door below, Mrs. B was next door below her. I remember Mrs. B invited me in for a cup of tea when I was first working on the house.

We had no water at the time, it was most welcome.

Above us was a chap I'll call Neil, a simple soul with some mental health issues, he lived with his elderly mother, who I'll call Elsie. Elsie knitted a yellow bonnet, when she found out that Wendy was pregnant with Adrian.

Across the road were a young couple who I'll call Stuart and Violet and behind them was a single man, I'll call him Rob, he was a hospital porter.

Next door to him was a couple who I'll call Sid and Kath. Sid was a Yorkshireman, a steel erector (scaffolding specialist) regularly away from home for the full week. He apparently, was one of the fastest steel erectors in the country. His skills were well sort after. Because of his skills, he earned a lot of money.

When he came home on a Friday teatime, his wife Kath, a Londoner, would be there waiting for him. They would both start on a heavy drinking bender from then, until late on the Sunday evening.

They would fight each other for most of the time they were together and they would knock seven bells out of each other, every weekend without fail.

Blue lights outside our windows.

On Friday, November 8th 1983. For whatever reason, I was stood outside in our little garden with Stuart, when Sid came home. As usual, Kath was already waiting for him outside, almost hiding in the entrance to their back lane.

Sid was carrying the usual two large bags, jangling with bottles. It was usually spirits, whiskey or brandy rather than beer.

As soon as he rounded the corner from the road into his back lane, Kath smacked Sid full in the face, with a lump of wood that she had picked up from behind the bins. It was around the size of a cricket bat.

He responded with a customary smack in the mouth, that was followed by a torrent of abuse aimed at and from, each other.

They then went indoors, welcome home Sid!

Later that night, at around eleven thirty, there was a commotion outside. I could see blue lights, they were flashing through the top of our bedroom curtains and dancing across the ceiling.

I looked out of the window, there was an ambulance, Jack was running and it wasn't like him to be running.

He grabbed the carry chair from the ambulance, and ran back in to Sid's house. When they came out of the house, I could see he was with Tommy, they had Kath sat on the chair and they were both rushing.

She didn't look good.

The morning after, we learnt that Kath had died and that Sid had been arrested for murder. He had stabbed her through the left side of her neck, through her lung and right into her heart.

It was bound to happen sometime. Stuart and I had seen Kath initiate the attack that night.

But they were just as bad as each other.

They were both to blame on many of the times, that Stuart or I, had to take one of them across the road to HRI for treatment. They had both injured each other on several occasions.

In the end, Sid was charged with manslaughter, not murder of Kath and sentenced to several years in prison.

CHAPTER 28.

FROM ONE EXTREME
TO THE OTHER.

Child death.

In the late spring of 1983 I think it was the spring bank holiday period, I was working with Mike.

We had known each other for many many years and we were of a similar age with quite a similar outlook on life. I had just got married, Mike was already married and he had a three year old daughter, Michaella.

On that particular day we got called to a job, it was late lunchtime. An ambulance staff's nightmare of a job.

The call was to a small child that had drowned in a garden pond. For once we were in the right place at the right time. We arrived there, in a matter of seconds literally. There was a woman present, she was slurring her words and appeared very unsteady on her feet.

She took us through her house and pointed into the garden. At the bottom end of the garden, the lifeless body of a little girl was still face down in the water. I was shocked that nobody had even tried to pull her out.

The pond was an irregular shape, but around four foot in diameter, it was only just above ankle deep. Mike stepped in and lifted her up and out of the water, she wasn't breathing. He started mouth to mouth breathing for her immediately, he then passed her to me as he climbed out.

As I took the child in my arms. I could see in the blonde haired, pony tailed little girl, Mike's own daughter. She was the spitting image of Michaella.

I carried on with mouth to mouth as I ran through the house with the lifeless body, Mike overtook me to open the ambulance doors. We both jumped in. Oxygen on and carried on with CPR. The woman stepped in to the back with Mike and her daughter. I jumped into the front to drive, calling a resus call in on the way.

The journey to hospital was only a few minutes. Hospital staff were ready and waiting for us. I stopped the ambulance and ran to open the back doors. Mike passed the little girl to me once again and I ran into the resus room at the bottom of the corridor, maybe fifty yards away.

Mike brought the woman into the department with him, she had told him that she was mum.

She had also said to him, "I told her to keep away from the pond!" That was the only conversation that had taken place, with no emotion at all.

He said it seemed a very strange thing to say at the time.

We quickly passed on all the information that we had to the doctors and nurses, who were all rushing round like headless chickens to try and save the little girl. Despite all attempts, it was not to be. It turned out that the little girl had been in the water for well over an hour before being found.

Following a job under those types of circumstance, we would normally have grabbed a cuppa and then chatted about the job. That was our usual way of stress relief.

Not that occasion, where was mum? We had to find her.

We looked all over the hospital and its grounds. Hospital staff, porters and security staff were helping us.

Every ward was rung, looking for a mother in distress. We were concerned for her safety, it wouldn't have been the first time that a distraught parent had gone and tried to commit suicide following the death of a child.

She was found about an hour later, when she walked, or should I say staggered back in to the hospital. She was fine. Not in any danger, she had simply been to the pub across the road from the hospital, she felt that she needed a drink.

Not only was she unsteady on her feet, she was ranting and raging incoherently. She was extremely drunk and blaming everybody else for what had happened.

I know I will never forget her.

Mike never discussed the job with me, but I'm sure that, if I could see his daughter's likeness in the girl. He must surely have seen and felt the same, probably far worse.

Danny in a fix.

September 1983, and another M62 job.

Called to a traffic accident, I was working with Danny. Danny was a little feller, rather portly, like I am now.

If you remember the TV show, "it ain't half hot mum". Danny was a dead ringer for "lofty" played by the late Don Estelle.

In those days, our motorway wear, our PPE, (personal protective equipment). Consisted of a black waterproof coat, if raining of course and some waterproof trousers, again in black.

To make us more visible, we had rolled up in our kit bag, a fluorescent vest. It was yellow in colour, with a single reflective band around the bottom.

On the way to the job, the attendant, in that case, Danny. Would get the yellow vests out of the bags, there was a doorway through into the back of the ambulances then.

He would hand one vest to the driver, me, or place it on the dashboard in readiness. He would then put on his own and he was ready to jump out, fully visible to all.

Today, they wouldn't be classed as safe for a motorway. The yellow coats have to have reflective bands, on the bottom, the shoulders and at least two on the arms. Long sleeves have to be worn.

On arrival at the incident, the scene had already been cordoned off by the police, as was generally done. A police officer came towards the drivers side of the ambulance. I got out.

As I was donning my vest, he was telling me that although four vehicles had been involved, he didn't think anyone was injured. But would we please check them over.

One vehicle was partly obscuring the slow lane. So the police had blocked that one and the hard shoulder off for safety.

Once everyone had been checked and cleared, they would be able to remove the offending vehicles and re-open the lane.

As I walked round to the front of the ambulance, there was no Danny!

That was most unusual, the attendant is usually out first.

It is always extremely noisy on the motorway, traffic thunders down past you in the open lanes. There was a slight lull in traffic noise, when both the policeman and I heard a sound.

A strange sound, coming from the passenger side of the ambulance. A sort of muffled cry. I cannot describe that sound in words, it had to be heard to understand. But it was a very hoarsey, rasping "heeelp!"

We both went around to that side of the ambulance, then promptly fell apart in stitches.

The worst thing for Danny, was that even the victims of the traffic accident had also seen him.

Danny had got himself into a ridiculous predicament.

As he had fastened his fluorescent vest and they had a very large and strong, but easily closed whilst wearing gloves, zip.

Danny must have already fastened his seatbelt, before he put his vest on and pulled up the zip.

He had unfastened his seatbelt and as he left the vehicle, he jumped off the side step.

He then due to being still attached to the seatbelt, must have just spun round. His feet were still resting on the edge of the footwell, but his body was face down at right angles to the ambulance, suspended.

The seat belt was restricting his airflow, hence the rasping. It was one of the funniest things I had ever seen. His arms were flapping desperately, looking like a very distressed canary. He was trying to loosen the zip, but his whole body weight was preventing it.

As I got underneath his body and lifted, the policeman undid the zip.

Danny fell to the floor, in an unpleasant heap, still gasping for air.

Five minutes later, he was fine and able to laugh about it himself.

What a shame that mobile phones weren't as prolific then, I would have paid for a picture of that!

Carl and his turtle shell.

A similar funny episode happened a few years later involving my regular mate Carl. He also was a little short in stature.

We had been called to a disturbance in Lockwood, very close to the famous Dixon's ice cream shop.

"Weapons have been discharged", was the message given.

On each station were a set of stab/ballistic protection vests.

We were told to grab the set of three, one each for us and one for the operational supervisor.

We had two medium sized and one large. All were very generous in size, to fit over the top of our uniform. From the outside, they all looked exactly the same. The label was inside the vest, near to the bottom and very difficult to see.

Carl threw two of them into the ambulance cab. Before he climbed in, he put his own vest on. As he then sat down, he realised that he had put on the large one.

I could have died, so could he as it happens.

As he had sat down, the vest had pushed upwards, forcing Carl's arms into the air and into a "I surrender" position. It had also obscured his face, just the top of his head and his eyes were visible.

It was like a giant green turtle shell.

He screamed at me "don't you bloody dare set off!" He paused. "You are not driving down the road with me looking like this" he bellowed. He looked a right sight and yet again, I was unable to get a picture.

I had to stop, as funny as it was, it would have been dangerous to drive on. He couldn't move his arms to get his seatbelt on nor nothing. I had to undo the velcro straps to release him.

Animals.

We have now and we have had in the past, many staff who are frightened of animals, particularly dogs. Whenever we attend a house, one of the standard requests from Comms. Whilst still connected on the 999 call, is to put any animals away in another room.

That serves three purposes. If staff are frightened of a particular animal, it means that they can attend safely. It also prevents the little darlings from getting under the feet. The last thing is, if we are picking up the owner from the floor, or strapping them into a carry chair. The animals, dogs in particular, don't really understand that we are not a threat. If the animal is doing its job of protecting its owner, it may go for us.

Some of our staff are that petrified, that if they can hear a dog barking, they will not even enter the premises.

One of my first experiences with animals whilst dealing with a patient, was at a farm, Stubbing Farm at Denby Dale. The farmers dogs were fine, it was the geese that we needed to worry about. They had three of them, evil buggers as well.

Many an ambulance door had been badly dented by them.

My nemesis.

I have had many near miss experiences with animals, but only actually been attacked and marked/injured once.

I was working with a good friend Dana from Todmorden.

We were working in Huddersfield and had attended a job on Manchester Road.

The details of the job have long escaped me.

I just remember asking the family of the patient, about her prescribed medicines. A young boy told me that it was all in a dosette box in the kitchen. (Separate daily compartments in a dispensing box).

Without hesitation, he went to get it for us.

No sooner had he opened the kitchen door, there was a loud whooshing sound. My head was down at the time and looking at the patient. Before I had the chance to look up, something really sharp hit me hard on the top of my head and knocked me over onto my back.

At the same time as I felt the blood trickling all down my face and neck, Dana screamed "f-ing hell!!!" at the top of her voice.

Dana is someone who is brilliant to work with, at the end of the day, she is almost as daft as me. We get on really well together. We are of a similar age and have been in the service for a similar amount of time.

We are both, proper "old school" in our ways of doing the job and caring for our patients.

When I looked up, she was on her hands and knees crying her eyes out with laughter.

As I sat up, the blood still was running.

On the window sill, in all its glory and stood there proudly with its wings fully extended. Was the largest and brightest, blue macaw parrot that I had ever seen.

That had been my attacker, my nemesis, it had claws like something out of a horror film, they were massive.

Evil beast it was!

CHAPTER 29.

ADDITIONS TO THE FAMILY.

Let's go to Spain.

Wendy and I had decided to book a holiday to Saloo in Spain, for the summer of 1984. It was late in October 1983 and I had been lucky enough to get the first pick, on the holiday rota at work.

We had booked for the last week in July and first week in August for the following year. We were really looking forward to our first proper holiday together in the sun.

We're having a baby.

It was Christmas Eve in 1983. Wendy and me, were given some great news. It was early evening after the Doctor's surgery had closed for the night and also for the holiday period.

Dr. G of Meltham Road called in to see us on his way home.

He told us that Wendy's test result had confirmed things, yes, Wendy was pregnant and was expecting our first child.

That news, was the best Christmas present a couple could ever get.

The day after was obviously Christmas Day and as had been planned, we both went to my mum and dads house for our Christmas dinner. Wendy and myself were setting out the table.

For mum, dad, my two sisters and us. Six of us in all, but we actually set seven places.

We had a couple of funny looks. When mum asked us what we were doing, I just simply said that we were practicing for next year and left it at that.

There was a total silence for a few seconds whilst the pennies were dropping. If only I'd had the chance and taken a picture of either mum or dads face, they were both fantastic reactions.

What a way to break the news, it was magic.

I think it only fair to say that mum and dad were well chuffed. Lindsay and Diane were shocked, but happy too. Wendy's due date was expected to be the first week in August.

Hmmm, I think we were due to be tied up with something else at that time of the year. Therefore we had no option, but we had to cancel our pre booked holiday.

We would not be going to Spain.

Fortunately, as we had used Altham's to book the holiday, the insurance were very good. All monies that we paid were refunded in double quick time.

Our Lodger.

January 1984. My cousin Michael, who at the time, was living in Knaresborough. He came to visit mum and dad. He had been given a placement, lecturing at the University of Huddersfield.

He was a professor and he would be teaching electronic engineering there.

Michael was looking for temporary digs, on a Monday to Friday basis in the Huddersfield area. He was asking mum and dad, if they had any suggestions or recommendations for him.

Wendy and I were there at mum and dads at the time, perhaps we had the solution. We had a spare room.

He was wanting one for the new year term, until Easter, or perhaps just a couple of weeks into the next term.

As long as it was only until the baby was born, it wouldn't matter. We offered.

He didn't mind sleeping in a room decorated as a nursery and he decided to give it a go.

He arrived on the Monday evening. He didn't need feeding having already dined. Just a bed really. Once in our spare bedroom we would hardly see him.

He had his own key.

On a morning, he would be up early, make himself a coffee and then disappear. We wouldn't see him until late evening. He would go out on Friday mornings and not return again until Monday night.

It was an ideal arrangement, for all of us. He sorted all his own meals, it was rare to sit and spend any time at all with him really. The arrangement lasted just until the end of May, it was perfect.

It sorted Michael out at a time that he needed it and we were only too glad to be able to help. Without any disruption to our way of life at all.

As I said you wouldn't have known he was there.

Dad's comb over.

When I was young, dad started losing his hair rapidly. From as far back as I can really remember, he started having a comb over. He was a bit like Bobby Charlton.

The 1966 World Cup Final look.

The older he got, the thinner his hair was getting. It used to be quite a comb over, but it got thinner and longer as his parting got wider. Then, to keep the hair in place, he would plaster it down with Brylcreem.

The minute he went out of the door, the wind would catch it and lift the flap of hair. Then it drop back down over his ear, leaving it sticking out at the side.

In the eighties it looked ridiculous, it would be even worse now.

One day in May 1984, dad was sat in his chair in front of the window. It was a Sunday, all of the family were there for Sunday lunch.

Diane was in her punk era.

For some reason she plaited the comb over, it stuck out of the top of dad's head like some bizarre unicorn thing. Dad then fell asleep.

Diane, then started to dare Wendy to cut the tuft of hair off. Mum also joined in, go on, "it's time it went".

"He won't have a go at you, not while you are pregnant" they said.

Then it happened.

Wendy, heavily pregnant with Adrian, stood up. She looked at the "horn" stuck out of the top of dad's head, then promptly took out a pair of scissors and cut it off!

No way! Wendy, quiet and meek as a lamb had just physically assaulted dad. She had removed his pride and joy, he would go mad when he woke up.

We were all sat with baited breath.

Dad woke up and as a habit had been formed, his left hand reached up to smooth the hair from his left ear and pat it down. Back into position, over the top of his head.

It wasn't there!

Still half asleep, his fingers were tapping and searching all over his head, where was it?

He looked in the mirror. The comb over had gone, it was no longer. "Who the bloody hell did this?" He cried.

Straight away Diane grassed Wendy up, "it was Wendy, she did it!"

But, instead of getting upset, he laughed.

He had been wanting to get rid of that comb over for years, but hadn't had the guts to do it.

It made him look younger, a lot younger and far better, it suited him.

I still can't believe that Wendy did that, it was totally out of character for her. We blamed her hormones and the fact that she was pregnant.

CHAPTER 30

OUR FIRST BORN.

Was it Labour? Yes it's a boy!

July 1984. Wendy wasn't feeling well, we went across to the Hospital and they did some tests. Wendy had a condition known as pre-eclampsia. It is a possibly life threatening condition, that can affect the health and wellbeing of both mother and baby.

Wendy was confined to hospital on bed rest.

On Saturday 28th of July. The hospital staff told us that Wendy was going to be induced, our first born would be born later that day.

It was the day of the opening ceremony of the 23rd Olympic Games, held in Los Angeles. It was also the day after Huddersfield actor James Mason had died, at his home in Switzerland.

Adrian Lee Firth was born at 17:20 hrs weighing in at seven pounds and seven ounces. Both mum and baby were doing absolutely fine.

A couple of days later, we returned to our home in Wellington Street. Our faithful dog Gem was waiting for us. We put Adrian in his carrycot on the seat, in pride of place on the fireplace extension. Gem laid down beneath him.

That was going to be their spot.

Gem would stay in that very place, at any time that Adrian was in his carry cot. If any visitors came to our house, Gem would be there between them and our newborn son.

Adrian was a sleeper, he still is. He would fall asleep the minute he was put down, we regularly had to wake him for a feed.

Adrian's Christening.

Sunday 18th November 1984. That was the day of Adrian's Christening at St. Stephen's Church. It was just on the road from our house in Lindley, across from the local landmark, Lindley clock tower.

The ceremony was performed by the Reverend Michael Haynes, Vicar and Honorary Canon.

Adrian's Godparents were. Wendy's long time family friend Gina, my long time friend from scouting, John and a joint friend Alex (Alexandra).

We purposely avoided asking family members, that ensured that there were no accusations of favouritism.

Just to embarrass Adrian, if he reads this.

Everybody had met up at our house prior to the service. Adrian looked fantastic in his Christening clothes.

Then disaster struck. He decided to fill his nappy and it was full. Not only his nappy, it leaked out all over his nice new clothes.

What a mess.

Wendy and her mother were rushing around like scalded cats, to get him sorted. He was bathed, washed and changed. The clothes were washed and dried. What a last minute effort, but they made it.

The ceremony was wonderful, then all of our friends and family returned to our house on Wellington Street. Where we all had a good old natter and enjoyed some snacks, nibbles and maybe a drink or two.

The house was full to bursting, it was a perfect end to a perfect day.

Meningitis!

Early in the new year of 1986. Adrian was very ill one day, he was absolutely burning up. His temperature was too high for us to record on a "Feverscan" thermometer. That only went up to 41 degrees, he was above that.

Wendy was pregnant with our second child, Ben. We were frightened.

We took him to HRI to the A&E. I carried him across, he was absolutely on fire.

It wasn't long, before they told us that he was being admitted to the children's ward. He had been diagnosed with viral meningitis.

He was admitted to a side room on the children's ward. Adrian was laid there on his bed, in just his underwear. The windows were wide open and he had a cooling fan directed at him, to try and reduce his fever. Wendy and me were both shivering away wearing top coats.

He eventually settled with no lasting effects.

Serious head injury!

Adrian seemed to enjoy school, he always had plenty of friends. School life generally seemed to be fairly uneventful.

One day though, I received an early morning telephone call from the headmistress at Cowlersley Junior School. She was blazing, she was shouting, she was not happy at all.

The way she spoke to me was not acceptable either, I was a parent, not one of her junior school pupils. I had been working nights and I had only been asleep for about an hour.

It was only a quarter past nine.

The phone rang, I was half asleep and before I had even had chance to say "hello". A frantic voice was saying "your son has been involved in a fighting incident and it has left another child with serious head injuries, you need to get here now!"

She was almost screaming, then she put the phone down.

I had recognised the voice as that of the headmistress, but she didn't even have the courtesy to say who she was.

I wondered, what the hell was going on? I had no idea.

I raced up to school, Adrian was sat outside the office. Funny really, after all, I thought fighting was more Ben's style. Another boy was also sat there, he had a cracking black eye. The other lad was almost a year older than Adrian, who had just gone nine.

I asked for the headmistress at the reception. I was told to wait there, she would be out shortly, again treating me like I was one of the kids.

Five minutes later she appeared.

No pleasantries, she launched straight at me with. "Well? I want to know what are you going to do about it?"

I said that I needed to know what had happened first, before I could make any decisions.

I initially asked her what the lads had said. By that time, she hadn't even asked the boys for their version of events. All she had been told had been third hand, of what another child had said, to one of the other teachers.

The headmistress told me, that another member of staff had been told that there had been a fight and that Adrian had been seen repeatedly banging the other lads head on the floor.

While she had been talking to the other staff member the lad with his black eye, had been sent to reception by his form teacher, to see what first aid may be needed.

The first person to ask, I suggested was the lad himself.

The headmistress then questioned my ability as a parent. She intimated that I obviously had no idea how to bring up children.

The other lads' mother then arrived.

As she was already known to me. I spoke to her about the incident, and the allegations that had been made. She agreed with me, that both the boys' version of events was the correct place to start.

All of the people present, including both of the kids. Knew of the job that I do, a serious head injury to me is not a black eye, as good as it was.

The other boy explained that there had been a game of football in the yard, before school. Adrian had kicked him. It was well known that Adrian had two left feet like me and when it came to football, he was clumsy. It was never going to be his game.

The boy had then kicked him back, after all, his pride was hurt. Then, in the line up going into school, the lad had kicked Adrian again. He got shouted at by a teaching assistant and so in the cloakroom he went to kick Adrian again for a third time.

That last time Adrian had caught hold of the lads foot with his left hand, and smacked him in the eye with his right.

Good lad!

End of incident! As far as I was concerned.

Both the lads mother and me were shocked. If the original kick had been intentional, that would be one thing. But the whole situation had been blown out of all proportion by the headmistress.

The boys mum didn't want any further action taken.

Whilst this was going on in the office, the boys were laughing and joking together outside in the waiting room. That said, what more should we do? The headmistress then asked again, "what are you, proposing to do about the incident?"

I told her that I would be taking Adrian to town and buy him a book.

She was horrified.

I explained that as far as I was concerned, he had walked away from two deliberate kicks. When the third one came, he had rightly defended himself.

That is the way that I would have wanted him to behave. If it had been Adrian who had been nearly twelve months older, then, perhaps I would have thought a little bit differently.

Due to the fact that he was younger and smaller than the other lad, then bullying did not come in to it.

The headmistress said that she would not tolerate bullying of any kind.

I told her that it wasn't bullying, it was purely self defence, as agreed by the other lads mother.

I stood up and left and went back home to bed. I wasn't prepared to argue with the woman, silly cow! I never really had much more to do with her after that.

Adrian got his book.

After Adrian left Cowlersley, he went to Royds Hall High School. That was generally uneventful.

When he left there, he went on to New College at Salendine Nook.

That was my old school, although it was then a Sixth Form College, when Adrian went. He even had Mr. Crosland, who was my old physics and one of my form teachers, as his form tutor.

It turned out that like me, that college wasn't the right place for him.

After a year at the college, the subjects weren't really what he thought they were going to be.

He needed a different way of life.

You're in the army now!

After applying to join, and eventually getting accepted. In December 2001, Adrian started a completely new way of life. He had joined the Royal Logistics Corps, he was in the army.

We went to his passing out parade at Pirbright. In March 2002, Wendy, Ben, my mum and me.

We were so proud. It was such a shame that dad wasn't still alive, he would have loved it. Without doubt he would have been the proudest grandad.

Wendy's sister Lynne, her son David and her husband big David, also went down for Adrian's big day.

Our little family stayed overnight at The Old Wheatsheaf pub and restaurant in Frimley Green. Famous for the Lakeside Country Club, (opposite side of the Green from the pub), home of the World Darts Championships.

During his training days, Adrian met a girl. Jo, she worked as a civilian on the base where he was doing his training.

They were inseparable.

Following his basic training, Adrian transferred from the Logistic Corps, to the Royal Signals.

He was then going to be deployed to Germany, Jo as his girlfriend, would not be able to stay go him. They decided that if they got married, then as a couple, Jo would be able to live in the forces married quarters in Germany with him.

31st January 2004 they did get married.

Ben and his girlfriend at the time, Kelly, (Scott's mum), Wendy and me travelled down the night before. We had booked two nights bed and breakfast at a little guest house, not too far from where Jo's parents Nick and Carol lived.

All of our family got together to meet Jo's family for the first time, it was the night before the wedding. Apart from the obvious accent difference, straight away, we all seemed to get on fine. Nick and Carol obviously thought the world of Adrian.

On the Wedding day, Wendy's sister Lynne, big David and little David arrived for the ceremony and for the do afterwards. All of us had a great day.

Following their honeymoon, Adrian moved to Wildenrath in Germany near the Dutch border. It was a joint base for some of the U.S. Air Force and some of the British Army.

They had a lovely house on a large secure army site not too far from Adrian's works. Jo flew out and joined him out there not long after.

16th of July 2005, Jo gave birth to their first born Damian Reece Firth. We were lucky enough to be able to go to Germany to visit them in late September.

We flew to Düsseldorf airport, from Manchester. Our transport was a twenty five seater private business jet, from British Airways.

We had never known such luxury.

Adrian met us at the airport and took us to his home. We were only able to spend five days out there with them. But it was brilliant.

Whenever possible, Adrian took us to see areas of local interest, work permitting and along with his new family pressures.

Adrian left the army in 2006 and moved back to Britain. He and Jo lived fairly close to where her family were in Banbury. They would visit us whenever they got the chance.

Then on December 29th 2007, Jo gave birth to a little girl, Willow Trinity Firth.

Adrian was struggling to get work down south, and he and Jo were having marriage troubles. They had some time apart in the summer of 2008.

He came home to Huddersfield for a while, to sort himself out.

He didn't originally tell us, but he had applied and was successful in getting a job with the Yorkshire Ambulance Service.

He officially started his training in September 2008. He was one of the last groups to be taken on for the role as Advanced Emergency Medical Technician. Then after all his exams he qualified as an A E M T like me.

He and Jo separated in the October of that year.

Adrian and Laura.

After Adrian and Jo split up and he moved back up to Yorkshire.

He started seeing Laura. They had known each other through mutual friends in the past.

Laura is a lovely girl, and you just can't help but like her immediately. She is a good looking lass as well. Adrian seems to be besotted with her.

Laura works for West Yorkshire Police in a civilian capacity.

Adrian was based at Dewsbury Ambulance Station, so he rented a place, it was only two minutes away from his place of work. A lovely appartment, it had two bedrooms in a secure complex, with some absolutely stunning views from the large balcony area at the back.

Adrian and Laura were getting closer and they began living together in rental accommodation at Lindley. It was higher up the same street from where we lived when he was born. It was a large place above a workshop in an old Co-op building. It had a kitchen that Wendy fell in love with as soon as she saw it.

Then they moved to larger accommodation, an old weaver's cottage in Wellhouse at the top of Golcar, near to the school.

They bought and moved in to their first proper home of their own together in December 2015 at Salendine Nook. With accommodation on four levels, it has a small garden at the rear. A first for them and there is a possibility of a larger plot of land at the side.

They had been left with some unpleasant and hidden surprises with the condition of the house, but, when they have finished sorting it out, it will be a brilliant place to live, I am sure that they will be really happy there.

Adrian has still got a great relationship with his in-laws, he can go to see his children whenever he wants. He brings them up north to stay with him and Laura whenever he can.

Laura is brilliant with Damian and Willow, and both of the children seem to love her as well.

Since his split with Jo. Jo has a new partner, who she married and has had two further sons.

The latest news on Adrian and his family life, he and Laura went to Iceland for a weeks holiday, the first week in May 2016.

Adrian had been planning to ask Laura to marry him on the fifth of May, that was also the day of Laura's thirtieth birthday, (sorry Laura).

He wanted it to be all done in secret, the only problem would be acquiring a ring. How could he get a ring that Laura would like, without her input?

His devious side came to the fore. He asked me, if it would be at all possible to borrow his grandma Firth's ring.

Her engagement ring, would be so special to propose with.

I would not be able to keep that a secret, I would have to speak to my sisters.

I knew that mum had gone to her funeral with her Wedding ring on. The whereabouts of the engagement ring, I didn't know.

It turned out that it was at Lindsay's, the ring had been removed (not cut), when mum had broken her arms. Lindsay had been keeping it safe since then.

Both my sisters said that they were thrilled to bits for him. The thought of mum's ring being used, was fantastic, we were all so pleased.

By the way, Laura said YES!!!

My sisters also said that if the ring fitted, they would be honoured if Laura wanted to keep it and wear it with pride. If it didn't fit, or if it wasn't suitable, we would all understand.

If they decide to get another ring that suits their style better, then that is up to them. But we as a family would be thrilled if Laura wants the ring as a keepsake, a memory of the night Adrian proposed.

We are all more than sure that mum would have been over the moon, she would have wanted the ring to be used and cherished, for what it actually means. The love of two people, prepared to live their lives together forever, just like her and dad had done.

Mum had even kept the receipt for the ring, it meant so much to her. I have that now.

Once they got back from Iceland, we helped to celebrate by going for a meal with Adrian and Laura, along with her mum Diane and her step-dad Alex.

We have all met before and they appear to think as much of Adrian as we do about Laura.

CHAPTER 31.

HENRY AND LAWRENCE.

Death in the river.

February 1984. I was working with Henry, he was one of the older members of staff at the time. We were working a late shift from 14:00hrs until 22:00hrs. It was just around 19:00hrs when we received a call to someone, a female, in the river at Dalton.

Down at Dalton, the river or beck, as it is known. Well it's more of a large stream really, runs underneath the main road.

There is a large weir just upstream from the road, and although it is reasonably shallow, the water just there is around twenty foot wide.

Because of the weir, there have been some man made concrete edges, they then blend in to the concrete sides of the bridge for the road.

There was a small crowd gathered, the majority of who were family members of the lady.

A man met us saying that it was his elderly mother that was in the water, under the bridge.

The lady had been missing most of the day and had left a couple of very worrying notes.

The family and the police had been searching for her for some considerable time. Some of her personal belongings had been seen near to the bridge, leading to their upsetting find.

Two female police officers were with the family.

The only way to check on the lady was to get in to the water. It was an extremely cold February evening, Henry and I shimmied down the embankment and had to break the ice to get in to the beck. The water almost came up to our knees.

Even in the darkness under the bridge, we were clearly able to see that the lady was already dead. She had actually been dead for quite a few hours.

We needed to get her out of the water and up the banking.

By that time Mark, the Leading Ambulanceman (L. A.) had arrived on top of the bridge. We had to ask him to call the fire service for some assistance, in getting the lady out of the water.

After what seemed ages, we asked again, only to be told that they had declined to attend. (Due to some incorrect information that they had been passed. Under twelve foot of water, is significantly different to twelve foot away from the edge).

As the family were on the bridge waiting, Henry and I decided that it was our job to make a move. We got the scoop stretcher into the water and placed it underneath the lady. To fasten her on, there were none of the quick lock/release straps that we have now.

Oh no, we had a forty foot lashing, a rope to you and me. We had to try and tie her on safely. Mark was shouting orders as to which knots were the best to use.

He was a Sea Cadet Captain in his other life.

Our hands were blue, if it held, it would do. Simple as that. We then had to stand the stretcher, complete with our patient at the side of the river and somehow lift her five foot. That was up from the water level and up and onto the concrete of the embankment.

It was not an easy task for just the two of us to do, but somehow we managed. We both got soaked to the skin with the freezing water.

Once onto the embankment, we were able to cover the lady in blankets to at least try and preserve some dignity and modesty for her and her family.

The lady police officers, Henry and myself then scrambled with her, up the banking and put her into the waiting ambulance. I then drove up to HRI, with freezing, soaking wet feet.

It was only after entering the warmth of the A&E department that the cold really began to hit home.

Once certified by the doctor, we would have normally taken the patient round to the hospital mortuary. On that night though, Mark, our L. A. would have to do it, we were just too cold.

I lived across the road from the hospital, and Henry lived just on the road near to the Clock Tower. We went home.

Henry dropped me off to get a hot bath and a clean uniform, he then went on home to do the same.

When he arrived to collect me, Henry produced a flask of hot milky coffee. As we arrived to exchange the car with Mark, for our ambulance at the hospital. He poured me some of this welcoming coffee, along with a little "tot of the good stuff" in it, as Henry said.

It was brandy!

Henry didn't turn up to work with me, the day after the event, so I was sent up to his home to check on him. He looked awful, proper man flu. I called his GP for a home visit.

Less than two hours later, an ambulance was called for Henry and he was on his way to hospital. He was admitted for two weeks, he had got the startings of and then he developed full blown pneumonia.

Henry.

Another couple of memories of Henry. He was a single man, well known for being thrifty.

If he was working on a Sunday, he would bring his washing in to dry, in the centrally heated locker room. He would also have his traditional Sunday joint of beef in the oven. Why use his own electric and gas?

I called at his house one Christmas Day, our family were having dinner at my sister Lindsay's. I went across the road to see him. He and his butcher friend Eddie had just finished their Christmas dinner.

"Fancy a coffee?" Henry asked. Knowing his love of smooth milky coffee, I readily agreed. Then he poured out what was left of a rich onion gravy from a pan and he promptly poured in the milk. Not even rinsing the pan, never mind washing it.

The coffee though, was lovely, despite the occasional strand of onion floating about in it.

Another time on station, Henry had brought some of his mate Eddie's home made traditional Cornish pasties in. He got them out of the hot oven, where he had been keeping them warm and he gave one each to Tommy and me.

"They're a bit dry on their own" he said, and then he promptly poured freshly made porridge all over the pasty. It was a very interesting combination by the way, try it sometime!

Bluurgh!!!!

Ouch, I bet that hurt!

Another story involving Henry, it happened when he was working with his regular mate called Lawrence.

They were called to a sports injury on the football field at Oakes, just off New Hey Road, not far above the Bay Horse roundabout.

When they got there, the footballer was a twenty four year old lad. He had been involved in a heavy tackle and had suffered from an obvious fractured femur (his thigh bone), the longest bone in the body.

It was a nasty injury, even though it was a closed fracture. There can still be a lot of blood lost into the tissues, up to three or four litres.

The player had already been assessed and treated by a team of St. John Ambulance volunteers.

The first aiders, had used the post from the corner flag, as a makeshift splint. They had wrapped the muddy pointed end of the post in a triangular bandage for padding, and placed it under his armpit. Then they had strapped his body to the post, from top to bottom using the traditional method of several triangular bandages, nine of them in all.

The problem with that type of splint, is that you cannot shorten it.

The flag post stuck out way past where the lads feet stopped, the flag was still flapping.

The hapless ambulance duo placed him onto the stretcher and they put him into the back of the ambulance, ready to set off on the short quarter of a mile journey to hospital.

Lawrence stayed in the back of the ambulance with the patient and Henry jumped out of the back, he then slammed the door shut prior to driving off.

There was, according to Lawrence, the most horrendous and blood curdling scream that he had ever heard.

The patient became hysterical, Henry had already got into the cab and was annoyed at the screaming. He set off towards the hospital, as he did so, he shouted into the back to Lawrence, "tell him to grow up, it's not that bad. We'll be there in a minute!"

All Lawrence could do, was to try and console the young lad. As he was trying, Lawrence could see blood, a lot of it. It was appearing on the floor of the ambulance around his feet.

It was running off the end of the stretcher, had the fracture possibly developed into an open fracture?

I think that by now, you will have probably already guessed what had happened, Lawrence hadn't.

When Henry stopped at HRI, he opened the back doors.

The lad was still screaming at the top of his voice.

It was only as they side loaded the stretcher out of the back of the ambulance (no lifts or ramps), that they could see where the blood was coming from.

When Henry had shut the door, he had slammed it into the protruding end of the corner flag post. That had then pushed the muddy pointed end straight into his armpit. After dislocating his shoulder, the end of the post had then actually burst through the bandage, into the flesh and had come out of the other side.

No wonder he was screaming.

His injury was horrific. He needed several hours of surgery to remove the filthy post. It posed a massive infection risk, as well as adding to the original physical injury. He was in hospital for several months, he never did regain full use of his right arm. His leg recovered really well, even though that needed an operation to fit plates and screws.

Ouch!

Nearly got him!

Another incident involving Henry and his regulate crew mate Lawrence, very nearly resulted in them being the most famous ambulance crew in Great Britain, and even the world.

Probably!

Henry loved telling this story, it was one of his favourites.

It was just before eight in the evening on the 22nd of May 1981. Lawrence was driving their Bedford CA ambulance, fleet number 136. It had the call sign Hudd Amb 8. He was heading back to station from Huddersfield Royal Infirmary.

He had just nicely started going down New Hey Road, from the Bay Horse roundabout. When a dark figure ran from a gap in the hedge of

"The Portlands" a row of large terraced houses on the right hand side as you travel downhill.

The male figure appeared to be running for his life, he hadn't seen the big white ambulance, he was too busy looking over his shoulder.

Crash!

He ran straight into the side of the vehicle and fell to the floor. Lawrence stopped and got out to help the poor chap. Only to be met by a foul torrent of abuse.

Then as the man got back to his feet, he threatened Lawrence with a hammer.

The man was a thick set man with a lot of black hair and a goatee beard. Lawrence backed off quickly and got back in the ambulance.

The man ran off again, just a little further down the road and to the left, through a snickett that joins New Hey Road to Thornhill Avenue, where he disappeared.

At half past seven that evening, on the path that runs across the bottom of the playing fields at Oakes. Across from the Bay Horse pub, near to the roundabout. Not even a quarter of a mile away from the incident with that pedestrian.

A young woman called Theresa had been attacked by a man wielding a hammer. He had smashed it down several times, onto the top of her head. Before rendering her unconscious, she had been able to manage a scream. A scream so terrifying, that her partner Jimmy, ran out of the house to help.

As Jimmy ran out, the attacker fled. It turned out that her attacker was none other than the Yorkshire Ripper, Peter Sutcliffe.

In interviews following his arrest, Peter Sutcliffe admitted to police that he was very close to being caught that night. He stated that he was laid on the floor, hiding in some bushes by the playing fields. Jimmy had actually stood on his hand as he searched for him, in the still of the night.

Theresa survived her attack, but not without horrendous head injuries that changed her life forever.

It was the same man that had run into the side of the ambulance. If he had been injured by that slight collision, just imagine what fame and notoriety our ambulance couple would have received.

It was reported to the police, on the night of the incident. Initially, the police didn't link things at all. They had too much going on with the investigation into the assault on Theresa.

A couple of weeks later when her attacker was identified as the Yorkshire Ripper, the police were all over the ambulance station and our intrepid crew members.

If only heh! If only!

CHAPTER 32.

OUR SECOND CHILD.

Was it Labour again? Yes, it's another boy!

It was March 1986. Twenty one months on from the birth of Adrian, and Wendy was in the latter stages of pregnancy again.

From quite early on the Friday morning, I had noticed some changes in Wendy, I kept asking if she was ok. Although she said she was, something was not quite right.

She was actually in the early stages of labour, I was aware before she was. But, she hung on for most of the day.

I asked Mrs. T next door below, if she could look after Adrian for a short while, my dad was on his way up from Paddock.

I took Wendy across the road to HRI, it was late in the evening of Friday the 21st of March 1986.

In the early hours of the morning, a Saturday again, Wendy gave birth to Benjamin Brian at 3:15am, he weighed in at seven pounds and two ounces.

Mum and baby were doing great again.

It's a good job she was ok, we were in the middle of closing a deal on the sale of our house at Lindley. We loved that house and the area, but it just wouldn't have been big enough for us with two children.

Ben was only four weeks old when we finally moved, it was a very stressful time for all of us.

Ben's Christening.

The 5th of October 1986, that was the day of Ben's Christening, it was at Paddock.

All Saints Church at Paddock had closed and they were using the premises of the United Church, just a short distance higher up Church Street. They had both merged together and become Paddock Shared Church.

The Christening was performed, by the reverend David Earle.

Ben's Godparents were Alison, the wife of John and Mark, the husband of Alex. They were both good friends from the past, and were married to Adrian's Godparents.

The third was Alan, a good friend and colleague from the ambulance service. As with Adrian, we hadn't asked any family members to officiate.

After the service, all of our families and friends came back to our house for a bite to eat and a drink. A lot of chat and reminiscing.

A good old family gathering.

Screwdriver through his head!

One day whilst I was at work, when Ben was just two years old. I got a strange message. An ambulance had been called to our house for Ben, they were bringing him to HRI.

The girl on the liaison office desk was stalling and stuttering, in trying to tell me what had happened.

Eventually she came straight out with it, and said "I'm sorry, but the message that I have been given, is that he has a screwdriver stuck through his head".

How do you react to that?

I had been using my largest screwdriver the night before, the shaft of which was around two foot long. I had some wonderful images going on in my head whilst I was waiting for them outside A&E.

When the crew arrived at A&E, I could only see the handle of the screwdriver, it was pressed hard up against his cheek. The beauty of it though, was that from seeing the handle alone, I knew that it was the shortest screwdriver that I had in my toolbox.

The shaft of that one was only one and a half inches long from the base of the handle to the tip, and maybe a sixteenth of an inch in diameter.

Ben had found it under the edge of the sofa, I must have dropped it the night before.

Ben and his brother Adrian, had been larking about on the sofa. Ben climbing up onto the back of it. Why, I don't know, but he had the screwdriver in his hand. Then somehow, he had fallen over the back of the sofa onto the floor. As he had fallen, the screwdriver became embedded in his face.

On their arrival at the hospital, Ben was very calm and still.

I took him from Wendy and we all, Adrian included, went in to the casualty department.

Dr. Mike, the A&E consultant was there. When he saw me with Ben, he sent us round for x-ray straight away.

He told me that there are many facial nerves near to where the offending screwdriver was stuck. Due to that, he advised us to see a specialist in ENT (ear, nose and throat). They would be more aware and familiar of the facial nerves and would be more suitable to treat it, than he was.

At the ENT department, they looked at the x-ray and there were a number of options.

First, was to give Ben an injection to numb his face, that was very quickly ruled out. He has still got a phobia for needles, even then he wouldn't let anyone near him with a needle.

The second option, was to go to theatre, to have an anaesthetic and remove it. That would have been ok, but a bit over the top to be having a full general anaesthetic. For a procedure that would last literally a few seconds.

Or finally, and seemingly what would be the most practical, would be to swiftly grip the handle and with one quick pull, it would be over.

That seemed to be the most logical choice.

I was sat down in a dentists' type chair with Ben on my knee. A cloth was sprayed with ice cold analgesic spray and was then applied to the side of Ben's face.

Both the doctor and me were ready.

Just as Ben drew a sharp intake of breath, due to it being so cold. In one quick movement, the screwdriver handle was swiftly pulled and the item was gone.

The doctor dropped it beside him, and into a bin. That was when Ben uttered his first comments, "that's my daddy's, you shouldn't do that!"

Ben was fine afterwards.

His only problem to be, was that his first tooth in that area grew crooked, where the blade had stuck in and damaged his gum. His second, adult tooth was fine.

He is now thirty years old and he still has a little scar on his cheek, in the shape of a cross.

It was a "Phillips" screwdriver.

Self harm.

When Ben has been feeling depressed, he has resorted to self harming in the past. Sometimes superficial, but at other times, he has caused some severe injury to himself.

He has also taken to tattoos, including designing most of his own. He has had his own tattoo guns in the past and has performed them for his friends. He has even done more tattoos on himself.

I don't know how he did it, as he still has a horrendous needle phobia.

When it was coming up to one of my birthdays, Ben had said that he was going to get someone to do a tattoo for me. I did almost get one when I was around seventeen.

I had been rather drunk, in Blackpool and I had nearly got a scorpion on my back.

Fortunately I wasn't all that drunk, so I had decided not to through with it. Ben had actually dared me to have one, I don't think he really believed that I would go through with it.

We went to the tattooist in Todmorden, just a couple of miles up the road from Walsden, where Ben was living at the time. I picked out the scorpion that I had originally wanted, I elected to get it on my right shoulder.

Ben, Wendy, Kelly and Scott in his pram were all watching.

Half an hour or so later, I had got the birthday present that would be with me forever.

Fortunately as Ben gets more mature, the episodes of self harm are less frequent, unfortunately the severity of the injuries when he does, has increased.

Night terrors.

I have no idea or explanation why, but occasionally Ben suffered from night terrors, they started from around two years of age. It was definitely not sleepwalking, it was, absolute terror!

Ben would be in bed, Wendy and I would be downstairs watching television.

When all of a sudden the door would burst open. In he would run, he would bounce all over the furniture, his eyes wide open and staring, he would be trying to speak.

Some words were actually coming out, but not making any sense, he would be talking nearly as fast as he was running.

If we tried to stop him, to cuddle him to try and calm him down, it would only make him worse. We had to physically restrain him, to pin him down, until he came round, it could take anywhere up to an hour.

Once when we were on a cubs camping weekend (in a hostel), near to Scaleborough Park Mental Hospital, Burley in Wharfedale. It was late, all the kids were in bed. The adults were sat in the common room, it would have been around eleven o'clock.

All of a sudden there was a commotion. Ben who was nearly ten at the time, came bouncing down the stairs, he only hit about three of the fifteen. He ran through the common room, into the kitchen and then back out again. He was over the sofa's, he went up and down the steps two or three times.

Shouting, screaming, none of it was making any sense. The other adults were at a loss of what to do.

I tried to grab him, at that age he was very difficult to hold down and he was fast.

Eventually I did manage to get hold of him, he was in a right state. Sweating, burning up and he was flushed. He was like a beetroot!

One of the other leaders, Helen (who I had known from my schooldays at Paddock, along with her brother Peter), she took over and held onto Ben.

Helen was a relative stranger to him, but it seemed to work and he calmed down. She kept him cuddled tight to her until he went back to sleep.

We were then able to put him back to bed. The day after, he had no recall of the events whatsoever.

It was an experience for all to witness!

I wouldn't want to see it again, in fact I don't remember any more serious episodes, he must have hopefully grown out of it.

No more school.

Ben would be the first to admit that he is not an academic.

He is the practical type. Very good at drawing and very good with his hands.

He had a short attention span at school, that had got him in to all kinds of troubles.

He was eventually sent to Westfields PRU (Pupil Referral Unit for naughty boys and girls) in Batley. He actually seemed to enjoy his time there.

They did a lot of outdoor activities, including abseiling, canoeing, riding waterfalls, all sorts of adventures, it was right up Ben's street. But it was only a short term placement before going back to Royds Hall School.

Peter our next door neighbour on Manchester Road, is now the Deputy Head of Westfields.

Eventually Ben had to leave school, he was expelled due to his disruptive behaviour. Eventually, after a long while, he started with some home schooling.

His tutor at home was an older man, a retired teacher, a bloke called Patrick, he was good. Ben got on really well with Patrick, despite the age gap.

Although Patrick had retired from full time teaching, a long while ago. He was very active and a super keen cyclist. A couple of times they went off for a couple of hours on their bikes.

Ben still enjoys cycling now.

The pair of them had many similar interests. Unfortunately funding for that was stopped all too soon.

Reactions.

Ben was never happy with what he had, he always aspired to get something better. He was always wheeling and dealing, even now, he's always looking out for a bargain.

Those bargains always backfired. He bought something that he thought was cheap and hoped to sell it on for more.

Somehow, he was typical of the Firth family and he always seemed to end up losing money, it wasn't for the lack of trying though.

We used to get into all sorts of arguments at home, Ben and me. I was just as bad as him.

Neither of us were able act on any argument, we just reacted to each other and everything that was said. That was always making things much worse. Eventually, we were arguing that much, he had to move out.

Thankfully, things have really settled and we get on much better now.

Kelly and Scott.

Ben had moved to several places where he was on his own, none of them seemed to be right. Some places were no more than drugs and drinking dens.

He then went to Halifax, to live in supported lodgings. That was a house where he would lodge with the owner, Sara. She was a psychiatric nurse, at the Dales unit in Halifax.

It was whilst in Halifax that he got a position at Key Training, a placement to give him practical education and life skills.

Ben took up welding whilst he was there and he became extremely good at it.

He did other courses in health and safety, maths and English, all sorts of things. Then he ended up assisting and teaching the others. Ben has always been at his best, when he was helping someone less fortunate than himself.

Whilst at Key Training he met Kelly, she became pregnant with our first grandchild. During the pregnancy, her parents disowned her, they didn't like Ben one little bit. Both he and Kelly, lived with us for nearly all of her pregnancy.

Kelly went to Key Training with Ben while she was pregnant. I used to run them to Halifax before eight, every morning that I wasn't working.

Eventually, they got a little flat at Walsden, just the other side of Todmorden, on Scott Street. It was directly opposite Gordon Riggs' famous garden Centre.

It wasn't long after moving in, that their son, our first grandchild Scott was born. Scott Lee Firth.

The flat that they lived in, was only a bedsit, really it was only meant for one person. It was ok for a couple with newborn, but it wouldn't be suitable for a toddler.

It wasn't long after Scott was born, that they managed to get a two bedroom house in Halifax. That was ideal for them.

Dragon Art.

Ben carried on at Key Training, for a quite a while.

At the time and for a change, he owed me some money. Unable to pay me back in cold hard cash, he made me a dragon.

He had been making dragons from scrap bits of metal, both for himself and for sale at the training centre.

Some of them sold for up to £300.

They were entirely made from scratch and each and everyone of them was different. The one he made for me is over two foot six inches long from nose to tail. It was and still remains one of mine and Wendy's prized possessions.

Relationships.

Eventually Ben split up with Kelly, she and Scott still live at the house in Halifax. She has got married since.

Ben has had several unsuccessful relationships over the years. They have resulted in two more gorgeous little grandchildren that we see occasionally. Both are girls, Kacey and Kaira.

Kacey lives in Huddersfield and Kaira lives nearer to Doncaster.

As I write this, Ben lives in a little place called Camblesforth. It is just outside Selby, very close to the famous Drax Power Station.

He has Kaira to stay with him every other weekend. We pick Scott up once a month to spend some time with his dad. Ben sees Kacey when he can get to Huddersfield, but talks regularly to her via Face Time on his phone.

One day, one day, hopefully he will find the job he wants and he will settle down happily with someone for the rest of his life.

That's our hope for him anyway, fingers crossed.

CHAPTER 33.

ANOTHER MOVE.

Another new house.

We moved to our current address on Manchester Road in Huddersfield when Ben was only four weeks old.

Buying, selling and moving house is never an easy time, but heavily pregnant. Then with a new born child and a toddler in tow was a nightmare. We don't have any further plans on moving again (or any more children)!

Wendy has dreams, lottery wins etc. but other than that we are staying put!

Neighbours at Manchester Road.

We have had a selection of neighbours since we moved to Manchester Road.

We haven't had any problems with any of them really. We have a shared access across the back of the house, with the terrace next door for bins etc.

Sometimes the gates have been left open and we have had some occasional issues with visitors parking, but on the whole we have been lucky really with the neighbours.

Next door when we moved in, were a couple, a little older than us, called Jonny and Phillipa. He was a roofer. We once had a leak, somewhere between our house and his next door on the roof.

Was it his problem or ours?

He said if we could leave it a week or so, he would sort it out. He did, the leak was near to his chimney. So he took his chimney stack down and then he replaced the whole of his roof. He used the same tiles as ours and blended it all in together.

All the leaks were stopped.

Following those two, another young couple moved in. It was just prior to their wedding. They were Geoff and Sara. Both psychiatric nurses at St. Luke's hospital at Crosland Moor.

They then had a baby son Adam.

Geoff was a fanatical Huddersfield Town fan, along with his best mate Bobby, who used to frequent the Socialist Club where I became a member.

Geoff left St. Luke's, he became a "control and restraint" trainer, for dealing with violent or extreme psychiatric patients. He ended up setting himself up in business teaching his methods. Even working at the most secure unit of Rampton Hospital in Nottinghamshire.

Geoff and Sara moved to Almondbury.

After them, another couple moved in, I'll call them Janet and John. He was a stock car driver and an engineer, we didn't see too much of him.

His wife had a baby quite prematurely, I'll called him Timmy.

They then had another child, a little girl.

Some months later, they did a moonlight flit and the house was repossessed.

The Estate Agents came and were doing their survey with a view to sell the property on. They invited Wendy and me round, they wanted us to see what state the house had been left in.

It was was filthy, a disgrace.

Then they showed us the cellar. It looked like that whenever there had been any paper, cardboard, or other combustible rubbish to get rid of. It had just been thrown down the steps into the cellar and then it had been set light to.

There was a pile of ashes at the bottom of the steps, that must have been at least three foot deep. Even the ceiling of the cellar had been badly damaged. It was lucky that the whole house didn't go up in flames.

That could have had the potential, to spread to the rest of the whole row of terrace properties.

Then along came Lucy, her dad Joe was a driving instructor who used to renovate houses in his spare time. He had to totally shell the house from top to bottom.

Lucy became pregnant, and she had a daughter, called Milly. It wasn't long after that, she sold up to find a bigger place.

Then it was Charlie and Haley that took over. They were there for a while before they had their son Andy. Some years after when Andy had started school, they separated. Haley left the family home and her son Andy went with her.

Charlie still lives there and he has Andy to stay over with him for most weekends.

On the other side of our house in the bungalow, was Bob and his wife Penny. He worked on the oil rigs for three month on and then three month off.

When we moved in to our house, the building society told us that at the front of the house, the garden wall was in a very poor condition. It needed pulling down and rebuilding to meet the current health and safety conditions

One morning, when I was talking to Bob about it, he said that it would be just up his street. If we wanted, he would do the job for a very competitive price.

He gave us a quote there and then, that Wendy and me were only too happy to accept.

Only the next morning, when we got up, the wall had already gone. Within the next two days, he had built it all back up again and a damn good job he did as well.

They weren't at the house much longer, before Graham and his mum moved in. Graham was a single lad who looked after his elderly mum, she suffered with the dreaded Alzheimer's.

I'm not sure how old Graham was, I would think that he was about five or six years older than me, but he seemed very young at heart. He had an older brother who was married with a family.

Graham was a musician, in a band doing covers and comedy, a bit like the

"Grumbleweeds". Their drummer was a little person called Mark, who used to go to my school.

He was also an actor, he has played the part of an obnoxious little dwarf in some big films. The Lion, The Witch and The Wardrobe, the Harry Potter series of films and many others.

When at training school at Keighley, some fellow students and me went to the village of Gooseye for a few beers. There was a live band on at the Turkey Bar, a fun bar and club, run in a similar way to the old Amsterdam Bar of the eighties in Huddersfield.

It was only about four or five miles from the training centre. The band, on the night that we visited? Yes it was Graham and his, from next door.

Small world!

Graham didn't seem to have a proper, regular job, he did all sorts of building and landscaping working for himself.

He landscaped all of his own gardens and did all the work on his own house.

He got us all the red bricks that we used for block paving in our garden, from the old pavilion at the Fartown Rugby ground!

And he revamped us a bench that he rescued from the next door Fartown Cricket ground.

Aside from that, he did small acting roles. Most being one off TV commercials, usually he would be sat in a bar while the filming was done all around him.

Graham had another sideline, where he and a mate were amazing lookalikes of the famous Laurel and Hardy. I took some black and white promo shots of them.

One money making job that they had, was to be filmed for a chocolate advert in Switzerland.

Imagine being paid for that and an all expenses trip to boot.

He also had a long running, but non speaking, part in the prequel of Last of the Summer Wine. Known as not surprisingly, the First of the Summer Wine.

It started with a pilot episode, then two series of six episodes each. Graham, was in nine of the total thirteen.

Not long after Graham's mother died, he went to Cyprus.

He was going to work there over the winter. I believe he was going to be like a caretaker and handyman at a holiday flats complex. Doing all the jobs that were required prior to opening for the new season.

While he was out there, he met Thelma, they came back to sort things out financially and then planned to go back out there to live.

He sold the bungalow and left for Cyprus.

It wasn't long though before they were back in the UK. They found that in the summer months, it was far too hot for them to live out there full time.

Graham had sold the bungalow to Peter and Ruth and their daughter Miranda.

Both of them are primarily music teachers.

Peter is deputy headmaster at Westfields Pupil Referral Unit for difficult children, mostly expelled from a secondary school.

As already mentioned, Ben attended there for a time before being home tutored,

Peter also plays in a band, I think as a drummer and Ruth plays in orchestras around the county.

Inevitably Miranda has become a talented musician, playing anything she seems to turn her hand to.

She is currently away from home, studying at University. When she comes home she performs with her own band. Usually in the local pubs and clubs. What I've seen and heard of them have been covers from my era, they sounded to be quite good.

CHAPTER 34.

MUM, DAD AND EDDIE.

Pen friends.

Mum always had a love of letter writing. When she was a pupil at junior school. St. Thomas' Church School. The teacher encouraged the children to have pen friends in other parts of the world to write to. The teacher had put the children in touch with some schools from all over the world.

Mum absolutely loved it, she loved writing letters.

Over the years, mum lost touch with most of her pen friends, but she did always keep in touch with two. One lady Anneke lived in Amsterdam, Holland, the other lady was Edith in Australia.

Mum was still writing to Edith until very late in her life, I will go into a bit more detail of that story, later.

Mum and dad were going abroad!

In June 1996. Mum and dad finally accepted an invitation to go to Amsterdam and meet Anneke and her husband Aart.

That, I believe was mum's one and only trip abroad. They went to stay with Anneke and Aart at their home in Amsterdam, for a week.

The highlight of the trip for mum, apart from the obvious of meeting her long time friend, was to see the house of Anne Frank. Mum had always had an interest in her story.

Not only did they see where the house was, but had a full guided tour of the premises. She was absolutely amazed, she couldn't get over the cramped and overcrowded conditions that they had to live in.

For dad, the highlight of his week, was when they went to Nijmegan Bridge. The story was made famous from the blockbuster film A Bridge Too Far. Starring, Dirk Bogarde, James Caan, Michael Caine, Sean Connery, Edward Fox, Elliot Gould, Gene Hackman, Anthony Hopkins, Laurence Olivier, Ryan O'Neal, Robert Redford and many more.

During the Second World War, "Operation Market Garden" was the mission of saving the bridge. Allied troops were being massacred by the Germans and their snipers, from their stronghold position. All the area is still covered in bullet holes.

The trip even strengthened the bond of friendship between mum and Anneke.

Eddie.

One of my former colleagues in the ambulance service, Eddie was a glider pilot during the Second World War.

He was involved in both of the historic Second World War battles for bridges. Firstly, was Operation "Deadstick". It was over the 5th and 6th of June 1940. The mission was to save the river and canal crossings at the famous, now named Pegasus Bridge, after the Parachute Regiment's logo.

It was a major campaign as part of the Normandy Landings.

The story of Pegasus Bridge, was made into a film in 1962, the "Longest Day". Starring John Wayne, Henry Fonda, Robert Mitchum, Sean Connery, Richard Todd, Richard Burton, Rod Steiger, Peter Lawford, Kenneth More and many others.

Secondly Eddie was involved in Operation "Market Garden". That involved the bridge at Nijmegan. The story told as above in the film "A Bridge Too Far".

The gliders were made of wood to lighten them. Eddie's paratroopers had been dropped, but his glider was shot at and burst into flames.

The cockpit was badly damaged and it meant that Eddie couldn't escape, his only hope was to have a safe "crash" landing.

There were some German snipers in an elevated position, above the bridge. They were just picking off the allied troops, they were murdering them.

Eddie had to make a decision, he was going down in flames, he was very likely to die. Bravely, he decided to try and take out the snipers using his burning glider. He decided to crash into their elevated position above the bridge.

Unfortunately he crashed around ten yards short.

It was a heroic and totally selfless act.

In later life, Eddie was eventually rewarded for his bravery, by both the Dutch and the French governments.

It was only a couple of months after Eddie's his retirement, that some people in suits from the "home office" came to the ambulance station and wanted to meet him.

There was a representative from the French Government with them. I was the Station Officer at the time of their visit. I managed to get hold of Eddie and arranged for them all to meet.

Eddie and his wife were invited to a ceremony at Nijmegan, at the site of his crash and he was awarded the "Legion d'Honneur" one of the highest awards to be given to a foreigner. They went back several times before his death and he was awarded other medals by the Dutch royal family as well.

Well done Eddie!

How the hell did he manage to do that, there?

I can only remember ever attending to one job with Eddie. It was a tragic road accident on Bradley Mills Road. Near to Bradley Grange, the ICI Club. I think it was early on in 1982.

It was a Saturday, late morning. Bradley Mills Road is a busy road at the back of the old Huddersfield Town football ground and very close to the newer ground of today.

It is a narrow road up the hillside and always on a match day had been fraught with parking problems.

The police were as usual before a game, putting out traffic cones near to the bottom and the bend. The two women police officers doing just that, heard the accident and they called for us.

Eddie worked everyday on a outpatient minibus ambulance, he had no lifting. It was nice and steady away, leading up to his retirement.

To keep his "Millar" pay as a qualified member of staff, he and his mate, Hal, had to work one Saturday morning for four hours. Once every six weeks, they would work just four hours, from 09:00hrs until 13:00hrs.

Usually crewed up together, that was the only shift when they attended 999 calls. I was covering Hal on this shift.

When we arrived on scene, apart from some other police, we were the only ones there to deal with the crash.

An articulated lorry with an empty 38 foot long, flat backed trailer had been travelling down the hill towards Huddersfield.

Heading up the hill, towards Rawthorpe, was one of the old original Austin Mini cars.

For some reason, the car didn't give way to the lorry. The lorry driver braked and had to swerve, as he did he jack-knifed, his trailer overtook him.

There was only one place in the whole of the road where that could possibly have happened and it had.

Where the gateway to Bradley Grange is, the land opened out, just enough for his trailer to be able to make that movement.

The mini was still on its way up, the trailer swung all the way round and went straight over the top of it. The mini was well and truly trapped under it.

I had to crawl underneath the trailer, to get to the car. The mini roof had been completely removed in one movement.

There was only the driver in the mini.

How, I don't know, but as well as the roof, the top of this mans head had been removed. It was horrific.

On the back seat of the car, both halves of his brain were sat there, clear of his skull and intact.

The fire service arrived and rightly so, ordered me out from under the truck until it had been made safe. They quickly lifted the back of the trailer using airbags and then several of the firemen physically dragged the car out from underneath.

The man was still making a noise.

I could then examine him properly. As with old cars, the steering column had stayed rigid and didn't collapse as they do now.

The steering wheel had become embedded into his chest. As the firemen moved the drivers seat back on its runners, the steering wheel fell away from his chest, it had been bent into a bizarre saddle shape. His breathing was getting weaker, as was his pulse.

We lifted him out and onto the stretcher, oxygen was applied and Eddie and I lifted him into the ambulance. The fire brigade had picked up the mans brain and put that, and anything else that they could find, into a black bag. They had then put it into the ambulance for us.

Eddie drove at speed to awaiting staff at HRI.

In the ambulance on route, the mans heart stopped beating, as did his breathing. We didn't have defibrillators then. I had to use a bag and mask to get air and oxygen into his lungs, it wasn't working. I tried cardiac massage, but due to the steering wheel and its column, the man didn't have any rib cage left. It had been shattered.

All I could do was to squeeze his heart manually, through his skin with my fingers of one hand, it was awful. As soon as I stopped, there were no spontaneous signs of life and he was pronounced dead at the hospital.

The noise and some of the mechanics of respiration, had been taking place due to some basic activity still coming from his brain stem. That hadn't been damaged.

It was quite possible that he had collapsed at the wheel whilst driving up the hill, that might have been why he hadn't made any attempt to move or stop.

Freaky though, that was the only possible place on that road that it could ever have happened. Anywhere else the trailer would have hit walls or fencing and been unable to swing round.

20 yards of a one mile stretch of road.

If the accident had happened at any of the other 1,740 yards, the man may well have survived.

CHAPTER 35.

WHAT A GENTLEMAN!

Norman.

In 1986. I was working with Norman, from Honley Station. Norman was a very pleasant quiet man, he was a heavy smoker, boy did he like his cigarettes.

The one thing that struck everyone about Norman, he was always feeling the cold. No matter what the weather was like, he was always wearing his service hat and coat.

The coat at that time, was made of a black nylon waterproof material, it was quilted inside and fitted with a very heavy duty stainless steel zip.

One evening we were called to attend to a female patient who had taken an overdose of of tablets. It was in a house in the Newsome area of Huddersfield.

On our arrival, we were met at the door by a woman, who I think was in her early forties. She explained that it was her partner that had taken some tablets.

The partner was another woman of around the same age, she had taken an unknown quantity of a type of anti depressant tablets. On first impressions, the woman appeared to have suffered no ill effects. Not from the tablets, but she did appear to be worse the wear for drink.

As I was speaking to her, she looked up and seemed to take an instant dislike to Norman.

How anybody could do that I don't know.

Suddenly, she had a knife, it appeared from nowhere. It was a kitchen devil bread knife, the type with teeth on one side and serrations on the other.

A long slim blade.

She thrust the blade straight at Norman, I saw the knife disappear and her fist hit him hard in the chest. He fell motionless to the floor clutching his chest.

It was so quick.

As Norman fell, I ran to him. At the same time the partner of the psychopath, picked up an ornament from the fireplace and smashed it down on the top of her partners head. Rendering her unconscious.

I called for back up of another ambulance, and the police. Norman wasn't moving initially, he appeared to be unconscious.

As I unnervingly unzipped Norman's coat, not knowing what I was going to see, two pieces of the metal blade fell out from it. There was some blood, but only an extremely small amount.

Norman came round, he said he was ok and he was talking fine. He told me that he only felt like he had been winded.

Following some further checks, the blade was the type that had two short prongs like a fork on the end.

His bloody coat! That bloody zip! That coat, that he was so attached to had just saved his life.

As she had hit him, the two prongs of the knife had fortunately gone one either side of the heavy duty zip and then the flimsy blade had snapped.

It was only the two prongs at the end of the knife, that had actually pierced some skin. It was her fist and the impact of it that had floored Norman.

He was so lucky!

Several years later, I just happened to be working out of Honley station, with Norman again. It was early in 1990. We had been called to a road traffic incident on Dalton Bank Road at the back of the works known as the ICI, I think it's called Zeneca now.

It is a well known fast road with long open stretches and with several extremely narrow series' of bends. To make it worse, one side of the road has a severe drop down to the river. It is a drop of up to 200 feet in places.

Fate has a habit of rearing its head in our job.

A small light van, a Bedford HA, similar in size to an escort van. Had lost control, hit and gone through the wooden fence and dropped the maximum drop into the river.

A crew were already on scene, they had requested another crew to assist. They wanted them to collect a rescue stretcher, that was based on station, we only had one of them.

That was our job.

As we arrived, the police and fire brigade were already on site. Along with the first ambulance that had requested our assistance.

At the bottom of the steep banking we could see the van, one woman was making her way up the slippy muddy banking with the assistance of two police officers.

The front end of the van was in the River Colne, it was submerged up to the front windscreen.

The woman who had already emerged had been the front seat passenger. As she made her way up, she looked familiar somehow, I am one of those people who never forget a face.

Other than being soaked through, she had only sustained very superficial injuries.

As she reached the road, Norman was taking her into the ambulance to sit and wait for her friend. There she would be able to get warmed up. She was soaked to the skin from being in the freezing cold and dirty river water.

Jerry was down at the waters edge, he shouted up to me, for the Neil Robertson stretcher. We very rarely used them, but this job was the perfect occasion.

A Neil Robertson stretcher, was a six foot long piece of kit made up of dozens of long lengths of bamboo strips. They were all fastened together with a canvas material, it was like a giant corset.

When fastened around the body, it formed a very rigid shell. It was to immobilise the spine particularly to extricate someone.

There are handles all along the side to allow the patient to be carried. It even has a lifting eye at each end, to allow it to be lowered or lifted by ropes.

They have now been superseded and replaced with spinal boards. The Neil Robertson was not suitable for cleaning, due to the canvas material and they were far too expensive for single use.

The driver of the van, had been assisted from the drivers seat and into the back of the van. She had a fractured femur, (thigh bone).

It needed careful handling up the banking, you can bleed very heavily into the tissues with one of those injuries.

Placed into the stretcher, we were then able to make the slow ascent up the banking. Another ambulanceman, Jack had been sat in the back of the half submerged van with the woman.

The fire service had lowered ropes down to the van through the trees. As we and others had hold of the stretcher, there were others at the side of us holding on to those ropes and grabbing hold of us. Making sure that we didn't slip back down.

We inched our way slowly to the top of the embankment.

Pain relief in those days was limited to entonox. Our patient had chosen her own stress and pain relief, as was clearly shown in a photograph that was printed in the Huddersfield Daily Examiner.

She smoked a cigarette.

I was positioned near to the head end of the stretcher, I could clearly see the woman's face and I had recognised her as well. It all started coming back to me then.

They were the lesbian friends from Newsome.

Little did my colleague Norman, realise, but he was only sat alone, chatting in the back of the ambulance to the woman who had tried to kill him a few years earlier. The one that we were carrying, was the one that had struck her friend over the head.

I couldn't wait to tell him.

She had actually got away with any form of legal proceedings, due to her unstable mental state at the time that she had attacked him. Even though she had suffered a nasty head injury, she had made a full recovery.

When I got to the top and told him, he changed.

Norman had a look on his face, one that I had never seen from him. It was more frightening, than any face that I had seen Tommy muster up.

I do remember that shortly after I had told him, that Norman leaned right over to her and said something quietly in her ear. Her face changed immediately and she went extremely pale. She never said another word to either of us.

I don't know what he had said, and he wouldn't tell me either.

That was totally out of character for Norman.

Karma!

Early on in 2015. Norman was brought into HRI suffering with severe breathing problems. I hadn't seen him since he had retired and that had been many years ago. He was with his daughter.

Norman had got the dreaded Alzheimer's as well.

I promised his daughter that I would copy some photos of him that I had, sometimes they can help with memory issues.

I also told her about the stabbing and his bloody coat. She was shocked, he had never mentioned anything about that to his family.

Norman's daughter remembered the coat. She said that she never saw him without it, now she knew why.

I did get him some photo's, but he wasn't well enough to appreciate them at the time. He passed away shortly afterwards.

His daughter has them now and she is very proud of her dad. She learnt a few things about him that she wasn't aware of that day that I saw them both. All of it good though.

He was a gentleman was Norman, RIP.

CHAPTER 36.

HOME AND CHARITY CALLS.

Out of the mouths of babes.

On a Sunday morning, shifts permitting, we always used to go to mum and dads for Sunday dinner. We would walk down from Lindley, with Adrian as a baby, in a huge Silver Cross coach built pram.
Whilst there, we would do our washing in mums top loading twin tub, before the long uphill walk back home.

When Ben was born and we lived on Manchester Road, we had our own washing machine, but we still went to mum and dads for Sunday lunch whenever we could.

It was on one of our regular Sunday trips to mum and dad's and we were all sat down for lunch.

Adrian was sat at his own little table in the front room, the rest of the family were sat around the dining table in the kitchen.

Ben was only around four months old at the time, he was doing his own thing, in a baby bouncer on the floor.

The news was on the television.

The day before, the main national news headlines were of two young British Soldiers in Northern Ireland. They had somehow got lost and had unwittingly travelled into a well supported IRA area.

They had then somehow got into the middle of a provisionals funeral procession.

Although they weren't on duty, their car had a rental number plate, it was that that had given them away.

The crowd quickly became an angry and hostile mob. The two lads were dragged from the car, stripped and beaten to within minutes of their life and then they were left to die at the roadside as roadkill.

A priest was filmed, trying to give them comfort and administering the "last rites". They had then died as he was doing so.

It was awful, it was a most horrifying thing to see, or so I thought.

Adrian, always had good hearing, he even heard things that I didn't even know I had said. As it had been so that time.

The murder was being featured on the lunchtime news again, the two squaddies had been identified.

Adrian at the time was aged just two years and one month, came bouncing in to the kitchen, with his shoulders back and ready to make an announcement.

There tucking in to our Yorkshire puddings, was mum, dad, Lindsay, Diane, Wendy and me.

"Do you know what they are grandma?" He said proudly and with gusto.

"No love" mum said.

At the top of his voice he stated, "Them are f-ing bastards, they are!"

I tried to crawl under the floor, mum didn't like swearing of that nature.

I had obviously stated that the day before, I didn't remember though.

Her reaction was brilliant. I'll never forget the look on her face and what she said next.

She just looked at Adrian and said "yes love, you are probably right! Now go and eat your Yorkshire puddings".

End of incident. Not another word spoken.

Wendy's Fingers.

Our house on Manchester Road, used to belong to Wendy's brother Raymond.

The windows were double glazed units that had been placed into the sad old and dilapidated wooden frames. One of the sealed units in the kitchen had already failed, there was condensation between the two glazed panels.

My friend Ken had a son, also called Ken. Young Ken was a partner in, and worked at a glass company. He came and measured up for a replacement panel.

If I fitted the new unit myself, it would save me the best part of a hundred pounds. Ever a skinflint. How hard could it be.

I got the new unit home. I had everything ready, including a waterproof putty. I took out the old wooden beading, the failed panel lifted straight out from the frame.

It was then that I asked Wendy for help. I placed a thin bead of putty all around the frame of the window ready to receive the new panel. I was stood on a bench outside the kitchen.

I needed help in holding the pane still, up against the frame while I changed my position.

Then I could apply pressure all around the unit and press it home into the frame. Before replacing the old beading with some new.

I lifted the panel and was adjusting my position.

The unit, was around four foot tall by eighteen inches wide. There was some weight to it.

I asked Wendy to put her hand against the glass for support, as I lowered it into position.

Shit!

Blood squirted up the inside of the glass, Wendy screamed. She had misunderstood my directions.

Instead of placing her hand against the outside of the glass for support, she had put her hand underneath it just as I had dropped it into place in the frame.

I lifted it back out immediately, I was certain that I had chopped her fingers off.

"Get my fingers, get my fingers!" She repeated.

In shock, I was saying "where are they?" Looking all over the floor and the inside of the window sill.

"They're on my hand you bloody fool!" She said.

Her fingers were bleeding profusely, particularly her middle digit. There was a ruptured blood vessel, it was fair squirting. I bandaged her hand and then continued to fit the window.

What choice did I have? I couldn't leave the window open while I took her to hospital.

At the A&E, they sutured her finger, without using any form of local anaesthetic.

It hurt her and it hurt her a lot. Wendy cursed Dr. Hans, the German doctor who had stitched her.

Then, only the very next day he tripped and fell down the stairs and he broke his femur, his thigh bone.

Remind me not to mess with Wendy!

Race '87 for Children in Need.

In spring 1987. Manny and I met up with Tom, a local businessman who wanted to raise money for that years Children In Need Appeal.

It was his idea, to involve two ambulance staff, two firemen, two policemen and one of his colleagues. Thereby completing our team, with two businessmen.

We had several individual and joint events throughout the year, all of our efforts culminating in a race against time. To visit as many police, fire and ambulance headquarters that we could get to on mainland Britain, in just a forty eight hour period. We went over the border into Scotland and across the border into Wales as well.

Local man Dan, offered and supplied a full sized 55 seater coach. Along with five drivers, including himself, for the journey.

C J S offered the fuel. We did just over 1500 miles.

Through the National Ambulance Service Society. We met their main benefactor, Sir Jimmy Savile, yes that one. He supported our ideas and gave us a few contacts. It helped pull one or two strings.

One of the events that Manny and me arranged, was an ambulance pull through the town centre. There were several of the ambulance staff pulling a blue light ambulance, using large ropes attached to the front of the vehicle. Loads more of our ambulance staff in fancy dress, were walking alongside us, collecting money in buckets.

That event alone raised just short of £2,000.

On the 27th of November 1987 our gang of eight, along with our supporters went to the BBC studios in Leeds to present a giant cheque for just over £12,000.

Our year had been a roaring success.

That was actually one of the highest amount of money paid in by any one group in 1987, in Yorkshire, anyway.

Now some individual groups can raise millions of pounds. How times change.

Whilst at the studios, I was fortunate enough to meet Linda Lusardi the famous former page three model.

I was hoping to have a photo taken with her but she was due to go on stage. I had just taken a picture of her with one of the firemen in our group, but then she had to go.

She said that she would come back.

True to her word, not forty minutes later, my name was called out over the PA system. Would I go to the main exit gate. Linda was waiting and had come back looking for me.

I got my photo.

She was with Lord Montague of Beaulieu he had brought an old vintage Bentley car, like the one that Steed drove in the TV series "The Avengers". With them in the car, was Melvyn Hayes from "It Ain't Half Hot Mum", he was so miserable. She was lovely though. I had my photo taken on the back seat of the car with her.

Brilliant, it made my day.

More Charities.

As a follow up to that event, I arranged several other ambulance pulls over the years. So in due course several thousands of pounds was then donated to differing charities.

Including the Huddersfield Babies at Risk Appeal, the Cancer and Oncology Unit at HRI. The latter, a thank you for a friend of mine Jude, a cancer sufferer herself. She and her husband Sid, and her daughters were with us all the way on that one. Jude was with us when we presented the check for £2,500.

Sadly Jude passed away not too long after the event. I hope that she is at peace now. She suffered a great deal in life.

The last ambulance pull, was in aid of the Yorkshire Air Ambulance.

We pulled an ambulance from Marsden to Huddersfield. I had dropped collection jars in each of the hostelries along the route, about a month before. It was a poor day, but well worth it.

It coincided with the Huddersfield Town Centre's Christmas lights, switch on in November.

I even ended up stood on the stage with the Pulse radio presenters and the cartoon character, Bart Simpson, to press the large button.

Another £2,500 went to them.

- Thank you Huddersfield!

CHAPTER 37.

CHRISTMAS HOLIDAYS 1987.

Changes coming.

It was late in 1987. The West Yorkshire Metropolitan Ambulance Service undertook some major changes to its operations. As had one or two of the other ambulance services in Great Britain, we split the service in two.

There was to be the outpatient services, all the planned journeys, known as PTS (patient transport service) and the A&E (Accident and Emergency service).

It was a major, but successful and badly needed change.

Free pick up service, anywhere, anytime.

It was in the early hours of my birthday 22nd of December 1987, I think it was at around three in the morning. I was working with Alec.

We had just taken a patient home from A&E at Huddersfield, he was one of our regulars, I'll call him Ron. We had just dropped him off at his address in Longwood, near to the Slip Inn.

Naughty of us, I know, but we then decided to have ten minutes to ourselves.

We drove up the side of the Slip and parked up at the top of the hill on Longwood Edge Road. It was a wonderfully clear, but bitterly cold winters night, the views were amazing. As was the welcome flask of hot coffee.

We were only there for a few minutes, literally, ten at the most.

As we made our way down Bull Green Road and back to civilisation, we recalled an accident down that very road. Where two women in a small van had left the road and rolled down the steep embankment, almost all the way to Longwood Road.

It had been a drop of over a 100 feet, but they had escaped with only minor injuries.

No sooner had we said that and there was a lady of around thirty years of age, stood in the middle of the road. She was waving both arms wildly like some form of demented windmill.

She needed help, as she moved to the side, we could clearly see her predicament.

There was a white Mini Metro car, which is only a relatively small car. It's rear wheels were embedded in the branches of a tree, the front wheels were still on the road.

It was a learner drivers car, from a well known national company.

She was the instructor and had just got back from the company "Christmas do" in Manchester.

Her husband, had been sat in the front passenger seat. He was much the worse for wear, he had drunk a skinful.

On the way home, he had vomitted out of the window and it had gone all down the side of the car. As they had got back to their house, she had parked the car on her steep drive, it was at right angles to Bull Green Road. She went inside to get a bucket of water to throw over the side of the car.

Whilst in the house, her sleeping husband, must have depressed the instructors dual control clutch and he had also knocked the handbrake off. The car then took off down the drive at speed, it hit the kerb and bounced into the tree.

The back of the car was a good fifty feet in the air and it was resting on a large branch, but it was rocking as her husband tried to get out.

We had to call in to our Comms and reveal our secret, we didn't have tracking then, but we needed fire and police assistance to make things safe.

Aunty Vi was our dispatcher, a very well respected old school dispatcher. She knew what we had been up to, she wasn't bothered as long as you didn't go overboard and milk it.

The man climbed out of the car and we had one hell of a job grabbing hold of him to stop him falling down the big drop. Somehow though, we managed.

Then, the other services arrived, and made the vehicle safe until recovery could be arranged for the next day.

On my way home at the end of the shift, daylight had arrive and I had my trusty camera with me. The car was still in situ. So I took a couple of shots.

It was only in the new year when I had got the prints back, that I noticed that there was a slogan on each side of the car.

On the back wing of the car, just in the branches of the tree.

It said "Free pick up service, anywhere, anytime". I thought that that was brilliant.

Good job we went for a coffee!

Happy Birthday to me!

Aunty Vi.

Vi, had been a controller with the old Huddersfield County Borough Ambulance Service, based at Huddersfield Station. Before that she had been based at Banney Royd on Halifax Road, working for the West Riding Ambulance Service. Separate services until the reformation in 1974.

She knew the Huddersfield area like the back of her hand. Her local knowledge was second to none.

Vi lived at home with her mother, a mother who without Vi, would have been housebound. It was on her days off, that Vi would regularly take her elderly mother out and about in the car and at the same time get to know more of her area.

Vi would drive for hours. She would find every back street, visit all of the nooks and crannies. If she passed, or heard of any new housing development being built, she would pay it a visit.

All to enhance her already vast and wonderful knowledge.

Every one of the ambulance staff and ambulance officers (not managers then), called her Aunty Vi, out of utmost respect.

Her tone never changed, she was clear and precise. Always extremely calm and professional whatever the situation. Every message, was ended with the precise time, followed by "WYMAS out".

That meant that it was the end of any conversation, and that Aunty Vi was busy and had other jobs to deal with.

At other times, if she could, Aunty Vi would always pass on a few words of wisdom and experience.

She is very sadly missed!

In 1974, WYMAS was formed. Aunty "Vi" went to work at Central Comms at our Headquarters at "Threelaands" in Birkenshaw.

From there, Aunty Vi covered all the areas of West Yorkshire and she even got to know all of the area extremely well.

I was working with one of our Leading Ambulancemen, (L.A.) another Jack. He was an ex Military Police Sergeant, the units heavyweight boxing champion in his younger days. Jack was a no nonsense straight talking Yorkshireman, he never had a cigarette out of his mouth, even whilst driving the ambulance to jobs.

A few did that, in those early days.

It was a night shift, in 1984, just after nine o'clock in the evening. The tannoy sounded, it was Aunty Vi. Our call sign was named and then she said "emergency call at Thornton Lodge".

We got to the ambulance, I was driving for that job. Jack lit a cigarette up as normal and then he called in to say that we were mobile to the area. He asked if Comms had any further information available.

Aunty Vi replied, "you are attending a maternity call, pains every two to three minutes and the patient is full term. Oh oh! Further to that, this is the lady's ELEVENTH pregnancy, better put your foot down gents! Good Luck".

Jack looked at me, and said "Oh Shit!" He then replied to Aunty Vi in his usual gruff Yorkshire twang "they should sew the buggers up when they've had two!"

Aunty Vi, very quick as usual, replied. "I see, a stitch in time saves nine, 21:07hrs, WYMAS out".

Absolutely brilliant..

Christmas present for Wendy?

I was just going home from work, it was Christmas Eve 1987. I had finished at the station at Marsh at around 20:00hrs.

It was only a ten minute journey home normally, but there was a fair amount of traffic around that particular evening.

It had been snowing earlier.

There was no danger of having a white Christmas though, it had been very wet, mucky and slushy stuff. Then to finish it off, it had started raining heavily.

It had taken me about twenty minutes to get home. As I slowed down, I was just going to pull over to the left to park in between our neighbours cars, when I had to stop suddenly.

The car behind even blasted his horn at me. I jumped out of my car and I couldn't believe my eyes. There in the road in front of me was a bedraggled, wet and dirty baby, yes, a baby. I'll call her Maddy who was fourteen months old. (Obviously we didn't know that at the time).

She had been on all fours and had crawled, not walked, out from between the parked cars

As I picked her up in my arms, my car was abandoned with its hazard lights on. The driver behind me, was just stood rooted to the spot and open mouthed, he couldn't find any words to say.

I took her up to our house with me and as I entered, I shouted out for Wendy.

When she came over, I said. "You know that you said that you always wanted a little girl, I have just found one outside, for you!"

She took hold of the little one.

I parked my car up and then I rang the police. I explained what had happened and where I had found her, they came out very quickly. At the time, I hadn't had time to get changed. I was still in my ambulance uniform

Some of the police officers knew me. They were so happy that they could comfortably leave her with us, rather than trying to get hold of social services at nearly nine o'clock on a Christmas Eve.

It meant that they were able to concentrate on finding out where she was from. There were lots of police up and down Manchester Road, knocking on all the doors. They were also checking around all the surrounding streets.

At the same time, Wendy had bathed and changed the little one, she was a lot fresher and cleaner then.

I think it was almost two hours before the police were able to find the little girls family.

They lived on Radcliffe Road, the road running parallel with ours, nearer to Milnsbridge. The family had thought that little Maddy was safely tucked up and fast asleep in bed upstairs, where she had been put at 18:00hrs.

Somehow, she had managed to leave the house without them knowing and she had then crossed the little road, Radcliffe Road. A quiet cul-de-sac on an evening, thankfully, as there were heavy vehicles that used the goods yard during the day.

She had managed to get through somebody's garden and up the stone steps. She had then gone through a dark and narrow passageway, that ran between the houses opposite and unbelievably had managed to cross the extremely busy Manchester Road, without being hit. The visibility that night was extremely poor.

She must have managed to get up the passageway at the side of our house, but not got any further. Then she had crawled out of our gateway and into the very busy Manchester Road again. As I got there she had just appeared out from between two parked cars.

188

If I had not already been slowing down, if I had been going to carry straight on, I would not have been able to stop.

When the police had found the mother and brought her across, she didn't seem to show any emotion, I hope it was down to relief and shock.

The little girl ended up going to secondary school with my youngest son Ben. He has since been in contact with her through the wonders of Facebook.

I also used to see her mother occasionally in our Social Club, that was twenty plus years later. She used to jokingly say, that at times she had wished that we had adopted her. She had been a right pain in the arse growing up, a proper little madam.

She has a youngster of her own as well now.

Sleepless night.

I was working Christmas in 1987, with a second Stuart. The incident took place only a couple of days after finding the little tot in the road.

It was just about lunchtime on the Boxing Day, we had a call to a female pedestrian who had been knocked down.

It involved a small white Ford Escort van, it been travelling down a steep hill and had been approaching a sharp double bend.

As the driver made the first bend to the right, there was a family crossing the road, he braked hard and skidded. He lost control of the van and mounted the pavement, the front of the van had hit the young seventeen year old female and had pinned her up against a wall.

She was still in that position when we arrived.

She was stood upright and was fully conscious, but in a lot of pain. Once we gave it to her, she was taking the entonox like it was going out of fashion, she was really puffing on it. It was helping take the edge off the pain.

She was trapped by her legs.

As I looked closer, and examined her. The flesh on her left leg had split wide open, from her hip right down to her ankle. There was a lot of blood, it was from a burst blood vessel and it was a spurter, a serious bleed. She had suffered several fractures and you could see every bit of bone in her leg, each fracture was totally visible.

We had to move the van.

I must admit, that my main fear and I had convinced myself, was that as we eased the van away from the patient, I was certain that her leg would fall off. Not kidding there. It looked to me, as though that would really happen.

Several bystanders were present. We got them all around the van, so that when the handbrake was released, there would be no movement that could cause her further damage or injury. Also, so that we could move the van backwards inch by inch and be able to stop as soon as needed.

As soon as the van was clear, we were able to ease our patient onto our stretcher. Thankfully, with her leg still attached. She had some horrendous injuries to that leg, everywhere else appeared to have escaped injury.

Her flesh had virtually exploded on impact, it had opened wide, like an unfastened long trench coat. Something that I had never seen before, were the little bubbles that can appear when fatty tissue is exposed. If squeezed, they burst with quite a "pop!" Like "bubble wrap". They had appeared everywhere, the thigh muscles are extremely fatty.

She also had a blood vessel that had ruptured, it was squirting blood everywhere, it was her "popliteal" artery, the one right at the back of the knee. I could actually squeeze the blood vessel at the site of the rupture with my fingers, that stopped the bleeding, until Stuart was able to place a pressure bandage on it.

In the ambulance, I had to cut all the clothing off the bottom half of my patient. What was left of her skirt, her boot and her tights.

All to get to the mass expanse of wound.

We put incontinence sheets, plastic side to the flesh and tied them with bandages, to try and hold her leg together. All the left thigh and hip had torn, and needed dressing. Her femur was in at least three pieces and her kneecap was almost at the back of her leg, that was what had ruptured the artery. Her calf muscle had been completely removed, we could then see that her tibia and fibula also had multiple fractures. Even her ankle was fractured and dislocated.

I have never seen a leg with as many injuries, I was sure that it would be lost.

We got her to hospital, the trauma staff were all ready and waiting for us and fortunately with it being Boxing Day, most people had avoided going to A&E. For once the department was not at capacity. (We never say the Q word). Our patient was handed over unto the expert care and it was time for us to go home.

We were on a 06:00hrs until 14:00hrs shift. By the time that we cleared, it had got to 14:30hrs, so it was time to go back to try and celebrate what was left of the holiday with our family.

That night, I had a sleepless night. I was tossing and turning all night, thinking about that poor girl. Not, would she lose her leg? Not would she survive?

No!

I had done all that I had done to her, I had undressed her almost completely. I had then put dressings on wounds, all around her intimate areas and I hadn't even asked her name. It really bothered me. I had actually got quite upset about it.

What on earth would she have thought about me? How unprofessional was that?

The 27th of December, that was my day off. I don't think I had had more than an hours sleep, due to thinking about her.

When I did wake up, from the little sleep that I had, I decided that the only thing to do was to go and visit her in hospital.

I waited until late morning, I think it was about 11:30hrs when I walked in to the orthopaedic ward. As I was in civvies, I asked the ward sister if I could call in. I explained to her who I was and why, even though it wasn't visiting time.

As I was asking, a little voice from down the corridor was calling to me. It was her, she had recognised me. The sister was more than happy for me to go in.

The girl, although she was in bed and rigged up to a weights and pulley system over it to keep her leg in traction. Was pleased to see me. She threw her arms around me and gave me not just a hug, but a great big bear hug. She said that she couldn't thank me enough. Her mum was there and she was saying the same. She also told me that because of what we had done, the doctors were of the mind that her leg might be saved.

They were both amazed that I had taken the time to visit. When I explained my real reason for being there, they both laughed. I really apologised for my poor behaviour. They thought it was hilarious, how could that affect someone who does our job for a living?

Well it does! I don't know why, but it does. Me anyway!

Her name, here I'll call her, Yvonne. I will never forget her and I'll never forget to ask a patient's name, ever again.

She showed me her leg under the bedclothes, they hadn't closed the wounds. They had fastened a pin through her ankle, and then the weights were stretching her leg to keep the bones from rubbing together.

To help the wounds, they had taken some skin from her right thigh. Then put it through a machine, something like a pasta maker and formed the live skin into a large open weave latticework. That skin had then been stretched across the open wounds to keep her skin alive at either side of them, with a good blood supply.

Despite Yvonne's injuries, there was reason that they had left the wounds open, it was so as to fix the bones with grafts first.

Then if the bones were healing, they could then fix the flesh and skin wounds later.

Within twelve months, she was walking around without any sticks.

Her leg had been saved, whether she would ever wear skirts again, I don't know. She had been left with some horrendous scars..

But at least she could walk and work independently.

My pal with no legs.

It was New Years Eve in 1987. I was sent to see one of my first regular patients from 1981, he was a double amputee patient I will call him Bob, he had suffered a fall.

Bob lived close to Huddersfield. He smoked like a trooper, probably thirty or forty a day.

As he would say, what else was there for him to do. He would sit in the same seat from his carers getting him up in a morning, until they put him back into bed at night.

He couldn't go anywhere on his own.

So he would look forward to his twice weekly trips out by ambulance. He would occasionally go for a full day out at the limb fitting centre, at Chapel Allerton Hospital at the far side of Leeds.

That was like a holiday for him.

We used to go for Bob to attend physiotherapy classes at HRI. It was hard work to deal with Bob. The fact that he had no legs, but was still a large bloke, meant that his centre of gravity was all wrong.

To get him out of the house, we used to use our folding carry chair. An ideal piece of kit when a patient's weight is evenly distributed.

To get Bob onto the chair, we would stand either side of him. We would go one under each arm and he would lift himself up and swing between us from his chair across to our chair. Sometimes he would be in his own wheelchair, that was so much easier.

We would take him out to the ambulance, lift him and the chair into the back of the ambulance, then he with his powerful arms would lift himself across and on to the stretcher.

He would go to physio twice a week for a few weeks and then he would be discharged for a while, to try and manage himself. They were trying to get him to walk on some prosthetic legs.

Both of his legs had been amputated well above the knees due to circulatory/vascular problems caused by his diabetes.

The physiotherapy just wasn't working. No matter what Bob did, it wasn't going to work until he lost at least six or seven stone.

Bob was in his predicament due to his own mis-management of his insulin dependent diabetes. I went for Bob on and off for at least the first seven years of my service.

I liked him, he was quite a character. Always full of beans with a beaming smile on his face that would light up any room.

Following that background. Back to why I went for him that one day in 1987, New Years Eve.

The doctor had been out to see him following the fall, it was the doctor that had called us. Bob had managed to get up off the floor by himself, but had suffered from some nasty skin tears. They would need cleaning and dressing properly in A &E.

Apart from the obvious injuries, he looked awful. That beaming smile had been replaced by a frown, a serious frown.

"What's up Bob?" I asked.

He was grumpy and bad tempered, he replied. "That bloody Doctor, gets on my nerves he does".

When I asked him why.

He told me that his regular Doctor from the local surgery, had been out to see him due to the fall.

Apart from arranging the ambulance, the doctor had told him that the hospital were going to refuse him any more physio, unless he stopped smoking and that he as his Doctor would have to take him off his books if he didn't help himself.

Bob had been piling on more weight, and his diabetes was far from under control. I had to say to Bob that I could see where the Doctor was coming from.

Bob was getting angry then. As he said, his trips to hospital, were his only time away from his four prison walls. Smoking was his only stress relief.

He told me that he was feeling very low and that he had even contemplated suicide.

In his usual black humour, that matched mine perfectly, he said "but I couldn't get up to the loft hatch to tie the bloody rope".

In the ambulance service, we say all sorts of things to patients to try and get patients out of their dark places. Sometimes it goes wrong, even when we mean well.

That day was going to be one of those.

I said to Bob, "it's all very well for the Doctors, but they don't see what life is like in your shoes. Get on to him, see if there is anything else to occupy your time. Challenge him!"

Bob looked at his stumps, "my shoes eh! Always the wise guy you are!"

I hadn't seen Bob for around another eleven or twelve months, I didn't even know if he was still alive.

Then one day I was working with Mike, I got a call to attend at a familiar address.

It was to help out by taking a double amputee patient to attend at a presentation, wait for him, then return him home.

It was a most unusual job, really it should have been a private detail, but it was being done as a favour.

I had been asked for personally.

I walked in to the ground floor flat, what a shock! It was clean and newly decorated, there was no blue haze of cigarette smoke. It was a different place altogether.

There in a wheelchair in the corner of the room, sporting his familiar beaming smile, but much less of a man. It was Bob alright, but about four and a half stone lighter.

"Come here you, buggerlugs!" He shouted. "I've been dying to see you!" He continued, "It's all your fault this". I walked over to him, he grabbed my hand and shook it violently and then pulled me to him and gave me a crushing man hug.

Bob had taken me to heart, he had gone back to his Doctor and he did challenge him.

His Doctor had always been very well respected, he's retired and really missed now. He didn't like being beaten, so he searched for alternatives for Bob. He told him that if he did find an alternative, then Bob would have to respond by stopping smoking and losing some weight.

He had only got in touch with the Paralympic sports people. They then went to see Bob to see if they could help him out.

He hadn't looked back since then. He was doing archery, discus, shot putt and rifle shooting.

"I failed the time trial for the 100 metres hurdles" he laughed. Bob was certainly back to the Bob that I knew.

The presentation was on behalf of the Great Britain Paralympic Team, they were going to arrange the transport for "Bob", he had asked them to try and get hold of me. As he had said, it was me that had thrown him the lifeline.

Bob had won two Silvers and a Bronze medal in his first international competition. He had also been to Europe, several countries on a tour. He was preparing to go to Canada. Further trips and competitions were in the pipeline.

To cap it all, Bob had stopped smoking completely.

My sporting hero!

CHAPTER 38.

A YEAR OF DISCONTENT.

The National Ambulance Dispute of 1989-90.

In the winter of 1989, there were some major disruptions within the ambulance service. Bigger than anything that I had ever seen.
We had tried to get a pay increase to give us parity with the other "emergency services". Especially following the major shake up and reorganisation that we had gone through. We in West Yorkshire had already split into the two branches of planned working PTS (patient transport service) and frontline A&E.

Margaret Thatcher's government at the time, told us in no uncertain terms, that we were "not" an emergency service. We were "glorified taxi drivers" and that "you do a worthwhile job, but it's not an outstanding one".

I believe (apologies if I am mistaken) that those comments were made publicly by Kenneth Clarke. The then Secretary of State for Health. They were certainly in the national press, attributed to the Conservative government at the time.

He said that we were only "professional drivers" despite the fact, it was disclosed that his own "driver", was on more than twice the money that we were.

At the time we were on a pay scale the same as council manual workers, bin men, road sweepers, gardeners etc..

Those comments made, was the red rag that had been waved once too often.

The whole of the ambulance service, throughout the country for once, were totally united.

The following item, was an item published in the Daily Mirror, on Wednesday January 17th 1990. It was following its original publication in the Guardian Newspaper, letters section just the previous day.

I am not a midwife
But I deliver babies
I am not a doctor
But I make decisions on medical conditions and treatment
I am not a surgeon
But I treat trauma and mutilation
I am not a nurse
But I nurse and give succour to patients
I am not a psychiatrist
But I take care of those suffering mental illness
I am not a social worker

But I help heal domestic disputes
I am not a counsellor
But I comfort and reassure the distressed and bereaved
I am not yet a paramedic
But I possess life-saving skills
I am not a firefighter
But I work alongside them and perform rescue, sometimes in their absence
I am not a police officer
But I frequently work amidst abuse and violence
I am not one of a team, subordinate to an officer
But I work with my partner making our own decisions
I am not used to clean, clinical surroundings
But I work in the dark, cold, rain and mud at the roadside. I also work in your home
I am not paid as a member of the emergency services
But I will respond to 999 to help the sick and injured people at your emergency
And after that, help "the old lady next door" to her appointment, as well
Finally, I am not just "a professional driver"
But I do drive with professionalism and skill under stress
I am an Ambulancemen
Some say, "a worthwhile job, but it's not an outstanding one".

Written by Frank Orr, aged 27, of Londonderry.

Kenneth Clarke.

That had been written in direct response to the public comment made by the then conservative health secretary Kenneth Clarke, of Margaret Thatcher's iron fist government.

It was during the long running ambulance dispute

Does that sound familiar to you? It does to me.

It sounds just like the current conservative Health Minister, Jeremy Hunt. He actually used the same comments, almost word for word in a national newspaper in April 2016. (Perhaps he can't speak unscripted).

Despite all the progress in training, skill levels, treatment and vehicles that have gone on since that dispute. Paramedics have to have a university degree now.

The ambulance service workers, are still treated with utter contempt, as manual workers who "do a worthwhile job".

They, the conservatives, still have a total disregard for the everyday working man. Even today.

Nothing has changed, they will get rid of the Health Service as we know it, without doubt. They are depriving it of funds now and they treat all health service workers, including the junior doctors with a total lack of respect for the skills that they have.

I am glad I am at the latter end of my career, when the health service is being privatised.

They are bloody welcome to it!

The young man from Ireland's comments sum up just about perfectly the the whole of my 36 years that I have worked for the Ambulance Service so far.

Local effects of the dispute.

It was a long and extremely bitter dispute that had started and inevitably services were disrupted nationwide. The public were kept fully informed, and the overwhelming support that the ambulance service were given by them, was nothing short of fantastic.

In some areas, ambulance staff lost thousands of pounds as they were prevented by their management from performing their duties. The army was brought in with their military ambulances and the police were taking patients in the back of riot vans to hospital, not a pretty sight.

At home in West Yorkshire we kept an Emergency service going throughout, although we did have days of action where non emergency journeys were suspended.

Those actions were fully supported by the public, donations were brought in to all ambulance stations around Great Britain. To assist staff that had lost wages.

Even in Huddersfield, many thousands of pounds were given. It was humbling for all of us, we hadn't thought that we would be so well supported.

Due to the split in services already done in the West Yorkshire area, none of us here in Huddersfield were financially out of pocket. The only money lost was in a lack of overtime, we wouldn't do any!

We worked our contracted hours only, and not a minute more.

I can assure any of you reading this, that not one person claimed a single penny back for lost overtime.

It seemed to work. After the long running arguments, the successful dispute came to an end in 1990.

The dilemma of what to do with the money came to the fore. It was decided in unison (not the union, it hadn't been formed then) that the only answer was to use it to benefit the public of Huddersfield.

We couldn't give it back.

In 1990 we were having events all over West Yorkshire, to raise funds to buy defibrillators to be placed on each of our ambulances. At the time they were just over £5,000 each to buy. Now they cost nearer to £15,000 each.

With the donated money, we bought three of the lifesaving machines.

Then every single member of staff was provided with a top quality stethoscope and a sphygmomanometer cuff (blood pressure monitor). We were the only station in the West Yorkshire area to be fully kitted out with them as personal issue.

Subsequently we would be able to use the equipment to treat and help the people that had donated them.

Again, that action was publicised in the Huddersfield Examiner, the public support was tremendous.

I can personally fully guarantee, that not one member of staff in this area put a single penny in their pocket. None of it was used for any financial gain.

Here is an official report of the History of the National Ambulance Dispute 1989-1990.

"Unity Through Trust. Comradeship".

"WITH DIGNITY, DEDICATION AND HONOUR THEIR FIGHT WAS NOT IN VAIN"

Public support for the ambulance workers was the hallmark of the most high profile dispute since the year-long miners' strike. The seeds of the dispute were sown in the spring of 1989 when the Department of Health made a pay offer of 6.5 per cent.

Ambulance workers rejected the offer in May by a three to two margin, and then by two to one in July. The unions were claiming pay parity with the hourly rate of the fifth year fire fighter and a pay formula.

In September 19,500 ambulance workers voted four to one for a ban on overtime and rest day working. Industrial action began on 13th September as Kenneth Clarke, the Health Secretary, rejected the unions' offer of binding arbitration. The 3,800 ambulance officers and controllers voted to join the industrial action at the beginning of October.

To the embarrassment of the Government the unions revealed an 11-year-old letter written by Mrs. Thatcher's Private Office in which she said ambulance staff, fire fighters and the police deserve a pay formula linking pay to national price or wage rises.

At the end of October the unions intensified the industrial action by banning non-urgent clerical work, refusing to transfer non-urgent patients from hospitals and rigidly adhering to a 39-hour week.

Meanwhile, unsuccessful peace talks were held at ACAS. (Advice Conciliation and Arbitration Service).

October saw London crews begin a work to rule, refusing to use the new radio call system, prompting the use of police vans as ambulances for the first time in the dispute. Police withdrew after agreement on emergency cover was reached between LAS crews and management.

At the end of October the Union banned all non-emergency work.

The government told local chief ambulance officers to dock the pay of staff refusing to work normally and, if necessary, to suspend them. Ambulance crews responded by threatening to declare themselves suspended if any union member was penalised, but agreed to provide emergency cover without pay. Suspension of London crews witnessed the use of army ambulances in London on November 8 for the first time since 1978-79 "Winter of Discontent".

In mid-November the Government made a new offer worth 9 per cent over 18 months funded by £5 million brought forward from 1990-91 budget and a further

£1 million to pay paramedics an additional £300 a year. Unions rejected the offer claiming it was ""old wine in new bottles".

Later that month ambulance crews in different parts of the country were suspended and the army used.

London controllers refused to put 999 calls through to the police and army.

Kenneth Clarke attempted to bypass the TUC unions by recognising the "Association of Professional Ambulance Personnel" for pay bargaining and offering them the 18 month deal rejected by the unions.

The Government was hit hard when just before Christmas APAP threw out the 9 per cent deal and voted to join the action when Clarke refused further talks.

In mid-December fresh peace talks between the unions collapsed after less than two hours and the army moved into Birmingham and West Midlands. Throughout that period ambulance workers on suspension continued to provide 24 hour emergency cover without pay.

At the beginning of January Kenneth Clarke started a blazing row by describing ambulance workers as "professional drivers". The argument was fuelled when it became known that his Department chauffeur earned £25,000 a year - more than twice as much as an ambulance worker. Frustration among ambulance crews leading up to Christmas came to a head when Glasgow crews went on all-out strike for a few hours.

By January, ambulance workers in West Sussex disappointed by the lack of progress went on all-out strike, to be followed by only three other services.

But public support had been unwavering. In December ambulance crews delivered to the House of Commons a petition of more than four million signatures - (the biggest ever gathered) - supporting them.

In mid-January the TUC held a major public assembly in support of the ambulance workers. Over forty thousand people in Trafalgar Square came to show their support.

On 30th January, hundreds of thousands of people nationwide stopped work at midday for 15 minutes to show solidarity with the ambulance workers.

The dispute went on for another three weeks until 21st February when, as a result of an interview by ACAS, both sides met to discuss a new offer.

Although not including a pay formula, the offer was a substantial improvement on the 6.5 per cent on basic rates, increases ranged from 17.6 to 23.6 per cent on basic rates, an additional 2 per cent for local productivity and a lump sum.

Ambulance workers, in a secret ballot, accepted by four to one the offer and returned to normal working at 07:00 hours on Friday 16th March, 1990.

This badge (a proud possession of mine that was accompanied by the certificate from where this report has been written) is dedicated to the men and women of the ambulance service for their determination, devotion and dignity throughout the epic struggle and to the public for their splendid support.

The unions involved were GMB, NUPE, T&GWU, COHSE and NALGO.

All of the above words were written and presented with a boxed commemorative badge. Available to all who took part in the long running battle for recognition.

A point worth mentioning here, although there was a large increase on the basic hourly rate of pay. The annual salary only actually increased by one half of one percent.

That wasn't made public at the time.

We used to have enhanced rates of pay for Saturday's, of time and a half. On Sunday's and Bank Holidays, we got double time. All the rates were consolidated, so working Christmas Day, or a night shift on New Years Eve attracted the same rate of pay as any other shift of the year.

We won the dispute for recognition, but the Conservatives screwed our bank balance.

Parity with the other services has never, and probably never will, be achieved as we are under the Health Service and not the Home Office.

CHAPTER 39.

HE SURVIVED THAT!

170 units of blood required!

It was March 18th 1990. In the early hours of a Sunday morning. I was working out of Huddersfield station with a member of staff from Honley station, she was called Joan.

We were called to a food takeaway on Chapel Hill, just outside the town centre. It was a call to a young male who had been stabbed.

When we got the call, we were actually fuelling up, in the Shell filling station at Marsh. I was driving, it only took two minutes from there. The takeaway was on our side of the road going down the hill.

There, our victim, I'll call Charlie was sat on the steps leading into the takeaway. He was bleeding so profusely, there was even blood coming out of the lace holes in his shoes.

It turned out to be one of the worst injuries that I have ever dealt with, where the patient survived.

I lifted his shirt to look at the wound, that was a big mistake, his intestines fell out and into my hands. I had to push them back into the large hole that had been created.

We then placed a large dressing across his abdomen, tucked his shirt back into his pants and were about to leave. Then his mate came running up, his thumb had been almost severed and he had a knife wound across his chest. It was bleeding, but it was relatively superficial.

We took them both to awaiting staff at HRI, Charlie's wound was so bad, that according to the Huddersfield Examiner. A report given by the Consultant at HRI. Charlie was in theatre for over seven hours, and had to have 170 units of blood transfused.

His liver had been slashed and his spleen had been cut completely through.

Charlie had been out with his friend, they had been drinking in a club across the road from the takeaway. A club with a poor reputation at the time, it was always having its license revoked, due to "dodgy dealings" and violence.

As Charlie was about to leave the club, he had picked up his coat, and knocked over the drink of another customer. He had apologised and then bought the man another drink.

He thought that was the end of it. After all, it was an accident.

On his way out, the man approached him and as Charlie had thought, punched him in the stomach.

It was only when he had got across the road to the takeaway, when he felt and then saw, all the blood. It was everywhere.

The man that had hit him, had actually stabbed him by hitting him in the abdomen, with a Stanley knife. The extremely sharp blade hit Charlie at the side of his ribs. From there, it went up along the edge of his lower ribs, met at the sternum and then back down the other side.

It had fully opened his abdominal cavity. Hence everything in there, wanting to fall out.

His mate had actually seen the attack and had managed to wrestle the knife off the attacker. His injuries, although serious, were not life threatening.

They never found the perpetrator, he got away with it.

Charlie spent an extremely long time recuperating, it took him over two years to recover.

I saw him again, it was just over three years later. I was with Carl that time. We had gone for a male who had split his head open, banging it on a shelf in a pub in the town centre.

The patient was being helped by one of his mates. In the ambulance, it was the mate who asked me a question. "Can you remember a stabbing in Huddersfield three years ago?" I said that I had dealt with several, so I couldn't possibly remember.

The lad then lifted his shirt and showed me his scar. I recognised that wound straight away, there was no doubt, it was Charlie.

That second meeting, was actually Charlie's stag night.

He told me that he was getting married to one of the nurses, who had been looking after him while he had been in the intensive care unit. He showed me a photograph of her, I recognised her straight away.

They had had two children together the last time I heard anything of him, but that was a while ago now.

Initiative, or was it?

Autumn 1990, I was working with Danny, he was driving, it was a VW LT35 ambulance. They had to be one of the poorest quality vehicles we have ever had to work with. They were absolute "rust buckets" and were so sluggish in accelerating.

On the way to a reported cardiac arrest, in a Romany gypsy caravan, on a makeshift campsite off St. Andrews' Road. He had lights flashing and sirens blazing, he was racing down the Castlegate ring road, to the junction with St. John's Road. At the junction, the accelerator pedal fell off!

I saw a police van coming in the opposite direction, so I flagged him down.

Armed with oxygen, bag and mask and defibrillator. I asked him to take me to the campsite, it was on the site of the old Huddersfield cooling towers.

No problem, he put his lights and sirens on and off we went.

On arrival, unfortunately the man had been dead for most of the night. He certainly fitted the criteria of our "yellow card". Rigor mortis and "post mortem staining" were definitely present.

The police officer took over, dealing with the sudden death. Eventually Danny turned up, he had managed to re-attach the accelerator pedal himself.

When we got back to station, our boss Bert, was not happy.

He said that we had no right to flag the police down, and that we should have called for another ambulance.

Our main problem in those days were communication issues. We didn't have hand held radios, or mobile phones. I didn't know if Danny would have been able carry on and get to me, or not.

I did explain to our boss that if the man had still been alive, I would have readily put him into the back of the police van, to transport him to hospital if necessary.

He went ballistic at that.

I was happy in my own mind though. If it had come to it, I could have stood in the coroners court and hand on heart. I could say that I had tried my best.

To put a tin hat on it, the police superintendent rang our boss to thank us for our initiative, for our insistence to try and save life. He was glad that his passing officer had been of help.

I was still in the office at the time, getting my telling off!

CHAPTER 40.

A BIT CLOSE TO HOME.

Dad's stroke.

Spring bank holiday Monday, 28th May 1990. Mum and dad were out and about on a walk, dad was still recovering from a nervous breakdown.
He had been so bad, that at the end stage, he had to be sectioned under the mental health act. He was formally confined as an in-patient at St. Luke's Hospital in Crosland Moor. He had to spend almost five weeks there.

When he had been in hospital for only a couple of days, it was evening visiting time, dad was displaying some slight features of a stroke. It was simply dismissed by the staff as dad being tired and exhausted.

It was the first day that dad had been taking the medication, fortunately, all his symptoms had gone by the following morning.

Dad had been taking medication in the hospital, he was on 75mg of dothiapin three times a day. That was the maximum dose of that type of anti-psychotic medication.

He had been put on such a high dosage straight away, it should always be administered using a phased introduction.

It is well known that the main side effects of suddenly starting, or stopping that medication could be a cardiac arrhythmia.

Dad was discharged on the Friday 25th of May, he was told to continue his medication until his supply was finished, that would be his night time dose on Sunday.

Then he would not have take any more.

Monday lunchtime, mum and dad were up near the Golcar British Legion Club on Scar Lane, when dad was taken ill. My mum had to get an ambulance, dad had suffered a stroke. Another George and Jerry were the crew.

Fortunately, it was a minor stroke, (also known as a TIA, or a Transient Ischaemic Attack). It had been caused by having an an extremely irregular heartbeat. Without doubt, it was as a direct result of a sudden withdrawal of the medication.

Dad then had to take beta blockers and isosorbide mono nitrate for the rest of his life to help regulate his irregular beat.

He had several more of the TIA's over the next years. He could have two in a week, or not have one for up to two years, they were so unpredictable.

Our little angels!
I think it was 1990. When the boys were young, they were around six and four

years of age respectively. The back bedroom that they shared at the time, was more than an adequate size for the pair of them.

I had built the boys, some bunk beds myself, from scratch. Not your traditional bunk beds, no, for a start, they were at right angles to each other. The top bed had a platform with a storage and play area to the side of the mattress. The beds each had a full single bed size mattress.

The window sill in the back bedroom was very low, it was less than a foot from the floor. So to keep the boys from standing in the window bottom, I fastened an extending wire mesh fire guard all across the frame for safety reasons.

One day the boys were upstairs playing quietly together. That was unusual for them. In that one, they were quiet and two, they were playing together. We were a little worried, but when something like that doesn't happen too often, we didn't want to disturb them and spoil it.

Wendy went into the kitchen to put the kettle on to make a cuppa. Then I heard her scream. I ran into the kitchen, thinking that she had had an accident, maybe scalded herself or something.

She was just stood, riveted to the spot and pointing out of the kitchen window.

What was it?

I had to go and look outside, I couldn't believe it, the little buggers!

There was a large pile of their things outside the kitchen window. The pile consisted of toys, books, teddies, clothing, bedding, quilts and for God's sake, even their bloody pillows and the mattresses from their beds.

We ran upstairs, there in the empty, bare, bedroom. Two mischievous smiling little buggers, looking at us as though butter wouldn't melt, stood right there on the window sill.

They had managed to rip the fire guard off the wall at either end, pulled it completely away and removed it from the window frame. Then not only that, they had managed to get the safety and security catch off the window latch.

It was supposedly child proof, a knob that needed to be unscrewed first. It should have just spun round freely, the only way that it should have come loose, was by using a square ended key to turn an internal thread.

They had removed the knob, releasing the upper opening part of the window and between them had thrown everything they could possibly have got their hands on, out of the window. I can't even imagine how they managed to get one, let alone two single mattresses out of the small window opening.

No wonder they were quiet, it had taken some doing.

To add insult to it, it was pouring down with rain outside. Some of the stuff was completely ruined. I still can't believe what I saw that day.

Swines!

Not only had they thrown their stuff out of the window, they had managed to fully block the toilet. They had filled it with as many of the smaller of their stuffed toys that they could.

CHAPTER 41.

A DREAM COME TRUE.

Grandad's Dream.

Wendy's dad John, had a dream. He wanted to take all his family, and his grandchildren and to see them enjoy themselves at the original Legoland in Denmark.

Unfortunately John passed away in 1989, he didn't manage to realise his dream.

In 1990, Wendy's family decided to follow his wishes and to arrange the mammoth trip. To carry out their dad's dream.

John had worked for the Huddersfield Corporation as a bus driver, working his way up to be an inspector. He had heart trouble and had to give up the driving side of buses, but he still managed to work for the company, changing as it did to First Bus at the time, until he retired.

It seemed logical then, to book the trip through them.

It had been decided, that none of the children were going to know anything about the trip for as long as could be possible. As far as they were concerned, it was just going to be a family day out on a coach.

The whole family, including John's wife Dorothy. Julie and John with their two sons John and Paul. Suzanne and Michael with their two daughters Joanne and Leeanne. Wendy and Ian (that's us) with our two sons Adrian and Ben. Raymond and Linda with their two sons Matthew and Adam. Lynne and her son David.

That was one big family outing.

We all met up at Huddersfield bus station at the allotted time. Apart from our big group of nineteen, there were only two other small families on the bus.

A conversation took place with the bus driver and the parents of the other two families. They were put in the picture that none of our children had any idea where they were going.

We arrived at the ferry terminal in Hull.

The bus driver had to leave us alone, while he made the necessary arrangements.

On his return, he said that he had been to have a word with his mate, who was the captain of the big ship. He then asked if everybody wanted to go on board and have our picnic lunch on the ship.

Unanimous. The kids thought that that was a fantastic idea.

Once the coach was on board, we all went up to the main deck where we could watch all the other passengers and vehicles of all sizes, driving on board through the giant doors at the back. We all then got together and as planned got out our picnic lunch.

It was at that point, that to anyone who wasn't a babe in arms, it was obvious that the ship had started moving. Not a little, it was proper moving. It was moving further and further away from the quayside. Then some of the kids started panicking.

One or two of the adults left "to see what's happening" to appease the children.

The kids were then told that we had been too late to get off the ship, so we would have to spend the night on board and as it was a very long crossing. (Expected 22 hours). We had all been allocated a cabin, so off we all went to settle in.

Meeting back at the restaurant at teatime.

A beautiful ship, it had all the facilities that you could imagine. For the children, it was a self contained town. We had some food and then we went exploring.

Some of the brighter children started to notice things were a little bit different in the shops. It was a DFDS, Scandinavian Seaways ship, the money in the shops was Danish Krone at the time. A lot of the products had similar labels to ours, but had funny names on them.

Adrian asked me, "is the ship Danish? and due to the length of time it is taking, is it going to Denmark? And, if it was, would we be able to go to Legoland?"

I had to reply that I didn't know.

We were of course going to Denmark, to the port of Esbjerg. At that time, we thought our little plot was going to be exposed sooner than we were hoping for. We told the children that we would have to ask the bus driver in the morning.

We all met up at breakfast, we the Firth clan, along with some of the others. Were dressed in our up to date, state of the art "shell suits", we thought we were the bees knees.

If only we had known how bad they looked.

Breakfast was a very expensive affair, it wasn't included in the price. It was 1990, I can't remember all the details. Except that our four breakfasts, had cost us the equivalent of sixteen pounds each.

The one item that I do remember the price of, as I had nearly had a heart attack when I had gone back for a couple more. The individual little Lurpak Danish butters that you see in cafe's everywhere, were SEVENTY FIVE PENCE each. Nearly thirty years ago!

Ouch!

All of us trooped back on to the coach. As soon as we got on, some of the kids were giving the driver some hassle. Knowing then, that we were in Denmark, "would we be able to go to Legoland?"

"No", was the short answer.

We were going to Vejle and staying in the Vejle Center Hotel for the night, wouldn't that be an adventure enough for them.

To make matters worse, we had to travel through the town of Billund, that is where the Lego factory is located. We were travelling right past the front of it.

Outside the factory gates was a pile of three super large Lego bricks, brightly coloured, each brick, as big as an average house. The children thought that it was Legoland.

When he was asked to stop, the driver said that he couldn't and to add more insult to injury, he put on a video for them to watch.

"The Lego Story".

That went down like a lead balloon. It caused a lot of tears.

Not only among our family, but also the children of the two other families, who thought they knew where they were going. Then, they thought that they wouldn't be going either.

Cruel, but it worked in our favour.

We stayed in the Vejle Center Hotel. It was a massive place, a hotel and conference centre. But it was lovely. We were unable to do much sight seeing due to the time that we had got there, it was after six in the evening and already dark. Once fed and settled in the rooms, it would be too late to go anywhere off site.

Or so I thought.

I had seen as we were arriving, that directly across the road was a local Fire and Ambulance Station. I had to go for a quick nosey. It would have been rude not to.

It was a one ambulance and one fire appliance station, run by a company called Falck, (falcon).

The place is now the international headquarters of Falck, one of Europes biggest agencies. For providing medical cover, doctors, nurses, ambulances, fire appliances and security services.

They are actually one of the biggest private ambulance companies, who are working across our region at the moment of writing. Particularly in the Huddersfield area.

What a small world we live in.

I literally knocked on the door and was met by a man who could speak very little English. He warmly welcomed me, and invited me in. The other members of staff there, weren't much better with their English either.

I was no good, didn't know any Danish words at all, (other than bacon!).

No matter, he managed to tell me to sit down and have a coffee and he would make a telephone call.

Within ten minutes, another member of staff arrived in his civvies. He was on his day off, but glad to be of help. He spoke perfect English.

We English, as a people, are so embarrassing with our lack of communication skills.

He showed me all around the ambulance station. A lot of their equipment was exactly the same as ours and it was even made by Ferno, or Ferno Washington as it was known then. In Cleckheaton!

He explained that in Denmark, the two services were run together, but each of the branches had different staff. They didn't work for both sides if you like.

He also took great pains to explain to me the costings. It wasn't a private health care, all the costs of calls were decided every month.

It was sorted out by a committee that consisted of two people from the police, two from the fire and two from ambulance services. There was also two drivers from a local taxi company, two people from an insurance and claims company, there was two doctors and finally two people from the courts. I believe those two were like our JP's or magistrates.

Fourteen people who went through every single fire, and ambulance call in detail. From their meetings, then the charges for all calls would be decided.

Briefly, if the call was to an accident and someone had been hurt enough that justified ambulance travel, then there was no charge. If an ambulance was called out in good faith, for an accident or illness but not required, then again there was no charge.

But on the other hand, if the ambulance was called for a patient who could quite easily have managed in a taxi, then the charge was double what it would have cost by taxi on the day.

The main usual difference was for when young children and elderly were involved, they were not often charged. Not unless the family could have quite easily have done the transporting. Then there would be double the taxi fare as a charge, just as the young normally fit adults would have.

If the incident had been self inflicted, either through drink, through drugs or self harm, that was looked at differently. That then would incur a charge of four times the taxi fee, to be imposed for a first offence.

All details were kept on an up to date database. If the same patient then had a second self inflicted call, the charge would be doubled again to eight times the taxi fare.

Following on, on a three strikes and you're out basis, a third call and criminal proceedings ensued. That was not usually to gain custodial sentences, the Danish were very big on their environmental issues. So instead of being locked up, you would provide many hours of "community service".

In the autumn months you don't see leaves all over the pavements, in winter time it's not treacherous under foot for pedestrians due to ice or snow.

No, that was when the most used form of community service punishment came in to its own.

All the leaves or snow would be cleared away, by those on community service orders, as soon as it was possible.

Any non-compliance and a custodial sentence was the next option. It would be for twice the duration, of the complete community service order.

I liked it!

We should bring that in over here. That would certainly sort the majority of the problems that we have within the health service.

And no mistake.

The next day and all of us got back on the coach. We were driven past the factory gates yet again, then back on the bus' television with the video.

I have a picture somewhere taken from the front of the bus, talk about long faces, not one child was looking at any of the tv's.

As we approached the actual Legoland park, the driver, as I had requested had given me a five minutes warning.

I was stood up at the front of the bus again, I wanted to get a picture of the kids faces.

The trip could not have gone any more to plan, or could it?

John, Wendy's dad would have loved it.

What I, and none of the others knew at the time, was that directly opposite the park was an airport. It was only a small one, but nevertheless it was an airport.

As we approached the entrance to the park, a plane was landing. I have a superb photograph, quality not the best, but the subject was absolutely perfect.

All the kids, including the other families. Were all looking at, or pointing at a little plane coming in to land. They all had miserable, blank looks on their faces.

At the opposite side of the coach, clearly visible on the photo is the large, brightly and multi-coloured entrance to Legoland.

Not one child, not a single one of them saw it. Only a few of the adults did, what an absolutely perfect distraction.

Thirty seconds or so later, on another photograph. We had done it, their faces on the second photo say it all. Those were smiles to die for, fists raised in jubilation, every one of them on their feet.

We had got all the way and into the Legoland compound without any one of the grandchildren knowing anything about it.

Absolutely brilliant!

John, I do hope that somewhere you were watching us that day. What an achievement!

You would have loved it!

I don't know how to describe the day at Legoland.

Did the children enjoy it? I do hope so. If they enjoyed the place a tenth as much as I did, then they had a fantastic day.

Everything that you hear about the Legoland Park is true.

It is done to perfection.

Everything has been thought about. There were even wheeled carts to pull young children around, or to put picnic baskets in. Train rides, boat rides, car rides, it caters for everybody. Disabled or able bodied alike. There is something for everyone at Legoland. There are so many rides and attractions for all ages.

There was of course a Lego shop. The prices in the shops, are governed world wide. So even though Denmark was far more expensive in general, the Lego itself, was just the same price as back home.

Inside the shop, as well as selling every available Lego product, there was a swimming pool sized pit, around two foot six deep and it was filled to the brim with individual Lego pieces.

The children were given a standard sized green base board. They were then each given an hour to jump into the "pool" and build something of their choice. Every hour throughout the day, prizes were awarded for the best.

There were eating out places, picnic areas. Indoor and outdoor seating areas, all of the seats and furniture was decorated as Lego bricks.

All around the park were little side shows, puppet theatres, face painting, all sorts of entertainment. Something on every corner.

There was the famous driving school, a large area where children could drive themselves around roads. With street signs, traffic lights, roundabouts and of course other cars. They could even "pass their driving test" on the course.

It was a little confusing for our kids, due to the fact that everybody was on the wrong side of the road.

If you were a fan of Lego as a kid, or still are as an adult, you would love it.

Even if you weren't, I'm sure you would still love it.

I haven't been, but the UK versions have got rave reviews as well.

The cost would be a lot less to get there too, Scandinavian ferries are so expensive, it would have to be a once in a lifetime visit to Denmark.

I can't remember much of the return journey, it was much of an anticlimax really. You couldn't top the day/experience that we had just had.

I do remember that the ferry crossing was a really rough one though.

I could see out of one of the side windows of the ship. All sky, then all sea, that was the sideways rock. Then there was the front to back ups and downs.

Lots of people were suffering from the effects of sea sickness. It didn't put the dampers on the trip though.

It was one of the best!

CHAPTER 42.

FAMILY TIMES.

A Firth family holiday in Great Yarmouth.

Summer 1991. Wendy and me had booked a static caravan on a Haven Holidays site in Great Yarmouth.

I had a tow bar on my car, at the time, it was a Lada estate. I had earlier bought a trailer from Ernie at work. We had put all our gear in it and I had added a wheelchair for dad.

It would be a true family holiday.

As a treat/break for mum, we had decided to take them both with us. The car was just a bit too small for all of us to travel all that distance. So mum and dad went on the train with Adrian. Wendy, Ben and me travelled in the car.

We had set off in the early hours of the morning and when we arrived we got ourselves set up in the caravan. Our static caravan was very near to the beach. We were in the first row of vans next to a quiet road and then only across the road and the sand dunes was a private beach.

The site had all that you could need. Cafes, restaurants and bars for adults. Kids activities, a pool and of course, all of the usual amusements etc.

The area around Great Yarmouth, was very flat, it was great for dad. He didn't need a wheelchair for everyday use, but it was good for any long distances. We went into town regularly, there were buses right outside the camp gates and they were cheap and regular enough.

Most of the time it was easier to just leave the car where it was.

All in all it was a brilliant family holiday. The kids had enjoyed it, we enjoyed ourselves and more importantly mum and dad did. It was good for mum to have a break from caring for dad too.

Station Officer.

In 1992. The ambulance service were about to face yet another major reconfiguration. Following the great dispute, the government couldn't afford for us all to act together again. It was decided that they would split the national ambulance service up, into twenty two individual Ambulance Service Trusts.

The rota's changed yet again and I was even further away from getting a position on the main rota. My only option to get a rota position, or line as it was more commonly known. To then be able to know for the first time since 1981, what I would be working well in advance. Was to apply for promotion to the Leading Ambulance post.

The L.a. was in the process of changing to a Station Officer position. (The same job, just a different title).

There were carrots dangled, the Leading Ambulancemen were offered two pips. A rank uplift of two, to become Station Officers. It sounded good on paper, but to get the uplift, there were consequences.

The L.A. had to sign over to the individual NHS Trust's conditions, away from the National agreements run by the Whitley Council.

On paper it was a better deal, but financially there was minimal benefit.

As a Station Officer, I would be earning just short of a thousand pounds a year more.

That was before tax, than if I stayed where I was.

It was purely personal choice to join "The Trust" or for the time being, stay as you were.

I was ready for the challenge and some responsibility.

I applied for the job.

I was shortlisted for it, then I had an interview and eventually, I was selected.

Mum and dad were so proud.

I had two shiny silver pips on my shoulders, but more than that, I had finally got the regular shift pattern I had been craving for.

There were five Station Officers at Huddersfield, one on each eight hour shift, therefore I had a straight forward repetitive five week rota. Mark, Ray, Stuart and Gerald were the others.

We looked after the station between us. Stores, fuel, time sheets, A&E, PTS and to the general running of the station.

Even small disciplinary matters, if we could sort them out, it would prevent any management involvement.

Things were finally looking up.

We had a manager at the time, by the name of Bryan. He had two understudies Darren, ex Comms and another Brian. William was also around at that time as a relief manager.

William was the man who took over when Bryan retired, only to be shafted later. When they introduced a PTS manager to Huddersfield and brought him in to work above William, as A&E manager.

His name was Bobby, he was not a bad bloke, you hardly ever saw him. But he was very approachable when you did.

If you had any questions, Bobby didn't like to be beaten, he would always get you some answers. I always found him fair and straight talking. Personally, I think he would have been respected more, if he had spent more time informally with staff.

Bryan was the last actual ambulance officer, he had worked on the ambulances as part of a crew, in the Wakefield area. Now they are called managers. A lot of them, haven't even been ambulance qualified.

Bryan would spend time with and getting to know his staff, whereas, Bobby always stayed upstairs in his office. I personally believe that it was the wrong way to do things, but I'm not a manager.

The manager that we have now though, is a different matter. Let's just say that I don't particularly see eye to eye with him. He is a paramedic, a good one. I worked with him on the road several times. Since he became a manager, we seem to have a difference of opinions, I'll leave it at that.

We can't get on with everybody. That's the way this world works.

Family minibus trip.

We as a family, had the use of the Paddock scouts minibus from time to time. As a Cub Scout leader myself.

In the summer of 1993, I borrowed the 17 seater bus and took all of the family to Withernsea on the East coast.

There was, mum, dad, Wendy and me, our sons Adrian and Ben. My sister Lindsay and her husband Gary, their children Elliot and Laura. My other sister Diane and her husband Stephen (they are not together now, she is with her partner Tim), with their children Laura and Jack.

For Jack the youngest of all, it was his first trip to the seaside. It was also the only time I can remember, that the whole of the Firth clan (Turners and Gibsons included), ever went on a trip all together.

I parked the bus in the main car park at the southern end of the beach and then all of us walked to the central area, it was near to the old coast guard station.

Whilst playing on the beach, we were all laughing and having a damn good time. Everybody was collecting pebbles for our garden. We had loads, a ridiculous amount, some really big ones as well.

One minute, dad was stood up talking and laughing along with the rest of us, the next he was laid face down in the sand. He had collapsed, he looked as though he had suffered another stroke.

He came round fairly quickly, it didn't really look as if it would warrant an ambulance call. I was fairly happy that it was another TIA. It is potentially dangerous as it is still a cerebral malfunction, but dad had come round and he didn't want to go to hospital anyway. Certainly not to one in a strange area.

The hospital was not far away, I decided that I would go and get the minibus. If dad was still fine when I got back to them, we would take him home. If he wasn't, or if he had got any worse, then the local hospital in Withernsea it would be.

I spoke to the Coastguard, I explained to him what had happened and where our transport was. He was on his own, otherwise he would have run me to the car park. He said that while I was gone, he would clear the area.

Then I would be able to bring the bus right up to the slipway and be able to reverse down it, to the beach, it would save dad a walk.

I ran to the car park, it was a longer run than I had realised. If it had happened today, it would have been me needing an ambulance. I was knackered then, now it would kill me. I raced back to the coastguard station with the mini bus.

When I got there, dad was feeling fine. He was feeling cold, even though the sun was cracking the flags, but he was cold. That had become a normal thing for dad.

The first TIA, had aged dad twenty years. He was only 60 at the time. He had no weakness to either side of his body, or speech deficiency, but he had become frail.

He was always feeling the cold. He wore a thick body warmer all the time, a bit big for him, it was like a giant turtle shell.

His short term memory had also deteriorated.

We all climbed into the bus and began the trip home. Dad was fine all the way, no more episodes on the journey, but he went to bed earlier than usual.

An abrupt end to it, but otherwise, it had been a brilliant day.

When Wendy and I got home, we had the task of unloading half of Withernsea's pebbled beach into the garden.

Crackers, all of us!

CHAPTER 43.

CLIFFORD.

Defibrillator.

The first time I had a successful outcome from using a defibrillator, I was working with Clifford, not to be confused with the other Clifford from when I started with the ambulance service.

We had been called to an address off the Wakefield Road out of Huddersfield, a male had collapsed. The address was at the beginning of a short and quiet cul-de-sac, with a large turning area at the far end.

I dropped Clifford at the house, then I went up the road to turn the ambulance round. On my return, a young boy was waiting, he said that Clifford had asked for our new machine.

Immediately I knew what he meant, and duly ran in with it. We had only been using defibrillators for around a month.

Clifford was at the side of a man on the floor, he had a bag and mask fitted with 100% oxygen and was pounding on his chest. I connected the defibrillator up, he was in asystole, that is a "flat line". A stopped heart, with no electrical activity.

Today we would be able to give some stimulating drugs to help start the heart. In those days, we could only carry on with CPR, luckily, the heart started to fibrillate. That is an uncontrolled fluttering, but it meant that we could charge the machine, ready to shock.

Although it is powered from nine volt batteries, the machine delivers an initial direct current shock of 200 joules, or an equivalent of around 3,750 volts.

I charged it up, then shouted the warning to "stand clear!" Then I pressed the button. It wasn't successful, so another greater shock was needed, the heart was still fibrillating. I then turned up the power to 360 joules, the equivalent of 5,600 volts.

"Stand clear!" Bang, another shock was delivered. Stop, look, on the screen there was some activity. Double check, yes he did have a pulse. (Although similar in principle, the methods and timing of resuscitation techniques have changed since. They are constantly being updated).

Still very ill, but a pulse and he had also started attempting to breathe for himself.

It was the time to load and go, to put the foot down, using blue lights and sirens all the way. Pre alerted staff were waiting in the HRI resus room.

The patient survived his ordeal and was admitted to the CCU, (coronary care unit) at Huddersfield.

It was a couple of weeks later that Clifford and I saw him on a general ward, his wife was with him. She then said proudly to her two young children, aged around seven and nine. "These two men are the heroes that gave your daddy back to us". That was just about the best complement that I have ever had. A proper lump in throat moment.

Man eating bed!

A funny moment with Clifford was in a very old cottage, near to a local landmark, Castle Hill.

There a man had fallen in his bedroom, he had suffered a possible broken neck of femur, (NOF). That is where the head of the femur, the ball joins into the socket of the hip.

Not that the incident was funny, but it was what happened next.

The bedroom or box room was very small, just big enough for a single bed and nothing else.

The man was laid on the floor, at the side of the bed, under the window. To get our carry chair into the room, we would have to lift him up from the floor and on to the bed.

I had the head end, Clifford got the man's legs, we lifted him level with the bed. I then put my knee on the bed for stability, that was my big mistake.

It wasn't a single bed at all, it was only a fold up bed, that had a single mattress laid on the top of it.

Then the inevitable happened, I had placed my knee just where it folded, snap! The bed folded in half, the combined weight of the patient and me caused it to clamp tight shut.

All I could hear from there, was the patients cries of pain and in the background Clifford was crying in absolute hysterics.

He said afterwards, that from where he was, all that he could see were four legs sticking out and unable to move.

If only he had a camera.

He had to get the man's three sons to come upstairs and help.

Embarrassed or what?

Not Harrods again?

Another shift in 1991, with Clifford. We were both still relief staff at the time and with no shifts allocated. Normally we would go in and work a nominal shift of eight hours, nine till five.

On the Thursday of that week, we were asked if we could come in early on the Friday morning. It was to do a planned, but emergency transfer to London.

The patient was needing some specialist treatment that was only available in London. We were more than willing, long distance jobs were very few and far between.

The treatment, was for a young girl with an advanced version of Crohn's disease. At the time, she was an inpatient at Dewsbury District Hospital.

Once leaving the care of the hospital, it would have to be a blue light and sirens emergency journey. All the way to the St. Mark's Hospital, Hackney in London.

The girl was to be accompanied by her mother and a nurse. We didn't have sat nav in those days. Due to the nature of the job, journeys like that were jointly prepared by our control room staff, in liaison with the control room and the Police from the area where we are travelling to.

On any cross boundary journey, all of the ambulance crews tune into the Emergency Reserve Channel, (ERC), always channel 1. That is the channel that is monitored 24 hours, by every emergency service in mainland Britain. It is also used in a major incident, to free up normal domestic radio use.

We were informed that we were to contact London Ambulance on ERC at around junction 3 of the M1 and give them a heads up. They would be arranging for a police unit to meet us at junction 2, to escort us straight in to St. Marks'.

As told, we duly called up at junction 3.

Disaster!

There had been a very serious road traffic incident on the M1 at junction 2, and there were reports of possible fatalities involved. All of the available police officers, had been tied up at the incident and there were no other resources available to help.

What the hell were we going to do? We didn't carry any maps other than an old Kirklees street map.

That was where Clifford came to the rescue, in his pocket, he always carried a diary to record his shifts. "The diary" was only around three and a half inches by two inches in size. At the back of the diary was a street map of the Centre of London. It was spread over around eight or ten little pages. It was so small, but it was a map, our only chance.

Using his map, Clifford was able to guide us almost all of the way. We were parked up at the side of the road, looking for clues to the last part of our journey, as we had got a little lost.

We had only been there for a couple of minutes, when a couple walked up to us. They had seen the "West Yorkshire" written on the side of the ambulance, they were from Castleford.

They wondered if we were lost, they were right. Thankfully, they offered to help. Luckily, they knew exactly where we needed to be. They pointed to a Church spire that we could see in the distance, it was about a quarter of a mile away. That was St. Marks Church, the hospital was at the back of it.

We arrived at our destination, it had been a long and stressful drive and we took the stretcher and our exhausted young patient inside.

Not to the welcome that we were expecting. The receptionist told us that she was not expected there, and we would have to take her back!

What? How could that be?

We had rung just prior to our departure.

We showed them the letter of authorisation, the address at the top of the letter etc.

Yes, the Professor named, was the right surgeon, yes he was based at that hospital.

But our patient at fifteen years of age, was classed as paediatric. They didn't have any paediatric services at St. Marks'.

That was when our patients mum sprang into action.

She ONLY happened to be, the President of the National Crohn's Disease Society, the famous society was chaired by our Professor himself.

She also had his own personal mobile number. She would ring him directly and find out.

Clifford and I left our unhappy little group in the office of the hospital administrator. Whilst things were being sorted out, we went for a quick, well earned and badly needed drink and a bite to eat.

On our return, the problem had been rectified. Although the letter was correct and St. Marks is where he was based. The telephone number that had been given by our professor. The number that we had rung in the morning, had been wrong.

Actually, it was that of St. Bartholemews' Hospital, and that was where he was expecting us. Unfortunately the correct destination had been omitted in from letter, simple.

We had set off at 07:30hrs in the morning, we finally got our patient into the right bed at St. Bartholemews' Hospital, at 15:45hrs in the afternoon. A long and arduous eight and a quarter hours later.

That wasn't the end though. We then had to find our way back out of London.

We were leaving the middle of the City of London at half past four on the last Friday before Christmas, known as Mad Friday.

Always known for the amount of people out and about, lots of them had finished work for the holidays at lunchtime. Alcohol had been flowing freely.

As well as avoiding hoards of drunken pedestrians, the traffic congestion was horrendous.

Out with the COHSE (Confederation of Health Service Employees) union diary, yet again.

The ambulances then, had an open doorway from the cab to the saloon area. Our nurse was sat in the middle, on a pillow covering a paramedic equipment box. Not strictly au fait with today's health and safety requirements, but we all did it then.

We commented as we passed, as to how good the Harrods store was looking in the early evening darkness with all their Christmas lights and decorations on and not forgetting all the other stores in the surrounding area.

All of the City of London was highly decorated, all the shops, the streets and even all the trees were fully decorated for the season.

It looked fantastic.

You can imagine our surprise, when after about half an hour of difficult driving conditions. There we were, back again, in Knightsbridge and passing the famous Harrods.

Some of the pages must have got stuck together. We persevered, still following the pages of the diary to the letter, guess what? Yes, another three quarters of an hour later, we passed Harrods yet again!

We were not doing very well, we were hopeless.

The diary went over his shoulder and straight into the back of the ambulance.

We would have to just trust to luck.

We eventually managed to find the M1, we were finally on our way. It was half past ten at night when we got back to station. Fifteen long and extremely tiring hours.

Still, seven hours of that was overtime at time and a half and we would each be able to claim for two subby's. (A tax free subsistence allowance, to buy food away from our base station). £3.75 each one.

Kerching!

Barked loudly like a big dog!

Another call with Clifford. It was at 04:30hrs, to an address in the Dalton area of Huddersfield. Clifford and me were working on the night shift 20:00hrs until 06:00hrs. The call was to a male with a badly broken leg.

It was as well, a right mess in fact. It was an open fracture with fragments of bone showing through the skin.

His story wasn't ringing true though. He claimed to have just fallen off the kerb edge and into the roadside.

There was quite a lot of blood around the wound, it was extremely dry and flaking. It hadn't only just happened as he said, it must have been a few hours ago.

I went to the ambulance to get some kit, as I did so, I heard someone whistle. When I looked around, there was a gentleman quite a few doors down the road. He was leaning out of the window of a first floor upstairs flat.

He asked "have you come for that lanky bloke with a broken leg?

When I said that we had.

He told me that he had caught the bloke in his flat at around midnight, a burglar. He said that he had just come home from the club when he could hear someone in his flat.

He had barked loudly like a big dog. He then heard our patient crash to the floor from the bathroom window.

I asked if he had rung police to report him.

He said that he hadn't bothered. "He hadn't chance to nick anything, I just thought it serves the bugger right and left him". He went on, "He's known round here, he's nowt but scum!"

It was then just after five in the morning, the patient had managed to crawl nearly a hundred yards to a friends house.

I called Comms and asked them to get the police.

Clifford and I stalled as long as we dare to await their arrival. We cannulated him and gave him intra venous tramadol for pain relief. We had put a splint on him, we did just about everything and the police still hadn't arrived.

At nearly six we had no choice left, but to set off to hospital.

The police were up there at the hospital, they hadn't told us, they just turned up.

Then they wanted statements and everything. We should have finished work at

06:00hrs, it was already 06:30hrs. It was a struggle, but we managed to persuade them to see us at the start of our next shift at 20:00hrs, that night.

The man that we had picked up, was a drug user and he was a known dealer. He was very well known to the police. He stood around six foot five tall, skinny and had the most ridiculous pony tail in his long hair. It appeared right out of the top of his head, not the back.

A couple of months later we had to attend an ID parade at the police station in Huddersfield, prior to attending at the magistrates court.

To try and disguise himself, he had shaved off all his long hair. It didn't work, he had distinctive tattoos on his arms and we remembered them from where he had been cannulated. Just for good measure, he had a tell tale full length plaster cast on his leg.

When we attended the Magistrates court in Huddersfield, he had to be removed from the court room during our evidence, due to his behaviour and threats of violence towards Clifford and me.

His case was referred to Leeds Crown Court and there he was sentenced to four years in prison, for the attempted burglary and several other outstanding charges.

I have seen him since on a number of occasions, clearly his memory is not as good as mine.

I have the advantage for the moment.

CHAPTER 44.

DISASTERS DO HAPPEN.

Disaster at Valley Parade.

Eleventh of May 1985. I was watching the television at home, the football was on. Although to be honest, I was not really interested in it, it just happened to be on. It was Bradford City at home to Lincoln City.
It was the end of the season and Bradford City had just been awarded the Football League Third Division Trophy.

I was due to start work at 18:00hrs that evening.

I could hear John Helms the match commentator, he was getting quite agitated and loud. A small fire had started inside the ground, it was at the right hand end of the far terrace. (From the TV camera angle). Then, within four minutes the whole of the 200 foot long stand had been engulfed in flames.

John's commentary haunts me and any other listener to this day, the poor guy was so emotional having to report on such a devastating and horrific event.

56 people of all ages were killed in the inferno and around another three hundred people were injured.

All the ambulance staff, like myself, who saw it happening live on television acted. They rang in to our Headquarters (at Birkenshaw on the outskirts of Bradford), and offered their services. Many of us, including myself, were due to start at 18:00hrs. The majority had already reported on station ready for work by 16:15hrs. It was unbelievable.

The fire had first started at 15:40hrs.

I wasn't actually sent to the ground at Valley Parade, selfishly, I am not sorry about that. My crew mate for that day was Fred. We were sent to work in the Bradford area.

We covered the Odsal Top and back towards the Brighouse side of Bradford. Any patients that we had, went to either Halifax or Huddersfield hospitals.

The Bradford Royal Infirmary was at an absolute standstill, many of the victims had made their own way to hospital. Also known commonly as self presenters.

Other help from Huddersfield, were our vehicle cleaners, volunteers only were asked for. As the ambulances were not in a very nice state. The Bradford Ambulance Station, was used as the temporary mortuary for all of the victims.

The smell that was in that station for the next few days, will never be forgotten. Even now when I go into Bradford station, the awful burning smell still comes back to me straight away. I don't think it will ever go away altogether.

A lingering, but very poignant reminder that something like that should never happen again.

The memory of those 56 tragic victims should not be forgotten!

Disaster at Hillsborough.

Another local and major football disaster took place at Hillsborough, in Sheffield. Liverpool were playing Nottingham Forest on the fifteenth of April 1989.

There was a large crowd of supporters, that were crushed in a surge inside the stadium. Crowd control fences, and "pens" were in position at most of the football grounds at the time. Due to football hooliganism and violence in the past. The "pens" were to keep rival fans segregated.

In the Hillsborough case, they were like cattle pens, keeping the people trapped inside with nowhere to go.

Ninety six people lost their lives and an unbelievable further seven hundred and sixty six people were reported as injured.

The ambulance crews on duty at the ground were volunteers from the St. John Ambulance, no professional ambulance crews or officers were present at the time of the incident.

The initial call to the South Yorkshire Metropolitan Ambulance Service (SYMAS), came from the police. It was more of a warning, saying that there was a riot taking place.

When the full scale of the actual incident came to light, the shit had already hit the fan. Nobody anywhere could have been prepared for what had actually happened.

Eventually several crews from the ambulance services in the surrounding areas were sent to help. My good mate Mike from Huddersfield and the other Bryan were working together out of Honley station.

They actually went into the Hillsborough stadium to help the injured and dying. Carl and I were sent to an ambulance station nearby. We were used on other emergencies and in taking patients away from Sheffield. To ease the workload on SYMAS and the A&E departments in Sheffield.

The enquiry into the tragedy has only just been completed in the last couple of months (April 2016), and that was decided by an agonisingly long and arduous court case. As a result of that, some justice has prevailed.

The survivors of the tragedy and the families of the deceased, have all done themselves really proud.

The case had been riddled with cover ups and corruption. Statements from police officers had allegedly, been altered beyond recognition, it had been an absolute travesty.

The South Yorkshire Police Force have been disgraced.

Further legal action against them, or individuals may still come to light. There have been calls asking to take legal action against the ambulance service. Would that be the St. John volunteers, or us, who knows.

Have there been cover ups there as well?

The Yorkshire Ambulance Service, as it is known now, were thought to have been in charge of the medical cover on the day.

That wasn't the case at the time, only basic first aid cover was provided and that, was by the volunteers.

Taylor Report.

The Hillsborough tragedy, triggered the Taylor report, published by the Right Honourable Lord Justice Taylor of Gosforth.

There were actually two Taylor reports during the investigations of the Hillsborough Disaster. The "interim", and then the "final" report.

His recommendations regarding the overall safety at all football stadiums nationwide, became mandatory.

It was a lengthy and highly comprehensive report. It was laying down literally "ground rules" for all sporting events, up and down the country involving "expected" crowds of spectators, of 5,000 or more.

It can be viewed publicly on the internet, it is both a fascinating and informative thing to read. It is a big document, there is a lot to take in, but it is amazing.

Unfortunately it has come on the back of such a horrific and tragic, hopefully never to be repeated, but will never be forgotten event.

The medical cover would have to be managed by professional ambulance staff, supported by the valuable work of the volunteer organisations, such as the St. John Ambulance brigade.

Huddersfield's Leeds Road Stadium.

One of the perks of being a Station Officer. Was to attend Huddersfield Town football and Huddersfield Giants rugby matches, in a safety and medical management capacity. My fellow Station Officer Stuart had been managing them for a while and he then got me involved.

It was down to the Taylor report, that our Private Ambulance service branch of WYMAS, provided the cover. They provided the medical cover for most of the sporting events in West Yorkshire and now they provide it for the whole of Yorkshire.

It meant that there had to be a manager present, trained in Medical Incident Medical Management and Support, in our case a Station Officer or above. He would be in charge of ALL the medical cover within the ground.

There would be a Doctor, with extra specialist training in trauma and major incidents, for the crowd only. The teams had their own doctors.

There would be a fully kitted regular emergency ambulance, provided with a registered paramedic crew, when crowds were expected to exceed five thousand. For the football matches, they now provide a paramedic, purely for the players as well.

Also voluntary services are present to provide the first aid cover, in the Huddersfield area, the voluntary cover is provided by the St. John Ambulance.

The regulations requiring a minimum of one registered first aider per thousand crowd. An officer in charge of them and a fully kitted medical room.

At Huddersfield's John Smith's stadium the system works great, we all get on extremely well together, including the stadium's safety officers and business partners.

The crowds in Huddersfield vary a lot, but usually there are 18 to 21 St. John volunteers. So that's nearly always more than the minimum requirements. They can call on other neighbouring groups for assistance for extra special occasions.

All of the events in our area, are co-ordinated by the Yorkshire Ambulance Service, Private Ambulance Manager.

Locally, it has been Mike, who used to be a Duty Manager for the ambulance service before going in to semi retirement. He is very well respected by all levels, clocking up a magnificent 50 years of service and he is still going strong.

Lately, he has been organising the medical cover for the Huddersfield and Bradford grounds, at Headingley in Leeds and for horse racing events in the area. Anywhere that crowds of 5,000 or more are expected.

Where possible, Stuart would cover the football matches and where I could, I would cover the rugby matches. We would then cover each other's events at times.

Mike mainly concerned himself with events at Bradford, again either football at Valley Parade, or rugby at Odsal. I did occasionally cover the rugby at Odsal Stadium in Bradford.

That part of the job was a real pleasure for me, even though it could be quite challenging. The doctors that we used, were all registered consultants in emergency medicine.

Initially, it was Doctor Peter, Doctor Mike, Doctor Niraj, and Doctor Mark, all of them consultants in their own right. With specialist emergency training for stadium events.

Occasionally, if it was to be a bigger crowd, maybe a cup match or an international match. Then there may be two ambulance crews and another doctor, sometimes twenty five to thirty St. John volunteers.

We occasionally had large scale music events, REM, Beautiful South, Bryan Adams, Elton John, Bon Jovi among others.

At those events, we had a few ambulances, three or maybe four. We had paramedics in the pit, the area stage front. We had a complete medical team of doctors from HRI, some were local GP's and we had hospital nurses. As well as all the voluntary services.

If and when Huddersfield Town start playing in the Premier League, the regular attendance, along with the medical cover will increase.

Come on Town!

A fantastic experience to be involved in.

Sadly Stuart was diagnosed with bowel cancer, he battled on for around five years. The latter year, he faded rapidly, he lost a lot of weight and became very frail.

Mike rang me one Saturday to attend a football match at Huddersfield Town, it was for that same afternoon. Stuart couldn't attend, he was gravely ill.

The other staff in the control room consisted of a Police Commander, usually a Superintendant. There were Safety Officers. Jim, or my old venture scout leader, another Jim, both were retired police officers. Radio operators, for both the safety officer and for the police and finally the camera operators for all the internal and external cctv cameras.

All of the people at the stadium, over the years, had become very good friends of Stuart. Not one of them had any idea of how poorly he had become.

He hadn't told any of them that he had cancer.

I had to inform them, not only of his illness, but also the sad information that I had been given that morning by Mike. That being, that Stuart was so ill, he wasn't expected see that weekend through.

They were all, as expected, extremely shocked and upset. Stuart had been a regular season ticket holder down at the ground for many years, his wife and daughter still are.

Stuart was well respected by everybody. He was such a Town fan, he probably had blue and white running through his veins.

I went to see him on the day after that match, it was the Sunday, I was shocked.

Stuart looked so frail, but thankfully, he wasn't in any pain. He had been sleeping propped up, but had slipped down in his bed, he didn't have the strength to lift himself back up.

He asked me to help.

As I pulled the bed sheets back, I saw for the first and last time how frail he really was. I was afraid to get hold of him, he looked like he would break. As I lifted him up the bed, I nearly threw him out of the window. He gave a wry smile, "less than four and a half stone" he told me.

He then wanted to be left to sleep.

I did as he wished.

I went downstairs and spoke to his wife Trudy. She told me that Stuart was on the verge of dying, that they had been hoping beyond hope for a miracle, but that his time had come.

I did say to her that I hoped that she wouldn't be offended, but I hoped that once he had gone to sleep, that he would not wake up again. He had suffered enough.

Trudy agreed.

He did wake up briefly, but only once that evening, his wife and daughter Ellie, were with him at his bedside.

He then went back to sleep, it was for the last time, he died the following morning, he didn't wake up again.

You are at rest now Stuart!

I carried on doing the managers role at the football matches, even after the ambulance service got rid of the station officer role.

Then out of the blue, in 2011, I was scheduled to manage a Boxing Day game, Mike rang me on Christmas Eve.

He said that there had been a mistake, and that he had double booked managers, he apologised and asked me to stand down.

That was the last time I was asked to attend at a sporting event.

As is the way of the now Yorkshire Ambulance Service, since our merger/take over with the rest of Yorkshire. Several people have no respect at all for the road staff, the "production" side of the job.

A few of the Managers treat road staff with utter contempt, keeping themselves to themselves, never the two shall meet.

Despite numerous requests, on and off for over three years. I have asked in person and sent numerous e-mails. I have made phone calls too, as to why I was no longer being used to cover at the stadium, after all those years. Why had I been removed from the Managers list? Why had my name been taken off the e-mail contacts list?

Unsurprisingly I didn't get even one reply. No courtesy. Not a thank you, an explanation, a kiss my arse, nothing.

Sheer, but expected, ignorance!

As far as I am aware I was doing the job right, I hadn't received any complaints. It hurts when you have provided a service for many years, to not be acknowledged as even existing. One of the people I asked was one of my own colleagues, he never got back to me with any answers. He is doing the job at almost every event now. Good on him.

They haven't asked me since!

I haven't been in contact with them either.

CHAPTER 45.

THESE JOBS ARE SERIOUS.

I thought he was dead!

It was around Easter time in 1992. I was working a shift with Station Officer Mark, it was early evening. We had to attend at a stone quarry on the outskirts of Huddersfield.

Reports there that a man had been buried under six or seven tons of pure Yorkshire stone.

When you get calls like that, you have no idea what to expect. I had some pretty imaginative ideas though, I had all sorts of images filling my head on the journey there.

With it being a works accident, the police are also sent. They act on behalf of health and safety, and factory inspectors. Just in case there has been any negligence and they have the powers to shut a whole factory down, pending further investigations.

On arrival at the quarry, there are several entrances to the site, our sirens had alerted the workers. One of them came out into the main road, and he flagged us down to the correct entrance.

We were sent towards a very large simply constructed steel and concrete building. It had an extremely high and wide roller shutter door, it was open, we were instructed to drive straight in.

We did as we had been told, parked where advised and walked over to where a group of people were standing.

On my approach to the group, I could see above them and attached to a steel gantry in the roof. There was a large, an extremely large, circular saw. The blade must have been nigh on twelve foot in diameter.

As the group separated a little, we could see on the floor a stack of stones.

They were a rough shape, but each were approximately eight foot by four foot, with irregular edges.

There was six of them, they looked to be about two inches thick. They had all been sawn off a large block by the big saw. The remaining chunk was still there.

The process of moving the cut stone, was to put wedges between each of the large sheets, allowing a large lifting sling to be put round them prior to lifting.

We were told that each of the slabs weighed in at over a ton.

As two of the men had been fitting the slings, the first stone had fallen over. The others had then followed, like dominoes, pinning one of the men underneath.

Fearing the worst, we thought that he was completely buried under the stone. Until we were sent round the far side of the pile.

The bottom slab was flat with the floor, but there we could clearly see a head and only the head of a man. It was complete with his hard hat, which hadn't even been dislodged.

The rest of the man disappeared under the stone. As I approached him, I got down on my knees, expecting to be pronouncing death. Surely he had injuries incompatible with life.

I had only just leaned over to move the hard hat, when the head turned and spoke to me in a really broad Yorkshire accent "orreight lad".

I jumped back, I fell on my arse cheeks and nearly shit myself. I didn't expect that. The others collapse about laughing.

"I've brock me bloody leg" he said. "Other na that I'm fine!"

Whilst I was in my ungainly position on the floor, I was aware of another person coming over to the side of me.

It was a female police officer. In those days, some of the women still wore the uniform skirts. That female officer did.

As she stood near to me, she was virtually stood right over the man's head. She was also thinking the worst.

When he spoke to her, Christ did she jump!

He said "bloody hell lass, I can see reight up your clouts" he followed up with "I like suspenders an all!"

She promptly spewed her guts up, all across the floor. To great cheers from the others.

It was after that, that he could start to explain. What really should have been obvious, but due to the circumstances had gone right out of the window.

Because of it being such a large saw, there had to be space below the stone for the blade to clear.

It consisted of a large trough, that also acted as a sump and was filled with water before operating. The water was sprayed onto the blade to keep it cool during cutting. It had an emulsifying oil added to it as a coolant, to stop the water heating up. It was the large trough that the man was laid in.

He had been lucky though, his head was right against the edge. Another couple of inches one way or another and it would have meant certain death.

It was tricky job to sling and lift each of the stone slabs without them slipping, and crushing him fully. It was all hands on deck to assist. It took almost an hour to free him.

He was right, his leg was broken. But not crushed. A nasty break requiring surgery, but one that would mend.

He was out and about, albeit on crutches, in just over six weeks.

About three months later, I was working with someone else. I had been called to an elderly man fallen in the street. The patient wasn't injured, he was just shaken and he didn't travel with us. We gave him the once over, before he went home with his family.

The man from the quarry, had been stood outside the working men's club, he came forward and made himself known to us. It was really good to see him on the mend.

He was a very lucky, lucky man.

Crown Court.

In 1992. I was working with Roy, we had a call to a private address in Huddersfield. We were told that someone there was suffering with severe burns.

On our arrival we were taken upstairs, to see a young male of around twenty five. He was laid fully clothed, in a bath of cold water. His friends explained that he had been in there trying to ease the pain for over four hours.

The man had extensive burns to his upper body and head. He had others as well, mainly to his hands and arms. We estimated that over 40% of his body had been involved, the majority of them were full thickness burns and they were life threatening.

Whilst we were dressing his burns, the house suddenly became full of police officers.

A man identifying himself as a detective sergeant, told our patient that he was under arrest for attempted murder. Then read him his full caution statement and then expected to take him away.

I had to say to that detective, due to the severity of the burns, that the only place the lad was going would be to hospital. First to Huddersfield Royal Infirmary and then he would probably be transferred to the specialist burns unit at Pinderfields in Wakefield.

The sergeant repeated himself and said that he had been arrested for attempted murder.

Again, I had to explain to the sergeant, that it made no difference at that time. The patient had a "right to life, he could be accompanied by a police officer, but he would be travelling in the ambulance with us and that would be final.

He very reluctantly saw my point and agreed.

Due to the fact that our patient was under arrest, he would have to be accompanied throughout by a police officer. That was fine with us, but we had to draw the line at handcuffs, our man had some of his most severe burns on his hands and wrists.

Roy and I continued to dress his extensive burns, due to the amount of full thickness burns and some severe blistering, we used up all our vehicles supply of specialist "tea tree" burns dressings.

Then Roy drove us to pre warned staff at HRI.

I was in the back of the ambulance attending to the patient, he was fully conscious and aware of everything around him. I both needed and wanted to know what had caused his injuries.

He was quite free with his conversation and the travelling police officer was eagerly writing everything down. Our Patient was after all under caution and that everything he said may be taken down and used in evidence.

He told me that he and a "friend" had been doing a "deal" over some drugs. He didn't say what, but that there followed an argument on price.

Then as if it was a perfectly normal thing to do, as part of the argument, one of them produced a can of petrol and they each poured it over themselves.

Doh!!!!!!!!!

"It was an accident" he said.

The other lad had already been picked up by ambulance, he had been treated and assessed at HRI. He had been transferred to the specialist burns unit at Pinderfields, earlier that afternoon.

I asked him "why had you been in a bath of cold water all that time?"

He said that he "thought that the cold water would have treated the burns!"

He had no context of the reality of what had gone on. Whether it was down to drugs, or shock, I don't know. He just hadn't a clue as to how badly he had been injured.

Following his initial treatment and assessment at HRI, he was then blue lighted across to the burns unit at Pinderfields.

After some lengthy treatment and investigations, a court case ensued.

I was summoned to attend at Leeds Crown Court as a witness. I had never been to Crown Court before, I had been a couple of times to the Magistrates, but that was different.

When ambulance staff have to go to Court, they are accompanied by someone, usually a manager. It is mainly for moral support. That day I was with a manager from Leeds, David.

We never attend court in uniform, it attracts the medical negligence parasites. Oh sorry, insurance agents. We always wear a suit and tie.

We were greeted by a member of the witness services, they are volunteers whose job is to help you through the daunting experience. The lady showed me an empty courtroom, she explained what would be going on and who sat where. A little about the protocols and etiquette that goes on in court etc. it was a great help.

Once inside the actual courtroom, I was escorted to the witness stand, David had to sit in the public gallery. It wasn't like what I had just been told.

The jury wasn't even there.

A barrister told me that there had been a bit of a mix up, and we first had to argue a point of law, without the jury's presence.

What followed was a nerve wracking forty minutes of cross questioning, then I had to step down and wait outside and be ready to go through it all again with the jury present.

I had to leave the courtroom, but David was not allowed to come out again, until my full evidence was over. I was left on my own. It felt like hours, but it was only about another forty five minutes. It was long enough though.

As my name was called for the second time, I was quietly confident.

How wrong can you be? The first experience was a bit of a doddle compared, things had become very serious.

The barristers, both prosecution and defence had a completely different attitude. The defence barrister was very arrogant. I was an innocent witness, but I felt very intimidated.

All I was there to do, was to tell them what I saw, what I heard and what I had done.

After all I wasn't on trial was I?

I was in there for a gut wrenching hour and a half. I must have lost a stone in sweat. I was shaking and stuttering. The defence barrister would ask me a question, then before I had finished my answer. He would be asking again, but using different wording, it was awful.

One of the questions, I couldn't recall what I had supposedly seen, I had to say "I can't remember".

He asked again and again, I still couldn't remember.

The question was straight forward in essence, it was regarding the presence of the police officer, but as he was trying to prove a point. He wanted a particular answer.

As this was an attempted murder trial, I don't think that I can say here what the question actually was. It doesn't really affect the feeling that was overwhelming me.

At that point, I still couldn't remember the answer and quite frankly I didn't care, I had had enough. I really was feeling awful, I was hot and sweating, my tie was choking me and I wanted to get out of there.

Just below me sat a court usher, I was told by the witness services lady, that I could ask the usher for tissues, etc. at any time

As the barrister was asking me again, all I did was, to ask for a drink of water. It came in a plastic cup straight from a jug filled with clear fresh water and ice.

I said "excuse me please" and I sipped the water, it was gorgeous.

The defence barrister shouted across, "yes Mr. Firth, ones mouth does get dry when one is lying, doesn't it?"

I looked up in disgust, he had got me. I nearly told him exactly what I thought of him, but out of the corner of my eye, I saw David. He had his head in his hands shaking it from side to side. Thankfully, that was why he was there. To stop me making a fool of myself.

I knew then straight away, that was exactly what the barrister had wanted me to do. I drank the rest of the water straight down. There wasn't a lot, but, "brain freeze". I thought I was going to faint, my head was spinning.

Then, before I had chance to regain the coordination between my mouth and my tongue, the Judge came to my rescue.

He addressed the barrister rather loudly and he said, "my learned friend, I think we can safely say that Mr. Firth has answered all your questions with absolute clarity and honesty" he went on to say. "Whatever was going on whilst Mr. Firth was saving your clients life, which as we are here today, he clearly did. Had no consequence or interest to him at that time. Please move on!"

The next statement, "no further questions My Lord".

That was music to my ears.

It was just what I had been waiting to hear.

The Judge then addressed me, he stated that he felt it right to clarify to the jury that it wasn't me on trial there. He also stated, that he had been watching me and that he had studied my body language. He asked if he could confirm that it was "the first time that I had ever been stood in that position, in a Crown Court room".

I answered that it was.

His next statement again I will never forget. "Well young man, you have conducted yourself admirably, well done! You may now leave my courtroom".

I didn't stop to argue, I needed a beer!

David could also then leave the courtroom.

"Christ" he said, "I thought you were gonna give that bloke a reight gobfull. I'm glad you didn't".

It was only the fact that David had been there and had done what he did, that probably stopped me. That's what those crafty buggers do to get guilty people off.

They try to trip up the innocent.

David took me to a local pub and he bought me that pint, my God did I enjoy it.

My patient was actually found guilty of attempted murder.

I have been to court on several occasions over my career, at both Magistrates Court and at Crown Court. I have also been once each to a Family Court and to a Coroner's Court.

None of them are a pleasant experience, but they are a necessary one at times.

I can honestly say that each time, the night before and the time at the court awaiting for your name being called, have been some of the most nerve wracking experiences I have ever been through.

Thank God I have only been an innocent party and only there to give evidence.

I can't imagine what it must be like to actually be on trial.

Sailing at Scammonden.

Another job in 1992, and again with Roy. Although it was a serious incident and it was very eventful. It turned out to be far more relaxing.

We had got a call to the main viewing car park above Scammonden Dam, someone there had broken their leg.

We arrived at the main car park overlooking the dam. Roy was driving, as I got out an elderly gentleman, told me that he was the one who had been asked to call.

A young lad had run up to him asking for help.

Then the man did something that I hadn't expected. He handed me a pair of extremely powerful binoculars and said "look over there in the far corner of the dam, you can just about see her".

I looked and sure enough, at the furthest point away from us. At the far side of the dam, near to the corner, where it runs next to the M62. I could see a young lad had his shirt off and was waving it furiously.

There was someone laid flat, on the bank almost at the waters edge. I could just about see them waving as well, from under a mountain of bystanders coats.

I grabbed the entonox bag, our pain relieving gas and air. Three blankets, my first aid bag and a long leg splint.

Roy said that he would have to drive all around the dam, up to near the end of the big road bridge over the motorway. A track runs down from there towards the dam. Not all the way, but it would be a lot nearer to her than where we were.

I set off on foot towards our stricken patient, as Roy set off around the dam. We didn't have individual radios then, only the one in the cab.

I eventually got to our patient, a spritely Irish lady in her forties, I will call her Nina.

She had slipped in some wet mud and gone over on her ankle.

X-rays were not needed there, it was definitely dislocated and possibly fractured.

The good thing was that it was pink. She had good circulation past her injury right to her toes. The long splint would be no good there. I had to fashion one out of a rolled up blanket. Old school splinting. I rolled the blanket up from each end towards the middle, to form two rolls and then placed one roll either side of the ankle for support. I then fastened everything together with a good old crepe bandage.

She was taking the entonox like a good 'un. Also lovely and warm, comforted by around eight or nine close family and friends. She had been wrapped in their kindly donated coats. We gave them back and then had wrapped her in some of our blankets.

I set off up the hill to meet Roy and get some carrying equipment. I met Roy half way. Yes he had got to the bridge, but there was a large padlocked iron gate. He couldn't get anywhere near to us.

The next plan, the boat club. From my scouting days, I knew that whenever anyone is out sailing, the rescue boat is manned. It could come right up to the waters edge, Nina was already only a few feet away.

She was a rather portly lady, (I hope she doesn't mind me saying that) and we could not have managed her all the way up the extremely steep and wet banking to the motorway hard shoulder.

On his way back round, Roy was going to get Comms to ring the boat club and ask for the rescue boat to be sent. They could bring the scoop stretcher and some more blankets. He did that as he set off to drive all around the dam again and to the club house.

Shortly after, I saw some welcome and familiar faces from my scouting days. They were coming across the dam in two boats, around eight of them I think in total. Graham one of my old venture scout mates. He brought the first boat, a flat bottomed one, aground.

The front, was then only around six foot from the patient. The other lads stepped out into shallow waters. Between us we managed to get Nina onto the scoop stretcher.

She was fitted with a life jacket, a comfort if ever I saw one. I'm sure she had already been through enough.

I had to put on a life jacket and Nina was placed across the bow of the flat boat. There was no sign of Roy.

Graham told me that he hadn't been keen to go on the water. He told Graham "there's probably already enough people in that boat without me. Thank you very much".

Then the fun part could begin. The boat was pushed out into shallow water, the motor started and we gently sailed across the full width of Scammonden Dam. Escorted by the rest of the rescue team in the second boat.

As we approached the landing ramp, I could see that Roy had reversed the ambulance right down to the waters edge. The water was actually splashing against the rear step. Roy was sat comfortably, with a pot of tea from the clubhouse and a cigarette.

The second boat had arrived first. Those boys were stood at the water's edge, waiting for us and there was a crowd of fifty or sixty folk who had come down to see what was going on.

The boat had managed to get so near to the ambulance, that we were able to simply slide Nina and the scoop off the boat and straight onto the floor of the ambulance. To some wonderful cheering and applause.

Once in the back, we took her off the bony scoop and sat her upright on the more comfortable stretcher.

Thanking everyone for their help we sat back and "enjoyed" the rest our journey to HRI.

What an adventure for a Sunday afternoon. Definitely one for the grandchildren that.

Shame no one got any pictures, or did they?

Off duty incident.

1993. That was also the year that I attended an accident on Manchester Road. It had the potential to have been one of the worst jobs that I had ever attended.

I had actually finished my shift, nights again and had gone to bed. I had only been in bed for an hour and a half.

I was rudely awakened by my eldest son Adrian. He had been on his way to school at around eight thirty and had seen that there had been an accident a couple of hundred yards away from our house, outside the local pub.

He had come to get me, it seemed as if it was a bad one, he thought I would be able to help. I ran on to see what I could do.

Oh my God! Little did I know what was to prevail.

A 38 ton articulated lorry, with an unladen 40 foot flat back trailer, had careered out of control and hit the hole/roadworks outside the pub.

In the hole were two men working on the gas mains.

Another one had just climbed out of the hole, he escaped injury, but will be definitely mentally scarred for the rest of his life.

As was their protocols, if something goes amiss, the priority is to get out of the hole and not to duck down. (I've been told since).

Stan was on his first day back on the job, following four years out of work, he was working with a colleague and good friend Jim.

They were about to cap off an eight inch gas mains, when they heard the lorry skidding. Jim had given Stan, a leg up, he himself then scrambled out.

Too late! Stan took the full impact of the lorry!

He was hit in the middle of his back. Somehow he ended up in an "S" shape around the front axle. His legs on the floor bent backwards and his head doubled over, almost on to his backside.

As I arrived, I could see Stan's head, I moved around into the road, and looked to see where his legs were. I could see legs, but unless Stan was fifteen foot tall, there was someone else underneath.

That turned out to be Jim.

Both of the men were in severe pain.

The off side wheels of the cab were in mid air, the near side wheels were still on the ground.

Every time a vehicle passed the truck rocked.

Jim was trapped between the sump of the engine, which was burning his back and the edge of the hole. He had been dragged along its edge for about twenty foot. Each time the truck rocked, he was in great danger of being crushed.

I managed to get passers by to ask each vehicle passing, if we could have their car jack. They managed to get eight in all. They were only one ton car ones, but placed around the cab, every little helped.

Thank you Tesco!

I was talking to both men and trying to reassure them that more help was on the way.

The fire brigade arrived first, they were led by their Station Officer gentleman Joe.

I got their oxygen on to both men, the smell of gas was becoming overpowering.

The third man jumped back down the hole, against all advice, but they had been unable to cap off the gas. He knew that he had to do something. The Stilson grips that he had been going for, were no good any more.

The valve top had been sheared clean off. All he could do, was to stuff their three donkey jackets up the pipe. He was using his feet, to stem the free flowing gas. He was then shoving blankets, coats, anything he could get his hands and feet on, up the pipe.

The first of any ambulance staff to arrive was my station boss at the time, Tony. He became the ambulance incident commander. Closely followed by, the first crew of Arnold and Annette.

A second ambulance then came, at Tony's request, bringing a full trauma team from Huddersfield Royal Infirmary. They were led by A&E consultant Dr. Mike. He had a consultant anaesthetist also called Dr. Mike with him, and an A&E Sister, Julia. The second ambulance crew was Jerry and Jack.

Then followed Paul, he was the duty ambulance officer, sent over from our headquarters at Birkenshaw, to oversee the whole incident.

Following a major struggle by all of us present, the fire service airbags managed to lift the truck enough to get Jim free.

His injuries were serious. He had burns to his back. But worst of all were the wounds to his chest, abdomen and thigh, where he had been dragged along the edge of the four foot deep trench. He required major surgery for internal injuries as well.

It took a lot more to get Stan free.

Although I was technically off duty, I drove the ambulance to HRI with Arnold in the back looking after Jim. Tony our manager stayed with Annette and the other crew.

Once Stan was out, his injuries were horrendous, including several severe spinal fractures.

During his stay in hospital, Stan was told that he was paralysed and would never walk again. His treatment was started at Huddersfield, then he was transferred to the Pinderfields spinal injuries unit.

Stan proved everybody wrong.

Within six months, all of which were hard slog, he was walking using a pair of crutches. He was going to the pub and then when he had consumed a few drinks, he had a habit of forgetting his sticks and walking home unaided.

I kept in touch occasionally with both of the lads, after all you don't often see end results. Whilst he was hospital in Huddersfield, I visited Jim a couple of times. What he told me, had me in stitches.

"What do you think of this?" He said.

He told me that his boss from the gas company had visited him and had brought him a present. "They are in that drawer there" he said. I opened the bedside drawer, then I nearly fell over laughing. Two wagon wheels, the chocolate biscuits. What a guy

"I wish I had thought of that" I said.

"He's just like you" said Jim.

More happened in the following months. I was nominated, with Arnold and Annette, for an ambulance service bravery award for the incident. We were put forward by our duty officer Paul.

I received my award during a lavish awards presentation at our ambulance HQ at Birkenshaw, the following year. It was presented in the form of a wooden shield, with the ambulance service crest on, with details on a scroll at the bottom. I was also given a Chief Officers Commendation, due to my services whilst off duty. They were presented by Sir Jimmy Savile.

Following on from the incident, the BBC series "999" recorded a TV programme of a reconstruction of the incident. The programme was presented by well known newscaster Michael Buerk.

It was filmed to be as accurate as possible, including interviews with both Jim and Stan.

Tragedy continued to follow Stan. Even though he did recover enough to walk unaided. He went on to get married and defied other odds. Stan and his wife Ella, managed to have a son, (always affectionately known as "Mucktub"). Little "mucktub" died, he was aged just two years, from meningococcal meningitis.

Life for Stan and his wife Ella, had to carry on and they had two more children, a boy and a girl. Eventually, the strain of life's events took its toll on their marriage and the couple split up.

Only recently, the family hit the national headlines again, when even more tragedy struck.

How could such tragedy possibly happen to one family?

Jake, the new partner of Stan's ex wife Ella. A very jealous ex policeman went berserk, he stabbed her frenziedly and killed her, before turning his rage and the knife on her two children. Fortunately their injuries were not life threatening.

The new partner had two children of his own from a previous relationship in the house, he left those two alone.

He was charged, found guilty and then sentenced to serve a minimum of 28 years in prison.

That wasn't long enough in my mind, for what he'd done.

Following an appeal, he somehow managed to get his sentence reduced to 25 years.

Stan has never been back to work. He hasn't wanted to. I couldn't begin to imagine what his mental state is though.

Jim on the other hand, has definitely had his share of psychological problems. As far as to say, I think that he has had a full personality change.

Eighteen years after the incident, I was returning home from yet another night shift. As I travelled through Milnsbridge, I was held up at some temporary traffic lights on Market Street, surrounding a hole in the road.

The lights went green and I set off. As I got level with the works, a man climbed out of the hole, I saw his face.

I thought "no, it couldn't be". I had to be sure, I drove around the block and returned.

Sure enough, it was Jim.

Amazingly, that was his very first day back at work. He was doing the same job, on the other end actually, of the same pipeline from all those years ago.

We had a good natter at the roadside and then arranged to go for a couple of beers at teatime when he knocked off. I met him at the Royal pub on Scar Lane with his wife Flic. I had quite few photos for him to look at. At times he was very confused, he didn't remember half of it.

I haven't bumped into him since.

Bravery.

Even though I received a Bravery Award for the incident on Manchester Road. Personally, that for me was not the bravest thing that I have ever done.

My biggest phobia in life, is a fire escape. I absolutely detest going anywhere near them.

The height isn't the main issue, it is the general design of the steps and being able to see through them.

My legs turn to jelly, and my stomach heaves.

My family would readily tell you of the number of times they have laughed at me when negotiating the entrance of Hubberton Trading, the army surplus shop in Milnsbridge. The door is at the top of a short fire escape staircase of around ten steps. I shake like mad just going up there.

On our holiday with mum and dad in Great Yarmouth, Ben went into a panic at the top of a huge helter skelter slide. It wasn't like normal ones where you sit at the top of a gentle slide and then slowly move off.

Oh No!

For that one, he was expected to just launch himself into a black hole, before sliding round and round the tower, finishing up in a polished wooden bowl at the bottom.

He was stuck at the top. He was only a nipper.

There was no other way down, even for any exceptional circumstances. I don't know how they would go on with a medical emergency!

There was a backlog of people behind him, they were getting wound up. I had to chase up there after him, I had to grab hold of him and then launch both of us into the hole. It was scary.

I have always hated fairground rides, they petrify me, but then an open fire escape staircase as well. Christ!

I thought I would die! But it had to be done. The tower was about sixty to seventy feet high.

In later life, nothing would phase Ben. Now if he had the chance, he would have gone out on the roof of it, just to have a look round.

On a similar fear, we had a family day out to Burnsall in the Yorkshire Dales. Over the river Wharfe, there is a footbridge.

It is a suspension bridge, consisting of four steel wires and a wooden floor. The whole lot moves when anybody walks on it.

I was stuck in the middle of it, when my two little darlings were bouncing up and down for all their worth. The bridge was up and down like a trawler on the North Atlantic, very much like my stomach was doing.

I hate those damn things as well!

Bravery on the job.

Once, whilst at work, we were dealing with a psychiatrically disturbed patient I'll call Shaun.

He had been a regular caller for many years, a self harmer. He cut himself and when he did, his self inflicted wounds were serious.

Often his wounds had been inflicted by razor blades, or his favourite choice, cut throat razors. They could be six to eight inches long, and have been a couple of inches deep and wide. Particularly on his thighs and abdomen.

When they had been stitched together at the hospital, he would simply cut the stitches and watch the wounds open up again.

That particular day, we had got him to A&E at Huddersfield, but then Shaun had got extremely agitated. We couldn't calm him down, no matter how we tried.

His language was foul and abusive towards the nurses, he was shouting loudly. Then suddenly and out of the blue, he produced a cut throat razor from his sock.

He was threatening one of the nurses with it.

The security staff then arrived, Shaun was immobilised and his razor confiscated. He was removed from the premises and taken just outside the A&E department by security staff, the police were called.

Whilst waiting for the police, Shaun ran off and climbed up the fire escape. It used to be on the end wall of Acre Mill, across the road opposite the drive to A&E.

He stood at the top, threatening to jump off. It was six floors high, the best part of eighty to ninety foot.

I was working with ex cadet Jean, she is now one of our managers, based at Halifax. Jean and I went up the drive to see what we could do to help.

The police were already there, then the fire service also arrived.

Shaun shouted that he would only let females ambulance staff up to talk to him. In those days, we had a blue jumper with the word AMBULANCE in large letters emblazoned across a horizontal white band at the front.

He didn't want anything to do with the police, so I swapped jumpers with a WPC. Then she and Jean went up towards a very excitable Shaun. The WPC was aiming to handcuff him to the railings at the top, stopping him from jumping, or accidentally falling.

She quickly managed to do that.

The fire service had brought the hydraulic platform, a police negotiator and a fireman were in the basket. All four of them were trying to talk Shaun down from his elevated position.

He was having none of it.

Two hours later, we were all still in the same position. My legs were shaking and I was stood on the roadside, at ground level.

It was the fear from just watching. I had had enough. I set off, and ran up all the flights. I grabbed him by the scruff of his neck, with the other hand I grabbed his pants and gave him the worst wedgie that anyone could experience.

The WPC then unfastened the handcuffs, I ran down the steps still hold of Shaun in the same way. I wouldn't, well actually I couldn't, let go. I was gripping him as though and it felt like it did, my life depended on it.

As we reached the bottom of the steps he was arrested, for possession of an offensive weapon, threatening behaviour and for a breach of the peace.

He was cuffed again and placed into the back of a police car.

The fireman from the platform went barmy with the police, he kept saying "you can't arrest him, I promised him that you wouldn't, let him go now! I demand it!"

That fireman was so lucky, he was a hairs breadth from being arrested himself. He had to be ordered away by his seniors, he was physically picked up and carried away by his colleagues, still swearing at the police as he went. There was quite a crowd of onlookers around, who witnessed everything. Today, that fireman's behaviour, would have been a dead cert for You Tube.

If he had got his facts right first and bothered to find out why Shaun was up there in the first place, it wouldn't have happened.

Typical firefighter hero!

That job, certainly for me anyway. It was the bravest thing I personally, have ever had to do. Not for some people, but it was a massive personal challenge in my life.

We all have our own phobia's in life. That was and still is, mine.

CHAPTER 46.

A LIGHTER SIDE TO THE JOB.

A Touch of Frost.

1993 was an extremely busy year for me. I was asked to be involved in some more TV work. I was with Mike, that time it was for the filming of an episode of the ITV drama series A Touch of Frost.

Season three, episode three "Dead Male One". It was part of the iconic television series and it was going to be filmed in Halifax, at the Shay. The football ground, home to Halifax Town FC.

The episode was to involve the local "Denton" football club.

A player was taken ill in the dressing rooms and then he collapsed. As part of the drama developed, was it as a result of an accident, or was something more sinister taking place? Could it be illicit drugs?

We spent all day at the Shay, the highlight of course, being the arrival of Sir David Jason. We had been asked not to ask him for autographs, apparently he would talk all day and they wouldn't be able to get any filming done.

He did however make the effort, to go and speak to everyone on set, including Mike and me.

At the same time as the filming, there were some shire horses and a dray waggon from Tetleys Brewery on site. I managed to get a photo of David Jason, stood with one of the magnificent horses. It was called Ben, like my youngest son.

The horses were present for photographs at the reopening of the newly refurbished Punchbowl Pub, just around the corner. It has since closed down, the pub and all its surrounding buildings have all been completely demolished.

David Jason, even stood on the pitch side and addressed the "crowd" on the terraces, he talked to them for the best part of half an hour.

The filming that was to involve us, according to the producer. Was to use the ambulance and a stunt driver, for scenes with the crowd and for us as a crew, to be on stand by in case of any accidents.

We had to explain to him, that we would not be able to allow the use of a stunt driver. It was down to insurance. Our ambulance, wasn't a private hire vehicle, it was an actual NHS emergency vehicle.

I would have to do the driving.

The scene, was that we had picked up the footballer from the dressing rooms, I had to drive the ambulance from the pitch side, with lights flashing. The sirens would be added later.

Then to drive at speed, through the crowd of supporters and as fast as I could, across and through to the far end of the car park.

It was a brilliant experience. To create more effect, I was asked to try and get some of the cinders on the old speedway track to fly, causing some dust. The cinders bit should be easy, the ambulance was a rear wheel drive Ford Transit, fitted with a 3.5 litre Granada performance engine in it.

As I drove out of the stadium, I had to head through a narrow gateway. I was told that some fans would be in the way and knocking on the side of the ambulance as I drove past.

Other "supporters" would be generally milling around, then I was to accelerate away from the gateway and through the car park.

It was the first of two attempts that was actually used on the television programme. They didn't use the bit with the wheels spinning on the cinders. I was really chuffed with it, I had created quite a dust cloud. I thought it looked great, but never mind!

Apparently there was too much dust.

That was it then for the first day.

The second day, we had to take the same ambulance to Killingbeck Hospital in Leeds. (Now demolished). There, one of the old wards was to be used for the studio version of an A&E department.

We had to load and unload the stretcher several times, until they were happy with it.

We had to take the trolley with our patient laid on it, in and out of the department a number of times, to give the producers a variety of shots to choose from.

Other scenes were being filmed at the same time in other parts of the hospital.

It gave us a real insight as to how TV programmes are made. The time taken actually filming, just to get two minutes on screen was amazing.

There were lots of "extras" outside when we first arrived at Killingbeck Hospital, they were all waiting to see if they could get a part in the programme. At the time, the going rate of pay for an extra, was eighty pounds per day plus expenses.

We had to wait several months for the screening. Finally, it was on and the whole family gathered round, dad was going to be on tele.

What a disappointment.

After two full days filming and all that time hanging about, we were on screen for less than a minute in total.

The person driving the ambulance was definitely me, but, due to the reflections off the front windscreen, it could have been anybody.

Neither of us were visible.

The hospital scene, was also disappointing.

In the hospital A&E entrance were several people walking about, including Sir David Jason and other cast regulars. Including actor John Lyons as DS Toolan and Paul Moriarty as Sergeant Wells.

The latter had spent most of the day with us in the ambulance, he never stopped cracking jokes with Mike and myself.

In the actual hospital scene, we wheeled our stretcher through the entrance lobby. We had our footballer, actor Jason Cheater as Adie Carr, laid on it. We must have been filmed at least twenty five times, from all different angles.

From the camera angle finally screened, you could see our feet as we walked into the A&E department. Again, it could have been anybody.

In a video playback, there are 25 frames used per second. After freeze framing the scene, there was only one part Mike and I were both fully visible, our faces included. That was with David Jason, along with all the main stars of the programme. The only hard proof that we were there.

We were visible for three of the twenty five frames, that is 12/100ths of a second. Not exactly our fifteen minutes of fame.

RADARS.

Early in 1994. The "RADARS" appeared. Not some supernatural alien event, but the introduction of the dreaded speed bumps.

The Rawthorpe and Dalton Accident Reduction Scheme.

I personally hate the damn things. In my own personal opinion, I don't think they do anything at all to reduce accidents.

They slow down the already careful drivers, but they can cause untold damage to wheels and tracking.

The boy racers, joy riders, whatever you want to call them. Or stolen car and motorcycle riders love them. They are a man made, illegal drivers theme park.

"In my own personal opinion" that is.

I have to say that, as I was hauled over the coals by our ambulance management later in that year.

I was a member of Huddersfield's voluntary road safety committee until it was disbanded in, I think the year 2000.

It was at one of their monthly meetings, that I was asked about "RADARS".

As a service, we had a policy statement about them. I read it out to the members. "Anything that is put in place to reduce the number of accidents, has to be given credit". The next important part was to say "if they prove themselves worthy, then the ambulance service will be fully supportive of them".

I was asked by one of the Huddersfield Daily Examiner reporters, present as usual at the road safety meeting. To describe to him, my own personal feelings on road humps.

It went as follows.

"Off the record". I "detest those things, whoever came up with the design, has a barbaric streak. There is not even one road possible to get to Kirkwood Hospice without bouncing the poor patient over them. They (the planners), must have only measured the front axle width for the speed cushions. The front end clears them easily, but the rear axle has twin wheels. It is much narrower and the back end of the ambulance will bounce un-ceremoniously over it. If the patient in the back of the ambulance, is in pain, as cancer patients often are. Their pain will be exacerbated (made much worse)".

The very next evening, on the front page of Huddersfield Daily Examiner, the main headline was in two inch letters. I quote. "Ambulance official attacks council!"

It went on to say "Station Officer Ian Firth of Huddersfield Ambulance Station said." And then a word for word account of my off the record comments. Not one word of our corporate statement.

Oh shit!

I got into work the next morning, our area director Stewart was stood bolt upright, at the top of the stairs. He was holding the Examiner aloft, front page showing.

"Well!" he said, "is this right?"

I had to explain myself. I was able to show him the transcribed minutes of the meeting. I had given the corporate statement to the committee. I was so lucky not to be seriously disciplined.

Following my serious talking to by our management. I was then invited by the then leader of Kirklees council, councillor Mel Munday, to a full council meeting at the Town Hall.

I always said that honesty was the best policy!

I attended the meeting, accompanied by my chaperone and that was my manager Bryan. Every time I was asked a question, he kicked me under the table and then winked at me.

I answered all questions as honestly as possible.

Then to Bryan's surprise, his face was an absolute picture. After I had answered my questions. I stood up, ready to address the assembled councillors.

I said. "Mr Chairman, may I please add a couple of suggestions, to alleviate the patients' suffering". I then suggested a couple of alternative alterations. One of which, was met with council approval.

Bryan then relaxed and he gave me a wry nod.

I was then formally thanked for my contributions and honesty, by the chair of the council committee. Councillor Mel Munday. Bryan and me left the meeting.

It was only couple of weeks at the most, the highways division of Kirklees Council started work.

Every one of the humps in Albany Road, running all down the side of the Kirkwood Hospice and all the humps in Waterloo Road, from the junction with Wakefield Road were removed.

I hadn't won the war, but I claimed "The Battle of Waterloo!"

Get it!

I claim full responsibility for that one.

Kirkwood Hospice once again had full access, even if was only from one direction, completely hump free.

I didn't receive one word of thanks or appreciation from the ambulance service for my actions, surprise, surprise.

I think Bryan was happy with the way I had conducted myself though.

Looking for my fillings.

Whilst on the subject of speed humps, they have sprung up virtually everywhere, especially in Kirklees.

One evening, in 2014. I was crewed up with Carrie, a paramedic, we received an emergency call in Birkby.

We were on our way back from Calderdale Hospital and were almost at Birchencliffe, when we were passed the job. It was for a female, a dialysis patient, who had collapsed in full renal (kidney) failure.

Carrie set off at speed, we were heading down Birkby Road, from the Cavalry Arms pub.

We weren't aware at the time, but some new speed humps had just been installed and they hadn't been highlighted by then. It was already quite dark. They were the full road width type, big buggers as well.

Carrie hit the first at about 55-60mph. We felt the front of the ambulance had taken off and then it felt like the back wheels had hit the bump, before the front end had landed. It was a hell of a bump.

We were still bouncing when we hit the next one. It felt as though the ambulance was going to roll over, it bounced that much.

We found out later in the evening, that even the rear number plate had been thrown clean off. It had probably landed in a hedge somewhere down Birkby Road..

We couldn't stop laughing though. When we arrived outside the house, I got my torch out and started looking in the door well with it. Carrie asked "what are you looking for?"

I told her that I was "looking for my fillings".

That was it then, Carrie was helpless, she nearly wet herself.

We both really struggled to keep it together in the patients house.

Quick outside!

I was telling Carrie of the above inclusion in my book. When she asked me if I had included another particular incident. Which to be honest, I had forgotten about. I'm glad that she reminded me.

She told me that of all jobs that we had done together over the years, and we have done a lot. Most of them, like the previous, we had been able to have a good laugh together. This was a serious one and it was the one that had stuck in her mind.

We had been called to an address in Lockwood, not far from Lockwood Police Station.

The call was from a male child to say that his mum was behaving oddly and then, while still on the call. In the background, there had been a loud scream and the phone had gone dead.

Comms had repeatedly tried to call the number back, but had been unsuccessful on each occasion.

Carrie and I were sent and we met up with the police at the end of the lane. Then we all went up together.

There were two WPC's and us.

When we arrived at the house, a woman answered the knocking at the door, but she wouldn't open it. She was speaking to us through the letter box of the locked door.

When I asked her about the child in the house, and if they were ok, she became very agitated.

From our Comms, we understood there to be a young child inside, the caller. "Probably of junior school age" we were told.

Obviously, once we had been able to speak to the woman, the child had become my priority.

Initially she denied any child being in the house. She was slurring her words and to be honest, she sounded to be in drink.

As I was talking to her, the police with us were asking for someone to back us up with MOE capability. (Means Of Entry, usually the big red universal key, in the form of a heavy steel ram).

We heard someone upstairs. Carrie backed off down the garden, to look at the upstairs windows to see if she could see anyone. As the police officers went around the back, to see what access would be like there.

The woman ran upstairs, she was screaming at someone to be quiet. Her language was appalling and she was very threatening in both manner and context.

That was when we heard the sound of breaking glass and a child screaming. The male officer had just arrived with his traditional MOE, but firstly, he opted for a size nine well positioned boot.

It worked well.

The policeman then rushed straight in and went upstairs, he was closely followed by Carrie and me.

Suddenly and out of the blue, the woman came running at us. She had something glinting in her hand.

I just had time to literally push Carrie, as I shouted "quick outside" and slammed the door behind her.

The two women officers were nearly sent flying, as they were just behind Carrie at the time.

The woman had got a large kitchen knife in her hand. As the policeman had gone upstairs, the woman had appeared from the darkness of the front room.

All I had for defence was my trusty first aid bag in my hand. Mind you, it was heavy and with a well aimed swing, I smacked her straight across the wrist. Yes! It caused the knife to drop.

I grabbed her right wrist and at the same time, I kicked the knife under the sofa. Just then, the policeman reappeared and grabbed her by the left wrist.

Between us, we manhandled her to the ground and were then in a position to call our colleagues back in from outside.

They went upstairs to see to the child, as we then had the female safely secured in handcuffs and sat on the floor.

The child turned out to be a male. He was actually fourteen years old, but was only the size of an eight year old, he had some learning difficulties and some mobility problems.

They were as a result of some kind of fancy named syndrome, we didn't find out what it was.

Other than being very frightened, he was fine.

The woman was in drink, and was promptly arrested for her threatening behaviour and taken by the WPC's to the cells.

Cassie and I waited with the boy, for the woman's parents. The lads grandparents were coming from Bradford to collect him.

It turned out that they were actually his legal guardians.

Due to his mother's heavy drinking and previous social services intervention, his mother only had occasional stopovers from her son, one night a month.

The social services were informed again.

Following on from then, the mother would only have access to her son under complete supervision. That would only be in a public place and only if there was no suspicion of any alcohol.

Apparently Cassie couldn't get over the speed that I moved her out of harms way and disarmed the woman. The element of surprise is usually a winner.

Cassie was married to Pat, also a paramedic at Huddersfield. As life has a habit of doing, things changed, Cassie and Pat split up and went their separate ways.

Whatever their reasons, it had got nothing to do with the rest of us. It was a matter that only those two could manage. I wish them both well.

Cassie left Huddersfield Ambulance Station in July 2016, and is hoping for a total fresh start. Still with YAS, but working on the North Yorkshire coast area at Filey.

I personally will miss her bubbly personality and the laughs that we had working together, doing a serious job.

I wish her all the very best of luck in her new adventure, I am sure she will do well, she has that sort of attitude to fit in.

I have met her since, she has got her mojo back and she is as happy as I have ever seen her.

Good luck lass, you deserve it!

Pat, is still at Huddersfield and he seems content again. Let's hope for new beginnings for the pair of them.

At least one of us can fire a bow and arrow!

In 1998. The police received some important intelligence, that there was to be a major drugs deal taking place in the Chapeltown area of Leeds, over the Leeds Carnival weekend. It takes place over the August Bank Holiday.

Second only in attendance numbers, to the carnival at Notting Hill in London.

It was to involve some major players in the serious drugs league and that several firearms were expected to be present.

The police were particularly interested in a couple of males, who had been closely followed by undercover officers from Interpol. They were believed to be flying out from Germany to Manchester, on the Saturday of Carnival.

Due the the vast amount of public expected over the weekend, a major operation would be put in place. It was to involve a large number of police officers, a lot of them would be none uniformed armed officers. With one ambulance crew and a manager.

The crew was to be myself and Ivan from Honley station. We would be working twelve hour shifts, from ten in the morning until ten at night, on both days.

It started with a full briefing session at Castlegate Police Headquarters on the Friday night. That was scheduled to last for about two,hours.

The briefing had to be attended by all concerned. We arrived as planned at eight o'clock, our supervisors were director Stewart on Saturday and manager Bryan on Sunday, all four of us were there on the Friday.

The seriousness of the incident was explained. The plans were to intercept the two individuals on the M62 between Outlane junction 23 and Ainley Top junction 24, before they got anywhere near Leeds.

The men were known as highly dangerous and they were not frightened to shoot their way out of a situation. They wouldn't be using toy cap guns either. Several automatic weapons of high calibre were already attributed to them.

Once arrested, they would be brought off the motorway and taken to Huddersfield police station for questioning. At Ainley Top roundabout, there is a slip road actually on the roundabout and a large parking area, for the Department of Transport Weighbridge. That was where we would be based, along with the prison van and several admin personnel.

If shots were fired and an ambulance was required. We would be in a position to enter the M62 and travel the wrong way down the slip road, and to whatever destination required, on a closed motorway.

The operation taking place that weekend, had been in the planning stages for months.

At the police headquarters and after all the operation had been explained, there was a request by the senior officer. "Are there any questions from the floor?"

One little feller stood up, he said that he had a couple of questions to ask of the "top table". That was occupied by several people, they were all high ranking officers.

His first question was regarding food and drink availability. His answer given, was that all personnel involved, would be given a lunch pack.

His second was regarding hot drinks. His answer given, was that the local police would try and liaise with the Hotel at Ainley Top. The Pennine Manor at the time, to be able to acquire some tea or coffee.

Thirdly, what was to be done regarding toilet facilities. His answer given, was similar to the last question.

The man, was a semi retired policeman who had spent many years on the force. All his questions were reasonable and valid, but the "top table" we're obviously getting a little cheesed off with him.

Several others asked questions, but then, he was off again.

"One final point if I may" he said.

"If we are to be parked at the Weighbridge, could we not use the building there. That has toilet facilities, it also has a small kitchen, where hot drinks could be made and it has space for up to eight people to be able to sit. Would it not be better to use that? Rather than leaving our post to attend at a local hotel, Sir".

His final question and following statement, was met with a very sullen response. That being, if his point had been brought up at earlier planning sessions, then perhaps there would have been a chance to arrange for something to be done about it.

"Leaving it until 21:30hrs. the night before, I am sure you will agree is a little stupid" he was told.

He was on his feet again, "my point Sir" he said. Was that "there are so many police officers involved in the organising of this event. From Assistant Chief down. All the Chiefs, but some little things. That I feel are important things, seem to get overlooked".

His reply was immediately snapped back at him, that it was "far too late to do anything now".

He stood again and said, "with respect Sir, as usual there are far too many Chiefs".

He then held his hand high in the air proudly, he was holding aloft a bunch of keys. He then had the whole room, except for the "top table" in stitches.

"I took it upon myself to ask them at the weighbridge last week. They are more than happy for us to use their facilities, Sir. Here are the keys".

He received a cheer from all around. "Never mind Sir, at least one of us can fire a bow and arrow," he concluded to rapturous applause.

I'll never forget him.

As an operation, it was classed as a huge success. Nothing at all happened on the Saturday. But at ten in the morning on Sunday, the men were spotted leaving a hotel in Manchester, near to the airport.

At eleven o'clock everyone was put on high alert, both of the target men were in one vehicle, with two other well known gang members.

At eleven thirty, the message came through that they had been apprehended, and there had been "NO shots fired". They had been isolated and stopped earlier than originally planned.

Perfect.

Then the prison van left us and went on its journey down the totally closed, wrong side of the M62 to collect four highly dangerous criminals.

Shortly afterwards, we were all stood down from the operation, but if possible we were requested to attend a debrief at Castlegate police station, in Huddersfield.

It had been a very costly exercise financially. Due to wages, manpower and resources etc, but it was a 100% successful. Both of the targeted men and two other major league players had been arrested.

Along with a massive amount of drugs taken off the streets. A large amount of cash was recovered.

An experience to be sure, although I can't say that it was the sort of job that would be my cup of tea. It involved a hell of a lot of waiting about, to me that was much harder work than working.

Never mind it ticked another box on life's journey.

We had an idea!

In the summer of 1984. One of our colleagues, Jack, fell off his motorbike at the bottom of Trinity Street. It was near to the Huddersfield town centre.

When Tommy and I arrived, he had only hurt his ankle, although it looked as quite likely that it could be broken. He didn't have any other injuries.

His only worry was his beloved motorbike, it was vintage, a collectors item. He wasn't happy to leave it so close to the town centre, he was frightened of it getting stolen.

We had an idea!

We were at a bus stop. That bus went directly to HRI, we lifted Jack onto the front seat and sent him on his way.

Then we put his motorbike into the ambulance, before blue lighting up to the ambulance station, where we dropped it off. We then chased after and caught up with the bus outside the hospital.

We lifted Jack off the bus and took him down the drive to A&E, to get his ankle sorted.

Yes, it was broken.

More than that, his beloved motorbike was perfectly safe in the ambulance station garage.

What a job!

Doing that sort of thing was very rare. It was naughty of us, I am sorry. I promise it won't happen again!

CHAPTER 47.

MUM'S LONG DISTANCE FRIENDS.

Pen Friend from the other side of the world.

As I mentioned earlier, mum used to love writing letters. She had two pen friends that she had written to ever since her junior schooldays.

Mum and dad even went to meet one of them in 1986, they went to Holland to meet Anneke and her husband Aart.

In the July of 1996, mum received a letter. It was informing her, that her super long distance pen pal from Australia, was visiting the U.K.

Edith and her husband Colin McDougal had retired from their enormous sheep farm in Australia.

It had been Colin's hobby, tracing his family tree and it had been his dream to meet some of his long distance family members, that were living in Scotland.

He had longed to visit the McDougal Clan.

Now that they had retired, they had the time and were planning a six month (almost) world tour.

As they were going to visit Scotland, they realised that Huddersfield is virtually next door, in the grand scheme of things. It would be the perfect opportunity for Edith and mum to actually meet.

They were coming to Huddersfield in the second week of August, they would be spending a week out of their tour in Huddersfield.

Back at home in Australia, Edith and Colin had been looking for accommodation for their mammoth trip.

For Huddersfield, they had been advised, to look on the Internet at The Croppers Arms pub at Marsh. It had been given some excellent reviews.

They liked the look of it, it was booked. A weeks stay at the Croppers Arms in Marsh, literally at the top of the road from mum and dads. It couldn't have been in better position for them.

The couple of Aussies arrived, it was an exciting time for mum.

An opportunity that she had never dreamed would come true, especially all those years ago when she had started writing.

Australia was literally at the other side of the world, it seemed like a whole lifetime away.

They met up, Edith, Colin, mum, dad and they all got on great. It was fantastic to see.

They had train trips to the Yorkshire Dales and went all over the place in the limited time that they had together.

Wendy and I met them a couple of times, in the evening and we all shared a meal at the Croppers Arms.

It was so nice to see mum and dad so happy.

When it was time for them to leave, I took them all to Huddersfield railway station. It was hard to see them saying their goodbyes, knowing that they would probably never meet again.

Little did we know.

That only two weeks later, dad would be very suddenly and cruelly taken away from us.

The worst possible news.

30th August 1996. The phone rang, it was early morning, I seem to remember that it was around half past five, I woke with such a start.

It was my sister Diane, dad had died suddenly.

He had been taken ill earlier in the morning, but wouldn't let mum call anyone. She wanted to get an ambulance, because his breathing was really poor, dad didn't want that. Mum had then rung my youngest sister Diane, at that time she lived just a couple of hundred yards away.

She was there in only a couple of minutes, they were both really worried, dad wouldn't let them ring me. So Diane had got the doctor out, (there's no chance of getting your own now).

It was his own doctor, Dr. Groves that came out, a lovely lady who was not far off from retiring. She straight away wanted to get dad to hospital, but that was the last place dad wanted to be and he told her so.

I raced across to Paddock, when I arrived, Dr. Groves was waiting for me, she had recognised a photo of me in the living room. She took me outside and explained to me. That dad had suffered from acute left ventricular failure. A sudden onset, resulting in severe shortage of breath. His lungs had then quickly filled up with fluid, due to his heart rapidly failing. The left ventricle in particular.

Even then, the ambulances carried some drugs, like frusemide. There were lots of things able to help, but that morning dad had been too ill for that. He had the sudden urge to open his bowels, a dangerous aspect of LVF, or any cardiac event for that matter.

He managed to get to the toilet, and more importantly for him, he got safely back into bed. He would have hated anything to happen on the toilet, he was very private man and very embarrassed over toilet functions.

Once safely back in bed, the doctor had again asked him to go to hospital, but he had still refused and he wouldn't let her "bother" me.

He told her that all he wanted, was to be "left alone" he just wanted to go to sleep.

She told me that that was exactly what he did, he went to sleep and he died.

I think that mum and Diane were disappointed that the doctor didn't try to resuscitate dad, by mouth to mouth or pounding on his chest.

I truly believe that the Doctor was right, she had respected dad's final wishes and she had done just what my dad had wanted.

In any case, as she had explained. All that would have happened, would have been to call my colleagues, they would then have had to stick drips in dad and fill him full of drugs.

Then to race him to hospital, possibly had to perform heart massage and maybe break a couple of ribs.

Dad wouldn't have wanted that.

The outcome would inevitably have still been the same. He might have had another hour, maybe two at the most.

He wanted to be "left alone", and he was.

He died peacefully in his own bed, mum, dad's only ever love and Diane were there with him at his side.

Dr. Groves gave my dad the dignity that he deserved in his last minutes, I will be eternally grateful for that.

I'm sure that mum, and my sisters Lindsay and Diane would agree now, now that they understand.

I will always respect her decision and I thank her for that, from the bottom of my heart!

It had been just two weeks since Edith and Colin had left for Scotland. I had to ring them while they were still there, with our sad news.

It was such a shock.

The blessing, was that dad hadn't suffered. He hadn't been physically ill for a long time, he had been frail, but he had been quite active.

The week with Edith and Colin, had brought a much deserved smile to both mum and dad. It was a privilege to see them both so happy together.

It had been a while.

We had been having a family joke trying to get a smile from dad. He had a permanent smile that week.

God Bless dad.

A slap across the face!

Not long after dad died, I was doing some work in the cellar for mum. I can't fully remember what I was actually doing, but I do remember the consequences.

Mum had never liked any bad language, ever and certainly not in her house. I would have been thirty eight years of age, I was nearly nearly forty, not a child.

I was smacking a stone chisel with a large and heavy lump hammer. I was really giving it some stick, when the inevitable happened. I hit my thumb on one of the strikes. Not only that, I trapped it between the hammer and the steel chisel.

It stung a little!

It had split the end of my thumb open all down the side of my nail and it was bleeding well to boot. The blood had run down my wrist as far as my elbow.

I ran upstairs, clenching my thumb tightly in my right hand to stop the bleeding. As I emerged into the kitchen, mum was there, she wasn't smiling as her usual self.

Before I had chance to show her what I had done, before I could say how much pain I was in.

Crack!

I was in even more pain. Mum had slapped me straight across my face, the force of the slap, almost knocked me to the floor. She said, "I don't want that sort of language in here".

To this day, I don't know what I said, but I can imagine.

Then, she helped me to sort myself out.

They always used to say, that you are never too big, to get a clout off your mother.

They, whoever they were, were absolutely right.

Ambulance Mates

Promotion to Station Officer

My Family

Colin Shackleton and me

Remembrance Day

Kaira

David Jason and Ben

Kacey

Mob-ability Ashraf

LEGOLAND BILLUND

Windmill Sunset

Joe McCafferty

Ben and Scott

What a mess

Longwood Sing

Laura, Willow, Adrian and Damian

Firthy's top knot

Oops

Some of my favourite animal pictures.

Photos

Top right & top middle: Photos Courtesy of The
Huddersfield Daily Examiner

Some favourite views

CHAPTER 48.

MURDER!

House fire, arson. "Little Jimmy".

Third of May 1997. It was early in the morning, just before five o'clock.
I was sat in the Station Office with my colleague of yet another night shift, Joseph, a relatively new member of staff at the time.

The tannoy sounded, which was unusual on a night shift. Due to the extremely loud klaxon noise it made. (We don't want to disturb the neighbours).

A voice message followed, "house fire, persons reported, Marsh". One of the worst things for any crew to hear. "Persons reported", is simply that, persons are reportedly inside/trapped.

I automatically looked out of the window, as we were already in Marsh and sure enough. From the window of the station office, I could see the smoke. A narrow, very black, plume of it. It was going straight up. There was no wind, and no deviation.

We raced to the address, I was driving, we were there in no more than a minute and a half. As I pulled up outside the address, there were no fire engines there.

I decided to pull up on the opposite side of the road, making sure that I didn't get blocked in by fire appliances when they did arrive. I had already planned my departure route.

From our position in the ambulance, I could see the front door of the house. I distinctly said to Joseph, "whatever happens, you don't go in there".

That fire was arson, even from where we had stopped. We could see that the PVC door had melted, leaving the handle almost suspended bizarrely in the air. You could also see that there were flames in the hallway, they were burning from up the walls, spreading down to the floor.

That wasn't a natural occurrence. Something had been sprayed or squirted in.

We ran across towards the house, the staircase was already black with a really thick acrid smoke crawling eerily down the steps.

Several people were outside in the street, one man shouted to us that "they've come out the back windows, there's three of 'em".

We ran with the man, down the passage between two of the terraced houses and around to the back. We were in a large communal area.

From there, we could see the state of the upstairs. The PVC window frames were warped and twisted, the glass had been broken and blackened by the flames.

On the floor, behind the houses, being comforted by neighbours. Was a woman, possibly in her thirties and two young girls of around twelve, or thirteen years of age.

267

The woman had some burns to her face and chest, she was covered in cuts from when she had smashed a window and she also had an ankle injury. Caused when she dropped from the first floor. The two girls were her daughters, they appeared to be reasonably okay, suffering with relatively minor injuries.

The woman told us that she had two nephews in the house and she didn't know where they were. She was hysterical, she had been trying to find them before being beaten back by the heat and flames. She had then smashed the window to get her daughters out, before jumping after them herself.

As I went around to the ambulance to get the carry chair for the woman, I again looked in at the front door. I could just about hear a faint crying. It was an eery awful sound, I could also hear sirens, where the hell were they? Usually the place is crawling with firemen, that day, we had arrived first.

I was so tempted to run upstairs. I had actually stepped forward to do so, when I felt the physical presence of someone grabbing hold of my belt to stop me. It really was strange, there wasn't anybody around, but it held me back, whatever or whoever it was.

The fire brigade arrived, the white helmet asked what we knew. I told him that there were two young boys still upstairs in the house, that I had just heard one of them and that we had three people who had jumped out of a back window, and that they were perfectly safe with us.

He straightaway detailed two of his lads with breathing apparatus, to go upstairs and find the missing boys, I returned to the back of the houses.

We wheeled mum, the daughters were able to walk. They were wrapped in blankets and supported by neighbours, back to the ambulance.

The mother was laid on the stretcher and the daughters were sat on the two remaining seats. Just as we were administering oxygen to all three of them, a man's voice shouted to us.

I looked up, it was a fireman. I stepped out of the ambulance, and he handed me a child, he was all floppy. "I don't think he's breathing!" He said. He was nine year old, I'll call him Neil.

I had to literally place him between his aunties legs, to be able to try and resuscitate him. Fortunately, it was only his upper airway that was full of soot and snot. I only had to sweep around the inside of his mouth with my fingers and use a suction unit, enough to clear his airway. It was only seconds, he started to cough.

That only took just a few seconds, but that cough was the sweetest sound to my ears! Just as Joseph fitted him with an oxygen mask. Neil said "I'm ok, I just need my brother".

Suddenly there was another shout, that shout was different. I jumped out of the back doors to see a fire officer with something in his arms. That was a shock, it was the other child, he had been wrapped in a blanket.

The man said to me that the child appeared to be dead. I had to have a quick check, he was right. Sadly, there was no doubt, his short life was over, there wasn't anything anyone could do for him.

He complied with the "yellow card". I couldn't tell the others.

I now know that it was the body of, I'll call him "little Jimmy".

My friend Alan, a long standing traffic police officer, came forward. He said "I'll take him with me".

We were the only ambulance present, we couldn't possibly have put little Jimmy in there with the others.

Setting off, with a pre alert for a trauma team to be ready. We made our two minute journey across to the hospital.

Staff were waiting for us, little Jimmy had already been transported by Alan in the police car.

We were then able to see in the clean environment of the resus room, the full extent of all our patients injuries. Other than those of little Jimmy. All the injuries that they had received, although some were serious and the smoke inhalation was very severe with all four of them. They were not life threatening.

In the days that followed, several stories of the events were passed around. The newspapers, the TV and word of mouth. All of the stories we heard were quite different from each other.

Even now, as I am writing this, the culprit for the proven arson attack has never been found. Despite the numerous appeals, evidence and items disclosed. The family are still no wiser, justice has still not been done.

I had my own personal suspicions not long after, about a young lad who had killed himself in Armley jail. He was as some described, "a bit simple".

About three months or so later, I met PC Alan, and he was telling me about it. He had also got a gut feeling, that the lad may have had something to do with little Jimmy's fire.

He was certainly known to be easily led by others, a few of the fires he had been caught for in the past, were the direct result of a dare by others unknown.

He liked to hang about to see the aftermath.

The fire that killed little Jimmy wasn't the lads MO, (Modus Operandi, or way of working). An occupied family property, just wasn't his style. He usually picked small, generally wooden structures. They would burn much better and much more quickly.

So why on earth would he have killed himself over such a small storage shed fire?

I, like Alan, do believe that he must have had something to hide. Did he have something to do with the fire at Marsh. I would really like it not to have been him.

My hope is that one day, the culprit could be caught and convicted, to bring some justice and closure for the family.

I personally, don't think that is going to happen though.

Alan, a wonderful man, died a few years after the fire. He had suffered from a short battle with cancer. As well as the cancer. I know that it had preyed on his mind for the rest of his life, that little Jimmy had died at the hands of some callous arsonist.

He never got over it.

I cannot take the hurt and despair away from the family. My next statement is not in any way trying to detract from their hurt. It is a true statement of fact.

It is not only the immediate family that are affected by that type of callous crime. All of the extended family, friends and neighbours. Yes, all of us, in all of the emergency services are very much affected by that type of incident.

It is very hard to come to terms with the fact, that another human being has carried out such a heinous act.

I was talking to my colleague Joseph recently, he still sees the face of little Jimmy on the journey to any house fire that he is sent to attend.

Never to be forgotten, "little Jimmy!"

Stress Relief.

I am sorry, for including the next story, but it is a fact of life. It involves my colleague Joseph.

It is what we do.

On a lighter note and following the tragic and unlawful stealing of a young life. It may not seem to appear appropriate to all. I cannot stress enough, that not one of us are making light of the job that we have just dealt with when it happens. It just happens. We would all end up in an asylum if we didn't.

After all, Ambulance staff are only human.

We would have to have some form of stress relief. Counselling, occupational health support, there are all manner of things available to us.

One of the ways that ambulance staff relieve stress, is to wind up, or play pranks on their colleagues.

I have to admit, that I have been one of the worst offenders for doing just that.

One that I remember well, was involving Joseph.

He was well known for going off on bike rides and not just five or six miles. Regularly, he would do fifty or sixty miles or more and that, following his eight hour shift.

We have ten and twelve hour shifts now.

I was one of the Station Officers at the time. One evening, as he left work at 17:00hrs. He told me that he was off out for a "good, long ride on his bike".

He hadn't been gone long, when his girlfriend of the time rang up to see where he was.

I told her of his plans with his bike, but she was very concerned that it was dark and he didn't have his lights with him. They were at home on the kitchen table.

I assured her that he would be fine, but to ring back if she became any more concerned.

When he arrived for work the following morning, I had my mischievous head on. I decided to try and wind him up a little, the results of which, went far better than I could have expected.

I asked him "why didn't you ring me when you got home?"

He hadn't a clue why.

I told him that his girlfriend had rung and that she had been worried about him.

I also told him, that I had asked her to get him to ring me when he arrived home and he hadn't.

The part of the rota's that I was working, meant that I finished work at 22:00hrs and had started again at 06:00hrs the next day. A good rest between them, eh.

He was mortified that she had rung, my plan was working.

I went on to say, that I had even had to put a missing persons report out on him, especially when she had told me that he didn't have any lights on his bike.

He had his head in his hands.

"I can't believe it" he repeated "I just can't believe that she rang" he continued, "she knew I had just bought some new ones".

I had him just where I wanted.

I told him that I had rung the local hospitals, that I had reported him as missing to the police and that all of our senior officers had also had to be informed.

Joseph went off to get himself a brew whilst he composed himself.

Just then, our divisional director arrived for work. At the time it was Stewart, another great bloke. He had worked "on the road" in Leeds.

He saw me in the office and instead of his usual "good morning". He looked at me and said. "What have you been up to?" He went on "you've got mischief written all over your face".

I told him what I had done to Joseph.

"Oh, that's a good one, I like that. Give me a couple of minutes and then fetch him upstairs will you? I wouldn't mind getting involved on this one".

He went up to his office, where he got Comms to send a message to his pager. They were before mobile phones. It was just to embarrass Joseph even further.

When I took Joseph upstairs, Stewart showed him the pager. He said "how do you explain this?" On his pager, it stated "Joseph, Huddersfield. Missing. Whereabouts unknown. Hospitals have been checked, and Police have been informed. Not rung in after arriving home, presumed still missing!"

Joseph nearly collapsed, he was so shocked. All he could say was "I'll kill her, I'll kill her when I get home. I'm so sorry", then he saw us. Stewart and I were helpless.

He called us "proper bastards!" Said with venom.

Joseph was young and naive at the time. He is a damn good and experienced paramedic now. Stewart apologised to Joseph, and then asked him if the prank had offended or upset him in any way.

Joseph answered. "Not at all, now, I really feel part of the Service".

That was exactly what it was meant to be, a bit of harmless fun.

It had been too good an opportunity to miss.

We've had a domestic argument.

One of the worst ever jobs I attended with Carl, was in May 2004.

It was for a "twenty four year old female, unrousable", that was the only information given by Comms.

We wrongly presumed, that at just after quarter past six, on a Sunday morning. That it would be as a result of her alcohol consumption on the Saturday night.

How wrong we were.

We were let into the house by a lady, possibly in her forties, she showed us upstairs to a small back bedroom. On the way upstairs, she told us that her son and his girlfriend had been having a domestic argument.

In the bedroom, a young female was laid on the floor, she was at the side of the bed.

She showed no signs of life whatsoever, there was no pulse, nor any attempt at breathing. At first glance, she appeared to us, as though she was already dead.

Apart from our patient, there was the lady who had let us in and a male sat on the edge of the single bed.

We knelt on the floor to assess his "girlfriend", he told us that her name was, I'll call her Diana. It was as we were fully assessing her, that the male stood up and he was looking down on us.

He was only average in height, maybe around five foot eight. But he was nineteen stone (we were told later), of pure muscle. He was dressed only in boxer shorts and he was glistening all over with sweat.

As he stood there his presence alone was intimidating. He was not threatening in any way.

He just kept asking if she would be ok. We attempted to resuscitate her, but to no avail. In our minds, we knew that our efforts were futile.

All we could say to him, was that we were doing our best. We both already knew that we needed to be wary of the job. It had become obvious very quickly that we were in the middle of a murder scene.

Her injuries were becoming more apparent.

They were horrendous.

The man said that they had been having an argument, a domestic dispute, but everything in the room was too neat and tidy.

Everything about the job was wrong, it was screaming out to us to get away, but what could we do?

It was murder, and no mistake!

How could we get help to us? without arousing his suspicion. I looked at Carl, he looked back at me. We had worked together for years, we both knew what we wanted, but how?

I had an idea, I desperately hoped it would work. I said to Carl, "I'll go and get the suction unit".

I knew we did not need a suction and so did Carl, his face was one of immediate relief. He knew that I was going for help, he didn't need to say anything.

I ran down the stairs ringing 999 from my mobile on the way.

I spoke to ambulance control, not the police, I needed speed. Ambulance Comms knew exactly where we were. I didn't need to say too much. Just that it was a murder scene, the murderer was still there and I needed help. Police, another crew, anybody!

And quick! Bloody quick!

The man had killed once, he might well want to do it again. He was still in there staring down at us.

If I had rung the police, I would have been tied up for ages, giving them thread to needle details, that alone would have aroused suspicion.

Call over, I grabbed the suction unit and went back in. Against our Comms instructions, they told me that under no circumstances was I to go back into the house and that was a "direct order"! (If a direct order is disobeyed, in normal circumstances, it could lead to dismissal. This was far from normal).

I couldn't leave Carl alone, we were mates.

Another ambulance crew arrived first, in minutes, two, maybe three at the most. Quickly followed by what appeared to be every police officer in Huddersfield.

The man was arrested and charged with murder.

The back up crew was Matthew and another Jack, formerly of Dewsbury station.

I had to go to Bradford Crown Court over that one, it was certainly not a pleasant experience.

The man himself had also stated (later in the proceedings, so I was informed by one of the police officers), in front of the courtroom. That if a female crew had been sent instead of us, he would have killed them on their arrival at the house

The Judge stated that the injuries that Diana had received, were much more consistent with those of a major traffic accident, than human intervention. The list of some her injuries was just far too explicit to put down here and too numerous to list them all.

I have since been made aware, via public news reports. That Diana had well over a hundred separate external injuries, as well as the multiple internal injuries.

Two examples. Her liver had been ruptured. The human body possesses 12 pairs of ribs, 24 in total. Diana had 38 individual rib fractures. Some of her ribs were in bits.

During the trial. The members of the jury, the barristers, the prosecution, the defence teams and me. Had all been given an evidence book. It was a ring binder completely full of evidence photographs. Each page had a large tag on it clearly marked with a number.

At certain parts of the proceedings, we were asked to turn to a specific page and that page only. We had not to look at any of the others in between.

Those photo's were of a very graphic nature and some of them even included details and images, of Diana's post mortem examination.

At the start of my questioning, I had to look at a photograph of the room, it had been taken from the doorway.

Diana's body, was still laid there on the floor. Apparently I was taken aback at that first photo and paused for a couple of seconds before looking back up to face the jury.

Even the Judge said to everyone in the room. "Ladies and gentlemen, as you were told at the beginning of this trial, some of the exhibits are very disturbing. As you have just seen, Mr. Firth, a medic of some long years experience was shocked by that. The first of many. Please be aware".

It was because I was then looking at the situation in the cold light of day, I didn't have anything to do, other than look. It seemed very harsh and cold somehow.

The man who was 27 years old, was unanimously convicted of murder by the jury. They were only out of court, in deliberation for less than four hours. He was sentenced to a minimum of 17 years and 127 days.

I remember reading in the papers, that the judge had told him that he would be in his late forties before he would even be able to apply for parole.

Not much of a consolation for Diana's family, but justice had been served.

Surgical Emphysema.

As well as the murder of Diana, I have been to one or two other murder situations and some attempted murders.

Here is the story of an attempted murder that sticks out in my mind. I attended to it in 2009, when I was acting as Operational Supervisor for Kirklees and Calderdale.

When we are working as an ambulance crew and even more so as a lone responder. We need our Comms to glean as much information as possible from the caller. When an incident involves assault, violence, self harm etc. Our own safety is of paramount importance.

The job came in as an apparently straight forward asthma patient, with difficulty in breathing. His girlfriend was with him trying to help.

It was near to Newsome. I was about a mile away, in Lockwood, on my way back from Honley Station. I had no hesitation about attending the job on my own.

I was there within three minutes, the girlfriend, around thirty something, invited me in to a ground floor flat. In the corner sat on the floor was a young male, who she described as "her toyboy", as he was only twenty five.

As he was knelt on the floor, he was gasping for breath. It was strange, for someone with asthma, he had no wheeze. But he was rocking backwards and forwards trying to force air into his lungs. His oxygen percentage had reduced to less than 60%. He was cyanosed (going blue).

I placed a 100% oxygen mask on him, then tried to listen to his chest with my stethoscope.

It was serious, he had no air movement in his left lung at all. His lung may have collapsed, his right side sounded ok.

On top of that, he also had developed another major, life threatening condition.

One that I had only heard about. I had been told many times, in training school, but I had never actually come across one. From there description, there was no doubt in my mind.

That it was surgical emphysema and it was widespread!

Just as I was about to ask for the location of my back up crew, they arrived, it was Gill and Charles from Halifax.

As I was verbally handing over to Gill. I saw a small spot of blood on our patient's tee shirt. It was only a spot, I took his shirt off.

He had two more spots. One was in the natural dip near his left collar bone, that one was bubbling. The other two were near his left kidney, those were just little spots of blood, but were starting to bruise around the centre.

It was then obvious, he had been stabbed!

I asked his girlfriend what had happened.

She just said that her boyfriend had been out to the shop and that he had run into the flat gasping for breath. Just like he was when I arrived. She said that she had just presumed he was having an asthma attack.

I explained that he had been stabbed, by something with a very slim blade, she claimed that she knew nothing about it. I immediately called for the police.

Then the crew had to make an emergency dash to the awaiting trauma team at HRI. I rushed along and followed them, in my Land Rover discovery. I took the girlfriend with me.

As the crew were unloading the stretcher with the patient, I ushered the girlfriend into the relatives room to await the police.

She became upset and agitated, I thought that it was the shock and upset at hearing of her boyfriends injuries.

She suddenly jumped up and ran towards me, she pushed past and was running out of the department.

As she pushed past me, a long thin, pointed "Phillips" screwdriver fell out of her coat. It had blood along the shaft. I kicked it back into the relatives room and then virtually rugby tackled her to the ground.

At that moment, the police arrived.

They were a bit shocked, that I was wrestling with the now screaming banshee on the floor.

They helped her up, as I was explaining the situation. She then admitted straight away that it was her that had stabbed her boyfriend.

She apparently had given him money to get some cider, but instead, he had spent it on and smoked some cannabis.

The weapon was now on the floor of the relatives room. The shaft of the screwdriver was fourteen inches long, but only about three sixteenths of an inch, about four millimetres thick/diameter.

The wounds to his kidney area were only superficial, the one in his shoulder had gone right to the full depth of the shaft. It had fully penetrated his right lung, causing a total collapse.

Air was also bubbling out into the tissues causing the widespread surgical emphysema.

They had told me at training school that if you came across that type of injury and then felt the skin of a patient who had developed the condition, it would be like scrunching a packet of crisps.

It wasn't a bad description.

My own take on it though, I would describe it as putting the flat of your hand into a bowl of rice crispies, without any milk and pressing down. There was absolutely no doubt though, what condition had developed.

In A&E he had a drain fitted immediately into his chest wall, that would drain any blood and let any air out. Hopefully that would allow the collapsed lung to re-inflate.

It certainly did.

He was then rushed into the operating theatre. There they could try and sort out the damage to his chest and his other injuries could be looked at more thoroughly.

He was seriously ill, but due to the timescale. He was operated on early and would survive without too many problems, other than the mass of scars from his operation.

I had been on my own, in a vehicle with a crazy woman, with a screwdriver in her pocket. One that she had already stabbed someone with.

It's a good thing to be blissfully unaware at times.

A Brutal Axe Murder.

It was the 23rd May 2001. Another memorable murder in the Huddersfield area, was attended by a Honley crew. It was nothing to do with me, but the story was well told around the local area.

I think you'll find it interesting.

It involved a horrendous murder that reached all the national and international news and newspapers. It could have been anyone of the crews in our area who had been called to attend. I felt it suitable to be included in my book.

Aiden and Annette from Honley, were called to an address not far from Flockton. Fairly close to the New Hall women's prison. It was to a very large, mansion sized house, a new property.

There, they met a woman I'll call Judith and her three year old daughter, they were both screaming hysterically. Upstairs inside the house, in the bedroom, the woman's boyfriend was dead. He had been brutally murdered, actually, he had been executed.

He was totally naked and blindfolded. He had been gagged, handcuffed at the wrists and his feet were bound with tape.

He had then suffered twenty heavy blows from a felling axe, (for tree felling, not a small wood chopper). When he was found, the axe was still embedded in his head.

The woman had come home from picking her daughter up from school, picked some bags up and was then waiting for her daughter's daddy to collect her for the weekend. Before leaving, Judith had sent her daughter upstairs to say goodbye to her partner.

The three year old daughter had found the gruesome sight. Obviously she screamed for her mummy and neither of them had stopped screaming since. Both Annette and Aiden were sat with mum and daughter in the ambulance. They were trying in vain, to console them a little, whilst waiting for the police.

They had got the doors of the ambulance, all locked and secure, after all, nobody knew the whereabouts of the assailant.

The police arrived and they took over the crime scene. The crew accompanied by a female police officer, took both of their screaming and shocked patients to the hospital, following their traumatic ordeal.

It was ages before the full story came out, but it turned out, that it was the little girls mum Judith. She was the one, who had meticulously planned and committed that most gruesome of murders.

To gain some form of warped credence to her story, she had deliberately sent her daughter upstairs to discover him.

How could she do that? Her own daughter! A child!

The story unfolded, that the couple liked to engage in some strange sexual games. Involving blindfolds, handcuffs, whips and other items. As well as involving many other people in their games.

They were active members of an apparently very large local swingers organisation and they were well known for their "dogging and piking activities". (Dogging, so I have been informed, is the act of having sexual activity publicly outdoors and piking is the act of going to watch the others performing).

The man had apparently been seeing someone else from the group, for his own private sessions. His girlfriend Judith, was having none of it.

She said in her statements that he had readily agreed to some bedroom activities, for just the two of them, before she had picked her daughter up from school.

That was how she had planned it, she lured him to his death. She had him where she wanted him. The axe had been placed in the bedroom by Judith some time earlier. She then used it to rain down the blows on her lover.

She calmly went to have a shower, where she had got rid of any incriminating evidence, or so she thought. Her daughter was out of the way at school while the murder was taking place. Judith then went to school to pick her daughter up.

Judith May have had a shower, but she hadn't flushed enough of the evidence away. Apparently there was lots of blood and trace evidence still in the drains, even several days after the killing.

The young daughter lost the two people who looked after her. She will also have life long images of her mothers partner, and the way that she had found him.

Neither Annette nor Aiden had any inkling of the woman's guilt, they were just as shocked as anyone else, when the truth came out.

They can laugh about it now, the day they were cozily cuddled up in the back of an ambulance, with a mad axe murderer!

It emerged in media reports, that the lover had threatened to kill the little girl and he had stated to Judith that he had killed children before.

That was it.

Enough was enough, as well as his extra curricular activities and his extremely violent and controlling behaviour towards Judith, his time was up.

Judith was convicted of manslaughter on the grounds of provocation, not murder. She was sentenced to five years in prison. That sentence, was reduced to three and a half years, after appeal.

Ironically the house that she shared with her lover, can be seen from New Hall Prison where she served her time on remand. She actually only served eighteen months, that's less than half of her sentence.

Murder. It's a small world.

On the 22nd of September 1990. I was asked by a friend, to photograph his best friends wedding. The wedding was of a local couple, I'll call them Linda and Dan of Slaithwaite.

At the time, as had been expected, it was a large family gathering. A brilliant day. Who would have thought then, on such a happy occasion what was to become in the future.

It was to be seventeen years later, almost to the day, that we would meet again. In fact, it was just one day after their 17th wedding anniversary. It was the 23rd of September 2007.

The couple had been going through a lot of difficulties and had separated only a few months before.

Over the years, the couple had three children together, I'll call them Sally aged 16, she was away for the weekend on a camping trip. Sarah aged fourteen and then there was Bobby, he had just turned four.

He had been spending the weekend with his dad, at the other end of the village.

Sarah had called round at her dad's place as planned. It was Sunday lunchtime, to collect her little brother, to take him back home to mum.

When she had arrived at her dad's, (she told us later), that her dad was in a strange mood, she was a little frightened of him.

He had suddenly picked up a large kitchen knife and began to stab his young daughter repeatedly. It was a frenzied attack, which resulted in Sarah receiving more than twenty, severe stab wounds. To her face, chest, abdomen and thigh. He also took a chunk out of her arm.

Despite her devastating injuries, Sarah had managed to escape her fathers evil clutches and had run almost the full length of the street to get help, to a local shop.

From there, a frantic 999 call was made. During the 999 call, details initially were extremely sketchy, there was a lot of panic and screaming around.

There was a short delay as is usual to determine safety, the location of the assailant etc. but an ambulance was sent. Whilst still on the call, the call taker thought that she heard the girl in the distance cry something about another child.

That information, was brought to the attention of our Comms Team Leader Theresa. A second ambulance was then sent to the scene, and that crew, was Carl and me. Along with William, then our Operational Supervisor.

Graham a paramedic and newly qualified technician Annie (now a newly qualified paramedic), were already in attendance. They were assessing and treating Sarah for her life threatening injuries. When they heard that there may be another child involved.

They asked Sarah, she was able to tell them of Bobby and his whereabouts. At the same time, the police confirmed that there was another child and that they were already in attendance at the scene of the attack.

Graham ran down to the other end of the road, he had to leave Annie on her own with Sarah.

When Carl and I arrived on scene, we stopped and quickly assessed the situation. I dropped Carl off to help Annie with Sarah. Then I drove up the road to assist Graham with Bobby.

When I ran into the house, Graham was on his knees using a bag and mask to breathe for Bobby. A police officer, was performing cardiac massage.

Blood was everywhere.

The only solution at that stage, was to scoop and run. Both Graham and the policeman, got into the ambulance with Bobby. I rang through to the HRI, and asked for a full trauma team on standby, giving a brief outline of the incident and severity.

As we raced through the streets, lights and sirens blazing, we had a police car escort in front of us. Annie and Carl with Sarah, were very close behind us.

On arrival at the hospital, all the staff were waiting. I picked Bobby up in my arms and ran straight into the hospital. Just inside the doors, on the outside of the resus room, were two highly distraught women. It was Bobby's mum Linda and her mum, little Bobby's grandma. I recognised them straight away from the wedding.

It hit me then who we had been dealing with. I couldn't believe that any dad could hurt his own children, let alone someone I knew.

The nurses, doctors and consultants worked on little Bobby's badly injured body for over an hour to try and save his life.

He had received nine forceful stab wounds, poor little mite was bleeding like a bloody collander, but only when the CPR was taking place.

He had to be pronounced dead, there was nothing more that anybody could have done for him.

The whole of the A&E department was silent, in the ever full waiting room you could sense the atmosphere. Even the patient's suffering from minor injuries or illnesses, realised that they were going to be sat there for a long time.

Those that could, left and went home, or elsewhere.

The whole place was full of police, trying to locate where Dan might be.

In the next bay to Bobby in resus, they were trying desperately to save Sarah's life. She was stabilised and then sent straight to the operating theatre. Several operations and a lot of treatment later, Sarah had managed to survive from her physical injuries.

How could she, or any other members of her family ever fully recover from it though?.

We as emergency services and the hospital staff, suffer greatly on those jobs, after all we are human beings with families of our own.

The man upstairs in the house was the man that owned the property, not Dan. Dan had just been staying there, he had only been renting a room from him.

At the time, the house owner had had no idea what had happened, he was just as frightened himself. After hearing all the noise and waking up to armed police in his bedroom. Then seeing the state of his home as he was led out by the police.

Following the incident, Dan had walked out and had simply gone down to a local pub, where he had a pint and then he had confessed all to a mate.

He was arrested in the pub, it was about an hour later.

On a normal Sunday lunchtime, Sally would have accompanied her sister Sarah, to fetch Bobby back to their home. She had gone away for the weekend.

Would her dad have attacked them both? Probably.

He didn't know that she wasn't coming until Sarah arrived on her own.

Eventually following court proceedings, he was found guilty of the brutal murder of his own son and the attempted murder of his daughter. He was sentenced to serve 21 years before parole would be even eligible.

All that to pay back his wife Linda, for an affair that she had allegedly had.

What a bastard!

CHAPTER 49.

_____

SPECIAL TIMES, SPECIAL MEANINGS.

Pride in Huddersfield Awards.

It was February 1999, Huddersfield Examiner was to hold its first annual community, Pride in Huddersfield Awards.

I had been nominated to represent the Ambulance Service, for the Emergency Services person of the year category, by one of my colleagues. I never found out who.

It was at the end of March, that I was told that I had been shortlisted for the award. There was a piece in the Huddersfield Examiner about each of the shortlisted nominees and a photo. A chance for everyone to vote for their favourite.

The final was to be held in the conference suite at Huddersfield Town's McAlpine Stadium. (John Smith's Stadium now).

It was a plush affair with dozens of people with their families all competing for several categories.

The master of ceremonies was ex Huddersfield Town player Steve Kindon. He was being assisted by Paul Clarke of the Huddersfield Daily Examiner.

I had been nominated mainly for my out of hours activities. Charity work, community events, public speaking etc. On the night Wendy and my mum were there as my supporters.

When our category was announced, all that Paul spoke of was an incident that had happened outside the Examiner offices in Queen Street South. One that I had attended with Carl, Ray and Danny. Paul had been there and done the original report on the incident.

That wasn't the community events that I had been nominated for, they weren't even given a mention.

As they read out each of the citations, the nominee had to stand and a spotlight was upon them.

Each category had three shortlisted. The winner of ours was announced, it was a Police Officer.

He had won, because he had done a lot of community and voluntary work.

Surprise surprise.

Never mind, well done him. I knew him well, actually. Joking apart, he was a good lad and did do a lot in his own time. At least I wasn't runner up to a bloody water fairy.

I would have died!

Tragedy outside Huddersfield Examiner Offices.

The incident that had been referred to at the awards evening, had happened a couple of years earlier. Two crews had been sent to an accident on Queen Street South in Huddersfield. It was a construction site, occupying most of the road outside the former Huddersfield Examiner Office.

The site seemed to be there forever, it must have been for at least twelve months.

In the middle of the site was a hole in the road. The hole was around twelve foot in diameter and thirty foot deep. Two men, a large pump, and a small digger were in the bottom of the hole.

As the workers were digging down, they were fastening a steel framework around the walls for support.

That involved a crane operator lowering some steel arched blocks that were linked and bolted in to place. He was lowering them down two at a time. Each weighed in at around fifty six pounds, that's nearly twenty five and a half kilograms.

The bottom of the hole had the compressor pump, because as they dug down it was gradually filling up, with dirty muddy water from the canal.

It was on one of the many block deliveries, that tragedy struck. Both of the blocks had dropped off the link and down into the hole. Like I mentioned, it was around thirty foot deep.

The two men had been hit by the blocks and had both been knocked unconscious.

To get us into the hole, a cage had been linked onto the crane, it was around four feet square and with a doorway/gate at one side.

Ray went down first with a fireman, to assess the situation. Both for the men involved and for the safety of the rest of us.

Then Ray needed someone else from the ambulance service to assist him. Danny hated lifts of any kind, I don't have much of a head for heights, so Carl was going to go.

I felt that I had to step in, it was pointless for both paramedics to go down there. When the first patient was out, he would have had to come out and travel with the patient.

I wasn't over happy, but at times, needs must.

I went down in the cage, it was very bizarre. It was very cramped down at the bottom of the hole. By then, both men had regained consciousness, one had a very severe looking head injury.

He had been wearing a builders protective hard hat.

As the block had hit him, the plastic strapping that supports the helmet, had sliced into his scalp and opened it right up into four separate flaps. It was rather like an open envelope. All scalp wounds bleed profusely, that one was no exception.

The other chap appeared to be paralysed, he had no feeling in his legs whatsoever. The block had hit him on the shoulder and knocked him sideways. We had to suspect a broken neck.

As a full precaution, due to how their injuries had occurred, (mechanism of injury). Both men had to be fastened onto spinal boards, with their head and neck immobilised with a collar.

The man with the head injury was to be extricated first, purely on a location point of view and to make more space to deal with his badly injured colleague. Once on the board, the cage was lowered and he had to be placed into the cage.

He needed to be kept flat, I went into the cage. Ray and I slid the board and the man, in as far as it would go, but about three foot of it was left stuck out of the gate. I had to hold onto a rope attached to the foot end to stop any movement or sliding. Then the patient and me, were slowly winched out of the hole. Ray stayed down at the bottom with the second man.

When we got to ground level, my nightmare scenario opened up even further before me.

To gain better access, the ambulance had been moved to the other side of the road. Instead of just emerging at ground level, I had to be raised up another fifteen or twenty feet, to get over all the construction equipment and swung across the road. Before being lowered to Carl and Danny and an awaiting stretcher.

I then went back into the cage to go for the second patient. Carl teamed up with Danny and they transported the first patient up to HRI.

Prior to leaving, they had got the other stretcher out of the second ambulance ready for my return. They passed me the second spinal board, I was ready, and off they went into the distance, as I went back up in the air.

At the bottom of the hole, the conditions were horrendous. We were both standing in above knee depth, of mucky and stagnant water. Ray was having to shout for "pump on", to clear the water. Then "pump off", to be able to listen with his stethoscope, for lung sounds and to take the patient's blood pressure.

It was most unnatural for the pair of us. Eventually we got the second man into the cage in a similar fashion. Ray and myself accompanied him, again holding onto the board using a rope.

Once in the ambulance, off we went. Me driving at speed to HRI under blue light conditions, to waiting staff in the resus room.

We were soaked to the skin and stinking of the stagnant water, when we wheeled him in.

The first patient had got away with minor injuries really. No broken bones, but had nasty lacerations to his scalp. A good seamstress was all he required to sew him back together. Other than scarring and cosmetic damage, he would be fine physically. Mental scarring of the incident may be more damaging.

The second man, was not so lucky, he did have a serious spinal injury. It was a badly broken neck and he was left wheelchair bound following the incident.

Careful and professional handling by us, prevented any further damage occurring from his spinal injury.

Oddly enough, my colleague Ray was also nominated for one of the Huddersfield Examiner Awards. It was about six years later, his citation also revolved heavily around the same job.

Ray won the award that year. To everyone's surprise, the people from the Huddersfield Examiner, had been doing their research. They managed to seek out the patient with the spinal injury and it was he, who came up on stage in his wheelchair and had the honour of presenting Ray with his award.

Yet another lump in the throat moment!

But, what a pleasant surprise. Well done "Ray".

Ambulance Technician of the year.

2005 saw the last of the WYMAS awards evenings. I had been nominated for the Emergency Medical Technician of the year, by my manager Bobby.

Wendy and I were invited to a swanky dinner at the Cedar Court hotel in Bradford. I had been shortlisted for the award.

The dress code, was a full dinner suit with bow tie for me and a posh frock for Wendy. We had booked a room to stay the night at the Cedar Court, following the presentations.

We were sat down for a full five course evening meal.

At our table apart from Wendy and myself, were. Bobby, my manager at Huddersfield. Janet, the manager at Halifax. Edward, assistant manager to both. Steven, training and development manager. June, our sub divisional admin assistant. Janice and her husband, she was from our resource office, she had been nominated as Support Assistant of the year by Janet and Steven.

Before the meal, ex Leeds United footballer Eddie Gray, did a speech regarding how proud he was to be there etc. Then between each course of the meal, he presented one of the award categories.

After the presentations were concluded, he did his full after dinner sportsman routine.

He was very interesting, if you had a liking for football that is. If you weren't interested in football, his speech must have been like having toothache, it went on and on.

I had been nominated in the category for Emergency Medical Technician of the Year.

After the shortlisting process, I was up against one other EMT from Leeds, I didn't know her at all. The third on the shortlist, was my old mate Neville from Dewsbury.

I pipped them both to the post on the night, and I won.

I was awarded with a presentation certificate and a wooden plinth with a brass coloured plaque, saying that it had been awarded to the Emergency Medical Technician of the Year 2005. Also mounted on the plinth was a £4.99 Corgi die cast model of a British ambulance.

Wendy was having a rough time through the meal, she was suffering, absolutely full of cold. Following the meal, Wendy made her excuses and went to bed early, ish.

The beer flowed well that night.

Not only of 2005, as those awards have not been held since. I suppose I am still the reigning Emergency Medical Technician of the Year. In my dreams anyway.

Medals and Long Service Awards.

I have been presented with three medals since I started working for the ambulance service.

Two were given out at station level. They were celebration medals of the Queen's Golden Jubilee in 2002 and the Queens Diamond Jubilee in 2012. They were presented, to celebrate her 50 and 60 years as our serving monarch.

They were awarded to members of all of the Armed Services and for members of the three Emergency Services.

The medal was also awarded to the Lifeboat crews, the Coast Guards and members of Mountain Rescue Teams.

The medals were awarded only to staff with a minimum of seven years service on the front line of the Emergency Services. The support staff, PTS, and control room staff, they were given a presentation boxed commemorative "coin".

In the year 2002, I was also presented with my Long Service and Exemplary Conduct medal. As it says on it, for twenty years service on the front line 999 ambulances, with an exemplary conduct record.

That was a more formal presentation, I don't know why, but it was held at the Fire Service Headquarters at Birkenshaw. Only a couple of hundred yards from our own headquarters.

Never mind! It was a lovely evening for Wendy and me.

I have three other medals that I can wear. They are commemorative items, rather than awards. One is the Association Of Chief Ambulance Officer's medal for long service, given for twenty years service. That was replaced by the Long Service and Exemplary Conduct award, but it is still an entitlement.

I also have the International Emergency Services Medal, and International Ambulance and Medics Medal. There is another, usually given by colleagues, on retirement. That is the Ambulance Medal, I might be getting that sooner than I had originally planned.

It used to be classed as a big thing when working for WYMAS, to achieve thirty years service. It was properly celebrated with an award, in the form of a gift.

The gift, to be chosen by the individual from a catalogue. All gifts/items were worth around £300.

You could get a gold watch, all engraved. A piece of art. You could have a wall clock, or maybe a barometer. There were all sorts of items to chose from.

You would then be invited, along with a partner, it was usually to our own headquarters at Birkenshaw. They would hold the presentations once a year.

Presentations also took place of the twenty year long service and exemplary conduct medal and any other awards were given out.

There would be a couple of slide show presentations and then a meal followed by the presentation of awards.

It became known via the grapevine, that when we had the merger/takeover with the rest of Yorkshire, the thirty year award was to be scrapped.

Not surprising with the way the ambulance service seemed to be heading.

Anyway, some wise guy found out that if we applied before the merger, we could get a financial award of £100 per ten years of service.

Better in our pocket than theirs!

I had twenty four years in, so I duly applied. Yes I could receive £200 for my twenty completed years. It was made fact that no cash could be paid, but a cheque direct to a company would be perfectly acceptable.

Wendy and me shopped around for some ideas, Until we settled on the idea of a gas fire, but one with a coal burning effect. We used Artisan in Brighouse.

We chose the fire that we wanted, from their showroom display. Then they came to survey our property and found that we needed a new lining to the existing chimney. It was all ordered and arranged.

When it came to payment, I explained the situation to them, no problems at all.

We rang our finance department at WYMAS from their office in Brighouse.

Then, because the total bill was for over the £200 they paid with a direct bank transfer, there and then. We just had to pay the balance. Once we had all the completed paperwork, I just had to forward it on to headquarters. The receipt was copied and all was returned back to us.

Sure enough, as soon as the merger happened. The £300 presentation, was as expected, discontinued.

I was invited to a presentation of my thirty years service award at Nostell Priory near Wakefield.

Wendy and me went to the swanky do in the Priory courtyard function rooms. We had wonderful food, plenty drink was freely available. I had to stick to one and then go on to tea or coffee, due to me driving.

There were a couple of speeches from our Chief Executive David Whiting and our Chairman Della Canning. That was then followed by the Lord Lieutenant of West Yorkshire. He is Her Majesty the Queen's representative. He did a speech and then he got on with presenting some twenty year medals.

Then there were further presentations. Our thirty year long service award, a few forty year long service awards and finally some awards for staff who had retired in the past twelve months.

My award, a certificate and a boxed and engraved Parker pen. Engraved with "30 years service for the Yorkshire Ambulance Service", but not personalised in any way.

For forty years, the staff got a cut crystal ball. Fancy cut with a flat bottom with the ambulance crest and "celebrating 40 years". Again not even with your name on it.

I just thought what skinflints the YAS were.

A good job we heard about the abolishment of the £300 in time. At least I got my fire and a £200 bonus towards it!

CHAPTER 50.

A TRYING TIME.

Wendy's fortieth birthday.

I decided to organise a surprise party for Wendy's fortieth birthday. It was going to be held at the Warren House pub on Manchester Road, at my local.
Joe and Tina the licensee's were more than happy to help me out. They would even sort out the catering for us, no disco, just a gathering of family and friends.

I also decided that as a present for the occasion, the eternity ring that Wendy had been wanting, would be the perfect solution. We went to JPB jewellers on Half Moon Street in Huddersfield.

Wendy had seen just what she wanted, but, they would have to make it for us. I had designed Wendy's wedding ring, and JPB's had made it out of platinum for her. It was based on a knot that I used to tie using string, or if I felt adventurous from rope. It was known as a "turks head". The eternity ring would again be platinum and set with "princess" cut diamonds into the front third of the ring.

Perfect.

On the very day of the party Saturday the 25th of September, the day before Wendy's actual birthday, everything that could go wrong, was going wrong.

The jeweller rang, the ring wasn't finished, he knew about the party, but all he could do was to apologise. The caterer had double booked us, so there was going to be no food. It looked as though it was going to be a complete disaster.

Not to worry too much though, looking on the bright side. There was going to be plenty of people there, it was good beer, we would have a good night whatever.

Wendy and me arrived at the pub as planned, at eight, the guests had been told seven forty five. The place was full of family, friends and work colleagues, Wendy was well chuffed.

Not only that.

Tina the landlady, her partner Joe and his sister Tracy. They had provided us with a brilliant array of food in the back room.

They wouldn't charge me for it either, "consider it a present for a good customer" Tina said. "Look at all the extra customers that have come in, it's the least we could do".

At quarter past eight the jeweller rang me, he was outside. The ring was finished and he had delivered it in person.

I bought him a pint, there's not many jewellers that I know, but he really earned that pint .

A perfect result, for a perfect evening. That night, we both went home very happy. I was so relieved that everything had turned around from earlier, and had all gone to plan. Oh what a night!

Stress, what stress?.

I woke up in the early hours of the morning following Wendy's party, it was her actual birthday. But I felt lost, I had no idea what was going on, all I could do was cry. I felt like a child, frightened and so far from home, but I was sat on my own bedroom floor!

It turned out that I was suffering a nervous breakdown.

I was given six weeks off work, I daren't set foot out of the house. I was in a right mess for a long while. My GP and the medication were helping, but only a little.

The best help of all though, came from a very unexpected source. A bloke that used to frequent the Warren House, he was called Pete. He was a Health and Safety Inspector for building sites.

My only connection with him, was that he had border collie dogs.

He saw me at our window a few times as he was passing on his way for a drink. He knew that it was unusual for me not to be attending at the Warren House. Some people had been starting to talk, they were wondering if I was ok.

He called at our house, he said that he could see that I wasn't well. He offered to help. He then told me, he didn't ask, he told me. That I was going on to the pub with him for a pint.

Just the one, he said. It would do me good.

It did, it was great. He spoke to me like a human being. Over the next few weeks, Pete and his wife Sally, would spend an hour or two every week with me.

That really helped. An acquaintance, not too close. Not a professional, and most of all, not one of the family. I needed to download to someone, my family had enough issues.

Carl my regular mate, as usual, was a tower of strength.

I eventually recovered. It was bloody awful, I don't ever want to go through anything like that again.

Most people who have a breakdown, go through one due to too much stress. Trust me to be different.

With the sequence of events changing for the party, all of my stress had vanished. I had nothing to be stressed or worried about, so I just lost it!!!

Typical Firth.

CHAPTER 51.

MORE EVENTS WITH CARL.

Do you know who I am?

In 2001. I was working again with Carl, we had been sent on a non-emergency call for an elderly lady.

It was to pick up a patient being admitted to the medical assessment unit (MAU), at HRI. She had received a home visit from her GP and he had thought that she needed admission for further investigations, regarding a possible infection.

Unfortunately for her, at the time that we had gone for her, there weren't any empty beds on the MAU. We were due to take her in to the A&E.

She would then be moved up and onto the ward, as, when and if, a bed became available.

There was a carer on scene at the house with her, she was very worried and concerned. She told us that the patient always had large amounts of cash and that it would be hidden all around the house.

The lady patient, was quite open about it and told us where all the money was. It was in drawers and cupboards upstairs and downstairs. Between us, we had collected a large amount of cash.

We placed all the money on the dining table and counted it, all four of us together. There was well over £7,000. We then put the money in a large envelope and all of us signed it, across the seal.

That was the patient, her carer, Carl and me.

In the ambulance on the way to hospital, the lady confided in me. She said that no matter what happened, she did not want her son having any of it, the money that was. She went on to say, that although he was her executor and that he ran all of her affairs, he always took every penny that she had. "As soon as he gets chance, he takes everything".

I assured her that under no circumstances whatsoever, would he get his hands on her money, if she didn't want him to. There was no doubt in my mind, that the lady, was of sound mind and had the full mental capacity to make that decision.

We, by law, have to abide by her wishes.

On arrival at the hospital, I handed the money straight to the nursing staff, with the same instructions that I had been given. A lady from the HRI General Office came down and the money was counted again. The office lady issued a receipt and handed that to the patient. The money would then be placed in the hospital safe, until the lady was discharged from the hospital.

She had been fully informed of those actions and was more than happy with the situation.

As I walked out of the cubicle and into the corridor, I saw a very smartly dressed man in a suit.

He asked if It was me that had brought his mother in to hospital. When I confirmed that I had, he held his hand out towards me and said "I believe that my mother had rather a lot of money with her when she arrived. I'll take that now".

I told him of her request and that due to his mother's mental state. I legally had no option but to honour her request and he would not be getting a penny of it.

He then very slyly said, "do you know who I am?"

I then answered, "yes, I certainly do. (I called him by his full name and title) But you still cannot have the money, I am sorry".

I don't know why I said that I was sorry, but that is just me.

He then said in a really condescending tone, "congratulations, I am impressed. I really thought that you would have given it to me. I would then have reported you".

He held out his hand for me to shake.

I looked at him with the look that I had learnt from my old mate Tommy and then, very proud of myself, I must admit. I just said "No thank you, I would prefer not to shake your hand".

I turned my back on him and I walked away.

His face was a picture.

That man, had been a well known personality on television, in the news and in big business circles. He had been working for the government in a high profile advisory capacity as well.

Clever bugger if you ask me, I took an instant dislike to him.

I told his mother what had happened, she laughed and she said that she was very grateful for what we had done.

Funny or what?

Carl and I attended many funny jobs over the years. One night shift, early in the morning, we attended to this one.

It was four thirty in the morning, the call was to attend to an elderly female having some kind of urinary problems.

The second page of our data dispatch system stated that, "every time she tried to sit up, she was passing urine". It sounded to be more of a district nurses job than an emergency ambulance one, to us.

The police had also been called to attend, to gain entry for us into the property.

Fortunately though, after shouting through the letter box. We managed to get the telephone number of a nearby neighbour, who was a key holder.

That would save any damage being caused.

Once we had got inside. Carl went upstairs, he had already heard a voice in the back bedroom, he stepped inside the room. Then he immediately came back out again, displaying the wonderful childish grin that he had perfected. It was one of pure mischief. He beckoned me to go upstairs, he whispered "you've got to see this".

The old lady had hurt her back a few days before and she had been sleeping in the back room, so as not to disturb her husband.

She had woken in the night, with a need to go to the toilet. But due to the pain, she couldn't get out of bed.

She had called out to her husband for assistance. He had come in from the front bedroom, but as he had tried to help his stricken wife to sit up, his back had also gone into spasm.

He was then laid across his wife at around 45 degrees. They looked like some bizarre form of a human starfish. Each time he tried to get up, he was pressing hard onto his wife's abdomen, it already contained a very full bladder. Each time he pushed to get himself up, the inevitable happened.

Although the couple were in obvious distress, for us and our black humour, it was priceless. The childish side of us only lasted seconds.

With our professional head screwed firmly back on, we went to work.

We sorted them both out, we managed to get the old gentleman back to his bed. We then assisted the lady to the bathroom where she could empty what was left in her bladder.

We took the bedding off the bed and placed it in the bath ready for washing.

Then we arranged for the district nurses to come and visit, to help wash and change the lady. Hospital treatment would not be needed and we had a lot of paperwork to complete before we left them.

As we were bidding farewell. It was then that I noticed the grin on Carl's face yet again. He had spied a wig on the bedside table. He put it on and then started bobbing up and down and waving his hands in the air, a bit like Al Jolson doing "Mammy".

Carl had a strange affinity for wigs.

Oh my! That would be for another story.

10 out of 10 for performance.

On yet another night shift, there was an emergency call to the M62. Again I was with Carl.

Reportedly a road traffic collision on the westbound carriageway, between junction 23 at Outlane and junction 22 at Windy Hill.

It was in the very early hours of a January morning. We had been called to a Securicor van that had reportedly overturned on the westbound carriageway.

There was very patchy sheet ice all over the carriageway, all three of the lanes had been affected badly. We had to be very careful on route. We actually passed five separate incidents on the way, all of those accidents were minor with no injuries suffered. We did briefly stop and check each and every one of them.

The police had already stopped all of the traffic westbound, between junction 24 and junction 22 and all the vehicles had been asked to leave the motorway for safety reasons.

There had been numerous incidents on the eastbound carriageway as well.

Some of those had patients, who had suffered injuries and required transport to hospital.

Resources from the ambulance services in West Yorkshire and Greater Manchester, were being pushed to the limits that night.

When we arrived at the incident that we had been called for. It was where the motorway separates for the second time, not where Stott Hall Farm is located, but just a couple of miles further on.

There was a Ford Transit Securicor van, it was in the middle lane and it was upright on all wheels. The passenger was already out of the vehicle.

He explained that they had been on their way from Manchester to Leeds, they had skidded and left the motorway. They had come from the fast lane and had somersaulted over and into the opposite carriageway. There they had ended up facing the direction that they had just come from.

If the traffic hadn't already been stopped, that could well have caused a major incident.

The driver was trapped in his locked compartment around the drivers seat, he was enclosed within a thick bulletproof glass box. He was experiencing some difficulty in breathing.

We were unable to access his little compartment, all the security measures had locked him in after impact. We did manage to assess him through the glass, we could see that he had a flail chest. (A floating segment of fractured ribs). He was also complaining of pain in his neck, that had resulted in some tingling in his right hand. We had to treat him for a full spinal injury. His injuries were time critical really.

To do that, we needed assistance from the fire service to extricate him from his little cocoon.

Whilst we were awaiting their arrival. We saw a large post office articulated truck that was heading towards Huddersfield on the opposite carriageway.

He started to skid and slide, it was obvious that he was going into the ditch between the lanes. He did and then the whole truck turned over gracefully and onto its side. His vehicle stopped there. That was just what the Securicor van had done prior to changing carriageways.

Carl stayed with our patient, I made my way across to the middle area, between the motorway to see that the driver was ok.

I could see the driver in his cab, he wasn't injured, he just couldn't physically get out.

He was stood on the drivers door, which had then become the floor, but he couldn't reach up to the passenger door to be able to open it.

I decided to climb up onto the top of the truck, then I would be able to hold the door open for him to climb out.

The only way to get up, was to use the tailgate lift platform as a ladder, easy.

Once on the top of the truck, which bear in mind was the side of it. All I had to do, was just had to make my way along the full length of it. It was wet and it was very slippy, I had only moved a couple of feet when I started to slide.

Brilliant!

I slid the full length of the truck, I bounced onto the cab door and then off and into the dirt. I landed in a crumpled heap, right in front of the cab.

Fortunately I wasn't hurt, just embarrassed. All I could do was to wave at the driver and then start again.

As I walked back, I could hear a lot of cheering. I looked across and near to our ambulance. There were two full fire crews, a few police officers and Carl. They were all laughing and joking, they had seen the whole thing.

I managed to get to and assist the driver at the second attempt, he was wetting himself with laughter like the others.

I was wet through as well, but from landing in the muddy grassed area.

As we met up with Carl and the rest of them, they were all shouting at me, with scores of 10/10, like a gymnast.

I had made their day.

The traffic on the eastbound carriageway then had been stopped.

The Securicor driver was released, from his little cell. We had to use a KED (a Kendrick Extrication Device) splint to immobilise his upper body and neck, he was unable to lie flat on a spinal board due to his breathing.

We set off to Huddersfield Royal Infirmary giving a warning for a trauma team at the hospital. My original ETA was of 25 to 30 minutes. It actually took us over an hour and a half to get there due to the horrendous driving conditions.

Time critical or not, it was simply unsafe to go any faster.

All told that night, there had been nineteen separate vehicle accidents, between the two motorway junctions. Sixteen people had to be taken to hospital by ambulance, for treatment of varying degrees of injury. Before the gritting teams arrived to make it safe.

Our patient was stabilised in Huddersfield with a chest drain fitted to re-inflate his lung, before being transferred to the spinal injuries unit in Leeds.

He had two spinal fractures, stable ones, but fractures nevertheless. One in his spine at the top of his thoracic (chest) region, the other at the base of his neck.

Dave Dee, Dozy, Beaky, Mick and Tich.

I think it was February 2010. We had received a call to an address at Paddock. There was a man there, who had a suspected broken ankle.

When we arrived at the house, Carl and me were met by a woman who said to us. "Do you remember the band Dave Dee, Dozy, Beaky, Mick and Tich?"

When we both said yes. She said that, "that one there, is the Dozy bugger".

Pointing to a man laid at the bottom of the internal staircase. Dozy had slipped on a loose carpet. On landing he had broken his ankle.

He still had extremely long hair and a long beard to match.

On the wall of the house were some pictures of the band in their heyday, included were a couple of framed gold discs.

They showed that without doubt, the man laid on the floor, was in fact Dozy. He used his real name was Trevor Ward-Davies.

Since the heydays of his fame and fortune, Trevor had fallen a little on hard times.

He did undertake some small amounts of teaching. Including several spells at the University of Huddersfield. Sometimes taking on occasional individual clients.

He taught the guitar and how to write music.

Trevor Ward-Davies died at the age of seventy on the 15th of January 2015.

The well known band, made famous for The Legend of Xanadu, Zabadac, Hold Tight, Bend It and many more.

It was originally Trevor's band, before being joined by Dave Dee (David John Harmon) who died in 2009 aged 65.

Carl's Retirement.

When Carl retired I felt lost, it was like I had lost a part of me. Each and every shift was strange without him.

Carl continued to work part time hours, but it was mostly on a car, an RRV.

He carried on doing that for another couple of years.

But the job has never been the same for me. The enjoyment and satisfaction has been nowhere near the same.

It's all about gone.

We had a retirement do for Carl at the Junction pub across from the ambulance station.

Where we had a presentation of several gifts. There was plenty of food and the place was heaving.

People, colleagues from work came. They were from our station, from other stations. Some nurses from the hospital and its admin staff, there were loads of friends that attended the evening.

That to me, showed how well thought of and respected, that Carl had been.

I had to make a speech. Writing it was easy, reading it out was one of the hardest things I have ever had to do.

The older I have got, the more emotional I have become, that was going to be a nightmare.

It would have to be funny, because that's how we were. I would really have to take the mickey out of him, because that's what we did.

It went fine, I had worried over nothing.

There were lots of laughter, there were some tears. But more importantly, it was followed by loads of cheers. Everyone was standing, applauding and there were more tears all around. I miss working with you mate!

A pre-emptive strike.

After Carl retired. His place on the rota and the position of my regular mate, was taken by Ellie. A younger and far better looking paramedic than he was.

I had worked with Carl, for a long long time.

I was hoping that Ellie was going to be good to work with. I had only worked the odd shift with her before.

Ellie was a damn good paramedic to work with, but and I'm sure that she would agree, she lacked a lot of self confidence.

Perhaps working with an older more experienced Advanced Emergency Medical Technician like me, would help her to gain in confidence.

I enjoyed working with Ellie, she was a scream. Although at times she could be a stereotypical blonde.

As I said though, she was a great paramedic, I hoped that my experience was of value to her.

One job I did with Emma that particularly stands out. Was to a young heroin user at a party in the Lascelles Hall area of Huddersfield.

We arrived at a house where a party had been going on, unfortunately alcohol wasn't the only thing being passed around.

Several illicit drugs had been available.

One young man there had started getting boisterous, that led to others getting involved and a fight had ensued.

The police had been called and the party was closed down. They, the police, then called for us as they were concerned for one young man's welfare.

He was anxious, he was obnoxious and he was arrogant. He admitted to injecting heroin, on top of drinking copious amounts of alcohol, which he seemed immensely proud of.

He was physically threatening.

Due to his general behaviour, he had been thumped in the face by one of the other party goers.

Not hard enough for my liking!

As Ellie was busy assessing the young man, he was making both inappropriate and offensive sexual suggestions towards her. We were both ready for leaving him there, he seemed fine, medically anyway. His injury was extremely superficial.

His behaviour though, was totally unacceptable. The police said nothing about it, neither to him nor anyone else, they just weren't interested.

The police insisted that he went to hospital "to be checked out". I don't know why, but they insisted.

Once out of the property, we got him in to the ambulance. He was still making lewd and offensive comments.

I said to Ellie, that I would go in the back with him. I didn't think it was either safe or appropriate for Ellie to be alone with him in the back of the ambulance.

I fully expected the police to come with us.

They had witnessed all of his actions and the comments that had taken place in the house. But no, as soon as the ambulance doors were shut, they were off.

I sat opposite the young man, he was staring, unblinking. He was trying to grind me down. I wasn't impressed, I had met his type before.

He made threats, he told me that he didn't like my attitude. He thought I was unprofessional and that I should show him respect.

I did explain to him, that respect was earned and that he certainly didn't come into any of my categories of respect. That his own attitude was totally disrespectful.

He was still agitated.

Because I wouldn't back down, he started making violent threats towards me.

I asked Ellie to get the police back, we had only come down Wakefield Road from below Lepton to just the Huddersfield side of Waterloo traffic lights.

That seemed to have pulled his trigger.

He said "I don't need the f-ing police". He snarled "I've got a razor in my jacket and I'm not afraid to use it! I'll slice you, you bastard!"

He talked like a big man, but his eyes gave him away. I was by then, almost in his face, if he was to make a move, I was ready for him.

As I was watching him, I saw his left hand reach for his seatbelt, his right hand then went for his pocket. Sure enough his seatbelt unclipped and he tried to stand.

As soon as he moved, I pounced. I hit him as hard as I could with my right arm, a good old "forearm smash" right to his jaw.

He fell to the floor in a heap. I dropped on him, he wasn't going to move anywhere.

Ellie was on the radio, I heard her cry out "get them here quick, Ian's going to kill him".

I was still sat on top of him.

When the police arrived, I lifted him up. I had hold of his jacket at both sides, just below his neck and threw him back on the seat again.

The police asked what was wrong.

When I told them what had happened.

They said "well he looks calm enough now!"

They were ready to leave again.

I said "you aren't going anywhere! You need to search him! He said he has a razor! He's threatened to use it on me!"

The young man shouted to them, "he's a bloody psychopath, he tried to kill me!"

It appeared that they were reluctant to search him, but I insisted.

In his pocket they found an antique cut throat razor. My heart sank. What could have happened to me?

What if Emma had been alone in there with him?

I insisted then, that if he was going to hospital, they had to travel to hospital with us. They did so very reluctantly. Less than two minutes after arriving at the Hospital, the police left.

Unbelievable.

The man quickly kicked off again, the nursing staff had to ring 999 to get them to come back. It was a different crew, they were taking things seriously.

That young man could easily have killed or seriously injured any one of us.

The new crew were disgusted with their colleagues, the first thing that they should have done, should have been a search.

He would then have been traveling with the police and it wouldn't have happened.

When he was examined in the hospital, the young man was fine from the original drink, drugs and assault. But he now had a broken jaw.

The only conclusion to be drawn, was, that I had done it. I had to give a full statement.

I used the legal phrase that I had employed "a pre-emptive strike". It was a single blow that I gave first, in the genuine belief that my safety had been compromised.

Due to the fact that he did have an offensive weapon in his pocket and that it had been found by the police, there was no case to answer. I didn't even need to attend court proceedings.

He was charged with several public order offences, including being in possession of an offensive weapon.

Is that my finger?

It was St. Valentines Night 2005. I had been called to attend to a male, outside a takeaway on Chapel Hill, Huddersfield. The takeaway is now Al Faisal's, I'm not sure if it was the same business in 2005.

There was a young man who had been shimming up a lamppost, outside the named property for a bet.

He had accepted the bet to impress the ladies who were present at the time. He had got well on his way up the post, when he lost his grip and slipped back down.

He had caught his hand on a traffic sign, that was located approximately 10 foot off the ground.

When we arrived, his hand was bleeding quite badly. As I was bandaging his hand, it was soon obvious to me, that he had lost the third finger of his left hand.

Once he was all bandaged up, I looked around on the floor for his finger, there was nothing to be seen. I then looked up at the sign, there it was, hanging from the retaining bracket of the sign.

That was when he said to me, "is that my finger?"

I climbed onto the roof of the ambulance and was able to reach it. There was what appeared to be, a cord hanging from the finger, it was the main tendon. There was approximately ten inches of bloody sinew attached to the finger, complete with a cygnet ring.

I returned the ring to him and then I ran into the takeaway, to get some ice to pack the finger in. They didn't have any ice, but I managed to get some from the pub, the "Rat and Ratchet" next door. We put the digit in a bag and filled it with the ice cubes.

Shortly after arriving at Huddersfield Infirmary and a quick assessment. Our budding street trapeze artist, was on his way to Bradford Royal Infirmary for plastic surgery, with a view to saving the finger.

Sadly, as the tendon had also been ripped out, too much damage had already occurred to be able to save it.

CHAPTER 52.

A ONCE IN A LIFETIME EXPERIENCE.

G8 Summit Edinburgh 2005.

A once in a lifetime experience arose, volunteers were required, it was to attend at the G8 summit in Edinburgh in the July of 2005.

During the summit meeting, in July, there was to be a protest held in the city of Edinburgh at the G8 worlds leaders conference.

Celebrity Bob Geldof was trying to get one million people, to wear white and to hold their hands together and to completely surround the perimeter of the City of Edinburgh.

Hopefully, the event would be seen from the air. It should look like one giant white ribbon of hope, all around the city. The whole event, was to be known as "The March Against Poverty". Other less peaceful protests were also planned for it.

There were to be an extra 1,500 police officers drafted in for assistance, from all over the United Kingdom. Medical cover was to be provided, and there would be an extra 70 ambulance staff drafted in. Ten of those would be from West Yorkshire. I applied to be one of the ten.

Pat also from Huddersfield and me were selected from our sub division. We all met at Gildersome ambulance station and travelled to Scotland in ambulance support vehicles.

On arrival in Scotland, we would all be staying at the Peebles Hydro. A massive, hotel and conference centre.

There we would meet our counterparts from Scotland and the support crews from the rest of the UK. All of us would be staying there at the same Hotel.

All 140 of us would be training together, because some of our individual protocols differed slightly, from within each service.

The first two days would involve training, to get everyone singing from the same hymn sheet, so to speak.

Then we were all going to be split into smaller units and spread around the Edinburgh region.

Amelia from Dewsbury and Gordon from Menston were part of my OSU (operational support unit). Along with Malcolm, as manager. There was Willy, Neil and Emma, all of them from the Scottish Ambulance Service.

We had three vehicles between us. A small transit support unit, which was full to the brim with extra equipment should a major accident be declared, (MAJAX).

We had the use of a people carrier, which the Scottish Ambulance Service used for on the road teaching. We used the people carrier, as our mobile base, for roadside breaks and generally whilst killing time waiting.

All of the vehicles were fitted with blue lights and sirens and fully marked up as Scottish Ambulance Service.

Then for the third vehicle, there was a Toyota Land Cruiser ambulance, with full stretcher and emergency transport capabilities.

The Toyota was used on a daily basis by Emma and Neil at their home on the Isle of Arran.

On the Saturday, the day of the march, we were all assigned to different areas of the city centre of Edinburgh. Our little contingent, were stationed on North Bridge, directly above the main Waverley railway station.

It was an extremely long, but a very interesting day.

For us, it was also very peaceful. Noisy and disruptive at times, but there was no malice, nor any violence shown of any kind. Despite the vast numbers of people around.

Hundreds of thousands of people were present, making a peaceful, even if a somewhat disrupting protest. To show to the world leaders and their public.

Some of the OSU's were called into action, but they were only called out for simple falls or minor illnesses, not for any major issues.

We remained on the bridge all day. We were not required to treat anyone, not even once.

For security reasons during the protest, there was only one entrance to the railway station left open and that was the main entrance off Princess Street.

As we were all in uniform and with our fully marked ambulances. Jo public assumed that we were all local people and would be able to direct them to the places that they required.

We stood on that bridge for a solid twelve hours, no medical actions, but we were regularly used for tourist information.

Not one person questioned "my" directions, they would believe anything I said, even with the Yorkshire accent.

Willy had come down to join us from the Outer Hebrides, he had battled cancer in the recent past and so he was semi retired. He, like me had thought that the event would be a once in a lifetime experience and he wanted to play a part in it.

He had a very dry sense of humour and he was a little older than the rest of us.

Me and him got on great.

He loved the way I was directing unsuspecting visitors, with a flair and conviction.

I may not know anywhere in Edinburgh, but by lunchtime, I could have convinced anybody that I did.

I had changed the names of most of the local landmarks, not deliberately, I just didn't know their real names.

For example, if I was asked how to get into the railway station.

I was sending people to "go down to the end of the bridge, turn left up the

Mall (Princess Street), then straight up the hill to the (we could see it from where we were and I would point to it) large Robert the Bruce statue. (Now I know it was the Prince Albert Memorial). You can then turn left again and head down Sassenach's Revenge (made up, as there was no name on the street) and then you will see the long ramp down to the main entrance".

Some people, following my directions, had asked if there was any quicker way to get to the station. I would get them to stand on a little step ladder that we had acquired and I would ask them to look over the wall. I would then say "you could try that way, it is much quicker, but it'll hurt!"

Over the wall, was the roof of the Waverley Railway Station. Lots of the glass panels were either missing, or you could see where they had been replaced. At the time, I hadn't been made aware that it was a local and common suicide spot.

We met two women who were in the Guinness Book of Records. There was the one with the most body piercings, she is called Elaine Davidson, originally from Brazil. At the time she was actually working as a nurse in Edinburgh.

A lovely person, but very strange.

With her, was the famous Isobel Varley from Stevenage in Hertfordshire, she was born in Yorkshire. Isobel was the woman who it is claimed, has the most body area covered with tattoos, for a senior.

She was very quick to show us, including to a very small area that had not been covered. All of that, in full public view, in the middle of the day on a busy street in Edinburgh.

She was not a young woman either.

Weird!

Just as I write this bit, I found out that sadly Isobel had passed away last year. On the 11th May 2015. She was aged 77 and she been suffering from Alzheimer's.

It's far more common than people realise.

The next couple of days were to be near the Gleneagles Hotel, where the G8 conference was actually being held. We had been briefed that some of the protesters attending the area were not going to be peaceful.

We were given lots of information from pre gathered intelligence. Who to keep an eye out for, but more importantly, who to be very wary of.

Some protestors had come from Italy, they were known as the "Black Block" they were both male and female. All of them dressed in black, wearing masks as well.

They had developed quite a reputation for using extreme violence.

In the hotel at breakfast, it was all over the news. That in Stirling, a small gang of the "Black Block", had surrounded a lone police van.

They were attacking it with pick axes, crow bars and scaffolding poles. It was frightening just to watch. What that policeman all on his own in the van, was going through, I cannot begin to imagine.

Further intelligence had come to light, it had come from police that had infiltrated the group under cover.

That, that particular group of the "Black Block" that had come to the G8 Summit. Had been planning to kill a police officer, "because they could".

Half way through breakfast at our hotel, the Ramada Jarvis on the outskirts of Edinburgh, an emergency call came in. Some of the protesters had broken through the security barriers at Gleneagles. It was all hands to the pumps, as quickly as possible.

Off we went, straight to the village of Auchterader, on the boundary of the Gleneagles estate. It had to be a high speed journey down the already closed and empty M9 motorway.

Some protesters were actually trespassing on the motorway, all at well spaced intervals. So for safety reasons, the whole of the motorway had been shut to all traffic, a major success for the protestors.

Peaceful, but extremely disruptive to everyday functioning.

We were ordered to travel the length of the motorway, to keep all our visible and audible warnings (blues and two's), on at all times. Under "no circumstances whatsoever" had we to stop.

If by any chance we collided with any pedestrians, we were told that they shouldn't have been there. It was not our problem, "if your vehicle is driveable, keep going". Any incidents, would be sorted out by the police and the local ambulance crews.

The Police, having the earlier issues in Stirling, would be around ten minutes behind us. So they couldn't provide us with an immediate escort. In hindsight, I think it worked better for us without them.

We flew, I was driving the land cruiser, I reached speeds of around 128 mph several times. At one point the Armco barriers had been dismantled and had been strewn across the carriage way.

In the distance, we could see that as we were approaching, some of the people were in the road throwing all the debris to one side.

They gave us a clear run through.

All of them were masked, but waved pleasantly as we passed. In the mirrors, we could see behind us, that they were blocking the road once again.

Once we arrived at Auchterader, a command post had been set up. We all met up there to await further instructions.

Then the helicopters arrived, they were the large chinooks, massive troop carriers.

When the four of them had landed, hundreds of well rehearsed police officers emerged. Their shields and batons at the ready, they formed a moving human barrier. To remove the marauding protestors from the grounds.

The atmosphere was very tense.

The police were battering their own shields as they advanced, it was a terrifying noise, a frightening sight and we were just the innocent observers.

An exhilarating event, the police managed to do their job, they met with very little real resistance. One or two of the protestors were arrested for public order offences.

After that, we could afford to relax a little and have some lunch.

We just had time to eat, before we could hear the next wave of people coming up the road.

They came in droves, we could hear very loud music and then saw dozens of decorated vehicles. All the people involved were in fancy dress costumes, slowly working their way up the high street.

Curiosity got to us, some of us went a bit nearer to the road. All of the people were happy, smiling and waving.

The next phase of the protesters, were all dressed as clowns. With unicycles, bicycles and even tricycles. There were jugglers, fire breathers and other street entertainers.

Again they were blocking the road, causing major chaos to traffic. But although extremely noisy, they were peaceful and showed no signs of violence.

We had got to the roadside and up close to them.

Then without warning, a lot of the clowns disrobed, they were all dressed completely in black and they had black face masks on. They were the ones that we had been warned about, the dreaded "Black Block".

Instead of violence, the music stopped and a very eerie silence became the order.

We had been told by the police intelligence officers, that if we were approached. We should answer questions calmly, honestly and politely and then at the first opportunity withdraw to safety.

I was stood there with Willy, when four of the people in black came towards us. I have to admit, that at that moment and for some reason unknown to me, my bladder wanted to suddenly empty.

One of the four stepped forward, it was a female. Then in perfect English, she began to speak. She told us that her name was Annabelle and asked us for our names.

We replied with our Christian names. She then calmly offered her hand to shake and asked us where we were from.

We politely shook her hand in return, I said "Yorkshire" and Willy said the Scottish Islands.

She said "wonderful" and that she and her three friends, one more female and two males had travelled from Turin.

They all shook our hands in a friendly welcoming manner. Just before we retreated, she politely asked if we would mind answering one more question. It seemed innocent enough.

She said "are you medical people here to attend to the protesters? or for the security services?"

I answered that one and I said that we were there for anyone that may need our attention, whichever side of the fence they were from.

She laughed at that and said "thank you". She then blew us a kiss and went off with her colleagues, dancing into the distance.

When I looked around again, the thirty or so people who had been standing alongside us. All ambulance staff, had gone. Willy and myself were all alone. Thanks fellas! Really appreciated!

We returned to the vehicles and were immediately pounced on by the police. We had been watched closely on camera, they wanted a verbal report of all events and a word for word account of the conversation.

That was an eye opener, I can tell you!

The rest of the day was peaceful enough. One protester had fallen, he suffered with a slight cut to his head, he was treated on site and sent on his merry way. Then we had one female teenager with suspected appendicitis, she was taken to a hospital in Edinburgh.

It had been decided earlier at the planning meetings, that Police would have gone to a hospital nearer to Glasgow, for treatment and the Protesters would be taken into Edinburgh.

That hopefully, would have helped to keep the two sides apart, and to keep confrontation to a minimum.

The next day, all hell broke loose.

It was the 7th July 2005.

Our little group, along with three more of the OSU's, were based at the ambulance HQ. The main control and communication centre, just outside Edinburgh city centre.

Our larger group's senior leader was the emergency planning officer for London.

Vic was our West Yorkshire's equivalent.

Bombs had gone off in London. What the hell was going on?

Nobody knew at that stage.

He couldn't have been any further away from his own service. He couldn't contact his family, all of the mobile phone signals in London had been blocked.

His wife was due to be travelling on the underground to her mums, with their two young children.

Where was she? Was she hurt? The poor man was in bits. He needed to get to London and quickly.

But how?

Very shortly after, we were asked to move the ambulances from the car park. No sooner had that been done and a jet ranger helicopter arrived to take him to London.

The president of the United States, George W Bush. Although he had Air Force One, on stand by. He also had some private helicopters for his staff, that one, we were led to believe was one of those.

Later on that day, I think it was nearly midnight and there was an announcement over the tannoy, in the hotel bar. Our colleague had rung to let us know that his wife and children were all safe and sound.

That morning, for some unexplained reason, they had been given a lift by a friend. And yes, they would have been travelling on one of the affected trains.

We didn't really know the man, but huge sighs of relief went round and a spontaneous round of applause and cheers as well.

The next day, that was our team's day off.

The gang took me to the Firth of Forth, over the road bridge and to look at the rail bridge. With a name like mine and I had never been to see either of the bridges.

All of us had our radios, just in case. It was an extremely tense day nobody could settle properly. After what had happened in London, what was next?

We were trying our best to relax, it was after all, our day off. Well, it was technically, but we had to be ready to respond at a seconds notice. We had to be in uniform and our vehicles kitted up and ready.

To be prepared in case any more of the brown smelly stuff, was to hit the fan.

We stayed in Edinburgh for the duration of the conference, ten days in total. Fortunately, we had no more occurrences of any terrorist activity, either up in Scotland where we were. Or thankfully, anywhere else where our families were.

It was an experience I am glad to have been part of. All emotions I can think possible were covered in those few days. I was glad it was over, I was so very tired, but I was so thankful for such a once in a lifetime experience.

Where the hell did that lot come from?

Writing about Pat from Huddersfield, going off to the G8 Summit with me, reminded me of a time I played a trick on him. He got me back though, big style.

We had played the same particular trick on several members of staff over the years, anyone who ever owned a motorbike, probably had it done to them at some stage.

That time for some reason, was Pat's turn. He had left his motorbike boots in the locker room.

They were unguarded ready and primed for action. We had a hole punch in the office, it was a large industrial sized one and it hardly ever got emptied. Until an opportunity like that arose. I seem to have a penchant for hole punchings, do you remember the Capri?

I emptied the hole punch of its contents straight into Pat's boots. With wearing thick socks, he probably wouldn't even notice them. The trick was to put a lot in, but not to go overboard.

It worked, at two in the morning at the end of his shift, he went to get ready for his journey home.

He put his socks on first, then his over trousers, followed by the boots. He was blissfully unaware.

He had all the way up the Dearne Valley to go, about ten miles to ride, it was late and he was tired. He got home and parked the bike. He took his boots off in the hallway, he went to the kitchen to get a drink and then he went upstairs to bed.

He was married to Cassie at the time, she was already in bed and so as we had hoped, he hadn't put any lights on.

It was Cassie that had got up first in the morning. She found all the white, plus a few coloured for decorative purposes, dots all over the place.

They were all over the bedroom, in the bathroom, all up the staircase, and all over the kitchen. She knew what they were and she had a damned good idea who might have done it.

She left them for Pat to find and clear up.

He came in to work later that evening for another similar shift, he never said a word about it.

About a week later, I was on a day shift. I had arranged to pick Wendy up from outside the Alfred Street multi storey car park in town, on my way home. She was there waiting for me.

Just after setting off, I was turning right from the end of Alfred Street, across the ring road, to join Manchester Road. As I did so, the sun was in my eyes, I pulled down my sun visor.

Christ!

It was like Niagara Falls, the buggers must have spent all week collecting hole punchings from everywhere. They had rigged up a tray on top of my sun visor, it was full of them. As soon as I touched it, the lot came down and kept on coming down, it seemed to take forever.

Brilliant, I had to give them ten out of ten for it. I was expecting some form of revenge attack, but I wasn't prepared for that. I had played with the bull and then I was feeling the sharp point of its horn on my tender posterior.

I knew that it hadn't been just Pat on his own, he had been working with Matt, he was a master of revenge.

When I saw Pat at work, a couple of days later. I shook his hand and I told him what had happened, I thought it was brilliant.

He told me about his boots and how he had felt uncomfortable all the way home. He said it was as though his boots were a couple of sizes too small. At that time in the morning, he hadn't even considered that they may have been tampered with.

What a laugh!

Little things as they say, little things.

CHAPTER 53.

FESTIVAL TIME.

"V festival" Weston Park Staffordshire August 2006.

After managing the medical cover, at many football and rugby matches in Huddersfield. I asked Mike if there was anything else that I could do as a bit of a challenge. He told me to have a chat with Dick, our emergency planning officer.

I knew Dick well from his time as a duty officer.

He was also my big ally in dealing with the blessed road humps. I had met him many a time over the years. I asked him for any suggestions.

He suggested that the first thing that I needed to do, was the Command and Control Course, on dealing with major incidents.

He put me forward for it straight away, within six weeks or so I had done the course.

Janet and Bobby our locality managers and other locality managers from around West Yorkshire were on the one day course. I was the only Station Officer on it.

They seemed quite surprised that I was there. It was set up generally for more senior managers, not road staff like me.

The whole day was spent discussing, using table exercises, all to do with organising multiple staff at the scene of multiple casualties. Not about the triage of actual injuries, but more of using the right resources for the right patient.

The day put a lot of things in perspective for me.

I had dealt with the scenes at the Huddersfield Town football stadium. With perhaps twenty to twenty five St. John volunteers, a double ambulance crew, at least one doctor and liaison with the police and safety officers.

Fortunately the incidents there, had usually been quite minor and generally easy to manage.

Following the course, Dick asked me to arrange some time off in mid August, he said that he had a treat in store for me. Duly arranged, I got the time off by using up some outstanding annual leave.

Dick introduced me to David, I do remember David from years back as a manager in the Leeds area. David was the one who had accompanied me on my first Crown Court appearance.

He was then in charge of the services provided by WYMAS Private Ambulance.

He said that Dick had told him of my wishes and that he had the perfect opportunity for me.

David had been looking for someone to help out, in the control room at the annual "V-festival" in Staffordshire. "Was I interested?"

Of course I was. I already had the time off and was available. My festival cover, was to be Friday, Saturday and Sunday night shift. Each shift was twelve hours duration, from 22:00hrs until 10:00hrs.

At the national music festival, there would be a village, all camping, of around 38,000 people on the one site.

There would be several NHS ambulance crews, even more St. John crews. Several paramedics and first aiders on foot. Both as "pit crews" and "crowd walkers".

We also had several doctors and nurses in a medical unit. Complete with x-ray, suturing and plaster room facilities.

Even a helicopter was based on site.

There would be hundreds of security staff, police and even their own fire service crews, all on site 24 hours a day.

I was under the impression that Dick would be in the main control room, with the controllers of each of the other services, acting as Silver Command. Then I would be in the ambulance control room, with Ellie as my scribe, me acting as Bronze Command.

That wasn't to be. As soon as we got on site, I wasn't supposed to start until 22:00hrs. We had arrived at around 21:00hrs. Dick was there, he took me into the main control room and he introduced me to the main site controller, the Gold Commander. Also in there was David, he was Silver Commander for the medical service. They were the biggest group of people there on site, aside from the security staff.

He was the day shift Silver Commander.

They were both explaining the role required of a Silver Commander and then they told me that it was my challenge. I had asked for one, boy oh boy was it going to be challenge!

Never fear, I was up for it. After all, if the mucky brown stuff hit the fan, Dick would be just next door to take over.

I took over Silver Command at 22:00hrs, I was in one portacabin, Dick was in the next door cabin. He was monitoring things. It was my decision which resources to use and when.

Dick was there to call in outside services, or if any patient was to be taken off site, he would be ringing the local hospitals etc.

At 22:45hrs, there starts a two hour total vehicle embargo. If any resources are required they must go on foot. In readiness for that, I had to utilise most of my professional and volunteer resources, leaving them at strategic positions around the whole site.

At the bottom end of the site, all set in the grounds of Weston Park. A large stately home with expansive grounds, there were five main stages.

Each of those, attended by thousands of festival goers. All 38,000 people would be in around fifteen per cent of the site.

At 23:00hrs the music was due to finish, then all the party goers would start making their way back up to the top of the estate, to the camping area. All moving in the same direction and at the same time.

Hence no vehicle movement for safety reasons.

If there was a life threatening emergency and it had been assessed by one of our medical staff as such. Then contingency plans were in place for transport, but it would have to be absolutely time critical.

We would then have to deploy already practiced, emergency procedures. It could be arranged, but it wouldn't be easy.

So, to avoid if at all possible.

At 22:50hrs. I had a call come in to the control room, there was a twenty four year old female collapsed at the front of stage number two. St. John staff were with the patient, but a doctor was required urgently.

I called for "Medic 1" to attend on foot. The doctor called back, "I'm not walking, I have a perfectly good four by four all terrain Land Rover vehicle and driver".

I had to be firm, "sorry, you will leave your vehicle in situ and walk as requested due to vehicle embargo". She wasn't happy. But did as was asked.

The patient was diabetic, she had gone "hypo", her sugar levels had dropped to coma stage.

The doctor had an assistant and she had her driver, Nick with her.

At the patient's side, "Medic 1" gave the patient an injection of glucagon and she came round fairly quickly. The patient then needed some food, in the form of carbohydrates. To restock the reserve tanks, that had just been drained by administering the glucagon.

Some sandwiches were made available.

By midnight the embargo was lifted, I then sent down an ambulance to transport the patient and our staff, back to the medical centre for a full assessment and for recovery.

At that stage, I didn't have any names for the people that I was dispatching, I just had call signs for my staff.

In the morning, we went to the meal tent (big enough for 350 people to eat at once) for breakfast. Dick went with some of the medical team on the first sitting at 06:00hrs. I went with some of the others for the second sitting at 06:30hrs. The rest of them went down at 07:00hrs.

That way, two thirds of the total medical cover was readily available at all times and the others were available on call, whilst having breakfast.

As I was sat eating, my colleagues at the same table suddenly stood up, as I was about to. I felt a hand press down firmly on my shoulder preventing me from doing so.

A strong and familiar female Scottish accent asked, if I was the ambulance Silver Commander.

It was our ambulance service senior medical director at the time, Dr. Amelia.

Her assistant was Jackie, our Chief Executive of the Ambulance Service, the big boss of the service. With them was their driver Nick.

Nick came over to the emergency side of the job and is now based at Huddersfield, where we work together on the road quite regularly.

Dr. Amelia asked if I would still have told her literally, to do as she was told, if I had known who she was. I had to say that it had been non-negotiable whoever it was.

They laughed, then she said that I had done well, for my first time in that position.

Nick and I became good friends after that weekend.

The rest of the festival went well, we did work twelve long hours, the first four hours of the shift were the busiest.

During the day, we went to the local university halls of residence where we had a bed for the day.

Back to the site at teatime, we would have a meal and then walk round the stages. Going to see any of the bands who we might know, we had unlimited access to all areas.

It had been the challenge that I wanted, although very stressful, I really enjoyed it.

V Festival 2007.

The following year, another manager. Darrell from Wakefield was put in charge, in the role of Silver Commander. I did the Bronze Commander role, it had a lot less stress.

He had to learn his new role by jumping in at the deep end, I knew how he felt. He did ok though, and he has since gone on further up the management ladder.

I had more time to think the second year, I had regular breaks, Dick would step in to either role for breaks, several times during the night.

I would have regular walks up the site, to the medical room. I was checking and changing radio batteries, making sure that everyone was OK. It was far more peaceful and I got to see other aspects of the festival.

That year, we all had to be put up in a Travel Lodge hotel, there were proper restaurant meals there and a swimming pool for relaxation.

The halls of residence at the university were being renovated, we were absolutely devastated by that, as I am sure that you can imagine.

The second night we were there, a call for help came in at two in the morning.

A young girl had been found down at the bottom of an embankment, she was laid in a stream.

The normal ambulances couldn't gain access to that part of the site, due to the extremely muddy conditions.

One of the men in our cabin at the time, was a senior Staffordshire officer.

He was also a senior officer in the local Mountain Rescue Service and he had his mountain rescue Land Rover with him. He said he had never been stuck in it.

He asked if I would go with him and we would go get the girl sorted.

Off we went, the vehicle was slipping and sliding all over the place, but we managed to get to the very top corner of the estate. I could see why the others couldn't get near.

The girl had managed to tumble forty foot down a steep, but obstacle free embankment and into the stream.

She wasn't hurt but was suffering from hypothermia and was exhausted from trying to get herself out.

I rigged a rope around me, Jim, my colleague belayed me down to the girl.

She was soaked, she had loads of layers and coats on, she must have weighed twenty stone or more. We got rid of three heavy overcoats, army greatcoat style, made worse due to being wet.

I was then able to lash the girl to me and with Jim's help, along with that of many of the other festival goers, they hauled us both back up to the top of the banking.

By the time we had reached the Land Rover, we were both absolutely soaked and caked in a thick slimy offensive smelling mud.

We took her to the medical room. The girl was confused and agitated, she had been in her predicament for up to two and a half hours. She was getting very ill at that stage, it was advanced stages of hypothermia.

The first thing that the young girl needed, was to get her undressed. Then wrapped in what is known as a "bear hugger", it is like a j-cloth material, a super lightweight air mattress.

That is laid on or around the patient, then a controlled but steady heated air supply is blown into it and around the patient. A fantastic piece of kit and the simplest idea. It warms a patient up in a well controlled fashion.

Due to the fact of how wet and muddy she and I were, she was asked if she minded me to help her disrobe. Dr. Amelia our medical director was there with her as a chaperone.

I helped the girl out of numerous layers of cold and wet clothing, until she was stood in her vest and knickers.

As she removed her vest, I could then see that the bedraggled muddy disgusting specimen that I had rescued, was an absolute stunner. She was gorgeous looking and with a figure to die for.

A thought came in to my head and has occasionally happened in the past, it came out. Although it came out much louder than I expected it to do.

Our medical director Dr. Amelia slapped me at the side of my head and actually knocked me over. She was laughing loudly at the same time, and said to me "I cannot believe you just said that!"

As I had seen the girl's vest come off, anybody, male or female, could not have missed the size of her breasts. They were huge.

The silly thought that came into my head and then straight out of my mouth. "How the hell have you got so cold with those things, they would have kept me warm for a week!"

After I picked myself up off the floor. I had to go and get showered and changed out of my cold, wet and very muddy uniform.

Later in the morning, as we were packing up from our night shift and our relief were taking over.

I went to the medical centre and enquired about the mud bunny. She was making good progress, she had been warmed up gradually and was feeling much better.

I was able to speak to her and I apologised for my statement.

She wasn't bothered and she hadn't been offended in any way.

It was only said in fun after all.

The next evening, our little group were passing the time before starting our shift.

Nick was chauffeur to the medical director again.

I was stood with him and we were near the front of one of the stages, Girls Aloud were performing. As we looked towards the stage, the "pit crew" were in the area between the stage and the barriers in front of the crowded audience.

A well known paramedic, who I will not name here, was there.

He was wearing his oversized ear defenders with built in microphone, he was bouncing up and down in front of the barriers, he said that he was dancing.

He thrives on being in the public eye, he was in his element. He just loves being watched, he thought he was the new John Travolta.

As we were looking around, Nick suddenly pointed out a young lad at the front of the crowd, he was being crushed up against the barriers.

As the audience were dancing, there was a pulsating crowd surge. The young man was trapped.

He was definitely going blue and his head was just flopping about, he was virtually unconscious.

Nick and I ran and pushed past "John Travolta", we grabbed the lad, just in the nick of time too. We had to literally drag him over the barriers, they were about four foot high.

We carried him to the side of the stage, he was floppy and his breathing was akin to mine when I'm laid on my back following a skin full of ale.

He was snoring deeply.

We turned him onto his side and he suddenly took a deep breath, it seemed to go on forever. If he had been a vacuum cleaner, he would have swallowed the carpet.

He came round a lot, Dr. Aaron, one of the A&E consultants from one of West Yorkshire's hospitals, was just behind us at the time.

He was one of our team, he examined the lad, before sending him by ambulance to the Staffordshire hospital.

It had been touch and go, I think it brought "John Travolta" back down to Earth with a bump.

His job as pit crew was to watch the crowd, not to pose like a peacock on heat for the ladies. He was where he was, to prevent that very kind of incident from happening, it shook him up.

Over the period of time spent at both those festivals, we met several of the famous artists, and were able to speak to them. Some we were able to have photo's with.

I met Paul Heaton from Beautiful South and Paul Weller from The Jam. Iggy Pop, all of Girls Aloud and Peter Kay, he was there to watch Girls Aloud. I even met Pink and many others, many I didn't even know.

I was showing my age. It was brilliant though.

Unfortunately for us, for David, who had run the medical cover for the event for twelve years. It was to be his last for YAS, he retired shortly after that festival.

When he did, the man who took over the private side of YAS, stopped doing it. He said that there was too much effort required, to cover such a large event.

What a load of crap!

The event was very well organised, well established and it made a large profit for our ambulance service.

David still does it now. In his retirement, he decided to start up his own company. He uses resources from private ambulance companies up and down the country, apparently he has quite a lucrative business going.

All thanks to the fact that the new man, thought it was too much effort.

A big loss to the YAS COFFERS.

I only went to two of the festivals, I wish I had got the opportunity sooner, it was a brilliant time and experience.

CHAPTER 54.

IT'S MY TIME, MY TERMS AND REMEMBRANCE.

Sharing my experiences, and giving voluntary assistance.

All through my time with the ambulance service, I have enjoyed sharing my experiences and talking to public groups.

I have given talks to countless numbers of schools, of all ages from nursery, up to and including colleges. D of E students, army cadets, sea cadets, scouts, cubs, guides and brownies and many adult groups. Even to "owls" groups for the over fifties.

I could actually join them now.

I was once invited to be an official after dinner speaker, at the annual dinner for the Association of Driving Instructors. Local branch.

That was some experience, it was in the function suite of the Huddersfield Hotel, when Johnny and Joe had the entire block down at Huddersfield's Beastmarket.

I was treated to a full five course meal, then invited to give a talk on my role in the ambulance service. Following a half hour talk, we had an extremely interesting two way questions and answers session for about an hour. They supplied me with plenty to drink and a taxi home.

It was a most enjoyable experience.

I have taught first aid to hundreds of people over the years.

Including various first aid badges in scouting and guiding, all over the district.

I was assistant Cub Scout leader to Malcolm, at Paddock, for many years and then Jane.

Taking over the cub pack and running it myself for a time. I even got my fifteen years long service award for doing so at Paddock.

As well as for several years I instructed the Service section, for the Duke of Edinburgh's Award, at both bronze and silver levels.

I even created the syllabus to silver standard for two groups of special needs students. Each over a twelve week period. Some of them went on to achieve their dreams and got their Gold Award.

I have been a civilian assistant with the local group of army cadets, attached to the Duke of Wellingtons Regiment in Huddersfield for several years. Both Adrian and Ben were cadets at that unit for a while.

I was a voluntary West Yorkshire Countryside Ranger, prior to joining the ambulance service. Helping the public, with guides on walks and local outdoor activities. Having times helping out reinforcing paths, making wooden stiles and even building a stone "clapper bridge". That was high up on the moors above Buckstones.

I have been a governor at Cowlersley Junior and Primary School, I was the early years governor.

That was the school that both my sons had attended. I have photos taken from then. One of the teachers at the time of my boys, was still teaching the early years there when, I had to resign from being a governor.

Ambulance rota's were not conducive to my attendance. I had to miss far more meetings and events, than I could attend.

It was great going to school though and sitting with the kids, finding out about their interests.

I can't forget the first time I was asked to visit the little ones, to be in my uniform and be prepared to answer questions about myself and my job.

The very first question asked, "what did you have for breakfast?"

Out of the mouths of babes, eh!

You can't beat 'em.

Another question and answer session that I remember well, was at Milnsbridge cub scouts. My colleague Aaron and I had been teaching them for their first aid badge. It was whilst we were sat down and asking the young ones about home safety.

One of our first questions, was to ask "what have you got at home that you and other people might find as dangerous?"

The first answer given, "my brother!"

Absolute quality.

Open days and charity work.

Alec, he was and still is an absolute crackpot, he is as mad as a box of frogs!

We became great friends. We did lots together. We had many a shift where we were working together.

We also got to loads of mischief together over the years. We even had an air rifle range at the bottom of the station garage.

Oops, another naughty secret revealed!

When I started, Alec was the regular mate of the legendary Cliff. When working with Cliff, Alec was definitely under the thumb. He wouldn't say "boo! to a goose".

He has certainly made up for it since, after Cliff went to the PTS side of the job.

Cliff once brought in some piccalilli sandwiches for them both. Alec said that he didn't like piccalilli.

"Gerritetten!" Cliff said, Alec did so without question.

We arranged two open days at Huddersfield Ambulance Station, for charity over the years.

Getting ready for one of them, the first one, in 1985. Alec and me, were in an old ambulance with Alec's brother Dan.

We had been going around all the shops and businesses in Marsh and Lindley, collecting donations for a raffle.

We were parked up on Abb Street in Marsh. Where we were marking up our haul of donated items, when we saw a bread delivery driver.

He was delivering to Marsh Conservative Club. He was being very professional. Wearing his clean and starched white clothes, including shoes, overalls, cap complete with hair net and even a pair of white cotton gloves. He would have easily got lost in the snow!

Eventually, one handed, he lifted up the large bread tray. He balanced it in the middle. As he turned, he caught the corner of the tray, on the edge of the van doors.

What a catastrophe!

All the teacakes and buns were thrown out of the tray, they went all over the road.

While he thought that nobody had seen him, he quickly threw them all back onto the floor of the van. He then carefully rearranged them on the tray and continued as though nothing had happened.

We had to let him know.

On A4 sheets of paper and in large letters, we placed a message all across his cab windscreen. "WE SAW YOU!" When he came back and saw it, his face was an absolute picture.

He jumped in his van and was off.

Caught ya!

While Alec, his brother Dan and me were out begging for donations for our open day. There was a shop, where "All About Flowers" is now. It was called "Bikes n Bits" then.

The proprietor promised us a racing bike for our star prize. Providing that we advertised his business on all of our promotional leaflets.

Fair enough, job done.

It was on the Thursday afternoon, only two days before the event and as planned, Alec and I went to pick up the bike.

What a disappointment, it wasn't a racing bike at all. It was a pink child's starter bike with a basket on the front, it had coloured streamers on the handlebars and it was fitted with stabilisers. It was just about big enough for a two year old.

They had been advertising an adult racing bike in their window, for the last four or five weeks, as the donation to our open day.

When I asked what had happened to that one.

He just said "oh, I sold that one!" He carried on "that's what's left take it or leave it!"

We so very nearly said "shove it where the sun doesn't shine!"

We didn't, we took the bike. Then we spent the next few hours on the phone trying to track down another bike. We had to get one, even if we had to pay for it ourselves.

We did it, it was almost tea time. We had managed to track one down, to a firm on Leeds Road. They didn't even want any publicity, in fact they insisted that we hadn't to mention their name at all, they were just glad to help.

After all, all the money we raised was going to "Huddersfield babies at risk appeal" for research into Cot Death. Or as it is now known Sudden Infant Death Syndrome (SIDS).

The second bicycle was a proper racing bike, with drop handlebars. It had fifteen gears, they even threw in a set of lights for it. They were fantastic and even now I am obliged not to name them.

Even though I would love to give them the credit that they truly deserve.

We managed to change our posters in all the shop windows and deleted the "Bikes n Bits" shop name from every one.

In the ambulance station, we had a stand with all the prizes on show and a card stating who had donated them.

On the stand for the bike, in pride of place, we put a large sign.

Stating that, "here is the Bit of a Bike" donated by "Bikes n Bits", showing the little tots bike.

At the side of it, a larger one. That was stating "and this is the racing bike, given in replacement by an anonymous benefactor, all thanks to them!"

Moral to this, don't even offer to help if you are not prepared to fulfil your obligations!

School visits and education.

Alec and me did numerous talks to schools, of all grades. We had perfected all of our routines. With regular visits to pre-school and nursery classes, right up to some kids in secondary school with challenging behaviour.

We did public displays for many years in Greenhead Park. We even attended many carnivals and joined in the processions. By following on behind the parade.

The main Huddersfield Caribbean Carnival, Paddock and Golcar Carnivals, to name a few.

We used to love it.

We joined a group, it was called "Prison me, no way!"

That involved going in to high schools, talking to fourteen year olds. It was run by the prison service. They took over that year of the school for the whole day.

The kids were to be the prisoners and they were treated as such.

There were lots of prison officers, police and us. The kids were given talks on the effects of drugs, joy riding and safety. They were talked to, by actual prisoners, including some life sentence serving prisoners. They even had a talk from some mothers who had lost their children. Through the effects of drink, or the result of joy riders, driving.

At break time they were "exercised" by being marched around the school yard, woe betide anyone with their hands in their pockets. They would be given twenty press ups to do, there and then.

One of the lessons took place in the back of a box Luton van. In the back, made by young offenders, it had been converted into an exact replica of a regulation sized prison cell. Complete with the furnishings that a real cell had, including a very basic toilet in the corner.

That van is still at HMP Doncaster Young Offenders Institution.

It taught them with the seriousness of the real world, the values of their choices, to take the right or wrong path in life.

Both Alec and I had been promised support to attend the events by our managers. It didn't happen.

As long as we were attending events voluntarily, all was fine, as soon as we needed time off to attend one, when we had been rota'd to work. We were unable to.

We were eventually told by our management, that the scheme had been ended and disbanded and therefore, we were no longer required.

That was not so, it is still fully functioning and is going from strength to strength, although it doesn't have any ambulance input!

It is in operation all over the north of England. We have been told that our presence is missed and that they would have liked us to continue.

Thanks YAS!

Kirklees Road Safety Champions.

Alec and I also worked with the Kirklees Road Safety Champions.

Now, that was a different idea, a true innovation. Different from anything we had ever been involved in before. There was to be a team of young people, of all senior school ages and from all sorts of class backgrounds. Educating other young people in road safety.

They (the young people were known as Champions), would be educating their peers. To educate them in road safety, by using their own ideas and methods.

They even came up with their own newsletter, it was involving cartoon characters that they had created themselves. The Champions, had developed their own slogans, and even made a few short films on "YouTube".

But they would be supported by adults and professionals, making sure that the advice that they were giving was correct. We would give them all the assistance that we could in a fun and enjoyable way. Through games, visual displays and practical involvement.

The Champions were involved in all stages, even playing the roles of patients. And the Police, Fire and Ambulance personnel, at the scene of a staged road accident.

We would use wrecked cars at the fire station and get the "patients" safely extricated. It was letting them see what it was like from our point of view, at an incident.

The scheme, was led by Siobhan (partner of Aaron, of Huddersfield ambulance station), for and on behalf of Kirklees Council.

It involved several members of the emergency services, yet again it was Alec and me that represented the ambulance service. We worked our magic to teach the young people, the Champions who would be doing the educating.

As usual, the senior management support was negligible. We attended many of the events, but only the ones that we could in our own time.

The police and fire services attended all the events and were paid their full rate for attending.

Bobby our locality manager at the time, did try and support us, wherever he could.

He even nominated us both for one of the Yorkshire Ambulance Service, WE CARE Awards.

We were runners up in our category, for our voluntary service.

I was presented with a framed certificate on behalf of Alec and myself at a posh hotel in Leeds, the Met Hotel. It used to be known as the Metropole Hotel.

The presentation was done by special guest Falklands hero Simon Weston and our Chief Executive David Whiting.

We did have some support from our Press Office, known as Corporate Affairs now. In association with them I had some cards made. Credit card sized giving basic CPR instructions. They made thousands.

Unfortunately the programme of the Road Safety Champions has run it's course and it has come to an end after a very successful three years.

A lot of young people had aspirations from their time with the Champions, including two wonderful young lads, twins. They had both decided early on that they wanted to work for the ambulance service.

They both got jobs for the YAS, at Huddersfield, PTS to start with. Their dreams are just beginning to come to fruition. Others champions have gone into nursing.

There were extremely positive results all round. It was a very successful initiative, winning awards for their initiative and inventiveness. Even meeting royalty, Prince Andrew the Duke of York presented one of their awards.

Young people, talking to young people and they were listened to. They were on exactly the right level to teach their peers, they were using the language that the kids of their own age used.

A brilliant concept.

Interfering trouble stirring vindictive sod!

Whilst attending one of the road safety champions events, we needed a vehicle. The only one available at the time, was the display vehicle used for our "Aspiring Foundation Trust"

That was housed in a converted "WAS" motor, an almost empty, full sized emergency vehicle. Save for some seats and a couple of flat screen tv's, to use for display purposes.

The vehicle was ideal for the type of presentations that we would be giving.

As usual people sometimes get the wrong idea.

Dean one of our Huddersfield paramedics rang me later that evening, he asked if I was supporting the Foundation Trust Application. I told him that it would be one of the last things that I would ever be involved in, to me that would be adding some of the final nails, to the coffin of the NHS ambulance service as we know it.

He explained that another member of our staff, who is not going to be named here. Had been sending messages via text and social media, that some of the messages were very derogatory statements about me and that some of them were very personal. He said "I think that you need to speak to him".

He seems to be proud of the fact that if someone makes a mistake, however large or small, he will promptly report them. He just cannot keep his big gob shut. He always has to interfere where he is most certainly not wanted.

He seems to think that it is funny.

I went into the station a couple of mornings after, he was there on his own and he never said a word. It was only when a few more people came in, he stood up, all high and mighty in the mess room.

He shouted my name, then he demanded. "I want some answers from you! Who do you think you are? Are you, or are you not, supporting the Foundation Trust?"

I ignored him.

He expected me to answer to him. Whether I support the foundation trust or not, has got sod all to do with him. Or anyone else for that matter.

The only time that I will ever answer to him, is when he asks for a lift back up off the floor, after I have knocked him on his arse.

I will answer him then. The answer will of course be, NO!

He has been very close to being "decked" on several occasions, mainly by husbands or partners of the female staff that he has upset, or offended.

He doesn't know how lucky he is.

Road Safety Week. Calderdale Roadshow.

In September 2015. I was asked to be part of the fire service roadshow in Halifax, for the annual Road Safety Week.

The event would be taking place at the Halifax Victoria Theatre in late November. I was wanted to go on stage and talk, to up to a 1,000 people aged 16-25 years.

They wanted a story of a job that I had attended, a story that had some personal connotations. Hopefully with a little drama and a twist or two in the story. To go into it in some details, details that may really shock the young audience into making the correct choices in life.

I wrote a story about a job that Carl and I had attended. It's timing and the patient concerned's choices, had become very close to me, too close in some ways. It became quite emotional and I didn't feel that I could stand up in front of so many people, I couldn't do it.

Alec had done the previous year's event, but he had retired earlier in the year and was no longer available. As we all knew, Alec didn't have any problems with talking, especially in public.

The talk would be in addition to a fireman and a policeman telling their stories.

Then the mother of a son killed by a drunk driver, her twist was that it was her son that had been the one who had actually been drinking. Followed by a young lad, Sam, who had been left wheel chair bound. He had become paralysed in a road rage accident, fuelled by drugs.

He was like me and couldn't tell his story himself, due to nerves. The fireman, Tom, did it. With Sam (better than I did) sat on the stage at his side, in his wheelchair.

For the next year, he plans to be on stage, with his mother as well. Not giving a speech, but to take part in an interview situation, to get their story across.

At the start of the event, as the students were filing in to the auditorium, there was some really loud bass music. Then the lights went out, there was a loud soundtrack of a car skidding. Then the tell tale sound of a crash. Smoke appeared from the stage, along with blue flashing lights and the sound of sirens. As the smoke cleared, the lights at the back of the stage revealed a wrecked car on its side all alone on the stage.

Between each of the guest speakers, some horrendously graphic videos and scenes of accidents were shown on a big screen. It was cold, hard and sharp, shock sequences. It had to be.

To put an even bigger twist on my story, I knew that I wouldn't have been able to stand there and do it myself. I got my eldest son. Adrian, also an Advanced Emergency Medical Technician (AEMT) like me, he was going to tell it. He adapted my story of the job and he made it his own.

His partner Laura and me were sat in the audience. He came on centre stage and confidently delivered the following, he was great. It came over very well.

This is my story, as told from Adrian's perspective.

A wrong decision!

Hello everyone, my name is Adrian. I'm an advanced emergency medical technician (but I prefer to just say "ambulance man") and I work for Yorkshire Ambulance Service. I'm here, along with all these other people, to try and deliver a message. Some of you may already be drivers, and if you spend as much time as I do on the roads, you'll no doubt encounter countless IDIOTS on the road every day! People, who for whatever reason, think it's okay to risk their own, and anyone else's lives just to get to wherever they're going. How can it be that important? Don't you just wanna drag them from their drivers seats, give them a good, hard slap across the face and tell them the error of their ways!? Well, think of this as a preemptive, figurative slap across the face. A wakeup call. We are not invincible. Nothing can be that important that we can drive at those speeds, pull off reckless and dangerous manoeuvres, drive while drunk, exhausted, unqualified or otherwise incapable, potentially at the gravest cost.

As you can probably imagine, in our lines of work, we commonly - I mean far, far too often - encounter incidents in the aftermath of somebody making a wrong choice. We do everything we can, what we're trained and experienced to do. We have to be professional and confident, no matter how adverse the situation. Sometimes, lives are saved. Sometimes, all we can do is "pick up the pieces". And yes, unfortunately I do mean that both figuratively and literally. We somehow find words to console and reassure family members in unimaginable situations, all because someone thought they were the only driver on the road that mattered.

After dealing with an event such as this, we have to carry on with the rest of our shift, go home to our own families and get on with our lives as normal. For some, this is much easier than others. I can't think of any of my colleagues who wouldn't have imagined "what if?" scenarios involving their own family members. Some may agree that this actually helps us to do our job well, helps remind us how all our patients are people and have their own families. I treat everyone how I'd want to be treated myself, how I'd want my own family looked after and cared for. So it's easy to liken patients to people we love.

The most frustrating thing, to me, about my job, is that we hardly ever find out how a patient is doing after we've finished treating them, be it referring them to another service or taking them to hospital. If we do, it's usually from staff at the hospital who dealt with them after us, but the information is limited. We might learn that a patient was discharged home, or that they were admitted to a ward, or in more serious circumstances, to the intensive care unit (ICU). After a patient has left A&E, where they've gone is almost always all we can find out about them, that is of course if they survived. There are very rare exceptions, where coincidences reunite us with the patient or their family, or they convey messages of thanks through letters or speaking to other health care professionals.

I'm going to tell you about a "job" from a few years ago that I didn't attend myself, it was a colleague of mine. This is his account of a young, fit and healthy lad who had everything to live for.

He was from a "broken" home. His dad had been in the army and they had travelled around a lot, it'd been very difficult for his family. His mum and dad divorced. He lived with his mum who had remained single. He spent as many weekends as he could with his dad and his new partner. This arrangement had been working well from around 7 years old.

At the age of 15, things began to change. He was going to do what HE wanted, he was nearly an adult! His behaviour changed, his schoolwork failed dramatically. He lost self discipline, normally he would take care of his appearance, now he didn't care. He was scruffy, his hair was greasy and unkempt, he developed an aversion to soap and water... he stunk!

He started hanging around with wrong-'uns, began stealing things - petty things, he'd tell himself, taking drugs - just weed, in his mind tame stuff. His parents didn't know how to handle him. He'd shut himself off from them, barely speak if he could get away with it, sometimes for days at a time. He developed a drinking habit.

At 16 and a half, his world came crashing down. His dad was killed, he was a pedestrian knocked down by a drunk driver. What was he going to do? Dad was his supporting crutch, cruelly ripped away from him. Mum was there, but she'd never been the strong one. His drinking problem worsened. He was on a downward spiral, brought lower by this tragedy. He couldn't carry on like this, he would have to change, sort himself out.

After thinking long and hard, he knew what he had to do. The Army, like his dad. The Duke of Wellington's Regiment, known affectionately around here as the Duke of Boots or the Havercake Lads among other nicknames, now part of The Yorkshire Regiment. That'd be it, a new start as an infantryman, to be challenged, they would make a man of him.

But he was knocked back at the first hurdle. At the Army Careers Office, they wanted people with potential. Not a scruffy, drug-taking, alcoholic teenager.

However, he was told that if he cleaned himself up, got free of all the intoxicants, that he'd be given another chance.

With the support of his mum and his dad's partner and with determination and willpower, he did just that. 8 months later, he returned to the Careers Office. Providing he passed his medical and his drug tests were clear, he'd be accepted to begin training. His dad would have been so proud. All the hard work would've been worth it. Soon, the letter arrived; all clear, of course it was. He was in!

He rang all his mates, this was cause to celebrate! He'd drive though, because he didn't drink anymore after all. Well they taunted him, "Just one pint!" and he was tempted... I mean it wouldn't harm, and it *was* his celebration. He'd earned it, he told himself. So that one pint led to another, and another... then some shots... before long he was out of control.

He didn't pause to think. He set off to drive, taking some of his mates home. Just before one in the morning, not even half a mile into the journey, the inevitable happened.

He lost control of his car on a downhill bend, hitting a wall full-on, spinning the car around 180 degrees across the road before hitting a concrete lamppost, which in turn snapped at the base and came crashing down, landing on and flattening the roof of the stricken car.

Unbelievably, all three of his mates managed to climb out of the car with relatively minor injuries. Our wannabe soldier was trapped in the wreckage. His unrestrained body was twisted grotesquely, his head and neck badly injured, bent bizarrely backwards over the drivers seat, his face pressed into the fabric of the roof lining which was saturated and dripping with blood. One of his arms broken and dangling unnaturally down the side of the seat, both legs crushed almost beyond recognition, both with multiple open and closed fractures, badly bleeding, trapped and hidden in the mangled wreckage of his car. The engine had been forced right back, pushing into the passenger compartment. Just to make matters worse, if they could possibly be any worse, it was pouring with rain AND... the live wires from the collapsed streetlamp were fizzing and sparking in close proximity to the vehicle.

As bleak as it sounds, this guy was still alive! After 999 was called, all the emergency services arrived, including my colleague. Over the course of the next TWO AND A HALF HOURS they all worked tirelessly to save this budding squaddie. My colleague and his mate had crawled inside the car and were tending to his breathing, restoring his compromised airway, his blood loss, trying to stem countless haemorrhages while getting him securely immobilised and treating other injuries. Other ambulance staff were outside, fetching more equipment as required. The police were piecing together information to establish what had happened while keeping the road closed so they could work safely. The fire service were making the lamppost safe, using special equipment to carefully remove it and the roof, bit by bit, before everyone was able to work together to carefully extricate him from the carnage. On that street, all soaking in the rain, there must've been up to 50 emergency services personnel all with a common purpose, saving this man's life.

It was only when he was brought onto the ambulance, strapped tight to a stiff board on a stretcher, that the full extent of his injuries could be properly observed. Still unconscious, gasping for breath, his heart, previously racing to compensate for all the bleeding, now slowing dangerously. Despite all the lifesaving treatment, he was dying.

The time had come for him to be rushed to Huddersfield Royal Infirmary, where a full emergency trauma team had been assembled and were awaiting his arrival, to continue his treatment. Eventually, he was stabilised, before being transferred by another emergency ambulance to the neurosurgical care unit at Leeds General Infirmary.

His life had been saved. Months in hospital, followed by many more months of rehab and physio at home helped him recover. But... he would never fully recover.

He lost an eye - it had to be removed in surgery. He struggled to walk, relying on crutches. He had permanent, disfiguring facial, head, arm, body and leg scars. But he'd been affected more than just physically. The severe brain injury he'd suffered caused a massive change in personality. He had uncontrollable mood swings, was often aggressive and violent, then other times becoming extremely paranoid and withdrawn. No more dreams of joining the army, if not for his disabilities, then for the criminal record he now had for drink driving - the very thing that had torn his world apart in the first place. He'd changed his life alright, but far from how he'd planned.

You might wonder why this account was so detailed, how my colleague learned so much about his life before the tragedy and what his life had become afterwards. Well, this was one of those "exceptions" where my colleague met his patient and his family after the incident. And not just the crew who attended the crash, many of my colleagues have met him. Again and again and again. Unfortunately, always in unpleasant circumstances. This man has racked up a great number of 999 calls either for being drunk and incapable, fighting, self-harming or even overdosing on tablets.

Now, for the last few months, none of my colleagues have seen him or heard anything about him. Since early September this year his house appears to have been let out to new tenants. I'd like to hope he finally managed to start turning his life round, but of course, a different, much sadder ending could also be the case.

What makes this story so poignant for my colleague is that 3 weeks before this young lad was accepted to start training for the army, his own son was. They are the same age, give or take a couple of months. His son went on to "serve Queen and Country" for 5 years, started his own family and later began working for Yorkshire Ambulance Service, like his dad. He's now been in the service 7 years and still makes his dad very proud.

If you didn't guess, that colleague of mine is my dad. He's been doing the job that I do now for over 36 years. He happens to be sat right there too, you might see him after this if you have any questions!

Just think... If he'd thought just a little harder that night, if he'd made the right decision, we could've ended up training together! He might've still been in the army now, could've been been making 40 grand a year and retired when he was 40! Or he might've left like I did, maybe become an ambulance man like me and make *cough mumble* and retire when he's ANCIENT. Or I dunno, become a bloody footballer or something?

We all have to make decisions all the time, and nearly all boil down to two choices; yes or no, right or wrong... sensible or stupid. Should I dye my hair for Halloween with temporary or semi - permanent? Should I volunteer to do something I've never done before and get up and talk in front of 700 people? Should I put ketchup or brown sauce on my bacon butty? (Brown sauce, obviously) But when one of the options can devastate or even claim your life, or that of your nearest and dearest, or a complete stranger's... we need to start choosing more carefully.

The choice is yours. ***Thank You.***

We attended the road safety event in November 2016. It was at the same location, the Halifax Victoria Theatre. That event was slightly more organised and more speakers were involved.

We even had some student actors in ripped clothes, complete with bloody make up, on stage at the beginning.

Our friend Sam with the wheelchair, couldn't face the public. He had to back down from it, he was embarrassed and couldn't continue. A shame really, he had quite a tale to tell.

None of us blame him though.

The stories are very personal, they are very hard hitting. The stories don't leave anything hidden, it just was too much for him.

Adrian did the same story again, it went down really well, he seemed much more confident the second time.

Throughout the whole performance, several students had to leave the auditorium feeling very overwhelmed and shocked. By what they were seeing, hearing and experiencing.

The comments, although the students had been extremely shocked, all of them seemed to be saying that it was a positive experience and that it had really made them step back and realise what can happen.

I suppose that is exactly the result we were after.

The next event, for 2017, planning is already taking place for an even bigger and better performance. The Yorkshire Air Ambulance are hoping to get involved as well.

We are going to pull out even more stops, effects and shocks next time.

Remembrance Sunday.
Since I started the Ambulance Service in 1981. Alec and me have attended to most of the annual Remembrance Parades, at the Huddersfield Parish Church. In fact, I have only missed three in all of those years.

We have tried to assemble larger groups to attend, the maximum we have managed to get was eighteen. Usually though, it was just the two of us. Occasionally we get a couple of hangers on, occasionally some retired staff that attend.

They can hang with us anytime!

Now that Alec has retired, it looks like it might just be little old me.

We do have an honorary member though, another Alec. He is a lad with Downs Syndrome. He has made countless uniforms, from his visits to charity shops. They are of all services, British and American and he is always a high ranking officer. Alec has a heart of gold and attends the parade every year.

In the run up to the parade, he will salute everyone and I mean everyone.

One year he saluted the Lord Lieutenant of West Yorkshire, who didn't see him. The Lord Lieutenant had turned, and he walked away.

In his own inimitable way Alec bellowed "Oi!!!"

The Lord Lieutenant turned round, when he saw Alec saluting him. He marched straight over and apologised to him. Then he stood to attention and performed his smartest and regimented salute, using his ceremonial sword.

Alec was made up, he hasn't been ignored since.

He is also one for the ladies, he will stop them, take their hand and kiss it like a gentleman should do.

Men not in uniform, well they are not ignored either. He will give a hand shake, a firm one, he grips your hand that tightly that he nearly breaks all of your fingers.

There can be no doubt, that the highlight of the day is when Alec is singing. That is something special to behold. Due to his learning disabilities, Alec cannot read. But he joins in loudly, with heart and soul wherever he can.

When the National Anthem is announced, Alec comes in to his own. He loves it. He is so proud to be there.

He roars out his own words, to his own tune and at his own pace.

It is sung with some passion, the only recognisable word is "Queen", and that comes a couple of seconds after everybody else's. A little like Corporal Jones in Dad's Army.

When the National Anthem is finished, Alec usually gets his well deserved applause.

Then he marches back to the Town Hall with us, his head held high.

To me that is done in the true spirit of the day.

Yes we do laugh, but you can't help it. Predominantly though, you are laughing with him as a character, not at him as a disabled person.

He loves it!

National Memorial Arboretum, Staffordshire.

A few years ago in 2012. Wendy and I attended a memorial service at the National Ambulance Memorial, it was held at the National Memorial Arboretum in Staffordshire.

A wonderful and moving experience, everyone there were wearing very smart uniforms. I was there in a fleece, it was a case of the Yorkshire Ambulance Service being the poor relations again.

I couldn't have felt worse if I had been in a flat cap and clogs, with a whippet on a lead.

I vowed that the next time (a two yearly event). I would have a proper green blazer jacket, look smart and present a poppy wreath.

I bought the jacket and the wreath, complete with Yorkshire Ambulance Service Crown Badge. (On both). But I was ill and I couldn't attend that year's event.

I decided to present the wreath at the cenotaph in Greenhead Park in Huddersfield, on the eleventh of November. I went to tell my manager Bobby of my intentions.

His next statement knocked me totally sideways. He told me that if I was to present the wreath, an official British Legion made poppy wreath, with the official YAS crest/badge. Then I would have to seek permission from senior directors. He warned me, that the permission may be denied, so as not to "offend" other races or creeds that work for us.

That, without shadow of a doubt was the most offensive thing that anyone had ever said to me. I dug my heels in. I told him, that I would not ask, I flatly refused.

I would DO IT, I would present the wreath at all costs.

If anyone wanted to stop me, let them try! And that would be the day that I would resign from the service, without any doubt.

I cannot believe that it had even been mentioned. I wear my grandad Firth's First World War medals with pride. What he did for us 100+ years ago, will always be remembered, and nobody will stop that.

And yes. "We will remember them!"

WW1 Medals.

Grandma Firth had been married twice, her first husband was killed in the Great War. The First World War. He had been dad to uncle James and uncle Bill. Uncle James was killed in action during the Second World War. Uncle Bill of course was very close to us, he had a son, our cousin Alan Collings.

Alan has been tracing his grandad's family tree and his grandad's War exploits. Including finding and visiting his grave in France. Between him and cousin Michael, uncle James' lad they have researched a lot.

When mum died in 2011. I acquired an old box, inside it was grandad Firth's medals. There was three more medals with them. Those were grandad Collings' First World War medals, Alan was absolutely made up when I gave them to him.

A magic moment.

Leonard McLean BEM.

Another remembrance story, this one is about an old ambulance man, Leonard McLean. He had heard that we were going to have an open day at the ambulance station, for charity.

He came to me prior to the open day in 1985, he had brought an old photograph taken of himself and his old mate Cess. It had been taken at the old Huddersfield

Corporation Ambulance depot on Leeds Road, behind the Peacock Pub. It had been taken in the year that I was born, 1958.

I managed to find out that Cess was still alive, although he was suffering from leukaemia. He lived very local to the ambulance station at Marsh. I got them to meet up at the open day. They hadn't seen each other since Leonard had left.

The photo that Leonard brought, I had sent it to be published in a book, one that was being produced about the history of ambulances. The man tasked with producing that book, although now based in the North East, was originally from Huddersfield.

He has a tradition that, whatever vehicle that he is producing a book about, he will find one image from Huddersfield to put in.

That picture was perfect for him.

I had managed to get both Leonard and Cess a copy of the ambulance book. Unfortunately Cess died from his leukaemia before I could get it to him. His wife Liesel (from Austria), was made up though, when I gave her the copy.

Leonard McLean had left the Huddersfield County Borough Ambulance in the 1960's, he had been presented with a Royal Humane Life Saving Award. It was for resuscitating and saving the life of a little girl from a house fire. He still occasionally sees the little girl, who is now a mum and grandma to children of her own. She still calls him uncle Leonard.

After he left the ambulance service, he worked at the ICI in their ambulance and medical room.

Leonard was awarded the British Empire Medal for his work.

I always used to see Leonard at Remembrance Day. He used to be at the rear of the parade with all the civil dignitaries and councillors.

As well as his medical jobs, he had been a driver for the Mayor of Huddersfield and he had been a long serving Justice of the Peace.

He told me that he was very proud of me, for attending the parades every year. He then asked me to accept his miniature version of the British Empire Medal, he said that there was no-one left working for the ambulance service of his era and would I wear it in remembrance of him, when he had gone.

A promise I readily made with honour.

Leonard at the moment of writing this, has been very ill, again with the unforgiving dementia. I have given him and his daughter many old photos that I have acquired of the old Leeds Road depot.

Sometimes, he does remember faces from the past, I hope the photo's help.

Here is an article that he wrote in 1970 for the ICI works magazine.

"So, you wanted to be an ambulance driver, did you?"

It was 1956 when I started ambulance driving. First of all I had to take a very keen driving test, because it sometimes meant that you had to be able to drive at excess speeds to get your patient to hospital, and you had to get the knack of missing grates in the road, so that you would not cause any discomfort to the people you were carrying. To make the ideal ambulance driver, it requires three things; Patience, Understanding and the Love of helping people.

I remember very well my first week as an ambulance driver. I reported at 08:15 am on the Monday morning, and my first job that came along was just a transfer from one hospital to another. The person who I was working with said it was the practice that the new man should act as driver, and I, having no first aid experience at all, could see the point in this. I was placed with a very reliable man who showed me how to carry, in certain ways, a person who was just ill and one who was seriously injured. It was a thrilling experience for me to drive that ambulance. 24 was its number, and NAN was its call sign. We had quite a lot of experiences together before I came to ICI.

As I said, I recall my first week; it was winter time and there was a lot of snow. Two or three days after starting I had to take some medical samples to Wakefield; Lord what a day it was, all the ambulancemen were run off their feet, with road accidents and people falling and breaking their limbs. When I left Huddersfield at 9:45 am the weather was really closing in and I had to go up the cutting known as Lepton Edge. It was snowing very hard and I had all on to keep to the road, in the end I had to come to a halt as the snow was just too thick. I could not reach my base by radio so I had to get through to a phone which was at a garage a mile or so away. The thought going through my head at that time was "so, you wanted to be an ambulance driver, did you?". The garage man thought I was the abominable snowman. They sent the Land Rover out for me because we had to abandon the ambulance at the side of the road, and there it stayed for three days. By approximately 2:30 pm, four and three quarter hours after I had left Huddersfield, I was back at the base. There was just time to grab a cup of hot tea, then the phone went. It was a maternity case at a farmers croft at South Crosland, which is a village just outside Huddersfield. We could not get any nearer the farm than three fields away, so my mate and I had to stumble and pick our way through as best we could. The lady wasn't quite ready for producing us with any kind of bundle of joy, but it was quite clear that could not afford to waste much time. We asked the farmer if he had a tractor, and he said not, but that he did have a horse. So we got old "Dobbin" fixed up with what was the back door, roped our stretcher to it and off we went through the snow to the ambulance. We did manage to get the woman to the hospital in time to give birth to a baby girl.

I would, at this time, say that in winter you hear of the buses and trains coming to a halt, but not for the ambulance driver. This also applies to fog. I once drove for a whole fortnight in black swirling fog, and more than once, I could have thrown my driving license on the fire. It did not stay winter all the time though, spring and summer came along. Gone were those dark dismal days and nights, and with them the first aid classes which we had attended in winter. I was also getting more experienced every day and was really settling down to the job.

Every now and then I still get a schoolboys kick out of ringing the bell etc. on emergency cases, but at the same time wonder what I will find, or see at the accident. One day we got an emergency call to go to the river Colne at Lockwood; a woman had fallen into it. When we got there, she was just sat on a small island under the bridge that she had jumped off. Luckily the river wasn't very deep, but we had to go and see if she was hurt. There were quite a few large stones for us to walk on in order to reach her, but I misplaced my foot and into the river I went, the cold making me catch my breath. The lady was not very badly injured, she told us that she had had a tiff with her boyfriend and so she had jumped off the bridge. I will not write what I was thinking.

I have sometimes seen my colleagues upset and put off their meals when we have had a child killed on the road. I myself, was called to a street accident where a small girl who had been playing at the side of the road had been hit by a wagon. Her little pants were black where she had been playing in the dirt; she had wet them just like any child does at that age. I picked her up and made her comfortable in the ambulance then raced to the hospital with her. I was just going through the doors with her in my arms when she died. The nurse told me to take her into the room and after I did, I wept unashamedly. "Could I have got there any faster than I did?" This is the sort of thing that goes through your mind after.

However, we do have a lighter side as well. There was the time that I left my mate at the hospital. As we did in those days, we had loaded up the ambulance, I thought that he had got in the back with the patients, so off I went. I was not aware that he was running down the road behind the ambulance, until the following message came over the radio. "Do you often let your mate run at the back?" I looked in the side mirror and there he was, jogging after me. I was anything but an ambulance driver when he caught up with me!

I have tried to outline the importance of being an ambulance driver. Every day is a new day with different people to meet and different jobs cropping up. Some people may think that we just sit waiting for calls, but I assure you that this is not the case, there are numerous jobs. There are the school buses to man, day patients to take to hospital and there are the infirm to take to handy work classes. Yes, it is hard work being an ambulance driver, but an exciting and rewarding one. Rewarding in the sense that you can help people, especially the old ones who look forward, yes, look forward to to you picking them up, because sometimes you are their only link between them and the outside world.

Leonard McLean BEM, 20th October 1970.

Leonard passed away on the 6th June, 2017.

His loving wife Steph, is aware of this story's inclusion. I have deliberately not altered his name, or any details, as a tribute to him.

God bless you Leonard, you were an inspiration.

CHAPTER 55

MY LEGACY TO FIRST AID.

Firthy's Top Knot.

One time when working with Carl, we had a call to an elderly male, he had fallen. Commonly known as a "grandad down", refers to male, or obviously "granny down" if female.

As well as falling, he suffered with dementia, a horrible, unforgiving condition of the mind.

He had the mental age of a young child.

His only injury was a long and nasty looking laceration to the top of his scalp. It was still bleeding, but not profusely. It wasn't a life threatening injury, but it would be needing several stitches putting in.

It was a nightmare to bandage, or to put a dressing on it of any description. He didn't understand what we were trying to do and as such, he couldn't keep still. He would shuffle and flinch every time we went anywhere near him.

Without putting on a comedy bandage, looking like something out of a "carry on" film, they used to do a comedy one for toothache. We decided that we had to leave it alone.

It didn't look very professional though, when we arrived at the hospital with the wound uncovered and open to infection.

It was shortly after that job, that I saw a little baby in an incubator, in the special care baby unit, (SCBU). To keep its temperature stable in the incubator, they had made a "bonnet" out of some tubi-grip support bandage.

That set my cogs turning, the old grey matter started to fry.

Why not?

In the A&E department, there was a more flexible, net based tubular bandage. It was used to hold light dressings in place on the arms or legs, it stopped the dressings being disturbed. It kept them neat and tidy when applied over the top.

I got hold of some of different sizes. It is supplied on a five metre roll, I got some lengths of maybe half a metre, in three different sizes. I got three of each. Three centimetres, two point five and two centimetres wide, from side to side.

If a knot was placed at one end and around twenty centimetres cut to length, then it could be stretched over the top of most sizes of head. If a dressing was placed over the wound first, then the gauze netting could be stretched straight over the top and voila!

A perfect scalp wound bandage, holding the dressing perfectly in place. If the netting moved at all, the weave was so open, that an adhesive tape could be applied to fix it more securely in place.

I could also see that the dressing could be utilised in numerous situations, even when a patient had a spinal injury. It can be applied whilst the patient is still and immobilised in situ.

Or even if the patient was already on a spinal board, there is no movement of the head or neck required to fit one..

The "Firthy's top knot" had been born!

"Firthy's top knot" has been used on several patients and even on a member of staff.

The dressing has even been featured on television, it was on a patient that we had taken on a spinal board to the LGI. A film crew were in attendance filming for a TV documentary, it was featured on the episode, even if it was only briefly.

I had applied a "Firthy's top knot" to a young lad, who had fallen down some rocks at a quarry in the Colne Valley and had been knocked unconscious for a time.

It was filmed and used on an episode of Yorkshire Television's Helicopter Heroes.

I have shown and explained the method to apply it, to several members of staff and doctors at A&E of varying grades.

Although I have never seen anyone else apply one. Every time that I have explained it, it has been met with unanimous approval.

One day perhaps!

For advice only.

I came up with the idea of credit card sized instructions for CPR, they could then be given out wherever we were.

Our Corporate Affairs department really approved the idea and said that they would fund them, once passed by our medical directors.

The wording was checked and double checked. The layout and design was fully approved and 10,000 of the plastic credit card sized instructions, were produced.

They have clear and concise instructions on how to save a life on one side. With a bit more of a detailed explanation on the reverse.

I was given 5,000 of them, they are ideal just to slip in a wallet.

Any time that I attend a public event, garden party or anything. I have my pockets full of them. I give them out to the members of the public, of all ages.

The instructions are very easy to follow for anybody.

CHAPTER 56.

FAMILY ACCIDENTS.

Mum's had an accident!

The 5th of May 2003, was May Day bank holiday Monday. I got a call from my sister Diane.
Mum had fallen in the street, outside what is a pizza shop. It used to be Haigh's mini market, at Paddock Head. Diane thought that mum might have broken her arm.

Luckily, I was at home, so I raced across to Paddock Head. Mum was still sat on the pavement. Both of her arms were broken and she was in a lot of pain.

When I arrived, the ambulance was already in situ. I'm really sorry, but due to my emotions running wild at the time, I only can only remember one of the crew and that was another Jack, being there.

They were struggling to lift mum and with having broken both of her arms, it limited some of her treatment. It is very difficult to cannulate someone with one broken arm, let alone both of them. Intra venous pain relief had to be ruled out.

Entonox, our gas and air comes into its own in those situations. After a couple of minutes, we were able to lift her up off the floor and onto the ambulance cot.

Mum was taken to HRI in the ambulance, Diane went with her, I followed in my car and my other sister Lindsay met us up there.

Following the x-rays, we could see that she was in a right mess. Her left wrist was broken, both the radius and ulna bones had been cracked clean across. She had also snapped her right humorous, the head of the bone had broken right off near her shoulder.

Mum had a bit more entonox, rather a lot really and that made her very drowsy. The doctor was then able to give her arm a short sharp tug, her wrist fracture had been realigned and a plaster cast was placed on it.

The other injury was far more more difficult to deal with.

The two options are, surgery. Which has its own risks and complications, especially with mum's long term breathing problems. Or to leave it to heal naturally, with rest and support.

The only support really available, is a collar and cuff sling.

The idea with that, is to allow the arm to drop somewhat naturally. The sling supports the weight of the wrist, the lever principle then allows some natural traction on the bone at the shoulder end.

That should then in turn, ease some of the pain, by not allowing the bones to rub against each other.

Healing takes its time, but it will happen naturally.

As well as the obvious predicament that mum was in, there were unseen issues. Her self care, eating, washing, drying, dressing and even basic sanitary care. Mum was going to be unable to do anything for herself, for quite some time.

Diane managed to get mum a bed downstairs at her house, mum would have to stay there. She needed twenty four hour care, for the next few weeks anyway.

The injuries were going to take some recovery. I was on nights the first particular week.

The Comms Centre were excellent.

I had explained the situation to them, that if mum had any problems. Even if she had only slipped down in bed, Diane was unable to lift her on her own. She would have to call me.

They were happy with that, jobs permitting.

It wouldn't be possible nowadays, we wouldn't have the time and probably wouldn't be any where in the near vicinity anyway.

Carl and I would go out, usually within twenty minutes or so. We would use our lifting aids to just simply "utch" her up the bed, sometimes it was twice a night.

There were some issues over compensation claims for mum, she didn't want to bother with a claim at all.

Don't think so!

Diane was there every step of the way. There was doubt over who caused the hole that had been left in the pavement.

I found an old photograph of Haigh's shop, from the days when the trolley buses were running. Clearly in the picture, was a trolley bus pole, it was there to support the electric cables.

At that time, it had belonged to Huddersfield Corporation, the council, so now it was Kirklees' responsibility.

The solicitor did the rest.

Eventually mum was awarded, I believe a fair amount of compensation, for her pain and suffering. She never actually said how much.

Mum stayed at Diane's for quite some time, it was a long recovery. Not just her arms, but her general well being and confidence.

Truth be known, I don't think mum was ever really back to her normal self.

There were other signs at the time, in hindsight I think that it was at that time, that the Alzheimer's was already starting to manifest itself.

Unbelievably, the house next door to Diane's became available to buy. It had belonged to the parents of Cliff, another of Paddock's former scout leaders. His parents had lived there, but unfortunately they had needed to go into care.

We looked at buying the house as a family, but to no avail, it was not in our finance bracket at the time.

Diane's boss from the Post Office came to the rescue, he agreed to buy the property and rent it to mum for as long as she needed.

What an opportunity!

If it hadn't have come up at that time, heaven only knows what we would have done. Mum moved in on 17th of January 2004. I remember the Asian lady across the road, brought mum a welcome pack. It consisted of fresh fruit and vegetables donated by mum's new neighbours.

Diane's caring was exemplary, Lindsay helped where she could, but nothing will ever take away my admiration for the way Diane looked after mum.

Medals should be issued there!

A previous fall.

Mum had also had a previous fall at home in 1991. She rang me to say that she had fallen and that her ankle was very swollen. I called in on my way to work to look at it and it didn't look good to me.

When I got to work, I had to explain to our Comms Centre what she had done. Ex cadet, Manny was to be my crew mate for that day.

Once we had clocked on duty, Comms passed us our first job, it was to go and get mum and take her up for an x-ray.

It was definitely fractured. She had to have a plaster cast on her ankle, she had it for about six weeks.

Once the cast had been removed, mum needed to have regular trips to the Infirmary for physiotherapy, by PTS ambulance. Sometimes it could be three times a week if she needed to see the doctor as well.

Dad used to love those trips out. Cliff was a star, he knew how frail that dad could be and wherever possible, he would keep dad sat on the ambulance with him.

He would take him all over Huddersfield, often stopping off somewhere for a crafty cigarette.

They were good company for each other, before Cliff saw him safely home at the end of his shift. That was great for dad and it was a nice break for mum.

I think I have said it before about Cliff, he was a legend.

Wendy's been knocked down!

16th November 2006. It would have been at around 14:00hrs. There I was, warmly tucked up in bed, fast asleep. I had been working nights.

There was a loud knock at the door, not a postman's knock, but a very persistent knocking.

I only had on my boxer shorts, instead of opening it, I shouted through the door "who is it?"

A voice said "it's Wendy".

A few more exchanges, took place. I was still half asleep, but I knew that it wasn't Wendy's voice, so who the hell was it?

Eventually I got my key and opened the door. It was Ruth from next door, she pointed to the middle of Manchester Road, she had a panic in her voice and an expression that I never want to see again.

That time as she said "it's Wendy!" She indicated to a lifeless body laid in the road.

My heart sank. I couldn't speak.

My life had just collapsed.

I ran across the garden, and jumped into the road. Holding onto Wendy, and keeping her still, was Joyce and assisting her was Dan, both of them were PTS ambulance staff. They had come across the incident involving Wendy and a car.

Wendy had stepped out between two parked cars, a car heading towards Cowlersley had to brake hard and stop. Wendy spun around quickly when she sensed it, her hands had just touched the bonnet of the car before falling into and hitting her head on the road.

There was a pool of blood coming from the top of her head, quite a pool actually.

Joyce and Dan went on to join the emergency side of the service, but it just wasn't right for them. Joyce is back and happy doing PTS. Dan went back to his former life of being a Huddersfield vicar.

At the time of the accident, as Joyce was trying to explain the events to me, Wendy was trying to speak. She was mouthing, but no words or sound were coming out.

There was a crowd around us, some offering to help, others were helping to direct traffic, all of them were shocked.

None as much as me though.

I am extremely sorry, but I have no recollection of who of my neighbours was there at the time.

If you happen to read this and were there on the day. Please, please, accept both mine and Wendy's sincere thanks for your help and concern, it was greatly appreciated.

Eventually, although it seemed to have taken ages, it was probably only minutes. I could hear the tell tale sirens in the distance. As the ambulance approached, I could see Nula driving, and Mike was sat in the attendants seat.

I had always said, that no matter what an arse Mike could be at times. If ever I needed an ambulance, I hoped that it would be him that came.

My wish had been granted, it was.

He jumped out and he took over immediately.

He whispered in my ear to "f-off", as I was "no good to Wendy dressed like that, in just your boxer shorts" and for me to "go and get changed". Whilst he and Nula were sorting Wendy out.

As I returned from the house, Wendy had been collared and boarded, immobilised and already placed in the ambulance.

Wendy, had just set off to go to town when it had happened, she still had her bus fare clenched tightly in her fist.

She received minimal treatment in the hospital, not even an x-ray.

Wendy was sent home battered and bruised, super glue had been placed in a small wound to her scalp.

Wendy is still convinced that some gravel from the road surface, may still be lurking just under the skin on her scalp.

There is a definite "spot" that is still very tender to touch. And that was ten years ago.

At the end of the day though, I returned home with the love of my life. Still walking, talking and appearing to be her normal self. No broken bones, or significant injury.

We were so lucky that the car driver was a lady with some road sense, not some stupid boy racer. I daren't begin to imagine how different the outcome could have been.

Down to the wood.

I had an extremely lucky escape myself, in the summer of 2007.

I was taking several loads of rubbish to the local re-cycling centre, including loads of garden rubbish.

Ted, Wendy's boss generously offered me the use of his old car to take the rubbish to the tip. The car was being scrapped at the end of that month and there were only a couple of days left. So it didn't matter if the garden rubbish was wet and muddy, or covered in creepies and slugs.

The only thing to remember, the gas struts that held the tailgate open on the Ford Mondeo estate, had failed. They both leaked, so the tailgate had to be held open with a broom handle.

As I was filling Ted's car with rubbish, I caught my arm on some of the thorns. Automatically I pulled my arm away, my elbow hit and knocked the broom handle away and of course the boot lid shut.

It was very heavy and dropped quickly. I had seen it coming, so I tried to jump back and get clear.

As I did so, I jumped into the front of the car parked behind me. It belonged to my next door neighbour, Peter. I then fell forwards just as the tailgate dropped, it caught me a glancing blow on the top of my head.

It still hurt and I dropped to the floor. I could feel the blood already running down my face.

I remember looking up, my son Ben had seen it all. He came running over our front garden and jumped off the wall and down beside me.

He had already rung 999 and he was still on the phone. I spoke to the call handler and explained that I was ok and that I really didn't need an ambulance.

My yellow shirt though was rapidly changing colour. I was bleeding a lot to start with, as scalp wounds do. I put pressure on the wound to stop the bleeding, when I removed the pad, the bleeding had almost stopped.

Ben took a photo on his phone. It showed clearly that I had a fifty pence piece sized lump of flesh missing from my scalp, the bone of my skull was quite visible.

As I looked around, I could see the piece of flesh hanging on the edge of the tailgate.

I lifted it off the car and put it in my mouth to give it a good clean.

Before fitting the piece back on top of my head, like it was the last piece of a jigsaw puzzle.

I then got Ben to put a proper dressing on it, before driving my own car up to A & E for treatment.

Initially the doctor, Giathe, was going to send me to Bradford Royal Infirmary for plastic surgery. I politely refused, I wanted to see if my own flesh would heal before resorting to that.

I had some steri-strips fitted over the piece of flesh and it was covered with a large white dressing.

Luckily I was in the middle of a few days off work, so I was able to wear a hat for a while.

It was a couple of weeks before the dressing was removed, but then it started to dry and heal properly. Eventually after a couple of months, it was barely noticeable.

Now, there is only a small white scar. It is about the size of a five pence piece now that can be seen. (That's how quickly money devalues). But only when I have a bit of a suntan, the scarred bit doesn't go brown.

It had tightened up and healed perfectly.

A full DIY facelift as well.

It was the edge of the boot lid that had caught me, if it had been the lock, it would most probably have fractured my skull.

I consider myself lucky on that one.

My leg's broken!

December 17th 2010, another day I will never forget.

I was working a day shift for a change, from seven in the morning until seven at night. I was the Operational Supervisor for the Kirklees and Calderdale area.

Mid morning, I was called to Longroyd Bridge, in Huddersfield. A body had been seen at the side of the railway tracks below the Springwood Bridge. Other calls stated that the person was alive and had been seen moving.

A crew and RRV had been sent from Huddersfield Station to attend.

Due to the fact that the patient was still alive. I was sent to ensure staff safety and to liaise with fire and police, on the treatment and removal of the patient from the site.

To also keep in contact with British Rail, again to ensure the safety of the crews.

I set off from Halifax ambulance station, blues and twos all the way.

I knew exactly where to get access, having been to a couple of railway suicides previously at the same place.

I parked at the back of what used to be the Albion Pub on Manchester Road, it's an Italian restaurant now.

I then had to walk up the hill and scramble up a five foot wall, to the British Rail fence. It was a two metre high, metal spiked top fence with a locked and barred gate, made of the same rails as the fence.

The Police were already on scene, but no fire service at the time.

The gate was still locked.

The only way past, was to climb over as I had done previously. I got on top of the fence and then had to pick my landing spot. There was the loose railway ballast all around, or a flat two foot square stone.

I plumbed for that.

On landing, I realised my mistake. The stone was only maybe a quarter of an inch thick, as soon as I had landed, the stone broke and my right leg went under me.

Oh shit!

The pain suddenly rushed through my body, I thought I was going to pass out. As fast as it came though, the pain went, my adrenaline had kicked in.

It's wonderful stuff that!

I had to walk at least another 250 to 300 yards up to where the crew were. The patient was a female 24 years old, she had jumped approximately 70 feet off the bridge fully intending to kill herself.

It turns out that the girl was known personally to me. She was the sister of one of my son Ben's friends. She had a lot of mental health issues and had recently lost a baby. She had become a well known drug user, an alcoholic and was a working prostitute to fund her habits.

She had obvious fractures to both her legs, a couple of them were open fractures. She had a suspected fracture of the pelvis and was being treated for head and spinal injuries as well. (Confirmation later at the hospital, she did have a couple of severe fractures to her pelvis, several fractures to various parts of her spine and a fractured skull).

We had been told via our Comms that all trains had been stopped and that we were safe to proceed. As I was speaking to the crew, another train went by on the lines. The patient was so close to that live line, that her jacket was nearly ripped off in the after draught.

I had an anxious call to make to the stationmaster at Huddersfield Railway station to ensure all lines to and from Manchester, Sheffield and Huddersfield were stopped and that no more trains would appear.

I needed full assurance of that fact.

He was asking me to tell him what colour lights were visible on any of the signals. Were any of them green? Some were. As we spoke all the signals around us finally went to red.

I was happy then, that was the confirmation I needed, that all trains were stopped.

The fire service had by then cleared the access road and by opening the gate, an ambulance could get to within 40 yards of the patient. There were three ambulance staff, two police and as many firemen as you could want, to carry the patient.

My role, there at the incident was over.

I started the long walk back to my Land Rover, it seemed to be taking forever.

A young female police officer saw me struggling. She asked me what was wrong, I told her that I thought I had broken my leg.

She lent me a helping hand, I could lean on her, it was embarrassing. We managed until we got to the wall and then she had to assist me to get down the that as well.

I said that I should be able to manage the rest of the way, as there were handrails either side of the path. Another 200 yards on and I would be able to sit down in my comfortable, Land Rover Discovery.

By the time I had got there, I was 100% certain that it wasn't a sprain, it was definitely broken. I tried to drive, no chance.

It was an automatic, but, the trouble was it was my right leg that I had hurt. With the other one I could have managed and driven myself to hospital.

I had to ask Kaley our dispatcher if she had another crew in the area, a non emergency crew would do.

Kaley wanted to know why, she said that the crew had already left the scene with the patient. "Why do you need another ambulance?"

I had to sheepishly admit that it was for me, I told her that I had broken my leg. There was a pause and then she said "I'll send one for you".

I heard them first, sirens blazing as they arrived in the car park. To the amusement of all around.

I hobbled into the back of the ambulance between them. The crew was Lisa and Janelle, working out of Halifax Dylan was out third manning, observing with them.

He took the Land Rover up to Huddersfield station and the girls took me up to A&E.

A&E Consultant Dr. Mark came and looked at me, he said straight away, even without x-ray. That as I had suspected, it was broken.

The x-ray confirmed, I had broken it, I had snapped the bottom outer end of my tibia off. I was placed in a plaster cast for six weeks.

Tragically while I was laid up my mum got very ill, she had started off with a urine infection and that had developed into urinary sepsis. She had also been suffering from Alzheimer's for a few years.

My sisters Lindsay and Diane will never know just how much I really appreciate, all that they and Diane's partner Tim, had done for mum in her latter years.

They, but especially Diane have been out of this world. Nobody anywhere in the world could have given mum any more love and care, I am so proud of my sister.

Treated with antibiotics, but not well enough to stay at home, mum was admitted to Green View care home. Whilst in there she had two falls, the second one broke her hip.

That was the last straw for mum, she wasn't strong enough to fight it. She had no idea what was happening to her.

It caused her so much distress, she was trying to remove her intravenous antibiotics. She wasn't getting any better, and inevitably, multi organ failure set in.

On the Friday the doctors asked the question about dignity and a DNAR (do not actively resuscitate) form. A legal document regarding the chosen care, if someone's heart was to stop.

That, for Lindsay and Diane, would be a most difficult and heart rending decision to even contemplate.

For me, trying not to sound callous, there was no issue.

I was happy (not the best word), to sign the paperwork. It would be the most humane thing that I could do for mum.

The hospital would then withdraw all active treatment and they would remove her drips.

Most of all though, mum would still be made comfortable with muscular injections to manage her pain relief, but that would unfortunately speed up the inevitable.

Mum wouldn't have wanted to go on like that, I'm sure that if she was aware, it is what she would have decided.

She had been an exceptionally clever lady, towards the end though, she had been reduced to the behaviour and abilities of a young child.

At times she even thought she had gone back to her childhood. Mum was worried that her dad was looking for her. She was seeing her long gone family members, in her current family, it was awful to watch.

On the Saturday and Sunday before she passed away, mum was a totally different person.

Could her Alzheimer's have suddenly gone? Could the doctor's have got it badly wrong? Had I made the wrong decision?

Mum was completely lucid and clear in her conversation.

She even asked to see my eldest grandson Scott, we hadn't let him see her before. That was in case seeing her with all the drips and extremely disorientated, had frightened him. After all, he had only just gone six years old.

We brought him in to see her, mum made such a fuss of him. And he loved it.

To him the only difference in great grandma, was the fact that she didn't have her false teeth in. A funny and pleasant, lasting memory for a young child.

As we went home from hospital on the Sunday night, mum had been so clear and lucid. We had been able to say our goodbyes. She was able to tell us that she wanted to be with dad, the love of her life, more than anything.

That was to be the last time we saw her alive.

I honestly believe that she knew and that mum died with as much care and dignity as was possible.

Since mum passed away, we have seen a remarkable amount of butterflies, they seem to appear whenever we are talking, or thinking about mum. The one that we seem to see most commonly, tends to be an almost kingfisher blue colour.

The butterfly is used in hospital, as a symbol for representing people with Alzheimer's, in our neck of the woods anyway.

They are used in over a hundred hospitals. There are different colours, to represent the severity of the Alzheimer's. Mum's was blue. It is a discreet way of informing the nursing staff, of what stage the patient is at.

Very apt.

Rest in peace mum.

You are reunited with dad now.

DVT?

When I had the plaster cast removed from my leg, it was heaven. My leg was thinner and weaker, but it felt so much lighter. That was on the Wednesday.

The following morning, I had a pain in my groin. I thought that it was due to the way that I had been resting and elevating my leg.

Then my calf muscle started aching. As the day progressed the pain got worse and my calf muscle had swollen up. It had got so tight, it was red and hot.

Whoopee do, it looked like I'd got myself a DVT!

That was just what I had needed. (A deep vein thrombosis). I went back to A&E, and yes, it was confirmed.

I had a CT (computerised tomography) scan, it showed that I had a large clot in my ankle. There were four smaller ones in my groin and a much smaller one in my right lung.

The cast must have been causing some pressure, which had been released when the pot had been removed.

I had to have daily Klexane injections, to thin my blood. They were self administered into my more than adequate abdomen.

The little sods, they're only a really small needle and you couldn't even feel it going in. You could certainly tell when you injected the liquid, bloody hell!

That stings!

I had to do that daily for four weeks, alternate sides of my generously proportioned belly. I ended up covered in little bruises. The injections were followed by a further six months on warfarin.

Initially, I was told that I couldn't have a beer, what was I going to do?

Then I was allowed to have just one pint a day, I managed to get my share.

Eventually I got some physiotherapy started at the hospital. I had been having severe hip pain, it turned out that I had been overcompensating, due to my big toe ligament being trapped in the scar tissue.

I hadn't been walking properly.

Following some intensive Physio, I returned to full duties at work, twelve months all but twelve days following my accident.

The works union that I am a member of is UNISON, they advised me to seek compensation for my injury. They sent me to see a solicitor. Our union solicitors, Thompson's of Leeds took on my case. They were first involved in the July, just over six months from the date of injury.

Eventually, after two years of investigations. They told me in a letter, that there was no compensation forthcoming. That they had exhausted all avenues and that there was nowhere to apportion any blame.

That was exactly what I had said, on my first meeting with them.

CHAPTER 57

ACROSS THE POND.

Supervisory roles.

I was a Station Officer at Huddersfield for sixteen years altogether, until the role was eventually eroded away. I also did nine years off and on, as Operational Supervisor, covering our sub division.

Based at Halifax we were responsible for Halifax, Huddersfield, Todmorden, Brighouse, Honley and Dewsbury stations and all the staff working there.

We were there to help at incidents and to look after the personal welfare of crews. That being both at work and at home if required. To liaise with the other services, to solve problems and to liaise with our Comms Centre.

Amongst many other tasks.

Visitor from the United States.

On one of my shifts as Operational Supervisor, it was the first Saturday in July 2008. I was assigned to look after an international visitor. He was Matt Zavadsky, the medical director of Tri States Ambulance Service, based in La Crosse, Wisconsin, USA.

We met at Huddersfield Ambulance Station. While there he spoke to Paramedic Pat, about his role. Pat was one of our RRV (rapid response vehicle) drivers. We then went to Halifax where he was able to speak to Paige, an ECP (emergency care practitioner). He was able to find out more of her role. A paramedic with extra skills, able to prescribe more medications, perform suturing and more.

He got quite an insight from them.

We then went to our HQ at Wakefield, he was given a guided tour around our Comms Centre by team leader Skye.

Skye then presented Matt, on my behalf, with a wooden shield with the Yorkshire Ambulance crest on it.

If you look closely, you can see one of them on the wall of the bar in the "Woolpack". The pub on the ITV television programme, Emmerdale.

We then returned to Halifax, for lunch, we had fish and chips from the award winning Stump Cross fisheries. Eaten straight out of the newspaper, with our fingers, no knives or forks and no plates. Then a cup of tea not coffee, that was all very strange for a health conscious American visitor.

It was a new experience for him. I told him that it was traditional Yorkshire fayre.

He said that he had genuinely enjoyed his lunch, but perhaps it wasn't going to be part of his everyday fitness regime.

Following lunch, I was sent to attend at a house fire in Todmorden. There had been reports that some of the occupants may have been trapped, inside the building.

During the journey with blues and twos, I was answering the phone (hands free of course). I was negotiating the heavy traffic and had an American at the side of me, banging his foot on a non existent brake pedal in the passenger side.

He asked me why I was travelling on that road and asked "why don't you use the main road?" He was extremely shocked to find that it WAS the main road, the ONLY road. The road down the Calder Valley is notoriously narrow and winding, with steep hills at either side.

Matt asked me how far it was to Todmorden from Halifax. I told him that it was just over twelve miles. He explained to me, that where he worked, the roads are so straight and flat, that he would have been able to see the fire from where he started his journey.

Welcome to Yorkshire!

Following his visit, Matt Zavadsky, then published an article in an American magazine. I believe it to be the equivalent of our British Medical Journal.

Here is the extract of that report.

We often talk about "Best Practices" in emergency medical services, but rarely look beyond our borders to gain insight into the most logical approach for how EMS could be more efficiently provided. I recently had the incredible opportunity to ride along with the Yorkshire Ambulance Service Trust, a division of the United Kingdoms' National Health Service. This experience provided a unique perspective on how the appropriate alignment of goals, coupled with a true 'global approach' to health system delivery, can be combined to produce a highly effective mobile healthcare delivery system.

Overview.

Yorkshire Ambulance Service (YAS) is a governmental agency providing mobile healthcare services to over 5 million people. They respond to more than 1,300 requests for service daily utilising over 1,900 field providers and 400 speciality vehicles. I use the term "mobile healthcare services" purposefully because not only do they handle traditional emergency ambulance responses using the local "9-9-9" system, but they also provide in-home medical services and non-emergency patient transports. YAS is one of eleven ambulance service trusts operating in the U.K. Over the past few years, the number of ambulance trusts has gone from 26 to 11 in an effort to create more efficient regionalised services - sound familiars?? Check the IOM report on the need for the U.S. To focus on regionalisation of EMS.

In a socialised medicine environment such as the U.K., the healthcare providers are government employees and the cost for providing services to the community is almost exclusively funded through taxes. There is no billing for the emergency services.

The experience started with my arrival at Huddersfield Ambulance Station (one of YAS' 61 stations). The first thing that caught my attention was prominent sign on the door leading from the crew's lounge to the ambulance bay which read that a 30 second activation time was the goal. Upon asking one of the crew members about the sign, he explained that funding is tied to operational and clinical performance. Reminders such as the prominently displayed goal statement help remind them of the need to continually strive to meet or exceed the performance measures.

Within moments I was greeted by Ian Firth, YAS' Clinical Leader for the day who began my "orientation" to the YAS district.

Vehicles and Vehicle Operations.

We started with a tour of the ambulances, rapid response vehicles and patient transport units. Suffice to say that in many respects, the U.K. vehicle design is far and away superior to anything here in the States.

The vehicle exteriors are designed for utmost visibility. By law the vehicles are adorned with lime-green reflective decals, overlaid with darker green reflective accents. You can most likely see these vehicles by day or night from the Space Shuttle. Even the interior of the doors have reflective tape.

The next most interesting feature of the ambulances is the integrated steps and ramps from the rear of the vehicle. Transport capable units are equipped with a winch as well, which makes it virtually unnecessary to lift the patient and stretcher into the ambulances. The ambulances are relatively small by our standards due to the 'unique' roads in the U.K. There is not a straight road in the country and the average two-way traffic road width is the equivalent to our one-way traffic road width (not including the fact that everyone in the U.K. Parks with one side of the car on the sidewalk and one side in the street). This makes for very challenging vehicle operations.

I'm convinced that the U.K. Medics are some of the best drivers in the world! During a response to an apartment fire, my friend Ian was travelling 60-70 kph on a street built for a single horse and buggy, passing cars and avoiding oncoming traffic while simultaneously checking the navigation/dispatch interface, talking on the cell phone, changing siren modes and shifting gears in his Range Rover (oh yea, did I mention that ALL the vehicles are STANDARD transmission!?). Ian is my new driving hero - he got us to the scene with all the decals still attached to the truck, despite the constant distraction of my right foot slamming on the floor where the brake pedal was supposed to be!

Clinical Services.

U.K. medics receive much more training than our U.S. Counterparts. Their EMT's (called Ambulance Technicians) are essentially equivalent to our paramedics in function. Paramedics in the U.K. Provide much more advanced clinical procedures than we in the States (routine pre-hospital thrombolysis and a drug formulary twice as comprehensive as ours for example). In addition to the traditional EMT/Medic ambulances, NHS employs Emergency Care Practitioners (ECP). These specialists operate out of rapid response vehicles and respond either alone, or with ambulances depending on system stasis (yes, they actually do system status management with "street corner posting" during busy times). This helps assure a closest unit response.

ECP's are paramedics with significantly more training. They are essentially akin to Physician Assistants here in the U.S. The ECP's perform advanced diagnostics, can do suturing and prescribe medicines. They are used to either respond to low priority calls, or come to the scene at the request of ambulance crews as an alternative to patient transport to the "Accident and Emergency Centre".

Skill proficiencies are closely monitored, but quite honestly, the annual patient:paramedic ratio in YAS is about 250:1, so these folks are HIGHLY utilised and subsequently have great proficiency rates.

Accident and Emergency Centres.

By U.S. standards, you might call the U.K. emergency departments "austere", however, I would call them "efficient". The patient rooms consist of basically a stretcher and a sink. Speciality equipment necessary to manage cardiac, neurological, orthopaedic or other categories of emergency conditions are brought TO the patient on carts. This prevents the need to have every room equipped for major types of emergencies. They do have code/trauma rooms, casting rooms and speciality eye treatment rooms. There are speciality hospital centres for trauma, cardiac and obstetrics. Patients are taken to hospitals and speciality centres based on their clinical need, not necessarily based on their choice.

Communication Centres.

YAS operates three communication centres in their district. The centre I visited was a combined "9-9-9" and NHS Direct centre. NHS Direct is the non-emergency information and referral department of NHS. At NHS Direct, callers can seek medical advice, ask for a referral to a practitioner, or request a home visit by a nurse or emergency care practitioner.

The three communications centres handle about 500 emergency medical calls and 5,000 Patient Transport Service (ambulatory/wheelchair/stretcher) requests per day. They do full emergency medical dispatch with pre-arrival instructions using the Priority Dispatch, Advanced Medical Priority Dispatch System (AMPDS). When I visited the Wakefield Centre, there were 7 dispatchers and 6 call takers on-duty, fairly typical staffing according to the centre manager. Doing the math that means call-takers average 13 calls handled per hour and the dispatchers average 10 calls handled per hour! Awesome work!

Helicopter Operations.

YAS operates an aeromedical programme for their large geographic coverage area. There is a unique twist however - NHS does not fund the programme. The entire cost of the operation, equipment, helicopter, salaries, fuel, EVERYTHING is funded through community donations. So, all you helicopter operators, imagine if you needed to fund raise your entire operational budget at the grass roots level - remember, NHS cannot bill for service, even helicopter transports!

Field Supervision.

During my ride time there were two field supervisors on duty (of course, one went home at about noon, leaving poor Ian to manage the whole district on his own for the second half of his shift). Ian fielded calls about every 5-10 minutes on his ever present cell phone. You can imagine the types of calls - vehicle and equipment malfunctions, personnel issues, staffing for the next day, dispatch concerns and vehicle placement for SSM, with a sprinkle of emergency responses thrown in (and some dang Yankee riding along who kept trying to get into the DRIVER's side of the Range Rover - the steering wheel is on the wrong side!). He handled it all with the grace and understanding of a well skilled mentor!

Granted, NHS is government run, but that in itself eliminates two main disconnects with our U.S. EMS systems. First, in the U.S. Many medical directors fear malpractice concerns, thus preventing true innovation in EMS delivery. Second, there is no incentive to bring the right services to the right patient at the right time and in the right setting. Conversely, we are incentivised to use the most expensive mode of transportation to bring the patient to the most expensive place to receive what is in many cases, simply primary healthcare. Just makes you scratch your head and say "Huh?" And we wonder why the Medicare system is failing?

Yorkshire Ambulance Service is a perfect example of a highly effective, efficient and integrated mobile healthcare delivery system. We Yanks would do well to try and mimic many of the outstanding systems they have put in place.

Now, if they can just do something about the weather - six hours of blue sky during a six day visit - YUK!

My personal thanks to Shirley Plummer and Robert Eastwood of NHS for arranging the visit and to Ian Firth for his hospitality and insight!

Matt Zavadsky, MHA.

Director of Tri-State Ambulance

CHAPTER 58.

STRANGE OCCURRENCES, OP-PORTUNITIES AND ODD JOBS.

YAA Photo Opportunity.

It was the summer of 2002, that was the second year of flying, of the Yorkshire Air Ambulance.

One of the first air crew members was paramedic Malcolm. I had worked with Malcolm on the road ambulances several times over the years, when he was based in Wakefield.

He was also a manager for the YAA, he knew that I loved taking photos and that I had already had several of the helicopter. As it was then, I had been to its Multi-Flight headquarters at Leeds Bradford Airport on quite a few occasions.

He rang me and asked, would I meet him at its base in Leeds and to bring my camera to take some more photos of our helicopter.

When I arrived, instead of going out onto the base. I went into the drew room. Malcolm told me that the helicopter parked outside on the apron, would be the one that I would be flying in and that I would be taking aerial photos of ours. The one outside, was a Bell, Jet Ranger helicopter.

It was privately owned by Multi-Flight, they had donated it and a pilot for the day. To follow the YAA, taking photos of the air ambulance helicopter over local landmarks. The idea was perhaps to be used for a fund raising calendar.

Nothing I do seems to be straightforward. Malcolm explained that they would be taking the door off the second helicopter and that I would be strapped to the outside of it, in a special harness to get the best results.

Now, I don't know much about aircraft design. But to me, if they are designed to have doors on, I don't see any point whatsoever of removing one.

Thank you very much!

I had never been in a helicopter and I was extremely nervous, but I wanted to be inside it. To be belted up and with the doors very well and truly locked shut.

The pilot who was to be my personal "chauffeur" for the day, a really nice bloke, explained to me the basics about helicopter flying.

He gave me a lot of reassurance and asked me to trust him. As I sat in the helicopter, he started the engine, I couldn't believe the noise.

We wore headphones with a built in intercom system. He slid my door open and fixed it back in the open position.

We took off, we had only lifted to about six foot off the ground. As the aircraft hovered there, he said "if you are not happy, you could simply step out".

Sure, I could, that was so true. He angled the helicopter over by just two degrees, it felt so strange. He then went up to about thirty foot, the height of the hangar roof, the door was still open. The second time he banked over to five degrees, again it was very unnerving.

He explained that it was because we were so near to buildings and that the perspective of the ground was very apparent, but that I wouldn't be able to connect the buildings and the angle of the ground the higher we went.

That was my introduction over.

We took off alongside the YAA, first stop Emley Moor mast. My local landmark. We hovered at the same height as the people working inside the top of the mast. As the YAA circled the top of the mast, we circled around the outside of them both. I had the whole of the back of the second helicopter to myself, scooting from one side to the other, taking dozens of pictures.

After refuelling, we went all around the rest of Yorkshire. Including, Harewood House, Bolton Abbey, Castle Howard, Nostell Priory, Fountains Abbey, York and Beverley Minsters, Goredale Scar, Malham Cove, Fylingdales, Menwith Hill, we were even allowed to fly over Flockton's, New Hall Prison and we flew over the Emmerdale set, in the grounds of Harewood House.

I took that many photographs, it's a wonder that I didn't have a blister on my shutter finger!

The climax for me though, was flying over the Humber Bridge.

To get the right angle to be able to see all of the Humber Bridge in one shot, the only way, was to slide the door open.

To use the full open aspect, instead of having to peer out through the little sliding six inch square window hatch that I had been doing.

What I did next was unthinkable.

I was strapped in securely, but I had to loosen/lengthen the strap so that I could put one foot outside onto the skid.

Jesus Christ, what the hell was I doing? But, what a bloody amazing feeling!

I took several pictures as we moved effortlessly around the sky, so high above one of Yorkshire's most famous landmarks. Then I shuffled safely back inside, and I locked the door firmly again.

I had done it!

The pilot asked me how I felt. I couldn't put it into words, I was buzzing!

He then said that at the point where I had opened the door, we had been flying at an altitude of over two and a half thousand feet. Then, to get the best position for my photo's, we had been banked over at forty five degrees.

No way!

He had been right, because my perspective with the ground was so far off. I hadn't even realised that we were at any angle, never mind forty five degrees and stepping outside.

What a bloody idiot!

I got some fantastic pictures though and what a day, I didn't want it to end. That must have been the most exhilarating experience I had ever had.

I loved it!

The Calendar idea had been scuppered. The photo's, were not going be used. In my mind, due to very petty political reasons. Anna the YAA fundraising manager at the time, said that. "We could not use the photo's for a calendar, purely and simply because we should have asked the owner or trustee of each of the landmarks for permission. Prior to taking the pictures. It was as simple as that!"

Surely even afterwards. If we had asked, for instance, the Earl of Harwood. Would he approve a shot of his home Harewood House, as a backdrop of the Air Ambulance, to be used in a charity calendar?

I'm sure that he would have been over the moon. He would then probably have asked for some to sell in their own souvenir shop as well. What a barmy state of affairs.

Still, it was a great day for me.

Sod 'em all I say!

Garry's luck ran out on Luck Lane.

Garry from Huddersfield, was acting up as the Operational Supervisor. It had been raining for a long time and there had been many areas of flash flooding all over the region. It was the 3rd of August 2004.

Garry was sent to an incident on Crow Lane, near to the school at Milnsbridge.

There were reports that there was a grandfather and his young granddaughter, that they had been buried under tons of stone, as a retaining wall had collapsed due to the weight of the water behind it.

Knowing Garry, he would not have been driving slowly. The child's safety would have been at the forefront of his mind, as he drove down Luck Lane, towards Paddock.

Just outside the old Hansons bus garage, the road was flooded. A good two foot deep, and more. Garry hit that water at "fifteen miles an hour", or so he claimed.

The bow wave of the water, caused by his vehicle, went as high as the gutters on the Victorian terraces at either side of the road.

He carried on for a short distance and then his Vauxhall Frontera came to an abrupt stop.

Garry was going nowhere.

Fortunately, as that was happening to Garry, the ambulance crew had arrived at the Crow Lane incident and other than a few bumps and bruises, both the man and his granddaughter had escaped.

They were "relatively" unharmed, get it?

That incident left the gates wide open for some prime mickey taking, Garry was going to suffer.

Over the next few days, whilst the Frontera was parked in Huddersfield ambulance station's garage. From unknown sources, little fish began to appear. They were well drawn and they had been carefully cut out and coloured. They ended up stuck all over the windows. Weeds and plants arrived next. Bubbles then appeared.

Even resussy Annie got in on the action. She was sat in the drivers seat with a mask and piping from an old style entonox set, looking like a scuba diver. Lastly a plimsol line appeared on one of the sides.

The vehicle needed a hell of a lot of money spending on it, before it could be roadworthy again. It had to have a new engine for starters.

Then my old mate, retired Tommy came up trumps, he lived in one of the houses at the side of the flooded area. He had been watching the events of that day and he had managed to get me a couple of photos of the incident. One of the great wave, and another when Garry had come to a stop.

Yes! I will treasure those.

What's the pervert been doing now?

In August 2006. I didn't work with Meg very often and this day, was to be one of those occasions. It was a Sunday morning, at around about half past ten. We had received a call to an address in the Rawthorpe area of Huddersfield.

A man upstairs in a house, had been heard by people in the street, screaming for help. We asked if the police were attending. They said that they didn't have anybody available.

When we arrived at the house, sure enough, there was a male voice upstairs shouting for help. I shouted back through the letterbox, he said that he wasn't hurt, but that he was in a "bit of a fix".

The doors were all locked. We still had to call police to be able to gain entry in to the property.

Fairly quickly, two female PCSO's arrived, they still couldn't get in. We eventually had one male officer turn up, with their universal key, a large red battering ram.

We told the man upstairs of the situation, he returned our requests with, "go for it!"

Once the door had been broken, the police women were looking around downstairs, the man asked for only male assistance to go upstairs. I went into the doorway leading up to the top of the stairs, they were wooden steps and there was no carpet. On the landing, the only thing that I saw was a black leather thong.

I walked through the door and into the front bedroom.

I could never, ever, have prepared myself for what I saw in there that morning.

There was a disused set of metal framed bunk beds to the right of the door. There was one man, in his early thirties, I would think. He appeared to be fastened to a home made cross, that had been made out of two ladders that had been lashed together at ninety degrees.

He was chained at the neck, both his wrists, around his waist and at his feet. All the chains were fastened with padlocks, they were around him and through the ladders. He was only wearing a pair of thigh high leather boots, complete with very high stiletto heels and absolutely nothing else!

The cross had been stood up against the bunk beds, but at some stage had fallen over. The top of the cross was resting on the window sill, the bottom against the bed frame, the man was suspended underneath.

He had been crucified.

He told me that there was a key to all the locks on his window sill. I walked in to the room, still very naive. As I was going past him, then I could see clearly what was going on.

I nearly died!

I jumped back and went out of the room. I demanded to know how to switch his televisions off. Only they weren't televisions, they were computer screens.

I had walked into an internet pornography scene.

There opposite the man, was a bank of six very large computer monitors and each of them had a camera mounted to the top. Each screen was divided in to about twelve smaller screens. On each of the small screens was a video image and on each one of those images, there was a different man in various stages of undress and pleasuring themselves.

They booed loudly when I went back in. I didn't switch them off, I just pulled out the plugs.

I then got the keys, as I was undoing the first lock, the male police officer came into the room. He had a pile of children's clothes with him.

"Whose are these?" He demanded.

I went cold, did this pervert involve kids. Looking around the room, there were a couple of boxes of children's toys and the bunk beds.

What the hell was going on?

The man was very candid and open, he didn't really have a choice, being locked in his position. He told us that the items belonged to his two daughters, he said that they were aged two and four years.

Once his wife had found out about his bizarre recreational activities, she had left immediately and had taken the kids with her.

He still had a few items, as once a month he had supervised visits from his children with a social worker.

If I had thought for one minute, that those things were for his own sick gratification. Or that God forbid, kids had been involved. I would have left the bugger crucified where he was.

I unfastened all the locks and made him get dressed and to get rid of those bloody boots.

He went on to explain that he could make an absolute fortune out of his once weekly performances. That it only usually lasted thirty minutes or so.

He would get everything set up, the keys were on a string suspended over a night light candle. When it had burnt through the string, the keys would swing across the room and into his hand, he would then release himself.

He had practiced and perfected his performance over the last 15 to 18 months.

This last time he had missed the keys, as he reached over, the whole of the cross had fallen over leaving him stranded. He had started his performance at around eleven o'clock the previous night, and he had been suspended there like that, for nearly twelve hours.

All the time he was being watched and cheered at, by his perverted paying public.

His hands were massive, they had ballooned up to three times their normal size.

Because of his predicament, he had urinated on the floor of the bedroom, to an "almighty cheer", he told me. That had been an unexpected bonus for his audience.

He was in severe abdominal pain and he was badly dehydrated.

He told me that because of the night's events, he had never made as much money, as he had "this time". He would "have to try it again".

He was welcome to it!

As we went downstairs, I flicked the leather thong from the top of the stairs, Meg reached out and instinctively caught it. Boy did she scream when she realised what it was.

As I took the man outside, I had to send her upstairs to see what had been going on she would never have believed it.

It was unbelievable.

As we were walking down the garden path, there was quite a crowd that had gathered outside looking on, due to the police and our ambulance presence.

As we got to the gate a little lad of around seven or eight simply said "what's the pervert been doing now?"

Due to the length of time that he had been crucified, he had developed kidney failure.

He was admitted to the intensive care unit in Huddersfield for a while, before needing a transfer to St. James Hospital in Leeds.

He was requiring dialysis treatment. The last I heard, he was still waiting for a kidney transplant, his own had packed up all together.

What a way to earn money!

Meg had to have a planned operation, and due to her sickness levels, her life was made uncomfortable at the Yorkshire Ambulance Service.

So, she left the service and has since got on at an ambulance service elsewhere.

I understand that she and her family have moved have to nearer her home town of Plymouth, where she has become qualified at technician level.

Here at YAS, she was a non-qualified Assistant Practitioner. Before that, Meg used to work in our Comms centre, until hating the atmosphere up there and coming out to work on the road.

I hope she does well for herself, she was made of the right stuff for our job.

We need help, how the hell do we deal with this?

2008, it was at about three o'clock on Christmas Day morning. I was working as Operational Supervisor out of Halifax.

The team leader from Comms rang me, she asked me to go and meet up with the Todmorden crew.

They were on a job at a farm, way out in the wilds above the Calder Valley, in the middle of nowhere.

She wasn't sure what was required by the crew as the patient had already passed away. "Perhaps there was something suspicious about it" she said. "They didn't go into details".

The details were sent to me via the two way data system, I set off.

On the way there, I rang the crew to let them know that I was on my way, it was Neil who answered, he is an experienced member of staff.

I asked him "what's up Neil?" He said "I'm not sure really, we just need a bit of advice and a little moral support Ian".

I told him I would be about fifteen minutes.

"Watch for the red light" he said.

Minutes later I was driving over the pitch black open moorland. There were no street lights and no house lights, no lights visible in any direction from where I was.

Then way off in the distance in front of me, waving side to side was a lantern, a red one. From where I was it reminded me of the old railway lamps. As I got nearer, I was shocked, the figure holding the lamp was a young girl, a very young girl.

I pulled up alongside her, the little girl came up to me and told me that it was her house I was looking for. It was at the top of the lane, then down the unmade road to the right.

The little girl told me that she was only five years old. She was dressed in her nightwear, her pyjamas and a very warm looking dressing gown, along with bright yellow wellingtons.

She got into the Land Rover with me and off we went. It was getting even more bizarre.

In a very matter of fact way, she told me that her daddy had just died. That is why they had sent for an ambulance, and that there was already somebody at the farm with her mum and her sister.

When I entered the farm, my little escort showed me upstairs. Neil was sat on the edge of the bed, he looked pale and confused.

"Where's your mate?" I asked. Then I heard her, another experienced member of staff, Mia came out of the "walk in" wardrobe. She was in tears, she was absolutely heartbroken.

What the hell was going on? It was certainly strange right enough. Neil began to tell me.

The patient, a forty two year old male. Had died on the bathroom floor, the bathroom was just in front of us.

He had been a patient who had suffered with kidney failure, he had then had to endure a long two years of dialysis, whilst on the transplant waiting list.

Eventually, he had received his transplant. On his routine six month check up, cancerous cells had been found. Sadly, the "new" kidney, without any option, had to be removed.

He was then put back on dialysis, but he would not be eligible for another transplant until he had been two years clear of any abnormal cells. He had been knocked back to square one, how much "bad luck" can one person have?

His time for review, was nearly up, it would have been in the middle of January. His name would be put back on the "list" to await another transplant. Because of his past, he would be classed as a priority case.

Only three weeks to go.

The man and his wife had two daughters, aged just five and seven years, brilliant for their tender years. They had had no choice in their short lives, but they had to grow up, right in the face of adversity.

They understood far more than any child their age should ever have to do.

Daddy had been taken poorly just a couple of days ago, with flu like symptoms. Both of his daughters knew that it could be dangerous for a man with his condition.

He had woken in the night to use the en suite bathroom, he had just got there and he had then suddenly collapsed, unconscious. Mum had called out for help and woke the girls, as she managed to turn her husband into the recovery position.

If that wasn't enough, he had then stopped breathing.

The eldest daughter had already rung 999 to say that her daddy had collapsed. Whilst still on the call, she then had to tell the call taker that he had stopped breathing, and had gone into cardiac arrest!

Adara at our Comms Centre, was the call taker who had received the 999 call. It was down to Adara to relay CPR instructions to the mother via her seven year old daughter. While at the same time, somehow reassuring them that help was on the way.

Due to the remote location of the farm and how notoriously difficult it was to find, even in daylight, never mind in pitch black. The youngest daughter was dispatched with the lamp to, stand and watch for the crew and then again for me.

Those kids were fantastic.

The crew, as experienced as they were, felt out of place, like they "were intruders".

It was a very unnatural situation and they had called me, because they just wanted a bit of additional support.

To talk it through with somebody.

Thankfully those unusual situations are very few and far between. But that was exactly one of the roles of an Operational Supervisor.

As with all sudden deaths, the police were called, to act on behalf of the coroner.

Not that there was anything suspicious in that instance, it was a very tragic and upsetting case.

Once the police had arrived and had been briefed by ourselves of the previous events. It would be customary for us to make our apologies and leave.

This part of the incident chokes me up, every time I try to talk about it, or as now to write about it.

I spoke directly to the mum, to express our sincere condolences at their sad loss.

Then to speak on behalf of both my colleagues and myself, I said that "dad would have been so proud of the actions of both of his two young, matured young ladies, who were not little girls any more and how they had handled the situation". I went on to say "how extremely impressed that we had all been and that how, they and you (mum) had coped until our arrival, we would never know".

They were brilliant.

Then the bomb was dropped!

We could never have prepared ourselves for the next comments. Mum first, said that she had appreciated all of our efforts and thanked us for trying.

That was bad enough, but then and without any prompting, the youngest, daughter. Only five years of age, bless her. She stood tall and ever so politely said "may I say something mummy?"

Mum nodded.

Then the little one said. "I would like to say, thank you very much, from my sister and me. For trying to save my daddy's life" and then if that wasn't enough. "I hope all three of you have a Merry Christmas and a Happy New Year. God Bless!"

I had just opened the door to leave, I tried to speak, I opened my mouth, that is as far as I got.

The tears flooded down my face.

I picked her up and cuddled and squeezed her, I could have brought her home with me there and then. That was all I could do, I felt so lost and useless.

All three of us left the house, not speaking, we didn't even look at each other. We each went to a different part of the farmyard and stood facing open moorland.

I know I cried.

We must have been stood for a good ten to fifteen minutes before we moved back together.

No answer to that one. Not one word was spoken to each other.

Eventually, I rang Comms. I told them we would all be going back to Todmorden Station and unavailable for at least half an hour, that we desperately needed a brew and a chat.

I also spoke to Adara and told her most of what had been said and done, and of course thanked her on behalf of the family and ourselves. I then promised her that I would call up and see her at Comms, later that night at the start of my next shift and to get the kettle on.

What a Christmas for those kids and their mum, they'll never forget it, how could they celebrate Christmas ever again after that?

Christmas Day night, I went up to Comms to have an informal chat with Adara. She was absolutely devastated as well.

She was explaining to me, how she had found it so very distressing to talk to the young girl. To keep asking if her dad was showing any signs of life, it was harrowing.

I then asked the Comms team leader to join us.

They needed to be made aware of what had happened.

I wanted it to be placed on record, how professional Adara had been on the call, how she had really tried to help that young family.

As a result of our conversation, we wanted to do something for the girls, something positive that they would be able to remember.

355

I even contacted ITV. The Noel Edmonds "Christmas Presents Show", were very interested to do something the following year.

On a closer note, Adara's mother lived next door to the mother of Kimberley Walsh, one of the singers in "Girls Aloud". They apparently would be more than happy to turn up unannounced, at the girls school in the Calder Valley. (Imagine that on return after the holidays) To perform an impromptu concert. Could that help?

You bet it could. Adara, Mia, Neil and me were amazed, what a surprise that would be.

Problems, problems, problems.

Nothing ever runs as smooth in the ambulance service as we would like it to be. It wasn't smooth, we had hit a downright rough patch. Although everyone it was mentioned to, without fail, supported the idea, it would not be possible.

To turn up at the school, announced or not. Would mean that someone had been discussing names, dates and personal details.

That would have been a major breach of patient confidentiality and as such, it is illegal, we would be breaking the law.

We could not go any further with our plans. Everybody involved, was so disappointed for the girls.

We hadn't actually breached anything at that stage, as no names or personal details had been discussed, just the nature of the situation.

The only two ways for anything to happen, would be in the unlikely event of the family getting back in touch with the service.

Then, and only then, would we be able to ask the thoughts of the family, and to be able to seek their permission to go ahead with it.

We could then arrange something with the school, it would have been a real experience for them.

The only other option, would have been if the newspapers had been contacted by the family, to perhaps do an official obituary on the fathers life and struggles.

We couldn't even approach the mother due to confidentiality issues.

Neither of those options happened, what a shame. If ever there was a time I would have really wanted to get involved, that was it. Those girls thoroughly deserved a treat.

I'll never forget that family.

Was it terror related?

In September of 2009. I had to make a call to our Special Operations Unit at Gildersome. That unit is now HART (hazardous area response team), and they have moved down the road towards Leeds, to a place known as Manor Mill.

They are used at major incidents, unusual incidents, chemical incidents etc.

They are also our team that would be called for advice, or to attend a CBRNE (chemical, biological, radioactive, nuclear or explosive) incident.

I was working with a great lad, (now working with Manchester area, he couldn't get on for training with ours), Garry.

We were to attend to a collapse call, at an address just outside Huddersfield.

On our arrival at the house, our RRV, Julia was also just arriving. Along with Community First Responder, (CFR), Royston, he was just parking up.

The patient we were looking for, had been expected to attend a birthday party next door, for his neighbour's young daughter. When he hadn't arrived, his friend had called in to see if everything was ok.

It wasn't, the man had found his neighbour laid on his bed, it appeared as though the man was dead.

It should have been a straight forward, with no complications, job. As you will have already read and gathered, I don't get many of those.

The neighbour told us that he had found the door already ajar, he had called out his neighbour's name. When he had received no answer, he had walked in. There he had found his neighbour laid on the bed, he was stiff and cold.

He left and had called us, he didn't know what else to do.

As we were entering the house, we all felt a shiver, it was unnaturally cold. There was a damp/wet cold air. It felt to be an extremely strange atmosphere.

I can't put it into words, but it immediately made my flesh crawl. My guts were rumbling again!

I felt really uneasy.

The first thing, the floorboards in the entrance hall and living room had all sunk between the joists, creating an undulating floor. The carpet was soaking wet through, in those two areas, sploshing as we walked. It had been wet for a long long time to cause the damage that had been done.

Then we passed the bathroom, that was even more eerie. There was an old style enamel bath, but it was full of ashes. It had been used for having small fires.

The bath was unusable for it's purpose, all the enamel coating on the inside, had been burnt away and looked as though it never had been used for bathing. Although a lot of burning had taken place, the polystyrene tiles above the bath were only slightly damaged. So there can only have been small fires, no raging infernos.

The toilet was something else. It was almost black, with some form of possible chemical staining. I suppose I would say it was actually etching into the ceramic surface, all down the inside and on the outside of the toilet bowl.

After all it was ceramic, that doesn't usually stain to that extent. It was like a black tarry colour, burnt in to the pottery.

At the side of the toilet and piled high up the wall, completely over the top of the sink basin and windowsill, were orange (all Sainsbury's) carrier bags. From the amount, the smell and the look of them. They contained all of the man's bodily discharges, from the last six months or more. The toilet had never been used for the purpose that it had been intended.

What was going on in here?

Next to the bathroom, was the bedroom, there was some music on a radio, playing very quietly in the background. The door had been closed to, but not shut.

We pushed the door open and there in the middle of the room was a large king sized bed.

Laid on the bed was an Afro Caribbean man, the neighbour said that he was aged around fifty. He was propped up on his right elbow, looking towards a laptop computer on the bed beside him.

The man had died, he had rigor mortis present. He was rock solid. We did what was necessary with our cardiac monitor, to be able to officially pronounce death.

We then retired to complete our paperwork and to inform the police, on behalf of the coroner. Apart from his living conditions, there didn't appear to be any suspicious circumstances surrounding his death.

Just to be nosey, I checked the kitchen, after all we had seen all the other rooms in the bungalow. The hairs on the back of my neck then really stood on end.

It was so wrong, it just couldn't be real.

The kitchen was full of items listed for us to be wary of following the bombs in London, from July 2005.

The alarm bells were now going mad. I showed my colleagues, it was time to go! Not only that, immediately outside, we had to consider evacuation.

Was it a hidden bomb factory? We couldn't take chances.

I rang our OSU and I spoke to the manager. When I told him of my fears, I could almost feel him shaking at my end of the phone.

Yes! It ticked all the boxes of terrorist activity. To get out of there, to advise everyone around to go indoors.

The specialist units arrived, including our own OSU staff and lots of police. Before we had left, an army bomb disposal team came from Catterick, near York.

It had turned into a surreal incident.

We had to give full and complete statements to the police. What we had seen, what we had done, had we touched anything? etc.

The added strange thing about it, the only mention in Huddersfield Daily Examiner, was regarding a road closure due to a police incident.

There has been nothing else mentioned anywhere, no newspaper or television coverage.

Any enquiries that we have tried to make, have just drawn a complete and utter blank.

Was it a terrorist in the making? Was it a plot that got thwarted? We will never know?

Always listen to advice.

Since I joined the ambulance service, I have been given hundreds of hints and tips to help me through my career. In turn, I have tried to help any new starters, by passing on a few words of wisdom, to try and prevent untoward happenings.

One example of advice, that was given to me during my early days. I have passed on to many, many people. Including to some experienced staff.

That being, when in a patient's house, always be very wary before taking a seat in a chair. There have been many ambulance people caught out and they have sat in a chair, that had been previously occupied by an unfortunately urinary incontinent patient.

As well as full time members of staff, we also have several volunteer staff, Community First Responders, (CFR), who attend emergency calls within their own local areas.

One such volunteer is Jed, he volunteers in and around Elland and the surrounding area. I passed on that valuable piece of advice to him, on one of the very first occasions that I met him. We have met up on many jobs since, over the years.

It was on one such occasion in 2009, I had been called to a male that had collapsed unconscious in the outer area of Halifax.

I was single handed working as Operational Supervisor out of Halifax. As I arrived at the address, Jed pulled up at the side of me. We went into the house together.

Unfortunately, our patient wasn't just unconscious, he had died.

The patient's wife had come home from shopping and founded her husband collapsed. When she had rung 999 and had explained the situation to our Comms Centre. They had advised her to get her husband onto the floor and they had then instructed her over the phone, to perform CPR.

Our initial examination showed that there were no signs of life, other circumstances allowed me to pronounce death, there and then.

I cancelled the backup ambulance crew and began the process of paperwork. That would be for the police and possibly the coroner. Jed was helping by putting all our equipment away and generally tidying things up.

As I sat down to start my form filling, I asked the lady where she had found her husband, prior to laying him on the floor.

Yes, it was the same chair that I was sat in!

I asked Jed if he could remember the piece of advice that I had given him, regarding sitting down at a patient's address. He just stood there and grinned, it was a really wide, teeth bearing grin.

Jed is a big lad, his whole body started to jiggle up and down, he looked me in the eye and simply said "you haven't?"

I nodded. I had.

The chair wasn't just damp, it was absolutely sodden.

My backside was soaked, the urine was running down the back of my legs. I had only completely forgotten one of the first and best things that I had ever been taught.

Too late!

After all the paperwork was completed, the police arrived and took over the situation, we made our apologies and we left.

Outside we both fell about laughing, he still reminds me of it now!

Explosion in a pie factory!

10th April 2009. Just before five in the morning, I was sat at my desk on Halifax station.

I was working the night shift as Operational Supervisor for Calderdale and Kirklees.

I received a call that there had been a gas explosion in Huddersfield, at a pie factory. A report that some people had been trapped inside.

I raced across to Huddersfield in my Land Rover Discovery, blue lights flashing. On arrival, there were firemen all over the place, in and around the collapsed building.

No other ambulance resources.

There had been a large explosion, windows and debris had been blown all across the road. I was met by Charlie, son of Ernie one of my retired ambulance colleagues. He had been working in the factory, when one of the ovens had exploded.

He told me that he and four other workers had escaped uninjured. That one man was at the back of the building badly injured. Two of his four colleagues were looking after him and that another man was missing. He was unaccounted for, somewhere in the debris.

Just as he was explaining that to me, a Bradford crew were the first ambulance to arrive, the paramedic and I ran with Charlie around to the rear of the building.

Another of the uninjured got into the ambulance cab, he directed the driver around the lane and to the back of the factory.

The man had been blown against some roller shutter doors. He had obvious head injuries, he had suffered from burns and was having difficulty breathing.

Those were his visible problems, others may be hidden and would have to be looked for due to the nature of the incident.

Another crew arrived, they wanted to place a collar on the injured man and to place him on a spinal board.

That was strictly the right thing to do, but I had to stop them. As Operational Supervisor, my role was to ensure that the crews were all safe.

From my position, I could see that the main concrete lintel above the shutter doors was badly cracked.

We literally supported the injured man and pulled him away from the doorway. In seconds, the concrete lintel about 18" square in thickness and about fifteen feet long crashed to the ground. It landed just where the injured man had been laid and where they were going to treat him.

How close was that?

He was then fully collared, boarded and immobilised, as he should be. His condition was then stabilised in the ambulance, before taking him to HRI.

The fire service were searching around inside the building, we could still hear more of the concrete and debris falling.

One of the firemen shouted to me, that they had located the missing man.

Now, who goes into the unsafe building?

Remember that there had already been an explosion. Transco the gas people had not arrived at that stage, gas may still have been leaking or even building up. Debris of unknown size and quantity could still be heard falling from above.

I had a paramedic crew still with me.

Do I send in the same paramedic? who hadn't noticed the lintel, or do I go in?

She was a young girl with very little experience of life, no disrespect to her. She seemed to be a good paramedic, who knew he medical stuff.

I decided that with my previous engineering background, those long boring wasted hours at technical college. I was a mechanical engineer, why did I have to study the construction of buildings?

This, was the reason!

The memories came flooding back. I studied what was left of the building and I could see a long large steel RSJ (girder) running from front to back of the building. Where the RSJ was located into the wall at each end, the surrounding plaster was intact, there were no signs of any cracks.

I quickly realised that it would be the strongest and safest part of the building. If I remained under it and stuck to that, I should be in a reasonably safe position.

I then asked the paramedic if she could whistle,

I think she thought I was barmy.

Not the slight whistle, to make a tune, no! A loud full volume "wolf whistle", using her fingers in her mouth.

Thankfully she was good.

I told her that if I left her line of sight at all, to whistle with all her might to let me know.

It only took seconds, I proceeded to go into the factory, it was a surreal sight. There was an oven, big enough to fit side by side and two deep, the large open basket type skips. Just like the ones in hospital that contain blankets, or ones that major supermarkets use prior to shelf filling.

The explosion, had blown the door clean off. It was that door that had forced the injured man into the shuttered door and had caused the damage to the lintel.

All of the inside of the building, was covered in a dusting of flour, it was still floating about in the air.

Hanging from every surface, shelf or fitting, were the soggy circles of the uncooked pastry pie lids. As they were uncooked, they were still soft and pliable. They had all stretched out of shape, bizarrely they looked like Salvador Dali's clocks. From his famous painting, the Persistence of Memory. They were just short of any hands.

The roof to the right of my safety girder, had collapsed. It was made up of concrete sections, they were roughly six foot wide and twelve to fifteen foot long.

Five in all I think.

The end wall had blown out, causing the far end of all of the middle three sections to fall into the building. The inner end of the blocks were still at roof height, resting on my safety girder.

The fireman pointed out a figure.

I could see that the feet of the man were towards me. I grabbed a long wooden pole, it had a brass "S" shaped hook on the end, used to open and shut the high windows. I was able to lift the victims shirt, I could clearly see that he had purple blotchy skin where it was at its lowest point, or in contact with the floor.

That certainly appeared to be blood pooling, it only occurs post mortem, (after death), where there is no circulation present. I had to move nearer, to be sure, there was a lot of rubble around, some of it was extremely large pieces.

I could then say, without fear of contradiction, that the man was dead. He definitely had "post mortem staining" as it is known.

I had only edged just that little nearer, when heard my colleague whistle, and boy, she could whistle!

It was time to make my escape.

There was nothing more that could be done at that time. I moved back out of the building, the crew and I returned around to the front of the premises.

We then moved our vehicles further back, to near a junction, about three hundred yards away, for safety.

A third ambulance, arrived, that one was from Honley station, they parked alongside us. The first ambulance and their patient was at the hospital, we were all out of danger.

The fire service though, they were a lot of firemen still milling about inside the building. My ambulance starting and school mate Gavin was their Watch Commander. I expressed my concern, particularly as no one from the gas company had been to safely turn everything off.

He said that they "know what they are doing".

Well if twenty firemen milling about aimlessly in a collapsing, unsafe building. With a still, potentially lethal gas leak, is "knowing what they are doing".

Then Fair enough, but it isn't the way that we work.

We were well away from it!

It was whilst there in our safe location, that we fully checked out the five walking wounded, they did not wish to go to hospital. Their only physical problem, was powder, probably flour in their eyes. That was washed out with copious amounts of saline.

We gave them each a few spare ten millilitre plastic bottles of saline to put in their pockets, should they feel that there was any more irritation in their eyes. They could start to rinse them straight away and then if need be, seek more assistance.

Psychological issues though, will be with them for a lot longer.

Our USAR team, (urban search and rescue) arrived. My manager and our resilience/major incident managers arrived. They should then take over management of the event.

Not to be!

I was nominated to carry on as incident commander from the medical perspective.

Whilst on the scene, I had written and completed a log. I had noted all the timings and events of the mornings incident, as they had happened. That was handed over later, to June, our admin officer, to be typed up clearly.

A clear report was then made available for the coroner, who would be organising the inquest.

Janet, my locality manager at the time, eventually took over. All of us from the ambulance service, were parked at my designated safety point.

Eventually the gas was switched off, specialist teams were called in to make the building safe, or what was left of it.

It would be down to them to arrange for the removal of the body.

I had pronounced that the man was deceased, or declared him dead, at five minutes past five in the morning.

It wasn't until three twenty five in the afternoon, that a ROLE form, (recognition of life extinct) was completed. It was to be another three hours after that, before it was safe enough to get inside and to get the man out.

It hadn't been safe, until around six thirty in the evening.

It was one of the most personally testing incidents, that I have ever attended. Something that I could really use the little grey matter in my head to deal with.

I really enjoyed the experience, (if you can understand that), that was what I would like to do for the rest of my career.

Not to be though, the ambulance service moved their rubber goalposts yet again.

The role, it was decided, had to be a paramedic, why I still can not understand. It is a role that I personally, feel requires years of experience.

Now, some of the young and recently qualified paramedics are taking on the role.

Edmund and Dan, both from Halifax, were perfect for the position. Not with the new system.

They were not deemed suitable, in the restructure.

They both seemed to be "pooped on from a great height".

In my mind those two would have been without any doubt the best people for the role.

After all, they had been doing the job for many years, from the inception of the role.

Dan said. "Stuff it then", and he took his early retirement. Early this year 2016, all being well, he will be off. Off to a new life in New Zealand. His wife Sara had worked in the NHS for a long time, in PTS ambulance and later, some nursing management positions.

Sara's daughter, a senior staff nurse, is going with them. They are hopefully setting up a retirement home for the elderly there.

Good luck to them in their new venture. You all deserve it!

We'll miss you.

Edmund has also taken early retirement. A major pattern seems to be unravelling, staff all over the division are leaving in droves to start new lives elsewhere.

Dad, can you lend me some money?

It was a Saturday night in September 2010. My son Ben had been ringing and asking me to lend him some money, so that he could go out with his mate, Mick in Halifax.

I was working at the time in Halifax as supervisor on a night shift that was from 19:00hrs until 07:00hrs in the morning.

I was tied up on a job at the time of his asking, so I had to decline. He was a bit let down, but I couldn't help it. He had been hoping to come over from Bradford where he was living at the time.

Later on, I think it was at almost one thirty in the morning. I was called to attend to a serious road traffic collision (RTC), underneath the North Bridge in Halifax.

The dispatcher said "I'm sorry Ian, it sounds like a really bad one, two have been reported as ejected from the vehicle and two or possibly three are trapped".

I said "oh brilliant!"

She went on. "That's not all. I don't have a crew available, the nearest one will be Todmorden, they are off their meal in fifteen minutes".

That would mean at least forty minutes on my own.

Sat with me on station at Halifax, was the PTS out of hours crew.

They weren't medically trained, but they cold do basic first aid. They had been employed to do discharges and transfers from the Calderdale and Huddersfield hospitals, only the non-emergency journeys.

It was Annie and Stefan. I asked if they had a fluorescent coat each, they nodded. I said "you'll have to come with me then!"

They did without question, they were working on a PTS minibus, I went in the Land Rover. The incident was only literally two minutes from the station.

From a distance, it looked like it was a major smash.

There was a small red hatchback car. It had gone head on, into a large concrete gatepost, then it had bounced off to some distance away.

Two lads were out of the vehicle, one was walking around and he had lifted the other one out. That second lad, had an open fracture of both the bones in his left shin. He was sat at the side of the road.

Hanging out of the passenger door, head first, was none other than my sons friend Mick. He said "Mr. Firth, please help me I think I've had a stroke, I can't move my legs!"

I cut the seatbelt that had become tightly tied around his thighs. He hadn't had a stroke. But he had dislocated and fractured his shoulder, it turned out that he had a fractured sternum (breast bone), as well.

There was another lad in the back of the car, he had some injuries. As soon as we had helped Mick out, he stepped out himself, with lots of minor cuts and abrasions.

Annie was then sat with the four lads at the side of the road. I had asked her to write down all their details, names, addresses, past medical history, current injuries, etc.

Stefan was with me, we looked back into the car. At first we thought it was all clear, then I heard a muffled cry. I looked again.

I could see just one eye, it was eerily looking up at me, out of the darkness. Slumped in the front passenger well, between the seat and the dashboard was an

Afro Caribbean lad. He was well stuck. I had to smash the rear windscreen to be able to get into the car behind him.

Then, the fire service arrived, the first officer came up and he said "we can have the roof off in a couple of minutes".

Why? Why do they always want to get the roof off?

I said "not now! I need some light, more than anything. I need to see the lad!"

Sure enough, they set up some arc lights.

The lad was underneath the dash, the glove box had split and the plastic had torn the skin from his neck. It looked like his throat had been slashed, but, it was only the top surface. The top layers of skin had come away and he was bleeding profusely. He had a piece of metal that had been in the glove box. That metal had gone in through his eye and emerged through the side of his head near to his ear. He was unconscious, when I first saw him. Shortly after, he was more semi conscious. A bit vague and drowsy. I couldn't see anything of his legs.

The fire service removed the passenger door and I could see him clearly then. Due to his neck injury, we had to be careful in applying a collar, so as not to cause more damage to his neck wounds. We delicately covered his neck with saline soaked dressings, applying them over the damaged area, before putting a collar on him.

By then, the Todmorden crew had arrived, alongside them came a crew from Bradford and then one from Huddersfield. The Tod crew were sorting out the lad with the broken leg. The Bradford crew were sorting out and then taking Mick.

Graham and Jan, from Huddersfield were helping me with my new friend Ed. He was by then, fully conscious, he had his designer stiff neck collar on. We then eased him out through the passenger door and onto a spinal board, that was by bridging the gap between the passenger seat and the stretcher. We were able to gently feed him down and then lay him flat onto the board.

Once out of the car, his injuries were more apparent.

He had definitely lost his eye, what underlying damage the metal had done would have to be found out later. He had his nasty neck wound. The left hand side of his body had taken the secondary impact, when the car had bounced from the first gate post and hit the other one side on, before bouncing off into the middle of the road. His left arm was badly broken, in several places. A couple of them were open fractures. Both of his thigh bones, (femurs) were badly broken, one of those was an open fracture as well.

He was in a bad way.

The three lads with the worst injuries, were taken in the blue light ambulances to HRI. Due to their traumatic injuries, the trauma team had been pre-alerted and were waiting for them.

Nowadays they would be taken direct to the Major Trauma Centre at the Leeds General Infirmary.

I asked Annie and Stefan to take the two walking wounded up to HRI, it would complete the job for them, giving them full continuity. They would then be able to see what happens in hospital at a trauma call.

Both Annie and Stefan, very shortly afterwards went on to join us, doing the emergency side of the job. If their actions that night had anything to go on, they would be a credit to the service.

Annie is currently doing her paramedic studies.

Stefan though has gone through a lot of health troubles, he was a "big lad" before, but he gained even more weight. He could hardly breathe and has since left the service.

Thank God I didn't give my son Ben any money that night, if I had, he would definitely have been in the car with those lads. He could have been sat in Ed's position. That lad is still a wheelchair user and probably will be for the rest of his life. He was only twenty four years old at the time of the incident.

The only good thing to come out of the incident. The driver, although showing off. As young drivers can do, was perfectly legal. It was his own car, the car and he were fully insured and he hadn't been drinking.

There will be payouts available for the injured.

Blondes do have more fun!

Cassie, was working with Jessie, they were both blonde at the time. They were working out of Huddersfield station. Cassie had called me as their supervisor to report a faulty ambulance.

I can't remember now what the fault was, but it was my job to liaise with our mechanics and to get the problems fixed.

Once she had reported it to me, she told me that they were sorted out and that they had already checked another vehicle. She told me that it was call sign 1455 and it was all ok.

"Is it?" I asked.

"Yes, we have both checked it" she said.

I asked again, "I thought that it was VOR?" (vehicle off road, for repair or parts).

"There's no sign on it (a yellow sign VOR, is usually placed on the windscreen), it must have been fixed" she added. "We've checked it top to bottom, all the kit is fine, we can't see any problems with it".

I then asked her to shut the rear doors for me.

"Oh!" She said, "there's no back doors on it at all".

Oops, typical blonde!

He might have a gun!

I was crewed up with Carrie in January 2012. There was thick snow on the ground and it was still falling fast and furiously. We had been called to some steps almost in Milnsbridge.

We had received reports of a young male, possibly dead, buried in the deep snow.

When we got there. Stuart was the RRV, he told us that he had only just arrived. He didn't want to go check on the man by himself, he said "you never know, he might have a gun". Stuart is a great character, but he can be such a wimp at times.

The weather was atrocious, it was freezing cold, most of the roads were getting close to impassable due to the heavily falling snow.

I went up to see our patient, the steps go up the hillside from the main road.

Partway up the path, there was a large mound of snow. As I got nearer, the mound was ever so slightly moving, in a regular rhythmical manner.

The man or whoever was inside, was definitely breathing. I prodded the top of the mound gently, the man was breathing, he was fast asleep. I woke him and I spoke to him.

The man had been there for a couple of days, he said that he had had a fall out with his wife and that he had left home.

Completely buried in the snow. He had all his belongings in a sleeping bag wrapped inside a waterproof bivvy bag, he was as warm as toast. He was absolutely fine and just wanted to be left alone.

There was no need whatsoever to take him to hospital at that moment in time.

He was going nowhere. He was really upset, as to why we were disturbing him, what right did we have to interfere in his life. He hadn't done anything wrong.

I had to agree with him, but because we had been called, we had to get involved. Morally I felt awful, but we do have a legal obligation of care.

We had to call the police, although he was happy to stay there, we couldn't leave him. Neither could we force him to do anything he didn't want to do.

If we had left him, even at his own request and anything had happened to him, we could have been out of a job. It had put everybody in a strange predicament.

The police eventually arrived, they weren't happy, they didn't want to get involved. In their own words, they said to him, that they had "better things to do on a night like this, than deal with an idiot like you"!

I personally think that really, they could have had a bit more patience with him. After all, he hadn't called them, it was us.

Eventually they managed to persuade him to go to his brothers for a few days until things at home had calmed down.

They gave him a lift there. He was not a happy bunny.

By the way, he didn't have a gun.

New lenses.

Carrie, had had her eyes done not long before that job.

She had a couple of operations, to have some new lenses fitted. One eye was operated on the first week and she had the other one done the week after.

Her recovery was extremely quick.

After the first operation, she was doing really well. It was whilst waiting for her second operation that she wore her specs with one of her lenses removed.

Carrie kept poking a finger through the hole in the frame, whilst driving down the road at speed, it was most unnerving.

That's Carrie for you though, she's nearly as daft as me. I think that is why we work well together.

It has seemed to have been successful though. She has had them both done, and she still no longer needs to wear glasses.

House warming?

Another job from January 2012, I was working with June, a true straight talking no nonsense Yorkshire lass. She is great to work with, with a great sense of humour. June has hell of a lot more patience than I have with some of the time wasters. She is brilliant with the elderly, or young adults with learning difficulties, she is a pleasure to watch.

We were called to an address in Crosland Hill. A young lad there, who was possibly not breathing.

We walked in, there was a lad of about seventeen. He was laid flat on the floor, he was obviously holding his breath. Every now and then, he was forced to exhale and then start again.

Another lad told us that it was a small gathering for his and his girlfriends housewarming. That it was their first house together, they had a new baby and that they had wanted to celebrate with their friends.

The lad was a friend of theirs, he had been invited. Then he had got himself extremely drunk and embarrassed himself. The couple and their other friends were at a loss of what to do with him.

He was mucking everybody about, June was just about to sit down on a large sofa. "Don't, he's just pee'd all over that!" The girl of the house shouted. "It was brand new as well".

June thanked her. She had seen enough.

It was time to stop messing about and get him up. As soon as we tried, the young macho male with no shirt, cried like a baby. Then he complained that he was having chest pains.

We got him up off the floor, we told him that he wasn't impressing us and that we could see right through him.

On the way to ambulance, he made one or two sarcastic comments and using colourful language, etc. He was winding me right up. June, was ever so calm and patient.

As he got in to the ambulance, he tried to sit on the clean sheeted cot and on top of the neatly folded blankets. June asked him not to and to sit on the seat to his left.

He said that he would sit where he "f-ing wanted!"

He was politely asked by June again not to do so, he then shouted "I've told you! I'll sit where I f-ing well want!"

Sorry, but that was one red rag too many, for me. I wasn't putting up with him any longer.

We as a service, have a zero tolerance approach, to verbal or physical aggression.

I reached up from the roadside and up into the ambulance, I grabbed hold of him and pulled him out.

June's face was a picture.

I said "I'll tell you where you can sit and it's not in my bloody ambulance! Get out!" and I launched him down the road. I went back to the house, and I explained to the couple what their guest had done and said to my colleague June.

Then I told them where he had gone.

The male who had called us was very embarrassed and chased after the lad and he gave him a right crack!

Served him right.

He even got up June's nose!

Working with June again. It was in August 2016.

We were called to a private sheltered housing complex at Dalton. Each resident has their own flat and can live independently, but there is a warden on site.

The warden checks on them a couple of times daily. There is also a community room, where residents can go and join in activities on a daily basis. They can even go to a dining room and have a pre-booked hot meal.

We had been called there, by a G.P. To see an elderly man who I will call John. He was an Alzheimer's patient, who had been getting increasingly confused. He had occasionally been violent and had been very verbally aggressive.

The doctor wanted John to go to the HRI, to have some blood tests. That would be able to tell, if it was his dementia getting worse, or if it was simply down to an infection.

When we arrived, John had already set his stall up. He was going nowhere. Each case we put to him, to justify his trip to hospital. He had his own perfectly rehearsed, but irrational reply as to why he wasn't going.

John's main argument, was that in his mind, it was his family that had deserted him and in his hour of need. He could not grasp why they wouldn't stay with him 24 hours a day. His brother lived in Lincoln, in John's perspective, it was less than an hour away.

His brother had been and he had stayed with him for three full days, but had then had to go home to look after his wife who was ill. He was an elder brother turned 80. John could not accept that his older brother had other priorities.

He told us that when he was younger, he was at work when his own mother was taken ill. She had lived in Dublin. He had left work and not having much money. He had hitch hiked, begged lifts, whatever, to be by her side.

He couldn't reason that age had crept up on him and his family and that it simply wasn't possible.

June, as usual was her wonderful patient self. Between us, we tried everything. June rang the brother and she got his side of the story. June actually knew John's niece, she rang her. The niece came down and she tried to persuade him to come with us.

We had been there for over two hours, but we were just going round in circles. The niece had to leave, as she had a family to look after.

Then John got really angry, he was very insulting and very personal to his niece. He said that she didn't deserve to have the same surname as him, that she had only got it by marriage and wasn't worthy of it. He told her to leave. He said that he

369

wanted nothing more to do with the lady, who had obviously done a lot of caring for him, it really upset her.

He was downright nasty to her.

That had touched a nerve with June, I could see that her attitude was changing. He had beaten her and not an easy task I can assure you. She stood up and left the room.

I for once had lasted longer than June. She kept popping back in, but she couldn't remain for long.

Eventually I called the out of hours doctors and explained the situation to them. Whatever it was, John wasn't fit to be left for long, he needed to be in hospital and we weren't the ones to get him there at that time.

I rang the call centre and told them of our predicament, they said that a doctor would ring back. He rang within five minutes, that alone can sometimes take hours.

The doctor readily agreed with me, that yes, John did need to be in hospital. That our presence at that stage, was actually aggravating him and making him worse. We agreed that June and me would leave and that a doctor would see John that evening sooner rather than later.

If needs be, a doctor would have the power to be able to section John under the mental health act.

I had to turn the tables and I had to be very firm with John. I refused to get back into an argument with him. I simply told him, that despite him saying that we didn't care. That we both had spent a long time with him, because actually, we did care. That it was he himself that was refusing all help.

We left and returned to station for our meal break, we had been at John's for over three hours trying to help him.

We had exactly thirty minutes on station, then a job came in, it was to go back for John.

The doctor had arranged for an ambulance again. There was no information that the doctor had even been out. After all, it had only been 45 minutes since we had left his flat.

All the way out to Dalton, we were both chuntering to each other. What would he be like now? We could have done without it! How long would we be there this time? All very negative things.

When we arrived, the doctor was waiting for us. He was a smashing Indian doctor, he had a wonderful cheeky grin. He explained everything that he had done and said. He was quite shocked, but really happy that we were the same crew. He said that he had fully read our paperwork, (always left with a patient that doesn't travel to hospital), before even speaking to John.

He told us that, because of everything that we had put on our paperwork, it had given him an insight as to what to expect. Due to that, he had approached John in a very serious and almost abrupt way. He had not given him any opportunity to even answer back, let alone get into a lengthy conversation.

He had told him straight, that an ambulance would come and take him to hospital. If he didn't like that, then it would be the police.

He then said. "I looked him in the eye and told him that I would speak to him again when the ambulance arrived and then I left John, to go and sit in my car until your arrival".

We went upstairs to the flat, knocked on the door and walked in. John looked at us both, he said "back again?" We could see that he was up for an argument. The doctor stepped forward, as soon as John saw him, he stood up and asked if he could have his jacket on first.

He told me where it was, I got it for him and he put it on. He asked June if she would mind getting his pills out of the kitchen and then he said that he was ready to go. He asked to be watched, but not helped down the stairs and then he asked if he could take my arm for support up the short path to the ambulance.

June and I looked at each other, where was the cantankerous old goat that we had left not an hour earlier, he was a very different and apologetic man.

He was lovely, that doctor taught us both a valuable lesson in dealing with typical John type characters. June was smiling again, we took him to get the treatment he needed. He was a perfect gentleman all the way to hospital.

What a change!

Under the affluence of incohol!

March 2012. This story, is another one involving June, although I wasn't working with her at the time. I wasn't even working.

I was the one that had rung 999 and called for assistance. I had been for an evening out at Milnsbridge Socialist Club and I was rather worse for wear, you might say!

Making my way home, I cut through the trees from Whiteley Street to Manchester Road. Using a well established snicket, it cut out quite a corner for me.

As I emerged from the snicket onto Manchester Road, I could hear someone crying out for help. It was around 01:30hrs and pitch dark.

As I looked around, about forty yards away from me, there was a young male. He was dressed all in black and laid in the middle of Manchester Road. He was struggling to get up. I offered my assistance, it was very clear then, that he had broken his leg.

I helped him to the side of the road.

Six young soldiers, all from the local area had been killed while out in Afghanistan. He was a young squaddy, and had been to attend at one of his comrades' funerals. He didn't want to go to hospital, he just wanted to go home to mum's. She lived near to the traffic lights at Cowlersley, less than half a mile away.

I told him that if he could stand, I would help him. He stood, then he screamed. I could see that his leg below the knee, was almost at right angles to where it should have been.

There was absolutely no way that we could manage to get him to his mothers, I rang 999 for an ambulance.

Then began the comedy saga.

First, when the call taker answered. She wanted an exact location of where the incident was, including the post code. I apologised for being intoxicated. I told her who I was, and that the young man was at the side of Manchester Road in Milnsbridge. That I would wait and flag down the crew on their arrival.

No, that wasn't good enough, she needed an exact location. I had to tell her, even though I apologised first, I knew that it was going to sound ridiculous.

I began. "Well, he is on Manchester Road at Milnsbridge, he is outside, what used to be St. Luke's Church. That is just next door to what used to be The China Rose Restaurant. It is just a hundred yards past what used to be the Warren House Pub".

I am sure that at first she thought it was a prank call, it must have sounded stupid. It wouldn't have sounded right if I had been stone cold sober.

God knows what it sounded like at that time.

Eventually I told her to "hang on a minute, and I'll drag him on to my house!" I would have been able to give her the full post code then.

She promised that a crew was on their way.

Firstly I saw the blue lights of a response car, it was Garry. The patient was by then fast asleep in a stupor, he was in a more drunken state than I was. Garry could see that the lads tibia and fibula (both bones of the lower leg), were broken.

The crew arrived, it was June and Garry.

As I was explaining what had happened to June, all she could do, was to join Garry in laughing at me. As Garry was speaking to the lad, he woke up and he was very aggressive, he thought that they were all laughing at him.

He suddenly threatened to stab Graham.

I just thought, well, at least I wasn't on duty. So I dropped on the lad and grabbed his wrists. I wasn't going to let go until the police arrived. All three of my colleagues were telling me to let go, but I wasn't going to do that. I had been caught out with that one before.

They were all laughing at me.

When the police arrived and had checked him over and searched him, he was lifted into the ambulance, again he was very verbally aggressive. I did pop my head around the ambulance doors to apologise to him, but that I wasn't going to let him harm my colleagues, whoever he was.

In the hospital, he was having a go at the nurses, he told them that he had been to Afghanistan and that he should be treated as a hero. His language was appalling.

However, the nurse in charge that night was Sister Theresa. She had dealt with his kind, many times before. Theresa is also a good friend of Staff Nurse Katie, whose son Gary had also been killed in Afghanistan. Theresa knew what it could be like.

She had the last laugh though. When she asked him what colour plaster cast he wanted, he retorted "put a f-ing pink one on!" They did, right from his toes, right up to the top of his thigh. He then had to go back to his barracks with it on and report to his commanding officer.

He would also have to explain how he got his injuries, and probably be put on a charge, for being unfit for duty due to alcohol.

As well as putting up with the piss taking of his squaddie mates for having a bright pink plaster cast.

It would only be for a few days though, because at some stage in the near future. Once the swelling had gone down, he would be needing an operation on that leg. It would need to be pinned and plated. He would be very lucky if he would be able to carry on his career in the forces.

Muppet!

Slow moving Police escort.

Rhian and Mitch, are both paramedics who were based at Huddersfield, they were a couple of the first of a new batch of paramedics. They had come through the university and on the road training, as student paramedics.

Both of them are extremely good at their job and they have the right attitude for it.

They are very confidant, but not in your face and are always very willing to learn. Out of work they are good mates with each other and they share the same sense of humour.

Unfortunately, they have moved on to other parts of the service now, they were disillusioned with how the job was going. I for one, have really missed working with them.

One day though, I was on duty with Rhian, Mitch was out third manning with us. It was as part of a return to work programme.

Our first job was to be a transfer from HRI to the Northern General Hospital at Sheffield.

It was a call for a male who had been badly injured, in a traffic incident earlier in the day. He was a motor cyclist, who had bilateral (both sides) fractures of his legs below the knees. He had a fractured pelvis, he also had fractures to the spiny processes on several of his vertebrae.

He would be laid on a spinal board and we would need to have a very slow and extremely smooth journey.

West Yorkshire police provided an escort from Huddersfield, they had then arranged for our escort to be taken over by the South Yorkshire police. We were going on the motorway, we had two police cars with us and were travelling at only 15mph.

When the South Yorkshire police took over, they had three vehicles. One in front, one behind and one in the middle lane, who was running at the side of us. We were maintaining the speed. The police were letting us govern that, they were watching us very closely.

At each motorway junction the front car sped off up the slip road and stopped anyone coming down the entry slip road and cutting us up.

The one behind slowed everyone down and the one at the side stopped any fast overtaking, therefore any undue rocking of the ambulance. As we got to the end of an entry slip road, the rear car swept past in the outside lane. He went up to the front, the first car then replaced him and joined on at the rear.

On route to Sheffield, the patients' pain was returning, he was in severe distress. He had already had 20 milligrammes of morphine, that was the maximum dosage that an ambulance paramedic can give.

Rhiannon rang thee HRI, to see if our patient could be given any more pain killers. Dr. Rob one of the A&E consultants, said that he could be given up to another 10 milligrammes in 2.5 milligramme boluses.

Rhian was about to give him some morphine. Then she realised that we had a problem.

Due to the security regarding the storage of controlled drugs, including morphine. They were kept locked in a metal safe, in a cupboard in the back of the ambulance.

The key, was on the ignition key ring (Since this incident, the key is now in the personal care of the paramedic).

Rhian was in the back and the keys were in the ignition, what could we do? It was not feasible to stop, neither would it be safe. We were causing major congestion on the M62 as it was.

There was only one solution.

Mitch was in the front passenger seat and I was driving. I had to get Mitch to lean right over and take over the steering wheel, as I was using the pedals to keep a constant and smooth speed.

I had then had both my hands free to reach down to the keys and remove the morphine key off the ring. Obviously leaving the ignition key in situ. It was such a good job there was three of us. In the old ambulances, the attendant would have simply stepped through the adjoining door from the saloon area.

The police officer at our side driving a Range Rover, spoke on his PA system. It sounded so clear, it was as though he was sat in the cab with us. He said "I don't know, I don't want to know and I don't care what you are up to, just be careful". We were still laughing when we left the motorway.

It worked though and the patient got his pain relief.

The police were wonderful, they provided a wonderful safe and slow journey. It is some experience to be involved in one of those transfers, especially when it goes well like that one.

Slow inter-hospital transfers at the moment, are fairly rare. I think they could well be become more commonplace in the future, when specialist care is regionalised more and longer journeys are required.

That same night was far from over! Bloody Vinnie Jones.

Once we had come clear and available in Sheffield, we were allocated another job. That patient was also taken to the Northern General. We were back there again.

We cleared at the hospital once more, inevitably the two way data screen was alarming for another job in Sheffield. As we read the details on the screen, our hearts sank.

We were going for a fifteen year girl old who had been found hanging, we were told that CPR was in progress.

We were strangers lost in an unfamiliar area, faced with one of the worst calls imaginable. Mitch asked over the radio if there was anyone else on the detail, maybe an RRV? The reply didn't help us. "I'm sorry guys, it is extremely busy you are on your own I'm afraid".

We have sat nav, thankfully.

On the screen though we could see the highlighted line of travel that the machine wanted us to take, but there seemed to be a road straight through the middle. That should speed the journey up and cut a great big chunk off the distance.

I made my way, straight for the direct route. It was a straight road alright, but, there were high kerbs and there wasn't much leeway between them.

Mitch and I then realised very quickly that I had gone down a guided trackway, they are designed only for the Sheffield trams. God help us if a tram was to come the other way.

Fortunately we got away with it and it saved us at least three minutes off our scheduled journey.

We arrived on scene to be directed upstairs where a man was performing CPR on his stepdaughter, I'll call her Bobby.

Bobby had been having a minor argument with her mum and step dad, following which she had suddenly stormed off and upstairs to her room.

She had then tied one sleeve of her jumper tightly around her neck and the other to the top of the bannister, she had then launched herself down the stairs.

When her parents heard the sound of that, they sent her younger nine year old brother to tell her to quieten down. They had thought the noise was from her stamping around in the bedroom, she had done that before from time to time.

Her little brother had found her lifeless body, it was laid in the stairway suspended from the bannister. He had screamed for help.

Dad was doing CPR brilliantly. When we took over, we were taking over from a completely broken man. He, his wife and their son were crying unconsolably.

We three, have really worked well together in the past. Especially in difficult circumstances, this job would be no exception. An RRV from Wath-upon-Dearne, (near Barnsley) turned up, followed by a supervisor and a trainee from Sheffield.

There was then six of us, that made it so much easier to get the right equipment into the house. I was doing chest compressions, the RRV managed Bobby's airway, Rhian had gained intravenous access, whilst Mitch drew up some life saving drugs.

There was still no output, no heart activity nor breathing.

The supervisor and her trainee managed to get the scoop stretcher into the house. Everything was all set up ready to go, for when we were.

We just needed a sign from Bobby.

Drugs were administered and I continued with the chest compressions.

It was then that I felt something that I had never felt before, I actually felt her heart start to beat, that was the sign we needed. Bobby's heart was beating. It was absolutely pounding in her chest. We were still ventilating her. But her heart was beating for itself at around 90 beats per minute.

We were ecstatic, but only for a few moments. Unfortunately her heart started slowing down, until stopping again.

We knew that she was fighting. More adrenaline, more compressions and it did it again. I actually felt her heart kick in and start beating. That time she was maintaining it, a steady heartbeat. Beating regularly at 90 beats per minute.

We knew then that it was the time to move.

Bobby was safely and securely strapped to the scoop stretcher. An oxygen powered respirator was attached and off we went. It was down the stairs, out of the house, across the garden and into the ambulance.

The supervisor took my keys, she would drive the ambulance and all three of us stayed in the back. A call was made to alert the paediatric resus team and away we went. Staff were waiting for us at the specialist Sheffield Children's Hospital. We would probably have gone back to the Northern General, that's where local knowledge comes to the fore.

They carried on looking after Bobby. We all went for a stress relieving coffee.

All six of us ambulance staff from three different localities. We had all been working together with the same objective in mind, using the same methods.

Each and everyone of us played a vital role. We had worked tirelessly together to try and save Bobby.

But we were well and truly knackered, it's not easy isn't performing CPR.

Whilst outside the A&E having the drink, the paediatric consultant came and asked one of us to speak to the family.

I being the oldest was volunteered. There were a couple of police (family liaison) officers already with them.

The family were in a relatives room. Mum and little brother huddled on a sofa, their heads were buried together in despair. Dad was pacing up and down he was devastated. He said that he had never done CPR before, he had never been trained.

All he had seen was "that bloody Vinnie Jones thing on't telly". He pleaded "Was I doing it right?"

I told him quite frankly, that although Bobby was clearly not out of the woods. And not by a long chalk.

The fact that she did have a heartbeat and had been trying to breathe for herself, was down to him and down to him alone. If he hadn't made the right start, Bobby would have died there and then at the house and no mistake. Now, at least she was in with a fighting chance.

Thanks to him and "that bloody Vinnie Jones".

I think it helped.

I told him that he ought to get in touch with the British Heart Foundation, if Bobby pulled through. Their story might be able to help others. I couldn't bring myself to say that if things didn't go well, the BHF would also want to know. That he had had a go.

That he had tried his best thanks to the video, and that "bloody Vinnie Jones".

I wanted to, but I thought it would not have been the appropriate time.

As we were all set to leave, the paediatric consultant came out. "Group hug guys". He then said, "come here and hold your heads up high, you've all done well tonight, thank you!"

A great gesture, it really meant a lot to us. But our heads were far from being held up high. Not at that stage.

We kept enquiring about Bobby, keeping our fingers crossed. Initially she was showing major improvement. On the fifth day though, we got some horrendous news. Bobby had suffered a heart attack. Despite all of the efforts to save her, sadly Bobby had died.

What an awful tragic loss of a young life, that would have such a traumatic affect on a truly loving family.

Where is the justice? Eh!

"Looks like a pig, pork".

October 2012, working with Carrie yet again. We have had some cracking shifts together and some brilliant jobs over the years. We had been called to "an incident" at Thornton Lodge. We didn't know what we were going for at that stage.

On arrival at the small back to back, rear terraced house. There we were met by a young lad, of around 20 years old. He told us that it was his father that we had come for, he had had an accident downstairs in the cellar area.

On the way through the house, there were several people of all ages. All of them were from the same family, they had only recently arrived in the UK from Poland. They were all quite obviously very shook up.

What were we going to find?

I very tentatively followed the lad down the cellar steps. In the cellar, were even more people in a state of shock. One woman perhaps in her forties, was trying to explain the situation in her own native polish language. She was doing a lot of shouting and a lot of arms waving, she was very excitable.

The son stepped in, he was almost perfect in his English speaking. The cellar was used as an extension of their living area. Dad was laid on the floor in the corner, he had a big smile on his face, he waved. He actually looked a picture of health.

As we approached him, the son removed a towel that was laid across his dad's lap. To the left hand side of his groin area, the man's jeans were ripped, there was a fair amount of blood.

The son explained to us, that his dad had been trying to repair an angle grinder. It was a large one, the nine inch diameter bladed one.

That one had a broken blade. There was a section of it missing. The best way that I can describe it, it was about the size of a "good sized portion of a nine inch pizza".

As he had been "mending" the machine, he had been sat on a wooden dining chair in the corner of the room. The grinder had been sat on the floor between his legs.

It was STILL PLUGGED IN!!!!!

Guess what happened next?

377

Yes. It started up, it had then bounced off the floor and straight in to the man's groin.

All legs crossed at this point!

I needed to examine him and the wound more closely. As I ripped his jeans further to have a look, the pizza sized missing piece of blade fell out of his pants. There was a large hole in the top of his thigh. It was not bleeding too much at the time.

I asked Carrie to quickly request a paramedic back up. If the man started bleeding again, then we could be swimming in the red stuff and he may bleed to death. (To exsanguinate).

A paramedic was requested.

When they had arrived they would be able to set fluids up. Primarily we would have venous access, just in case.

Whilst waiting, I carefully and fully examined his wound.

Firstly I exposed the area more. The wound was along the line of the elastic of his "y-fronts". It was a wide gaping, deep wound. I used a large wad of sterile gauze to soak up the pooling blood.

The extent of the damage was then very clear. The blade, although it was nine inch in diameter. It was only around an eighth of an inch thick, it was a cutting blade.

It had cut!

It had scored his femur (thigh bone) to a depth of an eighth of an inch, a line of around an inch long. Then fully visible and around the diameter of my little finger, pumping away, was his femoral artery.

The artery had been marked by the blade. It had a definite white friction mark across it. That meant that our patient had only been the thickness of the wall of his blood vessel away from certain death!

If it burst, then, he would literally only have a couple of minutes to live. Shit!

It was going to require extremely careful handling. The little grey cells were being exercised. To get him out of the cellar, we should strictly speaking, have carried him.

That would have meant him having to sit on our carry chair, with his legs bent at ninety degrees at the knees and again at the same angle at his groin/hip.

I felt that it would have put undue pressure on the already weakened artery wall.

Paramedic Ros, Manny's wife arrived. Once the situation had been explained and a large bore grey, (cannula) intra venous line inserted.

Fluid was set up, but not running. His blood pressure was fine at that moment, those things were all done precautionary.

I packed the wound with a large wad of saline soaked (to prevent adhesion) gauze. Then I put on a tightly bound pressure bandage.

If we could get the patient to keep his left leg straight, he could put his arm around my shoulder for support. That way none, or very little weight would be put on it. I was sure that we could get him upstairs. We did so, all the way to the ambulance, where he was laid down.

Thankfully, there was no further excitement on route.

The son travelled with us in the ambulance to act as interpreter. He told us that our calm and professional nature, had calmed all of the family down,and that they were very grateful.

Little did he know. My old mate Tommy taught me the "mucky duck syndrome" as he called it. "Keep your feathers all nice and smooth" he would say, "it gives a good impression" he went on. Then he dropped in the punch line. He said that if we kept that appearance up, the public would be fooled and remain calm. He said "it doesn't matter if you are paddling like buggery under the water, they won't see that!"

How true he was.

Once at the hospital, the doctors had a look, there had been no further bleeding. The sight that greeted us then, looked like something from a butchers shop window. As the son said as he looked, "oh! Looks like a pig! Pork!" It did, like a freshly sliced joint of raw pork.

He then touched his dad's genital area and laughed. "He's still got his bubbles!" He said. (Testicles, I think he meant). He had and they were both quite safe.

As Carrie said, it is at times like that, you can really see and understand the anatomy of the body.

To see a femoral artery under pressure is highly unusual. Normally, if we were looking at his sort of wound, we would have had a fatality on our hands.

Stop quick! I'm gonna be sick.

October 2012. We had received a call to Crosland Moor. It was early evening, perhaps 18:30hrs. Yes I was with Carrie, I was bound to be for this one.

This job will remain deeply rooted in my head forever. Unfortunately for all of the wrong reasons.

We had no idea what we were actually going for, all we had, was an address. It had been passed on to us, as a life threatening emergency call, from the shortly to be extinct NHS Direct.

There were no details.

As we pulled up outside the address and started down the short garden path, we looked at each other. From outside, the house looked no different to any of the rest of the long row of terraced houses.

It was the stench!

It hit you right at the back of the throat. We were both gipping from the smell and we hadn't even reached the door. We tentatively knocked.

A man in his thirties answered. Nothing unusual struck us about him, although at the time we were struggling to see through our painfully streaming and burning eyes.

When the door had fully opened there was nothing to stop the smell, it streamed out of the door, almost like a fog. It was an awful, rank, acrid, throat burning stench.

We had to step back. Neither of us could have prepared for that. It was awful. We tried again and went in. On the sofa was a woman in her late forties. She was extremely drunk.

We were told by another man in the house, her partner, that the patient was called Anna and she was alcohol dependant.

Anna had just had nearly three weeks holiday from work, yes that's right, work. When she had time off, she would go on a drinking spree. In all of that three weeks bender, not once had she left the sofa.

NOT EVEN ONCE!

The woman's partner had been catering for her demanding ways, or so he told us. He said that she was the one that makes him, buy her the drink. If he didn't, she would severely beat him.

On her time off that was all that she has been doing and that only very occasionally, had he managed to get her to eat something.

She hadn't even moved to go to the toilet.

Everything that had left her body over the last three weeks. Had been passed on to that sofa, just where she sat. It actually looked like she had not moved for the whole two years that she had lived at the address.

The sofa was without any shadow of doubt, steaming. All around the whole of the seating area, had a two inch deep cloud of steam hovering over it. The floor by her feet was two or three inches deep in the rank and festering mess.

We had to go outside again. We spoke to the partner and friend in the doorway.

Our main questions were, what had they rung for? What was it that they wanted us to do?

The answer, unexpectedly was. "Well she starts work tomorrow, she needs cleaning up before she goes".

I couldn't believe it. I then asked "how does that become a life threatening emergency call?"

He told us that it was NHS Direct that had made that decision and that they had told them that we would take her to hospital, to help her to get cleaned up.

I rang NHS Direct back, I spoke to the senior operator who had taken the original call. I asked what information had they been given? How did they come to that decision?

I was told that as the woman had been in that state, the original request for nurses to assist in cleaning her up, had been denied. They had told the family, that she would need to go to hospital, as her urine and faeces would have caused her some skin irritation and most likely an infection.

What a joke! No wonder the service was being shut down, it was a complete waste of time.

We had to get the lady out of the house.

Medically there was nothing wrong with her, physically there was nothing wrong, she was simply drunk and almost incapable. We stood her up to move her, as we did the stench again grabbed our throats. We had to keep going. As she moved, a sight met my eyes which again I will never forget, it was enough to cause nightmares.

Anna was wearing tights, all her faeces over the last weeks that weren't on the sofa, had collected in them. The mess, had been diluted with the most acrid, almost neat ammonia smelling urine.

Have you ever seen a beach when the tide has just gone out? All the sand worms leave their little spirals of brown wet sand. That was what was now appearing. All over her legs, as the wet stinking faeces was being forced through the mesh of the tights. We had to wait whilst most of the mess escaped, before she could move.

We had to retreat to the door again.

Eventually, between us all, we managed to get Anna out and into the ambulance. Despite it being warm outside and Anna was wearing a fur coat, we had to completely cocoon her in blankets.

I could not take any baseline observations, her entire body was covered in the stuff. She had somehow been putting her hands into the mess, then it had been wiped in her hair and all over her arms and face.

She needed to be dropped in a bath, her clothes would probably need to be soaked away from her skin and then incinerated..

I rang through to HRI to pre warn them of our situation and that the patient would need to go straight in to a cubicle.

Not due to her medical condition, but there was no way that she could be sat in a waiting room like that.

Carrie was driving at speed as I was in the back choking, my eyes were streaming, I really felt ill. I would have to ask Carrie to pull over I needed some air. I was going to vomit.

As I was in the process of asking Carrie to stop, I looked out of the window, we were already passing through the top end of Marsh. I told her to carry on. We had less than two minutes left of our journey, less if Carrie put her foot down.

We got our patient into a cubicle at A&E, they asked us to remove her fur coat. As we did, an enormous amount of her bodily emissions dropped onto the floor with a most sickening splat!

That was the last straw, we couldn't take it any more.

Carrie and I burst out of the cubicle and into the corridor that runs alongside. There were people just standing about and they were in the way. We had to just push our way past as we were coughing and retching all the way to the door and beyond.

I know it looked so unprofessional, but at that stage it was a matter of survival.

On the way to hospital, I was writing down our patients personal details, ready to book her in at reception.

Anna was a very arrogant person. She told me in no uncertain terms that she didn't have any skin sores and that the journey was a complete and utter waste of time. She said that she was perfectly capable of cleaning herself, and that WE were "making a mountain out of a molehill".

Not the best choice of phrase, particularly if you could see what I could see all over the ambulance floor.

Anna also said that she would not be admitted to hospital, as she had to go to work in the morning. I was curious and I asked her where she worked.

I was shocked again and not for the first time on that job. Anna was the **senior carer**, at two different residential care homes for the elderly.

It was a while later when I was called to the same address again, the circumstances almost mirrored that job. I put a report in to the social services, regarding her being a vulnerable adult, it was a safeguarding issue. I went on that without some considerable work done, that the house was unfit for human habitation.

Shortly after the second job, both of the above care homes were hammered by the CQC on inspection, (care quality commission). The management team went in and Anna no longer works at either of their care homes.

Both of the homes are dramatically improving in their standards now.

Moh-bility Ashraf!

September 2015. I was working a shift with Ash. He is well known in the area and not just at the ambulance station. It is for his part ownership of the Nawaab restaurant in Huddersfield.

Most of us have taken great delight in tasting samples or visiting the real thing, at some stage.

The particular day that I was working with him, was extremely windy and as usual we don't know where we will be or what we will see. That day was no exception.

We had been called to an accident at the side of the main Wakefield Road at Moldgreen, involving an elderly lady and a mobility scooter. She had been blown over by the force of the high winds.

On our arrival sat on the floor at the side of the road, along with quite a crowd of well wishers, was our elderly victim. She was badly shaken, but not apparently injured.

Her mobility scooter was in bits.

As we put her in the ambulance, to give her a full medical check up, a couple of lads stopped us. They worked for a firm specialising in mobility scooters, actually it was for a rival company. They still offered to help.

By the time we had sorted our patient out, the scooter had been fully reassembled. The lads had stuck a note on it saying "A ok, fully ready for use".

They had gone before either the patient or us could thank them.

True gentlemen.

The lady was still shaken and there was no need for any hospital treatment, she just wanted to go home. Normally she would have gone on her own way, but due to the wind, her confidence had taken a knock. We decided that we would take her home. It was only about a mile away, it would be safer for her.

Then we encountered a problem!

The scooter wouldn't fit in the ambulance. Even using the hydraulic ramp, the scooter just would not fit in.

Ash decided that he would drive it home for her, adding test driver of mobility scooters to his portfolio.

Off he set and what a picture!

I took the lady with me in the ambulance and we all arrived at her home together. The lady was very grateful.

A few years ago, we wouldn't have been allowed to do that.

Our only destination option would have been to hospital.

One move that we have made towards a positive progress, is to find alternative "pathways" for patients. To get the best treatment for the patients needs, or get them to the best place for their treatment. That might not necessarily be A&E.

Barnsley wheelchairs don't fit.

It was late October 2011. I didn't have a mate at Huddersfield, so I was asked to work out of Honley and to team up with paramedic Danni. It was for another night shift.

At around 22:00hrs, we attended a job in Penistone, for a large lady who said that she couldn't walk too far. Her sister stated that she was "simply too fat to walk".

Neither of us managed to get to the actual reason that she needed to go to hospital. We wheeled the lady all the way up through the communal car park and courtyard, to the top where the only access was for the ambulance..

We asked her if she could manage to climb the three steps up into the back of the ambulance, she said that she would try. She managed one and then she just threw herself to floor like a beached whale, she flatly refused to move any further.

We had a right time to get her to move, we had to physically lift all her body weight into a sitting position and then in stages get her to sit on a seat.

The whole time the back doors of the ambulance had to be wide open, anyone who looked out of their curtains would have been able to see the fiasco unfolding in front of them.

The woman was showing far more than expected, laid on the floor of the ambulance. Anyone looking out of their windows would have seen the unexpected full moon as her bare behind was revealed to all. It was embarrassing.

She was making a right spectacle of herself, her sister who was there with us the whole time, was disgusted.

After pulling and tugging for what seemed an eternity, Danni and me finally got her into a more dignified position sat in the vehicle.

We took her to Barnsley hospital with what we finally thought might be a slight chest infection, but we still weren't sure.

On our arrival at the Barnsley District General Hospital, we found a wheelchair for the patient. The wheelbase on the Barnsley chairs was much wider than the ramp of the ambulance. It wouldn't fit.

That meant that I had to plan another dismount.

I went into the A&E department and collared a Barnsley crew, I asked if I could borrow their WAS (the larger box style ambulance, with a hydraulic ramp on the back).

The crew obliged and gave me the keys.

I went outside, took their vehicle and turned it around and I reversed towards the back of our own vehicle. I dropped their ramp and placed a hospital wheelchair on it and then raised the ramp up high.

I asked Danni to open the back doors of our ambulance and then I reversed right up to it, dropping the ramp right inside and onto the floor.

We put the patient into the wheelchair, wheeled her back across into the Barnsley ambulance. I raised the ramp a couple of inches, then Danni drove ours away. We were then able to lower the ramp and the patient to the floor. No lifting, tugging, pushing or pulling involved.

When we looked up, there was quite a crowd of onlookers, mostly ambulance and A&E staff. All had been intrigued as to my actions at 23:30hrs on a Saturday night. We got a rousing round of applause for that one.

Even the A&E consultant gave us a nod of approval.

Andy Craft, the Pine Minister.

Danni, no longer works for the ambulance service. She is married to a good friend of mine Arran, they have a young daughter Merissa. Arran is an emergency care practitioner at Huddersfield, I work with him quite regularly.

We have a similar interest in woodworking, especially toys, but any sort of items that would give others pleasure and enjoyment. We both work from a shed/come workshop in the back garden.

Arran generally makes smaller, more modern and contemporary gift items. Whereas I prefer to make the more traditional games, older style items. Or larger items to use for fundraising events.

At the moment, Arran is doing particularly well, he advertises his work on Facebook, and that has inundated him with further work under the name of Andy Craft, look him up, he has some wonderful stuff on there.

He is almost ready to start his own web-site, under the name of Andy Craft, the Pine Minister.

Catchy eh?

Good luck Arran, I wish you well mate.

Motor cycle RTC.

In June 2013. This job was one of my last RRV shifts. I may do some more in the future, but who knows. (At the beginning of 2016, I have started working on the RRV again).

The job, although extremely disturbing was not the reason that I gave up the car.

That was all down to the politics of the service. It was getting to the stage where responders were regularly being left on scene with poorly patients for well over an hour. I wasn't prepared to put up with it any more.

At the time of this particular incident, I was mobile to a roadside standby and heading down the road towards Huddersfield. I had just left one main road and taken the slip to join the other main road, when I was called regarding a road traffic collision (RTC).

I didn't need any further information, I could see it. It was involving a motorcycle, the riderless machine was spinning out of control right before my eyes.

I made an illegal u-turn from the slip road and there in front of me, laid still in the road was the motor cyclist.

What I saw was horrific.

Do not read if easily upset. The upsetting text is between the asterisks.

*******Laid motionless in the road was a male in full motorcycle gear, it looked good quality stuff. Out from his helmet was pouring a river of blood.

Bearing in mind, that the accident had only just happened literally seconds in front of me. The blood was flowing downhill and it was actually flowing, there were ripples as it went. The flow had a width of at least eighteen inches and had already travelled at least twelve to thirteen feet.

Believe me, that is some amount of blood to lose in such a short time.

As I approached him he was unconscious, he was laid almost in the recovery position. I didn't get any form of response. I couldn't get to his wrist, or anywhere clearly to check for a pulse. I had my cardiac monitor with me, I was able to apply the spots under his leather jacket and on to his back.

That showed me that he did have a pulse, he had a pulse rate of 138 beats a minute. I was using the suction unit through his open face helmet, as I was trying to clear his compromised airway.

The suction unit holds half a litre of liquid.

I filled it and had to empty it out into the road. Three times I did that. As I was doing it, his heart rate was decreasing until it stopped.

Just at the same time as he went into cardiac arrest, the first ambulance arrived and also another RRV pulled up on the opposite carriage way.

The crew were Paramedic Danni, who is married to my mate Arran, she was working with an ECA from Wakefield, I'm sorry, I didn't know his name. The RRV was Paramedic Tony, from Huddersfield.

As we were log rolling the patient onto his back, consultant anaesthetist and Basics Doctor Jed arrived. He was on his way to work.

All that help and within two minutes of the accident happening. We had to remove the bikers helmet, that was a tricky joint procedure. Jed then RSI'd the patient (Rapid Sequence Intubation). That involves paralysing the patient, taking over his breathing with a tube inserted into his lungs and then manual ventilation.

Using what appears to be a small electric drill, (which in effect, is exactly what it is). Danni, used the kit for her first time, she drilled directly into the patient's shoulder and into the bone marrow. That left a cannula in situ, via which life saving drugs could be administered.

It is needed when there is no blood pressure left to keep the blood vessels open and the veins shut down, making it impossible to insert a normal intra venous cannula.

He was lifted using a scoop stretcher and put into the ambulance and rushed to awaiting staff at HRI. If his breathing hadn't been compromised, for that type of job the patient would go to a major trauma centre. Our nearest being LGI. He wasn't stable enough to travel that distance. To all intents and purposes he was already dead.

Any drugs that were given to him had no effect, the ventilations didn't save him. His injuries were far too severe.

He had exsanguinated, (he had lost all of his blood volume). He had literally bled to death right in front of us, despite all the extremely quick interventions.

All the blood had left his body from his head. It turned out that the carotid ventricles in his brain had ruptured, that resulted in a catastrophic blood loss via the ears and nose.

It took less than four minutes for all of his bodily fluids to bleed out, there was nothing more that we could do for him at the scene.

He was pronounced deceased, only shortly after his arrival at HRI.

For that patient, he could not have had any more help, any quicker than he did. Despite all the stops being pulled out, it just wasn't enough.*******

Only seconds after the incident, I was there. There were already off duty police officers present, who had been on the other carriageway on route to start work. They including Wendy's cousin Brian's daughter, Tracy, she was the first to make a 999 call. Several other calls followed in the next few moments.

Merry Christmas 2013. I've got my eyes on you.

It was Christmas Day 2013. I was happy to be teamed up again, with my mate Carrie. We were on an early shift, that involved a six o'clock in the morning start.

Happy Christmas to us and our families!

Actually it turned out to be one of the best shifts that I had worked for a long long time.

Less than ten minutes in and we were sent to the Colne Valley area of Huddersfield. It was for a lady fifty years of age, having a possible heart attack.

Already there was an RRV, it was paramedic practitioner Garry. The lady was having a "barn door" MI, that is an obvious full blown heart attack (known as a myocardial infarction). The treatment for her was pain relief and monitoring, and then a blue light run straight to the LGI.

At the LGI we took her into the Cath Lab, where they were ready and waiting for our patient. We took her directly into the operating theatre and there the procedure called PPCI, (Primary Percutaneous Coronary Intervention) to unblock the arteries started immediately.

It involves a catheter being introduced into the main artery at the right wrist, it is then passed all the way up through the blood vessels and directly into the heart.

A dye is injected first and that shows under x-rays, where the exact point of blockage causing the heart attack has occurred. They can then insert a stent. For lack of a better description, a stent is a bit like a flat coiled spring. It is inserted into the point of blockage and then as it is opened up, the blood flow can hopefully return to normal.

If the procedure is done quickly, it can prevent any scarring or further damage of the heart. Under an hour from the pain starting, to the procedure is perfect.

Soonest done, least damage done.

The procedure can be watched by the patient on the screens at the side of them. They are fully conscious throughout.

Our lady was in Leeds, in less than one hour from the pain starting. She was successfully treated, there was no lasting damage done and she had three stents fitted.

On the way back from Leeds, and with it being Christmas Day, Carrie had a blue Santa's hat on whilst she was driving. I had a red and white one, complete with a long white beard.

Comms called us, it was a good friend of ours, Josie. She was working on our bay with Theresa, another good friend. (I took her wedding photos).

Josie said "Ian, please tell me that you are not driving an ambulance wearing a Santa's hat and beard".

I wasn't lying when I replied "I can promise you that I am not".

Apparently we had been seen by the motorway police, they had rung our Comms Centre. They had said that they didn't think that it was appropriate behaviour for an ambulance crew, especially with us being professional people.

They didn't know the half of it.

We were waving to children in cars as we passed, it appeared to be bringing a smile to everyone, unless you happen to be working in a police car apparently.

Good job they weren't in Halifax later, I found out, that I could play jingle bells on the bull horn.

Mint!

Another call, that one in the Queens Road area of Halifax. We were not sure what we were going for, the caller hadn't been very clear. It was a complex of flats and entry was to be gained via an intercom system. We buzzed the wanted flat.

From the reply on the intercom, we knew that it wasn't going to be a straight forward job (just for a change).

"Whaaat!" The voice said very loudly.

We replied "ambulance".

"Whaaat!"

Again, "ambulance".

"Whyyy!"

"Please let us in".

"Whyyy!"

"Well it was you that called us" we replied.

"Whaaat fooor!"

We were getting nowhere.

Another resident happened to open the door, as she was making her way out. We wished her a Merry Christmas and then we seized our chance, we grabbed the door and entered the complex.

We got to the numbered flat and knocked on the door, we were let in by a lady.

The male occupant of the flat looked at us, well we think he was looking at us. The unfortunate man had what we call in "the trade" as Leeds-Bradford eyes. One looking towards one side of the room, Leeds, the other eye looking to the opposite side, Bradford. Also known as east-west eyes.

He appeared to be around the mid sixties in age.

His first comment to us, was more of a demand than a comment. "Well, which of you two ladies is gonna put my sock on?"

I said to him politely, "excuse me, but who do you think you are talking to?"

He screamed back at me, "well, I'm looking at you aren't I?"

I thought I was going to start laughing there and then.

I asked him if the reason that an ambulance had been called, was simply to put his sock on.

He yelled back, "well what am I supposed to do? I've got one on I can't reach the other!" He was shouting at me at the top of his voice.

I told him that we were from the ambulance service, we do not respond to 999 just to put someone's sock on.

He shouted back "you might as well now, you've nowt better to do!"

I asked him for the reason he couldn't get the second one on.

He showed us. It was like a scene from a comedy film. He bent down fully to the right foot, he could reach that one perfectly. With the other he just sighed and said "I can't do it, I can't bend down like this" as he bent down and touched his toes on the bare foot.

I said to him "is that leg longer than the other then?" He didn't answer.

It went on for twenty or more minutes.

He obviously hadn't had a stroke or anything.

After a while he started shouting even more. He told us that if we wouldn't put his sock on, to get out of his house. "She called you" he shouted. "I didn't want you, I knew you wouldn't put my bloody sock on".

I asked him, if the lady (Susan Boyle with no make up on, wearing a hat rejected by a charity shop), was his wife. He said that he didn't even know her and that she was only a neighbour in another part of the flats.

The man had a large collection of die cast metal trucks, very detailed models of Eddie Stobart's and such. Due to his poor vision he had made his own way out of scale number plates, out of bits of cardboard and stuck them with sellotape all across the front of each truck.

Everything in the flat was just not right. If you had been there, like us you would have sworn that it was a set up.

We left, he was still screaming down the corridor for us to leave.

The next job was in Illingworth, further up the hill from Halifax. Again it seemed to be perfectly set up as a comedy sketch.

There was so much nicotine in the house, the tar had liquified and was running freely down all the walls and windows. It was actually dripping off the ceilings in strands, like a dark treacle.

There were two brothers in the house, one of them was having chest pains. The RRV from Halifax, a young paramedic called Jack was on scene. He was trying, but really struggling to get a full history.

The brothers were both wearing light coloured trousers, that were absolutely rank, they were filthy. Covered in food stains from Christmas 1948, by the look of them.

One of the brothers had cut his own hair. As professionals, we shouldn't laugh, but it was impossible not to.

If he had cut it using a knife and fork held between his toes, he couldn't have done a worse job.

I have never seen anything like it. He had obviously been looking in a mirror, but he couldn't see the back or the sides, there he had just guessed where to cut.

It looked bloody ridiculous.

As Jack was treating the one with chest pains, we asked the other brother, how things had started.

He ignored that completely, he just stated to us that they would have to miss their Christmas dinner.

I asked him where he would have been getting it.

He told us that he would have been cooking for them both.

The only cooker in the house, was a two ringed electrical hob, sat on top of the kitchen surface. That looked like it had been just used as an ash tray since the day the house had been built.

There were no signs that there had ever been any cooking done in the house. There was a mountain of ash and filter tipped cigarette buts on the actual burners.

There was a twin tub washing machine in the corner of the kitchen that had a recessed top, which was full and overflowing down the sides of it with the nicotine tar.

We told the patient, that we would take him to A&E to check his chest pains out.

The brother said that he would travel with us, he told us that the casualty department would have to make them a full Christmas dinner, seeing as they couldn't get one at home.

We did explain that it wouldn't be happening.

They were both very disappointed and couldn't understand why.

Then he asked if the buses were running.

I told him that with it being Christmas Day, there were no buses running at all.

He said that they would take their bus passes just in case, as they would have to get the bus back home.

It was very strange.

We tried to explain the details of the last two jobs to our friends in the Comms

Centre. Josie, Theresa, Carrie and me, were helpless, we were all in stitches. We were laughing so much that we were in pain.

We did attend to other jobs that day, but they were not really significant from our point of view, they were everyday run of the mill jobs.

Definitely a day never to forget!

Completely and utterly hoodwinked!

It was early September 2014. I was working with a new to Huddersfield paramedic, called Richard. He had been qualified in the North West Ambulance Service for about twelve months, before he transferred to the Yorkshire Ambulance Service in the July of 2014.

It wasn't often that I worked with a qualified member of staff, so even though I didn't really know him and he was a "comer in" I was looking forward to the shift.

I enjoyed working with him, he seemed a nice lad. Richard lives in the Halifax area and so has moved to be able to work nearer home, fair enough. He was not quite the "comer in" I was led to believe.

We had a nice steady day. We didn't have anything too special to deal with until half past five, we were on a six o'clock finish.

It was a call to an address near Mirfield, we knew then that we were going to be late off.

We attended to a lady in her seventies. She said that she "just didn't feel right" with no specific diagnosis. It is very difficult to assess medically someone who "just doesn't feel right", although it does seem to be a very common condition.

The patient had a long and very complex medical history, including a previous stroke. She was diabetic with a heart condition. Just to finish off, the lady was blind and had anxiety issues.

We assessed the lady and although we could find nothing specific. There was definitely nothing acute, but both her and her husband wanted her to see a doctor at the hospital.

Due to her combined medical conditions, we reluctantly agreed.

She had suffered from several UTI's (urinary tract infections) particularly due to her immobility.

Where she lived was only around seven minutes from Dewsbury District Hospital, we thought it would see us off nicely. We could finish at the hospital for around six o'clock, we should be home for not long after half past. That's near enough to on time these days.

Then the sob story started, both the patient and her husband begged us to take her to Pinderfields in Wakefield.

It went on for ages.

The reason being that they had suffered several "bad experiences" at Dewsbury. She said that she had been left on a trolley for hours on end, that they hadn't catered for her blindness. The husband went on with several other plausible reasons as to why the Dewsbury Hospital wasn't suitable. The woman was in tears and her husband was pleading with us to help her.

The couple had a support worker, I rang her. By then it was already after six.

The support worker told us that the family GP, district nurses and she herself, we're putting together a care package. That would be of health and support to the patient, but that it hadn't been sorted out fully at the time. The GP surgery had closed and as such, we would have to take her to hospital to be fully assessed.

We took them to Pinderfields, knowing that we would be having a very late finish that day.

As we arrived at Pinderfields A&E, Richard went to hand over to the "triage" (sort and prioritise) nurse. While I waited with our couple in the corridor.

When he came back to us he had a shocked look on his face, he had also written a sly message for me on his gloved hand. When he showed it to me, I too was extremely shocked.

The couple had been taken to the A&E department at Pinderfields over a 100 times already that year.

The Dewsbury hospital had virtually told them that they were wasting time and were only seeking attention. That they had not to visit again, unless it was something life threatening.

The couple hadn't liked that.

Pinderfields were in the process of doing the same.

The care package that was being formulated, will have all of the lady's problems listed and her "normal" observations noted. It will help to sort the issues out once and for all. If all her basic observations match the ones documented in the care package, hospital can be ruled out. It will save many wasted ambulance journeys to hospital.

We will still be going to the house though.

Only new, or sudden changes in her condition would require a trip to the "nearest" hospital. Those care packages are becoming quite common now.

I think that the staff at the Dewsbury hospital were so right. Richard and me, had been well and truly conned!

I normally think that I am a good judge of character, but these two had completely beaten me.

A young lad relatively new to the service and me the old hand, we had both been absolutely completely and utterly hoodwinked.

We finally finished after half past seven that evening, what a shift.

Is that a flat tyre?

It was the Easter weekend 2015, I was working with Shelley. It was Saturday, our third of four shifts together. We were working a twelve hour shift, from 08:00hrs until 20:00hrs.

The woman on our dispatch bay had been awful, she had a really bad attitude towards us.

It certainly wasn't the way to make many friends.

At 19:57hrs, three minutes before our finishing time, she was giving us a job out at Holmebridge. That was a good eleven miles away. It was to a pregnancy related problem. That meant that the designated hospital would have had to be CRH in Halifax, that would be eighteen miles from the patient's address.

I asked her if she could please send a Honley crew.

She snapped back at me, that they didn't start their shift for another three minutes. I explained that they were six miles nearer to the job.

Her answer, "and your point is?" and then "just do the detail!"

I was furious, they were six miles nearer. My point was, that meant at least ten minutes closer to the job. They would also be the most appropriate crew. Not one nearing the end of a twelve hour day, with the prospect off a further minimum of two hours to be added on to the end of it.

Before we had left the station, Shelley went to get James our clinical supervisor. He was further down the garage. Shelley told him that she was concerned about me and she thought that I was going to end up having a stroke!

The dispatcher was unrelenting, saying that it was me that was delaying the emergency call.

Our 20:00hrs start crew were on station and they had offered to do the job, but she wouldn't let them. I set off, my blood pressure was going through the roof. By then it was 19:59hrs.

At bang on 20:00hrs our night crew of Clifford and Chris were detailed to it, we were then stood down.

I asked her why she had sent Huddersfield's 20:00hrs crew and not Honley's.

She replied, "they shouldn't have clocked on yet then should they!"

She had no excuse. The Honley crew were just starting, like Clifford and Chris and as such, were much more appropriate. As well as being far closer to the job in both time and distance.

Unfortunately if you question any of her decisions, you know there and then that's you late off.

I went home fuming, all night long I was seething. No sleep for me the night before an early shift, yet again.

The next morning was Easter Sunday, another 08:00hrs start, I was determined that our dispatcher wouldn't get to me that day. I was working with Shelley again on that Sunday morning.

The first job, was to an elderly people's complex in Marsden.

The patient there had only wanted a GP to visit, she had rung 111 to try and get one, but they had sent an ambulance. We checked her over, but she was not going to hospital anyway, she had only wanted to speak to a Doctor or get some advice.

We were able to liaise with 111 and we were able to arrange for a Doctor to visit her at home. That was just what she had originally requested, they would visit within the next couple of hours.

As we left, one of our front tyres appeared to be very low on pressure. I was determined that the dispatcher would not wind me up again. I saw my chance to chill out.

I drove around the corner and parked up outside the Riverhead Brewery, overlooking the weir and the ducks.

We were not going any further.

I radioed the dispatcher and told her of the flat tyre, that we needed ATS to come and replace it. I knew that it would take some time, particularly as it was the Easter Sunday.

Shelley and I had a walk up through the village and yes, the cafe was open, bonus. We had a cuppa, with a nice home cooked full English breakfast, followed by another cup of tea.

We then walked down to the weir, where we watched some children feeding the ducks. It was cold, but glorious sunshine. Some motorcyclists had converged on the quiet parking area. There was a wide variety of machines to be looked at.

All together, a very interesting three and a half hours, then the tyre truck spoilt things by arriving to sort us out.

We called up Comms to say that we had been sorted. It was by then lunch time. The dispatcher had no other options available to her when she said "return station, you are due your meal break now".

I bet she was choking!

The rest of the day, we had a lovely time. We even finished on time for a change.

There is a saying within the ambulance service, "if you want to play wi't bull, be prepared to get its 'orns up yer arse!"

She did that weekend, she had waved one red rag too many.

I've been working for the service far too long to be messed about by folk like her.

Spine exposed!

It was a sunny Saturday lunchtime, in June 2015. I was working along with Aaron.

We received a call to attend at the Grove Pub in Springwood, near to the Huddersfield Fire Station.

The details that came through on the screen, made us look at each other in disbelief. We both said straight away "as if!"

The call was for a male who had fallen in the beer garden, and that "his spine is exposed".

When we arrived, we were shown around to the beer garden at the back of the pub. On the floor laid face down was a young lad, I think he was nine years of age, I'll call him John.

He was wide awake and very calm, his mother was knelt beside him. She was holding a clean dressing over a wound in the middle of his back. It was mid lumbar region.

John explained that he had launched his model aeroplane, but it had landed on top of the wooden smoking shelter. To retrieve his model, he had climbed onto the stone wall behind the shelter. As he reached across, he had fallen down the narrow gap between the stone wall and the wooden wall of the shelter. He had felt his back snag on one of the stones.

He calmly walked around to where his mother was sitting and he told her what he had done, then he laid down and stayed where he was until our arrival.

When his mum had lifted his Huddersfield Town shirt and she had seen the wound, she rang 999 before applying a sterile dressing from the pub's first aid kit.

I looked under the dressing and sure enough, John's spine was indeed exposed. The wound was around seven centimetres in length, it had opened up widely. Two of the extremely white and shiny, spiny processes of his backbone were quite visible. There was very little blood loss.

Aaron and myself were quite shocked.

The stone wall did have an edge of one of the stones jutting out and it was covered in an awful slimy green moss. Fortunately for John, the material of his shirt was so fine, it had kept all the dirt and slime from his wound.

I must admit to being unsure at that stage, as to whether John might have had an underlying spinal injury. I checked him fully for sensations, or lack of, both above and below the site of injury. He had no neurological deficit (loss of feeling, sensation or mobility).

He was only in a little discomfort and he declined any pain relief. He had full sensation and movement in all four of his limbs.

Another check for nerve function in a spinal injury, is to be able to clench the buttock cheeks together. John didn't understand my question, his mother also tried to explain, he couldn't get it. I borrowed the walking stick of a gentleman at the side of us. I asked his mum to lightly touch John's backside with the end of the stick, he felt it alright and he clenched his buttocks tightly together.

Test passed perfectly.

We were then happy that it appeared to be just an isolated wound, rather than a spinal injury.

We got him up to his feet, where I could dress his wound. I replaced the original with another, but adhesive dry sterile pad.

He got into the ambulance.

Before leaving the pub, I pre-alerted the hospital to John's injury. Not for a resus call, it was a courtesy call. Due to John's injury, just to inform them of the location of the wound and our subsequent clinical findings.

I was told that the A&E consultant was already in the department and that he would see John in the resus/trauma room.

In there, John could be fully assessed again. He could be x-rayed in the same room, to hopefully confirm our findings, but making sure that nothing had been missed. After all, we don't take chances where the spine is concerned.

Once at HRI, the staff were waiting. Calderdale consultant Dr. Andy assessed John with a welcoming smile. "Let's have a look at this spine shall we" he said.

I'm not certain that he believed us.

He then took some photo's of the wound. After all it was an unusual thing to actually see the spinal bones. As he explained to John, "that is what camera phones were invented for". John asked for some copies of his war wound, so that he could put them on Facebook. He got his wish. He got his pictures.

He was absolutely fine, he just needed a little sewing work done. At the mention of that, John asked for some local anaesthetic. He had some muscles stitched together just below the surface, then several sutures on the surface. He calmly sat through it all. He would have quite a battle scar to show his mates.

The landlady of the Grove Pub, treated John on his tenth birthday to a course of some "proper climbing lessons" at Huddersfield Leisure Centre.

Within a very short space of time, John was back competing in his beloved Tai Kwan Do martial arts competitions. No lasting problems for him. He was a very cool, calm and collected little lad. Very mature for his years.

I'm sure he will make a full recovery and very quickly.

Boom! It's all gone.

Valentine's Day, 2016. It was a Sunday. I was working with a lad who calls himself Scooby, on a twelve hour shift, starting at 06:00hrs.

At twenty past seven we went to Halifax, to back up RRV Edmund. He had been called to a male slumped at the wheel of a car.

As we approached the scene, all of the roads at the top of Halifax Town Centre had been closed off. We had to meander around a little.

When we got to Edmund it was almost a quarter to eight.

The male, 23 years of age, was absolutely paralytic drunk. Edmund had already been there since 06:55hrs.

The lad had been trying to drive his car after a full night out on the town. Edmund had removed his keys.

We were stalling him and delaying things, to await the police who had been requested a long while ago.

As we were talking, Edmund explained that the cordon was an area around the multi story car park. "They're going to blow it up and demolish it this morning!"

Once the police had finally arrived and arrested the man, we thought that we would go up and have a look for ourselves. Just as we set off, we heard a klaxon sound. We ran up the last bit.

"That's the five minute warning" we were told. I had my camera, Pete had his phone, he set it to video.

Whilst we were waiting the five minutes, some "anoraks" were there. I didn't know that there was such a breed of people, but some of them said that they were "demolition spotters".

One of them came up to talk to me as I was in uniform, as they seem to do. The man, had got his eleven month old daughter with him. "It's her first demolition" he said very excitedly. "I travel all over the country for them". He said "I've seen hundreds". He then got out of his rucksack a tripod and a camera. Then he brought out a pair of bright red ear defenders for the little one.

More klaxons sounded, each one of the site men had a horn to press when his area was fully clear. Once every one of the all clears had sounded, the final countdown began.

First a loud crack sounded, then a massive knee trembling bang. It was one hell of a noise, the whole street floor vibrated from it. Only a few seconds passed and the whole of the four storey building had gone in a cloud of dust.

The little girl never flinched.

It was a marvellous experience, I hadn't seen a live demolition before. I don't think I'll be travelling the country looking for more though.

Oh well, back to work!

Have you got anything for diarrhoea?

During the Easter holidays of 2016. It was at the start of my RRV shift, early on a Saturday morning. I had a call to see a young lad in Moldgreen, he was a student at Huddersfield University.

He had got himself worried and had rung 111, the advice line for assistance.

Following their questioning, they had over egged his complaint into being a catastrophic rectal bleed. An ambulance and a rapid responder had been sent, as a priority life threatening purple emergency. The highest grade of call, akin to a cardiac arrest.

He did have a bleed from the dreaded back passage, but it was nothing to be majorly concerned about.

He had been to his local chemist shop the previous evening, due to suffering for 24 hours from a rather heavy dose of diarrhoea. He had wanted some medication to take, to help his condition.

The pharmacist had given him a supply of medication. It hadn't helped, if anything, it had increased the problem ten fold. He had spent nearly four hours glued to his toilet and in his own words "had nearly been turned inside out".

It is at times like that one, where a full history of events can be so important in diagnosing a condition. When he had arrived at the pharmacy, he had spoken to a young girl on the counter and he had briefly told her of his predicament. She had then used her own words to the actual pharmacist and had been given the wrong medication.

She apparently had gone to the pharmacist and asked specifically "do you have anything for diarrhoea please?"

They had exactly that, they had only given him a medication that causes the condition, a medication that purges the system completely.

It is usually reserved for patients being admitted to hospital for planned bowel examinations, requiring the said organ to be totally devoid of contents.

It had not only exacerbated his problem, but the excessive "thrutching" had caused his already inflamed anal tissues to bleed from undiagnosed haemorrhoids.

It was them, that he actually needed treating for. The crew took him to the hospital for treatment.

The effects of the medication had rightly frightened our budding science student, causing his call to 111.

No colonic irrigation for him in the near future.

Our human emotions.

Occasionally our emotions can get in the way of the job. Experience can help you deal with things a little easier. As I have got older, the more emotional I have got. Tears can flow at the most inappropriate time, I have to try and manage those emotions at times.

As I become older and more experienced, I have seen other members of staff struggling to come to terms with their emotions.

From being a Station Officer and Operational Supervisor, part of those roles was to try to help and support staff. We held induction days for new staff.

I used to make sure that they were aware, that in the ambulance service we used to have a fantastic occupational health service. They worked for staff. They would keep you up to date with immunisations. Help with any personal medical issues. Perhaps best of all, if you had a traumatic job, or had private individual worries, or concerns. We had our own internal counselling service.

Fully confidential and free.

I say that we used to, because now the ambulance service doesn't have an in house service. We use an external private company. They are employed by management. A manager will refer staff to them, to make sure they are fit for work.

Another added pressure.

If you have been off sick, you will be sent for a medical to see if you are fit to practise. Managers will tell you that they are there for you.

They will help and they will council staff, but only if it will get you back to work. If you are sick, you have to ring them and you have to then ring again when you are fit for work.

When I have dealt with them, the ones on the phone were up in Scotland, they had no idea of what we did in our job. The first time I spoke to someone, they were amazed that we were emergency crews.

They rang me once at nine in the morning to arrange an appointment I had the choice of going to Wigan or Doncaster.

That would have to be in my own time at my own expense, a distance of around 40 miles each way. For something that could have been done over the phone.

I asked the person at the other end of the line, if he had looked at my rota before ringing me.

He said that he hadn't, had there been a problem?

I said that there had. I had only been in bed an hour, after being nearly two hours late off from a night shift. He had to say that he wasn't aware that we even worked shifts.

If you went to see our old service, you would be given a copy of any reports that were sent to your manager. Now it costs, yes costs, to get a copy of a medical report done about you. It will cost £25:00 plus VAT, £30:00 in total.

Although, a good manager should print you a copy, for nothing.

I have always encouraged our staff to talk to others, it is never any good to bottle things up. We have a stressful enough job, without creating more. Chances are, that there will be someone around, who has been in the same situation. From my experiences, they will be more than happy to help.

I will give you an example of one such bottling up of stress. I came back to Huddersfield Ambulance station, it was mid afternoon. Stood outside the back doors of the station, having a crafty smoke, was Miranda from Halifax. She had been in the service for around nine years.

I saw that she had been crying, being ever tactful, I asked her straight out if she was ok.

"It's my hay fever" she said.

I said to her "hey! you're talking to me now, that doesn't wash. I've known you long enough. Come on, what's the matter?"

She filled up again, then she began to tell me of an incident that she had just attended along with Stew, one of our paramedics. Miranda was classed as an assistant practitioner then. She herself has just recently qualified as a paramedic.

Good on her, she'll do well!

She told me about the job that they had just attended. It was to a very frail old man, he had been a perfect gentleman. Even apologising for calling an ambulance, "not wanting to be a bother".

Then without warning he had suddenly collapsed and he suffered a cardiac arrest. Miranda immediately began chest compressions.

Unfortunately, to do compressions efficiently, the chest really does have to be compressed. As people get older, their bones get more brittle, it is most likely that ribs will break. That had happened, two or three ribs had gone as Mandy had tried to save his life.

Stew had been setting up the defibrillator, only one shock and the man had come round. That is the beauty of a witnessed arrest. The patient has a much greater chance of survival.

The patient had been sat talking to his family when the crew had left the hospital.

I said that she should have been proud of herself, "what was the problem?"

She replied that she had heard him say to his family, that he had a lot of pain from some broken ribs and that his statement had upset her.

I asked her how many successful cardiac arrests had she been to and she admitted that she hadn't seen many.

So I changed methods and asked her how many cardiac arrests had she actually been to. She had been to several.

I asked if she had ever cracked anybody's ribs before in the process, she answered that it had happened on nearly every occasion, but she was still upset.

I told her that unfortunately, it was part of our job. But how would she feel if that man had been her own father. If she had been called to the hospital because he had suffered a cardiac arrest. Her hopes of him still being alive would have been minimal.

If, when she got there, HE could tell her that a medic had broken some of his ribs. "What would that be like? Eh".

I said to her that because of her actions and her intervention alone. That patient of hers, "he could now tell people about his bloody ribs!"

She smiled as the penny had dropped, she had only been looking at the negative side of the job.

For me, it shows that Miranda has not lost her human side, she still has feelings.

We are humans, not robots and we do feel for our patients. When that feeling goes, it is time to give up.

We do have one or two staff that are totally emotionless, but they aren't so good at the job!

Miranda is!

What about our doors?

One bizarre job that comes to mind, involved a financial claim and complaint from a patient and his family. The only financial claim to filed against me, ever.

It was back in 1984. I was working with Fraser, normally he was Danny's regular mate.

We had been called to a house in Fixby, it was very near to the golf course. We had been given minimal information again.

Worried callers often think that the ambulance service have a crystal ball that tells us everything.

Other than that the woman of the house had rung 999 and was screaming hysterically down the phone. The only clear words repeated were that it was something about her husband.

We had been dispatched as a priority call.

On arrival at the address, it was an extremely large detached house with a large driveway. To the right of the property was a matching large detached garage, with two large double doors.

Each of the doors were of the type that consisted of several, possibly ten or eleven standard room sized doors joined/hinged together. To open them, they would all concertina to one end of the building, leaving room for two cars to get in and out. Four cars in all.

The woman came screaming down the drive claiming that her husband was in the garage. It was all locked up but she could hear an engine running, she was scared, understandably.

I wanted to know if the whole of the garage was one, or was it divided into two halves by a wall.

The reason for that, being that we could hear the car at the right hand side of the building, but one of the panels in the left hand door had been damaged previously. Some of the panelling was completely rotten with damp.

She said that it was all one large open space inside. That said, the damaged panel would be the easiest one to gain access through.

I kicked a hole in the bottom of the door, big enough for us both to crawl through. As I went towards the car, Fraser was opening the full front of the garage doors from the inside.

The man was inside the car sat in the driving seat, with all of the windows open. Both his car and the one next to it had their engines running, we had to cover our mouths due to the carbon monoxide fumes that had filled the garage.

I pulled him from the car, as Fraser switched the engines off. We both dragged him outside. Although he was a wonderfully healthy pink colour, he wasn't breathing. (Normal colouring for carbon monoxide poisoning).

We spent more than half an hour manually resuscitating the man on the driveway.

It was before defibrillators and drugs were available. We had to flush him with 100% oxygen and to physically get his heart and lungs working again. The only way to do that, was by good cardiac massage and forcing the oxygen around his body.

We must have been doing something right, eventually he started to come round. He was coughing and spluttering, we got him into the ambulance and raced to hospital.

His wife sat in the front with me whilst Fraser continued to oxygenate the patient. She told me that the patient had been a bit depressed that morning, but he did get that way from time to time. She hadn't been overly concerned.

The wife had gone out, to an appointment. On her return only an hour later, she missed his presence and had gone looking for him. That was when she heard the cars and had called us.

She hadn't suspected that he would do anything like that, but while we were resuscitating him, she had found a suicide note.

The man spent over a month in hospital, he had been critically ill for quite some time. But he managed to make a complete recovery and he had managed to turn his business around again (that was the source of his depression). His depression had subsided.

He was already a millionaire.

The point of my ramblings at this point, is.

Although we had saved his life. Only six months after the job, he put a complaint into the ambulance service. He said that we had been negligent and had caused excessive and criminal damage to his property while gaining access.

He also accompanied his complaint, with a bill for over £6,000 for having both garage doors replaced, due to the damage. Apparently they couldn't manage to repair one panel to match the rest and as such had to replace the whole lot, both sets of doors.

£6,000 in those days was a vast amount, when confronted about it I was "gobsmacked".

How dare he? Who did he think he was?

At the end of the day, I had kicked through a completely rotten and damaged panel. It had needed replacing anyway!

Some people!

Just because they have money, they really think they are above everyone else.

Not a word of thanks for saving his life!

The ambulance service to save any embarrassment, had paid him out in full for the cost of new doors. He had said that they had been newly fitted, and there hadn't been any rot or damage anywhere.

His comments were that Fraser and I were "hamfisted buffoons, with no respect for people or property".

The service didn't even send anyone out to see him.

The officers did say that as we had saved his life, they would not be taking any form of action against us. That was good of them wasn't it!

Should I have let him die?

I admit that the thought had crossed my mind, but I am professional and that is why I still do my job. I would like to think that I can hold my head high and say without doubt that I am a better person than him. Whatever he did for a living and however much money he had.

I wouldn't have minded being a couple of quid behind him though!

CHAPTER 59.

REGULARS!

Local characters.

Over the years, we at the ambulance service have had our fair share of regulars, each have been a character in their own right. Every station, every county and every service have them. Some have been funny and others violent, others have just made themselves a damn nuisance.

Some people do the strangest things.

Here are some of the strange things that people say, some of the things they do, or just some of the strange ways that they live their lives.

Here are just a selection of things that have happened over the years, to "normal people, living their "normal" everyday life. Even if it was not considered normal for us, who are we to judge.

What is normal?

We used to have a bloke I'll call Kevin from the Deighton area of Huddersfield. He came into the category of a complete waste of time. He was harmless, but a damn nuisance. He used revel in having fake seizures/fits. (Pseudo fits).

He was no more epileptic than me. We would go for him all over Huddersfield. At least it was always during the day and he was always indoors, if it was raining.

Kevin seemed to just simply disappear off the face of the earth, nobody seemed to know what actually happened to him.

Pseudo fits, seem to be a popular action of regular callers. We have had several over the years, who seem to get a bit of a kick out of collapsing in a public place. Another common event that occurs with some of the pseudo fitters that we have dealt with, is that when the patient suddenly recovers. They are not confused and they claim to have lost or had stolen, a large amount of money.

When recovering from a true epileptic seizure, the patient tends to have a phased recovery. Usually including a period of varying time of confusion, known as a "post ictal" (post-after and ictal-seizure) period.

Another regular of ours that did that, I'll call Claire of Huddersfield. She had a remarkable ability of letting a little notebook fall to the ground when she was having a seizure.

It had all her personal details in it. It had her date of birth, home address, relatives contact details and her full medical history of (none existent) epilepsy. When she suddenly recovered from her "episode", she would have everyone looking for a purse. A purse that would have contained lots of money. The purse would always be found nearby, but empty. It was the same story every time and always in an extremely busy place.

She actually suffered from a form of Munchausens syndrome, a constant need for attention.

Claire also used to take regular overdoses of tablets at home, to get attention in the hospital, but she went too far in the end.

Wrongly thinking that paracetamol was relatively safe. She had been regularly taking up to sixteen tablets, or one full packet at a time.

She had got away with it several times, but then she took a massive amount. 200 of them, she must have collapsed before ringing us.

By the time her parents had found her, the damage had already been done. Her liver and kidneys had already gone in to failure, she died nearly three months later at St. James's University Hospital in Leeds. What a horrible way to go.

Claire claimed that she had taken all those tablets whilst actually having a seizure.

Another regular patient of ours who does actually suffer from epilepsy, I'll call her Margaret, also from Huddersfield. Margaret although a regular, is a genuine epilepsy sufferer. When she had had a seizure she would, as most genuine sufferers be post ictal. She would be very confused when coming round, that phase could last anything up to an hour.

Many a crew have been for Margaret in the town centre, always wearing the same style and colour of red raincoat, whatever the weather. When coming round she would walk off in whatever direction she happened to be facing, leaving her shopping bag and purse behind.

The crew would have to follow her all over the place with her belongings, until she had come round enough to accept them back. Or be classed as compos mentis (being in full control of one's mind).

Unless she had injured herself, there was no way to get Margaret to see a doctor.

Then there was I'll call him Ivan, we had dealt with him from him being around fourteen years old. He was a very young alcoholic, who would take overdoses for attention. He was from the Dalton area of Huddersfield. He was a damn nuisance as well. He could get very angry at times, but he was small and skinny and not much of a threat. It was all verbal and for show anyway.

He would usually be in a public place causing a nuisance, the police would be called and in turn they would send for us, to "check him out".

For at least fifteen years we would go for him, until eventually he got taken in at a well known half-way hostel.

I'll call it Mary's. Mary eventually owned a full row of around ten terraced houses. It was a half-way house for all sorts of waifs and strays.

Fresh out of psychiatric hospital, perhaps had a spell in prison, or whatever. Sometimes temporary homeless would be housed at Mary's until they found their feet. Ivan managed to get a placement there and within six months, he was off all drugs and drink.

Amazingly, one day Ivan was found dead in his bed. He had died of natural causes. There were no traces of any drugs or alcohol in his system, he wasn't even thirty years old.

Following on from Ivan, we had two similar patients.

The first was I'll call her Joan.

She was a young black girl, also a chronic alcoholic. She would regularly collapse in phone boxes, or other public places where good samaritans would find her and call us.

She lived in the Huddersfield area, her mother also lived just outside Huddersfield. As well as regularly being drunk, Joan had a painful condition called Marfan's Syndrome. That meant that all of the long bones in her body were longer than normal, including her fingers. Giving her a very strange body shape.

Whenever we went for Joan, she had nearly always been incontinent of urine. She was getting more and more bloated. All her features were badly swollen due to a pickled and enlarged liver.

Joan could be nasty with ambulance crews at times. Generally though, if you were right with her, she would be no bother.

I once went for her on Christmas Eve, I was working on an RRV. It was late in the evening and she was at her mother's house. She didn't want to go to hospital. But she had bought a card and a brand new, sealed box of chocolates for the staff at A & E. She wanted me to deliver them. Within the card were some poems, very sad poems telling the story of her sad life.

They were good, very good, she was quite talented actually.

Tragically, it wasn't long after that, that Joan was found dead. She had fallen into the canal on the outskirts of Huddersfield. She was only thirty but she looked at least fifty, at times.

Still living, but a similar story is, I'll call him Cliff. He is a black lad, also an alcoholic.

When Carl and I first met Cliff, he was a fighter. A boxer, a big, lean and fit, fighting machine. He used to fight with travellers, bare knuckle fighting in his younger days. But then he became a heroin addict, hence our dealings with him.

If he was given "narcan" a narcotic antidote, he would get extremely violent, he could snap the old link type police handcuffs easily.

He was sent to a few years in prison for assaulting and hospitalising five police officers whilst on heroin. They cleaned him up in prison. In the last years, since his release from prison, it is the drink that has got the better of him.

He is in a sorry state.

Lastly, but the longest reigning of our regulars and there have been many others. But of all the regulars and perhaps the most memorable, is one who I'll call Kelvin.

He really gets right up my nose. I have been going for Kelvin since the day I started the service. He was just gone sixteen.

He was a heavy drinker and he was alcohol dependent, we would be called due to him being "drunk and incapable". We are still going for him now, when he is drunk and incapable.

He once clocked up nearly 200 visits to HRI in one year, he didn't wait to be seen on 168 of those occasions.

I dread to think how many actual ambulance visits he got in that time, because he very rarely travelled to hospital.

I have known of him making five 999 calls in one day. He can make three or four, several days on the trot. He will get told straight by the doctors, and will behave himself for a week or two, before starting again.

Nowadays what he wants is for the crew to just take his blood pressure, all that does is increase mine. It costs at least £400 for an ambulance to be called out. Then he sits there all smug and says, "just do my ob's (observations, pulse, oxygen levels, blood pressure etc) I'm not going to hospital".

He makes my blood boil.

We have been tied up with the waste of space for more than an hour at a time whilst we do his ob's and then have to complete all the necessary paperwork. He as far as I am aware, has been the single most drain on resources that we have ever had in Huddersfield.

He can be very threatening verbally, but far too drunk to carry out his threats physically.

A good thing for us warped and twisted minded staff, is that Kelvin also suffers from obsessive compulsive disorder (OCD). Everything in his house has to be just so. He has a glass topped table in the middle of his front room, he goes mad if you move anything on it.

One of the funniest things that I have ever seen, was when one of my colleagues removed the ECG dots from Kelvin's chest, he stuck one right in the middle of the underside of the clear glass table.

Kelvin went mad, but due to his drunken state he could not comprehend why he couldn't get it off the table. It would not compute that it was underneath. He must have spent twenty minutes trying to pick and scratch at it.

It was like my uncle Bill picking pennies up without the end of his middle finger, only better. He was screaming at it in the end, he threw us out for laughing. He then swore that he would kill us if we ever went back.

While we were on the phone to Comms, regarding his threats, he had already rung 999 again.

Whilst we were still sat outside his window.

They told us to go back in, despite his threats to us. As well as threatening us, he had told our Comms Centre that he would stab us both, if they sent us back.

We refused, it was a police matter then. They were requested, but didn't attend. The police just rang 999 and another ambulance was sent, yet another hour was wasted again.

Comms were regularly screaming out for crews due to outstanding emergencies, when we, and the subsequent crew were with him.

There should be a better way of dealing with these people. The drain on our NHS coffers, must be phenomenal. We are at a time when we have to save every penny possible, yet we are throwing away thousands of pounds dealing with wasters like him.

Admiral.

I haven't changed his name, due to the unusual circumstances of it. He was a local character in the area who caused never caused any trouble to anyone. Through choice he tried to keep himself to himself. He and his brothers were very private people, who lived a rather unusual lifestyle.

There used to be four brothers around Huddersfield, particularly in the late 70's and 80's.

Their father had been a Navy man, he had named all of his sons after high ranking officers in the Armed Services.

All four of the brothers lived an entirely separate life, but commonly they all lived on the streets, (of no fixed abode).

Each and every one of them was a well known "character" in and around Huddersfield at the time.

There was Major, Commodore and Brigadier, but the story concerned is about one of the brothers who had been called "Admiral". All of them, were their genuine Christian names.

Admiral used to live in the Lockwood area, I say area, because he didn't have a place of residence. He moved all around the area looking for shelter. Wherever he was, he would be seen with a pram. It wasn't a little pushchair, but a proper coach built old style pram. He had all his worldly possessions in that pram.

Admiral would wander the streets from sunrise to sunset, he must have covered many a mile every day. He would pick up small, even the most insignificant amounts of scrap metal, or rags.

Then he would take them every couple of days to a scrap yard at Moldgreen, it is still there just off the Wakefield Road. The yard collected the rags and clothing, you would receive a small payment based on weight. They would bale the rags up and then deliver the bales to to rag merchants.

When my mate David had collected the waste from the end of a jumble sale, he would take all the left overs to that place.

One day when we were dropping off the jumble sale rags, Admiral was there. He was "earning a bit" of spending money. He was stood in the large bale, compressing the stuff by treading it down.

He lost one of his shoes during the operation. On searching the bale he found one, it wasn't his, but it was much better than his own. He kept on looking until he found the other.

I met Admiral again, a couple of years later. He had been knocked down by a car, on Queen's Mill Lane. He was on his way back from the yard, to Lockwood. Ivan and myself were sent to the incident. As we approached, we could smell him before we saw him. He had a very distinctive "odour" about him.

The police were already there, they mentioned the "pram". They had looked in it and found a lot of money, several hundreds of pounds "so far" they said.

As we checked Admiral over, he was semi conscious and was not communicating with us. We straight away, could see that he had a broken ankle.

As I tried to roll his sock down to examine his ankle, I was extremely shocked. The sock didn't roll, it broke up and disintegrated into dust in my fingers.

Aargh!

Not only that, there was something stuck to his skin, it appeared that he had a plaster cast already fitted to his leg. It was all wet and extremely soggy. The cast went much higher up his leg than we could see. We placed him in the ambulance for a proper check up.

Amazingly, we found that his whole body was covered in the soggy offensive smelling mess. It was paper that he had placed inside his clothing to help keep him warm through the winter months.

It was only in hospital when they undressed him, that the lining paper, was found to be quality stuff. The paper was actually money. Yes paper money, 20's, 10's and five pound notes.

A lot of his money was found to be totally unusable. It had been there that long, that like his sock, a lot of it had perished. They removed it all in hospital.

They thought that in total there was over £7,000. Almost half of it was no good, or even unrecognisable. He didn't believe in banks!

Very expensive thermal underwear though.

Damart are a lot cheaper!

CHAPTER 60.

PEOPLE DO THE FUNNIEST THINGS.

There wasn't any running water, I thought that would do!

There are still some good Samaritans out there, not all of them are trained first aiders. I think he majority of people would still have a go, given half a chance.

In Huddersfield there is the Marina at Aspley. There are many narrow boats that are moored there and many others that pass through.

In the mid eighties, a company decided to build a restaurant and bar, the Baltimore Diner.

It was right at the very edge of the Marina, in a prime position. While it was being built, a small army of construction workers had descended on the area.

They had brought with them a large portacabin, which they used as a site office and canteen.

A homeless man from the area used to sleep in some dilapidated buildings, across the road from the marina. Where the Halls of Residence for the University are now.

The workers wouldn't let him sleep in the portacabin, but the builders used to leave him with a key. Then in payment for him getting the hot water going and making the endless brews, they would take care of his food requirements. Bacon sandwiches etc.

He would go into the cabin at about six every morning and get the hot water boiler going. The cabin also had a gas wall heater at one end, he would light it and be sat quite comfortably for when the men arrived half an hour later.

One freezing cold morning in January he was late. He had slept in, in his squat across the road. It was due to the cold. He ran across Wakefield Road, it was five minutes to six.

The second he lit the gas, boom!

It all exploded. The gas (bottled butane), must have been leaking during the night. As soon as he had caused a spark the lot went up. The cabin was blown to pieces and the man was blown across the car park.

It was witnessed by one of the workers who was just walking across the car park area.

He saw the homeless man up against a wall, every stitch of his clothing had gone in the blast.

He was badly burnt all over the front of his body, and some lesser burnt areas across his back. The man was a "qualified first aider", he knew that running water was the best thing to ease burns.

Not having any running water, he thought very quickly to himself and then he threw the man into the canal basin.

When Danny and I arrived we could see the devastated portacabin, from the main Wakefield Road. We were driving onto the site, just as the fire service were arriving behind us.

Stood by the edge of the water were three men. One other man was on his knees and he was leaning over the water's edge, he kept bobbing up and down.

As we got closer we could see that he had hold of the really long hair of our homeless man and was dunking him in and out of the freezing cold water.

We had to pull the man out of the water immediately, he was frozen. There was actually ice on the waters surface, he had obvious and already very severe hypothermia.

As we got the patient into the back of the ambulance. The first aider came and stood in the doorway. He very proudly told us who he was and that although he didn't have any running water for the burns treatment. He said "I thought that would do!"

We thanked him and took our man to the resus room at HRI. Once they had warmed him up sufficiently, he was transferred to the burns unit at Pinderfields.

The first aider probably had saved the man's life, from his injuries perhaps, but then he had almost killed him through hypothermia.

On the way to Pinderfields our patient was recalling the events, when he got to the part of being physically thrown into the water. He said "I thought that bugger was trying to kill me, I really thought he was trying to drown me for blowing up the shed!"

He tried, bless him!

Will chips do, I haven't got any peas?

Another shift in October 2002. That time with Carl, we were called to the Linthwaite area, just off Manchester Road. We had been sent to attend to a twenty one year old female, who was having some sort of seizure and was burning up.

Her mother had made the call. It was around four thirty in the morning.

When we got there, we could hardly believe our eyes. Laid on the sofa, absolutely stark naked was our young female.

She had a very pale white skin, with lots and lots of fiery red blotches all over her. They were on her face, arms, chest, back, stomach, groin area, and the tops of her thighs. None at all on the lower part of her legs.

She was laid there not responding to us, but was rambling away to herself and thrashing about. She was throwing her legs and arms into the air. Not only that, there were chips everywhere on the sofa. Not just a few, there were loads of them.

After talking to her mother, we established that the girl had been away at college for a while.

That she had come back for a visit and arrived in Linthwaite, only the night before.

She had borrowed a nightdress from her sister to sleep in. Not realising that it had been washed in a soap powder that she was going to be highly allergic to.

She had suffered a violent skin reaction, it had spread and was leading towards a full blown anaphylactic reaction. Her breathing was getting compromised.

Carl and I had to physically wrestle with the naked girl, until we could get a line/cannula into a vein. We could then inject some adrenaline into her body, that was then added to by giving her a salbutamol nebuliser via an oxygen mask.

We had to literally pin the naked girl down to treat her. She was fighting all the while.

Less than ten minutes later and she had all about calmed down. She was starting to come round. When she realised where she was and that she was as naked as the day she was born. She started ranting again, this time at us and her mother.

It was due to her state of undress.

We left the room while she got dressed, she didn't want us to see her naked. We hadn't the heart to tell her how long we had been there and what we had already seen and done.

She calmed down fully and we were able to talk sensibly. She had only had one of those reactions before. It had been many years ago and she had ended up in intensive care, she had nearly died.

When she had arrived home the night before, it was late and she had had a few drinks. She had completely forgotten about the washing powder that mum and all the rest of the family used. She had worn her sisters nightdress and due to the drink, had gone into a deep sleep.

She had been awakened in the early hours by her skin being on fire. The reason that her legs hadn't been affected, was that she had slept in her own sleeping bag on the sofa. The rash was only present, where the nightdress had touched.

Mum had panicked and rung an ambulance. Due to her thrashing about, the girl had ripped the nightdress to shreds in desperation, trying to get it off.

Mum hadn't realised that it was an allergic reaction and had forgotten that her daughter had carried an epi-pen (a measured dose of adrenaline injection) in her handbag.

We spoke about the condition, and how the epi-pen does its job without our intervention. We explained everything to them.

She wasn't going to travel with us, so we managed to get her an appointment with the out of hours GP.

Before we left, I had just one question.

What were all the chips doing everywhere? Our patient even had some in her hair.

Mum said that when she had rung 999, she had told the call taker that the girl was burning up and that she didn't need a thermometer to see that she had a fever.

The call taker had advised her, that if she couldn't get her to drink, which at the time would have been completely impossible.

Then to try and cool her down with something from the freezer, like a bag of frozen peas.

The mother then very innocently said to us, "I didn't have any peas in the freezer, but I did have four bags of frozen chips. So I poured them all over her to cool her down."

Both Carl and me were then on our knees in tears, it had been one of the funniest things we had ever seen.

We told mum, "we think they meant for you to apply the bags to her body, not to pour them over her, imagine where the peas would have gone". She just looked stunned and didn't reply.

After all, it was early.

As I said some people do the funniest things!

So, what do you think of that, then?

Another funny job, well it was to me. Was at nearly four in the morning. It was one Saturday in March 2011. All my best things seem to happen when I'm working night shifts.

A call came in to attend at the "Presbytery" at the side of a large Catholic Church, outside of Huddersfield.

As Stew and I pulled up outside the building, a rather red faced bloke wearing a dressing gown met us at the road side. He invited us into the house to explain things. On the way down the path, he told us that he was the Priest at the Church nearby.

In the house, we went into a ground floor bedroom.

He began explaining that he had only recently had an operation at HRI and that he had stayed overnight, before returning home yesterday morning. Which was Friday.

I asked him what the operation was for.

He told us that he had suffered from a hydrocele. (Water retention, like a cyst, in one or both testicles), just one in his case.

He had woken in the night to pass urine, which could be quite normal for him to do that several times during the night. That hadn't worried him. It was on returning to bed when he had seen "that", he pulled the bedclothes back and showed us a wet patch on his bed. It was a reddy pink in colour.

"Is that blood?" He asked.

It did appear that it was. He then took us by surprise. He opened his dressing gown, dropped his underpants and said "so, what do you think of that, then?"

As we looked, the site of his operation had a dressing applied. It had been leaking both blood and water from the hydrocele. We said that it can happen occasionally, especially when you have a wound that has got infected.

He covered himself up and said that we had made him start to feel a lot better. He admitted to being frightened, especially being alone.

We advised that he travelled with us, just to be certain and they would be able to provide him with sterile dressings and some antibiotics.

I was in the back of the ambulance with the Priest.

He said to me that he saw me smirk when I had checked his problem. He said that if I had found something that had amused me, I should share it with him.

I had found something funny, but it was sick humour. I couldn't share it with a man of the cloth.

No way!

He asked me again and again, I kept refusing his request. Apologising and saying that it was sick ambulance humour. That no matter how I tried to put it to him, it would seem offensive. I told him that I didn't want to offend anyone.

He persisted, but then he did make a comment that has left an impression on me regarding offensiveness. He said that "nothing is really offensive, unless it is intended to cause offence".

I assured him that I certainly did not want to cause any offence and I would still prefer not to tell him.

He then said "the more that you withhold it from me, the more intrigued I am getting and I will keep pestering you until you relent and tell me what was going on in your head when you examined me".

I had to give in, I did actually think that I hadn't let my thoughts show, but obviously I had. So I said to him, "I do apologise in advance, but unfortunately it is how my warped mind sometimes works".

I reluctantly told him. As a not very religious person, "it is not that often that I come into close proximity with a Catholic Priest. That we had all read recently in the newspapers of the scandals going on within the Church. Then the first time I deal with a Priest, he invites me into his bedroom. Then he drops his underpants and says, what do you think of that then?"

He started to laugh, then I finished and said "and you didn't even ask me my name!"

He really laughed, it was a proper belly laugh. He said that he "could see where that came from" and that "I am certainly not offended. I am a man of the world and I like to share a joke with the best of 'em". He then said that like me, he too "would have found it very hard to keep a straight face". He went on, "and if you don't mind, I'll share that with some of my colleagues". He finished "but might be best if I leave it out of tomorrows sermon".

I said that I was still sorry and that I should have been more professional, that it shouldn't have happened.

He told me not to worry and that I had given a very frightened man instant comfort and confidence that I knew what I was talking about.

To him that was "professionalism at its best. Thank you!"

CHAPTER 61.

JUST WENDY AND ME.

Anniversary surprise.

It was in the spring of 2008, that was the year when we would celebrate our Silver Wedding. It was a very special time for us, that year I wanted a holiday that would be perfect for the both of us. Not only would it be our Silver Wedding, it would be my 50th birthday as well.

We had had several holidays over the years, but not every year. We had been off as a family and just the two of us. We had been in the U.K. and abroad. We had been to Luxembourg, Ibiza to the same place three times, to Majorca twice and also to the Greek island of Corfu.

Although those were brilliant summer sun holidays, since the 22 hour long ship journey to Denmark with all the family. Wendy had always fancied a holiday on a cruise ship.

That wasn't really my idea of the best holiday type, but as I said I wanted it to be special for the both of us. The best option that I could see, would be for a cruise and stay holiday. We had seen them advertised and had discussed them in the past.

It would involve a week cruising around the Mediterranean Sea, docking at a new destination every morning. Having time to explore at each location and then to spend a week at a beach resort in Majorca.

Or you could have the beach stay first, followed by the cruise. It just depended on the itinerary, and the chosen dates of departure.

I decided that I would look into it and then I could book it as a surprise Silver Wedding present. I thought it would surely be a win win situation all round.

As we had done in previous years, I went to Althams Travel on Cross Church Street in Huddersfield. My sister Lindsay had worked there for her first job, her friend Karen still does. Karen had always been a great help in sorting out our holidays.

I had quite a discussion with Karen, but I was getting more and more out of my depth.

The more that I wanted to do it as a total surprise, we found more reasons that I couldn't.

There were several different itineraries with each one. Then the cruise ships docked at a different location and they all took a totally different route.

I needed Wendy to pick which one, i.e. did Wendy want to see Venice? Would she prefer to see the leaning tower of Pisa? Or would she prefer to visit the Coliseum in Rome?

It would have been wrong for me to pick. There was no option, I had to spoil my surprise.

I delicately approached the subject with her, I was met with a very cool and a most unexpected response. I was shocked. I tried again, I was still rebuffed, what had I done wrong?

Then she dropped the bombshell!

As I had been planning my surprise of a lifetime, Wendy had been up to some skullduggery herself. She had seen a friend and had organised the perfect holiday for me!

I had not only had to spoil my surprise, I had caused Wendy to divulge her secrets as well.

What a pillock!

Wendy knew that my ultimate dream was to go back to Kandersteg in Switzerland. Or if not Kandersteg, as I was nothing to do with the scouts anymore, at least to see the Bernese Oberland area of Switzerland.

She had only gone and booked a ten days Swiss Travel holiday based in the beautiful town of Interlaken. Smack bang in the middle of the area that I wanted to go.

In the past, Wendy hadn't really expressed that much of an interest in going to Switzerland. I had the opportunity that I needed to change her mind, I was sure that she would love it.

That trip, was already booked. We were going, she had made my dream come true.

What a wife!

Am I the luckiest man in the world? I think so.

I had spoilt things, but it really showed that we love each other dearly.

We're off!

The 1st of September 2008, that was the day of our departure on the holiday of a lifetime. We were going to Manchester airport and leaving the car there. Followed by a Swiss Air flight to Zurich.

From Zurich, we had a Swiss travel pass. That meant that we could travel First Class on any public transport from the airport to our destination hotel in Interlaken and on any route we wished that day. The same applied on our date of return from the hotel to Zurich.

The same pass also gave us a half price ticket on any form of public transport throughout our stay in Switzerland. Other than a private hire taxi. So all of the buses, trains, boats, and cable cars were half price on production of the pass. Over the next ten days, we would take great advantage of it.

Prior to going, we had discussed all the places that we would like to go to during our stay. We had a good idea of our intentions, although not necessarily in which order of doing them.

The beauty of modern technology meant that we could get a good idea of what the weather would be like, before setting off.

The first time that I had visited Switzerland, it was quite a gamble on any of the visits to the tops of the mountains. Now there were live webcams installed at most of the remote locations.

The weather was fantastic, the temperature regularly reached 25 degrees Centigrade outside our hotel. One of the days, our trip was to go to the top of Europe, at over 11,300 feet.

The top of the Jungfrau mountain. To get there, involved a train ride through some of the worlds most scenic countryside.

The train also went through tunnels leading up through the inside of the Eiger mountain. There is even a railway station inside, with large windows looking out of the North Face overlooking the beautiful picturesque village of Kleine Sheidegge.

If it was forecast to be bad weather, there was no point in going. The day was set. The weather was fantastic outside the hotel, 25 degrees. We looked at the cameras, although very cold and extremely windy up there at the top, it was going to be fine.

Trains ran from right outside the Hotel du Lac door. They were normal trains, through scenic valleys and villages, climbing to Grindlewald and Kleine Sheidegge. Then we went on a funicular, rack and pinion railway up to the summit.

On arrival at the summit, everybody was vetted. If you weren't geared up for the extreme cold, you weren't allowed outside. It was minus 25 degrees, the sixty miles an hour winds gave a windchill factor of minus 40 degrees. Neither of us had ever felt such extreme temperatures.

From the top, there was a short breathless outside walk to the rock. On top of which sits the Sphinx observatory, towering another 300 feet or so higher.

There was a lift inside, which went up to an outdoor open grid style walkway and viewing platform. It went all around the outside of the observatory and weather station at the top.

One minute the cloud was so low, you literally could not see your hand in front of your face. The next minute you could see all the way to Mont Blanc in France. The sky was so blue and the sun was really bright.

Then as quick as it had disappeared, the low cloud was back and eerily you couldn't see anything. It was like that every five minutes or so.

Due to the high altitude and the air being so much thinner up there, our oxygen levels were vastly depleted. My levels went to 68% concentration, Wendy's went down as low as 58%. She was quite cyanosed (blue) at that stage.

Slowly does it, no rushing around up there at the top. What an experience though.

Another day we were going up to see the Schilthorn, another high mountain.

At the top of which there is a rotating mountain top restaurant, the one made famous in the James Bond film, On Her Majesty's Secret Service. It is accessed by one of the worlds longest and highest cable cars.

I wasn't looking forward to that bit.

The last time that I had travelled in a cable car, I was sat on the floor. I had taken some good pictures though, by holding my camera up to window height to take pictures.

No, not this time. There was nowhere to hide, the glass walls went all the way down down to the floor level.

Not to worry though, I was fine, in fact I took some fantastic photo's.

The view from the top looking down the valley to Lauterbrunnen and all around the area was second to none. The sky on that day was perfectly clear.

We sat in the rotating restaurant and had a meal and a bier, it took just about an hour for the room to rotate the full 360 degrees. The views were fantastic in any direction.

On our way down, after the return cable car journey. We went for a spectacular long walk, all the way down the valley. It had a very flat bottom to it, with a small river running alongside the path.

There was some amazing rocky mountains and cliffs, they were all along one side of the valley as you walked down.

Occasionally there were some massive 3,000 foot drop waterfalls coming over the edge. At that time of year they unfortunately they only had a low water flow, still they looked brilliant.

The other side of the valley a typical vast, sweeping pine forest. From top to bottom of the valley, with its year round evergreen colour.

Occasionally you would hear screams coming from above, another lunatic would be launching themselves from the top. Hurtling down towards the ground at breakneck speeds, before opening a parachuteand then slowly and gracefully floating to the ground.

I will not be taking up base jumping, thank you!

Then we came across another village, with the famous Reichenbach Falls. One of Sherlock Holmes famous stories, where he supposedly fell to his death.

They are fantastic waterfalls of melting glacial ice. From the Eiger, Monch and Jungfau mountains, the amount of water was recorded as it fell.

At the time of our visit, it was flowing at over 20,000 litres per minute, all down the inside of a mountain. Nowadays, all of the inside of the mountain, had been navigated and lit. With fully serviceable walkways and stairways down to the bottom.

I bottled out of that, it was too claustrophobic for me in there. I felt that the water was trying draw me in and over the edge. I went back down in the lift and waited outside.

Wendy loved it.

We went everywhere we could. We travelled on boats across both of the lakes of Interlaken, Thun and Brienz. We went to large villages and smaller hamlets. Markets, shops, restaurants and even castles.

There was one area, that was even a complete history of Switzerland in a valley. As you walked around the valley reconstructions of buildings and lifestyles were all around. The whole area had been turned into a living and working museum experience.

Unbelievable.

Finishing at a rather welcoming building that was emitting a super enticing aroma, it was a Swiss Chocolate factory.

Now you're talking, wow!

On one of our walks, we headed up to a hidden valley where there was the marvellous lake Oeschinensee.

It was a long walk from the train, then we had a ride on Switzerland's last remaining open chair lift.

It was closing down at the end of that September and a proper cable car was to be built in replacement.

It was not nice up there, on that lift. I didn't like it one little bit.

The only thing keeping you safe in the chair was a piece of bamboo garden cane across the front.

There was a lot more walking, but finally, after coming round a pine forest wooded corner, Oeschinensee was there. In a most beautiful setting at the base of snow capped mountains all around. The lake was visible only from the one and only access path.

The path was unsuitable for road vehicles. Any goods taken to the shops or hotel were taken up that one entry path and that was only by a horse and cart.

Near to the lake was a souvenir shop, a cafe and restaurant. Then right at the waters edge, a hotel and restaurant with rowing boat hire facilities.

With its beautifully clear water. If you went out on a boat, you could see clearly every stone, rock and fish on the lake bottom. It was over two hundred feet deep in places. 213 feet at its deepest.

The day was completed by an even longer walk back all the way down the valley and into the even more beautiful town of Kandersteg.

Wendy and me, both looked around. It is one of the most gorgeous, picturesque towns I have ever seen. The buildings, every single one of them, are all different. It's an experience in itself.

The trains based there at Kandersteg are something else. They are covered wagons, where motorists drive on at one end and then off at the other end of the tunnel.

The Lotschberg tunnel goes from Kandersteg through to Goppenstein, and is just over nine miles long. It featured in a Charles Bronson film Love and Bullets.

I didn't walk all the way up to the scouts centre, that would have been another two or three miles further and then back again.

I would have liked to, but we had already covered enough distance for one day and the rain had started falling quite heavily.

I think it is fair to say that we saw everything that we had originally planned on seeing on our trip, and much more.

The day to leave and make our way home arrived, it was a sad day for both of us. There was so much more that we would have liked to have done.

Maybe another time.

Instead of going direct to the airport from the hotel.

We took advantage of our First Class transport. We caught the train to a place I hadn't seen on my first visit, to Lake Lucerne. Yet another amazing place.

The Lake and the city are fantastic, but best of all without doubt, is the wonderful covered wooden walkway bridge over the river Reusse. The bridge is known as Kapellbrucke, "Chapel Bridge" it is itself an ancient monument originally built in 1333.

Up in the eaves of the roof of the bridge were triangular iconic artworks, many of them had been destroyed by a major fire in 1993.

Thanks to modern technology, most of them have been reproduced digitally from the many archive photographs. Once the replacements had been placed back on the bridge, they looked brilliant. Good, but not quite the same quality as the originals.

We finally headed off back to Zurich and then made our way home via Manchester.

What a fantastic holiday, the best ever!

Switzerland is simply another world. It is unbelievable how clean the whole country is. The houses are all in traditional style wherever possible, even new builds are strongly governed.

In the outlying mountain villages, they are all timber chalet style buildings, absolutely covered in the most vibrant blooms.

If ever I get chance to return, I would without hesitation and I'm certain now that Wendy would feel the same.

Ten days just wasn't long enough.

Paris, a romantic city.

At home one evening, Wendy and I were talking about holidays, it was February 2014. Wendy mentioned that many many years ago in 1977, I had gone to Paris with Richard, one of my mates from scouting.

I had talked about that holiday over the years, on many occasions. She said, "you promised me that you would take me to Paris sometime".

Right, no time like the present.

I started browsing the web. This time, I fancied a coach trip. When Richard and I went all those years ago, we followed a coach trip itinerary, but on foot. I'm too old for that now. Paris is one of those places, although a fantastic city to see on your own, a good guide can make it even more interesting.

I found a holiday with Shearings. For five days and four nights. A fully guided coach tour, with many optional excursions or self viewing times available.

I booked it there and then. I even booked the back seats of the luxury coach. The hotel where we would be staying, was just outside the city centre. I had booked to start our trip on the 8th of June 2014.

The day arrived, we were to be picked up from Huddersfield bus station and then transported to Shearings distribution centre at Normanton near Wakefield. There we would join our luxury holiday coach.

It was a very smart and modern fifteen seater minibus to start with, we were the only passengers. That was until we picked up a few more of the passengers at Wakefield bus station, before heading off to Normanton.

At Normanton, we were directed to a large comfortable 55 seater luxury continental coach. By the time we were ready for off there were only a couple of empty seats. The back of the bus had a row of five seats, Wendy and I were sat at the right hand side and there were two ladies to the left, we had plenty of leg room. It was comforting to know that there was also a toilet on board.

We went to Dover to catch a cross channel ferry. Our coach driver was deaf with two hearing aids, he also had a major speech impediment. He was difficult to understand in the early stages, but as time went on we got to understand him and he had a great dry sense of humour.

We had a perfectly smooth crossing and the weather was perfect. We arrived in Calais and began our long and tiring journey to the hotel, that part of the journey seemed endless.

The hotel was a large place, the room was small but nice enough. The facilities were good downstairs, a bar, tea and coffee facilities.

Nearby was a railway station and a sports stadium next door that was under renovation. We didn't have any noise or disruption from either of them.

The only drawback with the hotel, was the evening meals. We were treated separately from the other hotel guests. All the Shearings travellers were sat down at a separate sitting, we didn't have any choices.

It was a basic set, two course meal. Some days it was better than others, but it was nothing special. One evening was fish and if like me, you didn't like fish, tough. There was no other choice. Those evening meals were the only spoiler of the holiday.

The breakfasts though, were a true continental help yourself affair. There was certainly plenty of choices there and all you could manage to eat.

Each day we had early morning starts, we would set off on the coach and our driver was the guide. Over the next few days he took us to all of the major, well known sights and areas of interest. We had night drives, we had a long and informative trip on the River Seine. We had at times, ample opportunity to stop and shop, with plenty of time for ourselves.

Late on one of the evenings, there was a spectacular thunder and lightening storm, that storm lasted for a few hours. According to the hotel staff, a months rainfall had fallen overnight.

The day after the cloudburst it was still raining, but we still went on a full days tour. It didn't really spoil things too much, other than some of the distant views.

Although it could have been better.

That day we went to see the Sacre Coeur, the Church of the Sacred Heart. A beautiful place, but at the time we were there, it was extremely wet. It wasn't worth going up to the top due to the weather, the views would have been limited. The actual viewing area at the top, is all outside with no covered protection from the weather. That was the only of the day that the rain had been able to ruin.

We had plenty of time to walk around the area, and we went inside the Church. There was time enough to shop and to get something to eat, before meeting up with the coach again and resuming the tour.

The only sights that we would have liked to see but didn't, would have been a trip up to the top of the Eiffel Tower. The waiting time just to the first level was over seven hours. Then further long waits to go up even higher.

The driver arranged for us instead, to go up a new modern business tower with a spectacular viewing area on the roof. The Montparnasse Tower, standing at 210 metres high. The viewing area through the windows of a cafe bar, was on the 56th floor. Then above that, there was outside up on the roof.

On the very top there were some spectacular views all across the beautiful city of Paris and from every direction. Including exceptional views of the Eiffel Tower. Not quite the same, but certainly a fantastic experience.

The other trip that I really would have liked to have taken Wendy on, would have been to see the Palais de Versailles. Again, due to the length of the queues of people to see the gorgeous palace, we would have been limited to about an hour. That's all, to view the whole of the palace and its wonderful gardens, that would not be anywhere near long enough.

Instead, the coach driver took us to a lesser known, but a certainly beautiful place. There we had plenty of time to view most of the inside of the palace and it's beautifully ornate formal gardens. We even had time to spend and get some lunch, in the local village centre.

It was the Chateau de Fontainebleau, a former residence of the Kings of France. A marvellous palace with 1,500 rooms. A total land area, including the formal gardens and forest, of greater than the city of Paris itself.

All in all, it was a brilliant holiday, if we got the chance we would like to return and visit the sights that we hadn't managed. I think if we did though, we would need to go for a more off season time.

I would have no problems with recommending Shearings holidays. Our last time with them, was for our honeymoon back in 1983 and they had looked after us then.

The only real drawback was that the return journey took a really long time, because there had been an issue with the refugee crisis at the docks in Calais, that had caused us some severe delays.

Then there was some major traffic issues, that meant that our driver would be exceeding his driver hours. We had to wait for quite a long time in a service area for a replacement driver. It wasn't a fault of Shearings' it was just down to some unforeseen circumstances that we had been involved in.

A great place to visit!

CHAPTER 62

ACCIDENTS DO HAPPEN.

Ambulance accidents.

You can imagine, that working for the ambulance service that we can at times have a rather aggressive style of driving. Several of us have been involved in accidents up and down, some were quite serious. The majority of them, fortunately, have been very slow speed knocks, during manoeuvring. Many of them in our own station garage.

Here are some records of mine.

I have had an occasional contretemps with another vehicle, I have also been on the rare occasion, known to have clipped a stationary object.

Most of the bumps that occur within the service, are not as you would expect from high speed blue light driving. They are more likely to occur trying to gain access to narrow areas.

Mine have been just the same.

I have clipped a couple of wheelie bins over the years, including an industrial one left at a nursing home. It had a long metal handle on the back to allow it to be lifted by the refuse truck. I only just touched the said bin, but it didn't have its brakes applied. The bin rotated and spun round, and the metal bar came straight through the rear window.

Carrie was in the back with a patient, she just went "ooh! Ian!"

I said that I knew, "I watched it happen, on the reversing camera".

Powerless to do anything about it.

First bus and then a second one.

Another time when I was working with Carl, my lights and sirens were on, as we were on route to a road traffic collision. A single decker bus mounted a high kerb, to give me room to pass. Unfortunately that meant that the bus' wing mirror was sticking out more into the road with it being on an angle, I got it!

Bang his mirror broke.

Carl rang the supervisor as we should do, all incidents have to be reported. It was Edmund. "Bloody hell! I'll have to ring the bus company, which one was it?"

Carl replied that it was a "First Bus". Not a mile down the road on the same journey, the same thing happened again. It was in exactly the same circumstances, I got another.

It was our mirror that smashed that time.

When Carl rang Edmund, for the second time in five minutes. He said "Edmund, you'll never guess what Firthy's done again!"

Edmund, replied in his usual dulcet tones, "for Gods sake, what's he playing at? Was it the same company?"

Carl told him that it was. Edmund got back and said "you know things come in three's don't you, tell him to use the train in future, bloody clown!"

There have been a few other minor scrapes against walls and gate posts, all of which have been reported. I can hand on heart say that I have never just left anything for someone else to take the blame, like many of the others do.

Tommy! I've hit somebody!

I have had two serious incidents whilst emergency driving, one involving a pedestrian and another one involving a car.

I'll tell you about the pedestrian first. I had only just really started working for the service, it was in May 1981.

I was working with my mate Tommy, we had picked up a lady in her thirties. It was a serious suicide attempt. She had taken an overdose of tablets and had then poured a flammable liquid over herself and ignited it.

She was in a mess, her condition was without doubt, time critical. I had radioed ahead for a trauma team to be waiting at HRI, giving them a seven minute ETA from Dalton.

The patient was deteriorating. Tommy shouted from the back "put your foot down lad, we're losing her!"

I was putting my foot down, I was belting up Trinity Street towards the hospital. As I got close to the bottom gates of Greenhead Park, near to the traffic light controlled pedestrian crossing. I could see that there was a large articulated lorry stopped at the crossing.

As I got level with the back of him, the lights started flashing amber. The lorry driver leaned out of the cab window and he waved dramatically for me to go on past.

My two tone sirens (the old ones) were screaming, "NEE NAW, NEE NAW". I had just started to accelerate again and I was picking speed up to around forty five miles an hour. As I got alongside the cab of the lorry, I saw him. Out of the corner of my eye, I saw a man.

Then I heard an awful sickening crunch, I looked up. There were slices of bread all over the windscreen.

I shouted "Tommy! I've hit somebody!"

There was a stunned cry "Jesus bloody Christ, that's all I need! You'd better get out and have a look then!"

I did, I didn't know what to expect. As I rounded the front of the ambulance, there was a little old man. He was sat cross legged in front of the big lorry. In his hand were the two handles of a shopping bag, and nothing else.

I helped him to his feet, asking if he was ok. He simply put a finger to his ear and in a poor speech he said "I'm totally deaf you know, I thought he (lorry driver) was waiting for me".

The upshot was, as he thought the lorry was waiting for him, he had set off running so as not to cause any longer hold up. Being deaf, he had no idea of my presence.

Fortunately, I caught the shopping bag on the upswing. If he had have been any further forward, I would have without doubt, killed him.

Other than destroying his bag, killing half a dozen eggs and feeding half the birds in Huddersfield with his loaf of bread, he was unscathed.

The lorry driver said that he would take him home. I asked the driver to give the man our details and to call at the ambulance station for some reimbursement.

He didn't, I never saw or heard anything from him again.

The woman that was in the back of the ambulance, was eventually transferred to the burns unit at Pinderfields General Hospital. She went on to make a decent recovery, from the burns, I'm not sure how her mental state went on.

Boy did I learn one hell of a lesson. I had been doing the job for less than two months!

Now, I always make my own decision when overtaking anywhere.

Even when trusted colleagues say "it's clear" I always still have that final check.

I have never looked in the rhododendron bushes near to those bottom park gates. In fact I don't think I have ever even been through that part of the park. Tommy once told me that he had seen a pair of shoes and a couple of shopping bag handles sticking out of the flower bed. He reckoned that the man was still in there, waiting to get me back!

Wedding dress!

Another incident took place one Saturday lunchtime in April 1984. I was working with Karl out of Honley Station. We received had a call to attend at a baby not breathing. It was said to be in a pram, in the street, at the top of Almondbury.

A nightmare scenario, my adrenaline was really pumping. I raced over the top of Castle Hill from Honley, lights and sirens blaring. I was shifting I can tell you.

As I came over the top of Kaye Lane looking down the long straight road towards Almondbury Church, a large truck was coming the other way. He was right at the bottom near to the Conservative Club.

He pulled in to the middle of the road, to stop anyone from behind him coming past, he put his hazard lights on and flashed me to confirm what he was doing.

That was a clear indication to me, of his intentions.

There were cars all down the left hand side of the road parked up. There were some occasional cars parked on the right. There wasn't any room for two vehicles to pass by each other, anywhere along that road.

I then had a clear run.

Lights and sirens were still on, I made my way down the middle of the available road. I think I was maybe doing about forty to forty five miles an hour on that stretch.

I had got three quarters of the way down when all of a sudden, with no prior indication. A car pulled out from the left hand side of the road, right across the front of me. I couldn't avoid it, there was one hell of a bang!

I stopped as fast as I could.

I knew it was serious. My bonnet had come up to the top of the windscreen obscuring my view and the windscreen had shattered, fortunately it was a laminated one.

Karl and I got out.

The first thing that I saw was the car that I had hit, it had been totally destroyed. It had been forced into another parked car and both of them were then on the pavement.

It was a mess.

The ambulance was also a mess, my near side front wheel was pointing in a totally different direction to its counterpart on the other side. There was no front wing and all the radiator grill and front body panels were on the floor.

The other driver, a young girl of around twenty years of age, was just getting out via the passenger side of her car. She appeared to be uninjured. Her dad was already out from the front passenger seat, also thankfully with no obvious injury.

I got on the radio to Comms for a replacement ambulance to attend to the original call for the baby, as we were unable to go anywhere. I asked them to get on to the police and request their presence at our little contretemps.

After our brief initial conversation, it was apparent that none of us had been injured. That was the priority. Then we could have the formal conversation and decide what should happen next.

It was then, that the young girls dad suddenly went into overdrive. He was screaming and shouting. There was a lot of swearing, accusations, finger pointing and the occasional fist shaking.

He claimed that I "had been going well in excess of seventy or eighty miles an hour and with no visible or audible warnings on", as he described.

That of course was totally untrue.

The sirens were the old two tone, nee naw type and on impact the front of the horns had fallen off. The sirens were switched on, they were still going and making a noise like a child's squeaky toy.

The blue lights on the roof, the big bucket type were still rotating, minus the buckets. The grill lights were across the road somewhere, I didn't know, nor neither cared if they were working.

The man was getting very angry.

The girl however, was very calm. She told me that her head had been all over the place.

She had just been to the shop for the final fitting of her wedding dress. Ready for her big day, the following Saturday.

The police were very quick to arrive.

They were taking very brief statements from the other couple, while I was arranging for our vehicle recovery.

At sometime in the proceedings, the truck driver from the bottom of the road, came towards us. He stopped and passed me a business card, he said that he couldn't hang about, but that he had seen it all.

"Just ring the number on the card, I'll be your witness" and then he was gone.

By the time all of our details etc. were exchanged between us and the young girl, the recovery truck had arrived on scene. We then returned to Honley station with the police, to give my full formal statement. And most important of all, a cuppa.

Cures all!

The man from the car had made all sorts of wild accusations about my driving. When it boiled down to it, our investigating officer Mike, told me that we had had four independent witnesses who had all corroborated my version of events. There would be no further action by either the police or from the ambulance service.

Thank goodness for that!

Jack in the box.

On a funny note, if it can be classed as funny. Alec who could be known for his fast driving, was heading from the Shorehead Roundabout to go down Wakefield Road towards Dalton.

It was peak traffic and nothing was moving. There were some roadworks right in the junction at the end of St. Andrews' Road. Only one of three lanes were open at the junction, hence the hold up. Three lanes into one takes some time.

A couple of the workers stopped the traffic from coming towards us, from Wakefield Road at its junction with Firth Street. Alec then went down the wrong side of the central reservation, down the empty carriageway all the way down to the junction. He then had to negotiate the chicane caused by the works.

As he was negotiating the bends. Still at speed, sirens singing loudly, a figure appeared. It was one of the workers in the hole. He jumped up out of the hole like a "jack in the box" to see what all the noise was about.

Big mistake.

As he appeared out of the hole, he stumbled forward. It was just as Alec was going past.

Crack!

A sickening sound, the man was knocked straight back into where he had come from. His hard hat gruesomely bouncing down the middle of Wakefield Road.

Alec stopped, the man was unconscious laid at the bottom of the hole. He came round very quickly and although dazed, he got himself back out. As he left the hole, there at the bottom, imprinted in the soft clay was a full body impression. It was like something out of a cartoon.

It had been the wing mirror that had caught the man at the side of his head.

Fortunately his hard hat wasn't strapped on and it was only an empty helmet that bounced down the road.

We both, for a couple of seconds, expected the man's head to have still been in it.

We had to take him to hospital for a check up. It turned out that he was none the worse for wear though, following his excitement.

Truth be known, I don't think either he or Alec were far off a trip to Marks and Spencer's, for a clean pair.

CHAPTER 63.

ANATOMY OF A CAR CRASH.

In A Split Second.

This report, was given to me in 1984, by a friend of mine PC. Alex. He had been a Traffic Police Officer.

We were at a joint services talk at Colne Valley High School. At that time, he was a school liaison officer for the police. A role that the ambulance service have never actively encouraged, as an occupation, but have relied on the good will of a few volunteers.

Although there have been many steps to improve car safety. I think that this report is still just as poignant now, as it was then. And so my reason for including it.

This is the slow motion, split second reconstruction. It is of what happens when a car, travelling at around 55 miles per hour, crashes into a solid immovable tree.

A slow motion picture of "***Death on the Road".***

1/10th of a second.

The front bumper and chromium radiator grille collapse. Slivers of steel penetrate the tree to a depth of 1 and 1/2 inches or more.

2/10ths of a second.

The bonnet crumples as it rises, smashing into the windscreen. Spinning rear wheels leave the ground. The radiator disintegrates. The wings come into contact with the tree, forcing the rear parts to splay over the front doors. In this same tenth of a second the heavy structural members of the car begin to break up, at the same time acting as a brake on the terrific momentum of the body. But the driver's body continues to move forward at the vehicle's original speed. This means a force 20 times gravity; his body weighs 3,200lbs. His legs, ramrod straight, snap at the knee joints.

3/10ths of a second.

The driver's body is now off the seat, torso upright; broken knees pressing against the dashboard. The plastic and steel frame of the steering wheel begins to bend under his terrible death grip. His head is now near the sun visor, his chest above the steering column.

4/10ths of a second.

The car's front 24 inches have been completely demolished, but the rear end is still travelling at 35 miles per hour. The engine block crunches into the tree. The

427

rear end of the car, like a bucking horse rises high enough to scrape bark off the lower branches.

5/10ths of a second.

The driver's fear frozen hands bend the steering column into an almost vertical position. The force of gravity impales him on the steering column. Jagged steel punctures lung and intercostal arteries. Blood spurts into his lungs.

6/10ths of a second.

So great is the force of impact that the driver's feet are ripped from his tightly laced shoes. The brake pedal sheers off at the floorboards. The chassis bends in the middle shearing body bolts. The head smashes into the windscreen. The rear of the car begins its downward fall, with spinning wheels digging into the ground.

7/10ths of a second.

The entire writhing body of the car is forced out of shape. Hinges tear, doors open. In one last convulsion the seat rams forward pinning the driver against the cruel steel of the steering column. Blood leaps from his mouth. Shock has frozen his heart.

He is now DEAD.

This anatomy of a car crash, is based on a true post mortem of a traffic accident victim in the late nineteen seventies.

The cars then were made of solid metal, crumple zones hadn't been thought of. Now, the body work is designed to collapse in on itself to absorb the majority of the impact.

Steering wheels and steering columns were solid, the column would be left exposed. It was a spear at the ready to pierce any unsuspecting chest, age didn't come in to it. They are now designed to collapse and fold out of harms way.

Seat belts, although they had been fitted to all cars since 1972, they were very often not used. Since they were made compulsory in 1983, very few people go through the windscreen. When I started in the ambulance service, it was commonplace.

Those injuries are beyond words to describe adequately.

Speed reduction cameras, seat belts, child restraints, not drinking, not taking drugs and the use of mobile phones. All the safety measures are there for a reason, and for one reason alone.

That reason is to "save lives", not to ruin the enjoyment of driving.

Only just a little thinking is required to prevent some of the most serious of accidents from happening.

Thank you!

CHAPTER 64.

***

MENTAL HEALTH ISSUES.

Who is responsible?

Mental Health, has been one subject that has caused a lot of concern over the years. Several questions have been raised.

Who is responsible for the patient? Who is responsible for the transport? What powers do we have as an ambulance service, when transporting a patient under section?

A "section" is an order under the Mental Health Act. It is a legal document to allow the detention of a person under the powers of the Act, either for their own safety, or for if they pose a danger to others.

There are various sections, all accompanied by a number. For example section 136, that can be enforced by a police officer. It would apply to a person in a public place, whose behaviour isn't compatible with socially accepted behaviour.

That may be due to the effects of substance abuse, or it could be a mental health issue.

It means that the person would be detained under the order of section 136, until that person has been assessed by a medical professional for their mental wellbeing. It is a medical detention, not a criminal offence.

There are some other more formal sections, those orders can only be enforced by a General Practitioner, a Psychiatrist and an Approved Social Worker.

Those sections usually involve longer stays in a place approved for the treatment of the psychiatric patient. It could be days, weeks, months or ultimately a lifelong commitment.

There is also a voluntary section, where a person, who has probably had previous issues with the Mental Health Act. Can see their GP, or even a doctor at A&E. Knowing that they are deteriorating and are in an acute need of assistance. Those patients may be admitted to a psychiatric unit and as they are there in a voluntary capacity, they may leave at their own discretion.

In most of the cases, the ambulance service becomes involved as a transport provider. If the patient becomes violent, we have to ask for police assistance. Bearing in mind, that the person, is still a "patient" with an "illness".

The police are there for safety reasons. Wherever possible and practical, the patient will travel in the ambulance to try and decriminalise the situation.

There are occasions where the patient can become so violent, that the use of an ambulance just isn't a safe environment. That being for either the patient, or the staff looking after them. The police may then be required to provide a secure van. (As a last resort). Ambulance staff will then travel with the patient in the van, along with the Police.

If a patient is going to hospital under care of a section, there will be paperwork. The papers are the legal documentation required, for the powers to detain someone under the Mental Health Act.

Other than section 136, the paperwork would be held by the approved social worker. The papers must travel with the patient. The social workers used to hold on to them. Then they would be travelling with us in the ambulance.

Now they tend to travel in their own car.

That action, enforces the fact that the section papers stay with the patient. If the social worker and the ambulance got separated due to traffic conditions for instance, there are then no powers of detention of the patient.

Elderly.

Many years gone by, I think it was the spring of 1982. I was with Mike, we were sent to an address at Paddock. Where there was an elderly lady, who was extremely distressed. She was having to be removed from her own house, her castle.

It was a typical situation where someone needed to be helped, for her own safety. She was in her eighties. I wouldn't be surprised that if nowadays, she would be diagnosed as having dementia of some kind. It wasn't as well known then.

The lady had suffered from a major burst pipe within her home. It had flooded all the electrics as well, the place simply wasn't safe to be in.

She had originally let a plumber in at her son's request. As soon as he had mentioned that she needed to leave, she had gone berserk.

He had managed to get hold of her family, the lady was even more agitated then. The dangers to anybody else and herself were obvious. To that lady, everybody else was intruding and interfering.

The police were called. The lady hit the first officer on the head with a hammer. He needed hospitalising, she had knocked him out cold!

It had quickly escalated into a serious incident.

The longer it went on, the more danger the old lady would be in. The doctor was called. His only option was to instigate a formal section, generally, it can take a long time.

He tried to speed things up.

From the plumber arriving, to the patient being under section three of the Mental Health Act, had only taken around four hours. That was very fast under the circumstances.

When we arrived, it was going to be our job to remove the lady from the premises. Away from her own "safe haven".

She was elderly and very frail.

It had put everybody into a real predicament.

Nobody wanted to see her in handcuffs and manhandled out like some violent criminal, but she was getting more and more agitated and violent. The plumber had turned the water supply off from outside the property, the electricity board had done their bit as well from outside the property.

It was safe in the house whilst we were negotiating with her, but it wasn't habitable due to the damage already caused.

It had to be thought out very carefully. Mike and me came up with a cunning plan. It was not going to be very dignified, but sometimes needs must.

We discussed our plan with the family and we explained how our reasoning behind it, was designed for the safety of the lady.

It was agreed.

We got the daughter, a familiar face for the patient. The plan was for her to go to the front window and to bang like there was no tomorrow.

Hopefully, the lady would be shocked and distracted into running to the window, allowing Mike and me to pounce.

We had already prepped the ambulance. We had put blankets on the floor for padding, wrapped more blankets over any cupboard edges, etc.

As soon as the daughter banged on the front room window, as expected, the lady screamed and ran to it.

Mike and me were armed with a Health Service Blanket. It was the old type, a big one, a proper one. Not like the cheap tatty efforts available today.

We ran up behind her, and cocooned her in the blanket.

As the lady was standing, we went from either side and we had got her wrapped up in seconds. A couple of blanket pins were added. (Giant safety pins, made for that purpose) she was secure.

We sat her in her little cocoon onto a carry chair, then applied the safety strap. Although not happy, she was coming with us and she could do nothing about it.

The patient was put on a stretcher, where we loosened the blankets and made her comfortable for her journey to St. Luke's hospital

Success! It had worked a treat.

We used the same method on several occasions after that, it worked brilliantly. The patient was completely restrained without any harm done.

It doesn't work every time!

I had a similar incident a few years later, in 1987. That time, I was working with Graham. I explained in detail what I wanted him to do, but he didn't get it.

I got a police officer to quickly act as the patient, to demonstrate to Graham exactly what was needed.

It needed to be right and be done right first time for the safety aspect to work.

We were ready. We approached the patient from behind, blanket at the ready.

Then, Graham spoke to the patient.

He asked her "would it be OK, to wrap you in the blanket?"

The whole idea was for complete surprise.

It failed drastically. I had got the blanket over one shoulder, Graham dropped the other side.

The lady, a large lady in her sixties had got a hand free.

She hit me full in the face with her right hand, her hand contained her purse. The purse was full of coins, it might as well have been a brick that she had hit me with.

My cheek began to swell immediately.

She wasn't finished at that, she dropped the purse and then lashed out at my throat. She caught all across the front of my neck with her one inch long talons that she called fingernails.

They made a right "bloody" mess.

Graham is a lovely lad, but his politeness is his greatest downfall. He needs to assert himself occasionally.

That was one of those occasions.

Check the paperwork!

It was late in the year of 1999. I attended at an address with Carl, it was near Halifax. There was a lady in her forties who had become extremely violent, she was smashing the place up.

"The Place" being a refuge. A home, for people already with severe mental health problems.

On arrival there, we were met by the "approved social worker". She assured us that all the paperwork was in order.

That although the patient was under section 2 and she would normally have to be taken to the Dales Unit (psychiatric wards) at Calderdale Royal Hospital. She would have to go via A&E. She had some self inflicted wounds to both her wrists, they would require treatment first.

As we approached the patient, she had armed herself with a piece of wood. It was baseball bat size and she was lashing out with it, at anyone who went near her. The police had already been requested.

We decided it would be safest to await their arrival.

When they did, we had a right tussle to disarm her. For the safety of all concerned, she had to be placed in handcuffs. Her wrist wounds were higher up than where the cuffs fitted. Then her legs and ankles were also bound with velcro straps.

She was then physically lifted into the ambulance. Yet again, not a very professional looking removal, but it needed to be done. It was handled professionally, with safety for the patient and others paramount.

The social worker was adamant that we, as an ambulance crew, did not require the paperwork.

She said that we didn't even need to see it as it was confidential. That inside, the documents contained private and personal details of the patient.

I had to insist that either the papers, or the social worker with the papers, had to travel with us. That I wouldn't leave without them.

After some lengthy confrontation with her, we managed to get her to seal them into an envelope and we finally had them with us.

Two police officers had to travel to help restrain the patient.

On arrival at A&E, the charge nurse ripped open the envelope. He then started to sweat, "no wonder she didn't want you to see these papers, they have not been signed. They are not legal, you have all been guilty of a physical assault on the patient. I cannot accept her in my department!"

That put us all in a legal predicament. Where was the social worker?

Her phone number was on the paperwork, it was about the only bit that had been filled in.

There hadn't even been a doctor out to see the patient, looking at the information that we had..

When the police rang her. She told them that she wasn't "coming to hospital", that she had gone home and "rung things through to The Dales", and was "no longer required".

The policeman stated to her that our patient "will be released from our custody in ten minutes flat, so you had better get your self down here quickly". He then told her that if she didn't, "a warrant will be requested for your arrest, in connection with arranging an assault on a vulnerable adult. The clock is ticking madam" he concluded.

Like I said previously, section cases are a legal minefield.

Honesty is the best policy.

The majority of patients with mental health issues, can be dealt with without threats of violence and confrontation. If you are open and honest with them from the start.

Some social workers have been known to lie to, or mislead the patient, to secure a section. It is a dangerous thing to do, as it can have a serious knock on effect during their aftercare.

A lot of patients with mental health problems are poorly and may be vulnerable. Many of them are very intelligent people as well. Even just a small amount of deception can create a great deal of distrust.

Full length mirror.

One example in 2005. Was typical of the type of deception I mean. I was working with a relatively new paramedic at the time, Stew. We also had an observer, a university student paramedic I'll call her Hannah.

We had been called via 999, to take a section three patient to the secure unit at the Fieldhead Hospital in Wakefield. The caller had said, blue lights and sirens would be required. Then nearer to the scene, a silent approach was needed. That always puts me on edge. What hasn't been said or told to the patient?

We attended to an address, in the Wheatley area of Halifax. The social worker met us at the bottom of the street. Not surprisingly, she said that the patient was totally unaware of an ambulance arriving.

Why do they do that?

The patient had been told that he needed to go to hospital, but he was under the impression that his wife would be taking him.

We were told that he posed no threat whatsoever to male staff, but he had been verbally threatening violence towards his wife of twenty plus years.

As I spoke to the patient, he was laid in bed. My colleagues both stayed outside the room. It doesn't pay for us all to all crowd in.

I was honest with him from the start and I told him that he would be travelling in an ambulance.

He was very calm and not threatening in any way. But he did say that he would not be coming with us. He would be making his own way later on in the evening, with his wife.

I told him that although he was very amicable now, that he would not be making his own way. That when I left the house, he would be coming with me. Hopefully walking voluntarily, but if needs be, that the police may be called for assistance.

He seemed quite shocked at that and he said "what you are saying to me, sounds as though I have been sectioned. Until I have, I will make my own choices. Thank you".

I had to tell him, that he had indeed been sectioned.

He then continued, that the woman who was talking to his wife, hadn't told him that bit.

I asked him if he had seen any doctors recently. He told me most definitely that he hadn't.

I had to speak to the social worker again.

She then told me that two doctors had indeed been to the house, that they had spoken to her and to his wife. From their conversations, they had come to the decision to admit the patient under section three.

That although they hadn't actually physically examined the patient. They had clearly heard his comments and the threats towards his wife. He had locked himself in his room while they were there.

They had tried to engage him in conversation, but were loudly and firmly rebuffed.

They had retreated for their own safety.

I then insisted on seeing and checking the papers thoroughly. After previous events, I needed to be sure. It did not seem to be the correct way of doing things.

The paperwork certainly seemed complete.

I went back to see my patient. I showed him the papers. He was upset that they hadn't had the decency to explain it to him, but ok.

He stated that he was only in his underwear in bed and would I allow him to get dressed first. To try and keep what was left of his dignity, then he would come out walking.

I told him that It was the least I could do, but that he could not shut the bedroom door, just in case he tried to lock himself in again. I stood in the doorway and turned my back, to give him some privacy.

Once ready, he said "I can't believe that you trusted me to do that. You turned your back, I could have had a weapon. You don't know anything about me yet. Thank you for that".

He laughed when I was honest with him again. I said that "although I turned my back, I was looking in that full length mirror on the landing, I was watching you all the time".

He was my mate then.

We had quite a conversation about the build up of circumstances that had led to his incarceration. He was a highly skilled engineer, he was actually a bridge design engineer. He had been made redundant four months ago and it had been very tough.

He had been really struggling to cope. He was very candid and honest with me.

I asked him how long he had lived at the address.

He smiled, and said "why, did you know Tommy?"

I did, Tommy used to work for the ambulance service in Halifax until his retirement.

He told me that he had bought the house off Tommy three years earlier, and that Tommy and his wife had moved "down south" to live nearer to their daughters and their families.

He then asked me, if I had any idea how long he was going to be admitted to the Dales for?

I had to ask him who had told him that he was going to the Dales unit.

He looked at the social worker and said that "it was that woman there", directing his finger.

When I told him that we were going to Wakefield instead, his face changed. He raised his voice and he called the social worker a "lying two faced bitch!"

He said it with pure venom in his voice.

He went on to say to me, "that's Fieldhead, that's where the proper nutters go isn't it? They're real loonies in there. Am I really that bad?"

I tried to explain to him that although it was a secure unit. It was also the place you went, when there were no beds available at The Dales in Halifax.

As we got in the ambulance, he asked if we would stop at the shop for him to get some cigarettes.

I told him that under normal circumstances, that it would not be allowed to happen but, as we had Hannah with us. If he had the money, I would ask her to go to the shop for him. He himself would not be able to step out of the vehicle once we had set off.

He agreed to that.

He was very open with me on the journey, but he was very annoyed with the "underhanded actions" of the social worker. That he wanted to officially complain about the way that she had treated him.

I promised him that I would report it to the staff at Wakefield and that he would be able to get more information from them as to how to go about it.

The patient, was a highly intelligent man. He was having "serious issues" that were beyond his control and he knew that he needed professional help.

He told me that he knew he had been getting angry and upset and he was extremely distraught that his wife seemed to be frightened of him. He wanted to do everything in his power to rectify things.

On arrival at Wakefield, he was placed in a small sitting room. The door was locked, as I had told him would happen. As after all he was in the secure unit. I told him that as soon as that happened, I would tell the staff about the social worker and get him the cup of tea that he was "dying for".

When I returned to the room, a staff member came with me. With a cuppa and the two of them began to chat together. The staff had by then read his paperwork from the social worker and also my frank and open Patient Report Form, where I had documented everything.

It had happened before, I wasn't getting bitten a second time.

The Fieldhead staff were disgusted with the social worker, her actions and lack of information.

One of the staff told him that he would be transferred to the unit across the road, one that didn't have any locked internal doors. It was quite an open area, where he would be assessed. All being well, he would be going back to the Dales at Halifax within the next couple of days. As soon as a bed became available.

All the man wanted was to be treated with a little respect and a little honesty. As I was leaving him, he stood and then shook my hand. He thanked me for my actions and most of all my honesty.

He respected that!

No thanks to the social worker and her not giving him the correct information, it could have turned into a completely different incident.

He was a big bloke.

If he had kicked off, he would have ended up in handcuffs and possibly in a cage in the back of a police van. It is not the way to treat anyone with mental health issues.

Just be honest with people. It's not that difficult.

CHAPTER 65.

FIREARMS INCIDENTS.

What was it like?.

Whilst at the RATC (Regional Ambulance Training Centre) in Keighley, in February 1981. There as part of my basic training, we did some work around ballistics and firearms.

It was only very basic stuff, how to stem the bleeding etc.

The training is far more advanced now thank goodness, but firearms incidents were very rare in those days. Now you hear of one every week, if not more.

Not long after finishing my training, there was a shooting at a pub between Bradford and Halifax. It hit all the newspapers and television news.

I rang Mike at Brighouse station, he was one of my colleagues on starting with the ambulance service. He had attended the incident. I wanted to find out what the injuries actually were.

"What was it like?"

It had been a fatality, involving one single gun shot from a hand gun. It was to the back of the head, it was a murder, actually it was an execution.

He told me, that just as we had been told at the RATC. There was a relatively small wound on entry, but the wound at the front of the patient's head, the exit wound. Well, that was something else.

The exit wound had taken half of the man's face away. Some of his forehead above where his right eye should have been and most of the man's cheek had just simply been blown away.

Mike explained that death would have been instant, so there was nothing really for them as a crew to do.

The police had dealt with everything.

Is this the way to "cash and carry?"

My first shooting, was at a cash and carry warehouse, it had occurred during an armed robbery. I think it was 1990.

I attended with Alec, adrenaline was rushing through my veins as I rushed to the scene.

We got to a pub, less than a couple of hundred yards from the warehouse. There were armed police all over the place, a man was laid in the road with at least two armed police officers pointing weapons at him.

There was nothing there to cause us any concern, he wasn't injured, he was one of the robbers under arrest.

No, our patient was inside the the main building, he was in the large warehouse area.

We were escorted into the premises and down a long corridor through the offices and into the large open space of the warehouse.

At the far end of the room we could see lots of people, including several police officers, around the body of a man who was laid on the floor.

As we got closer, we could see and hear that the man was fully aware of things. He was telling the police everything.

The patient was one of the store managers. I'll call him Ronnie. He had been bringing all the days takings from the cash and carry's tills, and taking it back to the giant safe in the office.

When the robbers had entered, he had his arms full, carrying a large canvas sack. The sack was containing all of the monies, that had been separated into the little individual cash bags, before being put into the bigger one.

He was held at gunpoint by at least three masked men, one was pointing a sawn off shotgun directly at him. Another of the robbers demanded the money.

Now my understanding, if you are being held up. Even without a gun pointing at you, with the objective of being robbed. Is that the general advice is not to antagonise the aggressors, give them whatever it is that they want.

No heroics, give them what they want and scarper.

Not Ronnie, he told them that if they wanted the money, then they would have to take it from him. At that point the sawn off shotgun was discharged.

Ronnie hadn't seen the large area of plaster missing from the wall at the side of him. It had only been a warning shot.

Amazingly, Ronnie took the sack by the bottom edge and threw all of its contents in one sweep. There was thousands of pounds, all across the racks of pallets.

At the same time, telling the robbers "if you want it, you'll have to pick it all up!"

He then went for the man with the shotgun, disarming him and knocking him to the floor. The other two ran for it. It was one of those two that we had seen apprehended outside.

The robber had then pulled out of his pocket a pistol, he shot Ronnie in the left shoulder with it and then he fled.

While he was on the floor, Ronnie picked up a radio handset that one of the robbers had dropped. Whilst waiting for the police, he had kept the getaway driver talking in the car park. That robber was also arrested on site, still sat in the car waiting for his accomplices.

We examined Ronnie, he had a small entry wound from a .22 calibre pistol (we learnt that later), on the left side of his upper chest.

It was just off his left shoulder joint, below his collar bone. To look at, I can only describe the wound as looking like the hole in a cats bottom.

A small puckered hole, there was no bleeding whatsoever, that we could see externally.

However, internally, there was some severe bleeding. Ronnie's neck and throat were swelling at an alarming rate, as blood was filling the area under the surface.

He looked like a bullfrog on heat.

His right arm was blue and it didn't have a pulse. He had no feeling/sensation, from his shoulder down.

On examination, I could actually feel the bullet just under the skin resting against the top of his right humorous. As I moved his arm slightly to look for a vein for Alec to insert intra venous fluids, the circulation suddenly became restored. Ronnie instantly felt pins and needles in his fingers as the blood flow returned.

Alec had been looking for one at the injured side initially. Now that he had got the circulation back on his right, Ronnie had got veins like drainpipes. The cannula, a large bore brown one was inserted. Saline fluid was up and running, it was time to go!

We ran through the warehouse with Ronnie laid on a large flat warehouse trolley, he was taking gas and air for the pain. He had the saline running, to try and keep up and maintain his blood pressure.

Just before we left the site, we were told of another male who had been shot. That man, had been shot at through a reinforced, bullet proof glass window in the cash office. Although the glass had broken, it had done its job.

The man in the office, had only suffered dozens of minor cuts. Pinpricks really, from the thousands of slivers of glass that had been sent flying following the shotgun blast.

There was no threat to life there, not one of the wounds would have even required a stitch. The police would deal with him and transport him to hospital later.

I switched on the blue lights and sirens, we had an armed police escort and we were off. I called up for a trauma standby at the hospital, I explained briefly what had happened and then drove like there was no tomorrow.

Ronnie's wife, I'll call Frances met us at the hospital. She was a member of the hospital staff, a sister on the coronary care unit at the time.

Ronnie had to have several hours of major surgery, the bullet had actually ruptured his sub-clavian artery. That's the one that runs underneath the collar bone.

Hence the bullfrog effect going on in his throat.

He did eventually make a good recovery, but his promising career as a county squash player was over. His chest was so scarred. In his own words, he said "it looked like the surgeons were having fun playing noughts and crosses on my chest"

Firearms in public. 1.

I personally have been called to two armed incidents, where a member of the public has been shot by the police.

One was on a New Years Day in 1992, in Calderdale and another in Kirklees. In both those incidents, a member of the public had been threatening others with their weapon.

The man in Calderdale, had been seen firing a rifle out of his window, following a drunken row with a taxi driver.

There was a police stand off, lasting for several hours. Whilst specialist police negotiators were trying to persuade him to drop his weapons, and come out with his hands up.

The man then appeared a couple more times and pointed his weapon towards the police, those were to be his last movements.

A police marksman was given the order, crack! crack! crack! three shots were fired. The man flew back from the widow and disappeared out of sight.

The weapons turned out to be replicas, a very dangerous game to play, especially when under the influence of alcohol.

I was again with Alec, eventually we were given the all clear to enter the flat, primarily to confirm death. There was no doubt. The man had been hit by all three rounds, all in a neat grouping to the left side of his chest, his heart. He would have been dead before he hit the back wall of his living room.

Firearms in public 2.

27th December 1994. The man in Kirklees, was an older man, 44 year old. He had a hand gun, a Smith and Wesson cowboy style revolver. He had taken it with him, when he went out for a drink. Then he had fired a couple of shots in the car park before going home.

The police were called, Carl and I were stood by not so far off.

Just in case.

The man came out of the house, he had been drinking for about three hours prior to going home. He was very unsteady on his feet, and he was slurring his words.

Carl and I were brought in a bit closer, but we were still behind the police line. By that time quite a crowd had formed, most of the people knew the man.

He suddenly brought the gun out from inside his jacket. The mood changed. The armed police were not in the mood for playing games. He was drunk, he had a weapon and he was pointing it at the officers.

I remember him being told at least four or five times to "throw down the weapon, and lay face down on the floor!"

It wasn't a request, it was a blatant command. From a police officer with a loud hailer.

He was warned again, that time though, it was crystal clear. "If you do not comply, the officers will shoot! Lay down on the floor, now!"

He waved the gun menacingly, then he fired into the air in defiance.

He was shot and killed by a police marksman. One single shot and it was all over.

It turned out that the man was well known for his "quick on the draw" cowboy/western style competitions.

There was a public outcry. The gun was confirmed to be a replica, it only fired blanks.

It looked real enough to me! It sounded real enough as well.

I'm sorry, but those are dangerous games to play. If you want to play with danger, you have to expect the consequences.

Again, I'm sorry if I offend anyone. But I don't have any sympathy for him, or anyone else in that type of situation.

Drunk in charge of a firearm in public, is asking for only one outcome.

That time he got it!

Self inflicted shotgun wound.

Another firearms incident and this was a Saturday lunchtime. Carl and I were sat on station at Marsh, when we had a call to a police incident in Huddersfield.

It was in the middle of a local football pitch.

As we arrived there was a massive crowd and there were lots of police everywhere. There were armed response, dog units and the helicopter was flying very low overhead.

In the middle of the football field was an armoured Land Rover, similar to those used in Northern Ireland during the troubles.

Our patient was on the floor, completely hidden from our view at the far side of it.

One policeman who met us, asked if we were aware of why we had been called. When we answered that we had no idea. He said, "it's ballistics, and you'll need to run, the crowd are baying for your blood!"

We couldn't get the ambulance on to the field, we had to run with a trolley on wheels full of equipment through the mud.

Objects were being thrown at us, as well as verbal abuse. One comment that I heard was "pointless running now, he's already f-ing dead, the time it's taken you buggers to get here!"

He wasn't dead, he was desperately ill, but not dead. He had held a sawn off shotgun to his own chest and then pulled the trigger.

I placed a wound pack on his chest, Carl managed to get some fluid running and then we put him on 100% oxygen.

The fire service had arrived and removed the locks from the gates, I could then get the ambulance onto the field.

I had to run back, an armed officer was at my side all the way. We jumped into the ambulance and had to force our way through the mob. Bottles, bricks and other objects were being thrown at us as we went through.

It was purely load and go, well it should have been.

I had only got the ambulance stuck in the mud!

Of all the times for it to happen, that was not one of them. The crowd were going mad. The Land Rover that was on the field came to the rescue. He got close to the back of us and literally gave us a push.

Phew! Success!

It only took a matter of seconds, but believe me, I aged ten years in those few moments. Yet another police escort off the field, avoiding the missiles being thrown at us. They stayed with us, all the way to waiting staff at HRI.

In the resus room, they did a procedure that I hadn't seen before. The man was suffering from a cardiac tamponade, (whatever in his chest cavity that was bleeding, was pushing his heart way over to one side and crushing it).

The surgeon cut the patient's chest, from the sternum to under his arms twice. Then he got what can only be described as a pair of bolt cutters, he cut through and then completely removed two of the man's ribs. He then put a metal contraption inside and spread the ribs as far as they would go.

As the doctors looked into his chest, blood was everywhere. They had two suction pumps emptying his chest cavity. You could clearly see the left lung had been completely shredded, as also had the left ventricle of his heart.

There were loads of the shot pellets embedded in them as well.

The conclusion was, that the young man could not be saved, his injuries could not possibly sustain life.

The consultant in charge stated that fact to all present. He then said "are we all, and I mean all, in agreement?"

Every head in the room nodded in silence, but in unison.

Without the manual compression of his catastrophically damaged heart, and the ventilation of what was left of his lungs. Neither of them functioned, he was pronounced as deceased.

The night before the shooting, the young man had held up a post office at gunpoint. Discharging his weapon into the ceiling in the process, fortunately nobody had been hurt.

The police had been chasing all around Huddersfield looking for him. An ambulance with Danny and Gerald in tow, all through the night.

During the night, the young man had rung the police taunting them. He was saying that he would give himself up at twelve lunchtime on the football field. "Where there would be witnesses to see that the police didn't shoot him".

The ambulance wasn't called that time, perhaps it was thought that he would give himself up without a struggle, I don't know. We weren't called, until he had actually pulled the trigger.

I don't understand that. The amount of police that were there, the amount of members of the public and knowing he was armed. I wish that we had been stood off somewhere nearby.

Personally, I think that it would have been far better if we had met up with the police. It would have helped if we could have attended their briefing at Castlegate Headquarters, before setting off together to the location in Huddersfield.

Perhaps the crowd would have been less hostile towards us, if we had been in the vicinity.

In the end, what an absolute waste of a young life!

The next one will kill you!
Another shooting, this time I was working with Ray. We had a call that a man had been shot, somewhere near to the Asda supermarket. On route there, we were diverted. Apparently he had left the scene and run home.

He had run to an address a good mile and a half away.

At the new scene, was a young man in his twenties, he was well known to the police due to his drug related activities. He had been on a deal that had gone terribly wrong.

The police were already there.

Adrenaline is a wonderful thing. He had been shot at fairly close range with a sawn off, 12 bore shotgun.

On examination, he had a wound near to his right kidney. The hole was big enough to put your thumb in, that was surrounded by the peppering of pellets to an area the size of (for those of you who remember) a vinyl single record. They were 7" in diameter.

There was some bleeding, but not excessive externally, he was feeling very faint. He was an Afro Caribbean man, but you could still tell that he was very pale and he was sweating profusely.

His blood pressure was dropping. He should have collapsed there and then on site, but his adrenaline had kicked in and his survival instinct had sent him home to mum.

He was already in severe shock. Ray cannulated him with a big bore cannula. A grey one was inserted into his arm and I connected a litre of saline to it, to try and help improve his blood pressure.

Again we rushed him, Ray driving to waiting staff at HRI. All the way there, he was begging me not to let him die. "Not on my shift", I said, "there's too much paperwork for that".

He was literally frightened to death, but he was very candid in what he had to say.

A policeman accompanied us.

The man told us that he owed his dealer a lot of money. He had agreed to meet him to pay back some of his debt.

On arrival at his rendezvous, the dealer had upped his price.

The patient had tried to argue his case.

The dealer relented a little, he said that if he cleared the debt by the day after, he would call it quits. Then he warned, or he would be dead.

Our patient had agreed to get some more money. As he turned to leave, the dealer shouted to him "you've got twenty four hours!"

Then our man heard the shot, "the next one will kill you!" the dealer shouted.

The patient said that he knew he had been hit, but he hadn't felt any pain until he had arrived home.

The man had suffered a ruptured kidney, that would need major surgery at St. James University Hospital in Leeds. He was transferred within an hour of his arrival at HRI.

I don't know what happened over his debt. After all, he would have been out of action for several weeks, recovering from his surgery in Leeds.

I have seen him around since though. I once went for him when he had suffered a simple fall. He remembered me straight away and shook my hand. He said to me "you promised that you wouldn't let me die and you didn't. Thank You".

Triad gangs? In Huddersfield?

A last job involving firearms and it was involving the specialist tactical armed police unit. It was January 2010. I was working a half night shift with Adie, that's 16:00hrs until 02:00hrs.

Up until that job, it had been very "quiet" (not a word we use in the ambulance service, due to fear of death from our colleagues) for a Friday night.

At around 23:00hrs we received an emergency call to an area not far from Huddersfield town centre. The only information given to us, was that the police had found a male. The destination given was at a road junction, between two of Huddersfield's small side roads.

That was it!

I was driving and we were on the ring road returning from a roadside standby, when we got the call. So we were only a couple of minutes away. As I pulled up near to the junction, I couldn't see any police, or vehicles. It wasn't right, something major was going on there.

The Firth gut was telling me that I would be far better off at home. I crept further round the corner.

On the floor was one male and one female oriental in appearance, they were bound at the wrists and ankles with what appeared to be cable ties.

There were three armed men in gas masks and black helmets, dressed in all black clothing. They had bulletproof vests on and what can only be described as mini hand grenades attached to their vests. They were pointing weapons at the couple.

(I was told later, that they were officers from the Tactical Arms Group, [TAG] and that the "grenades" were of a stun or smoke variety).

One of the masked men identified himself to us as police, he pointed up to the corner terraced house. He said "your man is in there, the inspector will meet you".

The house looked like a scene from the Iranian Embassy Siege in London. Not one window had been left intact and the front door appeared to have been blown off into the garden. Smoke was emitting from all of the open accesses to the house.

There were other similarly dressed armed men up and down the street, with two more oriental looking men on the floor.

I looked at Adie and he looked back at me, "shit!" we both said in unison. What on earth was going on?

We approached the doorway, one of the armed men was stood there. He told me that he was the Inspector with the TAG. That the smoke was from stun grenades that had been thrown in to each room prior to entry. He said that it was clearing fast.

The inspector then told us that. "Upstairs in the house is a young Chinese man, he is eighteen years old. He has been kidnapped from London, and held for a ransom of $2,000,000 US dollars. He has been tied to a bed for at least five days. He has been beaten, drugged and he has a heart condition". Then he added. "But it's not life threatening".

As I started to go in, Adie had conveniently side stepped and let me go first. I felt a push in the chest. It was the Inspector, "where the hell are you going?" he asked.

I told him that we would need to examine the patient to confirm that it wasn't "life threatening".

He just said "I've told you it isn't, that's all you need".

As I argued with him, Adie was behind me, he was saying "go on Firthy, you tell him".

It wasn't to be, the inspector stood across the front of me and physically barred my way.

I asked him what we were waiting for, he said that we would be able to go in "when the local police get here".

Twenty minutes passed before the local CID inspector arrived. He asked how our patient was doing, as he thought that he was already in the ambulance.

He was amazed when I told him that "Arnold Schwarzenegger over there won't let us near".

He barged up to the inspector and told him in no uncertain terms to go away.

We followed on behind. As we went up the stairs, the new bloke just said "if you need to touch or to move anything, please tell me. Then I can photograph it first".

That wasn't a problem for us.

Upstairs in the attic bedroom, there was a single blue tubular metal framed bed and a small chest of drawers. Laid on the bed was our patient. He was eighteen and he was fully conscious. He was bound hand and foot to the bed frame with cable ties.

There was a really strong urine smell in the room and there were faeces on the mattress. There wasn't even a bottom sheet on the bed, let alone any other bedding.

The patient was only wearing a pair of well stained boxer shorts. He had been in the same position since Sunday evening, it was then almost midnight on Friday.

He had only had a temporary reprieve from his predicament earlier that evening. He had been released from the bed, to make a telephone call to his parents from a remote location. Then he had been brought back. He was only away for half an hour or so.

His hands and feet were hideously swollen. They were like balloons, we needed to cut the ties off and quickly. Photographed in situ first.

We asked the young man for his version of events.

He told us that he had come over from China and was studying at university in London. He had come to his present location with some people that he had just met. To look at properties in the area. He had no real idea where he was in the country.

Following initial pleasant times with them.

He said that he had been tortured and abused. He told us that he had not been fed, although he had been given water through a straw that had been forced down his throat. Through the same straw, his kidnappers had dropped some little white tablets right down the back of his throat, they had made him go to sleep.

The tablets were in a little bottle on the drawers at the side of the bed, all the writing though was in Chinese. We would have to wait till we got to hospital to find out what they were, or did.

He told us what the name of the tablets were in English, but the name didn't match anything that we have listed in the BNF, (British National Formulary).

He went on to tell us, that every night one of his captors, had rung his parents back in Hong Kong to demand money. That they would beat him with a baseball bat, or burn him with cigarettes until he spoke to his parents. The bat was under the bed.

His parents were shipping magnates in Hong Kong, they were multi millionaires. He told us that his captors were all members of a large Triad gang. Most of his story was corroborated by our CID inspector.

Although he had been through such a horrendous ordeal. Other than being extremely dehydrated, all of his observations were within normal ranges.

My two main concerns were; that I have come across the tied wrist scenario before and that patient had only been "tied to his fixture, for under twelve hours". He had gone into kidney failure and had needed dialysis and eventually a transplant. This lad might go the same way.

The other, we needed to know what sort of heart condition he had. His broken English wasn't clear enough. He was trying to tell us about some form of heart surgery, but he didn't have any scarring to show for it.

We needed to speak to his parents. They were aware that he had been found, but had no idea how he was.

That telephone call was made by the police. It clarified things for us and also put the minds of one terrified family, a little more at ease. The family got some very welcome news and long awaited reassurance. They weren't allowed to talk to their son at that stage. They would have to wait until he had spoken at length to the police.

It turned out that when our patient was a young child, he did have a cardiac problem, he had a hole in his heart. That had healed without any surgery and he had been able to live a normal life, it was of no concern now.

We were able to write that issue off, straight away.

We managed to get our patient down from the attic and into the ambulance. He was frightened that his captors would still be outside waiting for him. We did assure him that he was safe and that his frightening ordeal was over.

We told him that there were more armed guards outside for him, than Barrack Obama had. He smiled at that, until we stepped outside into the darkness.

They had all gone, there was just a very dark and eerie silence that met us. There wasn't even one curtain twitching, nosey neighbour, looking out.

He was fine though.

He was kept in hospital for a few days, he had developed a degree of kidney failure and was severely dehydrated. But because his captors had at least been giving him some water, he was expected to make a full recovery before too long.

At least they did that for him.

It must have been a frightening ordeal, I hope that he was able to recover from his psychological issues.

We were told during our statements to the police, that the captors were indeed a well known gang from China. That police from Hong Kong, Interpol and the UK had been involved in looking for our victim. There had been more than twenty people involved in the immediate gang, but only nine had been found and arrested. The others had just simply disappeared out of sight.

Both Adie and I were well suited when the letter arrived from the Crown Prosecution Service, to say that neither of us would be required to give any further evidence in court.

CHAPTER 66

FALLS FROM HEIGHTS.

Falls From Bridges.

There are two particular nasty messy types of jobs that we all hate getting a call to. One is to someone on the railways. The other is a jumper. More often than not, people who have decided to jump from something, usually just jump. They don't generally make a fuss and tell people, they just do it. They are always reported as a fall, until it has been proved otherwise.

I, unfortunately have been to several jumpers in the past.

A memorable lesson from the Coroner.

The first time I went to someone fallen from a bridge, was in the early 1980's. It was actually a call to an unknown incident, at Longroyd Bridge at the bottom of Paddock. I was working with Ray.

Further information came through and that said that a male had been found. It went on "it is believed that he might be dead, he has a head injury".

The call came in at about four in the morning, it had just started to come light on a bright sunny day. It was in the middle of summer. A postman who was on his way to work, had found the patient.

When we got on scene, two policemen were already there.

There was a white male of around forty years of age, sat bolt upright against the wall with his legs outstretched. His head was slumped forward, blood had run from the back of it. Some of the blood had run down his face and it was all around his neck, down his chest and had pooled into his lap. His arms were just resting naturally to his sides.

The wall that he was leaning against, was one of the uprights of the viaduct. There used to be a little shop on that corner, a green grocers shop. It was called Carney's, it was built right up against the wall where he was sat. They called it a "lean to". It was demolished many years ago, there is still some discolouration of the stone where it was though.

The blood was dry, so it appeared that the man could have been there some time.

At the back of his head, he had a significant injury. There was a large wound, the area around it was a boggy mass, consistent with skull fractures.

He also had blood coming out of both ears, that again is a typical sign of a fractured skull, generally the base of the skull. His wound was fairly high up, on the crown of his head.

There was no doubt that the man was dead, he fulfilled the criteria on the yellow card. That was the tool used in the days before we had cardiac monitoring. He had already got signs of rigor mortis present and he had some evidence of post mortem staining.

We had to wait for the coroners officer. So we positioned our ambulance onto the pavement, the police were also in a transit sized van, so that was positioned at the other side of our victim. As such, we were shielding him from the view of passing traffic.

At that time, the coroners officer was a very experienced ex policeman named Bill, he was a lovely chap. Right down to earth, he called a spade a spade.

When he arrived, he listened to us and the police. We told him what we had found and seen etc.

Then Bill asked the question, "ok then, what do you think has happened here?" He went on "do you think he has been assaulted and hit around the head? Or do you think that he might have come from up there?" He pointed up to the top of the viaduct at that time. 70 feet above us.

The police, Ray and myself were of the first opinion. We were under the impression that he had been assaulted and we told him so.

"What makes you all think that then?" He said with a wry grin on his face.

We all agreed that in our opinion, if he had come from the top of the bridge. Which involved a fall of at least eighty to a hundred feet, surely he would have had more injuries. We didn't think that he would just be sat against the wall as he was, unless someone had moved him.

"Right" Bill said. "Let's have a proper look shall we?" The first thing he did was to step back, to take a good look at the scene.

Where the man was, was as near as damn it in the middle of the wall, and yes he was sat up against the wall. First of all, Bill mentioned the bleeding from the ears. He said that it was unusual to be bleeding from both ears, from a single blunt instrument trauma. That was more consistent with a fall from a height.

He looked around, there was an area just to the man's left hand side that looked scuffed. When Bill had pointed it out, we all agreed.

"Now we've seen that area" he said, "let's look at his jacket". Sure enough, all down the left side of the man's back, his jacket was covered in the same white dust.

He then said "now the proof of all proof". The next part of the statement is a little tip, that again I will never forget.

"Let's have a look at his belt shall we". We all looked at each other, "what is he going on about?" Bill lifted up the man's sweater, "just as I thought" he smiled as he said it. "Look".

The man's belt had broken, near to the buckle. It had snapped where the hole is for the tine in the middle of the buckle to go through.

"That's the weakest point" he said. "That can only happen when the body has fallen from a height of at least fifty feet. It occurs when the abdominal contents hit the deck. The abdomen becomes so large for a second, that something has to give. That is usually a belt, it wont happen at any other time".

A very valuable lesson from an expert in his field.

The man had then simply, but eerily, bounced into a sitting position.

When more police arrived, they searched around for, and subsequently found his car. It was near to the back of the Triangle scrap yard.

In the car, the man had left a couple of notes for his family, that were apologising for him taking his own life. From the car's registration details, they found out who he was and that he was from within a mile of the incident.

Unfortunately, it was a very sad, but a plain and simple suicide. Nobody else had been involved.

Ray and I gently lifted the man onto the stretcher and took him to the hospital mortuary.

Scammonden Bridge, the highest around here.

I have been to several people who have threatened to jump from the massive 120 foot middle, of Scammonden Bridge over the M62. Those people, mainly women, have been talked out of their actions by police negotiators.

Their actions cause absolute chaos, sometimes for hours. The motorway has to be closed in both directions, for the whole time the incident goes on.

They used to say that it cost the British economy around a million pounds for each hour that the motorway is shut. That was in the early 1980's, it has been quoted in 2016 that the figure is now nearer to a million pounds per minute!

I have also been to a few people, who hadn't stopped to tell anyone. They had just turned up, parked their car somewhere nearby and jumped.

It is one hell of a long way down. I have stood there and looked over the edge, I certainly couldn't do it. There have been a lot of people over the years who have made that horrendous journey, I haven't heard of even one survivor.

I personally, think it is an extremely selfish way to commit suicide. It affects the lives of not only the patients and their own families, but the lives of anyone who has either witnessed them, or had to deal directly with them.

If a body falls from more than 150 feet, it can explode on impact. You can imagine, someone jumping from the middle of Scammonden Bridge will never be a pretty sight. Witnesses see sights that no member of the public should ever see. Someone then has to remove the body from the scene, again a horrendous task.

Not only the people dealing with the aftermath, but there are literally thousands of people on the M62 at any given moment. A suicide from the bridge could badly affect each and every single one of them, for many years.

Either from them actually witnessing the fall, or from them being held up for many hours in traffic.

Those held up in traffic, are not only missing work, they could perhaps be missing holiday flights.

It has such an unbelievable knock on effect.

An interesting fact though, of all those who have leapt from the bridge at Scammonden. I think it is safe to say, that they have all have gone from the middle.

I have only heard of one person who has actually landed on the carriage way. All the others have landed on the hard (sorry about that, I didn't name it) shoulder.

Some have been a long distance from the bridge. The wind can blow someone a long way, especially when you see how windy it can be at Scammonden.

Quincy here, says he has come from the top.

Another bridge job was at Denby Dale, it was in 2009. There, a man had been found in an open area underneath the viaduct. A woman dog walker had found him, it was a cold and absolutely freezing January morning.

Carl and I had been sent, Nathan was the RRV. Both vehicles arrived together on that job. There was a police car on Denby Dale Road. As we stopped, the female police officer asked us to go round to the other end of the viaduct, on Barnsley Road.

We did as we were asked, on arrival there, there was another female officer. She pointed over the wall, there was a man laid out. He looked from where we were stood, to be in his late sixties. She said that he may have been there all night, but he had only just been found at around eight in the morning. By then, it was just after half past.

She said that could we just confirm death and because it could be suspicious, please could we try not to move him. She said he may have been assaulted and robbed, that scenes of crime officers (SOCO) were on their way.

I said straight away that he had not been assaulted, that he had definitely come from the top of the bridge. I explained that I could see the tell tale sign of a broken belt.

Like I said earlier, never forgotten.

The others hadn't heard the little snippet of wisdom before. Nathan went over to the man to confirm death, that was an easy task. Rigor mortis was fully set in. The man didn't appear to have any other injuries, but as requested, Nathan hadn't tried to roll him to look at his back for any.

When Arielle, one of the current coroners officers arrived. The WPC, who was a more mature member of staff. She had to be for her next comment, said to her that, "Quincy here says he has come from the top" and then she pointed at me.

Arielle asked me, "how can you be certain of that?"

I explained what her predecessor had told me all those years ago. She then replied with "you've been talking to Bill. That's one of the little tips he told me as well. You are absolutely correct, that's where he came from", and she pointed to the bridge.

Again an open car was found nearby, it had got some sealed envelopes for his family. Another sad day all round.

Tower block of flats.

My last personal story of a fall from a height, involves a tower block of flats near to Huddersfield. That was in April 2008. The call was for a young female, who was severely distressed and was laying on top of the barrier of the seventh floor balcony of a Huddersfield tower block.

Due to the job being an ongoing incident, the ambulance service were asked to stand off at a close distance, but out of sight. The RRV was Pamela, the crew was Nula and Annie. They were advised to approach from the back of the flats and to park up and wait. About a hundred yards away.

The police were on the phone to the young lady's sister, she was panicking. The patient was actually laid on top of the balcony's barrier with her arms and legs outstretched in a flying position, before falling to the ground.

When the lady actually came off the balcony and fell to her death, there were only two police officers at the scene itself. They had been stood in the doorway of the flats.

An ambulance just happened to be passing by at the time, it was bright yellow and it had a blue light at each corner. Although they were not flashing at the time and it said in large letters all down the side of it "emergency ambulance", the police flagged it down.

Unfortunately that day and it still goes on, the crew on the vehicle were a non emergency crew. They were at the time what was known as, an urgent tier crew. They were not medically qualified, but they were driving an emergency ambulance.

The crew were a nearly new starter Brendan and Aaron, on his very first day. On the way to his first, but routine patient. They both jumped out of the ambulance and ran to help. When they saw the lady and as was seen in the CCTV footage. They both put their hands on their heads in despair, what the hell could they do?

They did exactly the right thing and the best thing possible. They got a blanket and covered her up. The crew and responder came around the corner. Brendan and Aaron were so relieved, it was only a matter of seconds, but it must have seemed a lifetime.

I, as Operational Supervisor, then turned up to see if I could help. The incident had ended tragically, with the loss of a young life, she was the mother of a very young child.

If it is any consolation to her family, she did not suffer when hitting the ground, she had died instantly. As her body had hit the ground with such tremendous force.

The only part of her that I saw was her hand.

It was extremely windy and the blanket had started to lift. I had gone just to cover her again and to weight the blanket down to prevent any further exposure. A horrendous sight for anyone, let alone the first patient you had ever seen. If that was only her hand, then I could only imagine what the two lads had seen.

My job was to speak to all concerned, and to make sure that they were all ok. To spend a little time away from the scene and to encourage them to talk about it later over a cuppa.

The body, previously covered by a blanket, was covered by a pop up police forensics tent.

Our role at the incident, was then over, all bar the shouting as they say.

Statements had to be given. Brendan and Aaron's details weren't available to the police originally. As they weren't on the ambulance log, because they hadn't actually been sent to the job. So as far as the computer was concerned, they hadn't been there.

As supervisor, I was asked to view the CCTV footage. It had been synchronised with the 999 telephone call to the police. It was an eerie and disturbing experience. My job was to explain from a medical perspective, who was who. Why they had done what they did and when they had done it.

A tragic event with devastating affects on ALL concerned.

If you're gonna do it, do it right!

Another bridge incident that I wasn't involved in, but I knew the crew very well. If the truth had come out at the time, one or both crew members could well have been sacked.

It happened before I started, I believe in the summer of 1980.

The call was to a young man in the river near to Longroyd Bridge, outside what was then Charlie Browns Auto Centre.

He was stood in the water, which was only around eight inches deep. The bridge was about fifteen feet high from the river bed. He was a man in his early twenties.

The crew leant over from Manchester Road and asked him what had happened.

He told them that he had wanted to kill himself and that he had jumped off the bridge.

The only thing he had injured, was his pride. There were dozens of people gathered on the bridge, they were all mocking and laughing at him.

The fire service arrived, they lowered a ladder and the young man climbed up without any assistance. He would be going to hospital for a psychiatric assessment.

When he was getting into the ambulance, one of the crew jokingly said to him. "If you are wanting to kill yourself, that bridge won't do any good. Go and jump off that big bugger there". Pointing to the 70 foot high railway viaduct, just a hundred yards away..

The man was taken up to A&E at HRI. Then later that afternoon, he was transferred to St. Luke's Hospital at Crosland Moor for a full psychiatric examination.

He had been in there for less than half an hour, when he absconded. He walked down the road for about three quarters of a mile.

Yes you guessed it.

He had climbed onto the railway bridge and jumped from the highest point, he landed on Longroyd Lane.

It was the same crew that had been called to attend to him earlier. That second time he didn't walk in to the ambulance, and he didn't go to A&E. The only place that he was going to, was to the hospital mortuary.

There is a need to bite your tongue at times, it is statements like that that can bite you on your bum later.

CHAPTER 67.

THE RAILWAYS.

Rail track incidents.

Another nightmare of a call. Is for any call involving a pedestrian versus a train, it tends to involve some catastrophic injuries. There have been many over the years. It is one incident where people don't threaten to do it, they tend to just do it.

A gruesome fact that has come to light, is that you don't hear of one for a while. Then (pardon the pun) like buses, three will come along at once.

I have been fortunate in the fact that I have not been called to many. The ones that I have been called to, all except one, have involved a human fatality.

Only one person that I have dealt with, has survived.

There was another rail track incident, but that one involved an animal. A large dog, the dog survived and kept on running.

Two of them were at the end of Springwood tunnel, just up from Longroyd Bridge. They were only fifty yards or so, from where the girl had jumped when I broke my ankle. She is the one that survived, but she wasn't "hit" by a train.

Both a fall from a height, and a rail track involved. It was asking for mayhem, fortunately, it didn't turn out that way.

Each one of the other above incidents occurred, when a suicidal patient had waited at the end of the tunnel leading from just outside Huddersfield Railway Station to Springwood.

As soon as the train appeared at the end of the tunnel, they had stepped out straight in front of it.

As you can imagine, a train at speed is not very forgiving. It will cause extreme injury. The sort of injuries that will only be seen at that type of incident, and nowhere else.

It nearly always involves "picking up the pieces".

Needless to say I will not go into too many details of the injuries seen at a rail incident. That is something that no human being needs to be part of through choice.

As well as concern for the family of the deceased, my heart goes out to the train drivers. How could they ever be the same again.

I have been for another rail track incident at Deighton. That was just off the end of the station platform, under the road bridge.

Again, the patient had waited for the train to arrive. Then as soon as the train appeared, he stepped straight out from the side of the bridge. The train driver didn't stand a chance.

A train, even though it has emergency brakes fitted, cannot stop in any where near the same time or distance as a car. From applying emergency brakes to stopping is still a phenomenal distance.

If the train driver has seen you, it will already be too late for them to stop, he/she will be unable to avoid a collision.

"We need a hand!"

The first rail track incident that I was called to attend, was way back in 1981. It happened between Paddock Head and the viaduct at Milnsbridge. The train involved, had hit a patient at a speed in excess of 55mph. The patient, we were told, had virtually exploded on impact.

We were the second ambulance to attend. The first ambulance, had collected and removed the body and then taken it to the hospital mortuary.

There had been a problem, the body wasn't complete, a hand and most of the forearm was missing!

When we got there, we parked at where the old Paddock and Milnsbridge Railway Station used to be on Lowergate, opposite the junction with Meg Lane.

The police were there still on scene and the train was still in situ on the viaduct. The front of the train had hit the patient near to the bridge where Clough Lane goes over the line. The viaduct, is where the train had managed to come to a stop. Well over a quarter of a mile.

Some distance eh!

The police had already been searching for about an hour, we had to help, to try and recover it. After around half an hour, my colleague Fred shouted out. He had found it. There had to be photographs taken at the location, before we could move it.

It was around three o'clock in the afternoon, and I remember it was a Saturday.

Due to all the emergency services activity, it had created quite a spectacle. There were many onlookers everywhere. They were leaning all over the wall from Lowergate. Particularly they were stood on top of Cuckoo Bridge, the pedestrian footbridge from the back of the old St, Brigid's Church.

It was close to that bridge that Fred had found the hand and arm. We placed it inside a pillow case and walked back down the tracks to where we had parked, carrying our gruesome find with us.

We didn't have a ticket!

This next job was in 2006, with my old mate Carl. We had started the night shift at 21:00hrs, yes another night. Shortly after starting our shift, a message came in over the radio.

Reports of "something" had been hit by a train, possibly human, somewhere inside the Springwood tunnel.

We had to rendezvous at the main entrance to the railway station in Huddersfield. When we arrived, we were met by the station master.

There were the police, British transport police and a fire crew. We were given a short briefing.

An express train from Manchester airport had arrived at Huddersfield Railway Station. The driver had reported that he had just entered the tunnel at the Longroyd Bridge end, when he thought that he had hit someone or something.

It needed checking out.

Carl and I armed ourselves with his orange paramedic box, containing life saving drugs, fluids and means of administering. A first aid kit, just in case. We also had our combined cardiac, defibrillator, blood pressure, blood sugar and oxygen monitor. We had a bag and mask to resuscitate, and were both armed with torches.

The station master received the all clear, all trains had been stopped from entering the tunnels from all directions.

We had to enter the tunnel from the Huddersfield railway station end and then search in the pitch black for a body. Hopefully still alive, but probably would not be. A party of us, I think there was fifteen of us in all. Set off and ventured into the darkness, the unknown.

Walking along the track is difficult enough, in the dark, it was nigh on impossible. We were carrying heavy tackle, shining our torch from left to right, up and down. Looking, in the hope that we didn't really want to see anything. The last thing that I wanted to see was a head with a pair of eyes looking back at me.

When Carl looked up, he stopped me. "Look, where is everybody?" I looked around, where were all the others searching with us? They were a hell of a long way behind us, we might as well have been on our own.

The tunnel is 726 yards long, almost half a mile, it felt a bloody site longer that night.

As we got around halfway, we walked under the Springwood ventilation shafts. It was a pitch black night, there wasn't even a shaft of light showing. But there was a sudden blast of freezing cold air, it didn't half make us jump.

As we jumped, we disturbed the bats. There must have been thousands of them fluttering all around our heads, it was a bloody awful experience.

We got towards the far end of the tunnel, probably the last fifty yards or so, when we found some blood. There was a pool around the size of my hand.

Everybody got together, the search became more intense. We saw more blood, not vast amounts, but enough to be concerned about. We eventually reached the far end of the tunnel.

There, in the blood we could definitely see paw prints. Then we saw it, a really large German Shepherd dog. It was limping. When it saw us, it barked a few times and then it was off.

Running like mad down the lines, towards Paddock and Manchester!

We had to call it quits.

We all decided that the dog must have been what the train driver had heard.

Wounded, but at least it was fit enough to run away.

On the other line, parked up outside the tunnel, was a train heading in towards the station at Huddersfield. We all thought that we would be able to just climb on board and get a lift back.

No such luck!

The station master said that we didn't have tickets, therefore we would not be insured, "health and safety and all that". He waved the train off and we had to watch the red lights on the back of the train getting smaller and smaller in the distance.

Before we set off towards the station, Carl and me hid our kit beneath the undergrowth, not too far from the bottom of Gledholt Bank. We weren't going to carry that lot all the way back through the bloody tunnel.

Our arms already felt like they were four foot long and that we were dragging our knuckles on the floor behind us looking like some green orangutan, in a hi visibility jacket.

We walked all the way back to the station and following a short debrief, we got into the ambulance and drove back to the bottom of Gledholt Bank to collect our kit.

We were knackered and frozen.

A short climb up the banking and we were reunited with our stuff.

Then back to station for a well earned cuppa!

Too many ego's and not enough care!

Another night in October 2015, it was a strange shift. I was working until two in the morning with a fairly new bloke, Evan. I had known Evan's dad from his time as a police officer. Since he has retired from the police, he has been employed as a part time bearer, based at the Taylor Funeral Service with Wendy.

We had a call to attend at Brighouse railway station. The call was very vague, it reported that a train had hit something or someone. That had happened somewhere at the side of the tracks, between Brighouse and Dewsbury.

The whereabouts of the victim were unknown.

Initially we went to the road above Brighouse Railway Station, we would meet there to liaise with the British Transport police. The police helicopter was overhead, using its heat seeking cameras to try and locate our victim.

A paramedic RRV arrived and shortly afterwards the duty Clinical Supervisor arrived. Straight away he questioned as to why we were not on the tracks.

At that point in time, we had no idea where the victim could be. The transport police were searching the track sides, the helicopter still had no luck.

There was also a similar search that had started at Mirfield heading towards us. After speaking to the train driver, that was as narrow an area as he could pin down.

After half an hour or so, a message came back to us from the transport police. The message was that a female had been found and that she was alive, but her arm had almost been severed. She was described as being conscious, but said to be in "EXCRUCIATING PAIN!"

The patient had been found a good three quarters of a mile away from where we had been parked, heading towards Cooper Bridge.

We moved down to the industrial estate and parked right next to the railway tracks.

The C.S. collared Evan and they took the large green medical bag and oxygen, then they set off on foot down the side of the tracks.

The RRV and myself were getting the rest of the required kit out of the vehicle. We got the cot on wheels and the scoop stretcher in case we needed to carry our patient for some distance. We took some blankets for the patient. We also had our cardiac monitor/defibrillator.

As we were about to set off down the tracks, two more paramedics from our Hazardous Area Response Team (HART) arrived. They asked what extra information we had got. After telling them, then they set off after the C.S. and Evan.

The RRV and I were able to wheel the stretcher along a path for about half the distance, then we had to carry the gear the rest of the way to where the patient was.

When we arrived, the patient had already had specialist dressings (celox gauze, impregnated with haemostatic granules to stem heavy bleeding) applied to her armpit. The wound which had been ripped open was where the wheel of the train had actually run over her arm. It was only the skin keeping the limb attached.

She was still screaming in PAIN!

There were four paramedics around the patient, the updated call that came in from the transport police. Before we left our vehicles, stated that she was in "EXCRUCIATING PAIN". Not one of them had taken any morphine along with them.

My personal radio went again, it was Dr. Andy, who is a local A&E consultant. He is also one of the doctors who work on the Yorkshire Air Ambulance. He, along with a couple of other doctors, will turn out from home to attend at serious accidents. Such as this one. He asked if he was required and if there was anything that he could bring from the car with him.

I asked him if he could bring some serious pain relief, either morphine or ketamine.

Our patient needed some desperately.

He was not happy, not one of the attending paramedics had been able to give the patient anything other than paracetamol and ibuprofen.

He gave the girl some ketamine.

Which is an instant acting and extremely effective, pain relief.

The patient, from being hit by the train, to being found by the police, had been over three quarters of an hour. Then, staff had been with her for another three quarters of an hour before pain relief of any substance, was given.

Up until the arrival of the doctor, she had only been given two paracetamol, and two ibuprofen.

That was simply not good enough! It was embarrassing and pathetic!

In my opinion, that was simply due to having far too many ego's, and not enough care.

It was then a mad dash to LGI for emergency treatment at our Regional Trauma Centre.

One of the HART team asked me to drive, "fast and I mean really fast" he said. As if I'd never done it before and then he said sarcastically, "can you manage that?"

I gave him the look that Tommy taught me so well. Who the hell did he think he was? Some of the HART team, (I hasten to add, not all). Have got their heads stuck that far up their own backside, that they forget where they have come from.

They are only a cog in the overall wheel of care, just like the rest of us.

No better, no worse.

I did drive fast to Leeds and safely, it took me just under seventeen minutes to get to the LGI.

He said "not bad, but it could have been quicker!"

I said "well I had to drive steady really, as two silly buggers dressed in green were stood up every bit of the way!"

His mate acknowledged that it had been a smooth ride, something I pride myself on. And yes they had both been able to stand ALL THE WAY.

I couldn't resist it, I shouldn't have done, but I did.

I then went on "and I was eating my sandwiches and didn't want to spill my drink!"

That was true as well, I shouldn't really admit to it though.

I had had my sandwich on the journey, but I had to get Evan to open my bottle, I couldn't manage that at the speed I was driving.

I managed to drink it all though.

CHAPTER 68.

THE DREADED DRINK.

Alcohol and ambulance staff.

We have had our share of drinkers in the service over the years. B had two litres of cider just to get out of bed. He would have another bottle mid shift and many a time, he would have had a third one before the end of his shift.

T came in to work one night when he was so drunk, that he didn't even see the pool table and fell right over it. Thankfully, his was only a temporary issue while going through a marriage break up.

D was so drunk one night whilst at work, that she couldn't be woken up, she had fallen asleep in a chair in the mess room. Mark, one of my fellow Station Officers at the time, had to bring two of the District Nurses down from their office upstairs to assist.

Another night, after drinking 12 bottles of Barley Wine, the same D was stopped by the police for speeding on Halifax Road. Unbelievably she was on her way to work. She didn't take kindly to being stopped, so she smacked the police officer right in the face.

That was the end of her service!

L was well known for his liking of a drink. One afternoon, (before my time), he was driving down Westbourne Road at speed on an emergency call, when a woman pedestrian stepped straight out in front of him. He stopped on a sixpence and avoided her.

It was witnessed by some police officers and he was congratulated on his lightening quick reactions. In his own words to them, "it's a good job I'd had a drink. If I hadn't have had a drink, I wouldn't have seen her!"

I am sure they thought he was winding them up, how little they knew.

Another time. L attended at a cardiac arrest patient. It was inside the indoor market in Huddersfield. They had been working unsuccessfully on the lady for some time and so L and his colleague decided that they would have to cut and run.

In those days, there were no lift or ramps fitted onto the ambulances. You picked up the stretcher with the patient on and lifted the whole lot up and into the back of the ambulance.

L had already had a couple of drinks and he couldn't manage. The lady was tipped off the stretcher and landed in a heap in the middle of the footpath. (Again, before my time). The shock had the same effect as the then, only dreamed of in the future defibrillator. Her heart started and she survived.

How could the boss sack him for saving a life? He managed to get away with it. It was covered up.

Nobody else got to know about it at the time.

The last and final time for L, he had called at a pub in Lindley on his way home from work. As he left to drive home towards Outlane, he saw the police car at the end of Laund Road.

They were waiting for him, he had been warned several times by "friends in the police" that he was being watched.

Thinking that he was being clever, he made the decision to pull into Maplin Drive. It was an earlier turning. He could wait there, until they had gone.

Wrong!

He had already passed that junction. He was in such a state, that he hadn't realised. He pulled off the road, he then crossed the grass verge and ran through a low garden wall. He and his car then dropped six foot onto the front lawn.

Get out of that!

The police saw what happened. When they arrived he was sat on the grass, still in his ambulance uniform. He had pushed his uniform hat to the back of his head, quite a signature move for L and had lit a cigarette.

He was arrested, charged with drink driving and then sent to court. He was lucky in the fact that as he had only three months before his retirement, the police managed to delay his case until he had actually retired. Therefore he had no loss of his pension.

He lost his license and was banned from driving for three years. He actually gave his license up, sold his car and never drove again.

We had a joint retirement do for L, along with Hal and Ivan. It was at the Commercial pub in Paddock. The woman from the indoor market in Huddersfield was a surprise guest for L.

H, was not so fortunate. Only a couple of months after L had retired, he was in a different pub in Lindley. He actually had a further distance to drive home, than he would have had, if he was to have walked.

Anyway, he unwisely decided that he knew best. After drinking several pints, he got into his famous old white VW beetle. As he pulled pulled out from the kerb, he hit a car and sent it crashing straight through the concrete bus shelter across the road.

It was twenty minutes to four in the afternoon. Only ten minutes earlier that very shelter had been full of children from the nearby junior school. The consequences just don't bear thinking about.

He was convicted, banned from driving and also sacked from his job. He had nine months to go to his retirement. The case couldn't be delayed so long. I don't know how much, but it did cost him some or possibly most of his pension, it was never made public what happened.

I can only say that he was very bitter against WYMAS for what "they had done to him".

There was only one person to blame there!
A whole career wasted!

CHAPTER 69.

———————

THE MEANING OF LIFE.

Childbirth.

After more than thirty six years in the service, I have been called to and have been involved in many, many maternity calls.
More often than not, a call to a woman in labour is just that. We pull up outside the house, we have a brief conversation with the patient and do a set of basic observations. Then they walk out, they sit in the ambulance and we all enjoy the journey to hospital. At the other end they walk out and into the hospital.

Known up and down the country among ambulance services for many years, as a "Maternitaxi".

Every now and then, for whatever reason, the mother gets herself caught out and we have a bit of a panic on. Again, usually we can get things sorted. Then we can have a pleasant, if perhaps quicker, journey to the hospital.

On a few other occasions, it becomes quite obvious that we are going to be getting our sleeves rolled up and getting involved in a wonderful adventure.

Every now and then, and thankfully it is only now and again, these wonderful events can end up becoming an awful tragedy.

Here are some of my most memorable events, as you will see, each of them has a different occasion to cover.

They are only the tip of the iceberg, there have been many more.

My first delivery.
The first baby was in 1982. I was working with Ray, it was in the early hours of the morning. We had been called to an address in Golcar.

As Ray pulled up outside the address, I was just about to get out of the cab, when I saw her. The woman in her nightdress was running down the street, with her hands between her legs, her legs bowed like she had spent all her life on horseback.

"Hurry up" she cried, "it's here". She had been to a pay phone, in a big red box up the road. Do you remember them?

We got her into the ambulance and she laid on the stretcher. It's quite a bizarre experience to ask a stranger to take her knickers off so that you can have a look. We did look and there were no signs of delivery at that stage.

Sighs of relief all round.

We set off to hospital, she was still laid on the stretcher. The lady was breathing deeply on the entonox (or gas and air, our analgesic gas). We had got a little nearer, "it's here now", she said.

463

Another look, it was her waters that had gone, there was a waterfall of amniotic fluid running off the end of the stretcher on to the floor. There was also a very small amount of blood and a little mucous.

Still no signs of baby, but we were getting a lot closer though.

By the Bay Horse pub at Lindley she really changed, her breathing altered. She was arching her back and she was pushing.

I asked Ray to stop, I couldn't see where we were. "Not stopping now" he said, "we're almost there, we're at the Bay Horse roundabout!" He did slow down though as I was stood up in the back. Ray asked for a midwife to meet us outside the A&E doors.

The lady was pushing harder and I could see the top of baby's head. It was a new experience for me. A couple more pushes and baby's head was delivered. She stopped and took a few more deep breaths.

I felt much better, then I told her to push again. "Harder, harder", sure enough the magic happened.

A new life had arrived into the world, it was a boy. I wrapped him in a nice warm towel, then handed him to mum. As I was looking at him, he started to cry, it was the most wonderful sound that I had ever heard.

Of course later that changed when I was present at the birth of my own sons.

I put him on mums chest and wrapped them both up even more. We were at the hospital and the waiting midwife stepped into our ambulance, where she clamped and cut the umbilical cord. She wrapped the baby up again and gave him to me to hold.

I was made up!

The midwife was then able to check mum. All was fine, so off we all went, up to the delivery suite.

Mum thanked me, she said "you were ever so calm, how many have you delivered?"

Tommy's mucky duck syndrome had worked again.

I said to her "including this one, one".

I never heard from, or saw either of them again, but I know I'll never forget them.

The strange thing at the time that stuck in my mind, there was no mention at any time of the baby's father.

Now it is quite common for the dad to have moved on.

She's in there, upstairs, I'm off!

Another time working with Carl, it was just after midnight. We had been called to the bottom end of Dalton, that was a maternity call. On the way to the address, I remember saying to Carl. "I hope she's not having it, I've got a blinding headache".

As we slowed right down and were trying to pick out the house numbers in the dark. We saw a man coming out head first through the privet bushes. He stopped us and said "she's in there, upstairs, I'm off". Then he was, off.

That looked ominous, I ran upstairs. As I looked into the bedroom, the man's wife I'll call her Sally was laid on her back. Her chin was on her chest, her knees were drawn up and she was screaming.

Carl said "I'll get the entonox and matty pack" (maternity delivery pack). Then he ran back downstairs. As I looked at Sally, she still had her knickers on. I helped her to remove them, then I shouted back to Carl "don't bother, it's too late".

The baby was already being delivered, there was no stopping her. Only two more contractions and he was there. It was another little boy.

Then the door burst open and it was her husband, he was back. He had been to get Sally's mum. They both stood there open mouthed.

Then another sleepy little face appeared on the landing, it was their two year old daughter. Her face was amazing, her mouth open that wide that she looked like she could swallow the baby whole.

She couldn't speak, she just walked into the room, there was not a word spoken from anybody.

Then we were all shocked into further silence.

The little girl leaned forward, she gently kissed her newborn baby brother on the forehead and simply said to him "hello".

Dry eyes? I don't think so, I didn't see one!

Selfie?

I used to see father and son at the Huddersfield Town football matches regularly. They were fanatics. It was always nice to see them. The young one always made himself known, he was growing up fast.

Just before Christmas 2015, I saw them both at HRI. The young one ran across the main entrance to greet me as he would normally do. That time he had a big bunch of flowers in his hand, I said the usual "I didn't know you cared!"

Suddenly he was in tears, they're not for you. "Come here, have a selfie with me" he said. I did, I'd never had one of those before.

As he took the photograph, "my wife wouldn't believe me without it" he told me. "She has just had our first child, two hours ago". It was a little boy as well. "We were all talking about you not an hour ago".

Wow! I was thrilled for them both.

Dad was struggling a bit, he was walking with two sticks and he was starting to look old. I congratulated him on becoming a grandad.

As usual I asked him to give my regards to Sally. She had been suffering with really bad rheumatoid arthritis and her mobility had been severely impaired, the last time I saw her.

We need the flying squad!

Mark and me were called to a possible miscarriage, it was at an address away from Huddersfield. The woman was reportedly only eighteen weeks pregnant.

As we stopped outside the address, the man of the house met us. "You're too late" he said, "you've missed it, he's just been born!"

Eighteen weeks gestation, is far too early. We both ran in and there on the sofa, was a woman holding a mini baby.

I had never seen anything so small. It would have easily fitted into one hand.

The baby appeared to be struggling to breathe.

In those days, we had a little plastic concertina bottle with the smallest of face masks fitted. It was called a "Samson" resuscitator. I connected it to 100% oxygen and gently squeezed it between two fingers and my thumb to aid things along.

Mark called for the "flying squad" to attend. That usually consisted of a paediatrician, a midwife and a small incubator. They would arrive in another ambulance.

As I used the oxygen to resuscitate, the baby seemed to pink up. Both Mark and I were beginning to think things were looking up.

The house was an absolute disgrace, there must have been a dozen people in the room. The room was full of animals, there were at least four cats and two dogs. The animal mess was all over the floor, which also had an animal hair carpet.

I was knelt on the floor, trying to help the little mite. The carpet was wet.

The team came in on the second ambulance, they had only taken about six minutes from our request.

It was an excellent response.

The paediatrician that arrived was a junior one, he only took one look at the baby. He clamped the cord and cut it and he then wrapped the baby in a towel. He said "I'm sorry but the baby has died, it's far too small to survive". Then he walked out with it.

That was it, he left in the other ambulance with the baby.

We were all stunned. The midwife stayed with us, the placenta was then delivered and we took mum to the hospital.

It bothered me did that, it bothered me so much that I didn't sleep at all during the night.

That doesn't happen too often, thankfully.

I was due at work at two that following afternoon, but I couldn't wait. I went in the morning, we still lived at Lindley at the time and so I only had to walk across the road to the hospital. I went up to the children's ward to see the junior paediatrician for an explanation.

He was dumbfounded. "I didn't did I?" He explained that because he was only a junior paediatrician, he had been on call and he had actually been on duty for the whole of the forty eight hours of the weekend. Not a wink of sleep, it wouldn't be allowed now. (Would it?). Even though, he said that it was no excuse for his actions.

He brought in his boss, the consultant paediatrician.

When he had explained to him what had happened, the consultant went barmy.

He apologised profusely.

I said that it was the family that needed the apology. I told them both, that the man of the house would have killed the junior doctor, if he had been able to get hold of him the previous day.

Before they set off together to see the family, mum was still a patient in hospital. It was explained to me, all about the lung development of a foetus.

They went on to tell me that what I had seen and thought was breathing, was actually blood flow from mum to baby via the umbilical cord.

The baby's lungs hadn't developed anywhere near sustainability at that early stage. When Mark arrived at work for the same shift, he greeted me with "you bugger". What had I done?

He told me that he hadn't slept all night and had gone to find that doctor. "You beat me to it, you bugger!"

It wasn't just me then!

It's like a bullfrog!

When working with Clifford, we had been sent for a maternity call to an address in the Newsome area.

When we entered the house, we were both taken by surprise. The woman was laid on the floor and she was already pushing. The baby was actually overdue by a couple of days.

It had been a planned home delivery. Mum had rung for the midwife, but she had been delayed on another delivery and so the ambulance was sent.

Birth was imminent, Clive turned up the heat on the gas fire. "No good bringing a young 'un into 't cold" he said.

Each time mum pushed, what appeared to be a bullfrog's balloon neck appeared. Her waters hadn't broken, the sack, under pressure was ballooning out of the woman. It was full of amniotic fluid. When she stopped pushing, the bag was sucked back up inside mum.

Do I burst it? Or do I leave it? Clifford was chasing the midwife up, over the phone.

After about fifteen minutes of the same thing being repeated several times, the baby's head was delivered. As soon as we saw the head, the sac disappeared again, leaving the baby with a bag over its face.

I knew then that I had no choice.

I tried to get hold of the slippery gossamer like skin. I couldn't grip it, no matter how I tried. Clifford said "use your teeth!"

I gagged, I thought I would vomit.

Then I remembered, my trusty Swiss Army knife, it's only little, but it does have a handy pair of super sharp scissors. I've had it for years, it has come to my aid so many times.

One little nick from them and the waters gushed across our makeshift sponge of towels. Most of the waters were soaked up, the skin of the sac burst open and the baby was born.

It was a little girl, "not another girl", mum said. "I've already got four of them", she had been hoping for a boy.

Then there was a little applause from behind us, the midwife had arrived.

I asked her "how long have you been there?" She replied "long enough". She then examined both mum and baby.

All was ok and they would be able to stay at home. Grandma brought the other girls in to welcome their new arrival.

I asked the midwife "when should I have burst the sac?"

She replied that we could have done that "at any stage, but once the baby's head was born". Then as I had thought, "there was no option".

It was a strange one.

That's asylum seeking!

The next maternity call, was one of the most emotional cases that I have ever dealt with. I was with Matt, it wasn't long before he qualified as a paramedic.

Our call was to a council property in Dalton. We were met at the door by a very tall, skinny and dark African man. He stood about six foot eight inches tall. He couldn't speak very much English, but he ushered us upstairs.

There was a lady on the bed. Obviously very heavily pregnant.

She was physically pushing with all her might. But she was completely exhausted, nothing seemed to be happening.

On a closer examination, the baby didn't even look as though it was engaged in the pelvic girdle. Every time she pushed, her whole abdomen tightened. The baby appeared to be getting pushed out to one side, over the top of her pelvis.

She was getting weaker and weaker with each contraction.

The community midwife had rung in to our Comms, she was still about twenty minutes away.

What could we do?

I had to try something. At the next contraction, I placed my hands on the bump. I could definitely feel the head, the back and its legs. The head was down but it was pushing sideways. As the next contraction started, I applied some gentle pressure to the baby as she pushed.

I wasn't sure if I should have been doing that, but I felt that I had to do something. Right or wrong, it worked, the baby definitely moved into a better position. It seemed to just drop into the right place.

It gave the mother some encouragement. She started to push again. At the second push, her waters burst with a gush and I could see the top of baby's head. Another push and things were moving. One more and the head was delivered.

The mother rested briefly, then another push and the shoulders were visible. I encouraged her to push again, fantastic. A little boy had been brought into the world.

The baby cried, boy oh boy, did he cry!

I got the sterile scissors, (not my trusty knife that time) and asked dad to cut the cord.

His face was a picture.

Matt wrapped the baby up warm and when he passed him to dad. That smile was the largest I had ever seen. Then that very tall African man sat down and he cried.

It was a wonderful moment.

He then started talking, although with broken English. He told us that they were French speaking Africans, from Ruanda.

His wife was a school teacher where all the troubles had been.

All of the children of their village had been herded into the school and were shot with machine guns. Following that, the building had been set on fire.

The lady and her eldest daughter, a fourteen year old had escaped. They were evacuated. Dad had managed to find them and they had sought asylum in the United Kingdom.

They had two younger children, they had been in the school when the massacre had taken place.

Due to the lady being in the latter stages of pregnancy, their asylum application had been very quick, it had been facilitated by the Red Cross Society.

The couple and their daughter had only been in Huddersfield for four weeks. Then just last week and out of the blue. The Red Cross had reunited them with one of the two younger children, their daughter. She had managed to escape before the fire, she had been shot, but it was only a minor glancing wound.

Their son sadly, had been killed.

The new birth had helped their family become complete again.

The midwife arrived and both mum and baby were checked over, they were absolutely fine. The placenta was delivered and we all went to HRI, just for piece of mind for the family. There were no real medical or physical needs, but after what they had been through, we thought it for the best.

That job to me, reflected MY true interpretation of asylum!

Back seat delivery.

One Saturday night, just outside the A&E department at HRI. A car pulled up extremely quickly, Carl and me were just putting our trolley back into the ambulance.

The driver of the car sounded his horn and shouted for assistance. His wife was having a baby. Carl went back into A&E, to bring a hospital trolley outside, he also brought out some nursing staff with him.

It was a health care assistant that climbed in to the back of the car. The next minute, I don't know how she did it, but she came out of the back door on the other side of the car. She must have climbed over the pregnant lady.

"She's having it, now!"

She was almost screaming.

I had a look at the mother, as Carl brought the trolley around to the far side of the car. She was crowning, I could clearly see the top of the baby's head. We had been hoping to get mum inside, before the baby was born.

As the woman dug her heels into the rear seat to lift herself out, the baby's head appeared, she was going nowhere.

The matty pack (a kit for delivery, sterile towels, waterproof sheet, cord clamps, cord scissors and even a tub for the placenta), was grabbed from the ambulance.

One of the nurses opened it. I don't know what she did, but it seemed to explode. The contents went all over the floor, it's a damn good job that we carry two of them.

There was by then quite a crowd outside A&E, they were wanting to know what was causing such a commotion. A couple of porters were holding blankets up over the car, to give the patient as much privacy as possible.

The baby, a little girl was delivered. I clamped the cord and cut it. Then I wrapped the baby up and ran inside with my precious little bundle, to a tremendous amount of applause.

Inside, a midwife had just arrived. I took the baby into the resus room, which was just inside the A&E doors.

I left baby with her.

Carl and the other staff, had got mum onto the trolley and were bringing her inside.

All the nursing staff took over then.

As we were cleaning up, a young lad, around twenty years of age came up to us. He asked where mum and baby were, we told him that they had gone up to the maternity ward.

He then produced a carrier bag, they had had a whip round in the waiting areas. There was over seventy pounds in the bag, for the new baby.

I took it up to the family on Delivery Suite. Dad then came back down with me to A&E, to thank everybody.

A couple of days later, the dad came back to A&E. He had been looking for me, but I was off duty. He saw one particular member of staff, who will still remain nameless.

However, the dad gave him a large bottle of Glen Morangie whiskey in a presentation tin. He then asked him to give it to me personally, as a thank you.

Instead of doing as he was asked.

Our wonderful paramedic, told every man and his dog about it first. Even though at that stage, I knew nothing about it. He told anybody listening, that I was accepting gratuities. He didn't give it to me, he gave it straight to my then manager, Janet.

She told me in no uncertain terms, that if I was to accept it as a gift. I would be in contravention of my conditions of employment and would therefore be subject to disciplinary action.

I told her that I would accept the gift, but that it would not be for me and that I would be using it for a charity presentation.

I personally cannot stand whiskey in any shape or form. That last bit being perfectly true, I can't stand the stuff.

It was then allowed.

What an interfering arse he is!

He was deliberately trying to stir up trouble. One day, one day. My time will come! The pointed horns of that good old Yorkshire bull, will be ready and waiting.

The planned charity event, fell through due to lack of support. All donated items were distributed to other deserving causes.

The cause to gain the whiskey, Carl's retirement do. Carl loved a wee dram now and again.

Stuff our nameless paramedic!

I went up to Marsden a couple of days later to see the family. To say thank you and I took them a "Para-Ted" teddy bear for the little one. I told the family to call the bear Carl, the same as I did with every "Para-Ted" that I gave out.

The family were thrilled with it, they even took my photo holding the baby and then sent me a copy.

Quick, the football's on, do you want a beer?

This maternity call was just crazy, from the word go. It seemed like I was being set up, for some crazy prank TV show.

The call was to a fairly new housing development near Mirfield.

A lady was having a home water birth. Unfortunately, the midwife's car had broken down and she was awaiting the breakdown services.

I was working as Operational Supervisor. The call was "would I go and make sure that everything was ok with the family and stay with them until the midwife could get there".

As I pulled up outside the house, I was met by the mother's partner, a very smartly dressed female. She was around thirty years old, she spoke English, but had a strong underlying foreign accent. That turned out to be from Finland, as was her partner.

I was welcomed into the house, the mother was sat in her dressing gown and they had both been kept fully informed of the situation. They were more than happy with me being there "just in case anything went wrong".

Yes they were a lesbian couple and they were very open about their relationship. The mother had conceived using a sperm donor.

At the back of the lounge was a large inflatable hot tub, normally seen outside on a decking area. Where this one usually resided. It was a jacuzzi type and was already bubbling away. (No soap though, just warm water).

The mother was already having slight contractions when I got there, they were every five or six minutes apart, but not very strong. Very soon, they were starting to get stronger and more frequent. She decided that it was time to get into the tub and did so. She was wearing a long tee shirt.

Not before insisting that her partner get me to help move the television.

The football was due to start. It was a World Cup qualifier Finland against Germany, they were both absolutely football crazy.

They couldn't see the screen from where the tub was and it would be easier to move the television than the tub.

I wasn't ready for what happened next. The partner had gone upstairs and when she came down she was stark naked. She was totally unashamed and then she also got into the tub. The mother removed her long tee shirt and she too was totally naked.

There were four seats in the tub, they were both sat there glued to the screen ready for the football.

It was so surreal, me sat watching football on the television with two naked ladies just at the side of me in a hot tub.

The whistle blew and the game kicked off, the partner asked if I would mind going to the fridge and bringing a couple of beers over and to get myself one if I wanted.

They were then both drinking beer from a bottle, I was getting even more sure that it was some kind of television prank show.

Surely it couldn't be happening.

Could it?

The mother started getting restless, her pains were getting stronger. She was not drinking the beer, but had started using the entonox quite vigorously.

She said that she was feeling the urge to push.

The partner then got out of the tub and then she said to me quite candidly. "Right it's your turn now, you need to get in with her".

That couldn't be right, I had only seen a water birth on television but I was sure that the midwife didn't get in the tub as well.

I was as sure as hell that I was staying dry on the outside.

I leaned over the side and checked on mum, sure enough, I could see the top of baby's head.

The partner, still naked, passed me my matty pack. Which I opened in readiness. I asked her to get me the blankets that were on the table and a couple of towels ready to dry the baby.

The partner by then had put on a dressing gown, as mum was starting to push. She was leaning on the side of the tub, in an all fours position. She pushed again, baby's head delivered.

Mum paused for just a few seconds before pushing again with all her might. Then it happened, the baby came straight out. I held the baby in my hands as mum sort of stepped over the cord, she repositioned herself back on one of the edge seats in the tub.

I was then able to offer baby up to mum's breast and she cuddled the baby to her. I was giving the baby a full check over, it was a beautiful and healthy little girl.

The partner had got naked again and had climbed back into the tub with mum. They kissed and cuddled with their new baby. I clamped the cord, then gave the scissors to the partner who eagerly cut through the cord.

The couple had a camera on the table and asked me to take a couple of pictures of all three of them together. One of the pictures had both of the women raising a bottle of beer celebrating the birth.

It was all very odd.

The midwife knocked on the door, I was so pleased to see her. I had been so much out of my comfort zone. The baby was given to me, to dry and then to wrap in the warm blankets. The partner got out of the tub and just sat on the edge as mum was being examined.

She then held the baby to her and was cuddling her, but she still had one eye on the football.

Mum was absolutely fine, baby was checked over next by the midwife, she was fine too.

I needed a wash myself. After asking permission, I went upstairs to the bathroom to get cleaned up. All over the house were pictures of the two women, they were nearly always naked. Both in and around the home and on holiday. The ones up the sides of the staircase were large framed pictures.

It turned out that they were both devout naturists and wherever possible, they spent their life in the nude.

As I was about to leave the house, I was given a bottle of beer to take with me, to enjoy later.

I'll be honest, after that, I was ready for a drink!

As I was leaving, the final whistle blew. Finland had lost 2-1 to Germany.

I had been there in that strange situation for just over two hours. What a strange world we live in. Some people have no shame.

I think I was the only one that was embarrassed.

Less than 800 grams.

It was early December in 2010. Another maternity call came in, to attend at a block of flats in Elland. It was another job in the early hours of the morning, at around half three or four o'clock.

I was working with Azim from Halifax. The message "BBA" (born before arrival) came down the mobile data terminal. When we got there, there was a taxi driver waiting for us. He had been called originally to take the lady to hospital, with abdominal pains.

When he had got there, mum had already delivered the baby in the stairwell. Then she had had to removed her nightdress to wrap her newborn up. She was sat there frozen and almost naked. The taxi driver had used his jacket to cover mum and then had called us.

The baby was tiny, mum had only been twenty two weeks pregnant. We had to run and quickly. The cord was cut and the baby was wrapped in a very warm blanket. I took the baby quickly into the warm ambulance. Azim was getting mum.

Mum was very matter of fact, she just seemed to cough hard and the placenta arrived. Then she just literally picked it up and walked out of the flats and into the ambulance with it.

After covering mum and baby with more blankets, she shouted her thanks and admiration to the taxi driver.

He had been brilliant.

A full pre alert was given to the birth centre at Halifax, I told them I needed an incubator at the door and that they only had four minutes to be ready.

We raced in, the baby was pink and mother was fine. Baby was breathing really well on her own, but I had placed some supplemental oxygen running across her face.

It was another little girl.

They were ready and waiting for us at the hospital. The midwife was Aggie, she was our midwife when Wendy was having Adrian.

The baby weighed in at less than eight hundred grams, that's about one and three quarter pounds in my language. She was really small and very premature. Eighteen weeks early in fact.

The next night, we rang the special care baby unit (SCBU), to see how the little one was doing.

The duty sister asked why we had rung.

I told her that obviously due to the little ones size, and her early appearance, that we were concerned.

Her reply, "you might be, but let's say that our consultants aren't!" She then said "does that make you feel any better?"

I don't think the conversation needed any more. Baby was kept in SCBU until her actual due birth date, then she went home and was absolutely fine.

Happy days!

Not everything goes according to plan.

2006. Yet again it was early morning, at around half past four. Carl and I were on another night shift and we were called to attend at a hotel at the bottom end of Halifax. Operational Supervisor Edmund, was also on his way.

The call was to a young, possibly eighteen year old female running naked around the hotel and screaming for help.

When we arrived, Edmund was already there. In his usual dulcet tone, he said "she's in there, she's running bare arsed everywhere. I think she said she's pregnant".

We went inside and at that moment, the girl was sat on the floor in the bar area.

There were just a couple of male late night drinkers in the bar.

We asked her what was wrong and she told that she was "having the baby now!"

She didn't know how many weeks pregnant she was, she hadn't seen a doctor or been to a clinic at all.

She claimed that she had only found out that she was pregnant that morning.

Then she told us that she was feeling the need to push.

There was something not quite right there, the Firth gut was grumbling at its best. We tried to get the young girl to put on a dressing gown and to cover up, as she was only embarrassing herself.

She refused and then she ran outside, it was pouring with rain. She laid on the floor in the middle of the road, she started screaming. "Get it out! Get this thing out of me, for God's sake rip it out!" Her knees were up in the air, she appeared to be pushing with all her might.

She was screaming abuse at the "thing" inside her and she was saying that if it lived, she was going to kill it. None of the things that she was saying was rational, she was rambling.

There was a strong possibility that she may have been under the influence of illegal substances at the time.

To look at her you couldn't even tell that she was pregnant, she was only very petite, there was no baby bump.

Was it a psychotic episode? Was she pregnant?

If she was, it must only be in the early stages. Surely she wouldn't be ready to deliver, would she?

We managed to get her into the ambulance. She was getting very distressed, she really wanted that baby out of her body.

We rang the delivery suite at Calderdale Hospital, they said "bring her in, we'll have a look and see what's going on".

When we got there, the duty midwife got out a foetal stethoscope. It looked like a funnel of sorts. Yes, there was a foetal heartbeat. It was very faint.

The baby must be extremely small.

The next time she pushed, her waters broke. There was only a cup full if that. Then the smallest head that I had ever seen, with a mop of jet black hair appeared. It was blue, really blue.

The midwife inserted two fingers just inside the woman and she looped the chord over baby's head. She did that another twice, the chord had been wrapped three times around the baby's neck.

Another push and a very, very small little girl was born.

So she was pregnant!

The cord was cut and the baby was whisked away to be looked after in the SCBU. It was extremely small, the midwife concluded that the baby may be only seventeen or eighteen weeks gestation. If that was correct, the baby would not be able to survive.

We didn't know the weight of the baby at that stage. By the time the placenta had been delivered, another midwife came back onto the ward with the sad news that the baby had died. It was nowhere near being fully developed and it's lungs were just incapable of sustaining life.

It's weight, a staggering 400 grammes, that is about 14 ounces. From the development of the foetus, the midwife then suggested that the mother might have been twenty two or more weeks gestation.

A blood test had revealed that there was a high concentration of heroin.

Poor little thing, it never stood a chance.

The mother was living in the hotel as a DHSS placement. It was a half way house for her. She had been living on the streets and prostituting herself to fund her drugs habit. Hence the reason for the poor development of the foetus.

She would be kept in hospital for a few days for observation.

Not everything goes to plan, it's a good job we don't know what is around the corner.

Born underneath a Christmas Tree.

The next one to write about, sorry for rambling, but they all have very special and individual memories for me.

This birth has something even more special, due to the on street location. It was Friday 14th of December 2012.

The weather had been particularly bad, traffic had been snarled up everywhere. It was due to thick and black ice. There had been numerous accidents all over Huddersfield and the surrounding areas. Not many were serious in nature, but they had been causing major chaos and lots of roads had become completely gridlocked.

I had just walked into station, it was around 15:30hrs. I was getting ready to start my shift at 16:00hrs. I had just made myself a coffee, when Elaine, the PTS supervisor came running in to the mess room.

"There's a woman having a baby across the road!" she said and then she left. As I followed her down the corridor, she said "a man has just been to the door, they need help". She then calmly went upstairs and back to her office.

I went across the road to see what I could do. The woman was in the back of a taxi, a taxi actually driven by her husband. It was absolutely freezing. They had taken just over an hour to do two miles from Crosland Moor.

They had been stuck in the traffic approaching Gledholt roundabout for over half an hour, when the lady had needed to push. The driver had pulled into the little car park in front of the Junction Pub across the road from the ambulance station.

As I got into the back of the taxi, the RRV arrived, it was Sid working out of Todmorden. The only available ambulance was a non emergency A&E support crew and they were stuck at the bottom of Gledholt Bank. I used Sid's radio, I had to tell Comms to get that crew to us.

I know that it is against protocol for them to use blue lights, as they are not emergency drivers. Due to the unusual fact that Gledholt Bank Road was virtually closed, they would have to use the blue lights as extra hazard warnings and come up on the wrong side of the closed road.

I told Comms, that if they didn't allow that to happen, then the baby might die due to the exceptional freezing conditions.

They did allow it, the little Asian baby girl was born. She was wrapped up warm and put into the back of the warm ambulance.

Mum was then assisted out of the taxi and she also got into the ambulance. Sid was to travel in the ambulance, Anil would drive the car, while his partner Joe would drive the ambulance up to the hospital.

I was going back to station for my coffee.

"They had someone looking after them from a higher source", one woman said. "That baby could have died" said another.

The nice part for me, the real bit that I remember, was the location.

When I had arrived at the taxi, I had to ask the driver. The baby's father, to move his car just a little further into the light. Just so that I could see a little better, as it was already getting dark outside.

The only light source available to me at the time, was from a rather special source. It was the multi coloured and sparkling lights of the large Christmas Tree. The annual one outside the pub.

Well, it made it a special one for me anyway!

I remember it every year when they put the tree in the same position, and switch the lights on.

You'll have to go to Halifax!

Only just recently, Thursday 31st of March 2016. A six o'clock in the morning start with a relatively new lad, Martin from Dewsbury station. I hadn't worked with Martin before.

We received our first call of the day, a maternity call at an address in Deighton. A 23 year old who was in labour with her fourth child.

As we went into the room, she was already trying to push. Her husband was on the phone to HRI Birth Centre, where the patient had been booked in. They said "sorry we are short staffed, you'll have to go to Halifax!"

It's not really that much further, but that was not what we were wanting to hear. It's another six miles onto the journey.

There was around two to three minutes between her contractions. Her pregnancy was almost full term, she was thirty eight and a half weeks gestation. Her waters hadn't broken, surely once out of the house we would be ok. We waited for the next contraction to finish, she got on the carry chair and we got her into the ambulance.

Delivery pack at the ready.

Mum on the stretcher, dad on the back seat, mum's sister sat in the front with Martin. I asked him to put his foot down and blue light us to the Calderdale Royal Infirmary in Halifax. We left the house at 06:46hrs. Hopefully we could make it to Halifax without too many problems.

No! That wasn't happening.

Our little baby didn't want to wait, less than two minutes later, our mum was pushing like crazy.

That's when her waters broke. What a mess, it went everywhere.

The baby's head was crowning. I opened our delivery pack and got things sorted. Only one minute later, baby's head had delivered, quickly followed by the rest of a beautiful little girl.

Born at 06:50hrs, travelling at sixty miles an hour heading towards the top of Bradley Road.

Baby had only got a very short cord. I wrapped her up in a warm pink hooded fleece blanket, that mum's sister had supplied.

Mum cuddled her new baby to her abdomen. Dad was in tears, he couldn't get over the fact that the baby didn't cry. She was fine though, she had already tried sucking her thumb.

Cruel uncle Ian had to stop her and wrap her arms, swaddled in the fleece. Mum was bleeding heavily and it was all over baby's hand. I didn't want her sucking on that.

Eurgh!

It was the short cord that had ruptured causing the bleeding. I clamped the cord as far as I dare from the baby and then again as close as I could get to mum. The majority of the bleeding stopped.

Still flying, Martin got us to Halifax at 06:58hrs, not bad going!

On arrival on the delivery suite, we were greeted with "it's a good job you delivered the baby, we are short staffed on here".

We used to have three fully staffed maternity units in Huddersfield and two in Halifax.

Three of the units have already closed down completely and on that Thursday morning, there were only three midwives to share between the whole population of the two great towns.

What a bloody disgrace!

Thank goodness our little tot had decided to behave herself and not cause us any real problems.

The cord was sorted out in no time by the midwifery staff, the bleeding was stopped within a couple of minutes of our arrival.

CHAPTER 70

I WATCH CSI! EVEN WITH MY GUTS.

A good handover.

Whenever an ambulance crew arrives at a hospital A&E department, a "handover" occurs. It happens at every single A&E department in the country, it will probably be the same all over the world.

It involves the duty ambulance clinician explaining either to a single member of staff, or to to a full team of staff in a resus room, the basic outline of the new patient.

They will relay what has happened and what they have seen. What they have heard and what they have done. Either to, or for the patient and the results of their actions in doing so.

It has to be clear and precise, so that continuity of care can begin.

All the information, is then written down in detail by the ambulance crew on a patient report form (PRF, also known as PCR, patient care record) and that is handed over to the hospital staff. It then stays with the patient's notes.

If anyone has watched 24 hours in A&E, or Helicopter Heroes, or any tv programmes of that type you will have seen what I mean.

The handover is of paramount importance to ensure the continuing treatment of the patient. It prevents mistakes and saves the time of not repeating treatment.

The other thing that I feel as one of the most important aspects of a good clinical handover, is what the clinician has seen on their arrival at the incident. That can sometimes have changed by the time the patient arrives in hospital.

For instance, with any head injury, pupil size is important. Especially with a brain injury, the size can change of one or both pupils in a short space of time. The size needs to be recorded and accurately, when or if any changes occur.

What can appear as slight bruising to a body, can end up as massive discolouration to a large area of the body. The initial bruising seen at an incident, may have distinctive patterns. That may indicate the cause of an injury, and that pattern may end up being masked. By the time the ambulance has arrived at hospital, things could have changed significantly.

All those long CSI programmes were not wasted!

One case in question, I attended at an assault on the outskirts of Huddersfield. Again, I was working a night shift. It was around five thirty in the morning. I was working with a lad called Neil, he was from the Halifax station. When we arrived on scene, the police were already there.

They explained in their handover to us, that the male patient had been found laid in the gutter at the side of the road, by a bus driver on his way to work.

The patient had suffered from some severe head injuries and some other less significant bodily injuries. He seemed to have been drifting in and out of consciousness.

As I was examining the patient, Neil noticed that the windscreen of the nearest parked car was damaged. A four by four jeep type vehicle, had a bullseye in it. (A somewhat circular area of damage, radiating from the centre out). That type of damage to a windscreen is usually caused by the head of an unrestrained person. It had been done from the inside of the vehicle.

Neil asked the police, if that vehicle had been involved in any way.

As we continued examining our patient, the police had been asking further questions and some more details had come to light. In that a group of young men, had been out the previous evening in that vehicle.

On returning home, our victim had been left alone in it. He had been very drunk and was fast asleep. He was barely rousable when they had got home, so he had been left where he was to sleep it off

It then transpired that when our patient had woken up, not knowing where he was, he had panicked and had been kicking and smashing at the windows to get out.

We were told that the owner of the vehicle had heard the commotion and he had gone outside. He had then dragged his "friend" out of the car and he had given him a "good hiding", for causing the damage.

The patient had then been left in the road to suffer.

The vehicle owner had gone back to bed.

Our patient was in a bad way, he had become deeply unconscious. I called for a paramedic to assist with further medical intervention. That was Carl from Honley and he wasn't long in getting to us.

Our patient was collared and boarded, I had put an artificial airway down his throat to assist his breathing, known as a laryngeal mask. He was on 100% oxygen.

He had already been placed in the ambulance when Carl arrived. He then fitted the patient with a more substantial airway, a full intubation, for our unconscious patient. He was barely breathing and he needed fully assisted ventilations.

As Carl was doing that, with Neil's assistance.

I was looking for further injuries.

The man had several scuffs and abrasions all over his arms and legs. His bones in his legs all felt in line and intact, his pelvis seemed stable as far as I could examine.

It was his abdomen and chest that concerned me. His abdomen was firm, not soft as would be expected in someone unconscious.

That suggested that there may be some possible internal bleeding going on.

On his chest, there were some marks, some unusual bruising. At the initial time of his examination, there were two lines of bruises. They were parallel to each other, around eight or nine inches long.

They were exactly the same width apart top and bottom, as the width of the full span of my hand from the tip of my thumb to the tip of my little finger.

Imprinted into the bruising were hundreds of little diamond shapes, they had seeped little beads of serous fluid. Not blood, it is an almost clear fluid. The diamonds corresponded to the weave in the material of the patients own polo shirt.

There must have been some sort of prolonged or intense pressure to cause that, it wasn't a fist or a boot that had done it.

I had an idea, I quickly looked again at the car and where our patient was laid. The tyres on the 4 x 4 vehicle were exactly the same width again as my hand. Where he had been laid was against the kerb of a bus stop, it had a raised and high kerb in readiness for the access bus for disabled users.

The vehicle seemed to have been abandoned at a weird angle. I reported my findings to the police. I felt that the vehicle may have been driven onto or over him.

By the time the ambulance had arrived at the hospital, the bruising had already changed. It had become enlarged and had extended to the full side of his ribs.

During my handover to the awaiting trauma team in resus, I told them of my initial findings. I then added the changes and told them my personal suspicions. I felt that it was important for them to know.

I was dismissed immediately. The duty consultant said to me "that's all very well, but let's concentrate on his head injury shall we!"

I felt that he wasn't listening. What I had to say, in my mind was critical to the patient's treatment. I had to speak up for myself. I said "I'm sorry, but in all examinations A,B,C's (airway, breathing and circulation) are paramount. His breathing is being compromised due to his chest, I think it is filling with blood!"

He came right back at me sternly and he put me down in front of everyone in the room. As he reminded me that "I am in charge, not you!"

I was disgusted and I had to step away and leave the room. If I hadn't, my next statement might not have been a professional one.

There was another A&E consultant in the department, I had to find him and tell him. I was sure a big mistake was being made. I did so and he listened, we both went back to the patient. It had only taken a couple of minutes.

Just as the second consultant and I went back into the resus room, alarm bells were ringing. The patients' oxygen levels had suddenly plummeted to less than 20%, his throat was very swollen and it appeared to be pushed over to one side.

That is an acute life threatening situation, it is called tracheal deviation. It needs surgical intervention and fast!

The team had to open up his chest, there and then. To clear out all the blood and to relieve the pressure on his airway and his heart.

If not, it would have quickly lead to a "cardiac tamponade". A crushing of the heart, until it was unable to beat. Death can then follow and very quickly.

I didn't need to say anything. The second consultant winked at me, he shook my hand and said aloud for all to hear, "well spotted you!"

He carried on with "that is why it is so important to listen to a handover, I think we can all learn from that can't we?" He directed the last comment towards his colleague.

The surgery to save him, was performed immediately in A&E. It was very successful, a long recovery ensued but he survived.

The police had listened, they had found our patient's DNA on one of the tyres of the four by four vehicle. The patient's so called mate, the owner of the car had driven it onto the patient. It was only the extra high kerb for the access bus that had saved the patient's life.

The "mate" was charged with attempted murder.

Watching all those long episodes of CSI, were not a waste of time after all!

One hell of a way to die!

I was working with Arnold, I think it was in 1992, but I'm not sure of the date. He was the longest serving staff member at the time, a notoriously difficult bloke to work with was Arnold. It was as though you had to prove yourself to him.

He had been in the service for around twenty five years at the time. He was good at his job and he was an excellent driver, but my God he could be a moody bugger. If he was that way out, you would not be able to do anything right, no matter what.

One particular day, it was mid afternoon, we had a call to a lady who had fallen on a bus. "An elderly lady" it said, "the caller is talking to the patient, she is believed to have a broken shoulder". It sounded straight forward enough.

As you will already gather, I don't get many straight forward jobs. This one, was to be far from straight forward.

Arnold was driving, he could get a shift on when needed. I asked him to, I told him that I was having a strange gut feeling, one that I couldn't really describe.

I expected to be mocked by him for that statement, but I was pleasantly shocked.

He suddenly turned to me and said "best get my foot down then, I'm a great believer in gut feelings. Always act on them and you won't go far wrong".

As we arrived, the bus was in the middle of the road. At the roadside was a human windmill, arms waving like he was landing a jumbo jet. "She's on this bus" he screamed. There wasn't any other buses that I could see. He very excitably went on, "I'm a qualified first aider" Then he said, "I think she's broken her shoulder, it looks like it's out of joint to me. It might be dislocated".

We thanked him for his help.

He then said "I've been talking to her all the time, keeping her calm".

I turned the corner and looked onto the bus, "Arnold, get the defibrillator quick" I shouted.

He didn't question it.

I asked our budding doctor, if whilst talking to the patient, had she replied at all.

"No, I think she is in shock. She has been conscious all the time though", he said.

What I actually saw on the bus, really shocked me. The lady was far from conscious, she was dead. As I have mentioned in other areas, she fitted the criteria as per "yellow card". She had injuries incompatible with life.

We had to get everybody off the downstairs of the bus. Thank goodness it was that bus, there were only around twenty five passengers on it and only eight of them downstairs. The next one would have been packed full of school kids.

The police had arrived and they organised the evacuation via the emergency door at the back. The people upstairs were asked to remain seated and to be patient with us for the time being.

The lady was laid in the doorway of the bus. Between the automatic doors and the drivers cabin.

Right at the front of the bus, in the middle, is a grill for the heater.

The lady had been sat in the centre of the back seat, she had been in the process of getting ready for her upcoming stop. Just as she had grabbed her heavy shopping bags, one in each hand, the driver had had to make an emergency stop.

The lady had then stumbled forward and hurtled like a rocket for the full length of the bus.

Where she had then gone head first into the grill at the front. Her head had gone completely through the cover, which was around twelve inches square.

The distorted looking shoulder, was actually the top of the lady's backbone. All of the bones of her cervical spine (neck) had come through the flesh and were there for all to see. Her neck had been snapped completely.

One hell of a way to die!

Thank goodness that she would have died on impact and known nothing about it.

The driver unfortunately was stuck inside her little cabin. We had to keep talking to her and asking her to look away, it must have been devastating for her.

Until the patient was moved, she would have to stay in her seat.

Arnold had got some blankets and fixed them over the now open doors, the kids were all passing on their way home from school.

Lots of them were expecting to get on the bus. We didn't want anyone to see what had happened, especially any children.

To actually pronounce death, it has to be proven with other tests, including an ECG (electrocardiograph). With at least thirty seconds of continual asystole (flat line) rhythm.

As we couldn't move the patient from her position, I placed the ECG leads on her back instead of her chest. I just placed them in reverse order.

With her injuries, there was no doubt, but that was a final confirmation that death had occurred. By then, a police inspector had arrived, to take charge. There were many other police officers present, including a scenes of crime photographer.

The Coroner's Officer had been informed of the tragic incident.

Instead of waiting for his arrival, the inspector said that it was "very clear to all concerned, how the lady has died". To "take some pictures of the body in situ and then remove her from the bus, as quickly as practicable". Then to "take her to the hospital mortuary and give her as much dignity as possible, given the present situation".

That would also allow the driver to be released from her little cell, where she had been kept as a virtual prisoner, with the deceased lady laid at her side.

By the time that happened, the driver had become extremely distraught over what had taken place. We called for another crew to take her to hospital once we had got our patient free.

The upstairs passengers were then allowed off the bus.

It was after Arnold and I cleared at the hospital, that he came up to me and shook my hand. He said that I had done a "bloody marvellous job under the circumstances" and that it had been a "pleasure working with you!"

Following that job. Every time I worked with Arnold, I had a great shift, with him. None of his moodiness or pig headed attitude. He even asked me to do him the honour of taking the wedding photo's, when he and Annette got married.

I was chuffed to bits to be asked.

Gut feelings.

Arnold's advice regarding gut feelings has remained with me ever since that day. Unfortunately there have been several occasions where gut feelings have come into place.

When attending to a seemingly straight forward job, I suddenly get the stomach cramps and a churning uneasy feeling. That has usually ended up in the incident taking an unexpected turn for the worse.

I have suffered for many years with gut problems, from as far back as I can remember.

Finally being diagnosed with diverticular disease in 2005. The diagnosis followed months of tests and after having several visits to A&E. With subsequent admissions to the surgical assessment ward at Huddersfield Royal Infirmary.

The symptoms being a sudden onset of relentless stomach cramps and severe pain. The symptoms are not too distant from my gut feelings that I get on some jobs.

As with the lady on the bus. I had got the sudden cramps, on the way to the incident.

Can we use the big room?

On another occasion, I was working with Carl. Yet again, it was on a night shift. It was the morning of my 43rd birthday, the 22nd of December 2001.

We were due to finish at 07:00hrs.

At six fifteen, a job came in to an area of Huddersfield, just outside the Town centre. For a 31 year old male with severe chest pains.

We both thought that the timing of the job, would just see us finished off nicely.

We got to the address and after knocking on the door, a female answered saying that we had come for her husband. He had got up for work, then he had suddenly collapsed to the floor clutching his chest in agony.

She had dialled 999 very shortly after he collapsed.

It had only lasted for around ten minutes or so.

At the time of our arrival he was feeling fine, the pain had gone just as suddenly as it had started. The wife said that she had never seen him in such a state.

Her husband was full of apologies, "sorry for wasting your time" etc. but that he was absolutely fine and he was going to go to work as planned.

My guts started heaving, it was bad. I had no idea what or why, but something was wrong, seriously wrong.

We did a series of checks on the patient, his blood pressure, his pulse and respiration rates, etc.

They were as we would have expected, all were slightly raised but he had just been through a frightening experience. We performed a twelve lead ECG, a full and detailed heart examination.

It showed nothing.

The man was calming down, his mannerisms were calm, but his eyes seemed to be screaming out for help. He had without doubt been scared out of his skin. The couple had two young children in the house fast asleep.

I tried to persuade him to come to hospital, I used all sorts of persuasion techniques.

Eventually playing on the wife's fear, that at least she would settle better if he came with us to see a doctor. I pulled on all of the heart strings.

With Christmas just around the corner, he also had his kids to think about, etc. etc.

He reluctantly came with us,

I pulled up at HRI outside the A&E rather quickly. Staff nurse Katie was outside having a well earned cuppa and a sneaky fag. She looked at me and said "what have you got for us?"

I had to admit that I wasn't sure, but I asked if we could go into the "big room" the resuscitation room.

She was surprised at that, to say the least, but no problem.

We, including our patient walked in. Scott the charge nurse saw us "what have you got?" he asked. Before I could answer, our patient who had just sat on the edge of a hospital trolley, collapsed.

He had suffered a full cardiac arrest. He stopped breathing and his heart had stopped.

Despite it being a witnessed cardiac arrest, one where the patient has the biggest chance of survival. Despite him being in a hospital resuscitation room and despite the immediate actions of the staff all around him. We couldn't save him, he died.

He was "worked on" for over an hour, but never showed any potential signs of life.

That was a sad occasion, one that I will never forget. Katie hasn't either, we still talk about it occasionally, even now.

One of the questions repeatedly asked of me, is "why didn't you put a call in for resus?" I couldn't, how could I call for a "full resus standby" when to all intents and purposes my patient was absolutely fine. It was my guts that were heaving, nothing else.

I would have been a laughing stock if I had.

My guts were off again.

Only a month later, to the day and another night shift with Carl. I got another set of severe stomach cramps. I arrived at HRI with my patient, Katie just happened to be outside again. She saw me pull up, she threw her coffee away and asked "not again?"

I nodded, "big room it is then".

That time Katie called via the tannoy system for a doctor to come to resus, "immediately please!"

A soon as our patient got onto the hospital trolley she collapsed, another patient with a full cardiac arrest! It was in almost exactly the same circumstances as before.

Our patient had started with the same, sudden and severe central chest pains. Shortly after ringing 999, the pains had gone.

This lady though, still had some electrical activity in her heart. Even though there was no pulse present, her heart was fibrillating.

She was shocked once with a defibrillator, and she came round immediately.

There was no need for any cardiac massage, no intervention with drugs either.

She went on to make a full recovery.

That patient was 86 years old.

It is so strange how things can happen. I have always been a believer in fate.

It's not always an age thing. If your time is up, it's up.

A Coronary Thrombosis.

Following a post mortem examination of our 31 year old man and a full examination of our 86 year old lady on the wards. They had both suffered from exactly the same thing.

A massive coronary thrombosis. A large blood clot.

In both cases, it was believed that they had suffered a minor coronary thrombosis. From a small blood clot and that had hit and blocked their heart, that had then caused the severe and sudden chest pains.

Somehow the blood clot had been dislodged and passed through the heart and then gone bank into the rest of the circulatory system. As the clot was travelling around the body, the pain and all associated symptoms had gone.

Only for it to arrive back at the heart with a vengeance and causing the heart to stop.

It was simply fate that decided which of our two patients was to survive their ordeal, or not. They both had exactly the same, timely and correct initial treatment.

Humour me, let's take you to hospital.

I have had several incidents since, where I have had that same gut wrenching feeling.

It is awful.

I have always had to somehow manage and persuade the patients to travel to hospital. Some have then had a stroke, others have had heart attacks, or other major events.

Either on route to, or on arrival at the hospital.

But, since that young man. They have all, fingers crossed, survived.

Not all have made a full recovery, but they have all definitely been in a better position than they would have been.

If I hadn't have had my gut feeling and as they had wanted, been left at home.

Due to them feeling "ok now".

It has been very hard at times, how do you explain to a patient that you have a strange gut feeling about them?

They'd think you were off your head.

It has been a matter of using my experience to get them to go for "a peace of mind check up", or to "just have an MOT done". Even, "look, once you've been seen by a doctor. Both you and your other half will sleep tonight without worrying, won't you".

I think over the years I have picked up on most of the excuses, for not going and I've had counter replies to give.

What's that noise?

Another strange happening, that as occurred several times over the years. I have heard a strange noise/cry being emitted from a patient's mouth.

It is an unusual noise that I can't possibly describe adequately in print. It is always the same, a high pitched and fairly quiet, but it is a prolonged and whining noise.

The only time that I have heard it and it can be male or female, is when being sent to a patient who has appeared to have suffered from a severe stroke.

Each time I have heard that noise, the patient hasn't actually had a stroke at all. They have all been a diabetic patient whose blood sugar levels have fallen so low, that the patient has gone into a diabetic coma.

It can mimic a very dense stroke. If not treated quickly it can and has caused a full blown stroke to have developed later.

The noise doesn't happen every time. But each and every time it has, my guts have started heaving. They have all appeared and presented with the same symptoms.

It is very rewarding to see the distraught family watch their loved one change, from a collapsed and unresponsive, stroke suffering victim. Into a fully recovered normal family member.

Following relatively simple treatment.

A quick acting injection, or intra venous glucose and within ten to fifteen minutes the patient is usually sat upright. Probably having a drink. Usually a cup of sweet tea and a sandwich, or toast.

Some carbohydrates to top up their reserve tanks.

I have never seen it mentioned in any reference books. It seems that it is just one of the many things that I have picked up over several years of watching and monitoring patients.

Fingers crossed my guts will carry on being right!

CHAPTER 71.

DEATHS OF COLLEAGUES.

Funerals.

At funerals, it seems to be the only time that the old staff and current staff get together, it's sad isn't it?

Cliff, he had been going to and from the doctor with gall bladder trouble for months. They eventually decided to operate on him. During surgery, he was found to be riddled with cancer.

Within three weeks of his diagnosis, we were at his funeral.

He had the largest guard of honour by ambulance staff that I can remember. His funeral, was at Park Wood crematorium in Elland.

The whole drive was lined with ambulance vehicles and staff, both past and present. A team of six pall bearers were selected, to take Cliff into the Chapel.

I had been asked by his daughter Deborah, to photograph all the proceedings.

It was a strange request, but as she said, it would be the only chance to see all of his colleagues together. Deborah then said that she would "probably not see many those people ever again".

Paddy, also had a good turn out. He had a full team of six pall bearers all in full uniform with white gloves.

My old mate Tommy was one of them, but he had been drinking. As he got to the graveside he tripped, he then fell partly into Paddy's grave. Ernie was sure it was Paddy that had tripped him up.

How embarrassing for everybody.

Stuart passed away following a long and courageous battle with cancer, it went on for years. He lived his life as full as he could, right up to the last few days.

Then only two weeks later, Mark suffered a second burst AAA, (abdominal aortic aneurism). Anyone is very lucky to survive one. Despite his size, Mark had survived his first and he even returned to work.

Not for the Ambulance Service, but for PenDoc, the local out of hours doctor service (Pennine Doctors).

He then had a second one, he was lucky to get to hospital. It was during a transfer to LGI for surgery, that he died. They had only reached Ainley Top, when he had a cardiac arrest.

He was being transported there by his regular mate Graham, they had to return to Huddersfield.

Both of those funerals were very well attended.

Arnold, he also had a battle with cancer. He had worked for the ambulance service for 38 years, when we lost him.

I asked our Comms if I could attend his funeral as I was on duty.

They weren't happy.

I came in to work early, I should actually have started at ten, the same time as the funeral started.

I was working with Phillip, who usually worked out of Halifax. He knew about the funeral and he agreed to come in half an hour early so we would be together as a crew.

We clocked on at 09:30hrs and headed up towards the crematorium at Fixby.

Comms tried to give us a job at 09:45hrs, I refused that one as I wasn't due to start until 10:00hrs. I was advised that I shouldn't have clocked on then. I had to as I was taking a vehicle out on the road.

But then I was given a job, bang on 10:00hrs just as the hearse and Arnold were coming down the drive. There were only about four ambulance staff at that funeral. How times have changed and that was certainly not for the better.

We had Hannah from Halifax, a very popular Scots lass, loved by everybody who knew her. She had also suffered a long time with cancer. At her funeral, priority was given to Halifax Staff and rightly so.

I was told that I could stand by at the entrance gates of the crematorium at Fixby. Leaving the drive available for her closest colleagues. We would be able to leave if the need arose.

Comms ordered me to go to standby at the roadside near to Asda, less than half a mile away from where we were. I asked to be able stay at least until Hannah's cortège arrived. My request was curtly denied, I was virtually told to do as I was told. Some respect eh!

Like I have said before, there is not much respect anywhere now. I was with June at the time, I stayed put. Hannah would have laughed if she had known.

There were three more crews parked up with us.

As a mark of respect, we all stood in silence in front of our vehicles with all of the lights flashing. Hannah's partner chuckled as she passed us on her way into the crematorium.

Bobby from Halifax, Joey and Ernie from Huddersfield all died in the same week. Funerals for Bobby and Joey were on the same day. Ernie was just two days later.

We don't provide guards of honour now, you are lucky if you are allowed to attend if you are on duty.

I have lost count of the number of colleagues that have passed away since I started on my journey with the ambulance service. If I were to mention them all, I would need to write another book.

As I get older, hardly a month goes by that I don't read another name in the Huddersfield Examiner. Another colleague from days gone by, who has passed away, it is so sad.

Please forgive me if I haven't mentioned them individually by name. I do remember snippets from some, full stories of others, but I can assure you that I will remember them. I have special memories of everybody that I have ever worked with at some stages.

Some are only fleeting images, others have made a massive impact, but they are inside my head somewhere.

A Special Nurse.

There was a very special nurse, I'll call her Alice-May. She was a nurse who worked in the casualty department at HRI, she died at a very young age.

I think she was only in her thirties. There were rumours that her death had been self inflicted. Or that she had turned to drink after being beaten by her husband.

All sorts of rumours, but not enough facts.

Whatever the reason for her tragic and untimely death, Alice-May deserves a special mention from me.

At her funeral a lot of us from the ambulance service attended, she was "A true rose among nurses". We placed a card saying those very words, on a single white rose that we had taken to her funeral. She was a true and caring nurse, she has been very sadly missed.

Alice-May was a very lovely caring person, I think that she was born to be a nurse. She had a persona, an aura, that shone when she was caring for somebody who was suffering.

Mike and me could have come a real cropper one day, if it hadn't been for Alice-May. A young Asian lad, aged only 21, was said to be suffering with chest pains.

When we got there, there seemed to be nothing wrong with him. He ran down a load of steps to meet us, he forgot his wallet and so he ran all the way back up. He got his wallet and then he ran back down again. He just looked a little pale and clammy, he told us that he had been suffering from flu like symptoms for three days.

Alice-May said that she had seen something in his eyes. She couldn't say what it was, but she would just do a double check.

I'm not the only one that has gut feelings.

Alice-May did a twelve lead, comprehensive ECG and a blood test. Then she sent him for x-rays.

It was a good job she did, the lad was suffering from an advanced case of cardio myopathy, (massively enlarged heart muscle). Only a full heart transplant would be the treatment to save his life. Unfortunately, I don't know whether the lad got his transplant or not.

Mike and me thought the patient was a bit of a wimp, with "man flu".

Wow! That's experience for you! If you act on your experiences and feelings, you wont go far wrong.

Bariatric Patient.

It was a Friday the 5th of August 2016. And yes, another bloody night shift. I was working until six the following morning with my good friend June. At just after twenty past eight, we were dispatched to an address on the Burnley side of Todmorden.

We were asked to get a bariatric (for very heavy patients) stretcher. As the patient that we were going for, was known to weigh around 230 kilogrammes, that's nearly 38 stones.

We immediately asked for at least one other crew to be sent for assistance. As usual, we had to explain and justify our request. Although anyone reading this would probably already have realised why.

We had the stretcher, but we still needed to get the patient out of his house and into the ambulance. THAT is where we would need the assistance.

We had to respond under blue lights and sirens for a whopping twenty five mile journey, the ambulance had actually been booked since 15:15hrs. that same afternoon.

A bit of a mockery there. If we were to have an accident, me as the driver would have to justify the use of the emergency warnings.

The patient was being admitted to The Royal Blackburn Hospital, due to having some breathing difficulties. It seemed to happen to him every few weeks where he would be admitted for a few days. He would be stabilised and then discharged home.

When we arrived at the house, I was shocked. Not only to the fact that the man appeared to be the largest person that I had ever seen in my whole life.

He was a past friend and colleague.

He was also called Ivan, he had worked at Todmorden Ambulance Station for nineteen years, prior to retiring on ill health grounds.

He was 65 years old.

Ivan had been in the armed forces for many of his early years, he was always a big, well made bloke. But very fit and active as well. For a time, he was one of the guards outside of Buckingham Palace.

You know the ones, with the shiny kinky boots and the highly polished silver breastplate and helmet with a large plume.

He had then spent a time with the Royal family's close protection squad, a bodyguard working closely with her majesty the Queen.

He then joined the ambulance service, for some peace and quiet.

I had worked with Ivan on many occasions in the past and had attended several training courses with him.

It was a shock to see him like that. His weight had ballooned since a broken leg didn't heal correctly, it had left him unable to weight bare. He had another operation and that also went wrong. His bones disintegrated, they had become so brittle. He became chair and then finally he was bed bound.

His weight had got massively out of control, he was classed as super morbidly obese.

He could not support any of his own weight.

Whilst laid on a double bed, if he was up against the wall side with his buttocks, his massive abdomen would be overhanging at the other side.

He was in himself, perfectly fine. His mind was as active as I had always known. We spent ages reminiscing and looking at old photo's whilst awaiting our second crew for assistance.

He wasn't particularly short of breath, despite being on 24 hour oxygen, but he was retaining massive amounts of fluid.

His right arm and his right leg and his abdomen had filled with so much fluid. To the extent that his skin was extremely tight, it was blistering, and on the verge of tearing.

Ivan even said that his forearms looked like "Popeye". He told us that he had weighed between 36 and 38 stones, but wasn't sure what he would be with all the fluid retention.

When we arrived at the Royal Blackburn Hospital, we would have normally pumped our hydraulic stretcher up to the same height of the hospital bed.

We would use the foot pedal, to pump the hydraulics. Then using moving and handling sheets, simply slide the patient across and into bed.

That time, even though we had our specially built stretcher with us. It was marked up as having a capacity of 400 kilogrammes, approximately 63 stones.

It wouldn't pump, we could not move it. The hydraulics just couldn't cope.

We had to get extra staff as well as the four of us. I think there were ten of us altogether, just to roll Ivan across from our stretcher and into bed.

It took a long while that job, even though we had all struggled and worked up a real sweat. Ivan had retained his good humour.

We left him to rest, it had already gone midnight. But not before exchanging telephone numbers and the promise that I would go and visit him upon discharge.

We would be able to share our memories and exchange some more photographs with each other, over a cuppa

He was in great spirits.

On Tuesday the 9th of August, I got a message to say that Ivan had passed away in hospital. I knew that he was seriously ill, but I didn't expect that.

He had suffered from complete heart failure. It just simply couldn't cope with the amount of weight that he was carrying. The fluid retention had made it even harder.

I hope you aren't suffering now Ivan, rest in peace my friend.

A shock for everyone.

I had finally come to a position where I thought I had finished writing my book and then on the 8th of September 2016, another event happened that I need to add.

No doubt over the next few years there will be more events worthy of inclusion. I have decided though, that now, enough is enough. I can even hear big sighs of relief everywhere!

I have probably tested your patience to the limits already.

It was an enormously sad day for everyone who worked on the emergency ambulances in Kirklees and Calderdale. But especially for the whole of the A&E departments in both Huddersfield and Halifax hospitals.

We were all stunned by the extremely sad and unexpected death of a colleague.

She wasn't ambulance staff, she wasn't a nurse, she was the manager of the A&E reception at both sites. Nevertheless, Tracey was a friend and respected colleague to all of us.

I was talking to her only the night before, she was getting very excited about her forthcoming early retirement. She was planning to enjoy the rest of her life free from the stress of work.

Tracey was physically counting down the days that she would have left to work. She only had eleven more shifts to do.

When Tracey finished on Thursday afternoon, she went home full of the joys.

She was expecting a central heating engineer going to her home. Then just a usual quiet evening at home, nothing special.

Her family found her later that evening, she had suddenly passed away at home.

Nathan, one of our RRV paramedics was called. He had the unenviable task of pronouncing the death of a friend and colleague.

You are ever a professional Nathan, I sincerely take my hat off to you.

Tracey's funeral was held at Huddersfield's crematorium at Fixby. The whole place was packed, there were even screens showing the service in the outer areas of the building.

It was a real family service and a complete celebration, telling the story of Tracey's life.

She had lived her life to the full, she had always done what she wanted to do and enjoyed her life. Tracey was always the life and soul of any party.

Tracey was an absolute Huddersfield Giants rugby fanatic.

Everyone who had any professional dealings with the A&E, at either of the hospitals, had the utmost respect for Tracey. She will be very sadly missed by all of us.

Rest peacefully Tracey. We all remember you with the respect that you deserve.

That was a story that I just couldn't ignore. Tracey had been such a presence for 30 years. It is hard to believe that she is no, longer with us.

Walking into the receptions will never be the same.

As described by one of her colleagues:
The sun rose on 14/02/1962, sadly the sun set for the last time on 08/09/2017.
Tracey Louise Eaton, sadly missed, never forgotten.

CHAPTER 72.

FOOD AND DRINK.

One for you, one for me and four for them.

When I first started for the ambulance service, my old mate Tommy once said to me. "Remember son, there are six wheels on an ambulance. One for you, one for me and four for them".
At the time, I hadn't a clue what he meant.

But as he explained. If ever you need to do something for yourself, be open, honest and ask. Generally, if you do, you will get your wishes granted.

Calling at home, at the bank, or more importantly for some fodder. If you don't ask, you risk the chance of being reported by well meaning members of the public!

If you have asked, you are in the clear.

Wherever I have worked, whichever station that might be. The person that you are working with, will always know all the best places locally for something to eat or drink. The best breakfast sandwich, the best pies, the best fish and chips or the best takeaway. Whatever, you'll never go far wrong.

In the Huddersfield area, especially in the vicinity of our base ambulance station, we are spoilt for choice. There is something for everyone, there is just about every type of food imaginable.

Over the years I have found favourites, unfortunately some have closed down due to retirement or for other reasons.

Some are still around over thirty six years later.

I have found the cheapest, the most expensive, the weirdest, the best value, you name it and I have probably been at some stage.

Even if it was only once!

Roadside stand by and what the purpose is.

It used to be common place to be sent out on a roadside stand by, when our neighbouring stations had been depleted of crews.

For example. If Halifax or Brighouse stations had become empty of crews, we would be sent to stand by at Ainley Top. If Dewsbury were out, we would be sent to Mirfield.

At one time, we had a five star point at Mirfield, in the form of the Little Chef restaurant. There we had drinks facilities and use of the toilets.

Standing by in a lay-by in Swan Lane at Lockwood, it was a lovely midweek summers day.

It would have been just before 14:30hrs.

Gerald was driving at the time. We had been sent to Lockwood to wait at the roadside, a common occurrence when our neighbouring station at Honley had been emptied.

Gerald had selected that particular location as it was directly opposite the long established "Dixon's".

Not the electrical retailers, but a well known local ice cream parlour.

What better way to finish off a late lunch, than with a large helping of wonderful refreshing ice cream.

We sat in the cab and we were enjoying our treat.

A short time later, I became aware of a commotion going on outside the cab windows. When I looked up there were loads of children laughing and making a fuss. I thought that I must have nodded off.

I had, not nodded, but I had been in a deep sleep. It was after half past three, we had been there for over an hour.

As I looked at Gerald, well what can I say.

There in the drivers' seat, he was fast asleep. His head back, mouth wide open and snoring. He really was driving the cows home.

Not only that, he had an empty ice cream cone bizarrely stood end up on his chest, with a congealed mass of ice cream and raspberry juice spread out underneath it.

No wonder the kids were all laughing at us.

I had to wake him, he put the ambulance in gear and sped off down the road. We had to return to the station for him to get cleaned up.

He was blazing, he never stopped swearing all the way back to our station at Gledholt. Not because he had been laughed at, but because he had barely tasted the delicious treat that he had been really looking forward to.

Sadly Gerald is now another statistic of ambulance staff to suffer with the dreaded Alzheimer's, he has now become a resident in a care home

We have lots of roadside stand by points now, not necessarily for when or where stations are depleted. It is more often because Comms cannot really allow two crews to be on any one station at the same time.

The stand by points could be anywhere, we are spoilt for choice. From Odsal Top in Bradford, Wyke, Slaithwaite, Milnsbridge, Great Northern Retail Park, Highburton, Kirkburton, Drighlington, anywhere that Comms deem fit to send us really.

Taste Buds.

In Huddersfield. One of the best value for money, eating establishments, has got to be "Taste Buds" at Paddock. An early morning and lunchtime sandwich bar.

It has been run since 2002 by an ex Huddersfield Giants and Australia, professional rugby league player Geoff and his wife Jodi.

Geoff lives up to his past, he is a giant of a man matched with a giant personality. He is some character, he is always there with the friendly cheeky banter.

Jodi is much smaller and petite, but has a personality to match Geoff any day of the week, they bounce off each other brilliantly. They have two daughters, aged eight and six as I write this.

I remember seeing Jodi at HRI when she was heavily pregnant with her first, she was apprehensive and she looked worried. I sat with her for a while, hopefully, just spending a little time chatting over a cuppa might have helped.

Now, down to the nitty gritty, their products!

Sandwiches, hot and cold, of any type. Plated salads, pies and pasties. Hot and cold drinks.

If they haven't got it listed, just ask, either of them would be more than willing to sort you out.

They have other staff assisting at times and they will always give you a very warm and cheery welcome on entering.

Geoff has a special, his famous Aussie Burger. As you can imagine, it is unashamedly loud and brash.

It is a burger sandwich bigger than any I have ever seen. It contains everything you would expect in a burger and more, even beetroot. It has to be tried. I really, really, struggled with mine to finish it.

It was gorgeous, but it was a lot to take in, in one sitting. Despite my larger than average belly.

Although I did see a former Giants player, a New Zealander, Stanley. He was sat at the small counter in the shop. He ordered his Aussie burger, actually, two of them. He made short work of them. He never even paused for breath, they were gone!

Whatever it is that you ask for at "Taste Buds", you can certainly be sure that the butty will be packed. Full of the filling of your desire, in your own choice of breads.

A great value, satisfaction guaranteed, belly buster.

In Leeds, I had enough meat to feed a family of four!

The only other one to match "Taste Buds", is a little butchers shop, not far from Leeds Central ambulance station. It is hidden away, I thought the way it was described, it would only be for locals.

How wrong could I be.

I was working with a young lad out of Wakefield at the time, he is now a senior manager in Leeds. His father also worked at Wakefield, he still does a bit of part time work. Even though he must be in his seventies now.

Named Stan, both of them. That particular day, I was working with Stan junior. He was relatively new to the job, but his old dad had taught him well when it came to searching for grub.

We had taken a patient over to the LGI, when he told me of the little butchers shop.

They only do two types of sandwich, beef and pork. Both carved off the joint, straight from the oven. Hot beef with onions and gravy, (definitely need a tray, and a knife and fork for that one). Or a hot pork with apple sauce and stuffing and a large lump of "proper crackling".

We pulled around the corner at the top of the hill, about half a mile from Leeds ambulance station. There it was, it was only a little shop and right on the corner. It was just as Stan had described.

But it was the queue, wow!

I wasn't ready for that, it went all around the block. People had come from miles away.

They were quick though, the queue was far from stationary.

Inside the shop, was a small skinny bloke. He was serving general butchers shop items, to his regular customers. At the other side of the shop, were two women carving the joints and there were two others serving up the sandwiches.

Stan had warned me about the beef in gravy, he was right. I could see the amount of gravy, that was dripping from the bottom of the bags of the eager customers.

I plumbed for the pork. The woman grabbed a handful of meat from the tray, I thought that it was for both of us. Wrong, she then grabbed some more and piled it all up onto the same large teacake. Then the stuffing and some apple sauce, she then tried to close the teacake.

It was then placed in a bag, with a lump of pork crackling nearly as big as my fist.

That was in the early nineties, the price, a whopping £1.70. What better bargain could you get. I had enough meat to feed a family of four.

I was picking out lumps of hot pork from the bag, all the way back to Wakefield. I was full by the time I got there, I hadn't even touched the bread.

Stan had bought two, he finished them on the way back to station. Both of them, boy could that lad "trough his food".

I had been telling my regular mate Carl about the shop. We never seemed to go anywhere near.

Then it was around ten years later, I think it was 2006. We were in Leeds and had to go to the ambulance station. We had to see the mechanics, for some minor repairs to our vehicle.

That was as good a chance as we would ever get, we called round.

It was just as I had told him, there was still a massive queue. Carl thought we wouldn't have time, but the queue was moving just as quick as it was before.

He got the pork, he couldn't believe the amount of filling that had been put in his sandwich. How the hell could they keep going at that price.

It had gone up in price, £2.60.

Wow! Still can't grumble at that. Anywhere else it would have to be at least twice as much, if not more.

It was a rare find, that little shop it is still going. Now you have to pay in 2016 a massive, but still very well worth £3.75. A sandwich that can last two or three meals, for me anyway.

They had made a slight, but welcome change to their presentation. They had decided to place the sandwiches in a polystyrene serving box. The gravy remained with the beef all the way home.

I love food!

CHAPTER 73.

INSPIRATIONS.

My heroes and inspirations.

When I look back on my life, particularly my time with the ambulance service. I have had lots of colleagues or friends that I have admired, or respected highly. Those who have had some form of direct impact on me, my personal circumstances or have been my inspiration.

From my youngster days, the first person. Other than obviously my own family members, to have made a direct impact on me.

Would have to be Terry, one of my scout leaders and a director at Shaw's Pickles.

For his time and patience in teaching me. He taught me outdoor skills, how to look after myself, cooking, first aid etc. All that helped to set me up for life.

I do still see him occasionally. Poor bloke, he has also got Alzheimer's. I won't go into detail now, I have spent time talking about him in other chapters.

I have always held him in very high esteem.

From my days at Brook Motors Ltd, it would have to be Stanley. He was a true inspiration. He was one of the company directors, but his feet were and had always remained very firmly on the ground. His apprentice roots had never been loosened. I have also talked about him at length in earlier chapters.

What a guy!

I have had several unspecified mentors within the ambulance service. Not one of them had been officially allocated as a mentor. There are those who I have watched, studied and learned from.

When I started, it was Tommy. He was the one that taught me my original groundwork and he helped me to fit in. He taught me how to handle the most stressful side of the job.

Away from the ambulances, he even taught me some basic building work skills.

Then, after Tommy retired, I struck up a great friendship with Alec. He was allocated as my Field Based Assessor (FBA). He and I went on many, many jobs and adventures together over the years. I'm a great fan, daft bugger that he is.

Of course then there was my regular mate Carl, we worked together everyday for fourteen and a half years. For another six years before that we worked together, but not quite as regular. At that time, it was for six out of every eight weeks.

As well as being a fantastic work colleague, we worked well together. We always supported each other through difficult times. A little fella, but an absolute tower of strength for me.

I felt completely lost when he retired, it was like losing a leg. We then started to go out socially, the two of us together with our wives.

For some reason, that contact has dwindled, we must both just be getting on with our lives. But it still hurts.

I wish them both all the health and happiness for a long time to come.

For some years, at Huddersfield we had a manager called Bryan. He was a man that had worked "on the road, in the front line". He had a wealth of experience and was well respected.

For instance, when dad died. I had no hesitation in going to the station to see Bryan. I had been at home for mum and my sisters, I just needed a little me time. Bryan was there for me.

I have never felt the same respect for any other ambulance manager or officer since.

Bobby was a nice bloke, he kept himself to himself. Very approachable when needed, but he was always in his office.

The one we have now is "different". He has suddenly gone from road staff to Clinical Supervisor and then he became a manager. I won't say any more.

I have a new FBA now, actually now they are called a CS. A lad called James, an ex postman.

He is a super bloke, he will help out in any way possible. Any clinical issues or new training ideas, anything you can think of. James is the man to speak to.

I trust and consider him to be confidential, genuine, honest and a friend.

He is ideal for the job. He could easily have gone for our managers post, but he cares for his staff, it wasn't the job for him.

Shame, I believe he would have been good at it.

Another of our CS's, is only a young lad, he has worked his way up from PTS. He was one of the first student paramedics to qualify via university. He is Dennis, one to watch in my mind. He is young, but has a very wise head on his shoulders.

I hope he'll go far, he deserves it.

Just as I thought, since I started writing this book, he has handed his notice in at Huddersfield. He applied and has been accepted for a job as an instructor at our training school. I'm sure that that is not the last move he will make.

Good luck and best wishes for the future Dennis!

My all time HERO though, is a lad from Dewsbury. Both he and his wife go far more than above and beyond the call of duty, all the time. Chas, is not only one of the finest paramedics that Yorkshire has ever had, he is an absolute gentleman as well.

Since we disbanded the role of Station Officer, Chas has voluntarily taken on the role, he looks after the station and staff whenever he can. Because Chas does it voluntarily, management will just let him get on with it.

He doesn't get any recognition for it, not that he wants it, he enjoys/loves what he does.

His wife Abby, she is also a fantastic paramedic and she is a wonderful human being. They are fantastic together.

Chas unfortunately a few years ago was diagnosed with Parkinson's disease. It is an unforgiving illness, but Chas has battled with the utmost dignity and courage.

He has carried on working, even still operating single handedly on an RRV. (Rapid Response Vehicle). At times, he tries to hold his left arm still by tucking it under his other, it is absolutely heartbreaking to see it.

When backing him up on jobs, I leave with a lump in my throat and tears in my eyes. How could that ever have happened to such a wonderful caring man. Everyone who has ever met Chas, have the utmost respect for him.

He always has a wonderful smile, I have never heard him complain, or seen him down. Neither has anyone else I have spoken to either.

If fate hadn't already dealt him the worst poker hand ever, it dealt him an even more crushing blow. His lovely wife Abbie in 2013, suffered from a life threatening brain haemorrhage, she very nearly died.

Thankfully she survived, not only that, Abby has made a complete recovery and she is fully fit and back at work.

A nicer, more professional couple, I guarantee you will never ever meet.

But Chas, mate, YOU are my all time hero!!!

As a sign of respect, my mate James. One of the CS's at Huddersfield, has run six, yes six, full marathons to raise money for Parkinson's UK. All in honour and respect of Chas.

He has run countless half marathons and many other fund raising runs, for all kinds of charities.

James I respect you enormously buddy, but Chas takes the biscuit, sorry mate.

CHAPTER 74.

LIFESTYLE AND RECREATION.

The Warren House Pub.

I have always liked a drink, a good traditional bitter or ale. I have never enjoyed any of the top shelf spirits. I can't stand neither whiskey, rum nor brandy. I am not keen on lager either.

I prefer a darker old ale, preferably from the traditional "wooden keg" from hand pumps for me, is by far the best.

The first time that I went purposefully to the Warren House at Milnsbridge, was the 30th March 1986, it was a Sunday lunchtime. Just a couple of weeks before we were due to move house.

It was the week after Ben was born.

Alec was living at Paddock and he knew that we would be going to mum and dads for lunch. He offered to take me across to the Warren House, he said that I ought to find out what my new local would be like.

We left Wendy, Adrian and newly born Ben, at mum and dads. Alec and I walked across to the Warren House, it was a Theakston's house. One of my all time favourite breweries.

They had my favourite drink ever, that is Theakston's Old Peculiar. They had only just had it installed, for some reason though, it was on an electric pump.

We drank four pints and then decided to set off home. As soon as I got across the road, I started to feel ill. I gipped, only once, but all four pints were thrown right over the wall in one fell swoop.

What a waste.

We moved to Manchester Road a couple of weeks later, in the middle of April 1996.

When I was around 16 to 18 years of age, the two pubs in the district, that were known as the "in pubs" to go to, were the Warren House and the Junction at Marsh, opposite the ambulance station. I had called at both of them on many occasions in the past, probably before it was legal for me to drink.

They used to be packed to the doors.

Again, how times have changed.

The Warren House was to become a large part of my life over the next twenty or more years.

I told the landlord of my trial experience with his Old Peculiar. He told me not to worry, it had become a regular on the hand pump. A wicket, a nickname for the handle of the hand pump. As in the cricket game.

The first landlord that I had dealings with, was Paddy and his wife Elise, she was Austrian.

Paddy was a smashing bloke, but my God did he have one hell of a stammer. If you were a stranger, he appeared to be very abrupt, he would bark "what d'you want!" Either that, or by the time he had asked you, you would have forgotten what you wanted and gone elsewhere.

I was sat at the bar one evening when a young lad walked in and sat on a bar stool at the side of me. The lad was called Nigel, when he asked for a drink, I nearly wet myself.

His stammer was just fantastic, not only did he have the stutter. His head rocked violently and his tongue came out, it was brilliant. After Paddy had poured him a pint, I had to say to him. "I can't believe you took the piss out of Paddy like that, it was so funny".

He looked me right in the eye, his tongue was hanging out, he nodded a few times and then said "he he he is m m m my d d d dad".

That was actually how he did speak.

Nigel and I became friends. I had another occasion to laugh at him over his stammer. It happened one midweek night. I was sat at the bar and there was about seven or eight other customers dotted about. It had been a relatively quiet and event free night.

Suddenly we all heard the sound of breaking glass at the back of the bar area, it had come from the gents toilets.

In an instant, Nigel had left the bar. Shortly afterwards, he was coming round the end of the bar and he had someone gripped at the back of the neck and by the seat of their pants. That man had been sat alone in the corner for a while, he wasn't known to the rest of us. Anyway, Nigel escorted him to the front door and with a flourish launched him straight outside.

He was given a round of applause from all of us. He then started to speak. His head started nodding really violently from front to back, his tongue was dangling out of the corner of his mouth, as it did when he got really excited over something. He started "i i i it w w w was qu qu quicker th th th than asking h h h him to le le lea leave".

Fantastic!

I met many friends at the Warren House.

Peter he married a Thai bride Pemika. There was Richard and Andrea. Young Ken and his dad Old Ken. Old Ken married a New Yorker, she was called Zaz. Hugh from the fire service. Little "ginner" Paul, also known as Ginger Pig. Another Paul, again small in stature. We called him "Crime". When he came into the pub, he would order half a pint of bitter. If anybody offered to buy him a drink, it would always be a full pint. We played all sorts of tricks in the early days, to get a drink back off him. It was quite an achievement to get one. Hence the name "Crime".

As a reference to the well known saying that "crime never pays".

Next licensee's after Paddy and Elise, were a younger couple Benny and Edith, they had a daughter of a similar age to our boys.

When they were in charge of the pub, they tried a few new ideas to pick trade up. Including using the pub for children's parties. For birthdays, Halloween etc.

Wendy made a few decorative cakes for them.

Benny had some big ideas, ideas that would just never work in that location.

He wanted to install a caravan park on the land at the back of the pub, where it was off a very steep hill. It was also very near to a blind access junction onto the extremely busy Manchester Road, it would never have worked.

Benny tried one or two charity nights. One of them involved a customer, Bob, he was a year older than me. He led a very slow and steady pace of life. He would come to the Warren House with his old dog Dylan, who at the time was nearly seventeen years old.

Dylan walked faster than Bob.

At work, we had raised money for defibrillators in the past. Bob's dad had been one of the first people in Huddersfield, to benefit and to survive from a defibrillator's shock.

That time at the pub, we were going to raise money for the ITV's annual Telethon. Bob had volunteered to have his super long hair and beard shaved off in public.

Benny contacted the television company, they wanted to film the entire event. Bob with his hair almost down to his elbows and a beard to match, being shaved completely bald on his head and chin.

We had planned to shave Bob's hair off in the pub, the week before the Telethon. Before even starting, we had raised over £350 for the appeal.

All told, we raised around £750. On the lead up to the Telethon, they showed short snippets of Bob on the television. It was on each night for the whole week, until the actual Telethon night when he sat there in all his glory.

That was a great success. Unfortunately though that was the beginning of the end. Sales depleted, custom dwindled and they decided to call it a day.

As the couple were about to leave the pub, Benny asked if any of us wanted anything as a souvenir of the pub. He thought it was going to be shut down for good then.

I did, I wanted the sign. The sign of the official seal of the Old Peculiar of Masham. That sign had been mounted on the gable end of the pub for donkey's years.

He said "if you can get it down you can have it", so I did.

I got my ladders and climbed up to the sign on the wall, it was bigger than I thought. It was around four foot six tall by three foot six wide. I undid the bolts, then I lifted it away from the wall. How I didn't fall off the ladder I will never know, but I got it. It is now in pride of place, screwed to the wall of my shed cum workshop at the top of the garden.

We had a couple of other families that tried their best to run the pub. As business improved, the rent from the brewery soared. So they left for pastures new. Nobody could blame them.

Then, Alan and Cheryl took over. They were at the Warren, for quite a while. He was an ex rugby league player, his wife was from a restaurant background.

Whilst at the Warren, they had a son Richard.

He liked the pub, but it wasn't quite their lifestyle, they really wanted to run a restaurant in a pub.

The kitchen at the Warren House wasn't practical. It was upstairs and far too small.

They left to take on a pub in Illingworth, near Halifax. That had a small restaurant, just right for starting out.

Eventually taking over The Withens, which was on the moors high above Halifax, there they had the big restaurant that they had always wanted. They also had a large petting farm there.

Whilst at the Withens, Cheryl became pregnant again, their family was getting bigger. They closed the pub, but carried on living there running it as a farm. I have heard since, that they split up and that Alan now lives in the south of France.

Alan's family had a long history of breeding and showing champion shire horses. He had gone back to that.

In the Warren House, we had an occasional customer coming in. He was named Dan, he was a blacksmith from up the Colne Valley.

He was a right character, he was born fifty years too late. He was a traditional blacksmith. He always wore his wooden clogs, complete with irons. He had a cloth cap, it was miles too big for him and always set at an angle on the side of his head. He completed his outfit by wearing a leather jerkin, leather chaps and a scarf tied around his neck. He wouldn't have been out of place standing in a corner at the Colne Valley museum.

One of his tales that he regularly told in the pub went as follows.

It needs imagination and to be read in a broad Yorkshire accent.

"It wor at t' Grett Yorkshire Show at Arrowgit tha no's. I wor wi Alan at th'enclosure, lookin at th'osses. This tarty bird kem up t'us. She spock all reight proper lark an all. She gi' Alan a reight shiney silver cup an sed, that's for t' best shire oss i't show. He wor all chuffed an all, wor Alan. So I sed to t'lass, ey up see, ya sees that oss theer, I shod that f-ing oss! She di'nt say owt back neether. She just buggered off. An du's tha no, that wor that Princess Anne tha no's, stuck up cow!"

That is exactly how he spoke, I could just see him saying that as well. It was Alan's finest achievement getting "Best Of Breed" for his shire horses at one of the years most prestigious events. He was mixing with royalty, then a mucky faced little urchin like Dan pops up.

Priceless!

One evening, when Alan hadn't been at the Warren House for long. I was sat at the bar, when he told me that when he was sixteen, his dad had died right in front of him. He had suffered a massive heart attack, Alan had to watch his dad die.

He was helpless, as he had no idea what to do.

He asked if I could possibly show him and some of the other regulars, what to do in similar circumstances.

I agreed to show people, but had to be honest, as not an approved instructor. I would not be able to examine them and issue a certificate or anything, it would have to be for information only.

I took an adult and a baby resuscitation manikin into the pub. I think there was about fifteen people in at the time. I went through the whole active resuscitation process with them. We did it very thoroughly. It was a Tuesday night. Everybody had a go and truth be known, everybody was very good, it was all taken in a serious context. Even when we'd had a few beers.

On the Friday of the very same week, Alan and Cheryl, had gone to attend at a weekend licensed victuallers' conference in Edinburgh.

They had their introduction meeting on the Friday afternoon and it was followed by an evening in the bar.

Whilst Alan was stood at the bar, a man in his mid sixties fell against him and knocked his beer over. Alan was just about to knock his block off, when he saw that the man was going blue. He had collapsed. He wasn't breathing, he had suffered a cardiac arrest.

Alan immediately sprung into action, he called out for someone to get an ambulance. Then he carried out full CPR on the patient. He had continued with CPR for well over twenty minutes. Then the man made an effort to breathe, he started to come round. By the time the ambulance had arrived at the hotel where they were staying, the man had fully regained consciousness, he was doing well.

Alan had managed to save his life.

The man was only, so I believe, a retired Chief Constable.

Alan was given a top award, something akin to the Royal Humane Life Saving Certificate. He had to go back to Edinburgh to have it presented by the Procurator Fiscal.

Alan was all over the Scottish newspapers. In an interview, Alan commented. "It's a good job my mate Firthy showed me what to do a few days before. Otherwise I would have had to stand and watch him die, like I had to do with my dad".

Alan did let me and some of my friends down once, I was absolutely stunned and disappointed by his actions. I told him so in no uncertain terms. It was only one event, but it did put a dramatic end to our good friendship.

I had attended to a road traffic accident on Manchester Road, it was just a hundred yards on the Huddersfield side of Cowlersley traffic lights. It was half past eight in the morning, a young lad had been knocked down by a car, on his way to school. It was the same time of day and location, that both my sons would be, on their way to school.

I was with Mike, we had come through Milnsbridge and up to the traffic lights at

Cowlersley and turned left. Near to the junction with new Street, there were several people surrounding the lad in the road.

It wasn't one of my sons, but it was a lad in Adrian's year, a friend of his, Jim. He was unconscious and his breathing was poor. He had obvious head injuries and he had numerous bumps and abrasions.

We had to collar and board him, to take maximum precautions not to disturb any unseen injuries.

In the ambulance we had to cut off Jim's clothes to fully examine him, including his prized Huddersfield Giants rugby shirt. He was wearing it under his school uniform. We then set off to HRI, we had only just got going when Jim started to choke.

I pulled in to the Warren House car park. Just as I did, he had started vomiting. Mike and myself had to lift and tilt the spinal board over, to allow the vomit to run free, he was still unconscious.

We then had an airway to clear before intubating him, giving him an artificial airway. His life was then hanging in the balance.

We set off again to the resus room and the awaiting staff. He remained unconscious for the rest of the journey, Mike was assisting his breathing on route.

A couple of nights later I went to the Warren House for a pint. Alan mentioned the ambulance in the car park below his window, he had seen me and so he was naturally curious.

I was limited as to what details I could tell him, other than it had been a local lad and that we had basically had to resuscitate him in the car park.

I knew by then, that Jim was already starting out on the road to his recovery. The doctors had put his sudden unconsciousness, down to severe brain shake at the point of his impact.

A massive kind of concussion due to his brain being knocked around inside his skull. He had a few broken bones, but none were life threatening.

I told Alan that Jim himself was more bothered about his Giants rugby shirt than anything else. Alan said to me, "leave it with me, I'll get him another".

With his rugby connections, he said that it would be no problem.

I was over the moon.

Several weeks later, Alan told me that he had got a shirt. It had been signed by the whole of the Giants squad and at that time it was away being mounted in a frame. He told me to arrange with Jim's family to come along for a fun evening and presentation.

They were all really excited about it, I had told Jim's parents, but they decided not to tell him.

Three days before the presentation, Alan put the framed shirt on the wall for all to see, it looked fantastic. That was a Tuesday. On the Thursday, Alan rang me, he said that we had to cancel Friday's presentation as he had "sold the shirt".

I was shocked, how the hell could he do that? I couldn't believe it. When I told the family, they were furious.

That was only a couple of weeks before Alan and Cheryl left the Warren House. It would have been a brilliant parting gesture from him, instead he left under a dark cloud. Everybody from the pub was in disbelief.

What a disgusting and selfish thing to do!

We had Joe and Tina next, they were a really likeable couple. They both worked hard to hold down a full time day job and run the pub in an evening. They were the couple who provided such a great night for Wendy's fortieth birthday.

Joe also let the kids of the area, our Ben included, use the pool table for a couple of hours free on an early evening. Soft drinks only, after all they were only fifteen or sixteen. Five thirty to seven thirty. It was good to get them off the streets. Sadly one of them spoilt things by taking alcohol in, it was stopped for all of them.

Eventually Joe and Tina parted company, Joe went on his separate way. Tina still carried on as the licensee of the pub.

Some time later her new partner Sam moved in. They eventually got married. I took their wedding photo's.

Their last twelve months in charge of the Warren House, became more difficult. There were waning customer numbers and increasing rents to contend with. But they stayed on till the bitter end.

The Warren House had to shut down. It was the end of an era. The license was revoked, the council stated that if the place reopened, it would not be as a pub.

It is now a place for aroma therapies and beauty treatments.

What a way to end!

We customers, had several visits to the Theakston's brewery over the years. All of the landlords arranged an annual trip. There was always plenty of free beers on those adventures.

It was always one of the old retired "coopers" (barrel makers) that showed us around the brewery.

It was on one of our early visits, that one of them introduced me to a new drink. It then became one of my favourites of all time.

Old Peculiar was a premium beer, not a session beer. It would sit very heavily on the stomach. He had suggested drinking a half of Old Peculiar, mixed with a half of bitter in a pint glass. It was gorgeous. It was just as full of flavour, but it didn't sit as heavy on the old stomach.

Back at the Warren House, the drink needed a name. A pint of "mixed", was already traditionally known throughout all breweries for a Mild and a Bitter.

This particular drink was "Old Peculiar and Bitter", I named it "mother in law". Sorry Dorothy, no offence intended.

It stuck, even at the brewery in Masham, North Yorkshire.

When I told the old cooper, he howled with laughter. It was the first time that he had actually heard a name for the drink.

A new name was born!

Refugees at Milnsbridge Socialist Club.

The majority of the last few remaining customers of the Warren House travelled a short way down the road and enrolled as members of the Milnsbridge Socialist Club at the bottom of Factory Lane.

We were refugees down at the little club. Initially, it was a thriving venture, but as with the rest of the area's pub trade, the club's clientele was dwindling.

We tried our best to increase trade, we included a massive range of real ales. Mainly they were local ones, but we tried some from further afield. Over three hundred different beers and ciders were sampled in just over four years. Some customers must have been coming in.

My personal input to boosting trade, involved bringing in some old style, but traditional pub games. I started a growing collection, including bar skittles, bagatelle, shut the box and shove halfpenny.

I even made my own bull ring, I had an adapted dartboard with a pool game board. A marbles game that I made larger and adapted it for the pool table.

We tried all sorts.

We had an evening of all the traditional games to raise money for the "Forget me not trust" for the children's hospice. It went down a treat. I even mounted some little trophies on hand made bases, engraved with the name of each game done by pyrography. (Burning). It was only a temporary reprieve though.

The Club declined even further and further into debt until it became no longer viable, it inevitably closed down.

The future of the Club and its premises has still not been decided, another group were paying to rent the Club to try and pick trade up for themselves. It has been run as The Red and Green Club, for the last three or four years.

It is run on a casual basis for holding meetings, presentations, debating society evenings, or for private functions. I have no idea how it is doing, you never see the doors open. They were supposed to be buying the building, but again, I haven't a clue what is going on. It seems to be dragging on forever.

I don't go out drinking any more. An occasional pint with a meal now is about my lot.

A big change from my younger days.

I should be healthier, I don't drink and I gave up smoking over four years ago. I was fine then. I am now relying on damned asthma inhalers. How the hell does that work?

I'm not healthier, I am a rotting relic.

CHAPTER 75.

UP TO DATE.

Current climate. As of February 2016.

At the moment, talk in Huddersfield is of the major shake up to take place between the Huddersfield and Calderdale hospitals.

These are purely my thoughts, for the people of Huddersfield who are "upset" regarding the proposed closure of A & E at Huddersfield Royal Infirmary.

Comments have been published in the Huddersfield Daily Examiner. That if you are seriously injured in an accident, the extra journey time to Halifax by ambulance could be enough to kill you. The same concerns if you are having a heart attack.

Well, if either of those events occur, it's not Halifax you will go to. The ambulances have to take you to the Leeds General Infirmary, or the Northern General at Sheffield. For specialist treatment, as is the case now and has been for quite a while.

The other concern that I feel that the people of Huddersfield need to be aware of, is that once the Huddersfield ambulance has gone out of the district. The crews already have an all out battle to get back to Huddersfield. They will still and are already being used to answer calls in Leeds and elsewhere. They may be out of the area for hours. It is not unusual for the majority of Huddersfield crews to be working in Leeds, Bradford, Dewsbury, Barnsley or Wakefield at any one time.

From many of the calls in the Dewsbury area, the patients are being sent to Pinderfields at Wakefield and that's now. The Dewsbury A&E limit what they will accept and that's before their A & E, all about closes to ambulances in September 2017. Pinderfields hospital cannot cope with the current workload and are regularly "on divert" sending ambulance patients back to Dewsbury, because they are overloaded.

The ambulances will be away from Huddersfield even more, no wonder the Yorkshire Ambulance Service cannot meet the eight minute target, the targets are being reviewed at the moment. Nowadays, twenty and thirty mile emergency runs are not unusual.

To try to alleviate the difficulties, YAS are using several "private" ambulance companies to provide a short fall for our NHS service. Even St John ambulances. All of the private crews, including the "Johnners" a voluntary organisation, are being paid at a much higher hourly rate than we are.

How much is all that costing?

Well it all appears to be kept under wraps, nobody seems to know, or maybe the authorities are simply not wanting us know. Just like the hospitals are using private "agency" nurses at exorbitant rates.

No wonder new staff cannot be recruited. Who wants to work for the NHS and get paid peanuts and then be treated like monkeys. When you can get more than twice as much, easily, by working for the private sector.

It's not just A & E, there are plans to move the intensive care unit over to Halifax as well. When the new hospital in Halifax was built, the ICU was a lot larger than that of Huddersfield. Half of it was never opened, the beds are still in shrink wrap, they have never been used.

They have never had enough funding to provide the staff to run them. It isn't really surprising then that Huddersfield Royal Infirmary will lose exactly the same amount of ICU beds, that Halifax will gain.

The latest proposals are to close the hospital in Huddersfield altogether and pull it down, then rebuild a much smaller one.

How will it be funded? Unbelievably, the same PFI that got us into the mess in the first place.

In my mind, these are not proposed changes, these were pre planned with the opening of the new hospital.

You'll see, mark MY words!

The CCG (clinical commissioning group) that are overseeing things, are blatantly trying to pull the wool over people's eyes. Originally, they were saying that the changes were not financially orientated.

The PFI loan taken out to build the hospital in Halifax, was going to cost £65,000,000. With the current interest rate that they are paying, it is going to cost well over £773,000,000. That is even more than a Wonga, Payday loan. If ever the interest rates increase, where will it end?

They have had to admit that this PFI debt has been a deciding factor. Since Huddersfield merged with the Calderdale trust in 2000, all that has happened is that Huddersfield have inherited the debts.

As one wise guy stated in the letters section of Huddersfield Daily Examiner. Why don't the people of Huddersfield ditch Calderdale altogether. Then that Health Authority would go bust.

If they were then to go into liquidation, as other big conservative backed companies have already done before. Then their debts would be completely written off. They could then start up again the day after, under a different company name. Perhaps it could be named Halifax Health Trust, instead of Calderdale? Why should the people of Huddersfield be liable for a debt that has nothing to do with them?

To anyone with any amount of common sense, it appears to be a deliberate act of making it impossible for the NHS to continue, using back door tactics.

Locala Care, is another prime example of a private company, are they taking over? They are in at Dewsbury, Huddersfield and Calderdale. Does Holme Valley hospital have any NHS control? The three letters NHS do not seem to appear anywhere on site. Locala is in abundance. They already run the district nurses, they are after midwifery. Not for profit?

Give me strength!

If they pull the HRI down as planned and then rebuild a new hospital, like it is proposed.

I personally would be certain that it would be run wholly by Locala. They received a 238 million pound contract to provide health care in Huddersfield and Calderdale earlier in the year. They have already got their eye on the already "shut down" Princess Royal Hospital.

Sorry it was confirmed in late November 2016, that Locala have bought the Princess Royal Hospital. That will cost Huddersfield another five million pounds a year in lost revenue. Figure stated in the Huddersfield Daily Examiner.

The NHS bites the dust again.

As I edit and rewrite this, the four main executive directors of Locala, have just awarded themselves a two and a half percent pay increase, of their £130,000 + salaries. None of the other employees will be getting a penny increase this year.

Jobs for the boys yet again!

That is exactly what the conservatives have been trying to do since the great and fully supported action by the National Ambulance Service dispute of 1989/90.

Do not let it happen!

Please save our HRI at all costs!

Sorry for going on, but, my feelings are very strong about it.

Is it a ward or not a ward?

February 2017. There is a private company who have started up in Halifax. They have been employed to look after the people who are taking up hospital beds, known as "bed blockers". They are people who really do not need to be in hospital, but are not fit to look after themselves at home.

To make a complete mockery of the NHS, they have taken over a hospital ward to look after their patients.

So they are still taking up hospital beds in a hospital ward. Being cared for by a private company, paid for by the NHS. But according to the manager, it is not a hospital ward. It is a separate unit. It just happens to be on a hospital ward. Inside a hospital building.

Do the people of Huddersfield know? Do the people campaigning to save HRI know that we will be paying for the private company within our own property?

What a bloody joke!

To make matters even worse, if it was possible. If one of the patients on that facility becomes ill, because they are not part of the NHS, they have to ring 111. They cannot ring for a doctor within the hospital.

When they do, 111 will inevitably ring an ambulance.

Nick and me were called to ward 4 at CRH, it was a call via 111. For a patient who had suffered with angina chest pains, but was now back to normal following her taking her own GTN spray. The appropriate initial treatment for angina.

When we got there, we went in the lift up two floors. The patient said that she was feeling absolutely normal again. We did all our checks including blood pressure, heart tracings, blood sugars, temperature and oxygen saturations, all of which were inside normal ranges.

The manager of the ward was on duty at the time we were there, he insisted that the patient was taken to A&E. to be "checked out".

We took the bed that she was in, complete with NHS linen, and a Calderdale and Huddersfield NHS Trust label on it's frame. We put it in the lift and took her down the two floors to A&E, as we left the lift area we bumped into the hospital matron.

She asked us where we were going with a hospital bed.

When we explained where we had come from.

She just said "oh yes, that's what they have to do. So why isn't the patient in your ambulance?"

I simply said that the ambulance wouldn't fit in the lift.

The patient wasn't going anywhere near the ambulance, we were just being used as blue light emergency porters.

Outside the ward entrance to the hospital was a private ambulance, the crew were sat in the cab reading newspapers.

I asked matron "why didn't the company use the private ambulance?" The answer, unbelievable, but expected. "They would have to pay for that crew, but if it is called via 999, or if 111 send it. Then that is free".

Another absolute example of the health care professionals, completely abusing an already overstretched and under resourced ambulance service.

When I asked if they would be ringing 999 when the patient was ready to return to the "not a ward, ward". I was accused of being facetious.

If only the people of Huddersfield knew!

The Ambulance Service Today, February 2016.

As I have previously mentioned, since our merger, actually it was a complete takeover, by the rest of Yorkshire. (We are not "allowed" to say takeover). The service morale has been completely eradicated.

A job that I used to love, I now hate with an absolute passion!

Sorry, I will rephrase that sentence.

I do still love my actual job, that I am employed to do. But I do hate with a passion the political overtones behind the running of the service.

I have dedicated over two thirds of my life to the ambulance service and to the people who require our services. The pleasure that I have got in the past cannot be put into words.

How can you in all honestly drive at speed to a cardiac arrest, but take eight minutes and just one second over, to arrive? But then go on and save the patients life. Yes, that is classed as a fail! We haven't achieved the required time standard. Yet if we arrive in just one second under the magic eight minutes and the patient dies, according to our statistics, that is a resounding success.

I am totally baffled by it, but I am certainly not alone.

We have had a series of Chief Executives, none of who seem to stay long.

Not since the great days of John Davis, he was the Chief Metropolitan Ambulance Officer. Note the word ambulance officer there, it's not used now, it's manager or director.

We are working longer shifts and we very rarely finish on time. Twelve hours can regularly be now thirteen, or fourteen hours or more. Meal breaks are consistently out of their window. (Late).

We are supposedly to have a half hour break between the fourth and sixth hour of the shift, many a time it is nearer seven or eight hours without stopping. It has not been unknown to be eleven and a half hours on a twelve hour shift.

We are supposed to have twenty minutes to check the ambulance for its consumables, it's drugs, safety features, lights, tyres pressures, wheel nuts etc. I can't remember the last time we had the full twenty. Usually the station tannoy is calling bang on the start of the shift for us to get outstanding jobs.

In the last couple of weeks of February 2016, we have been ordered to have a mandatory six minutes check before we can be called. Allegedly that was due to two of our ambulances losing a front wheel.

As soon as we get to hospital, we clock in on a screen. As soon as the patient has been handed over to nursing staff, we clock in again. We then have fifteen minutes to then clock in again, as available for work, or face questions.

It is push, push, push all the time.

There is no friendly banter on station, we are never there to talk to anybody. If we are not actually on a job, we have to go on a roadside standby.

As soon as the meal break is over, we are sent back out, to the second, thirty minutes and that's it, there is no time for hot food to digest.

More than fifty per cent of the time it is to another area.

We have had at least five different private ambulance companies attending to jobs in Yorkshire. There is Falck, they are a company from Denmark. There is Jigsaw, they say they are here to pick up the pieces, ha ha God love 'em. Trust Medical, ERS, and even the St. John ambulance.

Even a simple invite to attend training school, contains threats.

You usually have to complete a workbook prior to attending. That officially should be done in works time, while on station.

Not a chance! We don't have the time, we're never there.

If you do not complete the workbook and accompanying question paper, the letter states that. "You will be classed as non compliant. We will write to your manager and inform them of your non compliance, this will then be escalated under current procedures!"

I find that treatment disgusting. I am an adult, a professional adult, not a six year old child at bloody Junior School.

(Sorry for swearing, I'll probably get 100 lines for that as well).

CHAPTER 76.

AND FINALLY!

Privileged.

I have been so privileged, yes, I do feel privileged. To be invited into people's lives, to witness all kinds of tragedy and happiness. Sometimes right down to the very depths of deepest despair.

Every day has been totally different.

As a member of the ambulance service, you have no idea from one minute to the next, where you will be going, or what you will be going to see.

I have also met some wonderful people and I have met some awful nasty people. I have at times been physically assaulted, threatened and verbally abused.

Thankfully, not very often.

I have always been of the opinion that whatever grade of staff that you are. Whatever the illness or injury that you are dealing with. If you arrive at hospital and the patient is smiling, then you have done your job.

All members and all grades of staff in the NHS, are ultimately one single tooth in a large cog wheel.

From building and vehicle cleaners, to all ambulance staff, A&E or PTS, Comms staff, Paramedic or Technician, Doctors, Consultants and Nurses, any maintenance or domestic staff. They are all there to provide the smooth running of the NHS.

As soon as any one person thinks that they are better than anybody else, that tooth in the big wheel gets too big and the whole job becomes unstable. If everybody stuck to their own task and stopped interfering with others, we would all be much better off.

The way that I describe to others, to be able to have dealt with my job. Is that there is always a barrier between me and the patient. If I know the patient, the barrier reduces. If it is a member of my own family, the barrier has gone. Then, I am just the same as anyone else. I am human, I still have feelings and emotions.

If I can see a reason for something happening, I can accept it and deal with it. If there isn't a reason, that hurts.

In the early eighties, Kirklees had one of highest concentrations of "cot deaths" in the country. At the moment, West Yorkshire is at the top of that list yet again.

I have no idea why.

Every single one of the babies that had suffered from "cot death", that I have had dealings with. They have all had the same facial expression. It is of complete blankness, one that shows no feelings or emotions. There isn't any sign of pain, discomfort or even peace.

In October 1984. One of my colleagues and I, had to deal with five cot deaths in four days! It was at the time when my youngest son Adrian was only three months old.

The very same age as the majority of the "cot death" victims.

We were both ready to give our notice in to leave the service, Bert, my boss refused to accept them.

We both went to the Junction Pub across the road from the station and got very, very drunk.

I couldn't say anything to Wendy, how could I. I spent most of that night, prodding and poking Adrian, making sure that he was breathing.

It took me a very long time to get over that.

All of the babies had died of an unknown and unexplained problem, all of them at around three to four months of age. It was put down to "cot death" or as it now known, as "sudden infant death syndrome". (SIDS). Not long after that event. We as a station at Huddersfield, raised a lot of money for the SIDS charity with our open day.

Funny.

I have lead an interesting life, it's been an absolute pleasure for most of the way so far.

There have so many comical moments, usually they are a result of off the cuff remarks.

A classic one involving Mike and me. We once had an old man wearing the thickest glasses that I had ever seen, they were real proper jam jar bottoms.

Mike, suddenly and out of the blue, said to the man. "By 'eck lad, tha must ave good eyes to see through them. I bet tha can see Castle Hill wi them on! An' I bet tha dunt need matches either, tha cud light fires wi them buggers".

The man didn't even crack a smile.

I did!

We have played a lot of practical jokes on each other, it has been a right laugh.

Graham, our very own "Forrest Gump". I mean that, wholly as a complement. A lovely bloke, he sees the world wholly through the eyes of an innocent. He cannot see any malice in anybody.

In his younger days, he was extremely naive and was often the butt of many jokers.

If he tried to get payback, something always went wrong.

One day though, he was passing through the door to the station kitchen from the mess room. He hesitated, a look came over his face. A look not seen on him before, it was one of pure wickedness.

His regular partner was a lady called Jan, she mothered him, perhaps smothered him was more appropriate at times. Although they really seemed to get on well together.

This was his day though, Graham was going to get his own back.

Jan had fallen asleep in a chair, she was all curled up. The chair was next to our water cooler.

The large bottle type on a stand.

The tap had been broken. So Clifford had ingeniously rigged up a temporary solution, by using the set that was used to administer an intra-venous drip.

That had caught Graham's eye. The giving set (as they are called), was a thin plastic tube normally about three foot long. That one had been shortened a little, towards the cooler end was the roller. Slide the roller up to let water flow, slide it back down to stop it, simple.

Graham's face was a picture. He carefully inserted the end of the tube into the sleeping Jan's trouser pocket. Then he gently turned the roller on and ran away into the kitchen to wait.

Magic!

It wasn't very long, the ice cold water seeped through Jan's pocket. It went right to her nether regions, what a scream. She shrieked loudly and ran off to the ladies bathroom.

The few of us in the room were in uproar. Graham, our hero who would have thought it?

Memoirs.

My mum wrote down a lot of her memoirs. An everyday life of a first class mother. My dad tried his best to write his, although it was a much shorter version. They are both extremely valued possessions of mine.

It is as a direct result of those, that my family had been pestering me to write mine down for future generations. I kept saying that I would give it a go.

Eventually.

I have tried to cram a lot of things into my time on this earth, I think it is fair to say I did my best.

I married a wonderful woman, who gave me two fantastic sons. I love them all dearly.

The boys have provided me with five beautiful grandchildren. Damian and Willow are Adrian's little darlings and then Scott, Kacey and Kaira are Bens little darlings.

Unfortunately as some of them live away, I don't see them all as much as I would like to do.

I can't say that I enjoyed school, in fact, I absolutely hated it.

But I will say that I had a great childhood, particularly after joining the the scout movement.

I had the opportunity to "play" at being a fireman at Brook Motors Ltd., and there I also completed an engineering apprenticeship.

Whoopee!

Since then, I have had an absolutely fantastic time with the ambulance service, if only the politics hadn't come into it.

It would still be, fantastic.

I have spent many of my years as a first line supervisor for the ambulance service and I would like to think that I can be trusted. When needed, I have provided a shoulder to cry on. I am as honest as the day is long.

I have been fortunate and I have had many many letters and cards of appreciation over the years. I have only ever had three complaints from members of the public, one was classed as "unjustified complaint". The other result was, "there is no case to answer".

The third one was resolved with a face to face meeting of the complainant and me. I gave a verbal apology to the patient, who had misunderstood the comments I had made. Perhaps, I should have made myself clearer at the time.

The only other complaints, I have already written about, they were all submitted by Station Officer "Sam" of West Yorkshire Fire and Rescue Service.

In my view they were a kind of sour grapes revenge attack. They were all written off as "unnecessary and unjustified" as well.

Rewards.

The heartaches have been many and the rewards have been but few. But to see patients arrive at hospital, that might not have done so. Without my own and my colleagues intervention is reward itself.

Thank you gifts can cause nothing but trouble, as I have already mentioned. But those two very little words, "thank" and "you" can and do, mean so much.

Tommy told me once of a thank you gift that he was involved with. The patient was my own aunty Joan, my mums older sister.

She had suffered a very severe and dense stroke. It had left her severely physically disabled.

It was many months later, that Tommy and another of my colleagues Ernie, had gone to take my aunty Joan to hospital for a routine outpatient appointment.

Straight away Aunty Joan had recognised Ernie, he was one of the crew that had been for her when she had suffered the stroke.

She asked Ernie if he would move the television and stand away from the cupboards in the corner. Underneath the cupboards were three drawers, he was asked to open the bottom drawer.

She then said "can you see a blue tin at the back of the drawer?" She went on, "if you can, will you pass it to me please?" Tommy was watching with baited breath, what could there be in such a tin? So well hidden from prying eyes.

Aunty Joan's stroke prevented her from opening the tin.

She then asked Ernie to open it for her. When he did so, it contained "penguin" chocolate biscuits.

She said to Ernie, "because you saved my life, you can have a biscuit, if you like". He did, he took a prized "penguin" from the tin and then he proffered the tin to Tommy.

Before Tommy had chance to reach and get one, aunty Joan shrieked "what do you think you're doing?" She then shouted, "you can't have one, you weren't the one with him!"

What a price on life!

Tommy didn't know when he was telling me that tale, that aunty Joan was a relative of mine.

We had a proper giggle over that.

My monologue.

As I have repeated several times, Wendy and my family had been trying for years to get me to write some of these things down.

The time felt to be the right time.

So in February 2016 I started my epic monologue.

In doing so, the looking back has been a treat. It has been a wonderful therapy for me, especially during times of feeling low. It has really lifted my spirits.

I have suffered heartbreaks and some bad times over the years, but looking back, I suppose I could say that the sun's been shining brightly on me really!

The writing and the memories, have made me laugh. Sometimes out loud. It has also left me in tears several times. But, that's life and it has been my life.

I would like to thank you for reading my ramblings and I hope that you have been entertained.

If not, then really, I don't give a damn! After all it's been my life not yours!

Cheers everybody!!!

Ian.